My Dear Boy

A Family's War-Time Letters and Memoirs
from 1915 to the Kosovo Conflict

Brad Bird

with

Bil Bird

Order this book online at www.trafford.com
or email orders@trafford.com

Most Trafford titles are also available at major online book retailers.

Cover images: the large photo shows James Mackenzie Bird in uniform in October 1942 with his father, Dr. F. V. Bird, at their home in Boissevain, Manitoba. Lower left, Mack's brother Clayton, far left, with his air crew in 1944. Beside him are Ken Willis, Ted Larkins, Moe Cohen (now Conway), Jimmy Brooks, Keith Mosher and Ralph Pilkington, kneeling. This is beside the Halifax bomber they called Daisy Mae. Lower right image shows Clayton (left) and Mack Bird in Winnipeg about 1941.

Printed in the United States of America.

ISBN: 978-1-4269-4853-4 (sc)

Trafford rev. 03/04/2011

 www.trafford.com

North America & international
toll-free: 1 888 232 4444 (USA & Canada)
phone: 250 383 6864 ✦ fax: 812 355 4082

DEDICATION

To Doris Bird (nee Aconley, July 9, 1919 – Jan. 7, 1997) and Peggy Bird (nee Margit Hjordis McLeod, January 2, 1925 – July 10, 2008).

Also to John Dafoe, former editorial-page editor of the Winnipeg Free Press.

Other books written or edited by Brad Bird

Nickel Trip
Me and My Canoe
No Guarantees

He may be reached at birdbrad@hotmail.com

ACKNOWLEDGEMENTS

I wish to thank my wife, Karen E. Stewart, for her patience and assistance over the four years it took to produce this book, which coincided with the first four years of our marriage.

My brother Bil provided much-appreciated help with the Bird family history in the Introduction, of which he wrote a portion. I am also grateful for his solid help with editing and finding old images of Jimmy Jock Bird and Dr. C. J. Bird, among others, on the Internet.

Our uncle, J. M. Bird, who is featured in this work, provided great assistance and cooperation in the production of this volume, as well as permission to publish his war-time letters.

Thanks also to brother Bruce for helping to interview our uncle and for ongoing support. He and his wife, my sister-in-law Deanna Bird, also played a key role in proof reading.

My friend Martin Zeilig, a fellow journalist and canoeist, put the bug in my ear to produce my uncle's story in the first place. He did what a good friend should do – push a buddy to undertake and finish an important job.

Clayton Bird, our father, supported this effort before his death at age 87 on Dec. 17, 2006.

With a book of this scope some errors are bound to get through, and these are the sole responsibility of the editor.

– Brad Bird

CONTENTS

Dedication   v
Acknowledgements   vii
Preface   xiii
Introduction   1

SECTION ONE: GROUND WAR
Chapter 1   Clayton Bradley's Letters Home   39
Chapter 2   J. M. Bird's Biography   51
Chapter 3   Against War   53
Chapter 4   'You're Filthy!'   65
Chapter 5   Precious Freedom   73
Chapter 6   Growing Up in Boissevain   78
Chapter 7   The Haunted Estate   83
Chapter 8   In Holland, and a Friend in the Underground   85
Chapter 9   Afghanistan and other Thoughts   90
Chapter 10   'Life's Been Pretty Good'   96
Chapter 11   Mac Bird's Letters Home   103
Chapter 12   Over to England   115
Chapter 13   In Italy   132
Chapter 14   Back in the Fighting   141
Chapter 15   War Wraps Up   156

SECTION TWO – AIR WAR
Chapter 1   Frederick Charles Clayton Bird   171
Chapter 2   Toronto's Manning Depot, Early 1941   178
Chapter 3   Finally At Work   217
Chapter 4   Quebec City   229
Chapter 5   Dartmouth Guard Duty   239

Chapter 6	Victoriaville	252
Chapter 7	Solo -- and Married -- in Portage la Prairie	267
Chapter 8	'Going All Out Now'	277
Chapter 9	England	288
Chapter 10	Instructing at Cranwell	298
Chapter 11	Promotion	316
Chapter 12	Operational Flying, 1944	331
Chapter 13	More Bombing Raids and Home	343

SECTION THREE: WAR REPORTING

Chapter 1	Biography of Brad C. Bird	355
Chapter 2	Arrival in Athens	365
Chapter 3	Three Women, Three Lives	370
Chapter 4	Panos Manikis	378
Chapter 5	An Aussie Haberdasher	386
Chapter 6	Into Macedonia	392
Chapter 7	Canadian Troops in Kosovo	398
Chapter 8	Serbian Grannies in Pristina	405
Chapter 9	On Patrol with the Canadians	412
Chapter 10	A Second Patrol, and Don Cherry	419
Chapter 11	At Panos's Farm	426
Chapter 12	Thessaloniki, Then Istanbul	430
Chapter 13	A NATO Conference and Vedat Uras	437
Chapter 14	Alanya's 'Progress'	441
Chapter 15	Sevil	445
Chapter 16	Sanliurfa	449
Chapter 17	Police Come Knocking in Elazig	455
Chapter 18	Bus ride to T'bilisi	462
Chapter 19	Zia and Emzar near Chechnya	468
Chapter 20	More Refugees	473
Chapter 21	Back to Turkey, and Nina	480
Chapter 22	Return to Thessaloniki	483
Chapter 23	Painting with Ilhami Atalay	487
Chapter 24	Midnight Stroll	491
Chapter 25	Social Issues	494
Chapter 26	Athens Full Circle	496
Chapter 27	Landing in Morocco	498
Chapter 28	Moroccan Travels	508
Chapter 29	Algiers and the Polisario Front	520

Chapter 30   Polisario Schools   531
Chapter 31   Toward the front   539
Chapter 32   I Meet the Commander   547
Chapter 33   On to Tunis   552
Chapter 34   Interviewing an Ambassador   560
Chapter 35   Arrival in Malta   571
Chapter 36   Tripoli   582
Chapter 37   Generous Egyptians   587

Appendix

              "Jimmy Jock"   593
              An English Mother to Her Soldier Son   598
              Fleeing the Bombing   599
              Guerrillas intensify war against Morocco   602
              Maltese hope election brings end to violence   604
              'Seismic diplomacy' shakes Aegean   607
              Terrorist presence in Tunisia dwindles   609

PREFACE

My Dear Boy tells the story of the Bird family's contributions to the defence of Canada and war reporting. It spans four generations and 85 years, from 1915 and the First World War through the Second World War, to lesser-known conflicts in Western Sahara in 1987 and Kosovo in 2000.

The Introduction outlines the history of the family, which began in Canada with the arrival of James Curtis Bird at York Factory on Hudson Bay in 1788. He had been born and raised in England. Jimmy Jock Bird and Dr. F.V. Bird are other key figures in this chapter.

Section One, Ground War, looks at those who fought as soldiers in the First and Second World Wars. This section is chiefly about Lieut. James Mackenzie (Mac or Mack) Bird of the Princess Patricia's Canadian Light Infantry, who fought his way up the boot of Italy in 1944, surviving numerous close calls. His memoirs are riveting reading. Seventy-three of his letters are recorded here, as well as 10 letters by and about Clayton Bradley, an uncle of Mac and Clay, who fought and died in the Great War of 1914-18.

Section Two, Air War, offers 137 pieces of correspondence by and to Mac's older brother Clayton, a Halifax bomber pilot in Snowy Owl Squadron in the 1940s. This section is made richer by the excellent letters to the pilot from family and friends.

Section Three, War Reporting, consists of the memoirs of Brad Bird, journalist son of Clayton and nephew of Mac, who covered conflicts in the Western Sahara, Kosovo, Turkey and Chechnya for the Winnipeg Free Press and other papers as a freelancer. His efforts might be of interest to journalists today, since he started by typewriting and mailing or faxing his reports, long before e-mail.

But it's the letters from the two world wars that stand out. More than 200 in number, they shed light not only on what it was like to fight in the two most pivotal struggles of the last century but also to live in a different Canada from what we know today, a largely rural society. The correspondence from family and friends to the men overseas enriches our stock of social history of the period, providing everything from the state of Manitoba gardens and Prairie weather to the daily schedule of an RCMP recruit in training. It provides a glimpse into the life of a young female teacher in a rural and French-speaking part of Manitoba, and reveals the thoughts and concerns of a Brandon College student as she opts for nursing over teaching, realizing she couldn't face "the little brats" daily. This was the golden age of letter writing, long before TV and the Internet, when people penned complete and thorough accounts of what was happening in their lives. We are the lucky beneficiaries.

The writings of Private Clayton Bradley in the First World War speak of rats in the trenches, bullets whizzing by and casualties – but also of lighter things such as scrounging for firewood, visiting a local cathedral and receiving gifts from home ("I got a nice warm woolen muffler from the Daughters of the Empire in Montreal"). The young man's decency and love for family – and the incongruity of such a sensitive soul being sent overseas to kill an unknown and largely unseen enemy – shine through in his correspondence. When we ultimately learn his fate, it is hard not to feel like we've lost someone we know.

The next two letter writers were more fortunate. They survived, but not without scars. Like Private Bradley, Lieut. Mackenzie Bird, called "Jim" in the army (who was briefly a captain), while only 23, fought a ground war, but one much different from that experienced by his predecessor. His was a war not of trenches and attrition but of aggressive advances against the Nazis in Italy. At first, young Bird opposed war. But when he saw what Adolf Hitler was up to in Europe, conquering countries and enslaving their peoples, he saw the need to fight. And fight he did. Combining the hunting and shooting skills passed on by his father, Dr. F.V. Bird, and those taught by the army, Mac served as a model soldier, one committed to the fight, convinced of his side's moral right, and effective in his work. He survived, which is the ultimate goal of a soldier, but he also weakened the opponent to a degree far out of proportion to what he was – one man. Like most of his peers he won no special citations, no fancy honours, though perhaps he should have. His testimony, shared in tape-recorded conversation with nephews Bruce and Brad, is a rare and riveting account of a soldier's life:

being on patrol, taking prisoners, de-mining fields, killing the enemy. What others have shied away from Mac Bird openly reveals, for, as he says, he thinks it vital for people to understand exactly how horrific war can be, in order that they avoid it whenever possible. The fight for freedom is the only reason he can see for killing one's fellow man in this legalized institution of mass murder. His thoughts on Canada's role in Afghanistan will also be of interest.

Mac Bird's brother, Frederick Charles Clayton Bird (known as Clay), then 24, fought a different war still, one from the air. As the pilot of a Halifax four-engine bomber, Clayton Bird flew 34 operations over Occupied France and Germany in 1944. He'd always wanted to be a pilot, from the time as a boy when he heard about Charles Lindberg's first solo flight across the Atlantic in May of 1927, in the famous monoplane Spirit of St. Louis. The war allowed Bird's dream, and that of thousands of other young men in North America and Europe who wanted to fly, to come true. Like those of his younger brother, Clayton's letters start out upbeat and confident, but segue into a sordid sullenness and depression as time marches on and the harsh realties of war take hold. Separation from his new bride only two months after their marriage, when he is posted to England, underlies his worries, as she has a difficult time without him. A year of instructing – teaching other young men from all over the Commonwealth to fly – preceded his actual tour of operations, or "ops" as they were called. And since it wasn't clear that he would be sent to fight at all (the reason they all enlisted), his frustrations come through, as do issues of physical ailments linked to his work. Mac also had war-related physical problems. Unexpected by both, however, were the emotional and intellectual hurdles they had to surmount at the end, owing, we now know but didn't fully grasp then, to the stress of their service.

And service it was. A fine record of service attaches to both Birds. These are role models for today's youth, men who did their duty to Crown and country, stood by their comrades, lived by their principles, returned to civilian life and made their marks at home as family men and community leaders. The good name that Canada has today was forged by men like these and millions of their like-minded contemporaries. It is right that we honour their contributions by reading their thoughts and stories and remembering their concerns, their struggles, their sacrifices – but also their joys and triumphs.

Section Three, War Reporting, takes a different look at war. Here we have one man's experiences in the field of freelance foreign corresponding.

It follows the editor of this book from Kosovo in 2000, where he went on patrols with Canadian troops, to southeast Turkey and the Kurdish conflict, to Georgia and the search for Chechen refugees who fled from the war with Russia. It also looks back at his initial forays in the Western Sahara in 1987, when he traveled with the Polisario guerrillas who fought to free their land from Moroccan occupation. The focus is on the people he meets, civilians and soldiers. Through interviews and informal chats he reveals their hopes and struggles. From there we travel to Algeria, Tunisia, Malta, Libya (a rare visit by a Canadian journalist) and Egypt. This section provides a good glimpse into the life – the travels, triumphs and tribulations -- of an overseas correspondent. For this Bird, war reporting means giving voice to people struggling with life-and-death issues and is, to him, one of the more important branches of journalism. He's glad to have done what he did.

In short, *My Dear Boy* tells of an old Canadian family's multi-faceted service in time of war. We trust it will find some use among those interested in the fields of conflict studies and journalism. Having earned a master's degree in Political Studies in International Relations (U of M 2005, with a thesis on the war in southeast Turkey), as well as an MA in Journalism (Western Ontario 1984), the editor's own interest in these fields is keen. The letters in particular are valuable sources of primary research. Clayton Bradley's are 95 years old; the Bird brothers', 65. To the family members who preserved them and/or gave permission to use them (Mr. and Mrs. F.V. Bird, Clayton and Mac Bird) we extend our gratitude; for without their efforts, this book would not have been possible.

Brad Bird

INTRODUCTION

The Birds in this book are descendants of James Curtis Bird, who was born in England about 1773. He sailed as a youth to what became Manitoba, Canada. There are many Birds in Canada and the United States, especially in Montana and Saskatchewan, descended from James Curtis. Maybe there was something in the bannock, or something special in his loins, for he sired 19 or more children with his two or three wives (the record is uncertain as to the exact number of his native wives) and set the stage for the story about to be told.

Bird was born in Acton, Middlesex County, now part of London, in an era of great voyages and conflicts. Under King George III, England won the Seven Years' War (which concluded 10 years before his birth) but also lost the American colonies in the American War of Independence (1775 -1783). The Hudson's Bay Company, formed by Royal Charter in 1670, provided many youth with a chance to escape the often stifling poverty and horrible working conditions of Industrial Revolution England. There is rumour that James Curtis was a bastard, born out of wedlock, and we hope it's true, as it adds some spice to the account. In any case the lad of 15 years signed a contract with the HBC on April 23, 1788 and landed on the stony shores of Hudson Bay at York Factory later that year. This was 12 years after America's Declaration of Independence.

At the time, an estimated million or so Indians, as they were then known, or Aboriginal people as we say today, populated the entire expanse of what became Canada. Today, the City of Winnipeg has almost the same population. Toronto and Montreal have three or more times as many people as the entire country had in 1788. And so the continent to

1

which young Bird emigrated was green in a way we can only dream about today, its early peoples living in tribal units and by the chase, rudimentary agriculture, the fur trade, or some combination thereof.

The economic driver of the time was the fur trade, and to this young Bird devoted himself. A tenet of the trade was that to do well, one must link up with the local population, and what better way than to marry into it? Indeed as Sylvia Van Kirk notes in her excellent book *Many Tender Ties*, the fur trade was not simply an economic activity "but a social and cultural complex that was to survive for nearly two centuries." Having a native woman as your wife not only connected you to the trappers and food providers necessary for survival and success in the business; it also provided you with love and family. And if you fell ill, nobody knew more than the native peoples about plant-based remedies. Indeed the whole point was to stay well, and in this they also excelled. In winter especially in these pre-Wall-Mart days, a young HBC clerk needed a native wife to make him warm clothes and do sundry other tasks necessary to one's comfort and survival.

And so young James married Mary, a Swampy Cree Indian born in 1777, "after the custom of the country," meaning without clergy. Swampy Cree is a dialect of the Cree language spoken in what became northeastern Manitoba. James Curtis later married, also in the country way, a Cree lady he named Elizabeth, after his mother. Bird began with the HBC as a writer, what we'd call a clerk, and would spend hours adding sums and the like. After some years, in 1792, at age 19 or 20, he was sent inland with William Tomison, the HBC chief inland officer, to Cumberland House, Manchester House (near Standard Hill, Sask.) and Buckingham House (near Lingbergh, Alta.), likely with his new wife.

He rose quickly in the company. The following year he was put in charge of South Branch House on the Saskatchewan River, near Batoche, succeeding William Walker. In 1794 he established a post at Nepawi, near Nipawin, Saskatchewan, to compete with the nearby North West Company post. Explorer David Thompson mentions meeting him at Cumberland House on June 23, 1797. By 1800 he was at Edmonton House. There he directed the HBC's move farther up the Saskatchewan River to build Action House near their rival NWC's post at Rocky Mountain House. Bird also organized the 1799 expedition by Peter Fiddler north to the Beaver River and Lac la Biche, where Greenwich House was established.

The London committee of the HBC found Bird's efforts to extend HBC trade "most pleasing" and in 1803 placed him in charge of the inland

posts from Cumberland House, near the current Manitoba border, to the
Rocky Mountains, to succeed Tomison.

Here's a summary of what followed:

1803 – 1813	In charge of Inland Posts at Edmonton
1813 – 1816	Chief of District in Edmonton
1816 – 1817	Chief of District in Carlton House
1817 – 1818	Acting Governor of Rupert's Land

This last posting, Acting Governor, requires an explanation. He
assumed this role after Governor Robert Semple was killed at The Battle of
Seven Oaks, which took place on June 19, 1816 in what is now Winnipeg.
As a result of a dispute between the Hudson's Bay Company and the North
West Company, Miles Macdonell, the Governor of Red River Colony
issued an order called the Pemmican Proclamation which made it illegal
to export food from the Colony. His rationale was that the Earl of Selkirk
had set up a colony of settlers on Red River and all provisions were to be
kept for them. In fact he was trying to hurt the rival company and give
the HBC a monopoly on trade. He was also trying to dampen activity by
the fiercely independent Métis, the mixed-blood people who emerged from
white-Indian marriages. The Métis did not acknowledge the authority of
the Red River Settlement, and this stand was probably consistent with the
Royal Proclamation of 1763. The pemmican proclamation was a blow to
both the Métis and NWC, and it led to trouble.

In 1815 Macdonell resigned as governor of the Colony and was replaced
by Robert Semple, an American businessman with no experience in the fur
trade. In 1816 a band of Métis led by Cuthbert Grant seized a supply of the
Company's pemmican (which had been stolen from the Métis) and were
traveling to a meeting with traders of the NWC to whom they intended to
sell it. They were met by Semple and a group of HBC men and settlers, near
Fort Douglas along the Red River at a location called Seven Oaks. Semple
argued with several of the Métis and a gunfight ensued. Although early
reports state that it was the Métis who fired the first shot, it may have been
one of Semple's men who did so. Semple and his group were outnumbered
nearly three to one. The Métis killed 21 men, including Semple, while they
themselves suffered one fatality. They were later exonerated by a Royal
Commissioner who investigated.

Bird was named Acting Governor, and if the editor's high school History teacher had taken his lesson of the Battle of Seven Oaks one step further, he might have found a living link to the event sitting in his class. But he didn't. E. H. Oliver said the posting was "Superintendent of the Northern Department" rather than Acting Governor. There is some suggestion that his doubtful parentage got in the way of a full governorship, while one historian claims Bird's temperament was a problem. Whatever the case, he was effectively in charge of the region for two years.

In 1818, with the appointment of a new governor, Bird resumed his old post as Chief of District from Cumberland House. In 1820 he became Chief Factor at The Forks post (now Winnipeg) on the Red River. He retired on June 1, 1824. Considered by HBC Governor George Simpson as a "principal settler," Bird received a grant of land of 1,245 acres on the east side of the Red River, land which later became Birds Hill Park.

This is corroborated by a letter of Oct. 11, 1930, by the Manitoba provincial librarian to Anne McDonnell of the Historical Society of Montana, in which he notes that he spoke the previous day to James Roderick Bird of Hodgson, Manitoba, then or formerly superintendent of Northern Indian Reserves. Bird said his grandfather in retirement "took up land on the Red River, several miles below Fort Garry – his land extended back from the river to a height which is still known as Birds Hill." Another relative, a Mrs. Cowan, in *Women of the Red River*, said Bird had "3,000 acres extending back to Birds Hill."

Even in retirement James Bird was busy. He had been appointed a justice of the peace for the Indian territories in 1815, and from 1835 to 1845 was receiver of import and export duties and again, justice of the peace. He was also appointed a councilor of Assiniboia in 1839 and held this post until his death in 1856.

As a fur trader James Bird had been a key figure in the HBC's success in the Saskatchewan District. Colin Roberson noted in 1819 that Bird had "more knowledge of the internal arrangements of this country than all the officers put together." Nevertheless, "a high opinion of his own importance and a strong sense of self-interest, together with excessive caution and vindictiveness, marred both his career and his retirement," according to one historian, John E. Foster. "In 1820, in what was not an isolated incident," he writes, "the London committee found fault with Bird, noting that 'jealous feelings – and fancied slights and injuries' had clouded his better judgment. At Red River, in spite of his social prominence, Foster claims, he was not held in high regard. He was known to have physically chastised an elderly servant [and] to have harshly dismissed and sued for breach of contract an indiscreet serving maid...."

"Bird had married," Foster continues, according to the custom of the country, more than one Indian woman, possibly polygynously (more than one wife at once -- a sin to the white race but perfectly honourable and practical to the natives) before marrying "an Indian, Elizabeth, at Red River on 30 March 1821." According to another source, *The Selkirk Settlers of Red River and Their Descendants 1812 – 1992*, Bird and "Mary Indian" were married according to the custom of the country circa 1797, while he and Elizabeth were married about 1806. He married Elizabeth again, formally in a Christian ceremony, on 30 March 1821 in Red River.

Whatever the truth about the number of his marriages, the fact is James Bird fathered a large number of children, many of whom, including James, are mentioned in the parish registers of the Colony. Elizabeth died in the fall of 1834 and was buried on November 1. Like his fur-trade colleagues in retirement, Bird then sought an English wife. On January 22, 1835, in what seemed to some indecent haste, he married Mrs. Mary Lowman, the widowed governess of the Female Seminary and the only available white woman at the time. She received a grant of 2,500 pounds sterling in trust from Bird before this marriage, prompting some to claim she'd been bought. But this wasn't an uncommon arrangement. Mrs. Lowman, by the way, brought the first piano into the Canadian west. The social standing of the couple rose after their union.

But some were scornful. A contemporary of Bird's, Donald Ross, who was also an historian, wrote to James Hargrave on March 13, 1835: "You may easily conceive my surprise, nay vexation too – when I found our children's governess had changed both her name and her condition – the former Mrs. Lowman having become in fact the present Mrs. Bird; that old shriveled bag of bones having purchased this fresh morsel of frail humanity, soul and body, for the sum of three thousand pounds sterling [in fact 2,500 pounds], good and lawful money of Great Britain, made over to her and her heirs forever: - an old man's lust, is surely, 'that worm which never dies.'"

Do we detect some envy here?

The marriage obviously found favour with the Company, and those ruling Red River, because in 1836 Bird was appointed registrar for land sales and grants.

At his death Bird left an estate, excepting real property, valued at just under 4,000 pounds, the bulk of which was left to his daughter and son by his last marriage, Eliza Margaret and Curtis James. Jimmy Jock got nothing, which probably left him somewhat disappointed, as he had stayed in periodic touch with his father. James Curtis also had extensive land and cattle, among other real property. The village of Birds Hill, near the Bird property northeast of Winnipeg, takes its name from James Bird. Today, Birds Hill Provincial Park is appreciated by thousands of visitors annually.

J. C. Bird died in Red River Settlement on Oct. 18, 1856, at the age of 83.

* * *

Now, his children. There were a great many, but only two made names for themselves.

Jimmy Jock Bird

With Mary, James Curtis had 16 offspring, including James Bird Jr. or Jimmy Jock (1798 or 1800 - 15 Dec.1892), who went on to fame as a fur trader, interpreter, and Blackfoot chief. Jimmy Jock's life has been documented by John C. Jackson in his book *Jemmy Jock Bird, Marginal Man on the Blackfoot Frontier*. "Caught between the opposing sides of a dual heritage, Bird situated himself firmly in both worlds," the book relates. "Hired as an undercover confidential servant [of the HBC], he crossed into U.S. territory to bring furs taken by Cree and Piegan hunters to his British employers. Later he served both nations, and his tribal friends, in the negotiations of the 1855 Blackfoot peace treaty and the 1877 Canadian Treaty 7."

Jimmy Jock, or Jemmy Jock, was a war chief during the height of the Blackfoot nation's power; a practical joker who loved a good laugh; and a good interpreter who spoke seven native tongues. He was kind to his friends and ruthless with his enemies. "Bird spent the first 41 years of his life as a complete outdoor man," Jackson writes, "always on the move, living by the hunt, accepting responsibility for the well-being of his family and the security of his band."

Jimmy-Jock Bird

He was sent to England to study as a youth but didn't like it there and returned. About 1820, near the time of union of the two rival fur companies, HBC and Northwest Company, Bird was sent to open trade with the Blackfoot. He found he preferred their way of life and joined them. The HBC, after all, employed some very unsavoury characters, and didn't always treat their people well. About 1825 he married Sarah "Sally" Piegan, daughter of The Bull's Heart, a Blackfoot chief, in a union that bonded him to the tribe. For more, see the *Winnipeg Free Press* story about Jimmy Jock from 1930 in the Appendix.

Jimmy Jock went on to earn quite a reputation. Consistent with the ethic of the West, where organized law was unknown until much later, he would use violence when necessary, such as at Fort Hall in 1836, "with the colorful chief joining in the action by personally scalping one of his victims," according to Grant MacEwan in *Métis Makers of History*. The Blackfoot nation were among the most feared warriors of the plains, and it is certain that Bird would have proven himself in battle before rising to such a trusted position as war chief. It wasn't only a man's ability to kill the enemy and protect the tribe that earned him such a position; he also had to be a good provider, and generous with his harvest from the chase. Had Bird not been kind to those in need, he would never have attained such trust among the tribe. One should consider with skepticism the white man's attacks on his character, for Bird indeed had little use for the hypocrisy of white culture and often didn't present his best side in white company.

The artist Paul Kane was an exception. Kane found Jimmy Jock in temporary charge of Rocky Mountain House when he visited there in April 1848. Though missionaries had little respect for Jimmy Jock and gave him a bad reputation, Kane found him hospitable and trustworthy. He told the artist he'd been sent out by the Company many years before to learn the Blackfoot language and help with trade, but he had married a chief's daughter and liked the wild life so well he left the service to live with the Indians. Kane learned much of the customs of the Piegan tribe from Jimmy Jock who had lived with them for about 30 years. Thomas Pambrun, son of Pierre, called the tall and athletic Bird, with his long flowing tresses, "undoubtedly the finest specimen of a man I ever saw.....He had women and children in every tribe and wherever he headed was victorious. The association with his name was enough. He was therefore courted by all, even by the company who paid him stipulated sums in good annually to keep peace." Pambrun noted that Bird was known to go as far south as Snake River near Fort Boise in Idaho.

The late MacEwan notes it was as an interpreter that Jimmy Jock made his name on both sides of the border. Good interpreters were scarce and much desired, and Bird was in demand. He exasperated Rev. Robert Rundle, the first Protestant missionary in the Northwest, and Father de Smet of the Catholic faith, for sometimes he misled them for his own amusement. Bird was known to "hate everything connected with the French or the Canadians," including their religion. Given the scandals even today in organized religion, one can understand old Bird's position.

The Blackfoot Indians lived lives of great uncertainty. Starvation, sickness, attacks from other tribes – all could come without warning, as John C. Ewers writes in *The Blackfeet, Raiders On the Northwestern Plains*. Yet the Blackfeet did not face these dangers alone. They believed they were surrounded by supernatural powers much stronger than human ones which they could call upon for protection from evil influences, and to aid them in their own undertakings. The religion James Bird Jr. embraced, then, was far different from that of the white man, and it made better sense to him. As Ewers writes:

> These powers resided in the skies and in the waters, as well as on land. Sun and thunder were the most powerful sky spirits. Beaver and otter were potent underwater ones. Buffalo, bears, elk, horses, snakes, eagles, crows and other animals and birds of the Blackfoot country also could communicate their powers to humans.

For Bird and his Blackfoot peers, supernatural power was given to men in dreams by an animal, bird, or power of nature (such as thunder), who appeared and spoke. The spirit told him about certain objects sacred to it and explained how to care for them. These comprised the contents of his personal medicine bundle. These sacred bundles were symbols of power, not the power itself. Unless a person transferred their power by formal transfer, they retained it until death. Even it if were lost or stolen, the person could replace the contents. Even today, many people embrace these beliefs. This is but a brief account of the Blackfoot spirituality, but it helps us understand why Bird would dismiss Christianity. It didn't fit the Blackfoot culture, lifestyle or value system.

Returning to Bird's work as an interpreter, in September 1877 he filled in for Jerry Potts, who often didn't do justice in his translations to all that was said. Potts also liked to drink, which didn't enhance his effectiveness during the signing of Blackfoot Treaty No. 7. It is a credit to Jimmy Jock that in all the references about him, none suggests he ever drank. As Lieut. Governor David Laird reported: "The Commissioners at first had not a good interpreter of the Blackfoot language but Wednesday they secured the services of Mr. Bird, a brother of the late Dr. Bird of Winnipeg. He had been many years among the Piegans and Blackfeet, and is a very intelligent interpreter." At that point Jimmy Jock was 79 years old.

W. H. Cox of the Royal Canadian Mounted Police noted in his diary of 1889 that James Bird, "known as Jimmy Jock in the north country," came to Piegan and stayed all winter. "We were told to give him rations and treat him well as he had been of some use to the government in the making of the treaty with the Blackfoot," Cox wrote. "He was very old and blind. His wife, an old Cree woman, used to drive around from one reserve to another all over the country, even to Montana, with a Red River cart, the old man sitting in the back, the old woman driving. He asked me if I would always put a piece of liver in his pack as it was good for his complaint. He said, 'The old woman used to chew my food, but her teeth is no good now. A friend of mine in Prince Albert made me a present of a food chopper and I find it very convenient.'" This comes from a collection of papers compiled by Ruth Silde of Prince Albert, daughter of May Bird, granddaughter of John Thomas ('Jack') Bird, Oct. 25, 1850 – Dec.18, 1946. Jack Bird carried freight by oxcart and dog sled from Winnipeg to Prince Albert and later was a butcher. Silde credits June Kelly and Millie Bird, "kindred spirits" who helped in the task of starting a family history.

In the end, after a life of adventure, Jimmy Jock wandered the prairie alone, blind and incapacitated, with his last remaining wife. He spent his final days on Two Medicine River in Montana, some eight miles south of Browning near the Holy Family Mission and school. There he would have heard the children's laughter and smelled the baking bread. He would have considered the great days of the chase, when bison covered the plains, when he hunted and fought and traveled vast distances with his Blackfoot friends, living as free as the wind. Far into the north he ventured, and deep into the south. Freedom to travel and paddle one's own canoe has always been important to Birds, even those of today.

In the months before his death, in the spring of 1892, Thomas Bird, a grandson of Jimmy Jock and son of Philip Bird, had gone with his uncle and foster-father, Tom Bird, to Carlton, Saskatchewan, to bring his grandparents back to Montana. His grandmother, Jimmy Jock's wife, a sister of Three Suns, a Blackfoot chief, died on the journey at Calgary.

Thomas Bird stayed with his grandfather in the tepee in Montana to look after him and was with him when he died on Dec. 11, 1892. His coffin was made from the planks of his Red River cart, as lumber was scarce. He was placed in the Holy Family Mission cemetery. No stone or marker has survived. When cousin Roy Bird visited in June of 2010 there was no mention of James Bird Jr. When Bil Bird came by a month later, a sign at the cemetery entrance announced that he was buried there. Today, the surrounding area looks much like it would have when Jimmy Jock was alive -- wind-swept, grassy and lonely.

Photo by Brad Bird, taken in 1996, of Holy Family Mission Cemetery

Dr. Curtis James Bird

The other notable son of James Curtis Bird was Dr. Curtis James Bird (1 Feb. 1838 – 13 June 1876). Born at Marchmount House on the Bird estate in Middlechurch in the Red River Settlement to his white wife, Mary Lowman, C. J. Bird was educated at St. John's College and took his medical course at Guy's Hospital, London. He returned to Red River where he lived on the Bird estate, later moving to the new city of Winnipeg. He succeeded Dr. Bunn as coroner in 1861 and held this position successively under the Council of Assiniboia, Louis Riel's provisional government, and the Province of Manitoba.

As W. D. Smith writes, at one point during the provisional government Bird, concerned over the loss of life among the poor in the Red River Settlement, proposed a type of Medicare program whereby two publicly supported surgeries, or clinics, would be set up. This promising idea would find full fruition a century later, under the stewardship of Tommy Douglas, so Bird was very much a man ahead of his time.

Dr. C. J. Bird

Dr. Bird's political career began with his appointment to the Council of Assiniboia January 23, 1868. He served on the council until its dissolution at the outbreak of the Red River disturbances in the fall of 1868. During the unrest he was twice elected to represent the people of St. Paul's parish. In the fall of 1869 he was chosen to meet with representatives of the other communities to decide whether a provisional government should be formed. In January 1870 he was a delegate at the meeting that decided a "list of rights" should be presented to the government of Canada. In the convention that met from 25 January to February 1870, Dr. Bird was selected to serve on the committee of six to draft such a list, its other members being James Ross, Thomas Bunn (son of Dr. Bunn), Louis Schmidt, Charles Nolan and Louis Riel.

Dr. Bird was a businessman as well as a doctor. He operated the Apothecaries Hall, located at Main Street and Bannatyne Avenue, in the early 1870s. The first soda fountain in the Canadian West was installed in Bird's store in 1873, according to *The History of Pharmacy in Manitoba* by Dougald McDougall.

After the creation of the province of Manitoba in 1870, Dr. Bird continued his life in politics. He was nominated for the federal constituency of Lisgar in opposition to Dr. John Christian Schultz; he was also nominated for the provincial constituency of Baie de Saint-Paul. Following his victory in the provincial election of 30 December 1870, Bird withdrew from the federal campaign. He was re-elected in the same constituency in 1874 and remained a member of the Legislative Assembly of Manitoba until his death.

On February 5, 1873, Dr. Bird was elected speaker of the assembly and held this position until 1874. It was this role which brought him trouble. Early in 1872, a move began to obtain the incorporation of Winnipeg. This was led, in part, by a man named Francis Cornish. Ruth Swan writes as follows for the Manitoba Historical Society:

> An Orangeman from London, Ontario, Cornish emigrated to Manitoba in 1872 amid rumours of political scandal and corruption. Although he had an able reputation as a lawyer, Cornish had been accused of 'bigamy, assault, drunkenness and boisterous public disputes', and of padding the ballot boxes when he was elected Mayor of London. Cornish left his wife behind when he came out west, but not his bad habits, for he was soon involved in anti-French, anti-Catholic and anti-establishment shenanigans.

Soon after his arrival at Red River Colony, Cornish began agitating amongst the "Canadian" (Ontario) immigrants who were angry at not being entitled to vote in the federal election of 1872. They hadn't been there long enough to fulfill residency requirements. As Swan relates, "on voting day a group of Orangemen ransacked the St. Boniface polling station and burned the poll book. They fought a group of unarmed Métis with wooden wheel spokes and then returned to Winnipeg 'crazed with excitement and liquor'." Cornish sprang onto the back of a wagon on Main Street and harangued the mob, insulting the Governor, the head of the Hudson's Bay Company and the Sheriff. Indeed, Cornish played a prominent role in what became the "September riots," during which the offices of three newspapers were also ransacked. To the rising number of "Canadians" at Red River, he was a hero.

The bulk of the population remained Métis, or half-breed, and most were illiterate and unsophisticated politically, which is why they selected Louis Riel to lead them in their rebellions. He had been to school and was an intellectual; on the downside, Riel never in his life shot a bison or took part in a Métis battle, so Riel was not a well-rounded Métis man. Most Métis had taken part in armed fights with the Sioux and others. Not Riel. This hurt the Métis cause, because he didn't see fit to allow his lieutenant, the highly capable Gabriel Dumont (who *had* fought the Sioux), a free hand to attack Canadian troops in 1885, using guerrilla tactics. If he had, there is little doubt the Métis would have won military victories and wrested valuable political concessions from Ottawa. As it was, the Métis were defeated militarily, Riel was hanged, and a good people – the first true Canadians in the west, since they came from nowhere else -- found themselves belittled, leaderless and marginalized. Riel said he reined in Dumont because he'd seen enough bloodshed. But it was an armed rebellion, one step shy of civil war.

The incorporation of Winnipeg became a bit of a war, too, with strong emotions on both sides. One editorial writer wrote that "in the matter of incorporation, some people seem to be getting almost crazy. They seem to imagine that it only requires incorporation to make the hamlet of Winnipeg jump into a great … commercial city. For our part we cannot see it."

In November of 1872 it was decided at a public meeting (likely dominated by immigrants from Ontario and the U.S.) that an Act of Incorporation was necessary. Schultz, who was another prominent Orangeman from Ontario, and Cornish were among those in favour. A committee was appointed to draft a bill, which was introduced in the legislature Feb. 19, 1873.

The bill met with opposition and obstruction, as some feared, with good reason, taxes and onerous rules if it went through. In second reading, an amendment of "Assiniboia" for Winnipeg carried. Next day, when the house met, the amendment naming the city Assiniboia was defeated. It was then moved that "Garry" be substituted (it failed), then "Selkirk." This carried. To this bill the legislative council attached amendments which impinged upon the provincial government's taxing powers; Dr. Bird, as speaker, declared the bill out of order. Since a new bill could not be presented until the next session in November, the proponents were infuriated by his action.

Early in the morning of March 7, 1873, Dr. Bird was lured from his house on the pretext that a patient needed medical aid. While driving in his cutter to the patient's home, he was attacked, dragged from his cutter, and soaked with coal oil. This was a particularly heinous act, as coal oil clogs the pores and can kill. Bird would never fully recover. Though the government of Manitoba promptly offered a reward of $1,000 for information leading to the arrest of the offenders, they were never brought to justice.

In the spring of 1876 Dr. Bird was in poor health; and in the hope that a visit among old friends in England would improve it, he traveled to England. Instead of improving, his health worsened and he died in London on 13 June.

(This was the same year the Sioux destroyed Custer at his last stand at the Little Big Horn, which today is a drive of some hours south of Winnipeg. The truth there, by the way, according to Sioux witnesses, is that many U.S. Cavalrymen committed suicide, fearful of torture if taken alive.)

Did Cornish have a hand in the attack on Dr. Bird? The skullduggery involved was consistent with his *modus operandi*. It wouldn't be at all surprising if Cornish had played a role in the assault, perhaps even led it. No man was ever found responsible for the act. Cornish remained popular among the white Anglo-Saxon Protestants of the area and was elected the first Mayor of Winnipeg in December of 1873. He was also elected to the Manitoba Legislature the next year, and served until his death, at age 47, of stomach cancer. Cornish's father, by the way, was a physician.

A character by the same name, Francis Cornish, is the protagonist in *What's Bred in the Bone*, one of Robertson Davies' finest novels. Davies' Cornish is a painter and art forger; his life doesn't parallel Winnipeg's Cornish, though both were born in Ontario. If memory serves correct, Davies did, however, model his character after a real-life personage. The editor talked to Davies about 1993 when, as book columnist for the *Victoria Times-Colonist*, he interviewed him at the Empress Hotel. Needing a chance to meet the great man, he followed Davies to a restroom during the banquet and pulled up to the urinal beside him, introducing himself and asking for time with him later. "Of course," Davies said, granting him a full interview afterwards. Since he didn't know about the Bird-Cornish connection at the time, he didn't ask him if his fictional character had anything to do with Winnipeg's first mayor. The famous man of Canadian letters died a year or two later in 1995, age 82.

* * *

But enough sleuthing. What concerns us most for our purposes here are James Curtis Bird's progeny. More than just outlining the family lineage, we're describing the history and character of the Bird family to help the reader understand how Clayton and Mackenzie came to be such fine fighting men. They emerged from a long line of strong, publicly-minded men and women with an affinity for the land and an inclination to stand up for what was right. Their character was very much in their genes (including of course their mothers'), though it was certainly burnished by environment. Clayton and Mackenzie were Métis, one-quarter Cree, though this was hushed up in their youth. It's no wonder the boys fished and hunted and roamed in and around Turtle Mountain; it was in their blood.

But let's be clear: though they sympathized with the Métis, as adults they considered themselves Canadians first. They fought as Canadians for Canada; and when they returned to raise families they did so not as marginalized Métis people but as proud members of the mainstream society. Their father, who leapt from log cabin in 1885 to a doctor's accreditation 28 years later, is the most remarkable story in this regard. In one lifetime he bridged both cultures, native and white, modeling the best aspects of each. This contrasts sharply with his great-uncle Jimmy Jock, who embraced the native and rejected the white. Driven by steely ambition, Dr. Bird served thousands and shaped for himself and his family a satisfying life. In his own way, as a tribal chief, Jimmy Jock Bird also served a large community, the Blackfeet people, extremely well. If we're all here for a purpose, then Fred Bird and Jimmy Jock clearly lived theirs.

James Curtis and Mary, the Swampy Cree, produced Henry (1805-1893), who married Harriet Calder. Henry was Dr. F. V. Bird's paternal grandfather. If Henry was born in 1805, then he would have lived at Cumberland House, on the Saskatchewan River, as his father was in charge of all the HBC posts by 1803 between Cumberland and the Rockies. Henry would have lived in Carlton House when his father was in charge there in 1816-17. These were isolated wilderness points, bitter cold in winter, glorious in summer, where hunting and rough chores were part of growing up.

Even today, they remain out-of-the-way places. In Cumberland House many continue to trap and fish for a living, as they did in the 1800s. There is but one road in, 100 kilometres of gravel. Bil Bird visited the community and spoke with several residents who were helpful; Brad, living in nearby

The Pas in 1988-92 and working for the *Opasquia Times*, wrote an award-winning series of newspaper articles based on interviews with people in Cumberland House about how the nearby hydro dam harmed their trapping and fishing livelihoods. Carlton House is similarly isolated.

Henry was well into middle age when his wife, Harriet Calder, gave birth to John James in 1845. At this time the Red River Settlement was little more than prairie grass as far as the eye could see with a few buildings strewn about from Upper Fort Garry to Lower Fort Garry, a distance of some 10 miles. The English occupied the west bank and the French, the east, of the Red River. Ferries dotted the rivers, both the Red and the Assiniboine, for miles. Even today, notches in the banks can be seen where the ferries tied up out of the pull of the current.

John James Bird.

Henry passed away in St. Andrews, and is buried in the St. Andrews Anglican Church cemetery, along with his wife, Harriet (1809-1889). They were married at St. John's Anglican Church in the Red River Settlement, October 28, 1824. It is likely that Dr. Bird knew his grandfather; however, there are no records, letters, or stories passed down to confirm that. Nor do we know where John James lived as a child. It is apparent that Henry was a farmer, probably owning land near the Red River. The Red River Academy and other schools existed while John James was a child. He likely attended one of these.

John James towered over most of his contemporaries. Our father, Clayton, remembers meeting his grandfather in the 1920s and thinking he was a mountain of a man. There are reports that he stood 6'6", and his older sons stood as tall. (Bil's second son, Ryker, stood 6'6".) John James' eighth child, Fred, our grandfather, stood 5'11." He told us that his father didn't interfere when the older, bigger boys beat up the younger, smaller ones. From what we have heard, John James was a hard man in many ways.

He owned Lot 70 on the west bank of the Red River, two lots south of Hay Road. It is possible that this is the same lot that his father owned because, although John James was the sixth-born child to Henry and Harriet, he was the first boy. First-born boys usually inherited the family farm. The Bird lot ran west from the river for some distance into bush and prairie grass. The farm house and cultivated land remained close to the river.

Dr. Frederick Valentine Bird

In June of 1871 John James married Margaret Peebles, the daughter of a Scot who had taken a Cree wife. Margaret was born in 1845, which means she was 40 when she gave birth to Fred, her eighth child, on Aug. 30, 1885.

In an undated notebook Dr. Bird wrote that he was born "on the west bank of the beloved old Red River, quite close to old St. Andrew's Anglican Church. This was my people's church. The reader will note the year, 1885, the year of the North West Rebellion in which my father took part in repressing. The leader of the rebels was Louis Riel, who was captured and after summary trial executed in Regina, also in 1885. In fairness I think the rebellion was caused by failure of the government land-surveyors to explain to the French Métis the real purpose of the survey – the French Métis thought they were going to be pushed off their holdings."

"I well remember my earliest childhood days – our home was ... close to Lower Fort Garry which was to the south. Our home was within a few rods of one of my uncle's, James Reid, a retired chief factor of the Hudson's Bay Company. How I loved playing around and about the two homes. Around my uncle Reid's home was a lovely stockade fence about two and a half feet high and I loved finding and keeping pieces of broken crockery – most of it had a sort of Royal blue colour design. Royal blue has always been my favourite colour."

Fred's mother was born on the way down from York Factory in 1844, "perhaps along the Hayes River or Lake Winnipeg, and she died in 1939," Bird wrote. "My parents were married at St. Andrews. They had the following children: Henry James, John, David Edwin, Mary Louise, Andrew, Hannah Margaret, Charles Calder, Frederick Valentine, Walter Benjamin, Rose Alice and Harriet the latter two being twins."

Life on lot 70 in a log house wasn't easy. When Fred was little their barn burned down. "I was only five years of age when one morning I came down from my bed in eager anticipation of breakfast – I well remember seeing my mother standing and looking out one of the west windows – when she heard me come into the kitchen she turned and said, 'I am afraid it will be a sad breakfast this morning'; and I said why, mom: and she said, 'Come and look.' I did, and out beyond across the snow-covered ground I could see carcass after carcass of all our cattle and horses. All had been burned to death during the night when through some unknown cause our barn burned to the ground.

Fred Bird and his mother

"When the winter gave way to summer, my father proceeded to build us a temporary home where he homesteaded in the Clandeboye and Petersfield district – all unorganized at this time. (The temporary home was later replaced by a substantial one in which John James died, on Jan. 2, 1933, at age 90.) In early fall, my father brought us to our new home to make a fresh start."

The fresh start involved clearing land of its aspen, bur oak and ash, using a team of oxen. Over the years, Fred helped his brothers and father in this labour. (In fact he saved the horns from one of the oxen, and they used to hang in his Boissevain office. They measured 39 inches from tip to tip.)

The new district soon opened up with other families coming in to locate, so the need of a school became of primary importance. John James Bird assisted in organizing what was called Norwood School and for many years acted as its secretary-treasurer. It was this school, starting at the age of seven or eight years of age, that Fred attended. Like so many others, he and his siblings walked almost a mile to get there, "summer and winter, rain, snow or blizzard," he wrote. "And I took my appointed turn, in which we went to the school earlier each morning in order to make the fire in the iron-box stove, using wood; we had to see that school was properly warmed up in time for classes. For this we were paid five cents each morning – a rather handsome remuneration."

Fred held a special place in his heart for older brother Andrew, one of the giants. Bil Bird, Clayton's eldest son, grew up hearing a story of how Fred got into medicine. Andrew came down with typhoid fever and died in 1900, age 23. Andrew's headstone lists typhoid as the cause of death. Fred was so devastated at the loss of his favourite brother that he determined to study medicine to help prevent others from succumbing to disease. Family living still in the area shared another story: Andrew and an older brother had a quarrel – Andrew lost the argument, and his life. Fred was 15 at the time of Andrew's death and

Believed to be Charlie Bird

surely would have known the true cause of his brother's passing.

For various reasons, Fred chose medicine – or perhaps medicine chose him. He writes: "To me there was a charming incident – it happened on that lovely morning when I was about set to start to school on my first morning. I was 7 or 8 years of age; I was all ready and I well remember my elder sister Mary placing a cheap five-cent scribbler, a lead pencil, a wooden framed slate, and the old clay pencil in my grasp when she said to me: 'Now Fred, you are starting to school, and what are you going to be?

Without hesitation I replied, 'a doctor.' I had already formed my resolution to become a doctor from seeing the two doctors in our town of Selkirk – I thought they represented the highest of all callings in life as I saw it in my childhood."

Given his age, one wonders how much he'd seen those doctors at work. They would have come out to tend to his siblings and parents on rare occasions. Another story concerns his mother and her influence. One day when she was ill she instructed Fred, about 14 at the time, to bring a certain herb from the fields. When she recovered from drinking the preparation, Fred was so impressed he decided to learn more and to become a doctor. Much later Fred had the plant analyzed: it contained digitalis, a drug used to treat heart problems.

What would young Fred have done to occupy himself, cut off as he was from even a neighbour? He would have helped around the farm. Usually only the girls were allowed to remain in the house during the day, cleaning, mending, cooking, and setting up for meals. Boys worked outside. Fred would have gathered eggs and fed the chickens in the morning, and made sure gates were shut and locked down throughout the day to prevent animals from grazing in the garden that produced the vegetables the family ate summer and winter. He would have helped milked the cows, when old enough, morning and night.

Fred dreamed under the clouds and laughed when it rained. He may even have cried when storms brought lightning and thunder. He may have offered comfort to his younger sisters, especially if the older boys taunted them and worried them about the storm. These and other things brothers and sisters do and have always done. Evenings, when all the family was indoors and dinner was finished, dishes washed and put away, some might read, others would play cards or board games such as checkers and chess, before the sun retired for the day, and the kids went to sleep in their beds.

What was different for Fred, all his siblings and all children around the world in the 19th Century and before, was that there was no childhood as we know it. A cuddly, comfortable childhood with toys and full days of leisure was a 20th Century invention. In Fred's time, boys especially were valuable tools for helping a family make do, as they continue to be in many parts of the world. When Fred reached the age of nine or 10, his father would have given him more responsibility. He may have been asked to keep the birds from eating the feed grain that was stored in the barn, as Bil was asked to do at the age of 11 by Mr. Elliott, on whose Ontario farm the Clayton Bird family lived. Fred may have been handed a .22 rifle to help him keep the birds away from the grain that would feed the cattle during the winter. This job with the rifle was an excellent introduction for what would later in life become both a means of putting food on the table when there was no store at hand or too little money to buy meat, and a sport in which a man could take great pleasure. (It is possible that Fred used a rifle similar to the one Mr. Elliott handed Bil, an 1898 bolt-action, with which he felled more than 700 birds in about two years. In a letter to his grandparents in 1957, Bil told them about joining the rifle club on the Downsview Air Base in Toronto and achieving a 97% average in prone shooting.)

Fred also would have helped clean out the cattle stalls in the spring. Even 50 years ago farm labour was extremely physical. Fred's dad had no tractor to pile the manure in 1900; he did have many sons who spent days doing that job. The earliest tractors hadn't yet been invented. The automobile only began to catch on in the early 1900s, and then only among the wealthy.

Fred had no indoor plumbing until medical school, about 1909. The farm Bil and family stayed on in Alberta had none either, and that was 1954. He had a pan under the bed to pee in, another contained hot stones which first you put under the covers to heat the bedding, and when you went to bed, you placed the pan under the bed so any more heat might rise and keep the bed a bit warmer overnight. All beds in the house were heated this way as there was no furnace in the house but the kitchen stove. He had a pitcher and basin on a sideboard to wash up in the next morning.

Bil Bird, Clayton's eldest son, a fine swimmer and all-round athlete.
He was born Oct. 15, 1946.

He hauled water from the well outside, before going to bed. He learned how to prime the pump before it would bring water to the surface, using the cup or pail of water present. There is a leather washer around the inner pipe that must be wet, and the container above it full of water, or air will slip past and no water hoisted. The handle of the pump was made for an adult. It took both hands and all Bil's strength to pump long enough on each stroke, and hard enough to bring water up. Then it was simple to fill the pails and bring them into the house for washing and cooking.

Fred did all of this and more. He slept well at night – mind clear from a full day's labour and a body fatigued from the same, and, in the summer, he could not wait for the sun to sink below the horizon before laying his weary body down and sleeping till sun-up, when he did it all over again. School, for some, would bring a welcome relief from the tedium of chores around the farm – until you reached the grade when times-tables arrived, and then many children began to long for the simpler days of home-life! But not Fred. He soaked up every piece of information he could find, studying and learning.

By the time Fred was a teenager, many of his older siblings had left home, married, and were raising their own families. By 1900 Fred's eldest brother, Henry James, was 28, had married Harriet Louis Palan, and had two children with another on the way. The second eldest, John, was 26, had married Euphemia Campbell, and had two children. Next was David Edwin, 25, who had married Christina Mattson, and had six children together. Bil remembers one of his daughters, Dorothy, and visited with her widower, Pat Ramsey, in 2007. Then came Mary Louisa, 22, who married James Edward Foster. They had one child, Edward. Hannah Margaret, 19, married George Edward Patton. Finally there was Charles Calder, 17, and only two years older than Fred.

Fred's younger siblings were Benjamin Walter, 12; Harriet Jane, 10; and Alice Rose, 10, who would marry Bill Engbert.

At school, Fred worked hard but was not an outstanding student, as he admits in his notes. "I had luck and took a grade a year, finally entered high school in Selkirk, where I further had luck in that my principal was that exceptionally fine man and able principal Mr. P. D. Harris. Without his help after school hours and his ever-present inspiration, I could never have made it. By his splendid assistance I finally attained all grades, including my pre-medical with Latin, etc. Because of the heavy fall work on the farm I had to keep at it and was always several weeks late in starting high school each term."

With the older siblings gone, Fred and the younger ones no longer had the older ones to worry about. But they still had their father, and he was a man accustomed to delivering physical abuse. Eventually, Fred's mother separated from JJ. She told him to leave the farm. Mary, her husband James Edward Foster and son Eddie stayed on to manage the land after JJ left. JJ not only had a vile temper, he also drank. He was more brutal when drunk, and, according to family, he was drunk a lot.

But he did help Fred at key points in his life, as did others in the family. "After finishing high school I went to normal school in order to take my third class teacher's certificate. I taught school for two and a half years at $40 a month, but I had great luck again, in that the dear old grandmother and her grandson, at whose house I boarded, gave me lodging and board for $10 a month. I used to go home every Friday evening until Sunday evening."

After two and a half years of teaching he figured he had saved enough money to scrimp through two years at medical school.

"After that I hoped to be able to work each summer to earn enough to complete the last three years – providing of course that I could pass each year. My father and brother on the farm made an agreement with me to the effect, if I worked on ·the farm for the summers until I graduated, they would finance me in medical college for the expected necessary three years. This I agreed to, and enjoyed every year I lived and worked on my father's farm."

Little is known about Bird's years in medical school, so we'll jump ahead.

Dr. Bird's Boissevain Years

In 1913 he graduated well up in his class from Manitoba Medical College in Winnipeg, attached to the University of Manitoba. On the advice of a professor Bird then set himself up in Boissevain, a town of maybe 400 souls south of Brandon, east of Deloraine in the heart of grain and cattle country. Small family farms were numerous in the area, and more people lived on farms than in town. Each farm typically had a dairy cow or two, pigs, chickens, horses, as well as vegetable gardens and crops, so there was great need for children as laborers, and families were large. Given also the physical risks of farming, there was lots of demand for doctors.

"I arrived in Boissevain on May 13, 1913, at 8:45 in the morning as nearly broke financially as it is possible to be," he wrote. "I engaged a boarding house – room only – opened a small and dingy office, all on credit, arranging for meal tickets at the Queens Hotel, and this on credit also. For some time it was disappointing: little business, debt incurred, more piling up. However, practice gradually came my way."

He worked steadily in those early years, but it wasn't long before affairs of the heart became equally as important as his patients.

In 1915 he was 30. Two years earlier the Rev. Percy Heywood had arrived in town as Rector of the Anglican Church. Two sisters of his wife came to visit, one of them being Irene Bradley, an RN, three years older than the doctor. She had graduated in 1911. Her father was Adam Bradley, a farmer near North Gower, close to Ottawa. As our father Clayton wrote in *Beckoning Hills Revisited* (1981, published by the Boissevain Historical Society), "So far as I know, they first met on a professional basis when he went to visit Mrs. Fred Mavis on Nov. 26, 1913." There may have been ulterior motives for using Nurse Bradley for this case, however, as soon he was wooing her. His letters to her often mentioned his practice.

One day, Charlie Raine and his father were working with some machinery on their farm south of town when something snapped and tore one of Charlie's index fingers almost off. They rushed into town and sought medical help. Bird told Irene about this in his letter of March 8, 1915.

"You want me to cut it off or sew it back on?" Bird asked the young man.

The terse question set Charlie Raine to thinking he might need that finger. And so he told Dr. Bird to "sew it back on." Bird told his beloved that Charlie was "doing fine and to all appearances would have a useful finger."

For her part, Irene wrote back and told him about herself. "My dear boy," begins her letter, for example, of Jan. 30, 1915.

Another week gone, another letter to look forward to – that is what I think each time I read your Thursday epistle. Strange how one measures time by the things that seem of the greatest interest and importance. Can you imagine it is only a little over two months since I left Boissevain?....And so you think I never tell you anything about myself – well, it is probably because there is really very little to tell. We live very quietly here [on the farm], and there is not much happens.

Her health was of concern to them both, and she notes that "there is certainly a steady improvement. I just noticed today, I am able to go through the day without lying down and feel fine by evening. Of course I am not on my feet so very much." Irene then describes a typical day. She gets up after 9, "never before," eats a big plate of porridge and cream, then helps with the dishes and makes up the beds. This is followed by a walk, and her "afternoon nourishment" of a glass of milk and a piece of cake. Then she sews or reads, eats a good supper, and plays cards with her father, who "finds evenings long sometimes." She's in bed by 10. This routine is occasionally altered by skating or dancing parties.

Irene does her best to cheer up her beau. "You have good cause to rejoice in the TB cases. Cheer up, you may find things pretty slow, especially now when you need a good business, but believe me, the time must come when people will get their eyes open and get the best man. I was telling my sister last night of some of your experiences with your opposition....It makes me boil when I think of it, when I think of where some of their poor victims are today."

In a letter of March 21, 1915, Bird wrote to "my dear girl" of his hopes:

"It must sure be fine to have a comfortable margin – I wouldn't mind if I could get into more comfortable means. I have had a hard fight for the business here but I feel hopeful that I am on a fair way to building up a decent practice. But now is the time I'd appreciate a little means whereby I could manage more easily. I have lived for this all my life, girlie, and I know there are not many can do the same as I have.....And even if I don't have money yet I have you girlie and I am young and healthy with fair prospects for practice."

The doctor also wrote about the First World War, which would claim her younger brother, Clayton Bradley, whose letters and story appear in Section One of this book.

"This war is a terrible thing. How I would like to go – I don't think that it would matter at all for myself, but I know it would likely be [the] finishing blow for mother; I am her boy I know and I cannot go because she does not want me to go. She is getting pretty well up in years and her health is becoming quite feeble so I am not going unless things go bad. I trust we have ultimate success and that many more will not be required. Nothing would suit me better if it had to be, to be a staff medical man."

In a letter of July 1915 he called her his "Wild Irish Rose," alluding to her background. It was not apparently English, as we had presumed until recently.

But the doctor had doubts about his suitability for Irene. He was of mixed blood; his beginnings were humble; he had a fiery temper. These doubts she quickly dismissed:

Do not worry, dear boy, that you are unworthy for I could never love an unworthy object. Of course we all have faults – would we be human otherwise? Are we not placed here to help one another correct his or her faults and so strive to attain that perfection that only One Being ever possessed?

Months earlier, Fred underwent an operation in Winnipeg. It was serious. At that point, Irene writes, she knew they must be together. "I suffered agony the day of your operation and I pleaded that you would be brought back to those who loved you." She tells him she likes this verse about home: a world of strife shut out, a world of love shut in. "Let that be our aim to keep it ever so and God grant the lines may never be reversed."

When Fred asked his father for help in preparing a dwelling for his bride to be, the old man came through. As Bird relates in a letter to his betrothed of July 3, 1915: "Our little house is papered all through inside and painted white on the outside with a dark roof: in the parlor, cream is the predominant color and I think the dining-room is the same. I'll get the measurements this week and take them along with me so that we can select our furniture to suit the size of the rooms. I am sending you a little plan of our house just to give you an idea of the plan. I wrote to dad some few days ago and he has promised me help for as much as I asked – that is alright, so I must say that dad is alright…. Dad is not a wealthy man at all and I asked for just enough to help me through with what I could round up myself."

His niece Kay Findlay, writing for the *Brandon Sun* March 2, 1974 ("Dr. Fred Bird – truly an amazing man") reveals how the proposal took place. The story she likes best, she says, is how he managed to get engaged to Irene without the third party present, her father, being aware.

"It happened in our parlor at the rectory in Boissevain," she wrote. "He resolved one night to call to propose. He hadn't counted on my father, though, whose mind was all right in most ways, but dense in affairs of the heart. Dad assumed his fellow professional had dropped in for a chat with him and so on and on he talked; just the three of them, very cozy. Time went on and so did my father, all about this newly installed coal and wood heater that looked serviceable but was cutting up. When dad bent down to fuss with its drafts, Uncle Fred quickly seized a Bible and leafed through the Old Testament till he found a passage about cohabitating – and there are some dandies – and showed it to Irene. She as deftly found Ruth, chapter one, reassuring him that 'Whither thou goest I will go….' When my father stood up minutes later, they had laid the groundwork for what was to be a remarkably happy marriage."

In 1956, Boissevain honoured Dr. Bird, left, with Irene, for his various services since 1913. At right are Clay and Mack.

Ella Irene Bradley and F. V. Bird were married Aug. 10, 1915, in North Gower. Their first-born daughter died within days, or hours, in 1918, a terrible blow. A year later Clayton was born, and then Mackenzie two years after that. Irene was an avid reader and book club member and a gracious host. In 1959 Irene received a postcard from a friend, Helen MacKenzie, who wrote from Scotland that she would "always remember with pleasure your garden gay with flowers, also your kindness to me." Irene loved her sons deeply and wrote dozens of letters to them in the war, starting most with the salutation, "My dear boy --", an echo from her letters to Fred. The loss of brother Clayton Bradley in World War One hit her hard, as we recount in Section One.

In 1919 or 1920 Dr. Bird went to New York to study post-graduate work in surgery. It was a difficult separation, as he left behind not only his wife but a young son, Clayton. But Bird had ambitions to start a surgery, and apparently he had ability, as the Mayo Clinic offered him a position, according to Clayton. He turned it down, partly because Irene didn't wish to uproot the young family. She felt their prospects were solid where they were, and she was right. But one can't help but wonder what would have happened if they had moved to the United States.

Unlike today, with our declining birth rate, much of the medical work early in the 20th Century involved pediatrics. Nurse Marion Hannah of Brandon recalls the birth of one of the many babies Bird helped deliver. She and the doctor drove by horse and sleigh about 15 miles to a home that turned out to be a one-room board shack. The patient was a girl in her teens and this was her first baby. She was terrified. The place was filthy and there was no water. "I was so impressed with the way Dr. Bird coped and cared for that frightened girl that, when he asked me, 'Well, are you going to stay with her?' I felt all Florence Nightingale and answered at once, 'Of course, I'll stay.' I had to sleep on a chair, though, the patient had the only bed."

Gentle when needed, Bird could also be harsh. Ida Smith told the story of her husband Lloyd, who caught his foot in a stirrup and received severe facial lacerations when his horse reared back. Doc Bird stitched him up without any freezing, saying it healed better that way. When Lloyd wriggled in pain, the doctor told him to "Keep still, dammit!"

In those years Dr. Bird served not only Boissevain but the whole of southwest Manitoba. Many times the weather was snowy and cold; many times he and his driver changed horses. Luta Orriss was 15 when her younger brother was born, and she recalled watching Bird and her father arrive at their Mountainside farm in a cutter. To her girlish delight the cutter hit a drift, tossing both into the snow. Years later Bird attended one of her own births with shaving cream still on his face.

Bird served during the flu epidemic of 1918, and also during the 1936 epidemic of infantile paralysis or polio. He and his partner Dr. Mackey sometimes worked two days at a stretch without sleep. The epidemic began about the middle of May and by the end of July the town had 11 cases, three people dead and two crippled by the disease. At one point the people of Killarney, Riverside and Deloraine were being warned by their councils not to go to Boissevain. Deloraine went so far as to impose an embargo on Boissevain people, forbidding them entry. In the *Boissevain Recorder*, the weekly paper, a Killarney pub asked Boissevain residents to please not drink in Killarney! There was a state of near panic.

Bird, the local health officer, asked provincial health officer Dr. Jackson for help, and he sent Dr. Elliott, who took a load off the local men. In August Charlie Lovell, Laura Clark and Duncan Armstrong succumbed, so that Boissevain recorded six deaths of the 126 cases of polio in the province. By September the threat had passed. Dr. Jackson wrote a letter to the *Recorder* commending Bird for his handling of the situation.

He didn't always succeed, however. Elma Mains, age 99 when interviewed in the mid 1990s, said Bird and his parter misdiagnosed her daughter's illness and she lost the use of her legs. But this hardly affected her opinion of the man: "He was our great doctor," she said. "We don't get doctors like that anymore." We do, but they function within a restrictive system. Boissevain's own Dr. A. M. Nell is a wonderful physician, and the town is lucky to have him. There are many other doctors of his ilk.

From 1941, when Dr. Mackey left for Winnipeg (likely to enlist), until 1947 when Drs. Don and Ethel McPhail came to town, Bird was alone medically. Those were busy years, but at least he was able to start digging out from the pile of debt he had accrued during the Depression. The Memorial Hospital was built in 1948 and the road system was rapidly improved, which made things easier for medical people. In those days house calls were the norm, both for doctors and veterinarians. Only since about 1966, when medicare came in nationally, did the custom change to require patients to travel to doctors. Prior to that, you often stayed home in bed and the doctor came to you.

Remember too that until medicare, medicine was a private business in Canada. Doctors were business people who charged fees for service. They had bills to pay and did not receive government money for their work. They competed with each other for clients. But the overriding ethic was one of helping the ill return to good health. To do this, and to make it easier for patients who too often had little money, Dr. Bird often relied on proven simple and affordable treatments, including his own pain-killing tablets.

A story shared by Fred's son Mac concerns his father's pain medications. A drug salesman was in Boissevain at the pharmacy and noticed medicines behind the counter labeled Bird's #1, #2, and #3. When he asked what these were, the druggist replied they were special remedies that Dr. Bird had prepared. The salesman bought one of each and, upon returning to Winnipeg, had his company laboratory analyze them. They each contained a compound derived from different roots, one of them being the same thing Doc's mother had used to help her heart ailment, digitalis. These were subsequently labeled as 272s, 282s, and 292s and mass produced, and Doc no longer had to make his own. He now had more time free to tend to his patients and his roses! As he was more healer than businessman, Bird may have missed out on a drug patent. This fits in with stories Bil heard as a boy that his grandfather had "invented" aspirin, which occurs naturally in the bark of willow trees.

He also ran for office, and served as a town councilor from 1924 to 1929, as Mayor from 1929 to 1940, and as councilor again from 1940 to 1944. In 1961 Council sent him a letter of appreciation and thanks for having served as town and municipal Health Officer for over 40 years since 1913. As a Liberal, he ran twice against A. R. Welch for the provincial legislature but was unsuccessful both times, in 1932 and 1936. The area is staunchly Conservative.

The Bird home, 710 Stephen St. Boissevain, about 1930.

One of Bird's speeches from his run for office in 1936 notes the deep sense of responsibility he felt as a Canadian citizen. He believed, he wrote, "that it is the duty of each citizen to offer his services to his fellow citizens and to his country. Should you honor me with election, I pledge to you, that whatever ability I might possess, the same will be devoted to your interests." He alludes to the deepening Depression. "Speaking as one who for the past eight years has deeply experienced the trials, the problems and the worries of public capacity [as Mayor], I desire to publicly express my great thankfulness for the consideration and cooperation of my fellow citizens; and most sincerely do I extend my deepest sympathy to those less fortunate than the average of us; those who, through no fault of their own, have experienced those conditions that test the spirit and morale of our manhood and womanhood."

He believed that successful agriculture "is the only sound foundation upon which a newer and better Canada may in course of time be built." To this end, he advocated "readjustments" to "assure the farmer that returns from his work shall be such that he can survive the lean years." Over the 62 years of his practice Dr. Bird helped many farmers. One of them was Dave Wall, a man of Mennonite background. Wall didn't farm long (he went on to own a TV repair shop in Deloraine and also built houses) but was working the land in the 1950s when he was hit by terrible pains in his abdomen. Dr. Bird advised him to get to a surgeon quickly, for he likely had a burst appendix. He was right, and Wall recovered. A great friend of the Bird family after that, he lived at Lake Metigoshe with his wife, Madeleine for years, a neighbour of the editor. Wall was also a good beaver and muskrat trapper, and he shared much of his knowledge in that field with the editor, over many great chats. Wall helped many people repair or improve their homes, often for little or no pay. Asked why he did so, the Christian man said the good he did would be passed along by those he assisted to others, and on and on.

As Clayton Bird wrote in *Beckoning Hills Revisited*, Dr. Bird's term as Mayor was particularly difficult. The Depression began in 1930, after the stock market crash of October 1929. Jobs and money were scarce and crops poor, due to drought and grasshoppers. "One of his reasons for running was his conviction that the Manitoba Power Commission, known as Hydro, should get the nod over its competitor, the National Utilities Company from the U.S.A. He fought for this several years," Clayton writes, "and, as Mayor in 1929, succeeded in getting it through Council." There's a story here as well. At one point a representative from the American company appeared in the doctor's office with a bribe of considerable size; Bird promptly threw him out the door. The MPC won out in the end.

Fred Bird also led council in taking over the cemetery from a private syndicate which had not looked after it very well. He even planned the landscaping of the cemetery – his and Irene's own yard was a showcase garden – and to this day it's an attractive facility. The fair grounds were fixed up, Clayton writes, and the tourist camp, all in his first year. After that came two of his favourite projects, the town trees and the concrete sidewalks. Much of the work in these projects was provided as employment relief projects, including the planting of the elms. The town had few trees before he became Mayor. His first attempt to get sidewalks failed when the voters narrowly defeated council's request for the money, but it went through the second time. "Before that Boissevain had wooden sidewalks, which could be very dangerous, or none at all, just mud paths...It was Dad's thinking that no one should have to be subjected to taking relief, but that anyone who wanted to should be given the opportunity of earning money for honest labour." Given the strong work ethic among the area's residents, this policy worked well. During the Depression Dr. Bird, like other doctors, received little cash in payment but lots of chickens and produce, for few had any money.

Despite his medical and public service work which ate up much of his time, Dr. Bird also took part in other activities. He was an avid hunter of deer and ducks and a keen fisherman. He loved to get out into the wilds of Turtle Mountain, with any number of friends, including A. B. Southon and M. Binnions. "In my opinion," Bird wrote in a notebook from the 1960s, "we will find higher and better human values when we associate ourselves more closely with wildlife and nature – that is my conviction and that is one chief reason why I am a conservationist. I think one should be able to go into the autumn woods for partridge, or later, into the marsh for a duck, or later still, into the mountain woods for a deer – and whether or not he comes out with a partridge or a duck or a deer, he should be able to come out from nature with his soul refreshed."

1942   Dr Bird   John Adamson   Earl King   Johnnie Adamson

Speaking of his soul, Dr. Bird was a member of St. Matthew's Anglican Church for 64 years, much of that time a rector's warden. He served on the board of directors of Brandon College for years. He loved dancing and attended many socials in the old country schools. He was particularly good at the waltz and he and Mrs. Myrtle Armstrong won prizes for waltzing. He had learned also the Highland Fling. For years his gardens were the showplace of Boissevain. One fall he told Clay he had lifted 3,000 tulip bulbs. In Canada's centennial year, 1967, he offered the town 50 sugar maple saplings he had raised from seed from trees brought from Ontario years before.

Many of the newspaper clippings in his notebooks pertained to gardening, fishing and hunting – lighter subjects. "Earthworm still most effective bait of them all," headlines a story by Red Fisher. Another entry is a clipped photo of a little girl with a bare bottom, wearing a life jacket, headlined, "Knocks bottom out of drowning!" (Aug. 4, 1966.) He had a great sense of humour and a big heart for little girls, related, no doubt, to the loss of their own daughter. Bird also enjoyed cooking and collecting recipes. He canned hundreds of jars of saskatoons and raspberries (before the province widened the road to Lake Max, destroying vast swaths of the plants). "Enjoy raspberries, the season is now," headlines a column called Cooking with Norah Cherry.

And he was always on the lookout for new medical advances and insights. On their visits, his grandchildren found medical journals around the big house at 710 Stephen St., underlined in red and open. He also clipped health-related items from papers, such as this one ("Always Tired? Maybe you're merely bored") from the *Winnipeg Free Press:*

> Feeling tired? It may have nothing to do with lack of sleep. You could be bored. People who lead the busiest lives – and logically should be the most tired – are the least fatigued. The reason is simple: they have plenty to occupy their minds. Doctors believe the best way to get the most out of life is to have plenty of interests – and exercise regularly....Music helps reduce fatigue and boredom arising from monotony....A good way to prevent fatigue is to plan your evening and have something to look forward to – even if it's only a good night's sleep.

Dr. Bird's contributions to public life were recognized publicly on a number of occasions. One was during the Jubilee celebrations in 1956 when, on July 13, his "babies and friends" honoured him at the Fair Grounds. Mayor Ed Dow spoke of his many accomplishments, and Mrs. Frank Barry (Laura Mildred Smith, his first baby, born Aug. 30, 1913) presented him and Irene with tokens of the community's appreciation. On Oct. 16, 1972, Manitoba honoured Dr. Bird at the Winnipeg Inn for "exemplifying a way of life that helps to make Manitoba a better place for all in which to live," when he received the Manitoba Good Citizenship

Award. He was also honoured on his 90th birthday at the Anglican Church. In 1983 he was inducted into the Manitoba Agricultural Hall of Fame.

In his later years, he often spent time in the home of friend Eddie Clark There he enjoyed something he'd spared himself earlier – an occasional rye. Clark was a businessman whose son Brian remains a friend of the family. Eddie and his wife's good counsel and friendship meant a great deal to the old doctor, as his own sons lived thousands of miles away, bound by family and careers.

At the age of 91, just shy of his 92nd birthday, Dr. Bird took ill and was placed in the town's hospital.

His grandson Brad, then 18, happened to be there, passing through on a road trip from Ontario to Vancouver. As the old man lay in his hospital bed, Brad remembered how his grandfather had cared for our bed-ridden grandmother for years, and dispatched robins with his pellet rifle because they ate his raspberries. "Who pays the taxes around here, me or the bloody robins!" he would bark at anyone who complained.

He remembered the joy the doctor expressed as he and sister Kim sat at his kitchen table and shoveled in his delicious saskatoon preserves. "You like grandpa's saskatoons, eh?" he would chortle. The place had a smell of its own, part carbolic acid, part dinners from decades past. It was a joy to visit there as a child.

The old doctor had wanted to die at home. The hands that had served so many so well, the strong hands that had helped in countless births, skinned out deer and broken new land, had gripped the stairway banister with all the considerable force they could muster. In the end he lost that battle. But his life had been a tremendous battle won.

As his face looked up from the white sheets, he said, meekly, "Clayton?"

Brad told him it was his grandson, one of Clayton's boys.

"Clayton?" the old man said again, peering into the eyes of his visitor.

Brad paused. "Yes, dad, it's Clayton."

Grandfather appeared to relax. His eyes closed. And he was gone soon after.

* * *

The funeral service on July 5, 1977 at St. Matthews Anglican Church was led by Rev. Murray Ames. Active and honourary pallbearers included Doug Opperman, Herb Barwick, Ed Dow, Cliff McKinney, Bill Eaket, Lorne Dunn, George Wright, Jack Moore, T. Henderson, Hec Couture, C. Armitage, Eric Gowler, W. Zeiler, Horace Clark, S. Maxwell, J. Pugh Jr., N. Opperman, Robert Barefoot and G. Carey. Among the 59 guests who signed the registry were Pearl Bird of Selkirk, Hattie Mogk (a next-door neighbor), Bill Bird of Petersfield, Irene Tillett (Patton) and Bernice Hawkins (Patton).

Dr. Bird was buried in Boissevain Cemetery.

Dr. Bird died June 30, 1977, exactly two months short of his 92nd birthday. Twenty-nine years later his eldest son Clayton would pass away Dec. 17, 2006, exactly two months short of his 88th year. Coincidentally, Brad was the only child able to attend to each in the hours before their passing.

– Brad and Bil Bird

SECTION ONE: GROUND WAR

CHAPTER 1

Clayton Bradley's Letters Home

Clayton Bradley grew up on the family farm with seven brothers and sisters near the village of North Gower, Ontario, in the Ottawa Valley. He was born in 1889 and was 26 when he wrote these letters home from training centres in Canada and the front in France in 1915-16. Tall, fair, blue-eyed and "slightly round-shouldered" as a friend described him, Clayton was a beloved younger brother of Irene Bradley, who married Dr. F. V. Bird in 1915, when she was about 33. Clayton wasn't a Bird, but his brother-in-law was Dr. Bird – and Clayton Bradley was the namesake of our father, Frederick Charles Clayton Bird. Clayton Bradley's sister Irene was our grandmother.

Irene and the rest of the family would have been deeply aggrieved by his death in June of 1916, when he was shot in the head by a sniper. As a result, Irene had serious reservations about her eldest son Clayton joining the air force when the Second World War began. He held back until 1941, not wanting to cause her grief, as he explains in his book Nickel Trip. (This may have saved his life, because the casualty rate among aircrew from 1939 to 1942 was high, about 75%. As aircraft and methods improved, the casualty rate declined.) In time, Clayton's mother came to see that his enlistment was necessary.

Clayton Bradley's life and letters are therefore relevant to the Bird family history, and what we know is shared in this section. His letters serve a second purpose as well: as a window on the world of a First World War Canadian soldier – his training, routine, thoughts and amusements. We think you'll find this section particularly interesting. The "Pearl" he writes to is, to our knowledge, a favourite elder sister.

Monday night. Jan. 17/15
[A training camp in Canada]

Just a line tonight to let you know how pleased I was to get your Xmas cake after coming into camp last night. There are nine in my section and we are all in a tent together. Some of the others got parcels too so it was "tres beans" as we say. We have a brazier in each tent. A brazier is what we use as a stove, a tin which stands about two feet high and 15" in diameter with a stovepipe made of biscuit tins. We are supposed to use coke in these, when we get it, but we have to rustle it, as we have not had our issue yet. But another chap and I went out today and got a good supply of wood, ammunition boxes and hardwood stakes, then we came across an old cook tent where we scraped up the remains of the coal and between coal and mud we got about half a bag.

Mother knows what a good fireman I am so I still have the tent good and warm. At present one of the boys is toasting bread on the coals and we are going to have some baked beans that we got in the YMCA tent here. This morning we had a bath and a change of clothing which was badly needed, as things are very much alive after being in the trenches. These baths were nice warm showers, but we had to make it fast as a new batch of twenty went in about every fifteen minutes.

I have not received any journals for ever so long, but yesterday I got three and today another. Also the OAC Review Xmas number. I see that the Mac girls have made seventy-five Xmas cakes for us but so far they have not been forthcoming.

The young fellow in our tent read of the death of his father some time ago in Saskatoon, but this was the first he knew of it. The toast is now ready. Bon soir.

Clayton.

The following letter was incomplete; just two pages were found in an envelope. He is likely still in a training camp in Canada in May of 1915.

...from the Capt. if he has any idea when we shall be going. Well I must leave now as our platoon plays platoon 15 at soccer on (16).

Thurs. May 6th. Well Pearl this is your birthday. I thought of it last Saturday evening, but we were busy or I might have sent you something.

Well our team lost 8-5. There were a couple of fellows didn't turn up and we had to pick up some others. Our Lieut. told us this morning that he expected we would go over to England when camp is over on the 15th. They are not sure but he thinks we will go as we will get better training over there. He said we were liable to go any time. So if you are coming here you had better come as soon as you can. We will be here till the 15th and I don't know where we shall go then. Perhaps we may stay here till we go.

Mess parade fall in –

Goodbye.

Clayton.

Stormcliffe

July 16/15

Friday 5 p.m.

Dear Father and All:

We have about half an hour before pulling out. This has been a very busy day as we were being equipped with several things we had not got before. Everyone is going with the exception of a couple who have sprained ankles. Only Captain Barclay and Capt. McDougall are coming with us. The officer in command will be an experienced man and so will the other officers. We are sorry our own officers are not coming with us, but I suppose it will be better to have old hands at the head of things.

I am sending you a pair of boots that I got to wear in the evenings or going downtown as the others are so big and heavy. I hope they fit all right. I know they were nice and comfortable for me anyway. The badges are our old university badges, and our present one and a stray 28th badge. I met a chap by name of Taylor from Boissevain. He said he was told to look me up. He is in the 27th from Winnipeg and is going over tonight too. There are 1750 going over tonight. Well we have to go now so goodbye and don't worry as I shall take good care of myself.

Hope you and mother are well. I got a present for Irene last night [his sister, Dr. Bird's wife] but hadn't time to have it mailed. So Mr. Dunton mailed it today for me.

Lovingly

Clayton.

41

Miss Pearl E. Bradley
RR#3 North Gower
Ontario Canada

PPCLI BEF France

August 31, 1915
[This is a postcard with a photo of a woman holding two flags.]

We arrived back at rest camp last night about 12:30. We shall be here for a couple of weeks. I received your letter of 8th when I came back here. There is not much news as things are about to pause here. We are back in the same place as we were when we left on Aug. 2.

Clayton.

The following letter was written in pencil in a fairly good hand on 8.5" x 7" sheets halved, though some words are unclear.

Oct. 15, 1915

Dear Pearl;

We just came back to the billets last night after being in the trenches for two days; we don't stay in so long now as we are nearer our billets here than before. The first night we were in support and had to stay out all night and it was a cold night too – in the morning there was a heavy white frost but we had a shack to go into where there was a stove, table, chairs, beds, a large mirror, pictures, curtains, etc., all this right in the trench – some class.

The French are great people for fixing up things and as there are several houses just near here I guess they got a lot of stuff out of them. We slept a good part of the day and in the evening we moved into the firing trench but it was warmer than the night before. The lines are not very close just here. We don't go to the same part of the line each time we go in. There was a pig in between the lines but poor piggie is now on the honor roll. There are lots of rats in the trenches.

One chap, a sergeant in the last draft, was relating his experience where the first bullet whizzed over his head and talking about how nervous he was. He was sitting in the trench with his back to the wall and what should happen but a rat jumped on his neck. Well, if he didn't make a jump to get away and made such a noise knocking over chairs and other things, and we were supposed to be very quiet.

I was on sentry one night and was looking out over the parapet with my head close to the trench side and a little mouse ran right under my nose before I saw it. One night in the billets one chap said he woke up and found a rat sitting on his face – I'll not vouch for this statement, altho he declares it to be true.

There were two of our lieutenants in our company were wounded by a shell. One, Belleuard, was pretty badly hurt. The other, Cawley, was not so bad. There is an Irishman has just joined us again after being in the hospital for some time, and I think he is half nutty – he is a comical guy and makes lots of fun. I had letters from Helen and Edna [?] lately, and they mentioned about the time you were in, also the ---. Were you in this fall? I don't think the trenches they would have there are like what we have here.

Had a letter from Mrs. Rogers acknowledging the photo. She says her husband has enlisted and is in the machine-gun battalion that Hamilton is donating (200 guns). Mr. Rogers also wrote a sheet and he says he likes it fine, but doesn't expect they will go to England till next spring. He would like to have gone last year. He is an American, too. The dilcher [sp?] is back again this summer with the same men except one – we have had nice weather for the past few days so that things dried up. But today it is raining again.

I suppose you are corn-cutting now. Let me know how everything goes. What is cheese selling for this summer? We always like to get Canadian cheese as sometimes it is not nice; but now in the cold weather it is better. In that newspaper clipping I sent we are somewhere above the ......[unclear] in the wood, France. The water is getting cold so that our swimming days are about over.

Here is a clipping which I found in a paper which I shall send you. Princess Pat worked the bagpipes. It is now much different to what it was in the beginning, as it has a few holes in it from shells, i.e. the Battle of Ypres. It is the custom of British regiments to carry their colours, altho I have only seen one a couple of times. Our badge is the sunflower which is said to be Patricia's favorite flower. You never said whether or not you got the book I sent father with the badges inside. I would be sorry to lose them, the McGill badge especially as they are very scarce. I sent them the day we left England 16 July. If you didn't get them I suppose the YMCA man has them, like the chap who has the other little things

I sent at Battalion. At least I expect that is where they went. A number of the boys say things they gave him to get censored and mailed never reached their destination.

Tell Gracie I got her nice letter and also post card. She is quite a correspondent. Well 'Mulligan' [stew] is up now so I shall have to dine. Hope all are well as I am, in fact we all are.

Lovingly,
Clayton

Another postcard followed.

Oct. 28, 1915

Miss Pearl E. Bradley
RR#3 North Gower
Ontario Canada

Rec'd yours of 22nd last night and shall write in a day or so. We are all well. This picture will give you some idea of the towns and villages out here. Had a concert last night in a cave about a mile from the firing line – had a mixed audience and had some good French selections.

Clayton

November 5, 1915

Dear Pearl;

It seems a long time since I wrote you. I hope you received my card, which I sent instead of a letter a couple of days ago. I think I left off in my letter to Percy by saying I intended going into town next day. Well, we went in on the train, left here at one o'clock and came back at six. First we went to see the cathedral. It is a very interesting building, with so many carvings and paintings, some of which are as large as 10' x 15'. The outside is all built up with sandbags, about 20 feet, to protect the walls from shells. We were all through the inside. It is very large and very high, and is very old too. I don't know when it was built, but there are several vaults of some of the old cardinals or whatever they call them.

After leaving the cathedral we walked around the town awhile – I went into a bank and exchanged a sovereign for which I got 25 francs in five-franc silver pieces which are about the size of a silver dollar. There were three of us together. We went into a jewellers where I bought a watch, a nice little one about the size of my gold one, with gun-metal case, for 18 francs. I think it is cheaper than in Canada. I lost my best watch before leaving England and this was the first chance I had of getting another. We were in some of the shops more for the fun of talking than anything else. We had a trip around the city as far as the car would take us and back, all for a penny. There we had supper, beef steak etc., two orders each, as we made this our dinner and supper.

We found our way back to the station at six and found our train. There are not many lights on the streets. The trains are very different from ours. The coaches are smaller and divided into two compartments, street cars same way. I have not been in Smee [?] as all passes are cancelled now, but I expect our company will go in in a day or so for a bath as some of the other chaps have been in.

We have had miserable weather during the past couple weeks. Scarcely a day passes that it does not rain. Sun shone yesterday for first time. We were to have battalion sports this pm but it rained, so they are postponed till tomorrow. There is great speculating as to where we are going. There are new rumors every day. Should you miss some of my letters don't worry, as we may be moving – during which there are no outgoing mails.

We received our issue of comforts sent out by people and societies. I got a nice warm woolen muffler from the Daughters of the Empire in Montreal. The issue consisted chiefly of mufflers, socks, handKs, wristlets, and a couple shirts. Then today we got a regimental issue of sweater, coats (the Bradley brand), and also Lady Farquhar sent us woolen gloves and neckscarves. So we are pretty well off for clothes.

Col. Farquhar was colonel of this regiment and was killed last spring. Did I tell you that Thos. Gedde's son is going to OAC? He was there last year and I never knew who he was till a few days ago. He is a clever chap and a regular young ---- from what the boys say. He has an autobile [sic] of his own in Guelph. He worked at the College on the bee dept. last summer. He is also a lieutenant in the OTC (Officers' Training Corp) at the College. Well I must close for tonight. This is Guy Fawkes Day. Anything doing around home?

45

Saturday 6th, Nov. 6/15.

This has been a nice day. In the morning we had a [mock] battle for the battalion and sports in the afternoon. We had a good afternoon's fun too, the chief items being a bomb-throwing contest, a five-leg race, potato race for UCDs, wrestling on horseback (one chap acting the horse), an obstacle race, [and] a Vic[toria] Cross race. This consisted of mounting a horse bareback and running about 500 yards, picking up a (supposed) wounded man and bringing him in. Then to top off there was a relay race which was most exciting. There were 25 men per coy [company], and our coy won, in fact they won in nearly all the events. I was in the five-legged race and the relay but our feet were of different opinions as to starting and so lost twice but we soon caught up and made good time, and although we didn't get in the first three we weren't last either.

All the officers were there and took an active part. The Brigade Gen. was also there to see the fun. Then there were the usual clowns to make fun. One came riding in on a great big old horse carrying a white flag on a long pole. He was dressed in white, at least what I saw was white. I don't know whether he was supposed to be a German or Joan D'Arc.

Sunday a.m.

(We ended up at a concert at night.)
The concert was a decided success last night, and the school room was crowded. The opening was a selection from the band, which consisted of 18, and they were dressed in all sorts of costumes. I didn't think they could find so much old things in a village like this, about the size of Gower. There were Frenchmen, Italians, a German, etc etc. There were even three or four girls, which showed the styles for the last few years. Then there were negroes galore. One of these worked hard on his banjo which was made of a board and a box and a few strings. There were several silk hats, too. The instruments were a flute, several tin whistles, two drums (large tea biscuit boxes) and the rest played on combo. They gave several selections which were really good. One comic one started very soft and gradually got louder till it reached a climax and then as gradually ended up as softly as it began. There were several good items which would take too long to tell about. At the closing Maj. Gault proposed three cheers for Princess Patricia and it would have done her good to have heard them.

Then we gave Maj. Gault three cheers. We were there early and had a good look around the school room. The seats and desks are built for three and are movable. There are a lot of maps and charts etc., an organ, library etc. I got a few little things — little dolls dresses that some of the kids had made, and I shall send them home if I get a chance.

There is a little black and white dog here that was tied when we came. He was very thin, evidently half starved. Well, since we came we give him all the bread and meat that we leave and it was wonderful how he filled out, and now he is as round as a ball. I see now that he has broken his chain and is running around.

I want to say that I got your letter, also ... of the 19th Oct. yesterday, also the shirt and socks some time ago. The shirt came in very good at the time as we were issued with underdrawers but no shirts. The sox are good too. I always keep a supply of dry ones on hand. I think I have told you nearly all, although I could tell you lots if I were talking to you but wait till après la garre finis. Am enclosing a couple of pansies that I picked in a garden here. There are lots of flowers still in bloom, dahlias, etc. and even roses in bloom. I had breakfast in bed this a.m. in fact most of us had. Got up at 9 for church parade at 10, but I guess the chaplain got lost in the fog. Love to all,

Clayton.

Have heard that the French had blown up those mines I spoke of.

Wed. night. Jan. 19, 1916

Dear Pearl;

Although I wrote you a couple of days ago I shall write another note tonight in case I don't get a chance during the next few days as we are going into the trenches tomorrow.

I received your Xmas cake which was very good. I guess I told you also from the College, and today we received a pair of socks and a few little things from Lieut. Dantos' people, he was our platoon officer but didn't come over with us from England. Had a nice letter from Jean Bradley saying she received the photo, strange they should be lost and found as they were. Received your letter of 31st and a card from Irene also today. Am glad you had a good time at Xmas; I had too.

47

So your concert was a success. I suppose you will take it to Pierces when the roads get bad. Do you know some parts of this country remind me of that country that night. The only difference is that there is about eight feet of cobbles in the centre of that road. I wish you could come to some of our concerts we have here. Just tonight there was one in the YMCA tent got up by the boys and was very good, chiefly vocal and instrumental, a few comic recitations, sword dance accompanied by the bagpipes. Then there was a sketch, "Sick parade in the army."

No matter what complaint a fellow has, from sore feet to a pain in the stomach, the doctor invariably gives a No. 9. I have been fortunate in keeping off those parades but that is what the fellows say. So it was a sort of take-off, then they operated on one chap who was all doubled up and they took out about three days' rations of bully beef, biscuit (hard) and jam. The instruments used were bayonets, small hatchet, wire cutters, and a saw. The latter was used to cut out a couple of ribs (piece of stick). It was little wonder the patient came out of the anesthetic prematurely.

Col. Buller sang "Yi-up I-addy I-oh" which went well with the fellows as the colonel is a fine man. The boys like him; he has a glass eye (right). Capt. Barkely also contributed. The best of all was a little Belgian girl ten years old [who] sang several popular songs of the soldiers in England, and was very good with the accent, "My Little wet home in the Trench," "Tipperary," "Copies to Guerre," and a couple of others.

The soldiers billeted here teach the kids English and it's surprising how quickly they pick it up. We are losing our one opportunity of learning French as the people here speak Flemish and can speak English fairly well. It was down south we learned quickly where the people couldn't understand English.

This is a forsaken country and I often think if I had it I would give it to the Germans. The people too are, some at least, disloyal, and you never know but some of them are spies, as some are. There are the loyal ones still sticking to their guns but there are others who no doubt have turned and seem to do all they can to make it uncomfortable for us, except get our money. For instance one place we were in they would take the plunger out of the pump so as we couldn't use the water for washing, and we would have to go and get it out of a shell hole or the ditch. Then they wouldn't give us straw, nevertheless we got it. Of course they are not all like that, and that is why we think they are pro-German. I often think there are too many so-called refugees living on the funds for the "poor Belgians" in England who should be out here, as there are a great many in England.

Must go to sleep now as this is the last night in nice warm blankets in a tent for a few days. We have had an easy time for the last four days and nice weather, lovely moon-lit nights. Suppose you have the same moon, as the kid said.

Am still keeping fine as usual. So goodnight.

Lovingly,

Clayton.

That is the last letter we have from Clayton Bradley. He died four and a half months later.

This is the first letter we have concerning his death.

Killed in Action June 1916

Havre   Oct. 2nd, 1916

PPCLI ?   Bradley L/Cpl C.A.
                                                                                                      A/11004

N. & M. June 2 – 4 – 16

I last saw him on the morning of 3rd June at Hooge [?} in our own lines, but we were nearly surrounded by Germans. He was wounded in the arm but able to carry on.

Informant Pte: R.A.S. Brown 1338,
No. 3 Coy. IX platoon PPCLI
Harpleus P.H.E.

* * *

On the back of the folded section of the piece of paper containing the letter above are the words: "In reply to Mr. Johnston's request for renewed searches. Rec'd by Luis Oct. 24."

This is the second letter.

9/10/16 Can. Red Cross Society
Information Bureau
1516 Coekspur St.
London, S.W.

Dear Sir –

In reference to the inquiries which we are making concerning L/E.C.A. Bradley A11004 etc. – I beg to send you herewith copy of a report which has just been sent to us by a searcher of the British C. Red Cross.

Altho it does not give any definite news we thought it best to send you a copy.

Perhaps you will kindly point out to relatives that it is simply a comrade's statement – and we cannot vouch for its accuracy. Please also assure them of our continued help and sympathy.

I am yours truly
Can. Red Cross Society,
Pen. Ermine M.K. Taylor.

France

N. & M 2/4 June 1916

I knew Bradley: he was a L/Cpl. In No. 4 Co. His number would start A-11… and I was told by a man whose name I forget that he was with Bradley and Lieut. Scott when Bradley was shot by a sniper in the head and killed instantly. This was in the afternoon of 2/6/16 up near Maple Cops whilst they were trying to get through. Bradley was about 5'11", slightly round shoulders, blue eyes, light moustache, and fair. I think he came from MacDonald College.

Reference:
Pte. M. G. Nilson
11082
No. 3 – 22 Geu.
Staples
A very careful and reliable witness.

CHAPTER 2

J. M. Bird's Biography

James Mackenzie Bird was born on January 6, 1921, in Boissevain, Manitoba. He is the youngest son of Dr. Fred Bird and his wife, Irene, and brother of Clayton. Mac was his own man, even as a youth. He wasn't musical like his brother, but he played organized hockey until about 18, a defenceman, which Clayton didn't do. Like his brother he hunted and fished from an early age, taught by his father. What follows is Mac's account of the period leading up to war, the war itself, and its aftermath. If it is sometimes stark in the telling, that reflects the man, who has a no-nonsense and up-front approach to life. During the war he was known as Jim Bird.

After the war Mac joined the civil service, Revenue Canada, and served for many years in various capacities, including head of information services, until retirement. He and his wife, Peggy, had a daughter, Karen, who today is married to Bob Watson, a lawyer, and they have a number of children.

As he explains himself in the latter part of the story below, Mac was an avid curler for many years until his knees gave out. He was a founding member of the Hollyburn Country Club near their home, which overlooks the Vancouver Harbour. At the time of writing in August of 2010 Mac was 89 and living on his own in the West Vancouver home that he and Peggy had built some years after the war.

The Italian Campaign, 1943-1945

A few words about the military campaign that shaped Mac's war years. The Italian Campaign was the name of Allied operations in and around Italy from 1943 to the end of the war in Europe. It was longer and more lethal than the Normandy invasion of France on June 6, 1944, but those who took part in it are generally accorded less respect than the veterans of Normandy, though this should not be the case. The fighting was just as intense, the struggle equally important. The Allies had to push the Nazis out of both countries, Italy and France, to win the war. In Churchill's words, the "soft underbelly" of Europe came first.

It is estimated that between September 1943 and April 1945 some 60,000 Allied and 50,000 German soldiers died in Italy. Total Allied casualties during the campaign totaled about 320,000 and the corresponding Axis figure (excluding those involved in the final surrender) was over 658,000. No campaign in Western Europe cost more than the Italian campaign in terms of lives lost and wounds suffered by infantry forces. By comparison, about half that number, some 425,000 Allied and German troops were killed, wounded or went missing during the Battle of Normandy. This figure includes over 209,000 Allied casualties, with nearly 37,000 dead amongst the ground forces and a further 16,714 deaths amongst the Allied air forces.

The Italian Campaign began with a combined British-Canadian-American invasion of Sicily on July 10, 1943 with both amphibious and airborne landings at the Gulf of Gela (American 7th Army, Patton) and north of Syracuse (British 8th Army, Montgomery). Forces of the British Eighth Army landed on the toe of Italy on September 3, 1943, the day the Italian government agreed to an armistice with the Allies. So the Italians did not fight the Allies in Italy, but the Germans put up great resistance, as Mac Bird testifies in the coming chapters.

CHAPTER 3

Against War

On Feb. 23, 2009, Bruce and Brad Bird interviewed their Uncle Mac Bird, then 88, at his home in West Vancouver. What follows is a lightly edited transcript of that two-hour talk.

When war broke out in September of 1939 I was 18 years old and living in Boissevain, Manitoba. I grew up in the town, which is south of Brandon near the North Dakota border. I was planning to leave to go to school because I'd finished Grade 12. I learned, however, that my father, Dr. F. V. Bird, was borrowing money to put my brother Clayton into Brandon College, and that meant that he would have to borrow more if I were to also continue in school.

I also learned that dad was heavily in debt. We'd had 10 years of disastrous crop failures around town, and everybody was broke. Few were paying their doctor in cash. Dad had $46,000 on the books when the Farmers Debt Adjustment Act came along about 1936 and knocked that down to $6,000, without telling those debtors they had to pay.

So I looked around for some way I could get out, and I got a bright idea. A cousin of mine was living in a building in Winnipeg where there was a business school, a correspondence school. The idea was I would become a male secretary and get into the business world that way, get myself attached to some business executive, and learn as I went along. It would only cost father six months' tuition at this school, and I'd be on my way.

The school was headed up by a guy named Walt Angus, who was a chartered accountant. I was only there a couple of months when he called me into his office and said, "I've been following your progress, and I think you should change course."

I said, "What do you mean, change course?"

"I think you should go into the chartered accountancy field. My friend in Fort Frances, Ontario, needs a man."

So I went to Fort Frances. It turned out this guy wasn't running an auditing business as much as a bookkeeping business, which is not what I wanted. So after a few months there I packed it in and came back to Winnipeg and went back to see Mr. Angus. He said, "Fine, I'll fix you up with Jim Mundy, a friend of mine." I stayed with Mundy for two years and got two years of my course completed.

Then the war came along, and in 1939 I was against war. I didn't want to go. But after two years of Hitler parading around Europe and raising all kinds of hell, it became obvious what was going on, so I had to change my thinking. I was in the Officers' Training Corp part-time while I studied, so I decided I would not only sign up, but do so with the family regiment, the Princess Patricia's Canadian Light Infantry.

Father had six brothers and three sisters. His younger brother Charley had put in three and a half years in the hell that was France in World War One, with the Princess Patricia's Canadian Light Infantry. I don't know much about Charley, and for some reason didn't visit him after my service in Europe to compare notes. But Uncle Charley lived to a ripe old age of about 94. [Ed.'s note: We have no letters from Charley Bird that I have ever seen, and very little knowledge about him has otherwise come to light. But he must have been quite a man to have survived for so long on the Western Front in the First World War, and we are no doubt missing a fine story. I hope this will encourage some input about him from those who know.]

On the other side of the family, my mother's, the Bradleys, her older brother Clayton died at Vimy Ridge in 1916, serving with the Princess Patricia's Canadian Light Infantry. So, it was the family regiment. He was shot in the head by a sniper in June of that year, the way I very nearly got killed. That's a story for later.

I enlisted in July 1942 and they sent me out to Gordon Head, a military camp near Victoria. This was an officers' training camp where we spent two months. We graduated and then went to Camp Shilo, near Brandon, and took more training there, and graduated as a full lieutenant. Then you could take any number of courses related to your work, like communications or first aid, anything that would help your ability as a leader.

I always did well in shooting. But it didn't bring me necessarily to the attention of my superiors because they still thought of officers as gentlemen. They didn't get their hands dirty.

I got my hands dirty. I was in Italy from January of 1944 and left Europe in early March of 1945. That was 14 months in Italy and two months in Holland. I was in France only in passing through. I did no fighting in France. But that's getting ahead of the game. Let's resume the story.

Mom never said anything when I joined up. Clayton had already enlisted and I guess she was resigned to the fact of my own enlistment. After Shilo I was in Winnipeg in training establishments there, came back to Shilo and took some more courses, and then in June 1943 I sailed for England.

Mac Bird and his mom, October 1942

I got over to England and thought I'd look up my regiment after I settled in. I made inquiries and was told you can't see them, they're on maneuvers. Well, surely I could see them on maneuvers. No, I'm sorry you can't. The maneuvers were, they were out at sea, putting up a diversion, because they were going in to the landing in Sicily and the attack on Italy. I never did see them until I got to Italy. I took more courses in England and stayed around there until the spring of 1944.

The diversion, by the way, was successful. Our flotilla got all the way into the Mediterranean undetected. When they landed in Sicily in July, the Germans were ill-prepared, and by mid-August of 1943 the occupation of Sicily was complete. I was not part of that Sicilian action.

I wasn't bored in England because they kept us busy with training. I took about four or five different courses. One was battle drill. That was the prime, useful one. In battle drill we learned how to kill. They showed you how to kill with knife, bayonet, even with your hands. We also took signals training.

The Allies moved over onto mainland Italy in September of 1943. By the time I got to Italy they were already on the main Italian peninsula, and they got stopped at the Ortona River.

I went out in January of 1944 and got to the base training camp in Italy and took more courses there, and exercises of various kinds. Then they sent me up to the regiment. They were in static winter lines outside Ortona. We were on the south bank of this river, and Jerry, our name for the Nazis, was on the north bank. It had been a river; the banks were about 20 feet high, but the Italians had dammed all of these side-flowing rivers all the way up the country, so what had before been a deep river was now a six-inch trickle. You could walk through it without getting your feet wet.

The activities we undertook were night patrol. On one of my early night patrols, one of the men behind me kept putting his hand on my shoulder. When we got back I said, "Why did you always have your hand on my shoulder?" He said, "Because if you got more than four or five feet away from me, I couldn't see you." I said, "What?" He said, "I can't see in the dark." I couldn't believe this because as I walked out there I could see three Jerry helmets over here, three more over there, three more over there. They were 120 to 150 feet away. I could see them. And this man couldn't see me when I was four feet away. So I asked the other boys; they were all about the same. They were night blind; I had night vision and had been born with it. Clayton had it too. So did dad. We three were about the same in many physical aspects, triplets. I was walking down the street in

Winnipeg one day and I met this lady and she stopped me and said, "You have to be Dr. Bird's son." Never seen the woman in my life. She had been visiting a friend in Boissevain, and this friend said you must see Dr. Bird about your problem. Dad fixed her up and she recognized me.

I was slated to take seven night patrols in the 15 nights I was there. I volunteered for three more because I was good. I could go out at night, see these Germans and walk between them. One of the things that strikes all soldiers of all nations is the fear of shooting one of your own. And at night, it's extremely difficult if you can't see. You can't yell out because that gives away your position. I learned a bit of German in one of the courses. I could creep up on a man, quietly, and use my commando knife, take him out, go inside the quarters he was guarding, and kill some of the troops in there. I would have three or four men with me. That was in the spring of 1944, when I was 23.

Here's one telling story about night patrols. There were three draws (or openings) in front of me, part of this riverbank formation from a million years back. The major and I didn't get along. He had told me to go in the second draw. As I was approaching these, I didn't like that one. I decided to go in the third one. I started up this draw when I saw approaching me a German coal-scuttle helmet. German soldiers are on the same trail I'm on. So I grabbed my three men and pulled them in behind me. Two of these men were scouts and snipers and my orders were to take them as far back as I could, drop them behind Jerry's lines, where they would find some place to hide themselves, and I would get back out again. By hand -- you can't speak -- I moved the three guys off the trail, off to the side, put them down, and with hand instructions told them to stay down.

I hunkered down, these two guys walk by, and my No. 4 man unfortunately grabs the first Jerry. Well, the cat's out of the bag. I jumped down and grabbed the second Jerry. Just hold them by the back of the tunic. They know they've been taken prisoner. No resistance, nothing. Then this Canadian soldier starts off back down the trail, going back home, with his prisoner. But he makes a fatal error. Instead of staying on the trail that took him down into the river bottom, he followed the first turn. That led them onto the ridge where three of the Jerries were in their slit trench. His prisoner said something in German and the guys in the slit trench opened fire, hitting the Jerry and also hitting the Canadian soldier in the leg. He stepped over to the side to avoid this fire and went ass over tea kettle down the hill.

I did the same thing, moved over to try to get a shot at the guys who were shooting at us and went tumbling down the hill, holding my prisoner. I collected myself at the bottom. The other two guys had followed us down, still on their feet. I got those three together, then moved back across the river, got to the trail that had taken us in, when I realized I was short one body. I put the guys down, whispered to them if I don't get back, take this prisoner up the trail and report in.

I then went back into No Man's Land, and as I was approaching the area where I knew our soldier was I saw the three Jerries had come out of their trench and were walking down into the area I was headed for. So I had to get rid of them. I devised a smart scheme in one sense, not very smart in others. When you throw a hand grenade you give away your position, because when you pull the safety pin the automatic spring in it goes Bing!, firing the ignition switch to ignite the grenade. You now have three seconds before it goes bang. But that tells Jerry there is a grenade coming, so they would drop.

I thought, I'll beat these guys at that. I stuck the grenade underneath my tunic near my armpit and released the firing pin. Slightly hazardous if anything goes wrong. I then throw it. So much time has elapsed that by the time it reaches the Jerries and explodes, it's still in the air. They start screaming, so I knew I'd made a big hit. I heard three voices, they'd all been hit. They quieted down, I approached them. They were almost all dead. I may have had to finish one guy off.

I searched them. They all had letters from home and were writing back to them. It was all in their pockets. Then I went looking for my man, found him, he'd been hit in the leg, couldn't walk, so I put him on my back and carried him back, picked up the rest of the troops and reported in. After hearing the story, the adjutant said, "I'm sorry, you've screwed up."

I said, "What do you mean I've screwed up? I thought I'd done a pretty good job."

He said, "You disobeyed orders."

I said, "I beg your pardon?"

He said I was supposed to go up the second draw, not the third draw.

I said, "Man, I'm the officer on the ground. You're telling me I don't have the discretion to make that choice?"

He said, "No. When we give you orders—"

I said, "Sorry, I'm in a learning process here. That's what I'm up here for, is to learn."

He said, "The thing is, you don't know what Canadian troops are going to be in draw No. 3 or draw No. 1 on the other side. We do. So when we tell you to go up draw No. 2, you go up draw No. 2. Because of that I can't write you up for the Military Cross because that's what you've just earned."

On another night patrol in February 1944 I had three men with me. We crossed through the water and I felt something wasn't right. I stopped, and pop! I knew what this pop was, a two-inch mortar. The Germans had fired a two-inch mortar. It would go up a couple of hundred feet, pop again, and a parachute would open up and a phosphorous flare would ignite and illuminate the area. So over my shoulder I breathed, "freeze." So we're standing there and this thing pops. I had shut my eyes to protect them from the bright light. I opened them just slightly and I could see the three Jerries over there, three over there, three over there, nine rifles pointing at us. So everything depended on the guys obeying my order. If anybody turned and ran, the Jerries would know, and they would open fire. Nobody moved. To pass the time and calm my own nerves I started counting. These flares would last 45 seconds. I got to 42 when they popped the second one. So I have 90 seconds of illumination. Believe me, that is a lifetime. When the 90 seconds was up, and nothing had happened, I just walked straight ahead, right between No. 1 and No. 2 groups, and took another prisoner that night, and brought him home. The other guys stayed right with me.

They saw me, but the thing about the human eye is when it goes from total blackness to sudden illumination it can see shape, but it cannot distinguish features. They couldn't even see what helmets we were wearing. So all they could see was four men, but whose? And again, don't shoot your own troops.

I had begun to establish a reputation. Believe me, word spreads when you're successful. One of my corporals said later, "Man, you always brought us back. We wanted to go with you." I only had five men killed while I was in command of a platoon. Only five men.

When I first joined the regiment I had this wonderful sergeant, Fred Snell, who explained the risks involved in taking prisoners. What would happen is, you'd have a group of German soldiers surrender and throw down their arms. And then somebody, the sergeant or lieutenant would say, "Bill and Joe, you take that group over there." They'd go over. Bill would stand there with his rifle on guard. Joe would sling his rifle, and he would pat everybody down. While they were busy doing that, another German soldier would appear from over here somewhere and he'd see these two backs turned towards him. So he'd just bang! Bang! And that would draw attention to him. He would drop his rifle, and we had to take him prisoner.

I took 54 prisoners. But if they had a gun in their hand and were swinging towards me, bam, they're gone. I was brought up Christian. I was brought up with the Sixth Commandment, "Thou shall not kill." And yet right from the day I arrived in Italy, I had one thought in mind: shoot first, shoot straight, and shoot to kill. I was the good guy. I was the guy who should survive. When you have a monster like Adolf Hitler, who could willingly condemn not one or two people to death but at least 12 million innocent people by the most horrendous means, then there's only one thing to do.

Each platoon had a lieutenant, a sergeant and three corporals. That's the command structure. There are three lieutenants in the company. You always leave out one lieutenant, one sergeant, two corporals, nine privates, pulled from the company. The idea there is, if the company in action gets wiped out, those nine men can form an experienced core around which raw recruits can be formed so that the company again can be activated.

I had no good friends on patrol. Favouritism is the kiss of death. I never became friends with any of my troops. And I didn't let them become friends with me. The same thing with me and the major. As I indicated earlier, he and I didn't hit if off. But I respected the guy. He was a smart man in many respects. He was a brave man; he had landed in Sicily and was still with us. But he and I disagreed and you don't argue with the major. I did unfortunately and it cost me.

The thing with leadership is, you are alone. The major was not friends with the other lieutenants. So you have this hierarchy. I could not be friends with my troops. The reason is quite simple. When you say, "Corporal Smith, go to the right and take action," and Cpl. Smith gets knocked down, you can't be buddies with him, because death awaits every move.

And yet you're a team. You fight for the team. The boys knew that I was going to be around for a while by this very simple factor: When I joined the platoon full time in May of 1944, I was the ninth lieutenant. When Sgt. Snell told me I was the ninth lieutenant, I said, "Wait a minute, you've only been fighting 10 months. What happened to these eight guys?" He hummed and hawed. I said, "Come on, I want the truth!"

Three were killed outright and five were wounded so severely they never did come back. I said, "That's insane. There's something very seriously wrong here, what is it?"

Again, out of support for those guys, he was reluctant to say anything. But he finally admitted: "They were officers and gentlemen and they were on parade."

I said, "What the hell do you mean by that?"

He said, "Three of them actually showed up for work on the battlefield in their dress uniform."

I said, "You mean all their gold buttons, their sambrown belts, and their hard hats with the silver badge and gold buttons?"

He said, "Yes."

"On the battlefield?"

"Yes."

Then I said, "And what kind of weapon would they carry?"

He laughed. "They carried that silly thing that you're carrying by holster." It was a six-shot revolver that was originally designed for the British Army for the Crimean War, .38 calibre. A useless thing. I could shoot at a German corporal from about 30 paces and be sure that I would hit him and knock him down. He could shoot me from 100 paces with his Walther. Lugers were carried by the officers and sergeants. Corporals had a Walther which was a cheaper version. We had this silly thing that could only shoot six rounds and then you had to break the thing open, pick the individual shell casings out, take a cardboard box out of your pouch, open the box, take one bullet at a time and put it into the empty chambers, snap it up, put the cardboard box back in your pouch. Now you're ready to shoot six more times.

The Walther had a 12-round magazine. I carried one, only for a short time. When I was in Boissevain one time, a guy there who had been through the First World War called me up one day and I went down to see him. He gave me a .455 Smith & Wesson, a totally different gun to the .38. If I could hold the gun steady enough, I could hit a German soldier at 100 paces and knock him down. It was a snubbed nose bullet and the shocking power of that thing was absolutely fierce. I had that advantage over my contemporaries. I used that gun in battle.

I also said to Fred, "How come your uniform looks so good?" The issued uniforms came in three sizes, small, medium and large. Sgt. Fred Snell was a big man, six feet, 249 pounds, fighting weight. That's a man. But he looked smart in this uniform. He and I would be issued the same uniform. I weighed 140 pounds and stood six foot two and a half. It would hang on me like a tent.

Fred was from Manitoba. His dad was a guard at Stony Mountain Penitentiary, and Fred later went into the service too. Fred was a great guy, a big man in every regard.

He laughed again. "It'll cost you a deck of cigarettes." I went to stores, I got two uniforms, Fred and I borrowed a jeep, went down into the village, to his Italian seamstress, and in 30 minutes she cut me two uniforms. They looked smart! I put a sleeve on my epaulet here, two pips (little round objects, indicating a full lieutenant. Three pips is a captain) on it, and the boys knew I was an officer. That was the only way I looked different from the troops. The same trousers, the same jacket. That was one thing that allowed me to survive. The snipers couldn't' tell that I was an officer.

My other weapon of choice besides the .455 Smith & Wesson was the Thompson sub-machine gun that was issued by the American Army. Again, a fantastic weapon. It also fired the .455 shell, big gunpowder load, snub-nosed bullet, same cartridge as my pistol. The shocking power of the Thompson sub-machine gun was fierce. I walked into one situation where I went into this house, I saw movement, I stepped into the first door, and there, six or seven feet away from me, was a German corporal with his hand on his pistol and his pistol was leaving his holster. So I squeezed the trigger of my Thompson sub-machine gun, hitting him with three rounds in the chest. Those three rounds picked him up and flung him back against the wall, four or five feet behind him. He hit the wall, slid to the floor, and his body was outlined in blood on the wall. I emptied the magazine into the seven privates who were swinging their rifles up to point at me.

On that particular show I'll have to go back to give you the full story there. We were moving up this ridge, and I was the tail platoon. Numbers 10 and 11 were ahead with the company headquarters. The major's runner came back and said the major wants to see you. "Jim, take your patrol in to the right, and take out a machine gun post."

I said, "Fine, where is it?"

The major said he didn't know.

"Well how can I take it out if I don't know where it is?"

"Just take it out."

"But you must have some idea where it is," I said. "It's pinned down 10 and 11 platoon, so why don't we bring the tank up and let him move in?"

"No!" he said. "Take your platoon out, now!"

I went back to my platoon, picked them up, started out. We were on this road. Ten and 11 platoons had gone around to the left. So he told me go around to the right. I told my boys there's a machine gun nest, so keep your eyes open. I said I've no idea where it is, but we're going to go to the right in the road and down into the valley and climb up.

The Jerry machine-gunner let us get down the forward slope. Then he opened up and knocked a couple of my men down, wounding them. Disregarding the major's orders, I jumped up and ran back up the hill. I'm going to get that blankety blank tank. That was a very stupid mistake because the German gunner put nine bullets through me. Three went through the blouse of my tunic beside my heart; two went through the sleeve of my tunic; two went through my mess tins that were hanging from my left hip; one went through my crotch, burning my leg about two inches from where my leg joins the body; and the ninth bullet went through my water bottle. But, they didn't touch me enough to do any damage.

I got back up to the tank. I spoke to him; he's got a telephone on the back. I described the shrub where he was, and so on; the machine gun's in that. I said, "Give me a couple of rounds, then cease all fire because I will be running back out in front of your tank."

"Roger," he says, "I read you."

So he moved forward, bang, bang, and I started to run. Just as I got level with the muzzle of his canon he pulled the trigger the third time. The side blast just about blew my head off. I screamed at him and heard a grunt from inside. I ran out in front, picked up my platoon. There was nothing left of the machine gun; he'd obliterated it, and the four men with it. I then moved around to the right of this ridge, and came in from the right. I saw five houses in a semi-circle. I approached them very carefully, nobody outside on sentry duty, even with all the noise around. That's when I went into the first house and encountered this German corporal and killed him.

In those five houses, I went in, the first man in each time. I counted 39 German soldiers. I killed 34 of them. They were all carrying guns. The reason I didn't kill the five at the second house is that they were sitting around a table and the only weapon they had at hand was a gallon jug of Italian wine. I didn't see a gun anywhere. And as I was approaching them, one of them turned from looking at me to the right, to a room, so I knew there was some action there. I jumped forward; a lance corporal and corporal were coming out, both of them carrying sub-machine guns. I killed them, but I took the five guys prisoner.

Five houses I went in, and each time, I was virtually unannounced. So I survived that show. At a regimental reunion about 15 years ago, I met four of my best corporals and big Fred Snell. They had come looking for me intentionally. They said, "We wanted to find you. We often wondered if you knew what your nickname was."

And I said, "No, I'm sure I had one. What was my nickname?"

They said, "Well, we didn't just call you Mr. Bird. We called you Mr. Killer Bird."

As I say, I took 54 prisoners. But I killed 1,273 German soldiers. Every man I killed had a gun in his hand. How I kept track of them all was a mental trick. You kept count because you wanted to know how many you took out before they took you down. It was a game; it was very much a game. How many could you take out, before they took you out? That was the game.

I believed I wasn't in it for the long run. With the way things were going on, there was no way you could survive. Remember, eight lieutenants before me had bought it. Why would I be any different? When the shooting finally stopped, in the regiment there were only five lieutenants, and I was one of them, who had more than 12 months' service. All the rest had one, two or three months, having replaced dead or injured predecessors. I shouldn't be here. I should have been dead 150 times. I think the Man upstairs had His hand on my shoulder.

CHAPTER 4

'You're Filthy!'

The morning after that ridge clearing with the five houses, I woke up after a nice sleep and went outside to see where my boys were, and there's 12 of them over in a hollow behind, cleaning their rifles. So I went over to talk to them. While I'm talking to them, I see this jeep on a ridge. It's driving up the road which runs on top of the ridge and it's driving at speed, and kicking up a cloud of dust, which is a no-no. It's sure to alert the German artillery and mortar batteries. This jeep comes screaming right up to our area. He sees us so he drives right up, jumps out. It's our glorious colonel. We'd had a wonderful guy as colonel before, and for health reasons he was moved out. This political appointee was put in command. His father was a deputy minister in the federal government, so he'd pulled strings.

But as commanding officer of the Patricias, the man had two problems. First he knew very little about the army. Second, he lacked judgment. He jumps out of this jeep and comes stomping up to the group. I immediately called, "Platoon attention!" We salute.

"Who's in charge here!"

"I am, sir."

"Who are you?"

"I'm Lieut. Jim Bird, sir."

"You're a disgrace to the regiment! You're dirty, you're filthy!"

One of my men the day before got shot. I'd grabbed his leg to shut the blood off. I got squirted. I was drenched in blood down the front of my uniform. I hadn't shaven, I hadn't washed. We'd been fighting for hours. I was tired, I was dirty, hadn't been fed much.

The colonel was beautiful. He was in a battle dress, but it was lined with buttons. He had his special belt on, pretty hat with badge, all his metal regalia. And he's standing there ranting and raving that I was a disgrace to the regiment and useless.

Standing orders in the army: when you're in a group environment and you're cleaning your weapon, you put a magazine of live cartridges into your gun. As you're closing the bolt action, you hold your finger down on the top shell so it cannot enter the firing chamber, and you slide the bolt down on an empty chamber. Reason: so you don't accidentally shoot your buddy. So, the four guys behind us had finished cleaning their weapons and had closed them up. First one, and then the second, ripped the bolt back, slammed it forward, one in the chamber.

Any man with any kind of grit would have turned around, stared those two guys down, and then demanded that I arrest them. He turned and ran to his jeep, shouting at me over his shoulder, "I'll get you for this! I'll court martial you just as soon as I get back!" He jumped in his jeep, he screamed at his driver, the driver burned rubber, they created another cloud of dust. The Germans saw this and sent over a mortar. They hit him. A piece of shrapnel scratched his shin, the sort of thing where you put a dab of iodine on it and put a band-aid on it and go on your way. He rushed into our local medical officer and said, "Send me down the line."

"What for?"

"I've been wounded!"

The doc looked at it. "I'll just put some iodine—" "Send me down the line!"

If you were treated down the line in a medical facility, you got the decoration Wounded In Action. You got to wear a Wounded In Action bar on your medals.

He said, "Send me down the line, I want to be recognized!"

Unfortunately what he didn't know was, the brigadier was looking for any excuse to bust him. The medical officer at brigade reported the arrival of the colonel with a scratch. The brigadier is reported to have said, "Great. Send the major – *send the major* – down to divisional HQ. You can inform him he is no longer in command of the Patricias." He got broken. That is the highlight of my military career.

The new commander was a Major Graham, a great guy. He commanded us right to the end of the shooting. A great guy: good field man, good personnel man, good period.

* * *

During fighting, you're not aware of rifle bullets unless they're very close. Then they have a very distinct crack! or snap! By the distinctness of the snap, you know whether it was six inches away or six feet away. I told you 34 bullets went through my clothing. The nature of the German machine gun meant that 340 bullets were aimed at me. It shoots en masse. Our guns would fire something like 100 rounds a minute. The German guns would fire 1,000. The problem was, they couldn't shoot an individual. They sprayed the area the individual was in. Their gun was great if 1,000 men were coming at you. By just spraying it across, they're going to hit 500 of those men. But if only 10 men were coming at them from 10 different directions, they had a heck of a time, because they had to aim it 10 different times; whereas our Bren gun was very specific. You aimed at one man and you hit that one man. They were two different concepts.

I had three Bren guns in my platoon, one to a section. I had a Tommy-gun, as did each of the corporals and lance corporals. All of the privates had rifles, or the Bren machine guns, or the mortar man, or the anti-tank mortar man.

In Italy, I never had much to do with the Italian civilians. They didn't approach us to give us food, because in most instances they didn't have any food to give. The Germans took everything they could find. The Italians were great at burying things. They buried everything: corn, grains, wine, whatever because they knew the Germans were going to take it. And they knew they had to have something to eat. The Germans took everything that was on the surface, including some of their livestock. So by the time we got there, there wasn't much for them to give us.

We heard about rape. The Germans committed rape. That's why we made it an absolute no-no for our troops. If it's consensual, OK. But if it is not, you back off, man. We told our troops straight out: We are not attacking these Italian people; we're attacking the Germans.

We met some of the Italian resistance fighters. Many of those people spoke not only English but four or five languages. Those brave souls were of all types – doctors, dentists, lawyers, and they organized. They protected

Jews. They would hide Jews in a valley, and they told us about that. I never got into specifics about that. Just, they had helped protect a group of Jewish friends. They didn't make contact with me. They would end up at regimental headquarters. Their information would be key to HQ, which would then pass out orders down to us.

* * *

I should have been dead 150 times, as I say. I've got big feet. I've walked 500 yards through a minefield. Where was that? We were told to attack this river crossing at night, and that was a very smart decision. I was chosen to lead the company through on this one. I walked up to the Jerries' wire, "Minen," with skull and crossbones on it to warn of what was there. With my commando knife I searched the ground until I found out where they put the mines. The German is a very methodical guy, and that was his undoing. I found no mines on the shoulder side of this roadway. This was a road that I was going to walk. But as soon as I got onto the roadway, there was a mine just six inches inside. I then reached forward a metre, and found the second one. I then went up beside that, on the roadway, got to the other path, there wasn't one right at the wire, but there was one half a metre up.

Methodical. And so, in front of that one, another one a metre up. So I'd established a pattern and knew where the mines were. I made some further checks, then I walked in, walking on the grass on the side shoulder of the road. Walked all the way up until I came to more barbed-wire tunnels. I thought there might be trip-wire mines but there weren't. So I was able to lift that wire and we crawled under it.

We moved forward and then came to an anti-tank ditch. I knew that would be mined. The mines, by the way, were only under maybe an inch of soil, and they were about two inches deep. I used the tip of my knife. They were easy to find with the knife. Once I located the first one, I put in a little flag there to mark it. Then I found the next one, one metre to the right, nothing in between, then moved forward, checking, oops, there's the next one, in the middle, one metre down, between these two I'd found. Again, check over to the right, another half a metre, another one. By that I was able to not go straight north through this, but go northeast, on a diagonal. I found the path, put the flags down, and I took the company through.

We only lost one man. He must have stepped to the side, and he stepped on one of the mines and fell down into the trench. The medics came up to get him out, and unfortunately one of the medics was our padre. As the medical corpsman was tying up this shattered leg, the padre, whose name escapes me, walked forward and knelt down to say a few words of comfort to the man, and knelt on another landmine. It blew away his leg and blew in his chest and he died.

Those were the only two we lost in getting the company through. We were then able to fan out and come in behind the Germans. They were in concrete pill boxes and so on. We just dropped hand grenades down the air pipes. About the mines, I passed along the information about the pattern. I hadn't been told about it. We did another four river crossings after that, and they were similar.

The Canadian engineers were very adept at that. They had mobile bridges. What they would do is come to an area and establish a bridgehead on which they could put down a piece of machinery, so it was solid. They would then put a bridge on rollers and build it in sections. They would bring section No. 2 up, bolt it onto No. 1, put a bulldozer behind it here, and push No. 2 and No. 1 out into the air. It would balance there. They would back off and put section No. 3 on it – and they could push quite a distance across a stream. The guys on foot would have already gone to the far side, the north side and put down a small section over there. Eventually you would push these mobile units onto that small section, and you could drive a tank across it. Within hours of hitting an obstruction like that, the engineers would have our tanks following us. The Germans were always there at the rivers. That was why we would go into these night attacks.

* * *

The Hilter Line was a famous battle in May of 1944. It was the one that I came up after. That was a close call for me. I was all packed back at the reinforcement depot in Avelino. I had my gear all packed, ready to move up. I was told I was going forward, when the runner came and told me to stand down.

"What's up?" I said.

He said, "I don't know, sir. You're not going."

So I took my gear off and went down to the orderly room. What had happened was, good sergeants who had been through the prior action were chosen, sent back to England and in some cases even sent back to Canada, trained and made officers, and were now being brought back. This guy had arrived on a draft at Avelino and he knew the adjutant and said he wanted to go forward. So I got bumped and he went forward. We had a large number of officers killed in the Battle of the Hitler Line, for the reason of senior stupidity.

The higher command decided that they would attack this fortified position in daylight. That was the 8th of May, 1944. They threw the Regiment and the Seaforth Highlanders into a brigade attack. The Patricias were virtually wiped out. I think it was only 91 men walked off that battlefield. Well, it was broad daylight. And you're moving forward against concrete pill boxes with machine guns and snipers in them, and sitting back behind them on another higher ridge was the German 88 anti-tank gun. It was a fantastic weapon. Our guns couldn't touch it. Our tanks could only take that gun out if they could get within 600 metres of it, but it could shoot them at 1500 metres. So they didn't have a hope in hell. We had a British regiment of tanks in support in that battle, and every single tank that they put into action was knocked out, never got into a position where it could be effective. The Regiment suffered something like 200 killed and 200 or 300 wounded.

I didn't experience that because I was back in Avelino. I was supposed to have been in that show. Then I came forward, and that's when I met this Fred Snell. That's what led forward to that, you see. I just couldn't believe that in just 10 months of fighting, 12 platoon could lose eight officers. It just didn't make any sense. There had to be some reason for it, and this was it: the officers were gentlemen, and they were on parade. I was actually disobeying orders when I refused to wear the regalia in favour of plain fatigues. Nobody said anything; and they eventually all changed. The military can be incredibly blind, up to a point. And then they see the light.

But this frontal attack, in daylight, was the height of folly. It was from that point on that we did all night attacks on these river crossings. And we were brilliantly successful in them. We Canadians would go through on these night attacks and fan out behind enemy lines, then drop a couple of smoke grenades down these air pipes at the bunkers. The Jerries would come out with their hands up and we would clear the line. No casualties, nothing.

We also captured the 88s. But we were unable to use them. You couldn't take one of those guns and mount it in one of our tanks. It had twice the barrel length and a lot more recoil. I felt for our poor guys in the tanks because they were just sitting ducks. They didn't have a prayer, which brings up another point.

I kept myself alive because I had good hearing. I would hear incoming mortar and I would scream to my guys, "Hit the dirt!" When you're flat, you're safe. We were in static lines one time; we had taken this position and were occupying a building. I was walking behind to go to company headquarters when I heard a mortar coming. I knew it had my number on it, I could just tell by the sound of it. I was behind a row of houses and I knew I had just a split second.

The Italian farmers created little paths three or four inches above their fields. The paths allowed irrigation water to flow water beside them and run into the crops. I thought, I need some protection, two inches. I stepped 18 inches to the side, dropped down. The mortar bomb hit beside my head, 18 inches away. If I had dropped where I'd been standing, I wouldn't be here. I'd be buried six feet under. The shrapnel scratched the back of my head. Three times that happened to me. Three times I had a mortar land beside me and scratch the back of my head. My helmet would bounce off when I hit the ground like that. That was another point. Don't wear your helmet when you're in that situation, get if off. It's no bloody help in that situation. But I've got a big nose. I dropped into the dirt, face down. I got my head scratched three times. Then I smartened up and put my ear to the ground. An inch shorter. I didn't get anymore scratches.

After that close shave with the mortar I was excited. This wasn't far from Florence. I lost my cool. I jumped up and started to run back to our camp. I didn't announce myself as I should have. The sentry pulled the trigger on me. Fortunately for both of us he left the safety on. The gun didn't fire.

The sentry was Willard White. His home town was Boissevain. We came from the same town! I had Willard in my Boy Scout troop. His family were patients of my father, the physician. Can you imagine if the gun had gone off? "I'm sorry, Dr. Bird, but I shot your son." I didn't even know Willard was in our company! This was shortly after I first arrived and I didn't know people.

I had at least 100 mortar bombs land within killing distance of me. I always heard them coming and was able to get down, so I'm here today. Thirty-four enemy bullets passed through my clothing. I told you about the nine. On another occasion, we were stopped by this machine gun. I crept forward and there was a little mound of dirt in front of me so I crept

71

up on top of that. I'm looking over the top of it with my field glasses, when all of a sudden out of the corner of my eye I see dirt flying up ahead. I take a quick look, and some fellow is shooting at me. So I hunkered down and pushed myself back down off that mound of dirt. Somebody else took care of this machine gunner and we moved forward and carried on.

That night, we just bedded down where we were. Tied to our back we had a plastic raincoat. It was called a gas cape in case we were given a gas attack, this thing was proof against gas. We used it as a raincoat. It was cold that night. So I untied this thing as we hunkered down for the night, and decided I would put it on to try to keep me warm. But – I took a look at it – there were 12 bullet holes through that little pack, where it was on my back. That guy who had been shooting at me put 12 bullets through that little roll of plastic.

Another occasion: we were moving forward and a sniper knocked one of my men down. I took cover behind a little stone wall, and I asked the boys who were with me, "Did you guys get any indication of where this guy is?"

No, no. OK. I stuck my head up above the wall, just my eyes. With my field glasses I was looking. One of the guys said, "Do you see anything yet?" As the sniper took aim, I pulled my head down to say, "No, nothing." His bullet went through my beret, taking my beret off my head. So I said, "That sonovabitch, he's ruined my new beret!"

This is how silly you get. "He can't do that to me!" is how I felt. I put the beret back on my head, had the boys line it up. I thought he was over to the left; no, he was over to the right. There was a little bush over there. I rigged up a blind behind me – again the plastic raincoat – had the boys stick it on their bayonets so it would act like a blind. The sunlight was from our rear. As soon as I stuck my head up, I was highlighted. The blind eliminated the light, so that we could put our heads up and look around without being seen. My machine gunner/Bren gunner put his gun on top of the stone wall. On the word go, he sprayed the area.

The sniper pulled his head down to avoid the barrage of fire. That enabled me to get up and run. I ran up the ridge and up to him, still hunkered down, and shot him. Snipers were not much loved by the armies. They were not well thought of. That's how crazy you get in those situations, though. Instead of getting scared, you get mad. This is the craziness of war.

CHAPTER 5

Precious Freedom

Part of my purpose in telling you what really happened is to explain to people that if you value the freedom you have here in Canada, be prepared to put your life on the line to sustain that freedom. The Dutch didn't understand at first. They said, why are you here? We said we're here because you people are in slavery and we're here to free you. That just blew them away. Hitler came very close to where his navy could take control of the oceans and he would have starved North America out and we would have had German paratroopers on our streets. That's the whole reason that I went to war. If freedom is threatened, then do your thing.

We have such a beautiful world here in Canada. We have a wonderful institution in this thing we call Canada. It really is a marvelous place. I was reading the other day about a small African country that's been taken over by the drug trade. The president was pushed aside and whatnot and drug barons were ruling the land. That's not life, that's not living, when you've got that kind of environment in your life, when you think of what we've got here, and what we've had right from the beginning. We get along with each other, we get along with Quebec. I walk along the sea wall here in West Vancouver and English is the language you hear least. People come here from all over the world because they value what we have. Well, there's a price to keeping freedom. That's why I fought and it's the only reason I would advise young men to fight today.

Getting back to snipers, when I met those four corporals and the sergeant, and they told me the nickname they'd given me, I said, "Well,

I admit to killing 1273, what do you guys admit to?" I don't remember the exact numbers, but the four corporals were 2200, 2400, 2500 and 2600 plus – each. And big Fred Snell, despite his size, more than 3,000. The six of us -- four corporals, one sergeant, one lieutenant -- 15,300-plus enemy kills. Just six of us! And killing was not our primary job. We were supervising the privates who had the rifles and the Bren guns, the long-range weapons. Our primary job was supposed to be supervising, but here we were with 15,300 enemy kills. The six of us.

That's half of West Vancouver. We were one platoon. When you think there are 12 infantry platoons in a regiment, plus the sniper platoon, plus some of the other killer platoons, the actual kills of a regiment like the Patricia's (he trails off). The Patricia's were recently written up in a military magazine as being one of the great fighting regiments in the world. That's the reputation that they have today. I and my little 12 Platoon helped create that reputation.

D-Day, June 6, 1944. The largest invasion force in history stormed ashore onto French soil. That was just a month after I joined the regiment. I joined it on the 20th of May, 1944, just after the Hitler Line wipeout. So I was on my way heading north, up Italy, in June. And you see, we were sent down to Italy originally for a couple of months. They wanted to give us some battlefield experience, then the entire First Canadian Corp was supposed to go back then to England and filter out through the other four Canadian divisions, giving them first-hand, battle-experienced, people. That was the concept.

The problem was we were too good. The American Fourth Army to whom we were attached said, "No bloody way, we're not letting those Canadians get away." And they wouldn't release us. "We need those Canadians here, we work too well with them." We would punch through the hole, and they would fan out through the hole with their armour. They were fully mechanized. Trucks and tanks. We had something like 15 or 20 trucks to a regiment of infantry; they had 15 or 20 troops to every truck.

I never saw Montgomery or Patton. The one I remember was Blood and Guts Volkes, the First Canadian Divisional Commander. We'd be on parade. He'd wheel out in front of us, bounce out of his jeep, jump up on the hood, "I want you to kick the balls out of those bastards!" rip-roaring and snorting, so we called him Blood and Guts. That's all he is. He talks blood and he talks guts. But he was a good leader. The troops loved him. He was their kind of guy. He could call a guy an asshole, shit head, or what have you. "Go and kick them in the balls!" The troops knew what he meant. He meant, right between the eyes. They loved him.

* * *

When I think of Italy, what comes to mind is the fact that for us, it was always uphill. We were never coasting downhill, it seemed, we were always fighting uphill. Even though we were on the flat, we were reaching these river banks, and Jerry was on the other side, so we had to get down and up again so we could meet them on even terms again. It was rarely on open ground. It was constant hills. Italy, you see, is a long, great boot, but it goes up in the middle. It has a ridge of mountains down the middle. And then you've got these rivers, which the Italians dammed for the electricity and water control to improve their farming down below. So the rivers that once were raging torrents are now six inches of water. You could walk, literally, all the way up north in Italy, and barely get your feet wet.

For us, Jerry always had the advantage. He could sight us in, and set up his machine guns in crossfire. No matter where you tried to enter, you'd be in crossfire from at least two guns.

We occasionally liberated some of the German weaponry. I brought five handguns home. I gave your father (Clayton) a luger. I left the others out in Boissevain. One day, some bad news got out about a hand gun. I became concerned that these hand guns were in father's gun case, and everybody knew he had guns. So I went out there one day to Boissevain on a trip, and I took those handguns out to the town nuisance yard and pounded them into scrap iron. So those guns are not available to anybody. I destroyed them.

The youngest German soldiers I encountered were 13 and 15, a lance corporal and a corporal. I caught them by surprise, saw them coming. I was hunkered down in a hedgerow. They turned to their left in front of me (to my right), so I let them get well over there. I then came in behind them and yelled out, "Deutschland soldat cammarad!" (German soldiers, surrender!). The eight privates behind them took one look, dropped their rifles and put their hands up.

But the two corporals were out in front. They both swung around. Even though any degree of common sense would tell you they didn't have a hope – here's me and my seven men with our guns pointed at them – they swung around with their machine guns. They're at this point maybe 200 metres away, but they swung around with their guns ready for a fight, so we took them out. Then I checked their papers for their ages afterward. Both had been in the army more than four years.

The eight privates they had with them were all conscripts from Austria. That's why they gave up as soon as they got the chance. One of the guys told me, "These guys, we're glad you killed them. They were real evil." Another man said, "That lance corporal, I crossed him one day. He got angry at me. He said, "You do that again and I will shoot you." He was 13 years old. He said, "I can shoot you and they won't do anything to me, they won't ask any questions."

You see, there was a generation of fanatical young Germans totally caught up in the racist Nazi dogma. That's why I had no compunction killing them, because those are the kind of human beings the world is better off without. Those were the kinds of people you didn't want going back to Germany to breed more.

On one of our last occasions, we moved into this area and hunkered down, and I sent out my scouts. One of my scouts came running back and said, "There's a big column of troops marching towards us."

I said, "What do you mean by big?"

He said, "There's 200 or 300. It's big."

I said, "Marching. What the hell are you talking about, marching."

They were four men abreast, and 30 to 50 deep.

I said, "Are there officers out in front? "Oh yes, there's half a dozen officers, plus quite a few non-commissioned officers."

So I set the guys up and said, "Now. If they turn left, and march towards us, we shoot all of the officers, and we shoot all of the non-commissioned officers. But don't shoot the private soldiers."

My analysis of the situation was perfect. Sure enough, they turned left and walked toward us. We shot all the officers we could see. The privates all dropped their rifles. Again, conscripts. All the privates were conscripts. I found out a captain was the officer leading them. He had been an office manager. He'd never been near the infantry. He didn't know what infantry was. And they'd put him in command, told him to march up to the front and attack the Canadians. He didn't know which end was up. And neither did the other officers with him.

The Nazis were desperate because we had eliminated a whole generation of military, of an age group from about 13 up to about 40 -- we, and the Russians on that terrible Eastern Front. That's why they had to bring these office types in. They still wanted Germans in command, but they were Germans who knew nothing about fighting.

A German soldier told us this: Whenever the Germans learned that the Canadians were in an area, they threw their best troops against us. We came up against the German paratroopers, and some of the other elite German infantry. We still destroyed them. We survived. Remember, we were the good guys. It wasn't us who were putting Gypsies, homosexuals, Poles, and other "undesirables" in concentration camps and starving them or gassing them to death. It wasn't us who were making lampshades from their skins. It wasn't us who selected a group of people – Jews – blamed them for Germany's woes and tried to wipe them off the face of the Earth. And it wasn't us who attacked Poland on August 31, 1939 and started the war. It was the Nazi government that did all that, Adolf Hitler. And Hitler had designs on North America. Not only other people's but our own freedom was at stake, our way of life. It was our job to put him out of power by defeating his military, and we did. Hitler started the war but we finished it. He committed suicide on April 30, 1945, when Russian troops, our allies, were fighting in the streets of Berlin.

There was never a moment in battle that brought me to tears. What I was doing was the right thing. We all thought that way. Those four corporals and my sergeant, Fred, none of us stayed in, none of us wanted to be professional soldiers, we elected to come home. We elected to get disbanded. We wanted to become civilians because that's what we were. None of us were military professionals before the war. All we went into uniform for was freedom: to maintain our own freedom, and to bring freedom to Europe.

By the way, this wasn't taught in our training. They didn't have to. That was why we were there. I was semi-educated, you might say, but my corporals, most of them finished Grade 12 and then went into the army. So they didn't have any higher education, but that was the only reason they were over there -- freedom.

CHAPTER 6

Growing Up in Boissevain

As a boy growing up in Boissevain I hunted. I owned my own .22 when I was 10. Dad was a doctor but also a hunter. He grew up on a farm near the Red River, so hunting came naturally to him, too.

As boys, my older brother Clayton and I were the bird dogs. Dad and one of his buddies would have shotguns on the side and we'd go into a field with a little copse of bush in a hollow. Clayton and I would go into these bushes, thrash around, and drive out any partridge and prairie chicken, and Dad and his buddy would shoot them. We did this from the day we could walk. Yes, we were out there when we were just toddlers.

I could shoot a gopher in the head at 100 paces with my .22. That's where I learned my shooting skills. Free-hand, standing up. The reason you shot him in the head was, a gopher had the instinct to dig itself down into its hole if it was injured. So you shot it in the head to stop it; you wanted its tail; you got five cents for it. That's where you got your cartridges. The farmers wanted these animals destroyed because their cattle would step in these holes and break a leg. And once a cow broke a leg, you had to kill it. You couldn't mend the leg. So they established this routine to pay us kids.

Clayton and I didn't hunt very much together. Clay and I were strange in many respects in that we never traveled together. On a Saturday morning when we would get up, Clay would say, "Les and I are thinking of going south." I'd say, "Fine. Russ and I'll go north." That was all there was to it. Russ Stevenson it was. I forget Les's last name.

Mack, left, and Clayton about 1933.

Turtle Mountain was on the American border south of us. Talk about mountains, it was only 600 to 800 feet high. But on the prairie you could see it forever. The Indians would have sat there, waiting to see the buffalo, and worked on making arrows. We found arrow heads. That was an Indian hunting ground, and it overlooked the prairie. Clayton and I found dozens of arrow heads. I also found a knife about six inches long, a piece of stone, but it had a very sharp edge to it.

After the war, when Clay and I got back, we found all our Indian artifacts were gone. All our clothes were gone. Our parents apparently didn't expect us to survive – or else the need for clothes in England was so great that they gave them ours. I had a lovely summer suit. My mother made a lady's dress and skirt out of my trousers and suit jacket. I had no suit when I came back. You were given two coupons when you came back, for suits. I had to buy new clothes before I could go to work.

Mom was a very strong person, very strong and very talented. She came from a large family; I think there were eight of them. Ella Irene Bradley she was, from the Ottawa area. They were farmers. But their father said that because of the family, each of you can only have one thing. So make up your mind what you want. Ethel, her sister, chose music. Give her a sheet of music, it didn't matter what it was, and Ethel could play it. But take the sheet of music away and Ethel couldn't play. My mother, who never took a single lesson on the piano, would watch Ethel playing, and then sit down at the piano and play it by memory. She had an incredible ear, and she could sing. She was in the church choir.

I nearly drove her crazy. Clayton joined the town band and learned to play there. He also was given piano lessons by a very bad teacher. Her idea of teaching was, if you weren't holding your hands right she would take a ruler and crack you across the knuckles. Clayton took a dislike to her. But he did learn to play the piano, and that got him into music, and then he went to the band. When he went to Brandon College he established an orchestra, and it was good enough that they were going to tour across the Prairies. The only problem was they couldn't find enough bucks amongst them to even find a car to get them around.

I said to Mom, Dad has a violin and I would like to learn. Dad had taken some lessons and practised a bit but it wasn't for him. There was a lady in town who just lived a couple of houses away, she plays the violin and could teach me. OK, you can have lessons. Well, I'm tone deaf, which I didn't know. Father is tone deaf; that's why he couldn't learn to play this violin, and it's why I couldn't learn to play it. I'm screeching away on this thing and my poor mother, with her beautiful ear, was listening to this. Finally she said to me one day, "You're killing me. I can't stand this. You'll never learn to play it, you're like your father, tone deaf. You can't tell a flat from a sharp or anything in between." And so I gave it up. To this day I have a collection of music, of CDs, some of the finest music you could ever listen to. I love it. But when I'm in a public gathering and start to sing, people get up and move away!

And yet I had a good ear when I was out hunting rabbits and gophers and deer. I had a good ear when I was in the army. I could hear German troops moving before I could see them. As a boy I could hear game. I got my first deer before I was legal. Both Clay and I shot our deer before we were legal. Father took us out with him. We were using a .303 Springfield rifle. We were taught guns early. One of his friends, Dr. Bigelow from Brandon, had a son Danny. Bigelow was a surgeon and had a clinic. He not only had more income coming in, but he had more people who paid him, because he was in a clinic. They always had cash. They would come with us hunting, and Danny had a little .410 shotgun, which fired a shell about the size of your little finger. You could only shoot partridge with it; you had to get within about 30 paces of these birds to have a hope of hitting them. We learned to use that shotgun, and again I would guess we were 10 or 11.

My grandfather, Dad's father, was unfortunately one of the many Birds who could not handle alcohol. As you probably know, we have an Indian heritage. He was John James Bird. The earliest memories I have are when I was four or five. We were in the farmhouse north of Winnipeg near the Red River, in the Petersfield area. Granny got up, went into the backyard, chopped an armful of wood, carried it into the farmhouse, and her 66-year-old daughter balled hell out of her and said, "Leave that to the men." Granny came into the living room muttering, "These young people don't know their place; how dare she speak to me like that." She was 92 or 93 then. Her husband, your great-grandfather, had not been living with them for four or five years. She had thrown him out because he was always drunk. Whenever he left home and got near town, he went into the beer parlour and came home drunk.

I remember Uncle Jack who was one of the other brothers. He was about three years older than Dad. I remember seeing him. We would drive into Selkirk. Dad would go into a beer parlour and pull Jack out. He would be roaring drunk. He couldn't handle his alcohol either. That was why Dad stayed away from the beer parlour. Dad loved his family and spent time with us, but his thing was the hunting.

That was the only time he had for us. He was on call 24 hours a day, seven days a week. Mels Binions had a farm a couple of miles from the American border. He became one of Dad's hunting buddies. He always took his dog with him so he never worried about getting lost. Mels would say, "Home, Jack," and the dog would just turn and take him home.

One of my deer that I shot in my early days was also an illegal shoot. I was legal hunting age I think by that time. I had shot this animal but I hadn't killed it. It was bleeding so I followed it. I came to this fence so I stepped over it and carried on. Eventually saw the deer, shot it, gutted it, dragged it back, got it back to where father was and he asked me where I got the animal. I told him that I'd jumped this fence. He said, "Do you realize what that fence was?" I said it was just another wire fence. He said, "That was the international border. You shot that animal in the United States of America!" He was pretty serious about it because it did have ramifications if any Americans had been around. I could have been in big deep goo.

A couple of things brought me to the army, rather than the navy or air force. First, it was the family regiment. Secondly, I had no inclination to go into the air. Third, when I thought of the navy, as a prairie guy, it just didn't seem to add up. When my buddy Russ Stevenson joined the navy, I said, "You're crazy, man. Every time we took you hunting in the car, you'd get motion sickness. Just riding in the car!" What did he end up in? A corvette, going into the attack on France. A small ship. He sailed across the Atlantic dozens of times in one of those floating bathtubs. And he got sea sick! No. I figured, my big flat feet were best suited to the fresh, friendly ground.

Dad couldn't go into the First World War because he was a doctor. He graduated second in his class. The top people are recruited by the medical clinics. Dad was never approached. He made the mistake when he was going through school of telling people he had Indian blood. Not a single offer came to him, from anywhere. So in 1913 he had to find a small town somewhere where he could move in. One of his teachers told him about Boissevain. There was an older doctor there, an English Army doctor. When World War One hit, this doctor said he'd been in the army in Africa and he was going back in, leaving Boissevain to Dad for a medical practice. There'd been two doctors in the neighbouring towns, Deloraine and Killarney, and both of them lost one doctor. So they were down to three doctors handling a large area of about 50 miles by 16 miles. When father decided that he should join the army, the medical people said no. Your place is here in Canada; you have to take care of this large territory.

He was upset about it because he was young, and his brother Charlie was in the Patricias. Dad felt he should be.

We faced no discrimination when growing up in Boissevain. I don't know that anybody knew of our mixed blood. Mom wouldn't let Dad say anything because she knew about what he had suffered already. I knew about the native blood, even when I joined the army. We'd had contact with Dad's family, so we saw. Peg asked me to keep it quiet, because there was too much prejudice.

CHAPTER 7

The Haunted Estate

I want to share the time I had a leave with Clayton. I was at Aldershot in southeast England, the base there, and he was at his airfield. Clayton had found this lady who had the estate. Her husband was off in the war somewhere. She opened her estate to service people, and she would have as many as six or eight staying with her at any given moment. While we were there this Australian was there and he'd visited many times, judging by the way they were friendly.

He was the one that warned me about the ghost. He said, "Don't get excited if you hear any strange noises at night, it's the ghost."

I said, "Oh bullshit. What are you giving me here?"

He said, "Oh no. This place has a ghost; it's haunted."

I thought it was all nonsense. We all went to bed. In the quietness of the night, strange noises started happening. There were three of us in this large bedroom: me, Clayton and my army buddy, Bob. I woke up and heard these strange noises and I look over at Bob and said, "Did you hear that?"

"Yeah," he says, "it's been going on for some time."

Clay was in the next bed farther over. He said, "That's the ghost."

I said my usual, "BS." Then "rumble, rumble, rumble." What is going on here? So anyway, we're talking about this. Then the Aussie comes along and opens our door and says, "Hope the ghost didn't disturb you."

I said, "What kind of nonsense is this, anyway?"

He said, "No, no, he does this every night. He goes for a walk." And then you heard, thump, thump thump. Thump, thump, thump. Somewhere, somebody was walking. "Yes, that's the ghost, he's gone for another walk."

What had happened was, away back in time, somebody had got murdered on the property, and this was him walking. He'd come back to haunt his killers. I didn't believe in ghosts then, and I don't believe in ghosts now, but that sucker was walking around out there, I heard him!

The room had a fireplace. Every room in the house did. One of the noises we heard was the fireplace tools banging together. There was a distinct metal clang. The Aussie said, if you hear a pistol shot, don't worry. I said, "Why?"

He said, "That's the only way to get rid of the ghost. I stick my pistol out the window and fire, and the ghost leaves." The guy might have been shot, and that's why he's afraid of the pistol. He did fire it, and the ghost left.

CHAPTER 8

In Holland, and a Friend in the Underground

Early in 1945 they said, "We're going to pull you out of Italy and consolidate you with the Canadians in Holland." We drove all the way up. We got into Belgium, and the company commander, the major and the captain, went off to England on leave, and left me in charge of Baker Company. We did our various training exercises in Belgium.

Then we got the order to move out. The major and captain were held up by bad weather, they couldn't get across the channel. I took the company forward. I was all ready to take it into the Eisel River Crossing. We were lining up at the bank, ready to load the boats, when Capt. Egan Chambers came back. I handed him the written orders, said, "Good luck, chum, I'm off to Blighty," and he took the company across the Eisel River and I got onto the first truck heading back and went off to England for two weeks' leave.

Then we really didn't do that much heavy fighting in Holland. We did some, but nothing compared to what we had in Italy. That was in early April, 1945, and on the 8th of May, the shooting formally stopped.

* * *

I did not experience any discrimination in the army. Yes, I was a little darker than most of the men. We Birds have the native blood. Dad was a half-breed and I suppose I'm a quarter. But I said nothing. I never mentioned it, because at every move I made through the army, the discrimination was there. Oh yes. I would never have been accepted into the regiment in the first place. I would never have been accepted into the Officers' Training Corp in the second place. No. I had Indians in my platoon. They did not appear to recognize my native blood, and I never told them. I didn't dare. They were good men, too.

I used anybody as the scouts. The scouts in sniper platoon was a special group. They had special abilities, and they were a power unto themselves. After the war, the sergeant of that scouts and sniper platoon told me he killed something like 5,300 men. Himself.

The Indians, or First Nations people as they're called today, in my command were treated fair and square. The discrimination was in the officer category. I could be seen to have moved up the ranks fairly quickly, but that was because I was assumed to have leadership ability because I'd been in the Officers' Training Corp in Winnipeg, whereas my brother Clay didn't have that. He went into the ranks, and got recognized from there. By the time I joined the regiment, I'd already been a lieutenant for 15 months. I started as an officer cadet when I went to Gordon Head.

At war's end, I was a captain for a few weeks. They caught me by two days. The army issued an order when the shooting stopped, cancelling all promotions retroactively. I missed my captaincy by two days. I received area medals: the war in Europe and the war in Italy. No others. Twice I was told I had earned a military cross, but they couldn't write it up because I had disobeyed an order. It's why I chose not to join the permanent force. You had to put up with a lot. To put it quite bluntly, you had to be a sucker – a bum sucker.

In Italy I never had a chance to befriend any Italian civilians. But I very nearly married a Dutch lady, Ans Anchelon. I got into Holland there, and the shooting stopped. We were at a dance. These three young ladies were there. I took a shine to this one. I asked if I could see her again. We hit it off, right from the start. We both felt the same way. We went together for a while. I knew that I was approaching the time to leave. I was adjutant then.

We got a few weeks' notice, and I told Ans, "I've got my orders, we're leaving in a couple of weeks." I said, "I think I want to marry you and I think you want to marry me. What about it?"

She said, "Well, I still have problems." She had been going with Franz. They were both in the underground. One day her boss came to her and said, "Come on in the back room, I want a quickie." And she said, "No, you know better than that. I'm going to marry Franz; I don't play around with anybody else."

He said, "I don't give a damn about you. I want a quickie and I want it now!"

She said, "No. Go to hell!"

He said, "I'll fix you."

He got on the phone and called the Gestapo. She grabbed her things, ran out the door and ran home and phoned Franz. Couldn't reach him. They had a code message. She left this code message for him. She was looking out the front window of her apartment, she was upstairs, she was looking down the street and saw this black car coming, and knew what that was. Civilians didn't drive those cars.

She had an escape route across the roofs and then went underground. She was underground for about two months. Then we arrived and the war was over, and I met her a few weeks later.

She explained this briefly to me and said, "I'm still involved with Franz."

I said, "I know, my dear."

She said, "I don't know if he's dead. Yes, he's vanished. I've searched for him, I can't find any trace of him. But, I don't know that he's dead."

I said, "Come on. You have to be realistic. The people where he was working said the Gestapo picked him up. I'm sorry. That's the end of the story. He's gone."

She said, "Well, I don't know that. I've signed up for the Dutch army. I'm going out to the territories for three years. I'll see you after that."

I said, "My dear, no. The war has cost me three years of my life already. I'm not waiting three more years on an 'iffy.'"

"Well," she said, "I don't think I can get out of the army."

I said, "I've heard that all I have to do is go to Queen Wilhelmina, and she will release you. She will give anything to the Canadians. So that's no excuse."

"Well," she said, "I'm not leaving the army. I'm going out to the colonies for three years."

I said, "Goodbye."

I would think her boss would have been executed. With someone like her, who reported him, and lost her fiancé, I'm pretty sure the Dutch people would quietly take him out somewhere and fix him.

She was a great gal. We didn't correspond. I told her straight, "I think I want to marry you, but, if you want to give it some more time, come out to Canada, work out there for a while, we'll see if things work out between us."

We were about the same age. She would be in her 20s. She was a good-looking gal. There again, her father was not a good guy. He started playing around on her mother so her mother divorced him. So she had a broken family life. And then she had this thing with her fiancé, and she didn't exactly have a happy, normal, adult life. But she was a wonderful gal. She was intelligent, she was good looking, a great swimmer, looked great in a bathing suit.

* * *

I never got back to Europe. Because of my nightmares, I didn't want to go near any association that would reawaken memories. I'd had two years of that hell. When Peg cured it, I didn't want to disturb it.

But I wanted to go back. We had some groups go back and they received a wonderful reception. The Canadians who go back, even now, today, they pave the streets in gold in front of them. The people I've talked to who have gone back can't believe it. The Dutch are deeply grateful.

The Dutch people I talked to while I was there could never understand why we were there. "Why would you come to Europe?"

We said, simply, one word: "Freedom." And this one girl said, "But you are already free."

"Yes, but you are not. We came over to bring you what we have in Canada."

They thought that was something pretty special.

You see, everything over there was conscript. But I said, the Canadian army you see here in Holland today is totally voluntary. The conscripts were coming in behind us, because there weren't enough volunteers in the end. In the beginning, it was all volunteers. And I doubt whether many of those Canadian conscripts saw action.

For some time, I kept a diary. I described in detail some of my early work in Italy. I found the padre one day going through a man's things, including his diary. I said, "You're not going to send that to his parents, are you?"

He said, "I have to. It belongs to him. Now it goes to his home."

That's when I destroyed my diary. I tore the bloody thing up. My mother, being the gentle thing she was, it would have killed her. It's sad. I think these stories need to be told. We have more than 100 men killed in

Afghanistan and people really don't know how they're dying. All they used to get in our war was a telegram, "We regret to inform you that ...."

What I should have done is leave my diary intact, and include a note: "In case of my death, this goes to my father only." He would have kept it from mother, and the stories would have been preserved.

CHAPTER 9

Afghanistan and other Thoughts

Afghanistan is not a place for Canada's military. The prime reason for going into a war is knowing you have a chance of winning and doing some good. You'll never win this war. Never. The Taliban are liquid. Whenever you try to stomp down on liquid, it squirts out. This is what the Taliban do. Whenever we move in and clean up an area, whoops, they squirt out over here, and over there, and they come back at you again. Also, when we were fighting, if I saw a coal scuttle helmet, I knew that was German. There was no question. How do you know what a Taliban is? What size, shape or sex? So how can you win against an enemy you cannot identify?

Afghanistan is what I call a totally dirty war. There is no winning it. And unfortunately, I don't know that we're going to do that much good. The people themselves that you are liberating have to want it very badly, to the point where they will take over and do what is necessary. The Dutch did that. The Poles did that. I don't think the Afghans will do that. They've never truly known freedom, so how can they want it? They are allowing the Taliban to sneak back in. Many of those people, most of the Afghans, support the Taliban. They want order and an end to the fighting. No, you will never win this war.

The Afghans who oppose the Taliban are afraid that if they speak out against them, one of their acquaintances will finger them to the Taliban and, phoot!, in the dark of the night. Not you, but your wife and kids. Because the Taliban don't care who they kill. All they care about is the message. Again, the little 10-year-old boy walking towards you. Friend or foe? You don't know. You don't know. But that bulge around his waist. He walks up to you and bam! And you're gone. The natural thing is you want to shoot him. But you cannot shoot a child. So as I say, you can't win this war.

* * *

In May of 1945 I was put in charge of the First Canadian Field Punishment Camp in Holland. I never got into Germany. The Punishment Camp was for Canadian prisoners, bad boys who had stolen the colonel's jeep, or reported for duty drunk. They'd get 10 days or two weeks or something like that. Our favourite treatment was to load them in full gear, except the gear was empty. Then we would load the backpacks and small front packs with rocks, 60 pounds of rocks, and then double them around until they dropped. Throw a bucket of water on them, get up and double again until they dropped again. We never killed anybody. They didn't want to come back. One guy told me, as he was leaving – I said goodbye to them all as they were leaving – I said, "I hope you've learned your lesson." He says, "You'd better believe it, sir. I am never going near a place like this again!"

The food parcels from home would come every couple of weeks. Other guys got similar packages. When I came home, I had between 2000 and 3000 cigarettes! They'd sent me so many I couldn't smoke them! Clayton got the same. And Clayton saved me. When I came home and had all these cigarettes, he said, "Throw them out, man."

I said, "You're crazy, I can't throw them out, I'm smoking 70 a day."

He said, "I threw them out, I quit."

I said, "You're kidding, you were a heavy smoker."

He said, "I know, but I don't smoke now, throw them out!"

I took those thousands of cigarettes out to the garbage pail and stuffed them in. And I never smoked again.

It was hell. Believe me it was hell. Withdrawal, wow. I never smoked before the war. I started in the army. Clayton also started in the war. Our dad didn't smoke, nor did he drink. I don't remember any of mom's people smoking.

I came back from that Punishment Camp job to half of the regiment. The other half, the guys who were staying as permanent force, were going into Germany as occupation troops. I elected to stay with the half that was going back to Canada. When I got back to the regiment I had a couple of Joe jobs, and then they made me adjutant. So I was adjutant, or chief administrative officer, of the half of the regiment that came back to Canada. I reported to the colonel.

It was a challenging job in more ways than one. I ended up as the commanding officer who took one half of the regiment into Winnipeg. What happened was, I had split everybody up into two parcels, because I was told that we were going to have two trains. I was on the second train. I had with me five majors and 12 captains and about 15 lieutenants. Just after we got off the ship in Halifax, a runner comes down from the major in command: "Tell Mr. Bird that the majors and captains are all going on train No. 1." They wanted to be the first into Winnipeg so they would be recognized. So they start off ahead. I'm in train No. 2 and the officer in charge.

I had no problems. I went through the train speaking to each coach. I warned the boys. I said, "I know how resourceful you guys are. We will be stopping. Unfortunately we won't know how long we're stopping. A freight train might come along and then we'll be back on the track. I know how resourceful you guys are and how thirsty you are. They told me that we get two bottles of beer. You get one with lunch and one beer with dinner. I don't want any of you guys nipping off the train to get some extra supplies." I said, "Just think of what your wife or your parents will feel like if I have to tell them that you stopped somewhere in the wilderness of northern Ontario, and I don't know where the hell you are (he chuckles). They'll be disappointed."

So anyway, the guys cooperated; none of them gave me any trouble. As we got into northern Ontario, train No. 1 developed a hot box, which is excessive heat in a wheel, on one of their coaches, and they got sidelined. We passed them. Train No. 2 arrived in Winnipeg with Officer Lieutenant James Bird in command. We stepped out of the trains, I lined them up along the platform, march them up on the deck in the Canadian National Railways yard, there's a big crowd of people out there, stand them to attention and announce to the crowd: "I don't know what the situation is, but this is train No. 2. I don't have any of the majors, I don't have any of the captains. They're on train No. 1. And so on." When I dismissed the troops, to the soldiers I said: "If you cannot find your family, come right back here. The legionnaires are in charge here, they will take care of you."

Made my little speech, "Patricias dismissed!" Saluted the last time. They all went off to their families.

I could see mom and dad over here, so I went over and talked to them for a few minutes, came back to the dais where the legionnaires were, and no soldiers had come back; they had all found their people. So we checked everything out, I went back to the folks. Clayton hadn't come over. We stayed at his place in Winnipeg that night, all of us. Then we got in Dad's car and drove out to Boissevain. That's how Lieutenant James Mackenzie Bird, officer commanding the Princess Patricia's Canadian Light Infantry, arrived home. It was an honour.

I don't remember seeing any photographers. They were expecting train No. 1. The railway knew where it was. They would likely have notified all the reception people, the dignitaries. I missed a bet. While we stopped in Kenora I got off the train to watch and see that none of the boys got off the train. I was standing and talking to a railroad man. I missed the bet, I should have told him, "Could you notify the Winnipeg Free Press as to when you expect us to arrive?" I didn't think of it. It would have been sweet to have been on the front page of the Winnipeg Free Press. I blew it! (and he chuckles.)

I came back in one piece but I tell you I paid a penalty for it. Many of the guys had trouble when they got home, for one reason or another. Here's an indication: towards the end, in Holland, I went to the medical officer and said, "I'm having problems. I can't believe this but I'm having problems seeing properly. I have to use my field glasses." He gave me a quick check and said, "Yes, you've got to see an eye man. But don't worry about it, the shooting's going to stop any day. I'll send you down to the medical people then." A couple of days later the shooting did stop. The only problem was, he went forward with the regiment, and they were stripping German units down. I was detached and put in command of the First Canadian Divisional Field Punishment Camp. So I never did see the eye guy.

At home I saw a lot of eye doctors. Finally the eighth one had common sense. He said, "I don't believe this. All 10 of your readings are different. They're all different. So what I'm going to do is give you an average." So he gave me a prescription that averaged the tests; I could use those glasses. I could work with them. I used them for many years. But after I got my glasses my eyes were still not strong. I couldn't work all day in the office and then study at night. My eyes gave me a bad time. So I never completed my accountancy course.

I got discharged and tried to become a civilian again and then I ran into my friend, Mr. Mundy. I went in to see him and said, "Well, Mr. Mundy, I'm back from the war, I'd like to start my course again."

He said, "You should never have left me in the first place. Why did you survive?"

"Well, I don't know that myself, sir."

Then he said, "I'll take you back as a first-year student."

I spent the first few months working with them checking additions in my head. Can you imagine? They didn't have machines. I checked the big sales registers and purchase registers of some big manufacturing corporations. Despite my previous time with the firm, I spent month after month doing nothing but checking additions because they hadn't been able to do this work. They didn't have a junior. I did it for six months. This was the Winnipeg office of a national company of chartered accountants.

Then the accountant's institute brought in a rule whereby we had to put in three years of apprenticeship. Because of the way Mundy had treated me, when they brought in this three-year rule, I went to him and said good-bye. "There's no point in my staying around," I said. "You don't think much of me, obviously, and I certainly don't think much of you." I was really behind the eight-ball because he taught one of the classes in the fifth-year course. I walked out and left him and went into private practice. I couldn't work, my eyes were bad, I couldn't study at all.

When I came back they put me in the veterans' hospital, the Deer Lodge Hospital in Winnipeg, and treated me there with shock treatments and so on. Useless. Absolutely useless. I started having problems (sleeplessness, nightmares, agitation) so the medics I was seeing put me into Deer Lodge. They put me through everything they had, but it didn't work. I had no more problems getting along with people than ordinary; it was mainly what was within me. And I couldn't concentrate because I couldn't see.

Then I started having nightmares. Those, believe me, were in Technicolor. They were awful. I suffered through those for nine years. Then I met and married Peg McLeod. I warned her about this, and she said, "Don't worry about it, we'll work through it." I would have nightmares in bed with her. I was thrashing around, swearing, cussing. She would wake me up, ask me where I was, what I was doing: she literally talked those nightmares out of my head. A few months living with her, the nightmares stopped, and I have never had a nightmare since.

Margit (Peggy) McLeod on 18 September 1955,
three months before marrying J. M. Bird.

A woman's instinct – the woman is the person who brings life into the world. We idiot men are the ones who take it out. Right? And a woman has that instinct. She knows how to preserve life, how to maintain life. And that's all she was doing, she was trying to preserve my life. And she did. She didn't know how she did. She had no formal training. Just instinct. But it worked, only a few months. We were married 52 years and eight months.

CHAPTER 10

'Life's Been Pretty Good'

We got married the 10th of December, 1955. Peg passed away the 10th of July, 2008. The great tragedy there is, one of my health letters told me, four or five months later, something that might have kept her alive. This doctor down south has found a way to rebuild a brain that has been damaged by stroke. He's had great success with it. He puts you in a plastic bubble, clamps it down air tight, injects oxygen in there and then raises the atmospheric pressure. What this does is send the oxygen into the smallest cell in your body, including the damaged cells in your brain. He claims that he has rebuilt brains. But by the time I found this out, Peg was so close to death that I couldn't move her. She was born in 1925; she would be 83.

Overall, life has been pretty good the last 65 years. Oh, I had some setbacks because of my eyes and couldn't complete my degree, which was always a disappointment to me. But we had Karen, who is a teacher, a mother and a wonderful daughter. She married a lawyer, Bob Watson, and they had two children together, Sam and Lauren. Peg and I did have two setbacks. She came to me one day during the second pregnancy and said, "I just dropped the baby." I said, "What do you mean? You're only three months." She said, "I felt I had to go to the bathroom, I went to the bathroom and plop, there was the baby." So, we went back to her doctor, and her doctor was blown away. He said there was absolutely nothing out of the ordinary; everything was kosher.

We got pregnant again, the third time, and the same thing happened. Exactly the same thing; she went to the toilet, boom there's the baby. So by that time she was going to be 41 if we got pregnant again. I'm old fashioned, I don't think 40-year-old women should be giving birth -- it's not good for them and not good for the baby – so we decided that we got one good first one, Karen, and we'd stay with her.

This house, would you believe, cost me 50 cents. When we decided we were going to build a house, I started looking in magazines. I found this magazine of house designs. They were sketches in scale. I was looking at it one day and said to Peg, "Look at this thing. What do you think?" She said, "That's ideal. That's what we want." We'd been driving around, she wanted to live in West Vancouver. She chose this spot here. I had seen these brick houses as we were driving around. We stopped at one and the contractor was there. Robbins, Jeff Robbins. "Could you build us a brick house?" Sure, he said. "Bring me your plans."

Made the deal with him. Found this 50-cent magazine, took it to him, said "could you build this house?" He said sure, no sweat, I'll take this to my draftsman. When he drew it up in blueprint, I said no, the dining room was too small. We added on two feet, and thank goodness we did. That's the only change we made to those 50-cent plans. We'd planned to have three pregnancies. The basement is twinned. The plumbing is here, and it's also in the basement; there's a kitchen down there. The bathroom in our bedroom is twinned in the basement. Everything twinned. But of course we never developed it because we ended up with just the one child. We only needed the one bedroom up here.

On one of my first dates with Peg we went to the home of one of her girlfriends. This girl introduced me to her father, a doctor. He found out who I was. And afterwards he told his daughter, "You warn that girl Peggy McLeod not to have anything to do with that man Bird." The daughter said, "Why?" "Because he has Indian blood in him." This fellow had been in Dad's medical class, well behind him.

My best job at the tax office, Revenue Canada office, was when I got to be Head of Information. I would hire sometimes 80 people. So I saw a lot of bodies. I would occasionally meet up with an Indian, but I didn't ask them about their ancestry, and they didn't volunteer. I hired by people's qualifications.

I haven't worn glasses now for about eight years. I bought a $65 course, about how to see well without glasses with eye exercises, and it worked. I put my glasses away.

* * *

In our letters home during war, we were told not to talk about the war and especially where we were. In my first letter, I talk about the training I'd just had. That was the only reference in all my 25 letters to the war. The others talk about the parcels from home, what had arrived and what hadn't. They put mom at ease; she was still hearing from me.

I didn't think I would survive, especially with the eight guys ahead of me going down. What right did I have to think that I would last any longer? I took that attitude that I was going down, but before I went down I was going to take a lot of these suckers with me. That's where the number counting started with me, and I found out a lot of the guys were doing the same thing. They wanted to know how many they got, before they got me. You had to have something to hang onto. You had to have some reason for what you were doing. Killing is not normal. It's the most unnatural thing there is, to take another human life. I've looked at men, and then pumped their chest full of lead. You see the fear come into their eyes when they see the bullets, and then you see the lights go out. It's like you've flipped a switch. Yes, the lights go out, and then they go down. And you see that. That records back here, in the brain. And you carry that with you. It took Peg to talk that out of my head.

When I got home, I got something from Dad that I'd never had from him before -- respect. I told him I'd had to kill, but I didn't say how many. Knowing him as a life saver – he birthed 2,300 and some babies – and here I am killing 1,273. When I told him I couldn't hunt with him anymore, I told him that when I look at a deer, I'm looking at a man. And he understood.

If we were just talking, and I gave him my opinion, I could see right away that my opinion was accepted. There was no argument, no resistance, it was accepted. Before the war, I was still his little boy. I was now his equal. It was satisfying, because being the stubborn Bird that he was, I never thought he could change, but he did change. I think he changed toward Clay in the same way, because he knew what Clay had gone through. That night of March 30, 1944, when 96 planes were shot down, Clay could just as easily have been one of them. When Dad and I met there at the railway station in Winnipeg, there were almost tears in his eyes.

Birds have always been stubborn. I don't know whether you guys have ever put that tag to yourselves. I can be as pigheaded as pigheaded can be. It can be a weakness, if you let it control you. I have tried very hard not to let it control me. Peg taught me a lot. She did more to improve me, if you know what I mean, than any other influence in my life. When she was growing up, one of her eye doctors told her mother one day, "Don't ever let this girl think about university; her eyes will never take it." So Peg was right off the bat precluded from developing her brain. That's why she went into secretarial school. It was only a six-month course, and then you started working.

But she showed her level of intelligence there. When I married her, she was executive secretary to the vice-president for Western Canada of the T. Eaton Company, who was resident here in Vancouver. When she was growing up she wanted to play tennis. She played it at home, so she joined the Jericho Tennis Club. She was on the board of the Jericho Tennis Club when I married her. So I take her back to Winnipeg for a year, and then we moved to Vancouver. Later on, a property salesman started the Hollyburn Country Club, just above our home.

The only problem was the municipality said no – no water, no sewer, no roads. So he was stymied. One of the guys who had signed up knew the British Properties. He knew that they were planning to expand west. And every time they created X acres of new housing, they must by codicil create a new recreational piece of ground. He went to the British Properties, and they said yes there is some property for recreation. We got the Hollyburn property for $65,000. It's worth today about $60 million. It's 15 acres or so. It's huge.

On the application form they asked you to put down any club activities you had in your past; Peg put down her activities with Jericho and others. I had been elected to the board of the Winnipeg Canoe Club and I was active on the board when I married Peg. So when the group that were trying to get the club going started looking over these resumes, they said these are two people we need. I was asked to stand on one of the committees and became active in it and friends with a chap named Bill Manson, who became the second or third club president. We were both curlers. I ended up on the board. Peg came home one day and said, "You won't believe this, but the group elected me chairman of the ladies curling section."

Mac Bird curling in Victoria, February 1966.

Peg had never thrown a curling rock in her life. When she questioned this, the lady said, "But Mac is a top-level curler. He'll show you." So I, on the kitchen table, got out some cans of Campbell Soup, which served as our curling stones. I said this is an in turn, and this is what the rock does when you throw an in turn. And I said, this is an out turn, and this is what the rock does when you throw an out turn, and I would turn the can down the table and make it turn to the side. I just took it step by step, the physical part of the game first, and then the strategy part. Many curlers make the mistake of when they're putting the turn on, giving the rock a push. That throws it off line. I showed her how to do the delivery out of the hack and so on, and then went to the strategy part, with last rock, and so on.

She took to it like a duck to water. She was a very smart gal. She was very level-headed in every respect. Right away, she was chair of that committee and she skipped a rink. You see, there was only a handful of the girls who had ever curled. She was terrified of it at first but she took to it like a duck to water. Fewer women curled in those days. This was 1963. We curled right up until my legs went bad. I guess it was 1989. I had my legs operated on in 1991.

I had a doctor who gave me drugs of the day that handled pain nicely, but what he didn't know, or didn't care about, was that these drugs handled the pain but they eat the cartilage in your body. The doctor who opened me up said no wonder you were having pain when walking, you were walking bare bone on bare bone. So he installed plastic and metal knee joints. They worked so well after surgery, I said I feel great. May I go back to curling? He said no; it's a walking knee only. But we had many great years of curling, Peg and I. She was a great partner and a great lady. I miss her terribly.

Wedding day for Mack and Peg in December 1955.
Brother Clayton is behind Mack's head; Doris Bird is also present.

Above, J. M. and Peggy Bird with daughter Karen on Jan. 15, 1968.

Below, Doris Aconley about 19 years old, before marrying Clayton Bird.

CHAPTER 11

Mac Bird's Letters Home

Like most people of their era, the Bird boys were letter writers. This was a very good thing, as they bequeathed to us a rich legacy of their thoughts, routines, frustrations and hopes as they embarked on the road to war against Hitler and Mussolini in the early 1940s. In this section we share the letters written by Mac, which he gave to his nephew Brad in 2008 with the comment they "might not be much good," because all he recalled writing about was food. Overseas, he did talk about what he was eating as a way of avoiding heavier topics. They were forbidden to record their military activities, locations, weapons, or to mention upcoming events. The fear was that letters could fall into enemy hands and jeopardize lives if such things were revealed. Military censors read every epistle with eagle eyes, cutting and chopping with abandon, using scissors and knives. As Mac told his nephews, he also didn't want to alarm his mother by talking about the uglier events he experienced.

These letters were therefore self-sanitized. They remain, however, of considerable value as social and military history, as you will see. In Canada during training the men were free to write whatever they wished. Together, the letters from home and abroad tell the story of men preparing for war and being at war. Mac was a lanky and observant fellow of 20 as his correspondence to his parents begins here late in 1941. He is a very busy young man – studying accounting at university, doing military training on the side, and working as well. Mac would eventually be sent overseas as an officer with the Princess Patricia's Canadian Light Infantry. His older brother Clayton preceded him to England as a pilot in the Royal Canadian Air Force, and in this first letter

Mac tells about seeing his brother off on the train to Halifax. Clayton and Doris had been married only nine weeks earlier. For the record, Mr. And Mrs. Bird's letters to Mac, and his letters from friends and other family, appear not to have survived.

November 30, 1941

Dear Mom,

I saw Clayton off Wednesday night and he sure didn't want to leave [he had received his wings, declared a pilot, on 6 November, a big day, nine months after enlisting]. Doris stood up to it pretty well but she was feeling mighty blue. I was talking to her last night and she said that Clayton was still at Halifax but expected to move any day [toward England]. As my Xmas present I gave him a pair of sunglasses especially designed for the Air Force. And speaking of Xmas, I have changed my mind about that new suit for the present anyway. I can get along with what I have now and it would be a white elephant if the government should suddenly wake up and take action on the conscription issue. A call came into the OTC the other week for seven officers for the Winnipeg Rifles which is a pretty nice regiment. I was sorely tempted to put my name down but decided merely to investigate. I saw Major Hopper, our O.C. [Officer Commanding] and he said that the present interpretation of the draft law in my case was that I could have my call postponed until I finished my University course. No one seems to know what would happen to us in the event of conscription but Alistair said that he thought that all Accounting students would be told to keep their jobs. I was rather shocked when Major Talinn told me that he would not try to influence any young man to join up when we have such a "gutless government" in power. That was his opinion of Mr. King's military policy and I imagine represents most military men's thoughts on the subject.

I write English and Auditing on the 6th and Accounting on the 13th and then a couple of months of well earned rest. It has been rather heavy going with both courses but I have rather enjoyed it. One thing it has relieved me of is women worry because I have no time for them.

That Swanson fatality certainly was unfortunate. You didn't say whether dad got a deer or not or who he was out with this year.

Doug and I were supposed to go to a special OTC church parade this morning at 9:15 a.m. but he forgot to turn the alarm on and we slept in until 9:50. Mrs. Morrison knew we were supposed to go and got up an hour earlier than she usually does in order to have breakfast ready. Doug asked her why she didn't call us when she saw we weren't up in time and she said that if we didn't have enough interest in it to get up on our own that she wasn't going to do anything about it. I was so mad when I heard such a stupid answer that I almost told her what I was thinking. It doesn't mean anything by our missing the parade except that the Major asked us all to turn out and show our appreciation for the privileges extended to us by the government. It also counted as an extra parade in case we were forced to miss any later in the next year. The fact that we haven't been to church in some time now made it very promising. Right now good old work calls me. Don't forget to send the weekly scratch [letter] unless it goes to Clayton.

Love Mac.

December 4, 1941

Dear Mom,

I have some good news about Xmas – I will be home on the 24th about 8 or thereabouts. And I don't have to be back till the 2nd. Pretty soft, eh!

I am glad the folks liked Doris because they really are crazy about each other. I have just been talking to her and she said she has had no letter yesterday or today so Clayton must be on the water [shipping out to England with other pilots]. She said he will probably cable when he gets there, but that will take almost two weeks. Please excuse scratch as am in hurry to catch delivery. Marion and Russell have definitely broken off according to Doris and M. is heartbroken. She really fell for him but I don't know why. Anyway she is getting a month's holiday and is going East. She may have a chance to forget him there.

Love Mac.

Then, for reasons unknown, there is a break in the letters until the following August. Some are apparently missing. Mac has given up university at this point and is in military training in B.C. Clayton, meanwhile, was a flight instructor working long and tiring hours at Cranwell, Scotland, which explains his irregular correspondence.

August 30, 1942

Mess 21
OTC (WC)
Gordon Head, B.C.

Dear Mom and Dad,

Yesterday we had completed six weeks or half our course but it seemed like a week or two. Our timetable is so full this month that we have no spare time. We have a route march and scheme every Tuesday and Thursday in the day time, a lecture from 7 to 9 and a night scheme from 9:30 to 12. Consequently, we are all so tired on the weekends that we have no energy for gadding about.

I have not been on the skeet range since my record performance because there is an exceptionally large Part 1 in camp now. Our officer promised to get us on both the skeet and a new pistol range but so far has not been able to arrange it.

It's Monday night and I've a few spare moments to finish this letter. I took it out with me on our march today but didn't have a chance to work on it. Our next two weeks will be spent in the field on various schemes. We leave camp at 8:15 or 9, march three miles to a lonely spot beside the sea, and spend the rest of the day discussing tactical schemes and carrying them out. We get about an hour and a quarter to devour a hot meal brought out to us at noon and served by CWOL's.

We have a much better officer this month than the old bear of Part 1. When I was talking to him tonight he told me that all my reports were very satisfactory except that I lacked voice control and volume. I am beginning to regret the error of my boyish days when I refused to go on the stage or in the choir. Also I understand that we are going to have a tough third month because of some complaints from some units as to the quality of some of the material [men] turned out of here in the past.

It does seem very strange about Clayton's silence but I can understand what he is up against if he is as busy as we are. Over and above our regular studies and night marches we get special assignments such as map enlargement last week which took four hours to complete. That and a week's laundry takes up most of Sunday which brings up the fact I have not seen the Julls [family friends] yet. I will try to make it next week but am not making any promises.

It's Thursday night and I'm going to try to finish this letter before we go on another night scheme. We should get some spare time tomorrow because another class graduates. We are still having grand weather and have only been rained on once in the field. I was afraid I was going to miss the corn and other vegetables that we had at home but today we had corn on the cob in the field and it really hit the spot. We are getting quite a bit of fruit and fresh vegetables now, and frequently run into vendors on our route marches.

I am enjoying the work very much now and find that my feet stand up very well under the marching. They will get a better test next month when we go on marches up to 20 miles long. I am afraid I will have to close because my time is nearly up. I will try to get my next letter off in better time, also that picture I promised you. I hope you have heard from Clayton by now and that all is well.

Love Mac.

September 1942

Mess 21
OTC (WC)
Gordon Head, B.C.

Dear Mom and Dad,

Just a little less than two weeks and we will be through here. It is hard to say just how I feel about quitting the camp because I have enjoyed my stay here. If only we had more time to ourselves there would be no doubt about it. We had an exam Saturday morning on the Tommy Gun and two-inch mortar and this time the whole class passed. Now we have only the hand grenade and three-inch mortar to get off our hands and we will be through with weapons. However, another important subject which is causing me no end of trouble is company drill. And the fact my regiment is known as Canada's best on the parade square doesn't help me any.

The major in charge of our wing was a sergeant-major in the Pats in peace time and is a past master at drill. He takes great delight in messing the company up on the square and then giving one of us the job of straightening them out. It really is the only way to learn drill but is very confusing when you haven't had much of it. They are still harping about my voice and one of them even advised me to take singing lessons. It does sound rather silly but if I am stationed in Winnipeg for any length of time I think I will, because a poor voice is quite a handicap.

Thursday night and your letter hasn't arrived so I decided I had better write. I would like you to send my Gladstone bag because I don't want to wear my uniform on the train and my trunk is getting pretty full. I have decided that I will go into Winnipeg before coming home even though Monday is Thanksgiving. Ruth would be terribly disappointed if I didn't show up. She asked me to stay in until Tuesday night but I don't think I will. I am anxious to get a crack at those ducks even if Billy [Akett] didn't paint a very good picture of the shooting in the last paper. I see my time is nearly up so I had better close. Hope you have had good luck, Dad. Try to have a feed ready for me for Tuesday dinner.

Love Mac

From there he went to Shilo and Winnipeg.

January 18, 1943

103rd CA(B)TC
Fort Garry, Manitoba

Dear Mom and Dad,

Please excuse the paper but I left my pad at Shilo along with several other things. Am I ever glad to be out of that place. This is "Paradise Regained" – that was simply "My Great Struggle." We are quartered in the large residence hall with only two men to a room, and we sleep in hospital cots – not double bunks. The batmen here are a revelation. At Shilo we had to chase them to get things done and usually the work was very unsatisfactory. Here they flit in and out like shadows quietly and effectively doing everything you desire.

The mess does fall down badly in one respect and that is the food. The rest of the camp is very efficiently handled but our cook just hasn't got what it takes. There is a very friendly spirit in the mess in contrast to Shilo. Here the lieutenants call the captains and majors by first names and everybody mixes. The colonel is a doughty old Cameron by the name of Younger. Four of us came in together from Shilo so that we were not strangers for long in the mess. We were told we were coming here for at least two months but some of the boys have been here for nine months so I don't know what to make of the situation.

It seems that every time I am home I forget something. As we have a very nice rink right here in camp I would like to make use of my skates if you please. I think they are in the outer kitchen behind the door.

I have not done any visiting as yet outside of seeing Ruth because I was not in the best of health when I arrived. My throat has kept me awake so much that I was dopey from lack of sleep and was running a temperature of 101. I saw the MO the night I arrived and he went to work. I spent the next day and a half in bed under medicine and certainly feel much better now. That will also explain why there was no letter. I went to bed early every night except Saturday because I just didn't seem to have any pep. As I have several lectures to prepare {for] I had better run. I received the underwear just before I left Shilo. Have you received the sleeping bag yet? One of the boys was to ship it collect.

Love Mac.

January 23, 1943

103rd CA(B)TC
Fort Garry, Manitoba

Dear Mom and Dad,

I hope you didn't get the snow we got in here because we got at least a foot. It was so miserable out last night that I decided to sleep at Ruth's from where this letter is also being written. We started for a show yesterday but no street car showed up for almost half an hour in Wpg.

I'm afraid I have some bad news about 48's home from here [two-day leaves]. They don't allow any extensions such as three or four day leaves. Now that the bus is gone I won't be able to get home by train on a 48. If that's the way they play ball in here I'm asking for a furlough pronto. Ruth's birthday is 5 February so I'm going to ask for it to start the following Monday, Feb. 7. I get a 48 every two weeks regardless of whether I want it or not so we went back and spent the evening here. This really is a grand little home. I wish you could see it sometime. I'm afraid Ruth and I will be losing it soon because the adoption papers go through in February and also Ruth's sister arrived in Canada to be discharged from the army. Her health is not very good and as she will have to rest for a month or two before going back to work. Ruth thinks they will take a suite downtown when Rita arrives.

I got the skates just as I was leaving the mess to come downtown yesterday so didn't have time to open the package. Thanks for sending them. I'll write Shilo about that sleeping bag soon.

Love Mac.

February 3, 1943

103rd CA(B)TC
Fort Garry, Manitoba

Dear Mom and Dad,

Ruth's sister Rita arrived here on Saturday and we have been partying ever since. She is a grand girl and has had some wonderful experiences over there [in Europe with the army]. They were not all for the best, however, because her boyfriend did not come back from Dieppe. I'm afraid this and a few minor tragedies have rather sickened her on the army and she is now anxious to get out. She leaves for Ottawa tomorrow where she will find out what her score is. I think she was shipped home when her nerves broke after Dieppe.

As yet I have heard nothing about my furlough coming through. It should only take 10 days and tomorrow is the 10th day.

[It goes on about a wisdom tooth he had removed and other minor items.]

Love Mac.

Good news: he's going home for a visit.

February 5, 1943
[On letterhead labeled "103 C. A. (B.) T. C.
Fort Garry,
Manitoba]

Dear Mom:

Just a note to let you know that my furlough came thru. I will arrive on Monday's train because I can't make connections by Brandon on the bus.

I am also getting a 36 but will spend it with Ruth as we are celebrating her birthday Sat. nite.

Doris heard from Clayton yesterday but I got the news second hand from Ruth so don't know what he said.

Love Mac.

Mac's doubts about his relationship with Ruth emerge.

10 March 1943
[same letterhead]

Dear Mom and Dad,

Ruth and I finally had a heart to heart talk Saturday night and thrashed our problem out properly. I only hope that our decision will be proven by time to be the only one. In view of the fact that I have consistently refused to enter into any long-term engagement, we decided that it would be only fair to her if she had the opportunity of keeping a larger circle of friends. Thus if anything does happen to our affair she will not be left holding an empty bag. Consequently we both agreed that it would be better for both of us if we saw a little more of other people and that is the way things stand now. I don't think that Ruth liked it very much – I know she would prefer something more permanent. But in all fairness to both of us I can't do it. I must say that she certainly took it with good grace. She is the most broad-minded girl I have ever met.

I know you both have been waiting rather anxiously for this but I did not want to write until I had thought the matter over by myself. Another reason leading up to my decision is that I did not feel my mind was absolutely clear of any doubt as to my feelings towards Ruth. Therefore it was for this reason that I felt that I should become acquainted with several other girls.

It is getting late so I had better close. I hope those extra vitamins will help keep the cold in check, mom. I am still taking my cold tablets and so far am still lucky.

Love Mac.

P.S. Dad would you please get that registration certificate for that pistol from G. Love [?} I have to register it here and police require old certificate.

Then he was shipped to the west coast. Notice below how it took seven hours to travel by ferry from Victoria to Vancouver. In 2010 it took 90 minutes.

April 18, 1943

Officers Mess
S4 CSAS
Nanaimo, B.C.

Dear Mom and Dad,

Just one more week to go and I'll be on the train again. I have received a 48-hour leave after the course and intend to spend one day in Victoria and the next one in Vancouver. As this will likely be my last trip to the coast for some time I want to see some of the folks in both places. I was in Victoria last weekend visiting Ruth's older sister and I'm afraid she took up most of my time. She is the dietician at the military hospital there but had not heard of Jack Findlay.

I really enjoyed the course during the last week because the stiffness had worked out of my muscles. I don't think I have gained much weight but if I can keep some this training up when I go back I most certainly will. Right now they are giving us too much road work to allow any weight to accumulate. Until yesterday the weather has been marvelous but the rain came and spoiled the weekend. I don't think I could put up with the weather out here when I compare it with the good old prairie weather. The spring flower out here is the daffodil and they spring up everywhere. They don't appear to be planted under control but spring up almost as thick as the lovely dandelion at home. I can see dad out on the lawn swinging his merciless "golf club" any day now.

I will leave Victoria on the noon boat Saturday arriving in Vancouver about 7 that evening. My train for Winnipeg leaves at 7:15 Sunday night and I arrive home at 6:15 on Tuesday night and start work next morning.

Bedtime so I think I'll turn in. Hope your knees are better now mom and watch those steps.

Love Mac.

April 26, 1943

Dear Mom and Dad,

I am writing this just as we are leaving Calgary…I hope you have heard from Clayton since Dad's letter. He probably is having one of his moody spells so don't worry if you haven't.

Love Mac.

Canadian Forces Base Shilo has been an important training facility since 1910. It is 35 kilometres east of Brandon, Manitoba, and only about a 90-minute drive from Boissevain, Mac's home town. He'd be eager to get home if possible, if only for the weekend as he mentions below.

April 29, 1943

Officers Mess
A15 Canadian Infantry Training Centre
Canadian Army
Shilo Camp, Manitoba

Dear Mom and Dad,

I am afraid the great moment is not many weeks away. When I arrived back at Fort Garry they told me I was to proceed to Shilo on overseas draft. We arrived this pm and I found out that I will not be leaving for at least three weeks but that I am definitely on overseas draft. The next few weeks will be spent in hardening up. I am going to apply for another furlough immediately but may only get a portion of it. Several of the boys on the draft just ahead of us were recalled from leave and I will probably get the same treatment. I am asking for a weekend tomorrow but do not expect to get it. If I do I will phone you. As I am very tired I will toddle off to bed.

Love Mac

Undated but enclosed in the same envelope:

Dear Mom and Dad,

I was quite right when I said we will not be leaving for a while because we still have no definite news. However, they still would not let us out for a weekend but tried to make us plant [word unclear] in front of the mess. One by one we slipped away to our quarters and refused to go out again. I was very glad I did because I have the best part of my stuff packed. Also discovered that I will not need the Gladstone so will send it to Heywoods and Dad can pick it up.

My address overseas will be:

    Lieut. J. M. Bird
    Serial No. 294A
    No. 1 C.I. R.U.
    C.A.O.

Just how long I will use that I don't know, but my luggage will go there so you can write me there. Don't send any mail here after Sunday because we should be gone by then. I hope you got the rain that we have been getting all day. We were fortunate in being inside most of the time. Today, however, was the first day we did any work. The other days we spent most of our time keeping out of the major's way because he was in a bad mood.

Bed time so I'll close,

Love Mac.

J. M. Bird, 88, and Brad's cat Jimmy, in 2009. Photo by Brad Bird.

CHAPTER 12

Over to England

Finally, the moment they've been waiting for, arrival in England.

Lieut. J.M. Bird
No. 1 CIRU
C.A. England

June 21, 1943

Dear Mom and Dad,

By the time you get this you should have my wire. We were very fortunate in our trip though they did manage to put our train through all the big cities at the most inconvenient hours. We arrived in Ottawa about 11:30 but they stopped the train some distance from the station so I had difficulty in finding a phone [to call his Aunt Emm, etc.]. Only gave me time to say hello to May and then I had to run. We didn't waste any time on the coast – just got on a boat right from the train and sailed shortly afterwards. The first two days were rather rough and I had a taste of sea sickness. However, I only threw one meal and ate soda crackers for the next three meals and then never missed a meal.

About two thirds of our guys were sick but this was partly caused by the fact that we had to supply 12 men twice a day for submarine/aeroplane watch. I was up near the bow and could see the big waves coming. I'm sure this didn't help my stomach any. The weather was perfect from our point of view -- foggy or overcast most of the trip. The meals were of the very best with the exception of the coffee. This was due to the English stuff.

So far I have little to complain about the rations over here. I imagine it is the lack of variety that gets the boys down. The bread is whole wheat, dark in colour and cooks with a very heavy crust. Personally I like it very much and I know you would, Dad, because it's the real thing for the teeth. We use margarine here and none of us knew the difference at first. Some of our draft left the port at night but our train left in the morning so we saw some of England. We had a short stop at noon for tea and I had to stay with the men while the other officers went for something to eat. One of the railroad guards noticed that I wasn't eating and asked me why. When I told him that we had not been issued sufficient rations he brought out his lunch and insisted that I take half of it. I thought it mighty nice of him, especially when two of the sandwiches were meat.

We didn't see a great deal of damage although houses burned out by incendiaries were in abundance. I don't suppose you knew that Ruth came out to Shilo to visit me. When I found we were CB I phoned her on Saturday morning and she came out on the evening train. She knows the matron of nurses here so I was able to get the room of a nurse who was on leave. Several of the boys had their wives out so she was not alone. Unfortunately we had to wait until 4:30 Monday morning for the Wpg train.

I will not get much leave for the present as the new setup requires that we take a course before we get landing leave. However, I may be able to see Clayton this coming weekend. Last night the big bombers were heading for the continent in considerable numbers. It certainly is nice to see them going that way. I have to write Ruth today also so will close now. Hope you are both well.

Love Mac

P.S. Let me know how long this letter takes. If it is satisfactory I may use them all the time. [It was stamped as arriving in Boissevain in the afternoon of July1, 1943, so it only took 11 days.]

In the following letter Mac talks about Clayton's skills as a pilot, a reassuring report for their parents.

Lieut. J.M. Bird
No. 1 CIRU
C.A.O.

30 June 1943

Dear Mom and Dad,

Got up to see Clayton last weekend and had a wonderful time. This was my first attempt at traveling in England and I had quite a time. I missed the late evening train and had to sleep four hours in a coach on a siding. Then someone woke me up to tell me I would have to sit up because the train was crowded. We left London about 4:14 and about 10 arrived in Sleaford. On inquiring about my destination I had trouble finding somebody who knew where it was.

When I finally did find him he was a very pleasantly surprised boy. He had received your letter saying that I had been home on embarkation leave on Friday morning and that p.m. my wire arrived saying I was coming. He was on duty but that did not interfere much. He took me up for a flight (my first) and I enjoyed every minute of it despite the fact that it made me sick. The air was horribly rough that day and we seemed to bounce all over the place. Clayton originally planned to fly me home on Sunday but refused after this affair. I was very much annoyed with myself but air sickness is very much like the sea variety – it just comes.

Clayton is an exceptionally good pilot and has passed the 1,000-hour mark now. I think you can stop worrying about him getting to operations because some brass hat told him definitely that there would be no transfers from that particular school. Clayton was going to the Lake District for a week's fishing soon, so he should be happy for a while. As they had just sent a school out, I was able to have a room right next to Clayton's and eat with him. They have a very nice setup there. Before I forget I have not received any mail yet but expect it any day as some of the boys have received some. I have started going for a run in the mornings because I found I was in terrible condition. I do feel much better for it although it is quite an effort to get up. So far we have done very little actual training, just recaps and tests to see now much we do know. Next week we will start on either a driving course or a battle drill course. Tomorrow, however, is being observed as a holiday but I don't know what I shall do. Probably just run up to a neighbouring town. Must write Ruth so will close now. Just remembered I ran into Doug Opperman [of Boissevain] in London.

Love, Mac.

Lieut. J.M. Bird
No. 1 CIRU
C.A.O.

8 July 1943

Dear Mom and Dad,

I received your first letter on the 5th which is very good time. It was written, I believe, the day after we left Shilo so your woman's intuition must have been working. The weather is still nice though it has managed to rain the last two days. We have been learning to ride motor bikes for the past week. I find it very interesting because I never did know much about engines. We spend each morning tinkering with our engines, and as each man is responsible for the welfare of his own machine, we take more interest in the work. The afternoons we spend either on the highway or riding in a sandy tank-testing area. Our instructors are all excellent riders and watch over us like mothers. There are several excellent theatres in town and they show some of the best pictures from Hollywood. However, being an officer rather cramps the fun for me because there are so many places we can't go. I have only had one dance over here and that while I was the guest of another officer at an officer's club – a very expensive one. I would like to join but it costs a lot and my stay here may be terminated any day. We have heard nothing definite but there is another rumor going round that we have to take a battle drill course. While I was at the club I also had several sets of tennis. Although my game was terrible, I enjoyed it because I never played much last year and was afraid this year was going to pass without my getting a game in. I am writing in the mess while listening to the radio, and it certainly is a pleasure to listen to a good musical program without being advised to try Carter's Liver Pills. We are having a dance in the mess Saturday night and through a mutual friend I arranged a date with a young lady whose parents are the old-fashioned dictatorial type. I had tea with the mother and Iylene the other day and the poor kid hardly uttered a word. I asked my friend about it later and he said that is always the way when he goes to their home. The girls have to be in by 10 during the week but can stay out till midnight on Saturday. Of course they are only 19 and 22 so I guess they can grow out of it. And now that I think of it I had better clear up the mystery of that photo from Kamsack. I imagine, from your description, that it is a picture of myself which I gave Evelyn.

These girls can cause awkward situations can't they? Hope you both are keeping well.

Love Mac.

Lieut. J.M. Bird
No. 1 CIRU
C.A.O.

18 July 1943

Dear Mom and Dad,

Well I finally received your wire acknowledging my letter and wire but they certainly took their time with it. You sent it on the 7th and I received it on the 16th which is slower than some of these letters. Clayton wrote me the other day but didn't seem any too happy despite the fact that he just came back from leave. I think it must be the "English" atmosphere at that school which affects him. I think I will try to see him again soon and maybe have him get Doug Noton down also. I think he is not far from Clayton's station. We had our dance here last Saturday and it was quite a do. I never saw so much food since I landed. Unfortunately the young lady I had was a Cinderella – we left at 12 on her mother's orders. She was not very attractive and a poor conversationalist despite a good education. Just another reason for not accepting blind dates. This afternoon we are going to another town in our third attempt to have our first riding lesson. About the only thing that should stop us now is rain. The last week has been quite moist although I did manage to get an hour and a half sunbathing yesterday.

Monday – We had our ride yesterday and I enjoyed it very much. I intend to keep it up until I get more proficient. Right now certain muscles in my legs and rear are quite touchy although not as bad as I had feared. My roommate and I are still carrying on with our PT and two-mile run every morning. Can you fancy me setting the example by waking him at 6:30 every morning? That little clock did the trick. I don't know whether I told you about my taking up the study of German but that is my latest fad. One of the boys here is quite a linguist and has promised to help me. Even if I never get far with it, what I do learn should come in handy, especially when I have no other language to fall back on. This chap can speak French and German fluently, has a smattering of Spanish and is now studying Italian.

Another group of lads arrived from home a few days ago but the only mail I got was one letter from Ruth. So far I have only one from her and two from you but I suppose they will arrive in a bunch soon. I do hope you have a few Sweet Caporals or Players on the way because these English smokes certainly do not stand up to ours. You didn't mention anything about the crops in your letter, only the tulips and peonies. I know the girls would be pleased if you sent them some tulips because I remember last year how they made quite an impression on the girls' friends. Hope you are keeping well.

Love Mac.

P.S. Be sure to use address as on back. In this way you can keep up with all moves.

28 July 1943

Lieut. J.M. Bird
No. 1 CIRU
C.A.O.

Dear Mom and Dad,

On the 24th I received three letters from you, one from Ruth and one from Doris [Clayton's new wife – families wrote to families in those days]. A few days before that I received Dad's fourth letter but seem to have missed one or two in between. I will let you know what the score is when I get back to barracks. Right now I am enjoying a rest in a military hospital after losing my tonsils yesterday morning. They had been bothering me ever since I left Canada so I finally saw a specialist and he said they should come out. I finished my driving course before I came in here. We are in a Canadian hospital with Canadian staff but I haven't met any nurses from Manitoba yet. We have a fine staff including one nurse who teaches German. I am going to have her help me when I am able to speak properly again. Right now my tongue is so stiff I sound almost tongue-tied. I had a local unaesthetic so was able to watch the doc struggle with the pests. He must have made a good job because bleeding was negligible. I didn't eat anything yesterday but couldn't stand the smell of food today without having some. I had some porridge and apple sauce for breakfast.

What do you people think of Benito's sudden descent from power? [On July 25, 1943, Benito Mussolini was summoned to a meeting with the king and told he was being relieved of his offices. Marshal Badoglio was chosen to form the new government. Italy surrendered and on October 13 declared war on Germany.] Over here opinions vary but most seem to think it is comparable to Petain's statement that "fighting would continue" and then France cracked five days later. Whatever it is looks good from here. I will probably get some sick leave when I leave here so may run up to see Clayton. I had hoped to be in condition for another flight when I saw him again but that is not necessary. Sorry to hear that the peonies took such a beating. It would appear that B'vain and district are in for hail every summer. Ruth mentioned receiving the tulips and also Doris's measles. Doris's letter was quite cheerful but was almost entirely concerned with Clayton. The nurse is making the rounds now and I'll close. She wouldn't let me get up today but maybe tomorrow. Hope you are both well.

Love Mac.

In the following letters, the frictions of living in barracks with all types of men begin to show. And, being a young man, he does look forward to dances.

Lieut. J.M. Bird
No. 1 CIRU
C.A.O.

4th August 1943

Dear Mom and Dad,

They let me out of the hospital and I sure am happy. I shall have to take particular pains not to get into a position where I would require hospitalization because I nearly went crazy with just one week of it. I was given three days light duty, which simply means that I lie around barracks for the remainder of the week and do not get any leave. That may be just as well because my throat still gets sore when I talk too much.

I suppose that by now you will have seen in the papers that my regiment is in Sicily. If I had arrived several months earlier I would have been in the reserves right behind them but as things stand right now may never see them. I can't explain the latter statement now but maybe I will be allowed to in time. The weather is still holding out so will have to start my morning runs soon. Right now a walk of one or two miles tires me out. My roommate now runs five miles in full equipment but I am not going to catch up to that. I have received all your letters Dad but your 5th, 6th, 7th have not appeared, Mom. They will probably come in the next group.

I am glad to hear that smokes are on the way as these English blends are not very good. Do not worry too much about candy because the mess has managed to get bars in several times in the last month and although they do not equal Canadian bars they help out.

We received a new roommate but he is rather queer. He is one of those youngsters with an over-inflated ego. I hope I don't have too much trouble with him but I dislike people of that nature, especially when you have to associate closely with them. We are having another big dance and supper here this coming Saturday and I am taking another blind date. However, I have received assurances that she is an attractive girl so here's hoping. Getting near bedtime so will close this one. Hope you are both well.

Love Mac.

16th August 1943

Lieut. J.M. Bird
No. 1 CIRU
C.A.O.

Dear Mom and Dad,

Life goes on as usual although we did have an alert yesterday morning. Nobody paid any attention to it. We just lay in bed and waited for the all clear. Nothing came near us and some of the boys who were up said they didn't hear anything. However, it was our first experience at listening to the "banshee" and I must say it is an eerie sound.

Lately the officers have not been attending PT classes and it came to the attention of the CO. As a result he had us put on special PT training which is twice as hard as before. I received a letter from Auntie Em [on the farm near Ottawa, his mother's people] on the 13th. It was written July 7. When it arrived here the PO sent it to the hospital, they sent it to the armoured corp for some foolish reason and they returned it to No. 1.

I was very much annoyed to discover yesterday that one of my roommates and regimental brothers had received some smokes about 10 days ago but had kept them very much to himself. He is a very childish and thoughtless person whom I have not entirely liked ever since I first met him in Shilo but I never expected him to pull a trick like that. I had reason to be annoyed because I had kept him in spending money for over a month because our bank accounts were slow in coming through and he had spent most of his money on a spree in London.

On Saturday afternoon I went on a tour to see the famous Eton College and it certainly is a marvelous sight. The original wing was built in 1440 and although slightly damaged by a bomb is still in remarkable shape. In one particular room the boys used to carve their initials and some date back to 1460. Amongst them are Shelly, Gray, Pitt, Chattam, Lord Halifax and his two sons. There is so much tradition packed into that place that we from Canada cannot grasp it. Although it isn't much I can say I have walked on the playing fields of Eton. Our guide said there are over 800 acres of them and that did not include the boating houses on the Thames. Windsor Castle is right near there and I intend to see it also. Last week we had one of your favourites, Dad, corn on the cob. Tonite we had a small beefsteak so I guess that you can't say that we're starving by any means. We have also had ice cream several times lately.

Love Mac.

He sees Clayton again and they "do the town" in Lincoln. We learn about practice with rifles and other weapons.

25th August 1943

Lieut. J.M. Bird
No. 1 CIRU
C.A.O.

Dear Mom and Dad,

Your letters are still arriving in remarkably good time due I think to a new service. Your #8 Dad arrived on the 23rd and your #12 Mom arrived the day before. As yet none of the smokes have arrived. None have arrived at the unit PO for two weeks now. However, I have found an English brand which tastes very much like Sweet Caps but I can't always be sure of getting them.

I managed to get up to see Clayton again but was not able to let him know I was coming. He was a way on a 48 himself but I got his address and took a line for the town – Lincoln. He was able to get me a room right next to his and we spent a very short time doing the town. We went to a dance that night and enjoyed a swim on Sunday morning.

I had to catch my bus at 1 and due to poor connections did not arrive home until 9:30 that evening. That is altogether too long to travel 160 miles, especially in this country. I wouldn't be surprised to see a serious cut in railway travel because the crowds lately have been tremendous. On my way down to London I rode about 60 miles sitting in the lavatory because the aisles were so crowded and smoky and my feet were sore from dancing and standing in so many queues.

My roommate and I had a chance to take a rifle out on the range today but all the targets were not satisfactory. I had a 2- 4" and a 2 – 8" groups at 200 yards but that can be improved. Our company has been training with other weapons lately and consequently we have not had much practice with the rifle. Tomorrow we hope to have around 60 rounds each for pistol practice. This is much better than Shilo where ammunition was regarded as sacred and untouchable. Don't worry about shortages of essentials such as toothpaste. There are plenty. Things are much better than formerly.

Love Mac.

He writes to his Aunt Em and uncle for a change. Note the story about the local ghost at a northerly estate on a trip with Clayton.

1 September 1943

Lieut. J.M. Bird
No. 1 CIRU
C.A.O.

Dear Auntie Em and Uncle Percy,

I suppose by now you had almost given up hope of hearing from me but I can explain everything. Your letter arrived here while I was in hospital having my tonsils removed. The PO here sent it to the hospital the same day I was discharged, and the hospital readdressed it incorrectly. Then it spent some weeks wandering around England before it got back to No. 1.

I have been able to see Clayton on two short leaves so far and as we are both due for a seven-day leave soon hope to be able to get up to Scotland for some hunting with him. However everything over here is "subject to the exigencies of the service" so I never count much on such plans made so far in advance.

[He talks about sickness on his first flight and Clayton being a "marvelous" pilot etc., which we heard about earlier.]

14 Sept. More excuses. I didn't finish this one on the evening of the 1st and next morning was told to take my seven-days leave then or never. So I forgot everything in my haste to pack and get away. I spent several days at Clayton's station and then we went up to Edinburgh. Somehow he managed to wrangle his leave on short notice and we planned to look for some hunting. We spent two days in Edinburgh and saw practically every point of interest thanks to a retired businessman who acted as our guide. Our tour included the castle, the Scottish memorial to the Great War, St. Giles Cathedral, the university, the House of Parliament, Hollywood house, which at present is the royal seat in Scotland. And of course we found many an ancient pub with goodly stocks of beer and whiskey [his father eschewed the stuff at this time of his life (he liked a rye now and then in his 70s and 80s) and wouldn't like to hear this, as one or two of his own siblings drank too much].

From there we went to Ladykirk, the estate of Lady Susan Askew. They had a very lovely place but unfortunately the hunting and fishing were both very poor this season and we were advised not to bother with either. We did have an amusing association with the local ghost which still puzzles me. My chum and I both woke up about 3 one morning to hear the irons on the fireplace being rattled furiously. After listening for a few minutes we turned on the lights and of course could see nothing. The irons also appeared to be in their proper place. A few minutes after we turned off the lights the noise commenced again but did not last long. I do not believe in spirits and neither does my chum but we are both at a loss to explain this incident. Clayton was in the same room but is a very heavy sleeper and did not waken.

From Lady Susan's we traveled to an old lady's estate about 20 miles away where we had supper. This was on Friday and afterwards we went to the Laidlaws' estate for the remainder of our leave. Ever since I have been over here I have wanted to meet some of the better class of people and I certainly had my wish on this trip. Everywhere the people were very hospitable and despite the rationing of certain foods we ate like kings.

I think I had better close now as I have about five thank-you letters to write. Hope you are both keeping well and please write occasionally. I won't promise to answer promptly because I hate writing but letters from home mean a lot over here.

Best regards, Mac

23 September 1943

Lieut. J.M. Bird
No. 1 CIRU
C.A.O.
[His ninth letter home, he notes]

Dear Mom and Dad,
   The weather has turned quite chilly now and although the sun is shining I have to wear a sweater in the morning to keep warm. If we have to spend a winter here I shall be very thankful for that heavy underwear I brought with me. ...I have only a few of these forms left and as they can't get any more for some strange reason I will have to fall back on ordinary mail soon. [Talks about letters received etc.]
   Right now I am on a short hardening course in preparation for a battle drill school that I have finally been accepted for. I asked for it when we first arrived and they finally took pity on me. It is a tough course but very instructive and just what I need. Hope you are both feeling well.
   Love Mac.

Below he's feeling down, but hopeful a battle-training course will fix that. It does.

October 1943 [no day]

Dear Mom and Dad,
   I received your letter No. 11 just before I came on the battle drill course. I guess I can explain that two-week interval with no letters by saying that I had been doing absolutely nothing since I came back from leave. You have no idea how depressing it is to report in day after day and receive the same answer – nothing doing, go back to sleep. Even though I like plenty of sleep it became very boring and I was very fed up until this course came along. It has the record of being one of the best schools in England so if I don't learn something it will be because I was too stupid. The course combines a hardening course and a lot of practical work, street fighting, clearing woods, handling and firing every infantry weapon, map reading, etc. It is a course I have wanted since I joined the army but I guess I'm too much like you, Dad, I can't get down on my knees to the people who control the strings. One of our regimental

126

majors was instrumental in getting myself and my two roommates on the course.

I'm glad you have heard from Clayton. He was down at my mess last weekend on his way to a ground school for air force officers. I think it is meant to give him an idea of army life and methods as well as a spell out of the air. You seem to be having tough luck with the radio but I know how you feel because ours was out for several weeks over here. I do wish you could send us a bushel of tomatoes because we only see them about once a week and the season is nearly over. As yet I have avoided any colds but I am keeping my fingers crossed because they are hard to break over here. I hope you have some more of that Vacasen [?] on the way because I have enough left to last until the middle of November. I want to get a good night's sleep tonight so had better close.

Love Mac.

Mac, 21, has been in England for four months at this time, and the wear and strain of training and waiting for the inevitable day under actual fire in Europe are beginning to tell. Like his pilot brother, he had periods of depression.

J.M. Bird
#1 C. I.R.U.
CAO

15 October1943

Dear Mom and Dad,

In your last letter you mentioned the possibility that I had gone "places" because I had not written. Please do not worry because these periods of depression come upon a fellow and there is not much one can do about them. I know now how Clayton felt and I must say I do not envy his long stay at one place.

Last week I received your parcel with the jar of honey and piece of cake in it and although the former did not last long we sure enjoyed it. There are fine "Pats" on this course so we share parcels. I also received 300 smokes from Mrs. Moore, Ruth's landlady, while in Wpg. She has been very nice to both of us while I was at Fort Garry, having had me in for supper several times.

This course is turning out to be a little tougher than I had counted on. This morning we ran about 14 miles in just under three hours. We ran across country from point to point as a platoon would in enemy territory and this made all the more work for us because we would run two or three miles and then crawl up on the position. My wind is in excellent shape and my old heart seems to take the strain without much effort but the hills bother my legs. However, by the time I leave here I expect to be in the best shape ever. The food here is better than at #1 so I hope to put a little weight on. I weighed in at 161 which is not enough in my opinion. Late lunch is being served so I'll have a bite and then turn in.

Hope you both keep well,
Love Mac.

28 October 1943

The family expects him to write home weekly, but Mac, like his brother Clayton, found that too onerous as the training intensified.

Dear Mom and Dad,

We are working four nights a week as well as the heavy day work and it does not leave one in a mood for writing. I have not heard from Clayton since he went on his course which I believe is over now. I would like to know what he thinks about army work.

What you have been saying about your garden certainly makes interesting reading because I have been rather disappointed at #1 in the amount of fresh garden produce given us. Down here it is quite different. We have at least two fresh vegetables both dinner and supper and frequently three. Also second helpings if desired and I have been taking full advantage. Instead of losing weight like so many of the chaps I have gained six pounds so far. Right now I am having some trouble with some strained muscles in my right foot and leg but hope that the MO will be able to loosen them up so I can finish the course without such a handicap.

The war news seems to get better every day but I can't help being slightly pessimistic. I can't see the Germans retiring in Italy without some real attempt at a crunching blow to our troops. Rommel is a brilliant soldier and no doubt has plenty of material to play with. As for the Russians, if they keep up their present pace, they will be dictating to us in a very short time. However, these Moscow talks may iron out some of the reasons for friction with the Russians. I had better close now and prepare for tomorrow. Hope you are both keeping well.

Love Mac.

14 November 1943

Dear Mom and Dad,

The mail has certainly been coming in much better since I got back here to #1. During the past week I received your letters 15 and 16 Dad and your 18 and 19 Mom as well as two from Ruth. I don't know why but since joining the army I have developed an insatiable hunger for chocolate and candy. Your parcels, plus our weekly ration of one bar from the mess, serve to keep me happy. I usually have the odd piece left over from the previous parcel whenever a new one arrives. Cigarettes, no.

We finished our course just a week ago yesterday and I am not very sorry. The muscles in my foot and leg were stiff for the last 10 days of the course and still have not returned completely to normal. The MO who examined me when I went to the hospital said it sounded like a fracture but nothing showed up on the plates. I am to have it X-rayed again although I think it is unnecessary. The fact that my foot is not yet up to normal is due to the fact, I think, that I was not able to rest it when the trouble first developed. I could have been sent back but that would have meant no qualification, hence I would have had to take the entire course again. Also the last two weeks were easier than the first three and much more interesting. We had several very good sessions using live ammunition and in co-operation with carriers, three-inch mortars, flame throwers, and on the last day carried out an assault with artillery in support.

Those gunners were magnificent. If any enemy had been in that position there would not have been opposition to our attack. This was also a marvelous battle inoculation as we advanced to within 150 yards of the edge of the barrage and as we lay there we would first hear the "whoop" as the guns fired, seconds later a weird whistling as the shells passed overhead, and then the "crump" as the shells exploded. This battle inoculation was the best part of the course. One of our officers back from Sicily told me that the majority of the casualties were men who had not had battle drill and became excited and confused when they came under fire the first time. Before I forget, Mom, that parcel contained the heading for my letter if and when…

Love Mac.

P.S. went for a walk today and saw the first snow over here.

28 November 1943

Dear Mom and Dad,

I seem to be slipping again but will try to improve. I'm just not very happy with my present employment and the only good thing about the immediate future is that I am due for nine days leave on Dec. 13th. I plan to have Christmas either with Clayton at his station or, if he can get away, with Dorie's folks [family near Driffield]. The government has laid down traveling restrictions during the holidays but I think my nine days will cover them.

The weather the last week has been very dull and wet and flu is reported everywhere. I myself have had a mild attack which concentrated in my bowels and resulted in my being annoyed by frequent attacks of diarrhea and cramps in the stomach. It is showing signs of clearing up.

Love, Mac.

Even in Canada, food was rationed, as he alludes to here.

9 December 1943

Dear Mom and Dad,

I was glad to hear you got your deer because it should be a big help to the meat ration. I had nine days coming up next week but it has been cancelled by the colonel until well after the New Year. Some officers here began acting up a few weeks ago....As a result the innocent must suffer with the guilty and I shall not spend Xmas either with Clayton or the Taylors. It is very annoying but nothing can be done about it. That slight case of flu I mentioned in my last letter developed and I decided I would be better off in bed. The MO agreed and I have spent the last five days in my room.

I have received several letters from Clayton since he was transferred, mostly dealing with leave. He seems satisfied with the work. He has not been off the station since he went there because he says it is really "in the sticks." He had bought something for Do for Xmas. I am glad you had a holiday in Wpg Mom because B'vain must get very monotonous with so many away.

Love Mac.

27 December 1943

Dear Mom and Dad,

Another Christmas gone but it certainly didn't have much of the real spirit. We served the men their dinner and it was quite a menu. They didn't have many turkeys but managed to get ducks, geese and chickens enough to give every man a good serving. To go with this there was peas, turnips, Brussels sprouts, apple sauce, sage dressing, mashed and roast potatoes and gravy. Pudding and sauce, mincemeat pie, beer, tea or coffee and free cigarettes finished off a grand meal. Each man also received a box of chocolates and a package of cigarettes from the Legion. I think you will admit that that was quite an excellent meal for over here. Our dinner was very similar but there were so many drunks that the dinner was spoiled. I have done very well as far as parcels go. Yours came quite early followed by others. There was cake in each parcel and it was all in good shape.

Love, Mac.

Two nephews, Brad Bird, 50, left, and Bruce, 56, right, flank their uncle Mack, 88, at Bruce and Deanna Bird's home in 2009. Deanna took the photo.

CHAPTER 13

In Italy

They are now in Italy — and the boat ride wasn't easy for the men. His description of Algiers is excellent. He turned 23 on January 6.

29 January 1944

Dear Mom and Dad,

I am sorry that I was not able to write you lately but circumstances did not permit it. In case you haven't guessed already, we are now in sunny Italy. Our trip down was uneventful and time dragged heavily despite the fact that we had a Canadian concert party on board. Our convoy was slow but very heavily escorted so we had no need to worry about Jerry bothering us. As usual I was not a good sailor and spent a good part of the trip in the horizontal position. I never actually fed the fish but felt like it so many times that it spoilt the trip. I would be feeling rather woozy at meal times and would bravely make the mess only to get that certain feeling about the time I was trying to put the main course away and have to run to my cabin. This kept up for the first four days and then I was able to hold my own.

We had very nice weather coming down the Mediterranean but a chilly wind prevented us from getting a sun tan. We passed Gibraltar at night so could only see the black outline. Algiers, however, was lit up like a circus and presented a lovely picture after blacked-out England. One of the vagaries of war is that the blackout is not enforced over here, the reason being that Jerry cannot tell civilian lights from military. The people seem to be rather badly off as a result of the war. Most of their clothes are badly worn, most of them wear wooden clogs, and I even saw some with their feet wrapped in rags. When our boat anchored in the harbour we were met by several small ships manned by ragged individuals begging for food. Somebody tossed some bread to them and even though some fell in the dirty harbour water, they fished it out and dried it on the seat boards. The Germans had made a thorough job of demolishing the city and people could be seen cooking their supper over fires on the street in front of their homes. Little children were filthy and invariably their only clothes were a dirty shirt. It was rather a depressing sight to me but the people themselves were cheerful under their hardships. We are quartered in modern buildings but again Jerry made sure we would be uncomfortable. However it is much better than canvas and I am happy about the whole thing. It is bedtime now so I'll take my leave for the time being. Hope you are both keeping well.

Love Mac.

Dances continue to be held, even near the war front.

13 February 1944

6 Coy. I.C.B.R.D.
C.A. C.M.F.

Dear Mom and Dad,

I have forgotten the number of this letter but it is my second attempt from Italy. As yet I have received no mail since leaving England but am not surprised. Col. Balston's visit may have resulted in a speedup somewhere but some lads out here have not seen it. One chap received 60 letters at once but he had been moving quite frequently. I think the blame rests with unit postal clerks who are notorious for their errors. The weather has turned quite ugly of late; rain, hail and snow have come in great quantities so that training has become quite uncomfortable. However we can be very thankful that we are in barracks and not under canvas. We have been getting stories back from the front about the wind and cold and they are not very comforting. I went downtown yesterday just to have a look at the shops for some souvenirs but the shops were closed. I don't think there is anything here anyway because Jerry cleaned the place thoroughly.

We are having a dance in the mess tomorrow night but we can only get 15 nurses. The remainder will be local girls but it is the custom here that several members of a girl's family accompany her when she goes out with a man. We are inviting 25 girls so it should be quite an affair, especially as only the very widely educated Italians can speak English. Most of them know French but that is no help to me. Even my high school Latin is not much good.

We had a grand mess dinner a few nights ago when one of our senior officers left. We are blessed with an excellent cook who does wonders with our bully beef, our staple meat ration. Our meals are rather monotonous on the whole because Jerry stripped most of the food, too. I wish you would enclose a toothbrush in the next parcel because my present one is rather soft. I'd better close now as I have to write Clayton and a few others. Hope you are both keeping well.

Love, Mac.

20 February 1944

Dear Mom and Dad,

Still no mail but hoping for the best. Some of the boys have received some so ours should arrive any day. Also the weather is still against us as it is still cold and we get frequent showers and snowflurries. I have not been doing any marching for the last few days because the tendon at the back of my right ankle swells up and becomes very sore. The MO said it was a common complaint over here and put it down to hill climbing of which we have been doing a lot.

A little financial job that you can do for me is in regards to a bank account in Wpg. I will send an ordinary letter next time in which I will enclose authority for you to close the account. I meant to do this before the last Victory drive but forgot. There is slightly more than $100 in it so you can pick up another bond on the next issue. I left it open because I thought it might come in handy, it being in the same bank as my English account, viz, the Commerce. I should have a sizable account by the time I get back to Blighty because I have only used $25 out of my January and February pay and don't see any prospects for spending much around here. I have been thinking of increasing my assignment but will let you know if I do. I believe I told you that I sent Ruth $100 at Christmas as well as flowers. I thought that she could use a gift of that kind more than some useless trinket.

A few nights ago we had a dance in the mess to which we invited 15 nurses and about 25 wops. I met a nurse who was stationed at Shilo while I was there so we had a grand time. I didn't bother much with the local girls because I can't handle their lingo yet. I was up to the hospital last night and boy does it sound good to hear Canadian girls' voices again. These girls came over on the same convoy as we did. Aside from a slight cold I am in the best of health. Hope you have avoided the flu so far.

Love, Mac.

Mac is pleased to be near the action, finally, and is soon to be on patrol himself.

5 March 1944

4 Bn 1CBIRD
CACMF
[In Italy]

Dear Mom and Dad,

Please excuse the writing because it is so chilly I can't get my hand warmed up.

They took our little stove away for another job. Since I wrote you last we have had several days of perfect weather but the rains came again last night and are still with us. I have the mud licked now because I scrounged a pair of gum rubbers and felt insoles. The other day we had a chance to go up to the front with one of our regimental officers who had seen action in some of the country we visited. It was very interesting hearing first-hand how the boys had fought here and there, being shelled while taking that place and so on. While we were talking just outside the last big town we took, Jerry started shelling the valley just in front, but it was just a few nuisance shots. We had hoped to see the regiment but circumstances interfered. On the whole it was an extremely interesting trip as we were passing through country recently liberated and the signs of war were all about us: blown bridges under repair, burnt out tanks, mine warning signs, bomb craters, shattered buildings, etc. It all seems so unnecessarily ugly because it is in direct contrast to the green grass and budding trees which hint at the approach of spring. Thank God war has not touched home!

I received a very pleasant surprise yesterday when Freddie Robbins [from home] walked into camp. He had been in hospital with his sinus trouble and is on his way back up. He has been fortunate in never having been wounded because he has seen a lot of action. He transferred to another regiment to come over here. He is so fat that I hardly recognized him. Another kid from home to pass through here lately was young Fred Venables. He was also out of the line through sickness. Fred had had later mail than I had so he brought me up to date. As yet nothing has gotten through for me and I am beginning to lose patience [he's been in Italy about six weeks].

I am enclosing a few pieces of the paper money we use over here. I'm sorry I can't find some better souvenirs but the Italians seem to have anything worthwhile hidden. I wish you would enclose a large tube of Barbasel shaving cream as I have started on my last one. Another thing I would appreciate is a box of 50 House of Lords or Tucketts Preferred Panetelas cigars. You can buy them the same way you get the cigarettes – through a local dealer. You might also change the secondary address from the Red Cross to the regiment so that if they miss me entirely the boys will get them.

Well it is getting too cold in here now so I think I'll make a cup of Oxo and bundle off to bed. Hope you are both well.

Love Mac.

31 March 1944

Lt. J.M. Bird
B. Coy PPCLI
CMF

Dear Mom and Dad,

Time flies so fast that I hadn't realized that I hadn't written last week. We have been very busy with patrols and guards despite the way the papers tell the story. The first night I was up here I was fortunate in being allowed to go on a patrol, acting in the capacity of a private soldier. I badly wanted the experience where I would have no responsibility before I had to take my own bunch out. We did get a prisoner and a very talkative gent too. He was badly scared and gave us all the information we asked for. We must have had Lady Luck with us that night, because, firstly, this chap had a bad cough which gave him away; secondly, Jerry was very slack that night and left this chap alone in an outpost; thirdly, Jerry sent up flares which helped us immensely but did not give us away and fourthly, one of our chaps developed a bark that I finally shut up with a package of Life Savers from one of your parcels. Don't take that as a hint to send more because we get a weekly issue. It just happened that I had those on me.

As yet I have received no parcels and no letters since March 10. We are living the life of Riley up here right now with nothing to bother us except guard duty and patrols. The weather seems to have definitely broken as we have had the sun now for three days running. It did snow one night but I was not out, thank heaven. It will not be long now before we go into summer kit and under canvas. We are living in partly demolished houses now but the hot weather brings out strange odors in this country. I have several letters to write so will close. Take it easy with the gardens this year, Dad, and remember, this is not a one-man war.

Love Mac.

Mac told me that by the time he'd written the following letter he'd already been on numerous patrols, taken prisoners and eliminated a number of the enemy. He does tell about the first prisoner he took while on patrol.

21 April 1944

5 Coy 2 Bn. 1CBRD
CA CMF

Dear Mom and Dad,

I have just received Dad's letters of March 19 in which you said you had not heard from me. I was very sorry to see that because I know what it is like to go for weeks without mail. The only reason I can give is that some mail going to Canada was lost shortly after I arrived and my first letters would be amongst them [in fact they got through]. I hardly know where to begin with the news. As you will see from my address I am back where I started from through no fault of my own. I started up the line and spent two weeks with the regiment on training increment but there was no room for me when my time was up so here I am. I did not see a great deal of action while there but was fortunate to capture a Jerry prisoner on one of my patrols. I believe I told you about him in my last letter but just in case it went astray I am mentioning it again. I am rather proud of him because some other officers who have been there for a long time have not had the same good luck. Also the men tend to look down on a new officer until he proves himself and that was my big chance.

I am afraid this letter is rather late but I have been kept rather busy since I came back. They now consider me a "man of the line" because of my two weeks up there and I am now training some of the recent arrivals from England. Our Victory bond campaign has gone well over the top both in the unit here and in the whole area. I have purchased $300 outright and $100 in installments so don't be too surprised when they arrive. I have had no chance to spend much in the last few months and found my bank account rising fast. How much did B'vain exceed the quota? Bob Gladstone [from Boissevain] is a lance corporal in our company here, as is one of the White boys. It's bedtime again so I'll close for now. Hope you have had several of my letters by the time this one arrives.

Love Mac.

5 May 1944

5 Coy 2 Bn 1 IBRD
CA CMF

Dear Mom and Dad,

At long last my mail is coming thru. I received five letters yesterday and three cigarette parcels, from you, Doris and the Moores and a parcel of chocolate from the C.P. Club and the one you sent on 13 Dec. The letter parcel just missed me at two of my camps which explains its delay. Your No. 34 letter Mom was stamped "salvaged from air crash" and there was an explanation in today's paper about the holdup when those planes cracked up [his older brother Clayton was flying operations and so this was a sensitive topic to raise with the folks].

I have not met any chaps, other than the ones I mentioned in my last letter, from home, but Freddie and I are still together. You would hardly recognize him he is so fat. And don't worry about drinking bad water – any time we are away from camp (where all water goes thru large purifiers) we are supplied with little bottles of sterilizing pills which are very effective. We are also supplied with anti-malaria pills, mosquito nets and cream and many other safeguards so that if a man goes down he has only himself to blame. This yellow jaundice is bothering a lot of the boys and seems to have the MO's baffled. They can treat it but they don't seem to know what causes it.

[Cousin] Emily wrote me to say she was working on those sox you mentioned Mom and they will be appreciated. I have a pair of Oxfords now for dancing etc. but only have that one pair of sox you sent in a November parcel. I am glad to hear that a few cigars are on the way as I do enjoy a change from cigarettes. A pipe seems a little too strong for my mouth and I have dropped it for a while. I was glad to hear of Do's [Dorie's] visit with Ruth as Ruth is about the only one that can handle her when her morale is low. [Dorie is Doris Bird, brother Clayton's new wife and Brad Bird's mother who gave birth to him many years later, in 1959, age 40.] As far as that goes, Ruth is good for anyone who is blue – I only hope that time and distance do not separate us too much.

We are having grand weather now and I am well on the way to a good tan. Do you remember how brown I used to get? I should have plenty of opportunity to get just as brown over here as the sun is quite high already. It's bed-time now. The bugler just sounded the last post. Glad to hear you are both in good health. We have been doing a lot of marching so I am in the pink myself.

Love Mac

P.S. don't bother sending soap – our canteens always carry Lifebuoy or Lud.

Parcels from home are safe and easy to talk about, and form a link with the folks at home who sent them.

14 May 1944

Dear Mom and Dad,

At long last the PO has found me and the parcels are arriving. With the last week I have received nine parcels of cigarettes and five parcels of eats, etc. I will list your smokes: D3A/141333; J4AA 03273; J4A06304; F4A 71183. The others were from Do, the Moores, the Ed Dows, the COTC and the Com. Parcels Club. The parcels came from the club, one of chocolates and one ordinary one, chocolates from Emily and two from you. The last one was the January 27th one with the lighter. I can't remember the date of the first one to arrive but it had a tin of pineapples and a tin of sandwich spread, choc bars, candy, etc.

There is still no sign of that writing case yet. Just when did you send it? You also mentioned a birthday cake which has not shown up. Your letters are coming thru in bunches also – last one from Dad is 36 and Mom 38. I received the pictures of you and the boys in good shape. Several of your letters had been burnt and soaked but were still legible. I thought I would not have room to pack all the good things you sent but the boys soon settled that score. Many of them had not received any parcels so by the time I had passed things around eight hungry men there isn't much left. They did the same when I didn't have anything and that's the way it goes – all for one and one for all.

The weather is perfect now. The whole country is very green and looks much better than when we first landed here. Nevertheless I am not very happy in this particular camp and would like to get back to the regiment. As you will have seen by the papers things are moving again so I may get out of here soon. We are wearing our summer kit now and does it ever feel good to get into shorts again. We are outdoors most of the time and battledress was getting much too warm. I had my picture taken recently and if they turn out OK I'll send you a couple of snaps. One thing you might include in the next parcel is a good sturdy flashlight and batteries. I lost mine some time ago. I hope you are both in the best of health and take good care of yourselves. Thanks a million for all the good things.

Love Mac.

CHAPTER 14

Back in the Fighting

He's back in the fighting now and avoiding all mention of particulars, preferring talk of the parcels from home and the weather. Clayton hasn't written because he's in the thick of the air war over occupied France and Germany, prior to the June 6 invasion.

B Coy PPCLI
CAO CMF

26 May 1944

Dear Mom and Dad,

As you can see I have moved again and am now with the regiment. I am certainly glad to be back because I was fed up with that 2 Battalion. We are in a much nicer part of the country now, not so many hills to climb. Also this part is not very heavily populated so we don't have to put up with the stench and filth that seems to surround every Italian community.

Just before I left I received two parcels from you, February and March. I forgot to notice the numbers, but each one had a package of serviettes, Oxo cubes, chocolate bars and candy. So far I believe I have received all of your parcels except the one with the writing case in it. I'm afraid we must presume it is lost. However, all the other parcels arrived in excellent shape so I can't complain.

I am still hearing regularly from Do and Ruth but as usual Clayton is lacking. He should have my address because I wrote to him from 2 Bn. From now on you may expect my letters to be short and possibly mixed up as to date and number because we will be moving forward and opportunities for writing will be few and far between. I shall do my best because I know what they mean to you. Please excuse the scrawl as I no longer have a comfortable table and chair to use. Chins up and don't worry about me. I have always managed to look after J.M. Bird exceptionally well in the past and will do so even more from now on. Love and best wishes,
Mac.

2 June 1944

Dear Mom and Dad,
We are enjoying grand summer weather now for which we are thankful. We have been camping out under the open skies for the past 10 days and not a sign of rain. We have no tents – just a cape and one blanket. The nights get surprisingly chilly here but I managed to scrounge an extra blanket or canvas tarpaulin to keep warm. Italy is a very lovely country -- provided you stay away from "civilization" – and we are gradually getting into the better part of it. I suppose by now you will have read all about the big show we had here lately. Censorship regulations will not permit me to say much but I can tell you that a certain officer D. Mc. was only slightly wounded. One of our boys was down to see him yesterday and said he was able to get up and walk around. Apparently they were only flesh wounds. Little Jim Gladstone came thru unscathed for which I thanked the Good Provider because Bob was just coming up about that time and for a while could get no word of him. But that is all behind us now and as you can see the war seems to be going well everywhere. The boys now joke about having their next leave in Rome but it is still some distance away.
The lighter is working like a charm. It fires in any breeze and keeps going too. It and the band-aids were about all I could bring with me because we are traveling light but I shall get into that candy and other goodies soon. I have not had any mail since leaving 2 Bn but cannot complain after what I received there. I do hope you have received some rain lately as it doesn't take long for things to burn. We have been having new potatoes, radishes, lettuce and the grandest onions. You would be in your element here Dad because there are plenty of them and they are not too strong even when they get to a fair size [likely code for "the Germans are here but we're more than holding our own."]. It is quite a change because

we had been living on dehydrated foods and they have no taste. From now on we will be much better because everything is starting to ripen or develop. I have to write Ruth now so I'll see you in the next letter.

Love Mac.

No mention below of June 6, 1944, the largest invasion in history, D-Day, when the Allies stormed the beaches of Normandy on the French coast. U.S. General Dwight Eisenhower had nearly three million men under his command. (It is likely that censors prohibited any mention of the invasion.) Old ships and blocks of concrete were assembled to be sunk off the beaches to serve as artificial ports. The British produced a range of specially modified tanks and other vehicles to help clear the beaches. The Americans, however, accepted only the tanks. Clayton was involved in the enormous number of air attacks prior, focused on bridges and railway points, to keep the Germans guessing about the actual location of the invasion. They never did guess correctly, and Hitler held back key divisions of Panzer tanks, which displeased Field Marshal Rommel but helped the Allies. On July 17, Rommel is wounded in an attack from the air. He is later forced to commit suicide after being charged with plotting against Hitler.

21 June 1944

Dear Mom and Dad,

If my writing fades blame it on this wop ink – it clogs my pen up. Our weather here has been very poor lately and just when we are trying to run a sports day. We have had four days of almost continuous rain and everything is soaked. Fortunately I have an old farmhouse for company headquarters so we can get dried out. I have had a touch of dysentery the last few days but these sulpha pills check it fairly quickly. Dad said in his 45th letter that he would forward my letters but I have time for a letter today thanks to the rain. I have also received two parcels lately. ….You will probably get my letter to Dad in which I told about seeing Rome on the sly. In case you don't here is the story – half a dozen of us decided we would like to see it so we climbed in a jeep and saw Rome. It was late at night so we didn't see much but we did see the Coliseum. It must have been quite a stadium when it was in good repair. Be sure to enjoy yourselves when back East and give all the folks my best wishes. I only wish I could be there too.

Love Mac

2 July 1944

Dear Mom,

Have just finished a letter to Emily but have time for another before I go on parade. We are having blistering weather at present but fortunately do not have to work during the afternoon. I was into Rome last week but unfortunately it was Sunday and none of the shops were open. The war simply does not exist for most of the Romans – shops are well stocked, the people well dressed and people can even hire the odd taxi for sightseeing. However our Yankee friends will likely spoil it as they spoilt London for leaves. We saw St. Peters and it is simply marvelous. The Germans never touched it which amazed me for there are several priceless paintings and other pieces of art that Goering would have liked. Guides took us round explaining the history and background of each part of the Cathedral. I was surprised at the numbers of people we met who spoke quite fluent English.

Your last letter to arrive was No. 47, the one with Leslie's picture. The boys all agree that she is the cutest baby they've seen in a long time. I will have to write Kae a line soon as she wrote me some time ago and I have never answered it. There seems so little of interest around here but I guess it is not the news that counts, just the letter. Will have to leave now so best of health and hope you enjoy your holiday.

Love Mac.

3 July 1944

Dear Dad,

I have written to Mom today so you won't have to forward this one. Your letter No. 45 arrived last week but I have had no mail since. I had one day's leave in Rome a week ago last Sunday but found the time too short to really see such a city. It has a rare combination of the old and the new without any apparent transition from one to the other. It was Musso's pride and joy and he made a good job of the modern side. Most of the points of interest are very well preserved and the Germans spared most of the historic sites.

I guess I started this letter too soon. When I came to the mess there were two letters from Ruth and your Nos. 46 and 47. That means a nine-day trip for the latter which is nothing to complain about. Glad to hear that the crops and gardens are doing so well.

I see where the Canadians in Normandy received congrats from Eisenhower on adding "new glories" to Canada's fighting record." I'm glad to see that the boys stood up under such a battle inoculation. Thank God my own has been very gradual compared to what that would be like. Well it's getting near bed-time and I have some work to do in preparation for the morrow so shall turn in. Take good care of yourself, Mac.

P.S. In next parcel please send steel mirror, preferably round and not too large.

Lieut. J. M. Bird
CACMF

30 July 1944

Dear Mom and Dad,

Sorry I can't remember the number. I let this one drag too long. There is so little to write about these days. [*He talks about parcels received with food and Emily's sox and about a Victory Bond he bought for $300, about $3,000 in today's money.*]

Yes I still hear from Ruth and will have to step up the tenor of my letters because she tells me I have strong opposition in Air Force blue. She said it's all on his side – he even went so far as to propose to her. I am not worried because although we have made no formal arrangements we have a mutual understanding which I think will weather all storms. She is working this summer in order to put herself thru and should be able to manage with what help Rita and I can give. I have not heard from Clayton for some time but wrote him last week. Will have to close now as I have many other letters to write.

Love Mac.

16 September 1944

Dear Mom and Dad,

At present I am down the line enjoying a rest after a rather strenuous time in the line. I have come to the conclusion, however, that war is not as tough or as horrible as it is generally made out. It is only certain unfortunate incidents played up by the press which create such an impression.

Your mention of all that corn on the cob, beans peas etc. makes me hope that I am home for Xmas because they should go nicely with that pheasant [he talks more about food]. I had better stop dreaming of all these niceties as my mouth is watering too much and dinner is not quite ready. We eat very well back here because the sergeant cook stays here to instruct new cooks and we sample their efforts, pretty fair most of the time.

Love Mac.

29 September 1944

Dear Mom and Dad,

Received your #57 Mom but can't remember Dad's last one. I have not received any parcels for some time but as far as cigarettes go it is just as well. I have been afflicted with some stomach disorder, mild jaundice I think, which so affected my mouth that I was forced to stop smoking for two weeks. Now I have very little desire to smoke and may be able to quite entirely. Consequently I think you should stop sending smokes – I'll rescind that. Cut down to 600 or 900. Someone is always running low. Then again my will power might weaken and I would have to rely on charity.

I was sorry to hear about John Kelly. An arm wound that would take you back to Canada might be rather an unpleasant one. I hope not in his case. I was also shocked to hear about Stanley Kenward – he was in the artillery and they suffer very few casualties. In the next few lines I shall give you some very bad news but you must promise not to divulge it until the people concerned have received official notification. Dougald McDonald had transferred to another regiment some time ago and in a recent action had the misfortune to step on a mine and received fatal injuries. I got this from an acquaintance of mine who is in the same outfit as Doug so I am sure it is true. However, though I know it is quite a shock when people receive such wires I shall have to insist on strict silence. Both the Gladstones are in our company now and young Willard White also but the latter is getting extremely nervous. In the next parcel I would appreciate some vitamin pills or something of that nature to counteract this tinned diet. When we are in action our staple food is bully beef and the doc thinks I am becoming allergic to it. We are on the beach again enjoying a rest but the water has lost most of its attraction because the air is too chilly these days. It looks too much like another winter here if Jerry doesn't crack soon.

Best of love, Mac.

Here, Mac mentions the minefield story which he describes in detail in his Memoirs. In a wonderful way, these letters supplement with detail and context the memories he shared in recorded conversation with nephews Brad and Bruce 65 years later.

5 October 1944

Dear Mom and Dad,

In case you didn't get my letter I have received the writing case and am using it right now. This bowel trouble has finally annoyed me sufficiently that I have given the MO the full story and as a result am now in hospital. The doc said it was only to get me away from the rough diet we are living on at present and also to have my stool examined to see if there is anything there. It has been bothering me too much of late to ignore it further so here I am. It will be a good rest although I dread the thought of working my way back up to the battalion thru those horrible reinforcement camps. I think I will try to talk them into sending me back direct as I have heard of cases where they have done that.

You have been describing some very poor weather over there in the last few letters but you are not alone. It has been cloudy or raining for the past week and everything is bogging down in the mud. It is very unfortunate because another winter here would be hell. A month ago we used to joke about Xmas dinner in Vienna but not any longer. The rain has settled the show here unless we get a dry break soon.

I was very sorry to hear about Victor Patton but we must expect these things [killed, no doubt]. I have never heard of Glen being out here.

I seem to be running out of news. It is so hard to find anything to say. And that article in the paper was laid on a bit thick. We did have to walk thru a minefield but didn't run into as much trouble afterwards. Losing the padre was the hardest blow of all. He had volunteered as a stretcher bearer and knelt beside a mine casualty and knelt right on a small mine. I found a sniper's rifle (he didn't need it anymore) and removed the sight. It is not a telescopic sight in that it has no magnification – it is a glass sight and serves to clarify the target. There are no cross hairs but three bars (-i-) as in the diagram and they are moved up or down to adjust for range. It should be ideal for the .22 to make a target rifle. I have not been able to find a Luger pistol as yet. They are highly prized as souvenirs. I did manage to get a good Swiss watch from a prisoner but gave it to my sergeant on the condition that he was to leave it with me if we ever parted. Unfortunately he was hit rather badly and I guess the watch was far from his thoughts for some time. Take good care of yourself and watch the cool autumn weather.

Love Mac.

The months of hard fighting have taken a toll on Mac's nerves. You can tell from the tenor of his letters, so different now from how they were at the start. His brother's letters shifted similarly, from upbeat and keen to discouraged and frustrated. The men became old for their age, as below.

14 October 1944

Dear Mom and Dad,

After a rather tiring trip I am now in a base hospital labeled "not yet diagnosed." They paid absolutely no attention to me at the first hospital – merely said they did not have the equipment and that I was to await evacuation. I waited a week or so really fed up with that outfit. I should get a real overall here because they are well equipped and have a reputation of taking more interest in their patients.

Parts of our trip were quite enjoyable, especially the boat trip. It was only a small ship but very comfortable and the sea was calm. We were a whole day on board before we reached port on the southern tip and still on the Adriatic side. There we were transferred to an English ambulance train for a very rough ride. First it took us 16 hours to travel across country and secondly we had to sit up all night. The jolting of the train bothered my stomach and I kept waking up. However I am now in a comfortable bed, have had a hair cut, wash and shave and dinner so now am ready for a short nap. I thought I had better get this written before it gets too dark as the lights do not appear very promising. I forgot to mention one of the highlights of the boat trip and that was a bath in a real tub filled with steaming hot fresh water. It was the first tub I had been in since I left 2 Bn last May and I really enjoyed myself.

I have really quit smoking as it is now nearly three weeks since I had my last cigarette. I wish you would continue to send me the odd package as they come in handy. Smokes seem to be always short over here. As for the cigars they are too expensive to bother with anymore. In your next parcel you might include a couple of my old text books – one a book on mathematics and the other one on auditing. I left them in a cardboard box, in the attic, along with other books and papers. I find that we have a great deal of spare time when we are in rest and would like to keep in touch with accounting. Well I have somebody else to write down East so will close. Hope you are both well and look after yourselves.

Love Mac.

Clayton and I have opened communications again. I hope we can keep it up. If he gets home for Xmas or shortly afterwards I am going to be awfully sorry that I did not try the Air Force too.

23 October 1944

Dear Mom and Dad,

Received your letter No. 60, the first since I left the battalion on the 5th. Moving from one hospital to another is the reason so my mail will be fairly constant now. The doc is quite convinced that there is no infection or foreign growth responsible for my trouble but blames it on nerves. I was quite surprised to hear this because my nerves have only bothered me once in battle and that was because of some very close mortar bombs giving me a bad shaking up. The trouble is not cleared up yet but I don't think they are going to worry much about treatment. I am taking pills which are supposed to "slow me down" and will spend three or four weeks here in convalescent camp before I start back. I imagine the rest and good diet are as much as they can do for such things anyway.

"Our suit" looks very nice on you Mom and I was glad to get the pictures. I wonder why Dad always squints when he has his picture taken outside. That phrase Mrs. White gave you was J.O.B. and means "left out of battle." A certain number of officers and other ranks are sent to a rear area before we go into a battle so that if the battalion is badly cut up there will always be a backbone on which to reorganize. It also serves to give the men an occasional rest or is a means of resting a man who is not feeling well but not sick enough to send to hospital. I did not get any sightseeing in except Ancona because I was sick most of the time. However I can consider myself very fortunate to have had my turn then because Rimini was very "sticky" as far as our boys were concerned. I lost many friends.

I was glad to hear Ruth had written you and don't be afraid of putting your foot in it. I never committed myself before I left for a number of reasons but we had arrived at "a mutual understanding." I have often thought that later events proved my theories wrong and that I should have married on the same gamble that Clayton did. For one thing, married men may get a preference on the discharge list, then there are many financial questions involved and last but not least the question of getting a head start on life when we do get back. And that brings another thought to my mind – you were wondering about my future whereabouts around Xmas. I can assure you it will be Italy and for some months to come. It is raining again and the real rainy season is fast approaching when everything bogs down. In my opinion the Italian campaign is all but mashed up – Jerry will be finished in Germany and certainly not in Italy. I have to run now so keep fit and good luck with the clinic, Dad.

Love Mac.

Next, Mac finds a cousin, the son of one of his father's brothers.

2 November 1944

Dear Mom and Dad,

I am now at the "con" camp but not enjoying it overly much. The weather has been foul ever since we arrived here but resulted in at least one very humourous incident. We were sitting in the canteen the night before last watching a film when the picture started to fade from our sight and it was evident that the power had been affected. The rain had been coming down in torrents for almost an hour so trouble was expected. The sound of the film had no sooner died away when a voice from the front asked if we had brought our swimming trunks. We soon caught on when someone turned on the lights – on a different hookup – and we realized that our feet were in several inches of water which was flowing in one side of the hut and out the other. How long it had been that way I had no idea but my feet felt damp when I got back to barracks. The food here is very well prepared but I cannot enjoy it fully as my bowels have not regained their former composure. The doctor's final verdict was "nervous tension" and that it was up to me to "grow out of it in time." He was quite satisfied that there were no organic troubles and went to great pains to be sure. He had several plates taken, had a barium enema and a rectum examination with an illuminated tube plus all the usual blood tests and stool specimens. In any event I am not going to try to rush back as life in the line right now must be hell with this persistent rain. I received the parcel you sent in August and thanks a lot. The chap who brought it to me on my last day in the hospital said that he had taken it to a Cpl Bird upstairs by mistake. I went up to investigate and found Everett who was recovering from jaundice [he is a cousin, son of Uncle Walter, one of Dr. Bird's brothers]. We didn't recognize each other at once because it is at least seven years since we met. He gave me Mac's address and also a hint as to where I might find Victor Patton when I get back up. All considered your parcel brought much more than you ever dreamed when you sent it. Thanks for the cigars but remember – no more. I have stopped smoking.

Love Mac.

P.S. In future mark my mail with "Not with unit" on left edge. This helps speed delivery and avoids confusion.

14 November 1944

Dear Mom and Dad,

I have now received both your No. 61 and 62, a parcel containing 20 cigars, a cake and many other good things, Sweetcaps No. 9-4-c 87355 and Buckingham No. S4-61832. The latter parcel I gave to Everett Bird, who is convalescing here also. He is looking well but I was surprised that he is so small – certainly not much more than a chip of Uncle Walter. I am giving all my smokes away because I know I will be tempted to start again and I would rather not for a while. I have no doubts that I shall when I return to action but until then I shall avoid it. I do not miss it now as it is six weeks since I had a cigarette. I was into Naples on Saturday afternoon but was very disappointed. I could find nothing worthwhile to send you for Xmas so don't be surprised if nothing turns up. I shall keep looking for a half-decent souvenir but the cheap trash they putting on the market here is an insult to a man's intelligence. I have seen bracelets offered at $40 that would not bring $4 at home and they are being bought. I was fortunate, however, in getting a ticket to "The Barber of Seville" in the San Carlos Opera House. It was quite an experience and I hope to repeat it soon as they have quite a nice program coming up. I have just noticed an error on my part. Those Sweet Caps are from the Com. Parcels Club so I shall have to write them tonite also. I received that clipping from the Free Press some time ago and it was a bit overdone I think. However that fighting during the first week in October was terrible and I was very happy to be left out of it. Also circumstances will keep me out of it for at least a month so don't worry about me for a while anyway.

Love Mac.

Just as his mother worried about Clayton's laundry regime, so too did she worry about Mac's. He gives her a pretty good answer below.

23 November 1944

6 Coy 2 Bn
1CBRD

Dear Mom and Dad,

I am feeling quite fit now that I am back at work but am still bothered by slight attacks of my old trouble. However, I shall have a good chance to rest before I have to go back up as I am now company training officer and should be here for several months. I am gambling on that anyway and you may have noticed the change of address. I would much prefer to be with the regiment, especially over Xmas and the new year, but do not want to go back until I am in top form. It won't be too bad here, however, as I know most of the men on the staff and now that I am an "old field man" I can more than hold my own with them, as many of them are too old to go to the field or have been categorized down here from the field.

You seem to worry a lot, Mom, about whether we get a chance to change our laundry when in action. While we are actually in the line we never get a chance to even take our clothes off (we don't want to be caught with our pants down) but when we go out for a rest, usually every week, our spare kit comes up and we change and wash. Mobile laundries and showers follow the fighting pretty closely and in the summer gave good service. Now they will have trouble in getting suitable quarters as the weather is becoming quite cool.

I have just finished an evening snack of bread, peanut butter and tea. The peanut butter is an American ration which we swapped for some whiskey. They have lots of things that our rations don't include but get no whiskey so the mess secretary makes a deal with them each time our whiskey ration comes in.

If Clayton had gone so far as to cable you that he was on his way he may be there by now, so tell him to write presto as he owes me a letter. If he is delayed you can blame it on lack of ships – that is the latest rumor around here.

I have another important letter to write someone in the East so will bid you good night.

Love Mac.

30 November 1944

Dear Mom and Dad,

Received your letters 65 and 66 Mom and yours 64, 65 Dad as well as a badly battered parcel you mailed in July. Some fool in the PO had stamped it "Addressee Returned to UK" and it had gone back to England and then back here. It is no wonder I was not getting the mail I should have. Some cigarettes, a letter from Ruth and a card from Wm Kings made up my mail for the week.

I still have upset spells but they were nothing like they used to be so I imagine another month here will probably see me 100% again. The news from the west coast looks like it might blow up a little trouble. Actually it does not upset the boys over here nearly as much as I expected. Most of them treat it as a joke but deep down I think they would like to go home for a few days and have some words with those boys [some type of rebellion?]. But whatever the damage done I think the ultimate good resulting from these reinforcements will be apparent, if not at home, at least over here.

I don't know where the politicians get their figures but I have never taken a platoon into action with the full number of men I am supposed to have and have often been down to 50%. This imposes an unnecessary strain on each man – with the possible exception of Prime Minister Wm. M. King. I only hope things smooth out now that the zombies are finally with us.

Don't worry about winter clothing as I have everything. I have two pair of long underwear that I brought from Canada. The army supplies us with plenty of sweaters, gloves, sox, etc. So don't worry on that score. Sorry to hear about Clayton's watch because I know what it's like to lose an heirloom. Years ago you gave me a four-bladed pearl handled knife Dad and several times it has disappeared but it always turns up again. I have carried it everywhere and feel lost without it. And don't worry about me forgetting that little girl – I have too many pleasant memories to allow that.

Love Mac.

Christmas is approaching and Mac is sad he isn't home with brother Clayton.

11 December 1944

Dear Mom and Dad,

My mail is coming fine now. I had a letter from Kay Findlay written while they were visiting you people.

The weather finally broke and the sun came out this morning in real earnest. But there was enough frost to freeze the ground and leave quite a snap in the air. We have a small stove fixed up so that it will burn either oil or wood as fuel of any kind is hard to get out here. The electric lights have been put in good shape so we are well fixed for the winter unless they call me on draft. We have been hearing some wild and wonderful rumours lately and don't even hope they are even partially true. Of course I can't mention them due to censorship but they don't mean as much as Clayton's good luck.

Several old "Pats" dropped in for a visit over the weekend and the boys had quite a party. I confined myself to two bottles of Canadian beer that I had been saving for a special occasion. I have not gone back to hard liquors as they are too much for my system in its present state.

Dinner time so I'll run along. I think I need a little real home cooking instead of this mass production diet. This will probably be the last letter to reach you before Xmas so enjoy yourselves and maybe next Xmas all the Birds will be home to roost.

Love Mac.

27 December 1944

Dear Mom and Dad,

Just a few hurried lines to wish you the best for the New Year. We had a pretty fair Xmas here but I feel sure it was nothing compared to the one you folks had with Clayton and Do. Boy did I wish I was there on Xmas day.

We had a big day here, the officers and senior NCOs serving a wonderful dinner at noon and then we had our dinner at 7 that night. The company commander and I "entertained" the boys in our room that afternoon as Xmas day is the one day of the year in which private Joe Soup of the Canadian Army is boss man. The boys all had a marvelous time thanks to plenty of Canadian beer, turkey, cranberry sauce, mince meat, cauliflower, potatoes, peas, dressing and roast pork, steam pudding with brandy sauce, coffee, nuts and oranges. Not a bad menu for this part of the world. Our dinner was the same except that we had a chicken broth to start with and a glass of port to finish. We had an Italian band supply the music in the men's mess while we had a piper in to play the various regimental march tunes.

I was a sober and upright young man on Xmas but cannot make the same boast for the mess dance on the 23rd. There was a shortage of girls and, not feeling in the mood to compete with the other wolves, I proceeded to drown my sorrows. Needless to say my old stomach rebelled and I paid for my folly in the usual way. I think I will celebrate New Year's with lemonade and something equally digestible. But I must run now and have my supper. Will write again soon.

Love Mac.

CHAPTER 15

War Wraps Up

Mac turns 24 on January 6, and is very much missing home. He's been in Italy a year.

2 January 1945

Dear Mom and Dad,

The day after and everything is getting back to the normal routine. For New Year's Eve I went down to the officer's club, which had advertised a good time, and after discovering that I did not like the concoction they chose to call a punch I brought the New Year in quite sober and upright. They had an Italian floor show which was fair and a very good dance band but again the girls were conspicuous by their absence. Icy roads were chiefly to blame there. We may have had a green Xmas but New Year's has more than made up for it as it is still snowing and the temperature is dropping. I had a lovely hot bath downtown today and decided it was a good time to put on my "snuggies." They certainly are the answer to these blustery days.

The officers' mess is the envy of the whole camp with its very efficient oil burner. We have a nice little stove in our room but fuel is so scarce that we can only light it occasionally. I have no complaints re my mail having received all my Xmas parcels in good time as well as plenty of cards and letters.

I was glad to hear that Clayton had a crack at the jumpers. I would dearly love to have been there but maybe next year. This country doesn't have any game but Jerry and he shoots back so you can't call it sport. I have never seen a game bird or animal since I have been here and that will be a year on the 28th of this month. Just between you and me I think I will be able to roost here until the weather breaks again. Right now it is pretty miserable at the front and I am not the least bit anxious to try my poor stomach and rheumatism against the elements. I picked up the latter in Fort Garry in the spring of '43 and it bothers my hips and knees when I get chilly in bed. As long as I have my sleeping bag I am OK but one or two blankets in a wet slit trench would be rough. Here's hoping for an early spring. Hope you are well and give my regards to all the lucky ones who get home.

Love Mac.

7 January 1945

To Mrs. A. E. Henderson of Boissevain, Man.

Dear Mrs. Henderson,

This will be my first letter of the New Year to the Community Parcels Club and in it I wish to thank you for the last parcel I received in the Old Year – my Xmas parcel. It arrived a few days before Xmas and in excellent shape.

Our Xmas here was much better than I expected thanks to a bountiful supply of turkey, cranberry sauce, pudding, etc. The officers and senior NCOs served the men in traditional army style and the men thoroughly enjoyed the day…..(He talks about the weather.)

Thanks again for the many grand parcels and cigarettes which you have sent me during the past year and may the New Year see so many of our boys at home that the Community Parcels Club will be able t say "A good job well done" and call it a day.

Yours Sincerely,
Mac Bird.

13 January 1945

6 Coy. 2 Bn ICBRD
CAO CFM

Dear Mom and Dad,

I have just been checking on the last few letters I have received and find I have all Mom's up to 76 and Dad's to 72. They still take too long for airmail letters, but if the weather in other parts of the world is anything like we are having here then I can easily understand the delay. Yesterday it rained quite heavily and it is still raining now (7 p.m.). And as there was a blanket of about five inches of snow to start with you can imagine what 48 hours of rain will mean. And last night I witnessed a weird phenomenon. I was walking downtown to my Italian teacher in a heavy snowstorm, when to my surprise the world was lighted up by a brilliant flash of lightning and followed a few moments later by peals of thunder. But there is a silver lining to almost every dark cloud – it is Saturday and I have been inside almost all day sitting beside my little stove studying my Italian and writing letters. I am becoming quite interested in the language and hope I can stay here long enough to gain a working knowledge of it.

Don't worry about that birthday parcel being late [he turned 24 on Jan. 6] because Tommy and I are still having late snacks on food received in our Xmas parcels. I received the first parcel of tomato juice and really enjoyed it. I have a cup of it each morning I think of it. Usually I am in such a rush that I forget it. Even the army has not changed my bad habit of staying in bed till the last minute and then bolting for breakfast.

I think Clayton is very lucky to be able to go back to university and hope he can clean up those supps. I have my texts here and occasionally do a little work but it seems so futile. Maybe the next few months will change that considerably. Before I forget I received 300 Buckingham cigarettes with a date stamped 8 Dec. 44. They must be this new fast system, because that is almost as the letters. Hope you are all well.

Love Mac.

25 January 1945

Dear Mom and Dad,

I am back at the battalion. As yet I am not on strength but on training increment, same as about a year ago only I won't be getting any patrols this time as I stay a few miles back of the regiment.

I was at a company smoker last night but managed to stay sober despite the well-meant efforts of some of my old friends to put me under. There is another tonight but I am not going. There have been many changes while I was away but two of the hardest ones to take were the deaths of my sergeant and batman, both of whom had been with me all the time I was in B Coy.

I am living in an Italian house and the people are wonderful when compared to those of the south. They have given us a spaghetti dinner, do our washing and help us with our Italian. One of the boys knows French so we use that as a medium of exchange. The people up here are more civilized than the south and give us a lot of help. They give us Partisans as guides and some of them are real headhunters and a big help. Will close now as I have to write that little woman in the East. Hope you are both well.

Love Mac.

4 February 1945

Dear Mom and Dad,

We are living like kings again with plenty of chickens, fresh beef, and some vegetables the Italians had stored up. I know you will probably think we are barbarians when I tell you that our company alone has killed 400 cattle within the past week but if you had been living on dehydrated mutton or bully beef for weeks on end and then a young heifer walked into your backyard – what would you do? ...I took over the post of chef for Coy HQ and do I ever wish I had paid a little more attention to what you did around that kitchen, Mom. I keep forgetting salt or don't know which way to cut the meat but we got by. We had some fresh liver and canned bacon, cornmeal porridge, coffee and toast for breakfast, steaks, hamburgers and roast for dinner with plenty of fresh onions and potatoes. For one supper I cooked 30 steaks, although there were only 13 of all ranks present. None was thrown out.

You will probably think I am crazy when I tell you we are in a front-line position and carry on in this manner but this is one of those phony wars right now with neither side doing much of anything. The weather is cool but usually thaws slightly when the sun is out. It will be terribly muddy when a real thaw comes. I am still on increment and may be sent back soon. I would rather be here than at 4 Btn. Hope you are both well

Love Mac.

17 February 1945 (his brother Clayton's 26th birthday)

Dear Mom and Dad,

Sorry not to have written sooner but I am rather fed up and there is nothing to write about where we are now. I am still on increment with no platoon of my own. I stay at Coy HQ and act as (illegible) which doesn't give me very much to do. I have retired as cook because one of the boys came back yesterday and as he used to be a cook I thought he'd better take over. The food has been rather grim in this position because there is no fresh meat available and we have to live on rations. ...

I don't seem to be in the mood for writing just now – even the radio playing some lovely music doesn't seem to help. I think that a few hours' sleep will go more good than anything so will sign off for now.

Love Mac.

30 March 1945

Dear Mom and Dad,

I don't know what got into me but I just could not get in the mood for writing letters. I sent a wire yesterday so I hope you will not be too worried. We are in Belgium now, as you have probably heard, and having a marvelous time. The people here are so radically different from what we have known in the past that I don't think I can describe just how we feel. Although they are short of some foods they still insist on giving us dinners fit for kings and wines that they have saved for years.

B Company's officers' mess is in the best hotel in the village and nothing is too good for us. We have maid service, sleep between fresh linen sheets, listen to the radio and piano, they assist our cook in preparing our meals and serving etc. In short, I have never seen anything like it since I joined the army, and officers who were with the regiment in England say that this supersedes anything they ever had there. The people in this village are so helpful and kind that it is hard to realize that there are such people. One family here were instrumental in helping many airmen to escape and we are helping them to contact the boys. We have the company billeted in ones and twos on the villagers and for most of the boys it is the first "home" they have been in for almost two years. They are behaving very well and seem to realize that it is too nice a setup to spoil by drunken rowdiness.

And speaking of drink, please stop worrying about me. Liquor will NEVER get a hold on me. At present I am in command of the company – the major and captain both being in England – and it is quite an experience. However, my NCOs are good and so I have little to worry about.

All my love,

Mac.

Mac wrote the next letter to an uncle and his family, but the letter was not in an envelope so we don't know who.

6 April 1945

Dear folks,

I am writing from somewhere in northwest Europe. Thanks for the parcel which I received the other day. It had done a lot of traveling around before it had caught up with me but it was in first class shape. I saw Ev shortly after he had come back up the line and he told me about meeting Clayton at a rest camp where he stayed after he had been in hospital. I hope to run into Bert one of these days if he is in this neck of the woods. I saw him once in England before I went to Italy.

It looks like the Jerries are on the run at last. It shouldn't be very long before the job's finished. I received a letter from home the other day. Dad sprained his leg but is back at work. Hazel quit work when Walter died, but has gone back again. One of the sergeants on the fitters staff knows you, uncle. Raymer and I knew each other quite a while before I found out he came from Boissevain. Well I must close for now. Hoping this finds you all in the very best of health.

Yours sincerely,

Mac.

8 April 1945

Dear Mom and Dad,

At present I am back in London on seven days' leave but I would have preferred to have spent it in Belgium. Never have I been dined and wined so well in all my life. They went to great pains to prepare special dishes for us and even the staple items had to be served in fancy styles and always on silver trays. They opened their wine cellar when we arrived (they had bricked it up against the Germans) and we had wines and champagnes as old as 1923. The hotel was called Vieux Chandron ("old cooking pot") and was well known in Brussels and Antwerp for its fine table and wine cellar. We only spent 12 days in that small town but a deep mutual friendship sprung up that will last a long time. Many of the boys are writing to the families they were billeted with and I hope they keep it up. It is nice to think that, in a least one of the countries in which Canadians have fought, the people were really grateful for our coming, despite the fact that our armies had been responsible for much destruction in their country.

I am smoking quite a bit now and would appreciate a few smokes each month. We can buy them over here now so don't think that I have been short. However, my cigars are all gone and I could use a few if you can possibly find any.

This leave is one of the best organized schemes I have ever seen in the army. From your unit you go to a collecting camp near a railway. After all your documents are checked you get on a train and travel nonstop to point of embarkation. Here they have washing and eating facilities as well as bunkhouses in case the tide holds you up. Upon arriving at a UK port you are hustled onto a waiting train which takes you to London, and from there you go your several ways. On the train you receive tea and cakes, the latest newspapers and a package of smokes. A walking information booth will give you train times, hostel addresses, what plays are on in London etc. When you reach the station and if you are staying in London your worries about a bed (the town is crowded as usual) are quickly ended when a loudspeaker directs you to a table where you receive a reservation in one of the many clubs in the city. Here you have a real bath, something to eat and then start your real leave. I plan to see some of the plays. Others on leave before me say they are quite good.

I slept in this morning and was quite tired after the long trip. Right now I feel the need of a little exercise before dinner so will sign off. Hope you are both in good health.

20 April 1945

Dear Mom and Dad,

I fully intended writing you whilst on leave but kept on the go so much that I neglected you again. I met a very nice young lady at the Overseas League Club and she agreed to be my escort around London. We had a grand time seeing several plays, moving pictures, dine and dance spots, the Kew Gardens, houses of parliament, etc. The last two days I spent at her place out at Peckham, a suburb of London. I had quite a time seeing her home each night. I could not go all the way because the tubes quit too early and it would have meant a four-mile walk for me. I have done that several times for Ruth but not for anyone else.

And speaking of her, she faithfully continues writing even though I sometimes neglect her too. But she still loves me so I imagine it will take more than a lack of letters to break it up. She has just finished her exams and is having a week's holiday before getting a job. I will be able to help her next fall but at present my bank account is rather low, as I have just written a cheque for a bond registered in your name, Dad, for $500 [about $5,000 in 2010 dollars]. That will help to explain why the certificates have not shown up. If you remember, an individual is only allowed to purchase $650 per year and when I reached my limit they turned my full pay into my account in r---- land. The letter informing me followed me around Italy for four months, hence the delay. I then made an assignment of $50 per month to you which I wish you would use to purchase bonds, possibly through the bank. When I think I am nearly due for discharge, then I can have you cancel that idea and build up a little ready cash. Hope this explains everything,

Love Mac.

29 April 1945

Dear Mom and Dad,

I am glad to hear that Cub and some of the other old-timers are getting back home, but it burns me up when they send men like Alex McDonald overseas again. That man left the regiment four or five times due to malaria and will probably suffer from it all his life....

Just heard over the radio that poor old Musso finally got his from his own countrymen. I didn't think they had either the brains or the stuff to

163

do a job like that but maybe I met the wrong type of Italian. Hope you are both well.

Love Mac.

Big news – the war is over in Europe! Mac has had enough and will not volunteer for duty against Japan. On May 4 Doenitz sent envoys to Montgomery's headquarters and German forces surrendered in Holland, Denmark and north Germany. Hitler and his lady friend committed suicide May 1, followed by Goebbels and his wife.

B Coy. PPCLI
CAO.

6 May 1945

Dear Mom and Dad,

We were playing bridge the night before last when the radio stuttered out something about more Jerries surrendering but no one caught the exact details so the game continued. Then the 9 o'clock news came on and we paid close attention. The war is over in Holland. At first we could hardly believe our ears but it is really true. We broke out the rum issue and after a couple of rounds and much speculation on what would be our next job, we went back and finished a couple of rubbers. The whole company received the news in much the same manner but some other troops did not and the sky was bright with flares and tracer fire. We have been waiting for this news for so long that it didn't seem possible to celebrate properly, particularly when there is still some fighting to be done. Don't worry about this soldier volunteering for the Far East. I have had enough; and although it isn't much compared to some men in the regiment, it is a lot more than our H. D. Army. Besides, my old flat feet are complaining too much lately and I plan to do something about it. I am listening to a rebroadcast of Jack Benny and it made me wonder when I could settle down in that old leather chair and listen to the radio.

....I had better sign off now and write the little woman in the East. Hope you sleep as well as we do tonite.

Love Mac.

19 May 1945

Dear Mom and Dad,

The good news for the rest of the world continues to improve but yours truly is in the blues again. Half an hour before the regiment pulled out for Amsterdam and other points I was told I was going the opposite way to become adjutant of 1 Cdn Div. Field Punishment Camp. What I did to warrant a job like this, and at such a time, I don't know. But I do intend to find out as I was quite annoyed at missing the victory ride through Holland.

Furthermore I imagine the people in those parts appreciate being liberated more than the ignorant crew that inhabits this part. There have been quite a few V.E. celebrations and we thought that they were really on our side but last the Anciliary Services put up a sign telling the people that only girls would be allowed in as the dance was for the soldiers. About 60 couples ignored the sign and walked in. The supervisor told all the men they would have to leave so all the Dutch got up and walked out. They collected outside and jeered at the supervisor when he appeared at the door and also at any girls who did not walk in with soldiers as escorts. By the time the dance closed well over 100 girls had seen the light of day and came in to dance but the crowd hung around to the last. I thought it an extremely poor show on their part, particular one remark overheard: "I wonder if it will be any better under the Canadians than it was under the Germans."

I would like to have been the person who heard that one because there would have been one very sorry Dutchman. I think it too bad that these people were not starved like some of their countrymen and maybe they would appreciate the smaller things in life. This letter seems to be full of grief and nonsense but I shall write again now that the camp is in full swing.

Love Mac.

2 June 1945
[On letterhead of Princess Patricia's Canadian Light Infantry]

Dear Mom and Dad,

I am going to use this paper as I think all mail is being flown home. I have been checking your recent letters and find that Dad's 91 and Mom's 97 are still missing. The rest arrived the last day or so. I am still at the F. P. Camp and though not entirely satisfied with the job feel that I am happier than I would be at the regiment as they are drinking pretty heavily and

I would be tempted to join them were I there. I am finished as far as any hard drinking goes as my old stomach rebels when I indulge. No regrets on my part as it is an expensive habit and smoking will cost me enough when I get home. I have no idea when I will be going but imagine I will return with the regiment in late August or September.

As I write I am enjoying one of those lovely cigars you sent me in April. They arrived in perfect shape and are quite a treat. I also have my bottle of beer for this week so I am content.

We have been having rather miserable weather lately, sun in the morning but rain in the afternoon or evening. As if the Dutch didn't already have more water than they knew what to do with.

Have not heard from Clay or Do lately but imagine exams are the big reason. I have been attempting to study myself but find it almost hopeless. It will be [sic] probably require someone cracking my knuckles to make me really get down to work again.

I don't seem to be getting along very well with this letter so will fold up now and try again. Hope you are both in the best of health.

Love Mac.

18 July 1945

Dear Mom and Dad,

I'm not getting any better with my letters but please remember that no news is good news. For a long time I was worried about being posted to the occupation forces but now that danger seems a thing of the past. Also I was getting fed up with that F. P. Camp job and finally managed a changeover so that I am now back with the regiment. For a while I was O. C. [Officer Commanding] B Coy [B Company] but we received several majors and captains today so I'm now assistant adjutant. I thought I was through with that type of work when I left the F. P. Camp but apparently my stay there was premeditated by the I. I [?] as they knew I wanted to go home with the regiment and wanted some officers trained in administration. It will be good training for me and will be quite a help in civy street [civilian life] to be able to say I was adjutant of the regiment, if only assistant adjutant.

I am glad to hear about all the rain as it seems to indicate a change for the better in our climate. We have been having our share of rain here but the odd sunny day helps out. I am trying to get in some tennis but I cannot find shoes large enough in the battalion [he wears size 12 or 13]. I have been sailing several times on a very nice lake nearby but the weather has not been very kind lately.

Please don't worry about my not writing much – I can't give you any reason because there really isn't one but I shall have to be much more punctual with my correspondence henceforth and I have just learned that the present adjutant is being promoted and I shall shortly become adjutant. I am rather pleased about it as it is a fairly responsible job and will take me out of the mental slump I seem to be in at the moment. I still hear regularly from the East but have rather neglected her [Ruth, who apparently loves him very much] also. However, she is a very understanding female and knows me well by now.

We have been told today that we may move anywhere around the 18th August but we are not counting on any date this far ahead as shipping etc. fluctuates from day to day. Have to close now as a job has turned up for me. Hope you are both well.

Love Mac.

This is the last letter we have before Mac arrived home. He's done a great job of documenting his time in the army, and that time is now at an end.

Sept. 25, 1945

Dear Mom and Dad,

Just a quick note to let you know I am on the last lap of the trip home. We move tonight and are supposed to sail tomorrow on the Ille de France. The date has been postponed three times now but it looks like it is the real thing now. In some respects I am sorry to leave as I have grown to like the English and particularly their country. We have had several days leave, most of which I spent in London. It is very expensive but seems to get into your blood once you get to know your way around.

I hope you have not sent those cigars you mentioned a few letters back as there is no chance of my receiving them now. I still have plenty of cigarettes as the authorities decided they would have to make them available because so many people had stopped sending them in anticipation of an early return of their boys. Must write Ruth now so will be seeing you.

Love Mac

SECTION TWO – AIR WAR

'Daisy Mae,' whose squadron letters were PT-H, at a Heavy Conversion Unit in 1945. The men in the photo above flew this plane in 1944. She made 62 trips and was powered by four Bristol Hercules 14-cylinder twin-row radial engines, each with 1650 horsepower. Maximum weight 6500 pounds. This is a photo of a photo that hangs in a pub near Tholthorpe, North Yorkshire, England, where the plane was based. It was given to Clayton Bird by Ted Larkins, flight engineer in Bird's crew and one of his life-long friends. Like brothers, the crew stayed in touch with each other all their lives. They are, from left, Clayton Bird (pilot), Ken Willis (wireless air gunner), Ted Larkins (flight engineer), Moe Conway (mid-upper gunner). The next two are likely Jimmy Brooks (bomb aimer) and Keith 'Lucky' Mosher (rear gunner), but the order could need to be reversed. Ralph Pilkington was the crew's navigator.

CHAPTER 1

Frederick Charles Clayton Bird

Clayton Bird was born on Feb. 17, 1919, in the town of Boissevain, Manitoba, near Turtle Mountain. Since his father, Dr. F.V. Bird, was half Cree, Clayton and his younger brother Mac were of mixed-blood too, or Metis. As we wrote earlier, their father had been born on a farm beside the Red River in 1885 near what had been the Red River Settlement. In 1873 it became the City of Winnipeg. Clayton's mother was Irene Bradley, a nurse from North Gower, Ontario, where her family farmed. She was of Irish descent and was the first white woman in this line of the Bird family since Mary Lowman, James Curtis Bird's wife in the mid-1800s.

Growing up in Boissevain was an interesting and active life, as Clayton recounts in his book *Nickel Trip*. He played saxophone in the town band, skated with girls to scratchy musical tunes at the local rink, swam in the creek on Musgrove's farm, explored the nearby ravine, collected Aboriginal arrowheads and other items, fished Lake Max for pike and pickerel, hunted rabbits and trapped muskrats, and served as "bird dog," along with his brother Mac, for his father. Indeed hunting was a big part of both boys' youth, and they developed keen eyes with a gun. One time Dad got three running jack rabbits with one shot each from his .22. Many deer and ducks also met the same fate. Hunting was a Saturday ritual, summer and winter, for both boys.

Clayton dreamed of becoming a pilot. He was a Boy Scout and learned woodcraft, Morse code, map reading and knots under Scoutmaster Alf Noton. When he was eight, his wooden carving of a plane won him a prize, the book *The Spirit of St. Louis*, at the Boissevain Fair. The book told the story of Charles Lindberg's solo trans-Atlantic flight. (Dad knew the judge, Teddy Brown, "who must have decided on a special category for my model," he wrote.) His dream was fulfilled shortly after Canada declared war on Germany on September 10, 1939. Listening to the exciting news of the Battle of Britain in the summer and fall of 1940, when Churchill's famous "few" defeated the mighty Luftwaffe, Clayton was more determined than ever to become a pilot, and preferably one to fly Spitfires or Hurricanes. As it turned out, he and thousands of others were more urgently needed in Bomber Command, as the war to destroy Hitler's industrial capacity and military installations heated up in preparation for D-Day.

Clayton as a teenager

Clayton Bird was 21 when he enlisted in the Royal Canadian Air Force early in February of 1941. Many months were spent in military training across Canada, as his letters reveal. A big day was September 13, 1941, when he married Doris Aconley, whom he'd met at a dance in Winnipeg. I believe she provided the incentive and inspiration for him to survive the many trials that lay ahead in Europe. Again, his letters reveal the depth of his love for her, and it only grew in time, he once told me. On his 22nd birthday, Feb.

17, 1941, he boarded a train with many other young men in Winnipeg and set off for Toronto's manning depot at the Canadian National Exhibition Grounds. That was the start of a grand adventure and 20 years of serving Canada in the wartime and peacetime air force. On March 24, 1944 his crew – Sgt. Ken 'Pee Wee' Willis, RAF, 19; Sgt. Ted Larkins, flight engineer, RAF, 19; Jimmy Brooks, bomb aimer, RCAF, 24; Flight Officer Keith 'Lucky' Mosher, rear gunner, RCAF, 20; and Ralf 'Pilky' Pilkington, navigator, RCAF, 21 – embarked on their "nickel," or first operation together as a crew over enemy territory. Theirs was a hair-raising journey as they were twice attacked by fighters, coned by searchlights and hit by flak, but they got home, six hours and a half after leaving base.

It was the first of Bird's 34 operations in a Halifax III, a new version of what had become a workhorse bomber. He did a number of hours on the much smaller Wellingtons, too, but never on ops (and wheedled his way into Spitfires and Hurricanes for some hours, testing them after repairs; if he hadn't done so, he'd never have flown them at all). Clayton praised the Halifax, which he noted was faster than a Lancaster to 10,000 feet, at which point the Lanc's turbo-chargers kicked in. The Halley also floated well when ditched and had more interior room than the Lanc for the men. You couldn't tell Dad the Lanc was a better plane; he knew the truth -- they were both exceptional feats of engineering. The Halley had brought him home many times against the odds, riddled with flak holes,

engines shot out, and he loved that plane. Once he got home and landed safely with two of its four engines gone. The boys had named it Daisy Mae, after the buxom girl in Lil Abner's cartoon strip. At the time of writing a model of it given him by Jimmy Brooks hangs in Qualicum Beach Legion 76, where he and Mom, and then Ena, spent many happy hours. Bil Bird picked up the model from Mosher's widow (for $100 — she'd asked $50) in Nova Scotia and drove it to Winnipeg. There it was boxed and shipped to Parksville. The real plane was written off in 1945 in a training exercise with a young crew, but the boys were OK.

After the war, Clayton rejoined his wife, our mother Doris, whom he'd married only weeks before being posted overseas. They had to get to know each other again, he said, as both had grown much during the war. But they made it work, started a family and had four boys and a girl. He worked at The Bay in sales for a while, but was happy to rejoin the air force in the early 1950s as tensions with the Soviet Union heated up, creating a need for plenty of pilots. Clayton worked for about 14 years as a flight instructor, rising to the post of Officer Commanding at Penhold air base in Alberta in the mid-1950s. (Brad was born in London, Ontario, near the base there, in 1959.) Clayton was held in such high regard that Wing Commander Joe McCarthy of Dam Busters fame, an American who served in the RCAF, asked him to check him out on certain aircraft. Dad said he enjoyed the air force partly because you were dealing largely with good men such as McCarthy. Bird wasn't one for putting up with nonsense at work; as part of a trouble-shooting team he traveled to various bases, diagnosed problems, and had to relieve men of their duties. At home, though, he was a patient and forgiving father who never raised a hand to us.

Until retirement in 1964 he taught wing commanders, men of a higher rank than he, at Staff College in Toronto, the only flight lieutenant to do so at the time. Then he embarked on a long and successful career teaching high school English and music, beginning with 10 years at Emery Collegiate, also in Toronto. There he renewed his love of music, polished his abilities with various saxophones and took up the clarinet. He played with the school band, much to the delight of the students. He also trained as a guidance counselor and helped many young men and woman get on the right track, including one boy who entered the military on his recommendation and became a successful surgeon, thanks to the training it provided.

Donny Walsh of Downchild Blues Band, his late brother "The Hock" and other musicians in the Toronto scene like Kid Bastian became good friends. Grossman's Tavern was a favourite watering hole where our parents had many happy Saturday afternoons or evenings. I recall the one time I was taken along; I was about 15. Dad sat across the table beside mom and was talking to a nearby musician when a slinky woman came up behind him and, to my amazement, slid her hands down the front of his shirt. It didn't faze Dad at all, who just kept talking. Mom ignored it as well. The woman, I recall, who'd clearly had a drink or two, said, "A girl's gotta cop a feel when she can, especially from such a handsome man!" Then she pulled her hands away and moved on. Dad indeed was a handsome man.

The late Jane Vasey and the rest of the Downchild band were visitors at the Bird home at 161 Grandravine Drive a number of times, including Christmas, when Mom made sure enough turkeys and trimmings were present for all. I recall the beautiful Vasey playing our piano in the front room. She was enchanting, slim and sweet, and boy could she pound out the blues! Such a sad day it was when she passed away young from cancer.

As an English teacher, Dad was practical in his efforts to encourage his students to read. His classes had youth who were struggling and not on their way to university. He went out and purchased boxes of used books about cars, planes, adventures, whatever young people were interested in. In this way he was ahead of his time, and earned the gratitude of his pupils. He told me once about a girl, about 17, who kept nodding off in class. He talked to her one day and learned she was struggling at home. She had to work to help make ends meet and then look after younger siblings, and this left her exhausted. So he allowed her to sleep in his class, and explained to the others why. His empathy won him their trust and respect. One year, class 11E presented Dad with a trophy inscribed with the words: "Mr. Bird, A Great Guy." I have it to this day.

He *was* a great guy. He and Mom took us camping and fishing, to Toronto Maple Leaf hockey games and Harlem Globetrotter events (with the hilarious Meadowlark Lemon), gave us opportunities; but most important of all they provided the love and stability at home that made all the difference. I always had the sense that things were good at home. Not once did I worry about that. This freed my mind to work hard at school and have fun with friends, and it played a big role in whatever success and happiness I've been able to achieve. No, we weren't often taxied to music lessons or hockey practice, as there wasn't any money for organized sport.

Like most families of the 1960s, ours was a one-income family, with Dad the bread-winner and Mom looking after us kids and making sure we had an orderly home. Nor was Clayton a man to hug his children, and I was fine with that, too. Hugging was Mom's job, and she did it often. I recall a rare hug one time from Dad when Keith Wright accidentally closed a car door on my fingers. No, he rarely if ever saw my evening softball games and never my high school sporting events. No, we never went to McDonald's or other fast-food joints and the only time we got treats like chocolate bars was when we went fishing. I didn't expect these things and don't believe my siblings did either. He was Dad, not our pal. My pals were my peers, Keith, Mark Davis, Louis Kay and others. We children knew, I certainly knew, that Dad had more important things to do -- such as earning a living and looking after Mom, who needed quite a bit of TLC -- than watching my games and wasting money at restaurants. In any case, it amazed me how foolish other parents could be at softball and hockey games, often shouting and embarrassing their children, my friends. Nor did Dad indulge himself much. His one major hobby was music, and every night after supper (we all ate together at the table) he'd head down to his music room in the basement and spend hours practicing his saxophones and clarinet. I loved the sound of it; and Mom certainly knew where he was! I asked him once why he never treated himself to golf the way other men did. "I had you and your brothers and sister and Mom at home," he said. "I felt that's where my time and money belonged."

Dad played a key role in helping Mom manage her diabetes through diet and supplements, and she lived to be 76. He spent many years looking after her. And though she was grateful, Mom wasn't always an easy patient.

For years Dad himself struggled with congestive heart failure. He amazed his doctor by learning probably more about the problem than the doctor knew, and they had long discussions about his findings and methods. His self-treatment, using Vitamin C and other nutrients, likely added years to his life. At one point the doctor told him there was no more sign of congestive heart failure. The inevitable happened, though. Dad died on Dec. 17, 2006, at the age of 87, exactly two months before his 88th birthday.

I didn't know it would be his final night – one rarely knows exactly when the end will come – but fortunately served him a supper of deer meat, one of his favourite meals. I'd done this many times in recent months, as well as T-bone steaks which he also enjoyed and simply couldn't get at Trillium Lodge. The man needed meat. He'd eaten a lot of beef and venison over the course of his life and his appetite was good to the end.

On this particular night he didn't eat much, however. A hockey game was on TV but he wasn't interested in that, either. He seemed weaker than usual and said he wanted to talk. He told me how pleased he was to have had five wonderful years with his second wife, Ena. He also said how much he loved his first wife, our mother Doris. He wanted to see her again. I told him it sure would be good for him to see Mom again. Dad had shared his final thoughts in a letter to all of us children, stressing the importance of love. He pointed out how we had never needed to say the words much, as we'd showed our love for each other in how we behaved. And so all the loose ends were tied up. This night he said again how proud he was of each of us, Bil, Bob, Bruce, Brad and Kim. We parted with our usual handshake and squeeze of his arm, for what turned out to be the last time. The phone rang later that night about 4 a.m. with the news Dad had died.

Clayton Bird loved to play his saxophones. Here he plays his soprano sax in the Parksville Fellowship Baptist Church in a Christmas program.

CHAPTER 2

Toronto's Manning Depot, Early 1941

As the letters begin, Clayton is 20 and selling life insurance in Winnipeg in his first real office job. He's excited about the prospect of helping in the war effort and is a confident and even-keeled young man. He's also well-liked, judging by the letters from so many.

208 Colony St.
Winnipeg, Manitoba.

Dec. 1, 1940

Dear Mom and Dad,

I was into the Air Force recruiting office last week, and Milton Culbert said he would get me in the next quota to come up. If there is a special quota before Xmas, I will be on it. If not it will be sometime in January. So it's not long to wait now.

But I really am sorry to have to quit the insurance business before I have had a chance to really get going. However if that is all I will have to give up before this affair is over, I will be one of the very fortunate few. Next spring is going to be a holy terror over there and I hope I won't be too long before getting into it.

I met Laverne Armstrong and Allen Kilmuray on Portage yesterday. They seem to be quite satisfied with their army life. But it must be admitted that neither one has an awful lot to compare it with. I am going over to St.

Boniface Hospital on Tuesday, I believe, and may look Audrey Armstrong up if I have a chance.

I saw Mr. Robbins and Iris by the Bay yesterday too but they were in their car and never saw me. I have yet to see Iris or Edith in here yet.

I almost forgot about the deer hunting, Dad. How did it go this year? If I had got into my new job a little sooner I might have been able to go out for it. I don't know for sure yet what time I will be going home, but I imagine it will be around the same time as Mac, on the 19th or 20th, perhaps sooner.

My new place is all that could be desired. If I had to stay in Winnipeg the whole winter I would want to stay here. I was pretty lucky to find it at such short notice.

After I saw Dr. Brock and he told me what the trouble was, I told Mrs. MacFadyen. It wasn't really her fault you know. I personally believe that one of the men who had first moved out brought them in [bed bugs?]. However she is a very careless woman. Anyway she herself suggested it might be just as well for me to move. I was going to anyway. But Mr. MacFadyen started to say something about the doctor not knowing what he was talking about. I am afraid that I lost my temper then. I didn't say much but he never said a word when I had finished. He is a lazy good-for-nothing anyway.

I can't think of anything else right now but may add something before I mail this in the morning. Thanks a lot, Dad.

Love Clayton

Wed. Dec. 4, 1940

Dear folks,

I couldn't wait to hear from you before writing again as I have a couple of special things to tell you. First I want to tell you Dad not to bother buying a turkey for Xmas as I am bringing one home.

The company has a turkey contest for the month of December. Agents who sell $6,500 insurance during this month qualify for a turkey. To date I have written up over $6,900 so am assured Xmas dinner even if I don't sell anymore. And I certainly intend to get some more in before I go home.

The other thing was for you Mom. I was talking to John Kelly yesterday and he would like you to write his mother. Here is the address: Mrs. John Kelly, 699 Brock Ave., Toronto.

Molly had something wrong with one of her lungs and had to have half of it removed. John didn't know what the trouble was. But it happened some years ago. The girls and Henry are all at home yet. Mrs. Kelly was over to Scotland a few years ago; at the time she wasn't feeling well and John said it did her a lot of good.

I was up to the Boy Scouts Assoc'n office in the Somerset Building this morning and was talking with Mr. Mills for three quarters of an hour. He offered me a place with All Saints troop as assistant scout master if I stay in Winnipeg. I would really like to take it because in this business something like that would be a big help, aside from my own interest in Scouting.

I sure do wish that I could keep in this business. It seems to me to be a real field but when the Air Force call comes I will have to forget it for a while. But I will go back to it, if possible.

Incidentally I am taking out a $50 policy with Northern Life. I made the premium $50 as that is a very convenient amount to have deducted from your pay envelopes in $5 lots when in the Air Force. It is what we call the Protection Pension at age 60, and really combines three policies in one. First I have $1,718 protection to age 60. Secondly I have an accident disability clause (for $1.72 per year) which means that if I am disabled for a minimum of six months, the policy matures for $1,718. And last, but not least, I have a monthly income of $17.19 for life or a cash value of around $3,000 at age 60. If you don't think that is a real policy, Dad, I would like to know why.

The other day I was looking through Stove and Cox insurance tables for Canada, 1940, and thought I would compare the rates of the other companies with our own. So I selected 20 pay life, $1,000 with profits. There was only one company that had a lower rate, at age 20, than Northern Life. It was National Life which I have never heard of. And the editorial write-up and opinion of the company was easily comparable with the Metropolitan or Sun Life. That means something when the relative sizes of the companies are considered.

And now I have to keep an appointment with a prospect, and I think a good one, so will close. Don't forget Dad to tell me how you and the rest made out on the jumpers. Was Southon out this year?

Love Clayton.

The following letter is from a friend called Wanda. She recently took up her new post as a teacher at a one-room school, and her accounts are interesting.

Laurier, Manitoba

January 10, 1941

Dear Clayton,

I received your letter the other night and was pleased to hear from you. It was the first mail I received since I came in here on Dec. 31st. I thought I'd better answer now when I have a chance. It is hard to say when I will get mail out again (post office is nine miles away). We're sure snow-bound in here like nobody's business.

New Year's Day was a wild one for the French in here! We all went to a big dance at night. We drove six miles through a blizzard by toboggan [drawn by a horse]. On the 3rd we had a dance in the school. By 5 a.m. we were still whooping it up. We are having another on the 17th and expect the place to be packed.

You must have had a lovely trip last summer [Clayton drove his parents from Boissevain to Ottawa to see his mother's family there.] I loved the East when I was down....

You certainly have had a variety of occupations, Clayton! [Vet's helper, relief camp manager, beet farmer, mechanic, roofer, insurance salesman, pilot trainee.] At least you should be worldly wise. Away out here I feel shut out from the rest of the world. I lead such a different life here but am happy. I have the dearest pupils. I had a close chum teaching in the next School District and every weekend we spent together on a cattle ranch. But she couldn't stand the country and the pupils and resigned at Christmas. Bill Miller (you knew him I think) was teaching just east of me and he too quit. Now I'm holding fort alone. You can never tell when a French person is going to declare their love for you or stick a knife in your back. Boring? Never!

There are three things I want to learn before I leave here – play the guitar, speak French and shoot. I often wonder if this is the same "me" that ran around Clear Lake. Can you remember some of the things we used to do? It seems centuries ago or else a dream – buying bars at the Wigwam, making cocoa without milk, listening to windbag Eric, the jamboree folks we knew, Mart Kenny's dance, the day Marion and I picked your camping site – oh gosh, I sound like somebody's grandmother! Must be sleepy. Would like to see you and talk over old times.

Am enclosing some snaps which you'll also have to return. Someday I'll buy a camera of my own.

Write soon. Mail keeps me in touch with the outside world.

As always,

Wanda.

P.S. Remember the ode to Clear Lake you once wrote? "Oh clear clear, clear lake?" I think I still have it. (Oh Wanda just shut up and go to bed!)

This letter is from a friend who is already in the service.

January 31, 1941

AC2 Graham,
No. 7 Air Observers School
Portage la Prairie

Dear Clayton,

I received your letter today and was glad you received your call. We are on guard here (15 of us), the other 15 that were here left for Regina. It is really a nice place. The meals are real good, 100% better than Brandon. We will be here for four or five weeks. I really don't mind it at all. We have 24-hours leave out of every five days so that is pretty good. It is really a soft job.

In regard to your personal things Clayton I would take your razor (they give you one but I think you will prefer your own, also your brush). If you have any black dress socks bring them and also your black Oxfords for dancing. If you have a white shirt it is also permissible to wear off duty. I would also bring your summer underwear as there are a lot of the boys never wear their winter issue at all. Personally I am not wearing mine now. If you have running shoes, bedroom slippers, bring them. Your radio would also be OK to bring but if I were you I would not bring your .22 rifle, especially while you are at the manning depot as I don't think they will allow it there. After you leave the manning depot you will probably be able to take it as they are not nearly as strict, at least they sure aren't here anyways.

If you have a large suitcase I would also bring it as you will find that you will have quite a few things, especially your personal belongings to put in it as the kit bags are quite awkward to be bothered with especially if you want something in a hurry, as they are usually in the bottom.

I would certainly bring your skates, sax and camera as you said you were. Well Clayton I am in a hurry so I guess I will end this ramble. We will probably run into each other at one of the Schools. I hope so anyway.

Yours,

Bud.

P.S. Write some time and let me know how you like it etc.

Toronto

Feb. 19, 1941

Dear Mom and Dad,

Well, the great day has finally arrived and I am now in the Manning Depot. We arrived in Toronto at 6:30 a.m. but didn't get off the train until about 7:30 and by then we had come right into the Depot. First thing we did was to have breakfast, and was it ever welcome! We had got up at 5:30.

They certainly have an establishment here. I can only guess at the number of men here, and there must be around 8,000, perhaps more. The dining room handles 5,000 an hour. In the last three days there have been over 1200 recruits come in and things are rather in a mess as they naturally aren't equipped to handle mobs like this. All the same, if a certain be-mustached Nazi could only see the gang here it would probably be a decisive factor in turning his hair prematurely grey.

I haven't been around after a uniform yet but may go tomorrow. Just whenever there isn't a crowd around. However we had two injections, or punctures, this afternoon, one in each arm and have a Dish test for scarlet fever tonight at 7. We finished supper at 5:30. The meals aren't bad so far but of course it is too early to really be able to tell.

I saw Wilbert and Mrs. Emery for an hour Sunday afternoon, after calling them up. He is with the Department of Transport yet but hopes to get a communication flight post with the RCAF [Royal Canadian Air Force] eventually.

I'm afraid I can't write much now as my right arm is too sore. I don't think that MD actually touched my arm with his hands. He just shoved the needle in and pulled it out again. There'll be more later, but for the time being this is all with love from

Clayton.

My address: F.C.C. Bird. A.C. 2
              No. R91897.
              #1 Manning Depot,
              Toronto, Ont.
              Toronto,

Feb. 21, 1941

Dear Mom and Dad,

We had Dish tests the other day as I believe I told you. As luck would have I was positive so here I am in isolation along with about 1500 others. Cub Brook and Bill Rosenberry were negatives but Jack Moore came in this evening.

It's all right over here but there is nothing much to do as they aren't organized to take care of situations such as this one. However they are rounding things into shape pretty fair. They are going to give us lectures as soon as possible and of course our various injections will be kept up to date.

One thing about it is we get out of doors more than we used to. We have to march over to mess for every meal and have a good bugle band to march to. The boys in the main part very seldom, if ever, get outside as we haven't been issued uniforms yet. I should get my fatigue clothes tomorrow as we had a clothing parade today. That is all I want until I get out of isolation as a uniform only means buttons to polish. I will be in here anywhere from one to six weeks, until my Dish shows negative.

Some of the boys do a lot of griping but from the looks of most of them they aren't up to much anyway. They give me a pain in the neck and I've told some of them so. Just as if the Air Force was to blame for them not being immune to scarlet fever.

We are in the Motor Show Building of the Canadian National Exhibition. It is a one-room affair, but what a room. They could put 2000 bunks on the ground floor easily. There is a sort of mezzanine balcony in which they have the various offices, canteens, etc. There is no hot water though and so far there has been no mail delivered so I don't know whether anyone has written me yet. It's a little early for that yet though.

I had a look at my papers on the way down through the officer not sealing my envelope, and I found that I am slated as the commission type by my interviewing officer. He thinks that I will absorb military life quickly. If he was thinking of isolation he was a long way out but I am sure going to try to justify his opinion of me. Anywhere from a third to 50 per cent of the air crew, especially pilots, get commissions anyway so I should stand a fair chance. My physical appearance is all for me too, which is all right. Both Cub and Rosie fell down on that. They were stated as not being of the commission type. Of course all this is strictly confidential as I am not supposed to have seen that report.

We don't do much over here. Get up about 7 or shortly after, parade for breakfast at 7:45 and after breakfast our time is our own except for the occasional parade for something or other. The long waits standing in line get me down. And my suit is beginning to look as though I had not had it [pressed?] for at least the past two months. But there is a couple hundred in exactly the same shape so I don't notice it so badly.

I've met some real fellows here. One especially who I am starting to chum with, Chick Harrison, is from New York State. There are quite a few U.S. boys here, from Texas, Mass., Georgia, and some other places. And there is no fooling in those boys. They want to get down to work. Chick has one year college and we figure on working together. Two brothers from Texas arrived in Ottawa with 38 cents between them. The whole works are just tickled pink to get in. But something that gets me down is the number of, to put it mildly, odd-looking guys. Some of them look too comical for words.

We are only a few feet from Lake Ontario in this building and believe me it looks cold. So far I haven't had a chance to do anything outside. All I know about the city so far is how to get downtown. I may never get a chance to look the city over either because if I am C. B. for three or four weeks or longer I will likely be drafted out as soon as I get my OK. However we shall see.

One thing I miss is my sax but it is just as well perhaps that I left it at home. However I may get it later. Well, I had better close now. My address is the same as before. I wrote Mac yesterday too.

Love Clayton.

Feb. 22, 1941
Boissevain

My dear Clayton --
Read your letter this a.m. (Sat.) and was indeed pleased to know you had arrived safely. What a mob that must be. I just cannot imagine 5,000 people being fed in an hour – well the whole thing is of a gigantic scale and that is just one part of it. Am sorry I did not write Mrs. Vale to meet

the train, but not knowing just when you were leaving Winnipeg I couldn't have told her what day you would be passing through Chapleau – had such a nice letter from her this a.m. She was so pleased to talk to you boys and would have gone to meet you had she known.

Suppose by now you are in uniform. Hope you can have a picture taken soon. Guess you didn't have any taken in Wpg as I haven't seen any in Free Press.

3 p.m. Daddy just came in – home from Wpg – he and four others went in Wednesday to a Board Trade meeting -- saw Mack – was glad to find your letter here when he came in. Hope your arms do not get too painful. Gordon -------- and Ken Woods are home. Ken said he would probably see you. Well, I bought my first war Savings Stamps yesterday. The IODE members are all pledged to do their bit so I promised 50 a month, not much but it helps.

The hockey team went to Minnedosa last night. Have not heard how they made out. It has been very cold here past week but much better today. How do you like Eastern weather? Hope you get in touch with Rowland Cherry so you will have some place to go when you feel you want some home cooking.

Am trying to talk to Daddy and write at same time, so is rather disjointed. He and Mack saw a hockey match, Monarchs vs. Portage, then went to Lees. Says the navy is growing quite a big boy.

Well my dear will finish for now and hope to hear from you soon again. Dad will write in a day or so.

Much love, Mom

Feb. 26, 1941
Boissevain

My dear son,

We received your letter quite recently and Mom asked me to write just now and she would be writing you later, probably during the weekend. We were, indeed, very glad to know that you and Cub and Rosenberry all travelled together. I am sure it was quite a surprise party when Jack Moore walked in on the gang. Yes, I am quite sure that with all the inoculations you will not have much opportunity of seeing much of Toronto. While the inoculations are on the program I think it would be best for you chaps not to have too much physical training anyway, as they tend to be a bit of a drain at times.

We are both well, though Mom had a bit of a headache today, but she went to bed early and is feeling some better. The weather has been quite cool since you left and quite a bit more snow, but a few more weeks will bring spring quite near. I was in the city for three days last week and spent a couple of evenings with Mac: we both went to see the final game between Portage and Rangers, which the latter won by 4-3. It was pretty fast hockey; that would be foolish to even try to deny; and it was anybody's game up to the last second. The weather was quite cold while we were in there and there was consequently not so much pleasure in the trip.

We were in on a meeting of the Western Associated Boards of Trade. One thing they are fighting for is the withdrawal by the government of military exemption to Mennonites and Doukabors. I was not able to arrange things so I could see Marion; having no car of four own while in the cit makes it rather poor trying to visit much. Neither was I able to see Dorothy Bird.

The town has been fairly quiet lately and I think the general prospects are for it to continue so for some time. There have been no big affairs or dances and not much general stir. The Boissevain juvenile hockey team took a 4-1 trimming from Minnedosa here in Boissevain and then travelled to Minnedosa and beat them on their own ice 6-5. They could have done same in Boissevain but were too convinced before they took the ice that they were licked. And that is the way they played until the last seven or eight minutes, when Boissevain did everything with the puck but place it in the net. I think Boissevain just had plenty of tough luck, as in my opinion Minnedeosa did not earn anything more than a bare win here. Boissevain is therefore through for the season.

Well son I hope you keep well and that the inoculations do not tie you up too much, I also hope you enjoy the training, and feel confident you will. Take the best care of yourself and remember me to Cub, Jack and Bill. Write to Mom and give us an idea at any time as to what we can best try to send you.

Very best of luck, Dad.

Toronto,
Feb. 28, 1941

Dear Mom and Dad,

I can't remember where I left off the last time, but one thing I do know. We have pay parade tomorrow night at 7. And I sure will be glad to get some dough, too. There are several books I want to get, besides other things. We shall be able to get out the odd night pretty soon. I believe they will leave us barracked here until our scarlet shots are finished, which will take nearly another month. Then we will likely be drafted out to serve our service guard which usually lasts six weeks.

Life goes on in here in a pretty lazy fashion, I am afraid. We don't have to get up till 7:30 if we don't have to shave or polish any buttons. There are very few fatigues, in fact I have only been on one, yesterday. I won't be on any more as I am now an acting corporal. It's a dirty little job that was wished on me by another corporal, only he has his stripes and gets corporal's pay. I don't get either.

My job is to look after the runners on the phones and front door. I have 15 to look after all the time. It doesn't require much time or work but I wish he had stuck someone else with his job.

Besides that I have only temperature and inoculation parades to look after. We have temp. parades every day at 4 p.m. I get "shot" about twice a week, for typhoid and scarlet. I have only one more typhoid but four more scarlet. I don't know what others there are but there are some. At any rate I am beginning to feel like a pin cushion.

We have voluntary lectures twice a day by a sergeant-pilot who is on overseas draft but was caught by the scarlet and found positive. Some of them are pretty good.

We have shows three nights a week, and there was a pretty fair amateur contest last night. The YMCA provides basketball, volleyball, checkers, etc. (and writing paper and ink) so we have plenty of amusement. I was talking to Bill Rosenbery and Cub Brook the other day and they had been on kitchen fatigue three days running and hospital duty the day before. They haven't had a night out yet, so in a way I don't mind being a positive. Our living quarters are incomparably better than theirs.

I got all my uniform yesterday except for hats and shoes. They couldn't fit me with either. But they had better pretty soon or my feet are going to suffer. I asked their flight sergeant this morning if anything could be done about it but apparently there isn't much that can. My tunic fits pretty well. The legs need shortening about half an inch I think but will know better when I get service boots. My tunic coat needs taking in a little at the waist and my great coat sleeves are a wee bit short. Otherwise I got a real fit. I think I will get a civilian tailor to do it as the RCAF man isn't very particular and in some cases doesn't make much of a job. I figure that if these are going to be my only clothes for the next six to eight months it will be worth a couple of dollars to get them fitted right. They can be cut to look really snappy and that's what I want. Some of the fellows look as though they had fallen into theirs and others look like baked potatoes ready to burst their skins.

So far I haven't received Dad's letter but I haven't been to the Post Office yet as I don't think it opens till 4. And then it may have been held up somewhere. It often happens.

Most of the boys are resigned to their fate by now and everything goes along fine. We have a dandy bunch of N.C.Os [non-commissioned officers] who are a treat. I have met some real boys down here too, most of them Americans. I don't know why it is but I like them. And I have a real decent bunk-mate from Sudbury. We make our beds together etc. and it only takes half the time. He gets me up every morning, too. I've been eating and sleeping like I never did before. Usually he has quite a job waking me.

Well I can't think of much else except that sometime soon I will be sending for a few things when I figure out exactly what I want. I may add more to this later so won't seal it now. Have to hurry to get this in next mail going out.

Love, Clayton.

March 1, 1941
Boissevain

My dear boy –

Am wondering if you are still in quarantine. It is too bad but just one of the things you have to take with a grin. I only hope you will not be there too long as you lose contact with the boys you went in with. What a mob to feed. Kay told us a funny one about the two recruits, who when asked by the major if there were any complaints, one said he objected to the rind on the bacon, the other that the cutlery wasn't shined enough. They were each given a week in the kitchen cutting the rind off bacon and shining cutlery – so beware. But I don't think you are that kind. It is generally those who had never been used to very much, who complain the most. Always use as much consideration as is possible and place yourself in the other fellow's shoes before you begin to criticize.

There are a few questions I want to ask you – did you have a berth going east? What do you use for pajamas as I found your two pair here? Will send them if you say so. Did you see the insurance people about changing that name? So far I haven't received it. I hope you have Daddy's letter by now. Also that you have a uniform, as I can just imagine how messy you must feel, wearing the same clothes you travelled in. Hope you didn't leave yourself short of shirts. Try to get rid of your overcoat there, as it is too bulky to ship back and you can send everything here and I shall send Mack what he can wear, and I shall clean your suit and put it away.

I spent an hour with Reg Noton yesterday. He is on his way to Nova Scotia, is an air gunner. Has three stripes and half a wing. He claims these accidents are mostly sabotage. They had proof at Mossbank, where he has been – controls filed to a thread – oil interfered with so that it splashed over pilot nearly blinding him etc. And the difficult thing about it is, it must be someone in uniform. Doug Noton is flying every day. Was one of seven out of a class of 30 who passed his exams. Guess they are pretty stiff. If you are shut up there long, try to get some books and begin studying. Of course you will not be able to get around to see any friends. Hattie sent me her sister's address, if you can try and see them. Bert and his wife live with her. They are just a young couple and he has a car. I wonder if I wrote them would they be allowed to see you if they called. Is there anything you need that you didn't' take with you?

Daddy has just numbered over 1000 tickets to be sold in a lottery. Old Mr. Hanley has given his beaver coat (probably paid $5 for it years ago) to be raffled. Proceeds to go to the Mayor's Fund.

Daddy said Rivette said he had a letter from you. He hadn't sold the pelts last I heard. Don't pile up a long correspondence, Clayton. Naturally everybody asks you to write and likes to hear from the boys, but it becomes in time very cumbersome – that is why I told Bill Brook not to feel he had to write me, as I can always hear through the family. And there is one lady I hope you do not waste time writing to and that is Roma Middleton. She has gone at least, thank heavens, overstayed her welcome if ever anyone did and has caused a coolness between Jack and his mother which worries the latter very much.

This is Mr. Henderson's 76th birthday. I must take him over his jar of corn on the cob. He must find the winter very long.

Am afraid Gartons are having trouble with Dick. There was a hockey match between Boissevain and Minnedosa a week ago and he took the car (his mother had gone to Wpg and left Mrs. Chandler to look after him) and got the batteries from Southern Motors and went down to Jack Gilling's garage and put a licence plate off his car and put it on his own. Some of the older boys went to Minn. with him and drove going over but he drove coming back (goes about 80 mph). Gilling in meantime missed the plate and notified RCMP. I heard his dad is coming home today. I 'm sure I don't know what the outcome will be. Do not mention it to any of our boys down there, as I do not want it coming from me. Will let you know later what the grand finale will be. I think likely the RCMP will put him on patrol for behaviour and if ever he repeats it, will mean a sterner sentence. He gave his mother an old key and kept the real car key. Don't know how he got hold of the batteries. Must close now. Best love and hope you will soon be "out" – Mom.

The following letter to Clayton is from R. Rivette (pronounced Reevay), a fur buyer and trapper.

March 3, 1941
Boissevain

Dear Clayton,

Received your letter the other day, just pleased to hear from you, pleased to hear you were well, hope you keep so. The weather here is terrible, snow and then cold. I went down to the bush yesterday and you would not no there had ever been any person there. I could not find 2 traps covered to deep in snow there was about 4" fell on Saturday night, it sure heavy walking. I went into [Lake] George and then took the sleigh road back to ---- through to Mud. That trap you had on the east side of Mud I could not find the tree that you stood up. There was only about one foot showing so I will have to go back later on. I sent the fox away but .75 cents apiece was all I was offered so I have still got them. Your Dad says he is going to tan them himself so I guess that will be best. There is no good in giving them away.

I am not going back to the bush until the snow is pretty well gone because the skunk will not start to run till then and I sure want to get some of them. I sure need the money. Business is rotten but I hope it will get better before long.

I am still not feeling just right yet but I hope to get over that to.

Well I guess this is all for this time write again. We are always glad to get a letter from you. And remember letters are always nice and good when in the Army. Be good and look out for the Black Marks. They are no good for ..... By By

R. Rivette. Remember me to Cub Bill and Jack

March 6, 1941
Christie Street Hospital,
The Annex,
Toronto

Dear Mom and Dad,

I intended to write you last Monday but wasn't feeling very well. On Sat. and Sunday last I had a temp and on Monday I tried to tell the M.O. [medical officer] that I was getting flu. He figured he knew better than I did or else didn't like being told and gave me some pills to reduce the temp. But on Tuesday he had to send me here, with bronchitis as he put it. But they call it flu here.

Another fellow had a sore foot and he was sent up by the same M.O. as having gout. The doctor here took a couple of looks at him and sent him into isolation. The guy had apparently had scarlet fever and is almost over it and they hadn't recognized it. I sure don't think much of that M.O. now. My temp had to go over 101 before he would any more than glance at me.

It's quite nice up here but until today I could hardly enjoy it. They give me pills every few hours which keep me in an eternal sweat. But I sure feel better than a few days ago. Last Friday night I phoned Roland Cherry and talked with him for a while. On Sunday night somebody came to see me, and I imagine it was him, but they couldn't find me. I sure was disappointed when the boys told me.

I haven't seen Bill or Cub for more than a week now, and I don't know what they are doing. They may not be here by now as their last inoculations were yesterday. I finished mine yesterday too. A nurse gave it to me.

Here are the answers to your questions Mom. Yes, we had berths and slept fine too [on the train]. It seems to me I could sleep in a cement grinder. I could use the pajamas but don't send them yet as there are a few other things I want and you might as well send them all at once. I left the policy with the cashier and they said they would look after it. Don't worry, as it might take a couple of weeks to go through.

Thanks a lot for the Recorders [local Boissevain weekly newspaper]. Jack and I really enjoyed them but that man W. V. [Udall, publisher/ editor] has a most highly developed practice of putting the least news into the most space.

And I don't know whatever made you think I was writing Roma. It never even entered my mind, although I got a picture of Don and a bunch of prisoners from Bill Emery. I will try to remember to enclose it. It came from an old Toronto Star Weekly.

I am sure glad to hear that Doug is flying. Most of those who flunk their exams must fail on the physicals because from what I have seen of the course, the main thing is to keep in A1 shape. Everything on the course is quite elementary. We had a graduate sergeant pilot giving us some lectures. He had finished his Grade XI and had worked in a bake shop for five years. I got through with no trouble at all. His theory was that those who had their noses in their books all the time got too nervous. And that is another reason for so many of the crackups.

We have had the severest weather here. Last Sunday was a beautiful day, temp 33 degrees and no wind. On Monday it rained all day and very cloudy. On Tuesday it was nearly zero F and quite a little snow on the ground. Today looks to be real nice out. We have one window open a little bit so as to get a little fresh air.

I have two roommates here, one of whom is a negro and a darned swell fellow too. Yesterday the chaplain dropped in and handed out cigarettes, which apparently he and the Red Cross do each week, and he gave me a package of Phillip Morris English Blends which I don't like. Lewis (the negro) traded me a package of British Conols without me even suggesting it. He is a soldier from the permanent staff of one of the trainees' camps near here. I'm a little tired now but may add more to this before it can be mailed.

Well, here it is Friday and I couldn't mail this last night as I had no stamps. Am going to try to get some though.

I am feeling much better but still have a little bit of temp now and again. They will likely keep me here for a week or so more and I hope they do. It will give me a chance to get over this flu.

I wrote Roland Cherry yesterday and asked him to bring me up a few things. There isn't much to do here except sleep. I expect me may be up tonight or tomorrow. The Red Cross ladies were up yesterday and gave us each 10 cigarettes and some candy. So far I haven't been able to get out to buy a thing and it sure means something when they come around like that.

I'm afraid that I haven't very much to say. Nothing ever happens around here and I can't think of anything else. Don't send any clothes etc. yet Mom as I don't need them in here and they would only be in the road. And for Pete's sake Mom don't worry about me, I'll be out of here in no time and may even get enough sick leave to get home. Anyway here's hoping I do.

Love Clayton.

P.S. Incidentally, the reason I use this Y paper is because I like it better than what I can buy.

The Northern Life Assurance Company of Canada
Winnipeg Agency,
300 Main St.
Winnipeg, Man.

March 7, 1941

Dear Clayton:

Received your most welcome letter yesterday and was glad to hear that you are stepping right along and enjoy your work. I was very sorry to see you leave so soon after getting started in a new career for yourself and opportunities it has in store for you but was glad that you offered your services to the country in time of need. I served 25 years ago and am unable to serve in the same capacity as you are now, but a[m a] willing worker for what has to be done to achieve victory at home.

Your contract will stay in full force throughout the entire period that you are on active service the same as if you were working steadily for the company and you will receive the same credit on any business that you have built up, renewals, and your position is open to you immediately on your return and discharge from active service.

In regards to Jack Woods' policy, I was up to see him and he told me that he was unable to do anything at the present time but he would definitely reinstate it at a later date. I explained to him the advantage of keeping the policy, also the low premium at his age and the small outlay monthly to meet. He said there was nothing wrong with the policy in any way but he could not do anything to look after it at the present time. Now a line from you, Clayton, to him about the last of March or right away, if you wish, stating that you had received a letter from me explaining that unfortunately he was unable to carry on his policy and that you wish that he would make an earnest effort to reinstate the policy by the first of April if at all possible.

If at any time you can interest your associates in a real saving and provide protection on their return, we will certainly appreciate the business, Clayton.

Hope that you will find time to drop us a line periodically and here's wishing you every success in the future.

Yours sincerely,

F. G. R----- (illegible)

Agency Manager

Also on March 7, 1941, Clayton's mother wrote this note:

My dear boy –

Was very pleased to get your nice long letter and to know you are not finding the C.B. too monotonous, also that you have your uniform – hope you have your shoes by now. How do you manage about your laundry? Be careful of those sox as wrong laundering will ruin them. You are to have another pair soon. Mrs. Ed Dow is knitting you a pair, so she told me a few days ago, which is very kind of her. She said Freddie Fox, her nephew from Regina, has been sent back to Regina with some others to recruit. Where are they putting them all anyway? You are only 60 miles from Brantford, so hope before you leave Rowland can take you over to see Irene H. Had a letter from her mother yesterday – was very pleased to get your letter. Said Pat had her diamond and she is thrilled – also they had a lovely photo of Irene and that Dr. Findlay was going to Wpg and expected to go overseas soon.

Saturday. Did not get this finished yesterday so will be a day late in reaching you. Irene Murray's sister Mrs. Munson of Wpg is visiting her and I had her over here yesterday p.m. to tea – then we went to Mrs. Dunn's for evening. Jack Murray wrote to Wpg and he had a letter saying he may be called in April. Jimmy McGregor still here. You may be seeing Jack Moore also, as he is to report Monday.

Daddy is working hard on the Carnival but unless it turns very cold I am afraid it will be very slushy. Is thawing fast today. It is to be next Saturday and a whole week can make a big difference. Irene, Verna and I are going to Brandon by bus next Friday to spend the day with the Heywoods – Verna belongs to the parish your Uncle Percy had in Wpg and knows them well – then she is going home from there. I had a letter from your Aunt Lill, Ottawa—said she hoped you would get in touch with Rowland. Red Walker and Jessie King were married last week in Brandon.

She works at Clements and he lives on his mother at home – nice prospects ahead for them both, eh!

Suppose you did not get a chance to see any of the hockey finals – that is Mr. Wakefield's son Albert who won the Manitoba game.

Well, my dear, there is not anything else I can think of. Hope you keep well and that your arms do not pain too much – am glad you are meeting such fine chaps. That is one thing, Clayton, I hope you will always be careful of – do not form friendships unthinkingly. "By your companions are ye judged" is an old proverb well worth remembering, and in such a large project as this, you are bound to meet all kinds, and there are always plenty of the fine type – so there is no excuse for getting mixed up with the wrong kind..

Bye for now,

Much love,

Mom.

[*The letter includes a newspaper clipping of March 7 headlined "Banquet to College Graduates" (likely from the Brandon Sun) with the lead:* "The 17 members of the '41 graduating class of Brandon college were honored at the annual Arts banquet Tuesday evening in the Cecil hotel. Dr. and Mrs. J.R.C. Evans received the guests, who were introduced by host and hostess Jim Nelson and Edith McFadden, and included faculty members and their ladies, members of the college board of directors, students and parents and friends of the graduating class....Ted Speers was toastmaster, and Dr. Evans delivered an inspiring message in his president's address."]

Toronto, Ont.
Military Hospital

March 10, 1941

Dear Mom and Dad,

It's only Monday evening but I thought I would write you again because I don't want you to be worrying about me. I figured you would get my first letter this afternoon. My temp has been normal now for about three days and I spend most of my time up and around now. I got Roland to get me a radio to while away the hours. It costs $1 week but is sure worth it. He and Margaret were around on Saturday afternoon and brought up some oranges, magazines and cigarettes.

I've been in here a week and if I'm in a week more I'll get four days sick leave. If I do I'll go up to Ottawa for most of it. I'm afraid that it will take the best part of a day to get the alternations done on my uniform. And of course the tailor will have to do it while I wait for him as we aren't allowed downtown in anything except full blues. But I still think it will be worthwhile getting the job done by a civilian tailor.

If I do get up to Ottawa I'll try to see everybody including Uncle Percy, Auntie Em and Uncle Allen. If I wiggle hard I might make it six days but there's not much chance of getting it long enough to get home. Besides the train fare would be prohibitive. I intend hitching to Ottawa. But don't get the idea that I'm broke. I've a $25.80 cheque here and a pay day coming up in five days.

Incidentally I haven't been able to get into the Records office to sign any of my pay over. But I'll try to send $10 home when I get the chance anyway when I get out. It shouldn't take all I've got not for the Ottawa excursion.

I wrote Irene Heywood this p.m. but haven't been able to mail it yet. Asked Roland to send me stamps but so far haven't got them.

The chap I came over in the ambulance with went into isolation next day with scarlet fever but my seven days are practically up so I don't figure I'll get them now. He comes from Vernon, B.C. and I had to write his folks to tell them as he can't write from isolation and didn't have time before he went.

We are in a military hospital and make our own beds etc. I spend most of my time out of bed now although I haven't got my outfit for doing it in yet. They call them "grays." So far we have been in semi-isolation and have trays brought up to us. But starting tomorrow I expect to eat in the dining room. Of course I have to get my grays first.

Mac sent my lighter about 10 days ago and I wrote him a while ago. It doesn't seem very long ago since I was home, but sure would like to get out there again. We have been having lovely weather the last week, but there is something about the West that gets you. Or maybe it's the thought of all those skunks running around with nobody to look after them [he trapped and shot skunks and other fur-bearers]. Incidentally it certainly would be nice to hear that Rivette had sold those pelts. You might as well keep any money there is, Dad, as I don't need it.

197

Well, will sign off now. It's getting on towards bed-time anyway (10:30). Keep yourselves well and don't worry about me.

Love, Clayton.

Also on March 10 Clayton's mother penned the following:

Boissevain

My dear boy –

Have just read your letter and we are indeed sorry to know that you are having such a tough time getting started in your course – no, I don't think that MD was very careful but of course you are not supposed to say anything. However, we were pleased it was not Spanish Flu or measles. And by now I do hope you are a lot better. Daddy will get some cigarettes and send them – how I wish we could drop in and see you but I am not worrying. I made up my mind when you enlisted I was going to be very sensible and so far I have kept my promise to myself and hope to do so all through. This thing is too important for individual self-pity and we are proud to know you are out to do your share.

This is awful ink but the bottle of good ink is about done. I just called the Brooks up and they had a letter from Cub Saturday – made no mention of being transferred, but said he hadn't seen you for a time and that he and Bill were going to investigate as they thought you must be sick. No doubt you have seen and heard from them since. Sleep all you can. The change in climate is partly to account for that. Saturday was very mild here but it is a little colder now.

Yes, it is wonderful work the Red Cross do. We had a display of work last Saturday at Miss Goodon's and it was a great sight. Daddy is going over town now so will close, as he is taking this letter. Best love and wishes for a speedy recovery, and I am not building too much on your being invalided home. It is a long journey, and you should be OK in a week. Love again my boy,

Mom

Next day, the following letter was written by an admiring cousin in Ottawa named Emily. She leads a fun and active life, as you will see.

Gatineau Power Co.
140 Wellington St.
Ottawa, Ont.

March 11, 1941

Dear Clayton:

So glad to hear you have at last made the Air Force. Have intended writing sooner but did not have your address. Mother was up at Auntie Em's over the weekend, so that is how I got your address. Clarke Bradley will be writing to you soon, as he also took your address. Did you know that he is in the RCMP? Joined just after the New Year. He was over Sunday night and he said he received a letter from the Air Force and also one from the Navy. Clarke has signed up in the Mounties for a year so I am afraid he will not be able to join the Air Force. I think this training will do him a lot of good and he will get out more. They have quite a number of parties at the barracks, and he takes them all in. He invited me to a skating party one night but not having any skates I didn't go, but he got somebody else. Two weeks ago they had a formal dance at the barracks and he phoned and wanted me to go but I had been (I was in bed) ill. Had a touch of the flu and was in bed five days running a temperature, but he took some girl who lives here in the city. I think she is from up around the Gower. 'Nuff about Clarke.

How do you like life in the barracks? Are there a good crowd of lads? Guess so. Clayton, if there is anything you would like in the way of knitted articles or food just let me know and I will be glad to help you out. When do you get a 48-hour leave? Any chance of you hitch-hiking to Ottawa? If so don't hesitate in coming. We can always find room for you, and if you would like to bring somebody along, OK. We would all be glad to have you and any of your friends.

Must write to Renee and perhaps she may be able to come down. Would love to see her. Have you called Roland yet? He would be glad to hear from you. I have a cousin living in Toronto, Bryce Seggie. He is about your age and I think he is working in Eaton's or Simpsons in the office, foreign exchange. I think you met him a long time ago up at McLaren's Landing. Oh, there goes 12:30 lunch time, must run.

Back at the old grind again. At last I have got my work caught up. We have been very busy here for the past three months. I have a little job to do but it can wait until tomorrow. What are you doing for excitement in Toronto? Is there any chance of you being transferred to Rockcliffe or Uplands? Are you going to take a pilot's course?

Badminton will soon be over. The club closes on the 19th of April.

The club tournaments are on this week. Last night we played ladies double and men's singles. My partner and I are I the finals of the doubles. My partner, Diana Lyon, was runner up in the singles of the Ontario Tournament which was held in Toronto in February. She is a grand kid, only 19, and we have so much fun playing together. Tonight I have to play singles and tomorrow are the mixed doubles. We play right down to the final round and the finals are scheduled for Friday night. Diana and I were in the semi-finals of the City and District tournament and were put out by the runnersup in the Ontario, Marg Robertson and Betty Snell. We defeated the runnersup last night of the City and District, Dot Renwick and Jane Caldwell. Marg and Betty won the City and District.

We had a tea dance at the club a week ago last Saturday and we had fun. There were a few going over to the Avalon Club (cross the river) after the party but our party (eight of us) were going to a little cocktail party first so we joined them later. There were 24 of us altogether. What a floor show. Clayton, imagine I was in the mood to jigger bug. Norm Fishbourne was in our party. He is still the same. Once in a while he asks me out for a beer but I still can't figure him out. Norm and I had a game on, singles, for the beer and I lost so I owe him a quart. He said he would collect it this week. We still carry on the funny conversations over the phone. There is another tea dance on the 29th, I think, or it may be the 22nd. Wish you could get down before the club closes.

How did you like that enlargement I sent you? Don't think you ever mentioned it. I haven't been doing very much skiing lately, but hope to get some more in now that the tournaments are over. You remember Elizabeth (Liz)? Well she is still as lively as ever. Her brother bought an old 1929 Ford sedan last fall and we have had more fun tearing around in that. What a car! Liz calls it "Effie."

Forgot to tell you I was in Montreal for a weekend and I had a grand time. Stayed with friends I met last summer. Mr. Howard has just put something on my desk so I had better get it done.

Best of luck Clay and write soon.

Love,

Emily.

P.S. I still think you had better forget the "Prairie Sunshine" now that you are in the east. Don't forget, if you get a chance to come home, come along.

On the same day, March 11, 1941, Wanda the young teacher in Laurier, Man., wrote him about the training planes seen over head, cutter rides, a visit home and other news.

Dear Clayton,

So the Air Force has claimed you at last? It is a long time since you first mentioned RAF to me. I am glad you like it so well. Liking what you have to do helps a lot. But how did you get the rank of corporal in such a hurry? Golly you're a fast worker ... or what was it?

Had a good laugh over your snap. After some pondering it dawned on me that Eric "Windbag" Littler took it (or am I wrong?) Surely that girl with you didn't used to be me!

The children and I see from 10 to 15 planes go over a day. They are from Dauphin Airport and the skies are surely humming with activity. It makes us all war conscious.

I have been busy teaching and dancing and gadding about the country and having the time of my life. (Remember the little girl who hated farms and farmers?) On Sunday this house was jammed with young folks. The boys played guitar, fiddle and mouth organ and we sang and spun yarns until later around Earl's old tin heater. Earl engaged three of the boys in whist and Eveline and Earl's sister knitted. We all had fun.

Two weeks ago I landed on the parental doorstep. I had one of my pupils in tow. "But how did you get out?" gasped the folks (as if I had been in jail). They hadn't expected to see me until the snow melted but I fooled them. On the Friday after four I went home with Eunice Benson, who lives by the lake, for we had heard her uncle was going to McCreary by cutter the next day. That night we danced at Balders under 4:30 a.m. and got up at 7 and went across the lake where we set out for a 20-below 15-mile ride. I hadn't seen a store since December. Then I wasn't satisfied. After much running around town with Eunice at my heels we got a ride to Kelwood. It was heavenly getting home. Eunice was tickled. She is 15 years old and *never* been farther than McCreary and Laurier and *never* seen skating, hockey, curling, etc. etc. Dad drove us back to McCreary at 9 p.m. where we met three boys from Sunrise, S. D. who had promised to wait on us and we left for the wilds again about 10:30. Five of us in a jumper, 30 below, the roads bad and the horses wild. Eventually we disregarded roads and went as the crow flies. The boys took us right to Bensons' – 12 miles out of their way. Oh mon dieu what a trip! I'm getting tough.

How do you like being 22? As for being 20 I feel sillier than I did at 16! I don't improve with age. I got a very encouraging letter from C. K. Rogers, superintendent of education. I guess they got a good report of me. I swelled with pride at "wonderfully good teacher" and "after your training see you give your talents to a larger school unit." I do so want to make good. But I know I'm going to weep more than a few tears when I have to leave these darling little brats. They're so cute.

I organized the junior Red Cross last week, Busy Beavers Branch. We're starting knitting soon. (Shucks, airmen aren't interested in knitting.)

Send me a picture of yourself in your uniform. I want to see what you look like. Don't forget please. [She places an accent < over the please and adds: "< emphasis – music training."]

I must sign off and write three more letters. Excuse the writing paper. Mine's done and I'm using the school foolscap.

Be good – write me about your Air Force life – and don't get up in the air and forget how to come down.

Yours, Wanda.

A day later, March 12, Clayton's mom wrote with news about the big carnival.

My dear boy –

I hope you are out of hospital by now and that you are not back in quarantine. Mrs. Brook said they had a letter from Cub last night – said he had not seen you or Jack for some days. He and Rosy are chumming up. Had 36-hour leave and decided to go to Niagara – got lifts there and back and last car took them home to supper. They are in Squadron 1.

Now my dear be careful and do not get fresh cold. Do not hesitate to wear extra clothes until you get back to normal. I am not worrying. I know you will have the good sense to see it pays to be careful, as every day lost means a tiny bit of advantage to Hitler and when thousands are held up it counts. Verna (Irene Murray's sister) knew that nurse Spafford who died in England – she is a niece of the Spaffords here in town. Well, the weather is keeping cold and really ideal for the big Carnival Saturday. The rink is being decorated with flags and bunting. The Scouts and band are to lead the procession.

Haven't heard if Frank has left Winnipeg yet. He was to report Monday or Tuesday. Do hope Jack Murray gets some satisfaction soon – he feels that it is taking too long – he fell on ice and hurt his back a few weeks ago and it has been bothering him ever since.

Did I tell you Edwin and Margaret are being married next month? They are going to live at home with Eddie's parents. Rose is having an experienced girl from Wpg to take Margaret's place. There is a girl in one of the banks who comes from Cloverdale whose dad played football with your dad when they were young. I am going to have her over for dinner some time.

Well, my dear, not much news so will close for now. Dad is out in kitchen folding flags and bunting and putting them in a suitcase ready for tomorrow to decorate.

Love and best wishes,
Mom.

Wed. March 12, 1941
Toronto

Dear Mom,

Just got yours this a.m. I already had the other written so opened it and am adding this. You shouldn't be spending your money on cigarettes for me. I have plenty of money and please don't bother with any more. It's been hard enough, and now that I have my first real steady job it's up to me to get along on it.

Don't worry about my health. All I want now is to get out there and to get going. Haven't heard from Bill or Cub but I am going to write them. Already have eight letters to be mailed. Incidentally thanks for the stamps. Roland sent 25 up. Was talking to Margaret on the phone yesterday. Am out of isolation now.

I knew you'd take it like a brick, Mom. After all there are lots who have no idea just how things lie. Take Olwyn for example. And now must close. Hope this isn't over-weight. Take care of yourself and Dad.

Clayton

On March 13 the Northern Life Assurance Company, Winnipeg Agency (where he had worked) sent Clayton the following note:

A.C. 2 Bird, F.C., R.-91897,
#1 Manning Depot, Toronto, Ont.

Dear Sir:

Government regulations require that all employers ascertain that all persons in their employ have been duly registered under the National Registration Act.

Will you please, therefore, write on this letter from your registration card the electoral district and polling division where you registered and return in the enclosed stamped envelope.

Yours truly,
Jack Durand [or similar, hard to decipher]
Branch Secretary.

Then a handwritten note: Clayton, excuse formality but I sent same letter to all those under contract. JLD.

Clayton wrote on the letter in pencil: 186 Wpg   58 North Centre.

March was a busy month for letters. Clayton's Uncle Percy, his mother's brother, wrote him from their North Gower farm near Ottawa on March 13, 1941. What's interesting is how people assumed a man in military training had time to sightsee and visit relatives. Also, there is no attempt to hold back bad news from a young man facing difficult times himself. Clayton is quarantined, frustrated and falling behind his chums on their road to becoming pilots.

RR 3 North Gower, Ont.

Dear Clayton:

I had a letter from your Mother saying that you were in training in Toronto – none of us thought when you were here last summer that you would be back to Ontario so soon again. I should think, though, that it would be more interesting than going back to Brandon. Toronto is a beautiful city; and you have your big Rowland to show you around and Margaret is equally as good.

Auntie Lill and I were there two years ago at Easter, for the week, and were able to see Wilbert Emery [sp?]—you will, no doubt, be a welcome guest there also. I mean at his sister's home.

I hope you will forgive blunders in this letter. We have all had a terrible shock, and it seems to be getting worse as time passes. Last night about this time (9:30) one of our neighbours (lives just back of our maple bush) and his son 14 years old were coming home from North Gower village and a car came up behind them – they were driving in a cutter. The horse was killed outright and carried 60 feet from the rest of the wreckage. The boy was picked up unconscious. The man was badly cut and bruised. Dr. Blair had them taken to the Civic (hospital) in ambulance where the boy died during the night. Today the father is more seriously injured than was first thought. The MDs fear his neck is broken. The driver of the car was a young man from Richmond, and with him was another young man. They were coming from Kemptville. The boy's mother is not well, HPB. This man is a brother of Collingwood Craig, who keeps the store up at Lansdowne.

We just got over worrying about Charlie Craig who lives next farm to the Cheese Factory, who was taken to hospital two weeks ago, and just the past two days out of danger. Your Mother knows these people, went to school with them all, so you might slip this letter in to her when you next write her. And I hope you will write her regularly and very, very often – even a card. She will miss you so much. You have been at home since you left college mostly [not true – Clayton was mostly in Winnipeg and Rivers working].

What a war. I am glad the Lend-Lease bill is signed, it will make Hitler shake in his boots. [The bill allowed the U.S. to provide military equipment to Canada, such as airplanes. They were flown to the border, towed over, and then flown on to airbases to be used in training. Some were taken over to England, as the bill also provided equipment for Great Britain, then fighting alone with the Dominions against the Nazis who had overrun Europe and North Africa.]

Your cousin Clayton Bradley has been in bed for more than two weeks with jaundice. The doctor told him he could get up last Tuesday, but he didn't feel like doing so, and he also had a slight temperature. So I told Grace to call the doctor and he came down. He's confident the trouble is his liver. He had "flu" up at camp, and had a layoff of two days. Finally he went to a doctor and to bed. He does not feel sick and has read several books. His Dad has the worst time getting help. The farmers are all certainly up against it there. There may be more when the men come back from the shooting if they don't go to the mines.

Well Clayton I hope you can read this. I have my wood to get out yet, when I can get some help myself.

Would love to see you in your uniform, and hope you will fly down to North Gower whenever you have an opportunity [at this point Clayton has never even stepped inside a plane, let alone become a pilot]. Take care of yourself. Love from Aunt E---- and Uncle Percy.

Also on March 13, Clayton's brother Mac, then 20, whose exploits as a soldier are recalled in detail in Section Two of this book, wrote to him as well. At this point, Mac is working days and studying nights in Winnipeg to be a chartered accountant, while also taking reserve army training. It becomes clear from these various letters that people were just as busy back then as they are today, maybe even moreso, as they had no TV to lure them to the couch.

511 Spence St.
Wpg, Man.
13-3-41

Dear Clayton:

Sorry to hear about the flu and all. It will sort of put you behind the rest of the boys but I think being tied down to a bed for a couple of weeks will do you a lot of good. Frank [Moore, of Boissevain] dropped in for a couple of hours on Sunday to tell me he was being sworn in Monday [Air Force]. He promised to give me a ring before he left town but so far I haven't heard from him so I don't know what has happened. He was staying with Stenie, and he only calls me up when one of Marion's friends wants a date. He tried it last Saturday night but I turned him down. I had been at the U "Color Nite" dance at the Royal Alex and was in no condition to go dancing again, either financially or sleepily. Don, Doug and I went with a trio from Sparling Hall and had a swell time. I arranged the date one night on my way to lectures and Doug and I decided to have some fun with Don and tell him his girl had a date and that my girl would arrange a blind date. At first we only intended to tease him but when he took it seriously we let it run. You can imagine the look on his face when the girls walked into the reception room Friday night.

My girl is Evelyn May MacDonald from Kamsack, Sask., and a Home Economics major. She is an exceptionally good skater, goes like a bat out of hell whenever she gets rid of me – about 5'8" or so and very nice company. I haven't seen either Marion or Doris [Clayton's future wife] since you left and I don't think I will be able to until after the exams. I still don't know when these are coming off but hope it will be late in April as I just can't seem to get down to work. I have been having some trouble with annuities and present values lately and decided to try to figure it out from the book. Now I am hopelessly mixed up as the book and the professor don't like each other and don't work together. A second-year student advised me to leave the text strictly alone and the prof isn't much help because he assumes so much that he only confuses us more.

I have been working at Radio Oil Refineries for the last 10 days and am finding out a few things about the cracking of oils, etc. I have also picked up a few more cuss words as the government oil controller has flooded the office with the most mystifying reports which usually ask to be filled out and returned within a week. The boss is just about ready for murder as he is the one they rely on to fill them out. I figure he'll be working another week on those reports alone and that will put the office schedule still farther behind. Also Thacker decided to get sick and has been away three days now. I think it's the measles as his girlfriend took them about three weeks ago. I hope I don't get them with exams so close. I have been looking for a longer week [more hours] for some time but the boss hasn't mentioned it and wouldn't start just now.

I have some English to do and so had better scram. Hope you are out of the hospital by the time this reaches you.

Mac

The following letter is from Clayton's Uncle Percy, his mother's brother, a high-ranking Anglican minister who would marry his nephew Clayton and his bride, Doris Aconley, in the not-too-distant future.

St. Matthew's Pro-Cathedral
Brandon, Manitoba
Ven. Archdeacon Percy Heywood, MA, BD, Rector

March 17, 1941

My dear Clayton –

We were all so delighted to receive your nice long letter, and I really intended answering it very soon, but after several days, here I am.

How are you now? The girls would say – "You poor kid" – being quarantined all this time, and I understand you have had the real thing [not true]. What a shame you had to go East and pick up all those germs; however, here is hoping you are over it all, and for all time. There is some consolation in knowing it is usually not a repeater. I suspect your Mother has told us she spent Friday last with us in Brandon, accompanied by Irene Murray and her sister Verna Munson. We all enjoyed a lovely visit, only very short.

I had to go to a meeting in the Baptists Church that afternoon where I saw your old chaperone Mrs. Darrach [of Darrach Hall, Brandon College most likely].

The day your letter arrived we had Jack (Dr. Findley) in to dinner, prior to his leaving for Wpg and joining up with the colours [military?]. Is staying at the Tuxedo Hospital, and poor Kathleen is hoping he may not be called on too soon to go overseas. He certainly gave up a splendid practice here, as he and Dr. Peters were working so well together – and may regret his leaving Brandon. However he felt it his duty to go over. His youngest brother arrived in England about Xmas time, so there is a link over there.

I am so pleased that you have such an interesting progamme of sports etc. when off drill. As your letter suggested something intensely interesting, I do hope you will not have to go out too soon, as so much standing and drilling will not do your muscles any good. Yes, the orchestra – I knew you would be there [Clayton played saxophone and piano]. Go to it, my dear boy, it will cheer you up, and many others as well.

Pat is busy as usual, having to work overtime, so many coming and going. Just heard today poor Bill has not been feeling well. Had flu and a bit of glandular trouble followed up. Renie is looking forward to seeing you – soon as you can make it – so hope Roland will be able to take you over soon as you are fit.

Love from Uncle Percy, Pat, and your Auntie [illegible scribble]

Clayton received a letter from a Brandon College gal named Ricky soon after hearing from the good Rector. This next letter carries a much different tone to begin with, but notice how it grows serious as she talks about her ill sister and the boys leaving for the war. It seems that sickness and war were on everyone's lips. In his previous year at Brandon College Clayton failed courses, which he had never done before. The war was on his mind most certainly, as he told me, but maybe this girl was too.

March 19th
Wednesday night

Dear Bird,

Mmh, what nice letters you write, my Butterfly. Of course I want to write to you even though it seems a letter won't be answered as promptly as it should be, but then you know well enough it's pure laziness. I would not want to lose a friend such as you for the world. Do you know, Bird, that last year was one of the happiest I've ever had. I can't say I'm unhappy for I don't know the meaning of the word but this year it's so different. I miss the laughing and fooling around. Remember those hikes – I think I was on one this year.

Last night I went to see Gone with the Wind. I liked it. When I came to ask for my night out – I didn't remember until going down for supper so had to ask Mrs. Darrach in the dining room. Lo and behold she told me I had my night out Monday. Immediately I piped up and said I most certainly did not. Well this considerably squelched me until I realized what she meant. Bernice had been in over the weekend and I'd taken a late leave on Friday night to be with her. Finally she was persuaded to let me go. You can imagine how mad I was – everybody looking at me and laughing. The show didn't get out until 12 and so it was 12:45 when I got home. Just as we were coming out I met my uncle from Deloraine – remember? What a surprise. I didn't know what to say. The boy I was with likely thought I was daffed (could be). This chap is in the Air Force, has been for six months. I used to know him at home.

Right now I'm rather blue this morning. I got word that my sister is very sick. My Dad has been in Winnipeg for the past week. I don't know anything except she is sick, and it worries me. Dad wrote just a short note and he took it for granted I would know. I guess the folks at home are too busy to write. If I don't get a letter tomorrow I'm going to phone. But I shouldn't be bothering you. There were so many things I wanted to tell you but I've forgotten them. Let me see, oh yes, you spoke of Pulfer and Paddy. Pulf got word today that Paddy cannot get her money through in order to get to Rochester [Mayo Clinic]. She'll be so disappointed. Poor kid, if only she could get those eyes of hers attended to.

Personally I hope you're out of the hospital and feeling okay again. This will surely get to you.

Dad sent a telegram and I met him at the train. I talked to him for almost half an hour; he was going home. Mother is in Winnipeg now with my sister – she is somewhat better. I just couldn't seem to settle down to anything – studying or letter writing. We start writing our exams April 2. Nice, eh? I don't know nothin' in Maths and I'm certainly going to see what I can do about it. With war 'n everything it seems terrible to be wasting time. Speaking of war there has been another one of the college boys who has joined up. Guess who? Jerry Old. Almost two weeks ago. He went into Winnipeg for the weekend and didn't return. I think he goes to Quebec or someplace in Quebec this week. One by one the army will call them just as it called you.

You wanted me to be frank and so this is what I want to say. I think you're swell and I'll always remember you and the times we spent together but we both know that all we can be to each other is the very best of friends. Please, Bird, don't think that I don't like you because I do.

Well, my dear, I must close now. Here's hoping you're feeling tops. I'll be waiting for another letter soon.

Bye for now,

As ever with love,

Ricky.

Next day, Clayton's mother wrote him again with an update about the Carnival. Nothing like a letter from home and questions about your laundry to make you feel better, and we're sure this had a cheering effect on Clayton. And what a blizzard!

Boissevain,
March 20, 1941

My dear boy –

Wonder if you are in Ottawa or Toronto but will address this to the usual place – we were very glad to hear you were recovering from the 'flu' so nicely and hope from now on you have no more setbacks.

Well, our Carnival last Saturday had to be postponed till next Sat. One of the worst blizzards I ever saw raged here from 3 p.m. till about 8 – no doubt you will read in papers of the lives lost in the West and in North Dakota – 68 down there and six in Manitoba. Daddy announced over loud speaker in rink [at a hockey game] that no one was to start home, that coffee etc. would be provided in town hall. It was terrible. I couldn't see the nearest houses at times. The weather has moderated and it is just right now (Thursday) so hope it continues till Sat.

Louie Moncur got highest votes for Queen. They have sold over 75 tickets on the beaver coat and 240 tickets to Carnival. They hope to make $400, all for Lord Mayor's Fund – Daddy is Chairman of Committees – he has also been given the job of Returning Officer for the coming election. Mr. McKinnon of Minto had the job for years, died last fall.

What have you done with your civilian clothes? Mack [spelled here as she spelled it, even though Mac himself and others leave off the k] spoke as though he could use your suit. Get rid of the overcoat down there, too bulky to send home. How are you getting along about laundry?

Mr. Garton has rec'd his Captaincy – do not know where he will be stationed. You remember the jam I told you young D got into. The case has to come before the Juvenile Court (I think in Brandon). He will probably get a severe reprimand – did I tell you Irene Murray and I went to Brandon on bus with Verna, her sister – had dinner at Heywoods – saw Pat's diamond and Irene's photo – I got a pair of shoes and a blue and white striped blouse for my blue suit – I do hope if you go to Ottawa to take the train – no hitch-hiking after flu.

Hope to hear from you soon that you are feeling tip top and are settled at your work – soon as that happens, we can arrange about our correspondence – you write a certain day and I shall do same so letters do not cross. Must go over town now. Have promised Dad fish and baked potatoes for supper. Lots of love,

Mom

Imagine knowing your town so well that you can rhyme off the names of the only "boys" who haven't yet been called up for service. That was the case for Clayton's mother.

Boissevain
March 22, 1941

My dear boy –

Rec'd your letter this a.m. (Saturday) and was indeed surprised to find you were still in hospital. However, I note you expect to leave today. I sent my last letter to your first address at the Manning Depot – you may not get it at all, but I thought you would be out of hospital long before or perhaps had gone to Ottawa. Oh well, no doubt the time seems wasted but one never knows – guess I am a fatalist, as I always feel these things turn out for the best in the long run. The other boys may be a month ahead but you may be spared something they will have to go through – am glad you have had interesting reading. You are a son of your mother's all right. I am never lonely if I have a good book – and remember there is one Good Book none of us read nearly as much as we should and never be ashamed to read a chapter when you get the chance.

Do you have a chance to go to church service? Take your communion when you can. It is a great help tho' when one is young and full of life, it may not seem so. I don't think the Padre would be very shocked if he found you doing nothing worse than playing a game of bridge – wasn't that some hand, 13 clubs. No wonder you were dazed. I know one person who got 13 spades and bid of no trump – of course didn't get a trick.

Mack warned us not to expect too many letters as exams are coming off sooner than expected but I hope he writes you soon. Jack Murray is staying in bed. His back is still very painful. I think I told you he fell on ice over a month ago. Never saw a doctor or had any treatment for two weeks [this was when you paid for each visit, long before medicare]. So no wonder it is taking a long time [she speaks as a doctor's wife]; ligaments were strained. I am taking him some books and do-nuts this p.m.—also your letter to read. He expects his call in April, so they told him. John Gardiner passed his medical and goes in Tuesday. Air Force – soon no boys will be left. Ned King, Elmer Walker and Roland Thomas are only ones here now.

The old boys still meet every Thursday and go through their gymnastics. So you think Eastern climate is feminine. Well, the West is a bit that way too. Yesterday snowed hard and today water is running in cistern. Am going over to Carnival tonight. Did I tell you they sold over 75 tickets on beaver coat and 238 Carnival – they hope to reach $400 for Lord Mayor's Fund. B'vain gave La Riviere a trimming last night on home rink – 17-4. They have met with great success this winter, but with three Mortons on [team], it is bound to be – must not write too much at one time.

Best love and wishes – hope in your next letter you will have full uniform and be started in your work. Don McDonald only got his Navy uniform about a month ago – joined six months ago, is still in Halifax. Love Mom.

On Sunday, March 23 Aunt Irene penned the following:

Dear Clayton –

As you see by the enclosed letter I had wonderful plans [to visit] a few weeks ago. Unfortunately it was all too sudden to arrange so I left it. I hope I can get in before you're posted. Or could you get out?

Was so sorry to hear you were in the hospital and have had such a dreary time since joining up – was very glad to get your letter. I heard from your Mom just a day or so back and she gave me news of everyone in Brandon – she probably writes you in detail so I won't repeat any of it. Perhaps you are on leave now – I hardly know whether to address this to the hospital or barracks. Please try to get Rowland and Marg to drive you down here some Sunday – I would love to see you all.

Irene.

While waiting to be called up after enlisting, Clayton worked as a roofer. "Steve," whose letter is below, is possibly one of the young men he worked with, judging by the "safety belt" reference. But he could also be Doris Aconley's brother Bert, a colourful character who was nicknamed Steve. Again, prepare for quite a shift in tone.

133 Chestnut St.
Winnipeg, Man.
March 25/41

Dear Bird:

How in hell are you anyway? You fugitive from a safety belt. Sorry I have been so long in answering your letter old thing, but due to my better half and domestic situation I am really quite busy. Was speaking to Mac on Saturday and was told you were finally out of the hospital, which is a fine thing, eh what? Some fun spending a few weeks in an isolation camp. However, you should have enough jack [cash] to go on a real binge or two.

Talking about binges, I was really on one last week. Marnie went to the Fort Garry with Bob Shields so I was so damned depressed that Scott (who by the way felt the same way) and I bought two 26's of home brew for $1.50 and so help me I don't remember giving any away, but in the morning I had the empty in my great coat, and honest to Christ I am just starting to see straight now. What we did or where we went is beyond me, but I did wake up in my own bed.

Marni and I have been over to see Doris a few times, but by the thumping hell where did you get the idea that I was over there alone, because as far as I know I haven't been.

We went to the Marlborough a week ago and had a hell of a good time only we weren't drinking – damn it!

This Saturday we are having our dance at the ship so we are taking that in, and on Sunday we are going to Mrs. Manson's [somebody's aunt] for dinner. Last week we had a smoker at the ship and 75 gallons of beer. Of course I sat right beside the tap and did all right.

I believe Ford is getting his discharge this week and wants to buy his coat back so I am perfectly willing to sell, as $10 is a handy thing to have. This past couple of weeks I have been leading a double life, taking Marnie home at 10 and buggering off to see a little blond out in Fort Garry, but she was getting too serious so I had to stop.

Say Bird, this Aconley woman really thinks you're the best, raves about you, drives us silly every time we go over, all she can think and talk about is you. Honestly I sometimes feel like telling her to get wise to herself, but she thinks there is no one like you (which I know damn well there isn't. After all they couldn't put two buggers like you in the same world) and just lives for each mail and when there isn't a letter she just about throws a kitten.

Q. Know what the street cleaner said to the horse?

A. That's enough out of you.

Silly isn't it but not bad either.

I don't know of a helluva lot more to say. Last night we were learning to sling a mic (hammock) and the captain was with us. After all the explaining one bugger said, "That's good for just about everything but a piece of tail." Well for a second there wasn't a sound, and then the storm came, resulting in us doing 30 minutes extra rifle drill. I really think it was worth it though. So long you old so and so because I'm not using any more paper on you. Your pal, 'Steve' xxxxxx *[an arrow points to the x's and he's written 'Bull Shit'].*

We haven't heard from this gal yet, cousin Marnie, one of his Winnipeg friends. What's important here is her comment about Doris, Clay's fiancé.

Victoria Hospital,
424 River Avenue,
Winnipeg, Man.
March 26/41

Dear Clayton,

At least I've really settled down to write to you but you can imagine now that you have taken up nursing duties – making beds etc.! How busy a hospital can get!

The more I see of this nursing profession the more I like it. It just gets you, and it's surprising what you can learn in six short weeks. Just imagine I'll have my cap in another month. Be a real genius nurse then and won't look so insignificant without a cap and bib!

I haven't seen Doris for nearly a week. Russ and I met her on the street Saturday night when she was on her way to the "drug stores" at the Bay. Sunday I had a 10-3 and slept – lazy eh! Monday, stayed in. Tuesday had a 4:30 off and went to a show at the Osborne, saw 'Foreign Correspondent.' It was really good.

Yesterday I had the afternoon off and Rigby and I went out to dinner and then to the Garrick 'Cheers for Miss Bishop'. Gosh it was good. Today I was lazy and stayed in and wrote letters, not that I haven't needed to for ages.

Last Friday I went to the "Grad's Farewell" at the Fort Garry, tails and evening gowns. My corsage was pale yellow roses. Had a grand time but the only hitch was that I had to be in by 12 o'clock. Real Cinderella, eh?

Guess it was Johnny that I was out with the night that Russ was over at Doris's. Yes I can well imagine that Doris would be easy to like – she really is a nice kid – and the more I see of her the more I like her.

Am going to the Navy dance on Saturday night with Russ. By the way my brother is in Toronto now – Bud -- working for Dominion Bridge Co. Ltd. Can't remember his address but will send it next letter if your brother hasn't already. Lights out in five minutes so will finish this tomorrow. Good-nite!!

Six bells in the morning. What a life, and I asked for three years of it!

1:30 a.m. Just got off duty so will add a few lines before I go out for a Coca-Cola. Yes I'm still at it dear cousin. Russ is coming over to me. He hardly ever sees my now that I'm a hard working girl!

By the way your old girl friend Kay Burgess is getting married this month, to Bob Barefoot or had you already heard. That is a surprise to everyone.

You certainly haven't seen much of the Air Force yet have you? Or Toronto – but will the sights be seen when you do get out, eh?

I guess I'd better close this again for the time being and get ready to go out. Had a letter from Mother this afternoon and all she seems to be doing lately is "trucking" around the town going to parties for Mrs. ....field – Aunt Margaret you know. Must close now and get this off in the mail. Love, Marnie

Write again soon eh!!

Jack is still sick in bed, and Mother said [illegible name] was over to see him and brought some magazines for him. Imagine!

P.S. How about a picture of you in your uniform when you get out of your hospital!!!

CHAPTER 3

Finally At Work

Manning Depot,
Toronto.

March 27, 1941

Dear Mom and Dad,

Well I am finally at work. It took a lot of thinking and plugging to do it, but I made it. Am too tired from today's drill to enlarge on it now but will tell you later.

Jack Moore is on overseas draft and will probably get home before this does. I got four of your letters and the cigs and Recorders at the P.O. when I returned. Also seven other letters. I don't know why they were kept here. Maybe there are some over at the Automotive Building for me. The orderly there didn't even know I had been away, let alone at the hospital.

You can send me my slippers, Mom, and a pair of pajamas. Also please include the crepe-soled Oxfords that I got in the States last year. I haven't been able to get my civvies away yet but will do so and just as soon as possible. Might as well send the overcoat as they pay the express anyway.

Didn't get down to see Wendel Wilkie as I was C.B. at the time. But the other night the Masked Wolf was in for a bit of wrestling on the sports card. If people will actually pay money to see such exhibitions of legalized mayhem, I wonder. It disgusted me so I left. But yesterday afternoon

Donald Dixon gave us a bit of a concert. Had a real good seat and really enjoyed it.

I was over to Rowland's Sunday afternoon and evening and went to church with them that evening. May Cherry might be down this weekend and I will have to be over to see her if I can. It doesn't look as though I will make Ottawa after all. Got letters from Auntie Ethel, Em, Emily, Mac, etc. in the last bunch.

Well I must quit now and go to sleep.

Love from Clayton.

Friday 1:15 p.m.

Was on drill parade three hours this a.m. and go on for another three hours in 10 minutes. Just got letters from Russell and Irene Heywood. And now I have to go. Will write again soon.

Love,

Clayton.

Boissevain,
March 28, 1941

My dear boy –

I wonder just where you are and what you are doing – I do hope you have fully recovered from the flu – it is such a treacherous thing one never knows how it will leave one. Hope you have been getting my letters. I sent most of them to the hospital and then one to your old address – also sent [Boissevain] Recorders [a weekly newspaper] and a [Winnipeg] Free Press. Had a letter from your Aunt Lill asking for you. Said Emily [of the Gatineau Power Co. office, badminton player] had written you day before she got yours and hope you got it. Mr. Brook said Cub expected to be moved at any time.

Well, the Carnival came off with a bang – made about $475 and will have $400 to send to Lord Mayor's Fund. Daddy was certainly pleased. He worked hard as did all the committees but as chairman he had such a lot of detail to attend to. Just now he is spending a few days in bed with a carbuncle on his right wrist. He went to Brandon Medical and Dr. Bigelow lanced it. It was a horrible looking thing but is healing nicely. I wish he could find out the cause of all this. He seems to have that kind of trouble so often. I wrote Mack and sent him your last letter, asked him if there was any chance of his getting home Easter. Have you all your uniform yet?

Would love to see you in it. Perhaps you would be having a picture taken, or you may be transferred west.

Isn't that grand news about the Slavs – all honor to them. If some of the others had had their (Daddy's word) "guts" they may not be where they are today. What a blow to Japan as well as Germany and Italy – and today Russia declared she would stand behind Greece and Turkey and the U.S.

Must go now. Not much news. Oh yes, who do you think is getting married tomorrow? Bobby Barefoot and Kay Burgess. Poor Bob – they are to live in top flat of Andrew's house. Bye bye for now. Write when you can. Love Mom.

Three days later, Mother Bird writes again and is still fretting about her son's laundry regime.

Boissevain,
March 31, 1941

My dear boy –

We were glad to get your letter Saturday saying you were out at last, started on your training. Yes, I have heard they all find the first few days' drill pretty strenuous, but it soon wears off. Expect your muscles will be pretty soft after being sick, and I can just imagine how you would sleep. Daddy and I have just parceled up the things you asked for – he mended your slipper – I sent the light-weight pajamas, as you seemed to find those heavy ones too warm. Did you take one suit with you? You haven't told me yet how your laundry is done.

If you go to Automotive Building you will find a letter from me and a parcel from Mrs. Ed Dow. She phoned me last week and I gave her your address. She is sending you a pair of sox – be sure to acknowledge as soon as possible. We had a call from the "Navy" yesterday. Russell had two days' leave. Looks well in uniform but thinner – said Mack is studying hard for exams. We are having gorgeous weather, but very dirty underfoot. Snow nearly gone. Haven't seen Jack Moore. If he came home he hasn't been around. I think Frank is in Brandon. Jack Murray went to Brandon today to have X-ray on his back. He sure has had a time. Stayed in bed for past week. Has to report on the 9th., but am sure will not be able to.

Am glad you could spend an evening with Rowland. Suppose June is quite a young lady. Hope you see May Cherry.

Must go over town and mail this and parcel. Mr. Southon is laid up with flu so I had Newby come over this a.m. to do the work – Dad expects to be out in a day or two – the carbuncle on his wrist was fine but he also had one just inside his nose and it was very painful – broke last night so he has felt much easier today – has breakfast in bed and comes down for other meals, but feels like lying around most of the time.

Has most of the voters' lists in, so is pretty much prepared should there be an election here, which I hardly think there will be –

Love and best wishes Mom.

On March 30, Clayton heard from his cousin Clarke Bradley who had joined the RCMP. He writes a fascinating and detailed account of life in the force in his first few months. You will soon appreciate why he opens by saying he is in a "leisure position just now," because the RCMP training day was jam-packed with work.

RCMP
N Division,
Rockcliffe, Ont.

March 30, 1941

Dear Clayton:

As I am in a leisure position just now, and with a little time on my hands after a lovely supper at Aunt Lill's, I decided to write you a few lines.

How are you getting along anyway? I hope you have completely recovered from your attack of the flu. It is a hard dose to get rid of, and we have had plenty of it around home from time to time.

Our Clayton has been sick too. He spent his 30 days training at the Camp in Brockville, Ont. He had a cold while he was there and a few days after he got home he went to bed and only just got up about a week ago. He seemed to take the measles first, but they did not come out on him or make him very sick. When he went to bed the doctor thought he had jaundice but later said his liver was out of order. He lost a lot of weight and was very weak, but I hope he is getting along better now. Dad had quite a time getting a man to take his place, but he has a Frenchman now, who is quite interested in the work and willing to stay all summer.

Mother is as well as she was in the summer, although her voice is very faint and it is hard to understand what she says. The rest of the family are quite well including Aunt Em and Uncle Percy.

I suppose you were surprised to hear that I was in the RCMP. Well, so was I. I did not think I would have made it, but they must have been wanting men pretty bad. I later learned that each one of us was thoroughly investigated before we got notice to come in to enlist, and we are all gentlemen, so they think. However we are a fine bunch of fellows, but each one has his differences or some little characteristic that annoys someone else and only today I heard two chaps talking about another fellow whom they both disliked. But that is quite natural in a bunch of 100 or more men.

Our men are divided into squads of 24 each. This is a nice body of men for a class, and also suitable to instruct in drill or P. T. We get a very stiff training schedule and don't get much time to slack off. I understand our three months training in drill (one hour a day) is almost equivalent to a year's training in the army.

We also have some studying to do. Imagine me with the Criminal Code. We have to know the meaning of each section of it, and where to find the different offences and definitions of certain crimes. We also have Rules and Regulations of the Force and the RCMP Act to study. They are about as tricky as the Code, but we are finished with them now. When a chap has mot done much reading for the last five or six years and then picks up an Act passed by the federal government, he has to do some thinking to grasp even the faintest idea of it. That is the position I found myself in, and when our marks came out, I felt as if I would be farming again after three months' hard work and small pay.

We also have to take typewriting. That's just in my line, I thought. Last November I could type 35 words per minute, but when I took a test in January on a different machine I could only make 16. It took me almost two months to get up to 40 wpm, which is the desired speed which a Mountie should be able to type. Some of the fellows who had never seen a typewriter before can type more accurately than I can, and one fellow got his 40 wpm almost as soon as I did. I think the class is doing very well, and our squad has the highest average of any squad there since the war started.

We get plenty of fatigue work to do also. Every morning there is a large stable of about 48 horses to clean out before breakfast. About 30 men have to do this; the other squad has to do inside fatigue, which includes sweeping, waxing and polishing offices, which with three others is my job, and emptying waste baskets and other cleanup jobs. We get up at 6 o'clock, our bugler went to Regina, and my God! are we ever relieved. It was worse than a bomb to hear that long drawn out Reveille every morning. Our role call is at 6:30 when we are assigned to our fatigue duties. Breakfast is from 7:15 to 8. We have an inspection at 8:30, just our uniforms. At 9 the classes begin. We have two hours at noon and quite at 5 in the evening for supper.

There is always a stand-to party of four and night guard of two. The stand-to party must remain in barracks all night and since the roads got muddy have to wash all the cars at 6 o'clock, and do any other necessary jobs in the evening. The night guard has to stay on all night and check everyone in at night and also see that the stables and LM stores are locked up and see there are no "saboteurs" around. We have a small hangar which holds at least one plane. All of our planes have been given over to the Royal Canadian Air Force since the war began except one. Our pilot was transferred from N Division a couple of weeks ago but I don't know where he is now.

The RCAF flying field is just near our barracks, and if you ever get here you will be able to see our barracks every time you take off. The condition of the runways now makes landing almost impossible, and flying is almost at a standstill.

Emily [who writes Clayton letters while working for Mr. Howard at the Gatineau Power Corp.] has just gone out with a lieutenant of the navy. He called her up about 7:30 and was to call in about an hour. She was all excited about him. He is a very nice chap too, but is much older than she is. She says she has quite a good time with some of the flying officers too.

I got word from the air force about two weeks ago to go in and have a checkup on my medical. I had a sore knee when I was in there in September and they wouldn't pass me, so I didn't go back after I got into the RCMP. But I let them know that I was engaged where I am for a year, and maybe I will be here for life. We can be discharged at the end of our three months training if we are unsuitable, and anytime during our service if we do something that we shouldn't do. We had one of our squad who deserted. He went to the States after the first pay day by walking across the ice to Detroit. Authorities got him there for illegal entry and sent him back to Rockcliffe where he was given three months hard labour in the County jail. Another fellow was discharged for flat feet, and another chap still, one of my best pals, had to purchase his way out because there was something wrong with the circulation in his legs and they pained him terribly, but X-rays would not show anything wrong with him.

You will want to know if I have done any riding yet. Well, riding has been discontinued until the war is over at least, and one-year men will not receive that training anyway. From all accounts it is the hardest training one can have, and God help the man who falls off his horse carelessly. When we do something wrong in P.T. we generally get about 20 pushups to do. If you do something wrong in riding, you have to throw your stirrups over the horse's back ("crossed stirrups" they say), and ride that way for an hour or two. Those NCOs (non-commissioned officers) are nice men while not on parade, but they drive us like hell when they get the chance.

Well, Clayton, so much for the RCMP. How do you feel about the Air Force? One of our chaps from North Gower got his wings earlier this month, and likes flying perfectly. I think I would have like it myself, but I know Dad did not want me to go in for it.

You remember the old Maxwell car? We got it made into a tractor last fall. It runs pretty good and has as much power as any tractor that you will buy for $1,000. Its cooling system is not quite as good as it should be.

Please excuse the disjointedness of this letter, and when you have time let me know how you are.

Your Cousin,
Clarke Bradley.

Tuesday, April 1, 1941
Toronto Manning Depot.

Dear Mom and Dad,

Things certainly have been popping around here for the last few days now. But first I suppose you would like to hear my experience in getting back into the Air Force after discharge from the hospital.

They sent me back here to the Manning Depot and told me to see the M.O., which I did. After that we got our own bunks and bedding. And then we were left to our own resources. The rest of the boys were OK but it was this way for me. My squadron was No. 6 and its orderly room was in the Auto Building. So here I was in the Pool with no orderly room and that is where you have to report for everything. The M.O. had given me three days off so on Monday I scouted around and found out what to do and when to do it. First I went to No. 1 Squadron orderly room and there was told they could take me on if I showed them I was Dish negative.

So I got a permit from them to go over to the Auto Bldg to get it. Had to wait till Tuesday to get that. The Dish tests were all given in the Auto Bldg. So I got the Dish on Tuesday and then went back on Wednesday to have it read. It was negative. I'd had a hunch it would be. I have only had two scarlet injections. Went around to No. 6 Squadron OK to get my card and found they didn't even know I had been in hospital.

However I got the card and came back. Then No. 1 told me that I had to have security guard training first. So I went down to the S.G.T. orderly room and got taken on after some talking.

The point is this. If I had left it up to them to get me placed I might still be wandering around here doing nothing. Or even have been sent back to the Auto Bldg to have my five scarlets over again.

Anyway, I still had no boots and there is a lot of drill in S.G.T. So on Thursday a.m. I reported on sick parade. The MO gave me an off-duty till I got some. I took that around to one of the sergeants in SGT and he went over to the stores with me and after some hemming and hawing and grumbling they finally pulled a pair of shoes out and they fitted. I haven't the slightest doubt but that they could have given them to me long ago. Even then they protested that they had none to fit me, but I just sat down and argued that I had to get some if they had to make them on the spot. The sergeant left it up to me.

The new batch of SGT had just started that a.m. so I was only three hours drill behind them. We get three hours each morning and afternoon except Saturday when it's only in the a.m. It was kind of tough at first, first being out of hospital etc., but was fine by Saturday.

We were issued our rifles yesterday a.m. but as pay parade was yesterday p.m. had no drill till this morning. Incidentally it took me from 1 o'clock to 7:30 to get my pay. Boy did they ever get mixed up over me. At that they sent a $5 cheque to the hospital and I have to wait for it.

As soon as I can I will drop into the pay allowances office and get my pay arranged. In the meantime I will send a money order for $15 as soon as I can buy one. I will need about $15 or so myself to last to the middle of the month as I had to buy a service cap. They absolutely didn't have one, I looked. I got it at Eaton's for $2.25. I think I should charge the Air Force for it and for six weeks rental on one pair Oxfords. Then I have to get me a grip, $5, and pay some insurance, etc. I will get $5 set towards my insurance per month. That will put me ahead $10 a year on my premiums.

Cub was posted to Trenton and left yesterday morning at 8 o'clock, the lucky dog. I would like to go there but would rather go to Regina or somewhere out west. The west is *definitely* my country. Incidentally, we are going to the rifle ranges for a little target work on Thursday. Our rifles are .30 Springfields, the same as Dad's. They weigh about nine pounds and we get a 16-inch bayonet with scabbard with it. I understand our targets are to be two-inch bulls at 30 yards. Should be a cinch, even offhand or should I say especially with those rifles, Dad?

I met a boy in the hospital who had a girlfriend in the East End. Her sister came up with her to see him in the hospital one day and although they couldn't get in, saw me at the window and was interested so asked me out to supper Saturday. They are very nice people, three girls and the mother. The father apparently died some time ago. I never asked. Their name is Tait and if the Boissevain Tait's name was Billie he was Mrs. Tait's uncle. She comes from the West originally anyway. Queer how people meet like that, isn't it? One of the girls and I went to a dance and had a pretty fair time. Then Sunday afternoon a couple of chaps from Long Island, New York, asked me if I wanted to go with them to the home of some people they knew.

The man's name is Frank Secord. He flew with the Royal Flying Corp in the last war with Billy Bishop and had a respectable score to his credit. He manages some theatres now. Has given the boys tickets to some of his shows and I think Jimmy and I are taking his daughter to one tomorrow night. They are a very interesting family, one of the most cultured I ever met and a lot of fun. Mr. Secord served us boys a highball before dinner and it was as smooth as silk but kicked like an army mule. Then we had a swell buffet supper.

Jimmy Allen was in France with the American Ambulance Corp and had quite a time of it. Was captured but escaped. He really wants to get going. Rawlins, the chap from New Orleans, was around to see me about going home with him the other day but of course I couldn't get a 10-day sick leave like he did. He is in pretty bad shape yet with laryngitis. Hasn't got his voice back yet.

However Jimmie wants me to go to New York with him this coming weekend if we can both get passes. It won't cost me anything for fare but am rather afraid of what it will be down there. Would sure like to go but will have to judge from the condition my finances are in. His family has money and he doesn't need to worry about it.

Haven't heard from Bill yet (at Borden) but am going to the post office as soon as I have finished writing this and there should be one there. Expect to hear from Cub in a day or so too. Have 14 on my writing list now.

I got the paper the other day (the Recorder) and it sure was a treat to see it. The papers down here give the news, I guess, but it doesn't seem the same. Dr. Easterbrook certainly deserved his fellowship. Have a good mind to write him and give my congratulations. He was one of the hardest working as well as one of the smartest men there. His wife used to make notes on books she read for him so as to save him time. They certainly did work.

Haven't looked the Kellys up yet but have really been busy. Will look in the telephone book soon and see if they have a phone. 599 Brock is the address if I remember correctly.

Tell Auntie Irene that Rosland and Margaret had asked me if I had seen or talked to Irene Seggic. Sure is a complicated family we have. Will be writing her one of these days.

Have found a good library about half a mile from here, on the grounds; I am going to spend some time there getting my navigation maths into shape. It's no wonder some of these pilots wash out. Was watching one write a letter the other day and he had to form each letter carefully and then go over and repair the job when he had the word finished. I wrote about four pages by the time he had half a page down and then I left. A lot of them were discharged yesterday.

Seeing all the chaps coming and going here makes me wonder just how things will end up. It's beyond me how national economies can stand the strain much longer if wars get as much more expensive as this is compared to the last. It's my opinion that a lot of things are going to crack, and I don't mean nerves.

Thank Mrs. Pugh, Mrs. Lovell and Mrs. Lowler very much again fort the sox. They are swell. Also Mrs. Dow. I got a blue woolen pullover from the Salvation Army Service Centre last night. Am going to give them my overcoat. They should be able to use it.

Well, have time to get to the post office before it closes. So long for now and Love

Clayton.

The following letter is from a member of his mother's Brandon family, the young woman, Pat, who was recently engaged. She sounds like a fine lady.

440 – 13th St.
Brandon, Man.
Sunday night

April 1, 1941

Dear Clayton:

We were certainly very sorry to learn of your succession of illnesses. That's pretty tough, almost like two months' guard duty for an impatient pilot.

I was so surprised to see you in the office, at first I couldn't' figure out whether you were a rookie to be in our station or just what, and knowing I would get razzed about you afterwards (which I did) stood there rather stupidly.

Perhaps you know that Renee was in to see you but couldn't, she was very disappointed, and I hope the next time she gets in you will be suffering from nothing worse than spring fever. Hope you have a radio in your ward. We listened to several good programs today, namely Dr. Stuart's weekly summary of the news, Bishop Wells on war services, Jack Benny and Charlie McCarthy. I thought C. McCarthy was the best with the bishop running a close second.

Tomorrow is pay day. Hurrah. One thing about being in the hospital, Clayton, is that you certainly receive a tidy sum of shekels when you are released, which will be lots of fun spending in Toronto, on Toronto femininity.

Your letter describing No. 1 M.D. was so interesting, Clayton, and I hope your attitude at the time of writing will not change. Manning depots and guard spots are particularly bad, I imagine for dissatisfaction, as they are not dealing with what they want to be , and having no patience some of the men will think nothing but bad of the place.

Bill was sick in the hospital for 10 days with an infected gland which broke internally so they didn't have to cut him. He lost 20 of his nice pounds (wish I could!) though and felt pretty tough in all. Having just received a baking set from a certain flour company, which I delight in using, I sent him in several boxes of things and reading material. Don't be surprised if after my next creative and artistic urge you receive some. They probably won't compare with your mother's, but you must get used to the break sometime.

Your mother and Mrs. Murray and Aunt Verna (Munson) were in two weeks ago and we had a nice visit. I thought Irene Murray was lovely and she told me all about the Department of Agriculture, which was very interesting, so that I am becoming more and more impatient to be in it and active, because this business of sitting 16 hours a day and lying down asleep for eight is believe me dull.

You have probably heard about my ring. It is really a beauty. I am so glad you dropped in that Sunday. We called at your place and you were able to at least meet Bill. There is nothing very definite about the date and as Bill's recent illness will set him back severely it is still more indefinite.

Well Clayton, goodbye for now and best of luck for a quick recovery. Love, Pat.

P.S. Dashed into Wpg while Bill was there, and was at Lee's awhile Sunday afternoon. Doug and his sailor friend were beating out a mean tune on all the different types of wood in the room. Uncle Archie was out of course. It was really funny. I wanted to hear them on the drums, but they assured me that the drums had been tabooed by surrounding tenants at an early date.

CHAPTER 4

Quebec City

No. 4 Manning Depot,
Quebec City,

April 3, 1941

Dear Mom and Dad,

Well, they pulled another of their little tricks on me Tuesday p.m. and I'm in Quebec City. Am going out tonight and am thinking of going to see the Chateau Frontenac. Until we actually got off the train here, we didn't know where we were going, so there wasn't much point in writing you.

This is a much smaller place and there aren't near as many here. There is a terrific barrage of French around us almost continuously. Am going to pick up what I can but don't expect to be here long. But then you never know.

On the way down we saw the wreck at Iuberman. You have probably read about it in the papers by now. The engine had piled right into the station, on its side. The load of army trucks was so much scrap iron. We left Toronto at 9 a.m. and got here about 10:15 p.m. I phoned Rosland twice but couldn't contact him so will have to write.

Our barracks are almost on the point formed in the acute angle where the St. Charles River joins the St. Lawrence. It is not a very choice site as right across the Charles is a junk yard and auto wreckers' establishment. And right here, if nowhere else, the St. Charles is a most unbeautiful sight, to put it mildly.

One advantage is that the living quarters are cleaner, so far. But I don't like anything else about the place as well as Toronto. But we will get some good drill training here anyway. We had a Commanding Officer's inspection at 2 p.m. today. Our Officer Commanding really complimented us on our appearance and made us an epitome for the others to follow. However he needed to as he had given us an awful talk in the a.m. Some of these fellows are pretty sloppy in their appearance.

Well I really must go now. I want to see as much of the city as possible in case we are moved soon. But I'll send a longer one in a day or two and tell you of some of the things I've seen and places I've been. So long for now,

Love,
Clayton.

Also on April 3, 1941, Cousin Kay wrote this letter. Again the news of young men enlisting etc. is at the forefront. Also of interest – the Aussies and Kiwis in Winnipeg.

50 Balmoral Place,
Winnipeg, Man.

Dear Clayton —

I guess this is the first letter I've written to you for years – since you were in rompers and I was using children's note paper with fox and geese for letterhead – and now we are both grownups (?) and out battling in the world. Was so sorry to hear you had such a nasty welcome in Toronto … and certainly hope you are all better now, because it sure would be hell to be locked up in hospital on nice spring days like these. Today is just beautiful, sunny, and warm and so none of the staff in this particular office feel a bit like working, and we're all bumming just now as the boss is out – nice people!!

I imagine you're liking it down there, yes? I've heard that there is so much to do within the barracks, i.e. sports, movies, all the (male) company one could desire etc. etc. that you don't have to go out to enjoy yourself – I heard this from the girl-friend's girl friend of a lad who went down the same time you did. Hope you've seen Renee by now, though with your being sick and her being terribly busy with a special drive of her little pots and jars of pretties, it's quite possible you haven't yet arranged a rendezvous over a mug of suds – to me that's the ideal rendezvous for two Manitobans not long in Ontario.

Haven't seen Mack lately, and the Lees only once, though I saw Uncle Archie in the distance at the Musical Festival on Monday eve, and in spite of my frantic gesticulations to try to attract his attention and wave hello, got no answer. Spoke to him briefly afterwards though. Enjoyed the Festival more than I expected to. The three adjudicators (all nerdy Englishmen) were particularly witty and informal, and there was lots of back-chat among them, and their adjudications were really quite good bits of humour. And to hear the Church choirs make a stab at sight reading was quite fun. The song they gave them was quite a rollicking DRINKING song, and several of them seemed hard put not to burst right out laughing.

Am looking forward to going home for Easter weekend – will you be going anywhere? It would be grand if you got leave and could go to Ottawa [to visit Cousin Emily and the other Bradley family, his mother's people]. What sort of duties do you have?

Perhaps with so many people to write, viz. our family, Mack, 7 – 10 girlfriends (or do I overestimate the number) you won't get around to answering my questions, so don't kill yourself to answer this preamble dear cousin. I'll get my news of you from Mother, who will get it from your Mother, etc. – the good old Bradley grape-vine.

Jack's been in town since March 1st, is a lieutenant in the RCAMC and of course (in my eyes) looks DIVINE in his uniform, not that I tell him that of course. I just confine myself to the remark that his hat looks too big for him and his darned brass buttons scratch me when we're dancing together. It certainly is nice to have him here though and we're having a lot of fun. He has a new musical instrument called a "recorder" with which he is quite enamored, so I accompany him and he plays nice little fluty pieces – that is, when we're over at his house where there's a much-used piano (there were five boys in the Findlay family, and each one just loved to "sit down to the piano"). Jack also has a cello, but has never performed for me to date. We went to a nice formal dance at Ft. Osborne Barracks in the Officers' mess a few Saturday nights ago. I was very excited because I was sporting a new white silk jersey evening dress, and J. bought me a gardenia to wear in my hair – t'was a good thing I felt like dancing with him though because most of the other officers were corpulent old things with not much rhythm and awfully big feet. The

231

orchestra was a military one and played absolutely no swing, but nice old-fashioned numbers like "After the Ball is over," etc. etc. Some fun! You'd have hated the music dear.

Pat's Bill was here in hospital with badly swollen glands for about 10 days and she was in twice during that time, risking her job in Brandon and her chances of a ride back both to some extent – LOVE is a wonderful thing isn't it? And she makes cookies etc. etc. for him. All I've done for J. so far is knit him a scarf for Xmas, but am thinking tentatively of kitting a sweater for him. But have just mastered the pearl stitch, and there is an awful lot of him to cover, so it will probably be next year's Xmas present if I ever start it.

By the way Gerry Old was asking for you – also Jean Duncan – Jean was visiting here last weekend and we saw her briefly Sunday evening, and all drove down to the bus with her. Gerry is in the army, Ordnance Corp, I think, but I'm so vague about units, ranks, etc. you shouldn't quote me on it. He doesn't seem to have many regrets about busting up his course, though, and seems glad to be in uniform.

Hasn't been much doing in Wpg to report of late – except that the Metropolitan store at Portage and Carlton and part of the Steele Block over it burned rather badly a week or so ago. The noon-day services at Holy Trinity Church, with a different speaker every week, have been really packed, and last Friday when we went we couldn't' get a seat – people turned away in droves!! Dr. Westgate figures the secret of their success is their brevity, and says parsons should gather as much and act accordingly. A lot of the people here are entertaining Australian and New Zealander airmen, and seem to like them, though have trouble understanding their very broad accents.

Well dear heart, the second mail has just come, and spring or no spring, DUTY calls your cousin Katie, to see what's in it.

Hope you keep well and have lots of fun, and if you ever get a spare moment drop me a line. I'll always be anxious to hear how you're getting along, and *how well* you're doing, and how many *good* marks you get for deportment, etc., and how *few* times you are "C.B." Love, Kay.

Also on April 3, cheerful Boissevain friend Jeffrey Moore, also in the Air Force, writes from Brandon Manning Depot. He's "rich" with $28.60 in pay, maybe $300 in today's money.

Dear Clayton: --

How are tricks? Are you happy in the service? Well I suppose you "get along" anyhow. Here in Brandon that's just about my attitude. I hope things will be better when I am "drafted" somewhere. I spent six days in the RCAF hospital – tonsillitis. Went back on parade today. My throat is still a little sore. Wish I'd had an operation and got rid of the beastly things!

Jack [his brother] arrived home last Saturday – he was in "town" last night. I had gone to bed early. He arrived at 9:30 p.m. and surprised me very much. I guess I shall see him before he goes back next Saturday.

I heard that you had a little "sojourn" in the hospital too! The week I was in Winnipeg when I enlisted, I stayed at the same boarding house as Russ Stevenson. That made things rather nice. He has changed a lot since entering the Navy – for the better I hope! Incidentally, he boards at 133 Chestnut St. in case you didn't already know [in those days before postal codes that is all the mailing address Clayton needed to write him].

This is a red letter day. After more than three weeks of financial embarrassment (I missed the first pay parades) I have finally reaped my golden reward of $28.60 – what a lovely feeling to be "rich" again! But what will be left when I pay off my debts?

I hope to go home Saturday. I hear that Cub [Brook] missed his "draft" – bet he swore. Here they have a different system, and that would not have happened. They have a "draft roll call" and if you are in the station or they can get in touch with you in any way you will be notified.

I was talking to Mack when I was in Wpg. He talked quite cheerfully of the staggering amount of studying that he faced preceding his exams. What a man! Did you ever try roller skating? I did in Wpg. It really is fun. Met a petite secretary; she works in same office as Verna Musgrove. Went to Wpg Roller Rinks -- nice place. No. of locals in this pool: Jim Noble, Allan Kilmurray, Murray Sexton, Bryant Howell, Frank Jenkins. Makes it nice for me! Write me a note sometime!

Sincerely, Jeffrey
AC2 Moore F.J.
#R95444, RCAF
Manning Depot, Brandon.

A few days later Clayton's father, Dr. Frederick Valentine Bird, 55, born in a log cabin in 1885 on the Red River, sat down and penned the following, a rare letter to his eldest son. He wrote in a beautiful hand in the standard of the day, a fountain pen. At this time he had been mayor for a decade, 1930 to 1940, during the Depression; a councilor for four years prior to that; and now served as a councilor again. He had lost a small fortune through the Farmer's Credit Rearrangement Act, which wrote off the debts he was owed by farmers in the government's effort to save agriculture. He is the area's medical officer, one of only two Boissevain doctors, the Electoral Officer, etc., well on his way to earning the provincial Good Citizenship Award and induction into the Manitoba Agricultural Hall of Fame he would later receive. He has served Boissevain as a physician for 28 years since arriving in 1913 out of medical school in Winnipeg. As chair of the carnival, you can't blame him for being pleased about its success. Boissevain is a little rural town of about 700 people north of Turtle Mountain, 15 miles from the North Dakota border, south of Brandon, in the heart of wheat and cattle country. As the following was written, its hard-working and durable people were just emerging from the dry and dirty days of the Great Depression, its young men eager for the work and wages provided by war.

Boissevain,
April 6, 1941

F.C.C. Bird,
AC2, No. R91897.
#1 Manning Depot,
Toronto.

Dear Son –

It is a long time since I last wrote you; it was much different from what I had planned, long ago. Before our Ice Carnival of March 15 I thought of writing, and then I thought I would leave it until after the Carnival was over, so that I could tell you about it. Well, March 15 started off as a perfect day and continued so until about 5 p.m. when, with a huge crowd in town, there started one of the wildest blizzards we have experienced here for years. I tried in every way possible to arrange that no one should try to leave the town for the country, out in the terrible confusion, [but] some did get away: two outfits came near being lost in the storm; in one case a family of three and in the other, a family of four; in both cases their cars stalled and they started to walk: they hadn't gone far when they were becoming exhausted, and by the greatest of luck, in both cases they stumbled into another car, stalled, and climbed into this. The storm abated about 9:30 or 10 and the community escaped without loss of life. By the time the storm had broken, the afternoon programs of hockey had been played. There was a huge crowd in town, so we decided to go ahead with the evening final game of hockey, but to postpone the rest of the program for one week....

Well, the Carnival eventually materialized on March 22. We sold so many tickets that we stopped because we did not want to exceed the capacity of our rink too much. I wished you could have seen the performances; I was directing it all by microphone from the ticket office. The old rink was a sight: I do not think, in fact am sure, I never saw a rink so beautifully decorated with ensigns, bunting, flags of all shapes and sizes, both British and American, and streamers of coloured lights. It was beautiful and very tasteful. At the west end, about 12 feet inside the big door, and setting with its front just bordered by a large line of colored lamps that ran straight across the rink from north to south, was the very beautifully decorated float about 18 feet long and eight feet wide, as you will see in the pictures we are sending you; it was draped with bunting and had a large union jack for a background; on the front over the canopy were strung colored lamp and rows of tinsel; and upon the platform were robes and rugs and chairs, on a speaker's chair for the Queen.

At 8 p.m. sharp I announced the bugle call which announced the coming of the queen and her retinue: Ralph Clark, as arranged, was standing at the west end door and sounded the flourish. Just as he finished, the big door at the west end opened and in came the brand new cars, the first one with the queen and the Mayor; the next one with the first two ladies in waiting; the next with the second two ladies in waiting; and the next car with the Reeve, the Archbishop, and the little flower girl: they all came in followed by the Scouts in full uniform and the Killarney band of 22 pieces; they circled the rink down by the north side to the east and up by the south; as they were approaching the west end the Scouts broke off and smartly formed two lines of guards of honor, entering from the platform about 10 on each side and six feet apart between their two lines; then the Band marched to the east and counter marched back to stand facing the throne; at this moment, the Queen's car drove up between the Scout's guard of honor and the Band and stopped: a Boy Scout stepped smartly forward and opened the door for the Queen and she stepped out; they all came to a salute; the Queen very sedately passed up between their lines and ascended the throne. She was followed, in their order, one by one, by the ladies in waiting, the flower girl, the Reeve, the Archbishop and the Mayor: all went to their respective seats on the decorated platform and instantly as they were seated, the Band struck up O Canada, and how – their performance at this stage started our Carnival off with a bang that never let up until it was all over – one of the finest nights Boissevain and Community has ever experienced.

After leaving their charges, each car was taken to the west wall where they caused no interference and everybody was able to be present. The Archbishop then proceeded to crown the Queen and in a very good voice that could be heard over most of the packed rink, read the Royal Proclamation; then the little flower girl presented the Queen with a most beautiful bouquet of roses. After this the Mayor presented the Queen with the box, covered in gold paper, containing the tickets sold on the beaver coat presented by Mrs. ... Hanley; the Reeve opened the lid and the Queen reached in and drew the lucky ticket, Mrs. Geo Donald and Love, who immediately put it up for auction sale by Roy Armstrong – right there it sold for $30 and we already had $89 cash from tickets on it.

After this came dress carnival and racing events -- all were really pretty – and entries included the neighboring towns. The rink was packed four deep from each end on both sides, the waiting rooms and upstairs were so packed, no more could get in, and there were 200 out on the ice; and still many were turned away at the door. We were not asking people for their tickets on account of the confusion because of the storm the week the week before, but many insisted on paying, and there were over 200 more tickets sold that night at the wicket. After the crowning, and all during the events, the band kept playing.

At the close, after the Queen and her ladies were presented with their prizes by the Mayor, all the other winners in turn were escorted up to the throne by the Boy Scouts and each winner was presented with his or her prize by the Queen. After it was all over, the decorated platform with the Queen and her ladies started around the entire rink with faces to the crowd; it went all round the rink to the accompaniment of the Band playing the National Anthem. So the big night was over. Everything went through in finest detail and after paying about $100 in expenses we had cleared $421.15 for the Lord Mayor's Fund. We are forwarding you three pictures of it taken by George Dring.

I hope you won't mind such a long write-up about our Carnival: but now for more general bits of news. First of all we are both well again: Mom has always been well but I had the tough luck to develop two carbuncles at one time; one on my right wrist and one in my nose. I am over them both but am feeling a little below par yet; with a reasonable chance I feel I will come up all right within the week. We had Jack Moore in to see us on Friday last: he was looking well and was leaving for Saturday, yesterday, for Toronto. I haven't been out much yet but I saw Rivette [the Metis trapper and fur buyer who wrote to Clayton] yesterday – had to have a hair cut – and he had just finished a course of Measles. The weather has been very backward, snow flurries, cold thawing, mud and slush, and generally poor weather.

We also had Russel Stevenson in for a short visit a few days ago – he is looking real well and I believe is taller. Mom will enclose a few lines in this letter. And maybe I should tell you that Miss Louise Moncur was elected Queen, Miss Hilda Chambers first lady; Miss Ealonas Hall second; Miss Myrtle Handover third, and Joan Gasoner fourth lady. The flower girl was Marion Crowhurst and the Archbishop was Mr. Littler. All performed their parts with distinction.

I am planning to take things as carefully as I can for some time yet: the weather is "rotten" and the roads are terrible. Well son I think I have told you most of the news. I trust you will take the best possible care of your health – another two weeks will probably bring some improvement in the weather [where he is]. The clothes you sent arrived OK. I hope you were not disappointed when your mail was so unfortunately withheld while you were in hospital. In the great rush of preparations and confusions that must follow at times, we must be prepared for occasional disruptions; but come what may, we won't forget, nor become careless: our thoughts are always with you; best of luck.

Dad.

[His mother adds in a note:]

My dear boy –

I see Daddy has written quite a lengthy letter so mine will be brief. Rec'd your nice long letter a few days ago and yesterday the parcel of clothing arrived – Dad tried on the overcoat and it fits him fine – will be just the thing to wear in car – Jack Moore called Friday so no doubt you will be seeing him – I asked him a lot of questions re laundry, food, etc. and he speaks highly of all – Mrs. Maxfield was down to see Les who was in hospital with pneumonia – Les is better but I guess was pretty sick for a time. Don't know if Mack will be home Easter – hope he can make it.

Well old Adolph [sic] is living up to his natural beastly nature, but I think Jugo Slavia [sic] will give him a run and will be strongly backed by a good many – Glad to know you are meeting nice people – it pays to be particular – think you ought to postpone trip to N. York [Gower? Where her family live] – it takes a lot of money and that would be too hurried a trip anyway – Don McDonald will be home in May – is still in Halifax. Love and best wishes, Mom.

The next letter he received was post marked April 9, 1941. Clayton did not open it. I opened it and it was from Wanda, his teacher friend in Laurier, Man. whom he met at Clear Lake – a simple card saying, "Happy Easter to you. May the Easter season bring joy to you in everything. Wanda." She never wrote again that I am aware of. Clayton had Doris Aconley on his mind and would soon act on that front, marrying her in September.

CHAPTER 5

Dartmouth Guard Duty

On April 9 his mother told him of a friend who got work up north with the Hudson's Bay Company, which at that time still traded furs with local trappers.

RCAF Station
Dartmouth, N.S.

My dear boy –
You certainly are moving some. They must be overcrowded in Toronto and had to move some of you. I do hope the weather is fair as it must be terrible drilling in wet and mud – we are having continuous rain here since Sunday – not heavy but enough to keep running into the cistern -- will make seeding late but better than dust storms. Did you get the parcel and pajamas and shoes? And I mailed some papers and snaps of Carnival. Dad stays in bed good part of time, but gets up to B.R. Guess the dampness was too much for his throat. It got sore. Roland Thomas has gone to Wpg – has an outpost job with Hudson Bay. I heard he applied for Air Force but one eye has only 40% vision and was rejected.

Heard the call for 60,000 men for army this a.m. and 2,500 for wireless, also for other branches. I do hope and pray the Slavs will be able to overcome those beasts.....Keep well and dry. Never neglect a cold. Did you get the sox Mrs. Dow sent you? I hope you will be able to go to church

Easter Sunday and take Communion. If you don't want to keep those snaps of carnival send them to Em. Best love, Mom.

On April 15 Clayton's Mother thought he was much too thin. She was probably right.

F.C.C. Bird, R – 91897,
RCAF Station,
Security Guard
Dartmouth, Nova Scotia

My dear boy –

Well, I wonder how long you will be at this address – you certainly are moving some – but glad you like the country – am sure it will be lovely later on at blossom time. It is famous for its fruit. Suppose you are on guard at an airport. That is what I imagine you are doing. Doug Noton had six weeks of it – he was home for Easter and has 75 hours flying in. Daddy and I were pleased to get the snap. But my dear, you are so thin. We were both struck by that and also your cap was too far down on your right ear. Is a bit hay-wire. However, the smile is there and I take it you are happy, so why worry about an ear.

Mack sent a half dozen pictures, the same size as your class picture. They are very good. I shall not send you one as no doubt you do not want to get loaded up with too much stuff – I forget if I told you, your box with clothes arrived. Be sure to tell me if you got Mrs. Dow's sox. They were addressed to Automotive Bldg.

How are the meals and beds? Suppose you are always ready for both – have you any studying? – if so there will be exams.

7 p.m. Nellie and Kathleen Brook came in while I was writing – Cub is in Picton, Ont. but expects to be back in Trenton. They told me that Doris Chandler, a Boissevain girl who used to teach school, is living in Dartmouth. Her address is Mrs. Chas-Baker, Cole Harbour Road [underlined in green pencil]. She told them she is always on the lookout for the boys in case there is anyone she knows – she is a very nice girl. I have never seen her since she was married, but I know she would give you a welcome. They live about a mile from the airport. You might get her through telephone.

Had letters from home yesterday and your Uncle Allen was much better. I think I wrote you since I heard he had a stroke April 6. They have a nurse, a daughter of Howard Bradley's. I must tell you what Nellie said when I showed her your snap: "I can't believe I ever held Clayton on my knee." Only you were in a baby carriage.

Elizabeth Gamble called last night to get her mother who was here playing bridge. She thought the snap was real good – but I still think you are much too thin – do you get lots of milk? Dad [age 56] said to tell you he will write in a few days. He went to the office a week ago Saturday and must have got chilled – developed sore throat so he has been in house all week. His stomach gets upset too [*which may be related to food rather than illness. Dad used to tell me his mother would overcook the wild meat they brought home, so he and his brother and father normally cooked it themselves*]. The weather is clearing up and today it was lovely; we were without sun for over a week and it was dismal!

Well, my dear boy, I must go down and mail this and call at office for mail. Hope you keep well and that you will like whatever you have to do. That makes everything so much easier, even turning out at 2:30 a.m. Hope you have a chance to go home to your friend's. Makes a nice change and be sure to look Mrs. Baker up. Love from

Mom and Dad.

On April 16, Cousin Emily from Ottawa brought him up to date about her badminton exploits and relationship with Norm Fishbourne ("I can't help liking him … I wish he was a couple of inches taller.")

Gatineau Power Co.
140 Wellington St.
Ottawa, Ont.

Dear Clayton:

Please excuse the pencil but this is the only way as I'd better sit at my desk and look busy. If I used the pen and ink I would have to go over to the other desk.

Anyway this is faster and I shan't have any dipping to do.

Sure glad to get your letter. You sure did excel yourself in describing Quebec City. My we laughed. The letter arrived Monday a.m. Of course I had to work so the family opened it as they wanted to hear all the news. So any time you feel like writing an "Extra Special" (with a few spicy words etc.) address it here. I sure enjoyed the way you described the streets in Quebec and the gals. So glad you had such a "rip-snortin' time." It must be nearly 12:30 by now, so will finish later after I've had my repast and walk.

Gee, I just hated to come back this afternoon. It's such a perfect day. I've started to get a tan already. So you like Dartmouth? Clayton, try to look up Ted Davis from Ottawa. I think he is still there. He lives just across from us and is a good head. Don't think I know anybody else just there, but I have some friends who just left for North Sydney, F/O Bob Thomas, his wife. Surprised that you were moved so soon. Bill Smithers is still in Regina. I'll try to drop Rowlie a line and tell him where you are as they will be wondering. They were down over the holiday. My I was disappointed you couldn't' get down as we would have had a good time. Was thinking of you last night. Was over at the Standish.

Tonight is the annual meeting of the Badminton Club. The closing dance is Saturday night, will just keep my fingers crossed. Would love to be going. Club closes on the 22. We won the Journal Trophy 8 to 1. Diana and I lost to Marg Robertson and Betty Snell in three games. Ottawa's just won the one event. Marg and Betty had a damn hard time to win so I didn't mind losing. We had our pictures taken by the Journal photographer and it was in the Journal. There were 18 of us on the team. The cup was filled with champagne and passed around to the players. I was asked to receive the cup from the sports editor of the Journal. The Canoe Club will be opening soon. We have started swimming again at the Chateau, was there Thursday.

Norm Fishbourne and I have had loads of fun this winter challenging each other to the best two games out of three for the beer. The first time we played I won, so down we went to the Chateau for the beer. The next time Norm won so I paid the treat and he took me to the Club for dinner. Last night was the final match. I won the first game 15-7 and Norm won the next two (boy, it sure was hot on the courts) so there I was again stuck for the beer. We went over to the Standish and sat upstairs overlooking the floor. Norm ordered and I put my dollar on the table but he insisted (he just called me now to see how I was feeling, the old dear, damn it I can't help liking him) on paying. Norm said I could treat him on pay days; he was paid yesterday. We didn't leave there until 1 o'clock. He was very interested to hear about your being in the Air Force. Told him I was just writing to you. We each had two quarts of beer. We always have so much fun together; I wish he was a couple of inches taller. Oh oh, I have to go and take a letter.

Am all through now, except my mail but will do that later.

How about sending me a snap taken in your uniform? Would love to have one. Do you need anymore socks (hand knitted) and how are you off for sweaters? If you want a sleeveless sweater I will knit you one. They are always comfortable under your coat. You will need one for the fall. I made Bill one. Just tell me the size and you shall have it. If there is anything else you would like let me know.

I wrote Rene yesterday and sent your new address to her. Clarke Bradley spent Good Friday with us. Rowlie drove Mom, Dad, and May up to Uncle Allan's. Did you know he had a stroke about 10 days ago, but is getting along nicely. They have a trained nurse with him all the time. Clarke [her cousin on the farm and in RCMP] has asked not to be moved for the summer in case anything happens to his Dad or Mother. You remember Uncle Jim, Dad's brother, who took you and your Dad fishing? Well, he passed away a week ago last Sunday. He had the flu in the winter and never really recovered. Took very ill and was taken to hospital and pneumonia set in. He was Dad's youngest brother. Dad is keeping very well and is getting out in the garden now. He has quite a tan. Mom and May are fine and so is the rest of the gang.

My friend Mr. Sanderson from Northern has just been in for his orders. He gave me an Easter bunny and a two-pound box of Laura's [chocolates] for giving him so many orders.

It is just about time to call it a day. Don't feel so hot, either. That Prairie Sunshine doesn't agree with me. And I smoked a lot. Laughed at Norm. He decided he would go all to ---- [her dashes] so he bought a large package of cigarettes and we smoked nearly all of them. He gave me some for today. How about another newsy letter from my big, dark, brown-eyed, handsome-looking air-minded cousin from the West? Better get the complexion on as it is fine to fine [?].

Love and best of luck,

Emily

[Written in pen across the folded paper] Hi! Just waiting for Elizabeth Lloyd to call for me to go up to the Club. Just finished doing my nails. Your Mother sent us a lovely photo of Mack. He looks so much like your Dad, specially around the eyes. Want to mail this tonight.

"Me."

Clayton's father shares his thoughts about fishing, politics and tulips.

Brad Bird

Boissevain, Man.
April 20, 1941

F.C.C. Bird
R-91897
RCAF Station
(Security Guard)
Dartmouth, N.S.

Dear Son –

It's a long way from here to where they have now moved you; but, as you said, it's a great country. We hope you will get an occasional opportunity to try conclusions with those different kinds of trout: I suppose they will allow their airmen to take privilege with fishing: at least I sincerely trust they will: you will most likely be able to get that chap whose home is down there to try to get you some fishing. The snow is all gone here – has been for about three weeks, but the weather has been rather cool and mostly cloudy. The geese are here, but, that is as far as most of us dare go. Today it is clear but the thermometer hovers around 32 [F zero C].

Jack Murray is having a rather poor time of it for the past two months – fell on the ice at a hockey game and hurt his lower back – he has been more or less disabled since – has had X-ray but there does not seem to be anything wrong: so I guess it is a matter of time and care: he has suffered plenty: I think he is coming along better now, and I believe that he is going to Winnipeg on Wednesday to be examined by the Air Force to see what they can do about his back as they want him in the force. Mom just told me now that Jack just left today with Robbins for Winnipeg. I am afraid that he cannot possibly be put in shape before another two months. You will be pleased to know that Jimmy [scribble] Greyons [?] has at last got his call for the Air Force, but we don't know just now where he is to go: I suppose a safe bet would be "somewhere in Canada." Oh well, the main thing is that he has received his call, for goodness knows he waited long enough, and spent much money on going back and forth. Several others have joined the Army; but I don't think you would know them: Chuck Anderson and Alex Gladeu are two you might know.

The elections are drawing to a close and in this constituency the coalition took politics out of politics, and there was no contest. In my opinion it was real smart; so smart, no time was given for any thought on action in reference to coalition. However, although it was quiet here, it was apparently pretty hot in other constituencies.

Although the weather has been quite cool, my tulips have been coming up in great bunches and some peonies are well up. I hope to do some gardening, in the way of general cleanup, this weekend, and perhaps to sow some garden peas, onions and cress. Things are rather quiet in the little old town, but I think it is the lull before the rush of seeding, which will likely be in full swing next week. Then there will be the gardening and general cleanup and perhaps some *fishing.*—here's hoping, anyway.

How are you keeping? I hope your health remains good and that you gain about 15 or 20 pounds. Take good care of yourself at any rate. Write to Mom when you write and I'll be writing you more frequently also. With all the new airfields being completed in Manitoba and opened up in May and June I would not be surprised to see you moved back to the West before long. Here's hoping.
Your Dad.

My dear boy —
Daddy and I have been studying the map a bit, to brush up our knowledge of the geography of Eastern Canada – you certainly do not seem to be very far from the Atlantic. Hope you are keeping fit and like the work. Be sure and tell me if you are having lectures or what you are doing in the study line. Haven't heard from Mack this week so presume he is hard at it, as he has exams on 26th. Well my dear there is so little to write about. Just now Irene Murray called – said Jack had gone to Wpg with Mr. Robbins – left at 1 p.m. Had a letter from Air Force asking him to go in and have a checkup. It will be much more satisfactory for them to see him, otherwise they might not give him a chance. Jimmy McGregor got his call at last – Frank Moore is at Rivers and has been made a signaler – Bud Graham is in Vancouver and Doug Noton goes to Carberry. There are planes go over here quite often, only one at a time.

Had a letter from Em saying Allan is much better. Can move his leg and arm and talks to them. I wrote Grace last week. Clarke [RCMP guy] gets up from Rockliffe quite often to see them. Hope he is not transferred to Regina until his Dad is better.

Well my dear, I have to write Mack, so will close now. Mrs. Brook said Cub had sent them a very fine photo, had it taken in Toronto. I would like to see you with some more flesh on your bones before you get a large one taken – but we have the little snap and the ones Mack sent on the Radio, where we can see them all the time.

Best love, Mom

April 20, 1941

RCAF Station,
Dartmouth, Nova Scotia

Dear Mom and Dad,

Yes mom, I got the PJs etc. in Quebec and the papers and photos here the other day. Also received Mrs. Dow's sox and they are A-1. It certainly is nice having plenty of sox. It means I can change often without worrying about washing too often.

The snaps were pretty good all right. Helen Cliffe looked especially good as John Bull. I'd like to have been there for it even though the weather was kind of miserable.

I know Roland Thomas has applied to the Air Force (and the RCMP) but couldn't make either because of his eye. He was lucky to get the HBC job though there's a lot of mud to wade through for a while I guess.

I'm very sorry Mom but Easter a.m. I got off duty at 6:30 which means getting to bed about 8 so I hardly felt like getting up to go to church. To tell the truth I was asleep. This job is hard on me as we go out at all hours of the night or day and never know more than 24 hours ahead what hours we will have. Consequently it means we are eating and sleeping at all hours and to sum it all up, I don't think I will put on much weight on this job. But don't worry about me looking thin. I weigh just the same as when I signed up in Winnipeg.

Thanks so much for the Easter card Mom. I'm awfully sorry not to have remembered but really in Quebec there was absolutely nothing to remind one that it was Easter. And we were so busy getting into the run of things here Easter weekend that we all forgot. And on this job Sunday is just another day on which we have to work. I was on 10:30 to 2:30 last night and slept in this a.m. as usual. This week though I am going on a special shift from 5 to 12:30 in the evenings. It will last the week. I don't know whether or not I'm going to like it.

Please get Doug Noton's address and regimental number from his mother as I would like to write him. I know my cap was away down on my ear in that snap but it was just one of those cheap little prints where they do them while you wait. I'll go into Halifax soon and get some real ones taken, maybe tomorrow.

Incidentally I intended sending $20 home last pay day, had it saved up, but they only gave us $5. They are full of little tricks like that. Then there is a $5 cheque following me, or supposed to be, from Toronto. Will go into Records and have $15 sent to you each month. We have had so much trouble with the different offices because of moving so much, both in Toronto and after we left, that I haven't wanted to bother them. But now I'll get it done and you should get $15 shortly after the end of the month.

Am glad my overcoat fitted Dad. That is something he needs in the little Ford. I had intended giving it to the Salvation Army in Toronto but was C.B. because of being on draft for Quebec.

As I have said, we are always ready for bed, and meals too. I had six meals in 24 hours one day, three of them while it was pitch dark. Have started brushing up on my maths and am going to get a buzzer if I can find the dough and get my Morse Code into shape.

Doris Chandler must have just got married a short while ago as I can swear I saw her in Brandon last fall, or was that Lucille. I'll try to look her up sometime soon. Don't forget to get Don MacDonald's address, number etc. for me.

Bill Kuzenko and Jack Moore may be down here now, or they may be on their way overseas. Find out from the Moore's if you can, as it would be all right to see them here before they went over.

If I was to write every Sunday I can get my letter on the TCA at 3 p.m. Could you get your answer back by Saturday? I'm afraid that the Boissevain-Winnipeg train ride will prevent it but we can try it anyway.

It is quite foggy here today and raining a little. The fog horns and bells are booming away. But it is quite warm and I haven't worn my great coat for some time now (in the daytime) although we really have to bundle up to go on at night, and some of the posts in daytime too. However I have started looking at the fishing tackle displays and am going to try the trout some morning early. Will only be able to get some line and a few hooks but hope to have some fun.

I am afraid this was kind of disjointed but there were so many things to say. I can't think of anything else right now so will sign off.

All my love,

Clayton.

Boissevain,
April 24, 1941

My dear Clayton – *[the first time his mother so addressed him; she is growing aware he is no longer a boy but a man of 22, what with carrying weapons and all. Middleton's death notice surely affected her too.]*

Daddy and I were glad to get your letter – They all seem to think the guard duty is the worst part of the training, but I suppose it may be necessary. I went down to Moore's today. Frank is in Rivers and has been home for a few hours, a few days ago. He told them he was doing guard duty too and that they carried arms – that was what moved me a bit, as at the beginning, in Brandon, they had nothing but their fists. Suppose they didn't have the equipment. Doug Noton just moved to Carberry today. Don McDonald expects to be home in May for holidays – he is a 'writer' – I saw a picture of Bob Moore, he looks well but very sober. He is in Wiltshire and working very hard on the wireless. Haven't heard anything of Bill Garton for some time. Saw in the Free Press today that Doug Middleton is listed amongst the dead. He is Olwyn's husband and poor little Wendy's Dad.

Jack Murray went to Wpg Sunday – the Air Force sent him to a Dr. Gibson who has him go in every day for X-ray and electric treatments – for last week or so he had a pain behind his ear – this turns out to be an abscess behind an eye. They told him if he hadn't gone in he might have lost the sight – also told him he would not be fit for duty under six months and perhaps a year. He will feel it terribly as he really has no prospects here and very little companionship. Eddy and Margaret are to be married at last in June and to live with Eddy's Dad and Mother. Don't worry about not getting to church Easter – I just wondered if you were able to make it. That would be Lucile Chandler you saw last summer as Doris has been married three or four years and has not been home since. Irene has just come in – is going in to Wpg tomorrow to be with Jack.

Must close now. Take care of yourself. Best love, Mom

She enclosed a note with the following:
LAC Moore, John T.
R 95106 RCAF
No. 1 Manning Depot Debert, N.S. 65 miles from Halifax

D.J. McDonald, V 16239 Lodge Camp,
RCN Barracks, Halifax.

G. D. Noton, R80094,
SFTS Carberry, Man.

Cousin Katie wrote from Winnipeg. Again, military news is central, if only about a young man in uniform.

From 50 Balmoral Place
But really from the office, again.
Friday, April 25, 1941

Dear Flighty Cousin of mine –

I was certainly pleasantly surprised to receive so FAST your nice, long, chatty letter – as I mentioned in mine, I thought your eight to 10 (or has it jumped to 15 since you met les Jeunes filles belles in Quebec) other correspondents would so occupy your spare moments that your cousin Katie would have to wait until perhaps next Xmas for some direct message from you – anyway here I am answering right away quick to keep the old ball rolling – I wonder which of us will get tired first?

I'm so glad you like your present place, or possibly the big moguls of the RCAF have by now moved you again from your nice view of the sea & your liberal rations at Halifax? You're certainly seeing the country anyway, and for one of your wandering feet and adventurous turn of mind I imagine it's just what you like, and incidentally of course you have the nice comfy feeling of doing your duty too. I'm afraid, dear, I have to admit to disobedience of your strict order not to show that picture of you with your hat hanging on one ear – so I showed it to almost everyone I know and Gerry Old, Jack, Pat, etc. all think it *very* funny, "Cute" (that from Pat) etc. etc. ad lib – so you don't find guard duty dull? I always feel sorry for guards walking back and forth, back and forth, for such a long time, and having to be on their dignity all the time, and not having anyone to talk to – and I don't suppose anything ever *does* happen to need guarding, does it? Or maybe in my girlish innocence I'm not up on 5th column activities in the Maritimes – anyway I hope you see the enemy before they see you, dear, and you being so good with a gun it would be your "coup," to use a little French word. How did you get along with your Brandon College and Boissevain High School French in Quebec? Patsy and I found ours almost useless when we were motoring thru' that country several years back, and had to go around behind the counter ourselves to get the groceries we wanted – the word for "strawberry jam" for instance was never in our grammars in school, nor was ice cream, two VERY necessary items in one's life.

I went home on Good Friday evening and stayed till Monday eve which was really a grand holiday to have. Jack came on Saturday by bus from Wpg and stayed till Monday, when he caught the 3:30 train for Souris where he had to go with Maris Garton (Dist. Recruiting Officer) to inspect men for the King's ranks. When seeing Jack off I bumped into Maris and we had a little chat – he'd been home for the weekend, but said he hadn't seen your Pop at all as he'd been home sick with those carbuncles. I guess he's better now though. Pat was terribly disappointed that Bill couldn't get up for the Easter week. And as the four of us had planned to raise a little mild fun, and we'd promised the boys breakfast in bed, and also had little sneaking notions about putting Easter eggs under their pillows, etc. so it put a damper on everything when B. didn't come. But the roads around Morden were absolutely washed out – that whole country was under water, etc. but is OK now. B. went to Brandon last weekend and he and Pat are both coming here tomorrow – joy oh joy and tonight one of the girls in our gang is celebrating her birthday, so it doesn't look as though I'll want anything more than sleep on Sunday and all next week.

It was my birthday last Friday and I had a good time in general. The night Before Jack and Gerry Old and I went to a good concert (mostly music, but all very good) at the Dominion Theatre, and we went back to J's and made quantities of cinnamon toast (my specialty) and had tea. Gerry was being moved to Portage the next day and hopes after three training here for months to be sent overseas. He and Dunc were at our house for Easter Sunday lunch (ye Swift's ham with pineapple, etc.). We warned Mum that Doug was a dietician, so she'd better be on her toes, so she was – and Pat had clipped a bit from a Swift's advert in the paper re the proper way to carve a ham, with a diagram, with ABC joints etc etc. so it was all done with due decorum. Hope you went to church on Easter Sunday? I went with Mum to the 7:30 (see my wings? Mostly on account of I couldn't sleep) and then we came home and Patty had painted all our breakfast eggs beautiful shades of pink, green and fuchsia, and they still tasted all right!

It was a nice sunny day that day too. Pop's garden though under glass is coming along, and the fertilizer he's addicted to just now sends a lovely

(?) perfume right through the basement – still everyone has their hobbies. The latest news from Renee is getting along well with her job, tho' it leaves her quite tired at times. She is still going with her Flying Officer, and it almost sounds at times as if she really likes him – ROMANCE is really blossoming in the Heywood family, at least. Guess for a while Pop [Rev. Percy Heywood who would marry his nephew Clayton and Doris] wondered when and if he were ever going to get rid of his three "graces." Renee sent me a pretty sweater and a little ornament for my birthday and Easter, respectively, and J sent me a lovely flowering plant, knowing how I love plants. My wandering Jew isn't doing so well lately, and the bugs have really set in in earnest to make it their citadel – guess I'll have to hang up the white flag. Wildwood Club is just now canvassing for tennis members, and as I'm a member of the membership committee. I'm having to badger my best friends and all my acquaintances to join and have fun at Wildwood. If you were here I'd work on you, too, and must get in touch with Mac. I guess he's still studying pretty hard, anyway I haven't heard a peep out of him for ages.

Thanks so much for your advice re paying Jackie (dear boy) lots (judiciously spread out though as you warned) of attention. I guess I'm just not built that way tho Clayton – i.e. re gushing about how nice he looks in his uniform, etc. I didn't realize how big a uniform goes over with some people until J and I were downtown in Brandon on Saturday night, and everyone, tho mostly females, darn them, gushed and oohed and ahed over how nice he looked – he does look nice of course, but I think he'd look OK in sackcloth and ashes, so never bothered to tell him I thought he looked WONDERFUL etc. Guess my technique is definitely not good tho. Will see what I can do to improve it, and try it out on you next time we see each other. Well, dear, figured I've rattled along long enough for one session so goodbye, and take care of yourself.

[*Unsigned, no name, but from Katie*]

251

CHAPTER 6

Victoriaville

Boissevain, Man.
April 30, 1941

My dear boy –

Am anxious to see your pictures and am glad you had them taken. Yes, I missed the last page of that letter and figured you had left it out. Have you located Don McD. Yet or Jack Moore: Just now Daddy has Keith Henderson out in kitchen putting him through an examination for RCMP. Russell S. is home on a week's vacation. Had a letter from Mack asking me to send your suit in so am going to see if Russ can take it. He is going back Friday. And where do you think your brown light-weight coat is? On its way to England. There was a call for clothing for bombed areas and mention was made that men's clothing was, as a rule, scarcer than women's or children's so I gave your coat. The IODE [International Order Daughters of the Empire] were collecting and were very glad to get it. I hope your ankle is better. It is miserable to have anything wrong with your feet. Why is the Air Force not popular there? If they behave they should be. Or perhaps they object to the planes roaring over their homes – have heard of some cranks doing that.

If you write every Sunday, I will answer day I receive it, so there will be no crossing. The Chalmers were in town last week. Mrs. C. told me Alf is in Ottawa in the electrical department of Air Force and Nick is joining up...Eileen Muir called to see us Saturday. She is teaching on permit near

Wawanesa and is going to Normal next fall. Allen is doing well, nurse has left, what a responsibility for those girls. Poor Clayton had a bad attack of jaundice – was just up and around when his Dad took sick. Well my dear news is very scarce. Will go over and mail this. Am out of stamps so can only put on three. Dad is feeling much better. Goes out round the yard but expects to be back on duty next week. Stomach flu was his latest and it knocked him out, as he couldn't eat regular meals. Is handling a bit of 'Scotch' every day – seems to stimulate him.

Best love from Mom.

May 4, 1941

My dear Clayton –

Rec'd your letter yesterday (Saturday) and will write some today. Have started house cleaning, so had better write while I can. Daddy being laid up has made me very late with things of that nature. He will be back at office tomorrow. The weather is grand but quite warm. We have had such lovely warm rains. The growth is just forging ahead – I believe the tulips will be in bloom in another three or four weeks. I am planning to hold a "Tulip Tea" under auspices of IODE May 31st, last Saturday of this month, and sell tulips – am sure we would make a nice lot of money.

We have been having asparagus for supper every day for a week. Wish I could send you some. So you feel like eating and sleeping – well that is quite natural, I should think – you are outdoors, I should think, most of the time, and with a change of climate it does make one drowsy. You do not sound very enthusiastic about the job or country. How would you like to be in Egypt, fighting in the desert. It must be fierce. Well, you have not much longer at the guard job and will likely soon be moved to a training camp – hope you are sent west as you certainly do not seem to like the East. Only my boy, I hope you do not get in the habit of grousing – it is like a disease and can grow on one – You are being disciplined (in case you don't know it) and no doubt records are kept and every grousy word will be chalked against you, and in the long run does not get you anywhere. You boys are lucky to be getting your training now instead of a year ago. The strides made in inventions etc. are tremendous and you will have the advantage of learning the mechanisms etc. of the latest types. You no doubt are missing the social life you had here in the West, but remember you have a big job ahead of you and a lot of study and concentration – so better just be content with doing your bit and doing it well. You are young and you have a great opportunity to make good, so make the most of it, my boy, while you can. And please do not write Jack too much of the dark side of the picture. None of the boys likes guard duty and after all it is only a small part. He is in Wpg yet but will be home soon. You must tell me when you need more sox – I can always get someone to knit them and I can buy the yarn here in town.

Monday

Has been raining almost all day – everything looks so green and is growing so – only the farmers can't get crop in. While I think of it, Doris Chandler's name is Mrs. Charles Baker. Be sure and look her up. I told her mother I had sent her address and she will be expecting you. Well, my dear, will close now. Dad will be going over for mail, and I will send this. Mack wrote his last exams Saturday so we may get a letter today. Russel said Mack was talking of joining Navy. Hope he waits another year. Best love and wishes, Mom.

On May 8 Ricky from Brandon College wrote again, with news of graduation and her career goal. She clearly has a shine for him, like some others.

RCAF Station
Dartmouth, N.S.

Dear Bird,

Your swell letter came while I was home for Easter holidays and was I ever delighted to get it. Of course you'd never know by the time I answer letters. Holidays were rather lonesome things, nothing going on, no friends dropping in – if anyone did come it would be for Mildred, the girl who works in the house. Isn't it funny how you lose contact with people?

Last night Ellen McFarland, new girl in Grade XII and I saw Mrs. Darrach go off dressed in her formal glad-rags so....Well anyway it was a good show – pure comedy, in fact sometimes Ellen and I were still laughing after the more sober people had quieted down.

There are only five of us left in residence, that is students, but this place is being turned into a shelter for old-maid teachers. We have six of them underfoot; probably next year there will be twice as many teachers as girls. By the way I don't think I'll be going teaching. I'm hoping to enter St. Boniface Hospital this fall or next March. I've made up my mind that I wouldn't like teaching impudent little brats. Are you surprised?

As I write this I'm wondering if you're still at Dartmouth. You certainly get around. Gee, did I ever laugh about your remarks about the girls in Quebec. Here's hoping you like Dartmouth and that the people are friendly. I bet you look nifty, I mean swell in your uniform.

The grads have been having their annual round of parties. I guess their marks will soon be out. Poor Paul doesn't think he made it. He and Paddy left right after he finished his exams for Weyburn. He did not attend any of the parties but they'll be having a much better time together. We expect them back today; they were coming last week but Doug has had the flu. He looked very thin and sick before leaving. I wonder if the two of them will ever enjoy perfect health. Paddy hasn't been able to go across the line [U.S. border] as yet but I understand her Dad is going to try again – if he hadn't been so stubborn she would have been over long ago.

The COTC boys left Saturday morn at 4 o'clock for Shilo. Wasn't that a horrible hour? It was a rainy, windy, ugly black night but they didn't seem to mind and marched off singing – their commands had awakened myself and other girls so we watched them. Gosh it gave me a funny feeling. On Sunday some of them came in for church because the grads were taking the service – Knip preached, Downing read the scripture, Bliss was in there too. Oh, were the kids ever sunburnt!

May 10.

The grads got their marks today. All the girls are thru', and Bliss , but Mooney, Pulf and Wesley didn't make it. Isn't that a pity! I feel sorry for them. Wesley went down in chemistry, the other boys in their bug-bear French.

It's only 6:45 and I'm here alone but I wanted to complete this and I have also to write home. Don't forget I look forward to your letters. Best of luck.

As ever, Ricky.

P.S. Where is Rosie and what is he doing?

Boissevain,
May 11, 1941

My dear boy –

Thanks a thousand times for the lovely message which I received Saturday morning as we were at breakfast. Mother's Day never meant so much to me as it did this year with our two boys away and one so far – Mack sent a very lovely card with such a nice verse and I do appreciate it very much from you both – I was sorry I did not get to church this a.m. but we had an unexpected visitor Saturday about 10 p.m. when Pat Heywood walked in [Percy's daughter, her niece, Clayton's cousin] – had come over with the Littler boys. She stayed overnight and today took the noon bus to Morden to visit Bill. She has tomorrow (Arbor Day) off so that she would go to see him. Did not seem very definite about the wedding day. He was in hospital two weeks – had an operation on his neck. Houses are very scarce in Morden and I expect they haven't a great deal of cash ahead to buy furniture and all the necessaries it takes to start housekeeping – Pat is looking very well and seems to be very happy. Yes, I know what good letters Kay can write as she and I corresponded when I was sick and I always got a great kick out of her letters. Irene hasn't been very well, had to go to hospital for a while but is better. Her job was held for her and she got two weeks' pay. Pat said she wrote you and sent a Reader's Digest while you were in hospital in Toronto. You have a very long list of correspondents but it sure is nice to get letters if one has time to answer them.

Am having Helen Corkish come tomorrow to wash and help with house cleaning – will likely be here all week. Expect to have the Tulip Tea about 31st if tulips are ready. They are earlier this year and I think there will be a great showing. Hope it is a nice day and that we have a good crowd.

I started knitting a scarf for you, so will likely have it ready by the time you have learned to fly – I can't knit too long at a time so it takes me longer than most. Dad and I drove out to Peace Garden after supper tonight – saw about a dozen deer and dozens of rabbits. They say Whitewater Lake has lots of water in it. Jimmy McGregor called to see us Friday. Left for Wpg Saturday and is going to Penhold, Alberta. He switched to radio but hopes one day to take up flying. Said he heard they were going to have an airport at Whitewater, but I doubt it [they never did]. Well, my dear, guess I will ring off and mail this. Hope to soon get your photos.

Best love from us both. Mom.

Boissevain,
May 16, 1941

My dear boy –

Rec'd pictures Wednesday and was indeed glad to get them – we think they are real good and are very pleased to see the improvement in your appearance. You certainly must have put on some weight, as your face looks much fuller than in the snap. Did you keep any to send away and is there anyone in particular you want me to send one to? I'm sending two East and took one to Ninette to Mack – he went there Sunday and expects to be there about two weeks.

Love Mom.

Hometown friend Frank Moore wrote from Rivers, Man.

May 22, 1941

Air Navigation School,
Rivers, Manitoba

Dear Clayton:

Very pleased to receive your letter two days ago. So you have had rather a rough ride since joining the marvelous RCAF. I, too, have had some fun. The past six weeks we have been "on guard" at Rivers – you know, that God-forsaken spot 27 miles from nowhere! Oh well, it isn't too bad, every fifth day is 24 hours off duty – leave station if one wishes. Since being here I have had two 60-hour passes, and I lit out for St. James. I know a cute little secretary there. Is she swell? I couldn't go back to Boissevain or civilian life under any conditions! Having too much fun in Air Force.

Expect to get drafted to Regina and I.T.S. (Initial Training School) any day – hope so anyhow! Rather dubious about making the grade as pilot but will I sure try hard??

We get quite a bit of drill and PT in day time here – a curse thinks I. But also get Morse code classes which I like – am getting on to code quite well. Our 45 men in guard are divided into five groups of nine each. It so happens that all the fellows in our group (B) are real good chaps – no hunkies, etc. That sure makes it nice. There is a fellow in the guard, "Adams" from a farm near Newdale or Minnedosa, who took one year at Brandon College, same time as you. He asked me if I knew you – foolish question! Do you recall him? (Tall, dark, thin, slow).

Guess your Dad has had a rather poor time in recent weeks, was very sorry to hear this, but I heard he's out and about now. So the gals down Quebec way are all right. They are all right in the vicinity of Brandon and Winnipeg too. Even Rivers can boast of a few neat numbers -- so I am told. Ann is history, but even so, she is still a very lovely red-head. It is said that Regina is simply paluted [sic] with swell numbers (authoritative report). Knew a red-head from there last summer – looking forward to seeing that fair city.

(On guard at wireless station, 5 p.m. to 8 a.m. consecutively, that accounts for the windiness of my letter – do you grasp my meaning?)

Guess Doug Noton is getting along fine in the service. Near to getting his wings. Allan Kilmury is out here with me. John Gardner will be called up for service next July. Have you heard from Albert Brooks lately – never heard about him for a long time. Robert Moore is now stationed with RAF in Devonshire, passed his examinations OK. He says the town where he is staying is lousy with beautiful girls. And I am stationed at navigation school in Rivers – unhappy fate!

So long for now. Hoping you have all the luck that goes. May run across you some time. If you can afford the stamp, write again.

Happy in the service, Frank Moore.

Then he got another letter from Cousin Emily, who stealthily writes from work despite the ever-present threat of discovery by her boss, Mr. Howard. She even includes some cute jokes.

Gatineau Power Company, Ottawa
May 27, 1941

Dear Clayton:

So sorry I can't brag about the weather today but we have been having beautiful weather of late. The weekend wasn't so hot. It is dismal and cold today so I can sympathize with you. There is nothing that gets me down so as having nice warm weather during the week when you have to work and then the weekends are miserable. Oh well, so much for the balmy weather.

I've had so many interruptions since I started this letter, phone calls etc. and Gwen reading jokes to me out of the Readers Digest. Mr. Howard is out of town today, hence the loafing, but I've plenty to do. About twenty requisitions have just come in and I really should type out the orders but they can wait.

Enjoyed your letter and sorry to hear that you are having such a hard time meeting people in Dartmouth. You mentioned that you may be transferred to Victoriaville, Que. It is in the Eastern Townships and is quite a hkie (that word is for you to unscramble, just got my fingers mixed up) to Montreal, let alone coming to Ottawa, but there is nothing like trying.

Clayton the reason why I asked you to send your letters to the office is because, well, just in case you happened to mention anything about liquor etc., I wouldn't want mom to know. Do you get me? She may take it as a joke and she may not. We have you and Mac sitting beside each other in the living room. Your mom sent us the photo last week and we sure were pleased to get it. I think it is very good but mom thinks your cap is too big, so I had to explain, that they were made larger in case the airman's head swelled, oh, oh, is that a nice thing for me to say? Just a wee joke or is it? Thanks just the same and I hope to get a few snaps of you and your gang someday.

Have just finished knitting a pair of army socks for one of the boys and started a pair of white socks for myself. Brought my lunch today so will be staying in to knit on a helmet for the navy. Can't neglect my knitting for the I.O.D.E. [International Order of the Daughters of the Empire].We (our chapter) are all knitting for the navy.

[The following is written in pencil]

- ! - We just can't depend on Mr. Howard. The old so and so came in this aft at 2 o'clock so I had to get busy. Luckily I had started to type the orders. Just heard this – why was the flower mad at the bee? Well, you would be too if somebody took your honey and necked it.

(2) What did one burp say to the other burp? Let's sneak out the back way.

(3) No, I can't tell that one.

(4) Why did the moth eat the hole in the rug? Because he wanted to see the floor show.

Clayton, you have never said what you are taking up or perhaps you can't tell. We've been wondering. Feel as though I haven't told you much news. May is feeling OK again and Dad and Mom are fine.

The Red Cross has been calling for blood donors so I went up for the test and passed so am waiting to be called. Les Lloyd is working in the Munitions Supply Board, so we can never count on her doing anything. She won't have time to play tennis as she has been doing a lot of night work and also working Saturday afternoons.

I haven't been near the Canoe Club this summer. Will not be playing tennis as my back has been bothering me. Am going to start taking treatments.

Guess you wondered why I deserted the typewriter but this is quicker and handier when Mr. Howard is in [her hand-written letter]. Can shove it under something. Am enclosing a pen holder Clayton that was given to me. Thought it may fit your fountain pen; if not give it to somebody else.

Perhaps you will be stationed somewhere else by the time you get this note.

There's a plane flying over. Do they ever fly low. Lillian's husband in Regina taking a navigator's course but is also learning to fly. Has been at the controls several times.

Write soon my tall, dark, cute cousin from the West. There are more gals arriving in Ottawa every day. Competition is dreadful.

Hope you will be up in this end of the country soon as it is a good place.

Love, Emily.

May 28, 1941
Boissevain.

Victoriaville, Que.

My dear Clayton –

Please excuse pencil but am writing in bed, and as my fountain pen requires to be dipped I frequently find pencil easier [this was before ball-point pens were available]. As to why I am in bed – nothing more interesting than an attack of Sciatica. You are too young to know you have a Sciatic nerve, but believe me, we older ones know when a pain hits it. You can imagine about six teeth aching from your hip to your big toe and you have it fairly accurately. However, I have an electric pad in bed with me and with Alice Corkish downstairs to run things, guess I shall be up and around some day. Daddy has been so very busy I just couldn't ask him to take time to write you boys, and I didn't feel up to it before. He had a bad case yesterday – two cars collided on Ninga Road. He has three patients at King's now, no fatalities. You will see accident in Recorder.

Will not send papers till I get your new address. Am taking a chance and sending this to Victoriaville. Did you know Cub and Rosie are there…. Did you see or hear anything of Jack Moore? Is nearly a month since they heard from him and are very anxious.

Isn't that grand that the Bismarck was caught? [Wikipedia reports that Bismarck, pride of the German Navy, only took part in one operation during her brief career. She and the heavy cruiser Prinz Eugen left Gotenhafen (Gdynia) on the morning of 19 May, 1941 for Operation

Rheinübung, during which she was to have attempted to intercept and destroy convoys in transit between North America and Great Britain. When Bismarck and Prinz Eugen attempted to break out into the Atlantic, the two ships were discovered by the Royal Navy and brought to battle in the Denmark Strait. During the short engagement, the British battlecruiser HMS Hood, flagship of the Home Fleet and pride of the Royal Navy, was sunk after several minutes of firing. In response, British Prime Minister Winston Churchill issued the order to "Sink the Bismarck",[2] spurring a relentless pursuit by the Royal Navy. Two days later, with Bismarck almost in reach of safer waters, Fleet Air Arm aircraft launched from the carrier HMS Ark Royal torpedoed the ship and jammed her rudder, allowing heavy British units to catch up with her. In the ensuing battle on the morning of 27 May, 1941, Bismarck was heavily attacked for nearly three hours before sinking.] Ross Henderson was called to military training and has decided to join Air Force (if he isn't too late). Yes, I think that is best thing for Mack to do. Be sure and tell me who you are sending photos to as I do not want to duplicate. I have just sent one each to Lill and Em and Mac and ourselves so may send one to Auntie Hattie. Les Maxfield is home but leaving for Flin Flon where he has a job. Fred is going to Nakomis, Sask. -- I imagine he is going to be married – anyway enlisting is the last thing either one will ever do, one reason why I favour conscription. My tulip tea was a huge success. Had it Friday May 23rd. – made $27 -- $11 at tea and sold tulips in bunches of nine for 25 cents. Over 600 cut that day and you can hardly miss them. Sold $4 worth Saturday and Sunday. People going away for weekend took them to their friends. Jack Murray has a job in Wpg, so we shall be losing them soon – Cyril Rankey has his job here. Have to shift my position so must close. Have to write Mack later.

Love and best wishes that your move be more comfortable than last. Take my advice and cut your correspondence list. You will not have nearly as much spare time and it is too important a job not to give it your 100% best as I expect and know you will do.

Love Mom.

P.S. Harriet Brook – her mother just called – H. leaves tomorrow for Vancouver where she is in training. They wished to be remembered to you.

Ricky from Brandon College wrote him next day.

Clark Hall
May 29, 1941

Dear Bird,

Both of your letters came last week and I decided to dash off a few lines tonight just before I start to study. Only 16 days before we write our first exam – history, by the way. Do I ever remember you helping me with those terrible dates. I must tell you I have managed to study.enough to pass at least history, but the others, oh dear, that's just another horrible dream. My folks are depending on me passing, but ….I hope wonders can be accomplished in the next 15 days.

I was home last weekend. We drove about 300 miles all in all. Gee I had fun. Last year when I went home it was dull compared to this. We went to a dance at Virden on Saturday night and got home around 1:30, then up at 8:30 and off to Deloraine for a dinner. I was simply dead tired when I got home Sunday night. Such a life is hard on an old woman like me who isn't used to such frivolity. Honest to Pete, it's as dead as doornails around here and I don't mean maybe.

Expected Paddy in today but I guess it's tomorrow she's coming. Pulfer got a job as an assistant chemist in a factory (or something) down on Georgian Bay. What will those two do separated – Pad said last week that they hadn't been apart for more than two weeks at a time.

You seemed rather in the "dumps" in your last letter. Is Nova Scotia that bad? Surely there's something nice about it. But gee, don't rainy days make one blue. Now let me see what I can tell you about the gang. Most of the boys are still at camp. For the past two weeks it's been Winnipeg. Betty, Phil and Marg McKay have also been in Wpg this week. Marg and Doug Wesley have been going together this year. They make a cute pair but I never thought Wes would go with Marg. Won't they be having fun. As far as I know Mooney and perhaps Bliss have jobs as instructors out at Shilo for the summer.

I might go home with one of the girls tomorrow night so I simply have to stop writing and get busy doing silly old maths. Gee whiz I'm scared stiff of these exams. Last year I didn't care but it's going to be awful this year. Oh dear, will I ever grow up and get some sense into my noodle.

Now I simply must go. Don't forget to write when you have time –I hope you aren't working as hard as a while ago.

The best of luck.

As ever, Ricky.

His father writes to share the news of his mother's maladies, the army's Victory Loan campaign, and other news.

Boissevain, Man.
June 16, 1941

My dear son –

I fully intended writing you yesterday but I was so busy; in fact I have been awful busy ever since I got over my illness in the spring. Am feeling very well, nevertheless, but I wouldn't mind getting away for a short visit. Shortly after I got around fairly well, Mom took Lumbago and Sciatica. I think it is going on three weeks for her. However she is feeling much better now and is able to sit up quite bit. We will have to be pretty careful, though, to see that she doesn't try out her back and leg too soon. I feel quite sure that the warmer and brighter weather will do much to relieve her trouble – the weather has been so damp and so cold – the nights were really bad, more particularly for trouble like hers.

I have been able to get my lawns and garden into pretty good shape and everything is looking so good. I don't remember when I have seen this part of the country look any better – I mean the crops chiefly: but lately there has been some report re cutworms, and I believe some damage.

We had a real night in Boissevain on Saturday past – the army was here in a campaign Victory Loan and Recruiting drive. There was a wonderful crowd and the main program was carried out in two parts – first, army battle maneuvers at the fair grounds; and secondly the public address system and band concert in front of the memorial monument, where two weeks before we erected quite pretty arches in triple form with a large flag pole in the cutter behind, and in this we were quite proud as community to fly our Victory Loan flag with honor pennants showing, the first to indicate we had reached our quota and the other five to show we had gone over the top by a quarter of our allotment, five times, and another full week to add to it. The arches were beautifully draped in bunting and streamers of colored lamps and small flags – it really looked quite smart at night, and I can take all credit for the entire design and with two others erected it entirely.

Well I am glad to know the gang is all at Victoriaville, even if for a while, and hope before long to see you moved west. The young fellows of the town are pretty well gone now – mostly only the two Walker boys, Red and [illegible] and Pender left.

I have a little time tonight after a fairly heavy day and so I thought would write you this short letter. I am expecting to be called on another case some time during the night. You do not need to answer this letter but simply mention having received it, when you write your mother. You will undoubtedly find you will not have the time to keep up too much correspondence because your studies will soon require a lot of your time. And I do not think son you can spare sending $20 each month out of your pay; I think you should rather try $15 – whatever you think best, though; and we shall try to keep it for you. Try to take good care of yourself and write to your mother regularly, as she looks for your letters. Best of luck, Dad.

P.S. This writing is not good. I broke my fountain pen and had to send it away for repair, and these old dip pens write so unevenly, even after constant dipping.

June 21, 1941

3506 University St.
Montreal, P.Q.

Victoriaville.

Dear Clayton,

I just saw Cub Brook on the Street; was very much surprised to see him. He was only I the city for a few hours, unfortunately. He gave me your address and said that you would be passing through Montreal in possibly two weeks.

It is certainly a long time since we've seen each other, and I would like to see you, and talk over old times. I've left my job at the chemical plant where I was working for B.A. in their Montreal East Refinery. Please write and let me know what time you'll be in this city, and I'll do my best to meet you at the train. Until then, best of luck.

As ever, Jack Garton.

Boissevain
Undated, but mid June 1941

Victoriaville, Que.

My dear Clayton –
The heat is so great. I can scarcely find enough energy to write, so it may be short. We got your letter from Cub and we are hoping you will be lucky as he and be transferred to a Manitoba depot – Virden was opened about two months ago. It is 80 miles from here, but hope you get Portage. Better chance of getting home often. Cub looks well tho thin. I am coming downstairs ever a.m. now, but do not walk very well as yet. I walk just like Mrs. Southon, you know 'hobble' but if I could have a few of her pounds it might help my poor legs. Irene Murray has been at Clear Lake all week getting cottage ready for renters; then she is coming back here Monday for a while. It will be nice company for me. Dad just brought mail in. A letter from her saying she will be here tomorrow (Sunday) instead. Looks like a storm – very oppressive – hope you can keep cool. Did you get the bathing trunks?
Hope to hear any day where you are to be moved and will wish hard for Portage – much love, Mom.

A mother's prayers must have helped, because a few days later…

Saturday, June 28, 1941
Victoriaville, Que.

Dear Mom and Dad,
We leave here Tuesday morning and are going to, of all places, Portage la Prairie! Please pardon the scrawl but you can understand that I am a trifle excited.
We were just told this morning, but had known for several days that we would be posted soon. We had to draw lots as there were too many wanted to go to Portage, but Rosie and I both made it. So the whole gang of us will be together again. But we almost decided to step out for Regina in order to be sure of staying together. It pays to gamble sometimes.
I was issued my complete flying kit the day before yesterday and the rest of the boys got theirs today. Some of the boys failed their exams, others their link, and one or two on medicals, but none from our immediate gang.

Bill lost a 14-day leave, though, when he failed his armaments. But he is going to Portage which helps a lot.

I doubt very much whether we will get any leave but we may get a couple of days. It's a pretty slim chance though because the other fellows are supposed to report at Portage on the third, as I understand it. That's Wednesday, and we should arrive in Portage that day, so....

Well it's dinner time now and I have some things to do and I can't think of anything else to say so will close. Don't write of course until you hear from me in Portage. I don't know what time the train hits Winnipeg but it would be between 12 and 8 p.m.

Lots of love,
Clayton

CHAPTER 7

Solo -- and Married -- in Portage la Prairie

No. 14 Elementary Flight Training School (EFTS)
Portage la Prairie,

July 4, 1941

Dear Mom and Dad,

We got here yesterday at noon and started working in the afternoon. Of course that is what we wanted, but it would have been nice to have had a few hours to get home on. I may have from noon Sunday to 11 that night, but can't rely on it. Of course that isn't time to get home so am going to Winnipeg, if I get it. Doris [first mention of his future wife] hasn't been well lately either.

Met Mac at the station and he looks OK in his new suit. Bumped into Charlie Patton at the Royal Alec too. He has just joined the Air Force as a wireless air gunner. He went to Penhold, Alberta, yesterday [where Bird would one day be OC, Officer Commanding, in the 1950s].

I was up flying for 25 minutes this morning but should get more tomorrow morning. We get up at 4:30 for a.m. flying but next week I will be on afternoons which will be much better. Bill got in two hours today; he's the lucky guy so far.

It sure is nice being with the gang again. There are six of us, two from Deloraine, two from Boissevain, one from Crystal City and Bill from

Winnipeg. The station is the best yet too and so is the grub. It really is all right for a change.

It is 9:50 now so had better get to bed soon. We had a terrible train ride down, no berths and I am still digging the grime out of my skin. I never saw Jack Carlton as we only had two hours in Montreal and we spent one of those eating. It was my first meal of the day (7 p.m.) or I wouldn't have bothered eating and would have found Jack. I was so excited about getting away from Quebec that I couldn't eat. Besides, the meals there were no incentive in themselves.

Well, must hit the hay now. Don't know whether I can post this tonight or not as nobody has any stamps and the post office on the station doesn't sell them, queer thing. But will see what I can do.

Love, Clayton

Boissevain

F.C.C. Bird
No. 14 E.F.T.S. (Elementary Flight Training School)
91897
Portage la Prairie, Man

July 9, 1941

My dear boy –

Dad and I were so glad to get your letter this a.m. and to know you are so happy with your work – what a thrill your first flight must have been – you didn't say how it affected you – did you feel dizzy or sick? Yes that does seem a shame you have to travel as you do and I can't understand why it should be necessary. However, let's hope you have no more of that part of the training (if it is a part). Doug Noton got his wings last Wednesday – he was 15th in a class of 60. He and his sister are going to Wpg Beach for a week (the Gardiners camp there every summer and he has a crush on Joan) then he reports to Halifax on the 19th and I guess it is overseas for him. I hope you will get a few days' leave soon – don't hesitate to phone home and Dad can meet you in Brandon. If you are given leave without much notice do take a bus. Don't wear yourself out hitchhiking. I am sitting out on verandah in the screened part. Irene is also writing. She goes to Wpg Thursday. Am so glad you boys are all together and hope you can remain so.

Glad Mack was able to meet train – am sure you were glad to see each other. Mrs. Blythe (housekeeper) is ready to go and I want to send this on bus, so bye for now – hope we may be seeing you soon – Best love, Mom

Portage la Prairie,
No. 14 EFTS.
9 a.m.

July 15, 1941

Dear Mom,

Well Mom, I made it today. In other words I sooled, in eight hours and 20 minutes. There is a minimum of eight hours dual before they are allowed to solo you so I wasn't doing too badly. Cub hasn't yet but has felt ready for it a couple of days now. It's a great feeling to be up there all alone. The Tiger Moth flies a lot easier with no one in the front cockpit too. I wanted to take her up for an hour now to practise take-offs and landings but it got too bumpy due to the hot sun. However that kind of stuff won't worry us a week from now.

We must have just as good a station as there is in Canada. The planes are all kept in good shape, the instructors are the best, and everything else is darned good except for the passes. We had to have quite a bit of flying time in by Saturday or we don't even get 24 hours off, which is the most we can get at the best of times.

I was darned sore when I got your letter saying you had met the bus in Brandon. They wouldn't give me a pass on account of my low flying time and I almost went AWOL [Absent Without Leave]. The only thing that stopped me was the fact that I would get three to four weeks C.B. [Confined to Barracks] and then wouldn't be able to get out. Now that I have soloed though I will really get in time and it will be the weather that stops me this weekend.

Right now I am sitting out in front of the hangar locker-room watching landings and take-offs. There are a number of Ansons here use the same field. They belong to an observer's school that is right here beside us. There are quite a few New Zealanders and some Englishmen besides Canadians at it. We are all Canadians with the exception of one Englishman, four or five Americans and several Frenchmen.

You may read in the papers about the number of accidents that take place at flying schools, but if you could only see the amount of flying that is done, you would find the percentage pretty low. And most of them are due to carelessness or foolishness. We had one last night in which I understand both the instructor and the pupil were killed. Incidentally the "pupil," an American, flew against the Russians with the Finns, got 13 bombers and the Finnish Distinguished Flying Cross in 65 hours of combat flying in a Curtiss Tomahawk. They were either flying low or stunting hard enough to fold the wings back but that kind of stuff is foolish in these little ships and those two should have known better. The instructors all swear by them as training planes and they really are good.

You should have seen [cousin] Emily when she saw me on the platform. Boy, I nearly had all the wind knocked out of me then [she liked her cousin Clayton very much and likely gave him quite a hug]. I sure wish that I could have got up there for a weekend. Emily is a lot of fun even if she has been pretty badly spoiled.

Well, I must send the news into Winnipeg [to tell Doris he is coming to see her]. Tell me if you are going to be in Brandon next weekend. If you aren't, I will phone around 7 or 7:30 p.m. Saturday if I am able to get away. If I can't, I won't phone. I would like to see Doug before he goes but in case I don't, wish him happy landings from me.

Love,
Clayton

Dr. Mackie is leaving and Dr. Bird will move his office into his home.

July 16, 1941
Boissevain

Portage la Prairie

My dear boy –

Daddy just brought your letter and I must at once correct the impression you have that we went to Brandon to meet the bus – no, it was the bus from Brandon when it got in here at 7 p.m. Knowing you do not get much notice, we thought there might be a chance you got off – however, the tin of pumpkin is still in the fridge and will be ready for a pie when you do come which I hope will be this Saturday.

And so you have been up in the clouds all by yourself. And yet I, knowing that day had to come, I will never think of you as alone – there is always a Higher Power watching over Mothers' sons and I am only going to feel proud that I have a son who has the courage and the wish to be a part in blotting out this awful scourge. No doubt the British are planning their offensive this fall and I think Germany will feel the weight of it right on their own soil.

I have always heard Portage is one of the best and Dad and I were so pleased that you were sent there – it must be a wonderful feeling and this a.m. I was resting on the chesterfield and heard a plane circling round – somehow I couldn't lie still – I had to go out and look at it and I just wondered was there a possibility of it being you.

We miss Doug's serenading but I really think he was taking chances, he was flying so low, and I am glad you realize the foolishness of any such foolhardiness – I too think a lot of these accidents must be due to carelessness.

No I don't think we will be in Brandon Saturday. It is to be a big day but I can't walk around well enough and Daddy saw the opening of Virden Airport so is not thinking of going, so if you phone we shall be here. Do not expect Doug will be back here again – is at Wpg Beach and has to report in Halifax on 18th so is probably on his way now. Mr. Littler said Evan is very disappointed – tried to get in as clerk but was turned down because he wears glasses. Think I told you that Dr. Mackie is leaving and that Dad is moving his office over here to the house – will tell you all about it when you come, which I hope will be soon.

Till then, bye and good luck.

Love, Mom.

Big news -- Clayton has decided to marry Doris Aconley.

Portage la Prairie,

Sept. 2, 1941

Dear Mom and Dad,

I got your letters yesterday at noon but was too busy to be able to answer them. There was a smoker last night too and the orchestra played for it so, after my weekend I was really played out. In fact this a.m. I felt so rotten that I went on sick parade and am now in the hospital which explains the pencil.

Now don't start worrying because all I need is a good rest and a chance to get into shape again. That's the trouble with this life, there is plenty to do but physically it does very little good. At any rate I would like to stay here till the end of the week and then I want the MO to give me a [leave?]. I will only get behind in flying as I can keep up the ground school OK. And I can catch up on my flying. Incidentally I soloed Friday in four hours. I have about six hours now on Harvards, and I like flying more than ever. These are real planes.

I thought that you would understand the suddenness of my decision to get married, but as you said, Dad, these are not normal times. Under ordinary circumstances I wouldn't consider it but as it is I don't think that we are doing anything crazy, or that we shouldn't. Doris is 22, about seven months younger than myself, about 5'7" in height, dark hair, brown eyes (to match mine) and at present is a little underweight due to a tonsillitis attack about two months ago. I am enclosing a snap taken in front of the Parliament Buildings in Winnipeg this spring when I was down east. It isn't the best, but may give you some idea of what she looks like.

We may have to change the date from the 13th to the 27th because ordinarily I am only entitled to a 36-hour pass on the 13th which wouldn't give us any time. Also I'm very sorry but I won't be able to get home for a while because all small towns are out of bounds to us till the epidemics [scarlet fever, etc.] are over. I most certainly won't get away this weekend as my flying time will be down and I am going to have to work to make it up. For the same reason I may not even get a 36 [hour leave] on the 13th [day of their wedding].

At any rate it's too bad all this had to happen but it was beyond our control. We got the licence and wedding ring on Saturday afternoon, and I don't know which of us was more self-conscious. I hope you don't mind my going ahead with things like this, but the way things are it's either do it now or do nothing. Yorkton, Winnipeg and Regina are the only places not out of bounds.

By a lucky coincidence Doris is Anglican and about all the arrangements we have made are that it will likely be in the Church of England Church in St. James. At first she thought it would be fine to have Uncle Percy officiate and then she got scared because she doesn't know him. I believe that I've told you before that she is a bit shy. You will probably understand anyway, Mom. Naturally I was a bit disappointed, but knowing her I can see her point. It will be a quiet affair all around too [Percy did the service in the end].

Well, lights go out in about a minute, so must close.

Love, Clayton.

P.S. I got my bathing trunks from Victoriaville today. No stamps on it or anything. I don't know how they got here.

Sunday, Sept. 7, 1941

Portage la Prairie
Flight School No. 14.

Dear Mom and Dad,

I thought that was a good idea of yours Mom to write Doris as she was wondering how you would take it, not having met her. Besides she is kind of shy and when you do meet her she won't talk much.

Incidentally I am still in hospital but should get out Tuesday. I was run down, from all appearances. That was my own idea too. If I get out in time we still plan for the 13th and thought perhaps Uncle Percy could do it for us. We were only going to have a very quiet affair anyway as neither you nor Mrs. Aconley is in the best of health and neither of us want it big and splashy. We were going to have a few personal friends at the ceremony but nobody but our own families at the reception afterwards.

I am writing Uncle Percy tonight anyway to see if he could work us in sometime. I imagine Kay's wedding will be around 3 or 4 o'clock. In that case he should be able to handle ours at 12 or 1 o'clock which would be fine. We are renting a car and are going somewhere out of the city for our honeymoon (which I am afraid is going to be of the abbreviated kind). We don't know ourselves where to go but that shouldn't be hard.

Incidentally Mr. Reeves of Northern Life gave me his congrats and offered the use of his car. He promised to scalp me if I didn't let him know when it happens. He was telling me that Mr. Martin, agency superintendent, had some kind of supervisory job lined up for me in the company. They are carrying on my contract and I am even in line (so far) for their pension plan.

Here is Doris's address: 234 Whytewold Rd., Winnipeg, Man.

I told her she could expect a letter from you. Had better write Uncle Percy now. Hope Dad can be there. It will seem quite queer if he can't make it.

Love, Clayton
P.S. Don't know what church yet.

273

Sept. 9, 1941

Dear Mom and Dad,

That certainly was a good idea of Mrs. Aconley, writing to you, Mom. I should have thought of it sooner but it never occurred to me. Now it looks as though everything is fixed up fine if Uncle Percy can arrange it. I think that idea of cutting out the reception afterward is perfect because she is in no shape to have to look after anything like that. It will make it a lot easier for you too and give you a chance to be at Kay's. Besides I wasn't looking forward to it, in fact suggested it not knowing whether it was the right thing to do or not. And, purely incidentally, it will sure save me some money.

Two o'clock in All Saints suits me just fine too, as that will give me some time to get ready which I won't get here. I am still in hospital but am glad of it. They are keeping me as long as they can and so long as my temperature and pulse stay normal I will have the best wishes of the MO and perhaps an extra 48 hours leave. Temp and pulse have been OK now for four days and I have been up and around for a couple now. I feel fine although a bit weak.

But that is only natural after a week in bed. Apparently I had a bit of poison in my system from that flu. I had been going around here since we arrived feeling really rotten, but foolishly let it go hoping it would go of its own accord.

I still have to get the C.O.'s permission but that is merely a matter of form and will be fixed up tomorrow. There is a form I have to get from Records office and one of the boys is getting it for me tomorrow morning.

Mrs. Aconley wrote me and told of writing you. I got it yesterday morning with your letter and must answer tonight. We had thought of renting a car and getting somewhere out of the city where it will be quiet. Of course I won't be able to do anything too strenuous as I want to take it easy for a while. However if I do get the extra 48 we may go to Boissevain for a short visit. That will have to depend on the money, too.

Dorie will work at Eaton's for a while anyway until I can see how things are going. I may bring her out here. Well I must get to work on the other letters now. Do your darnedest to be there, Dad.

Love, Clayton.

Portage la Prairie,

Tues. Sept. 16, 1941

Dear Mom and Dad,

I got your letter today, Mom. Mac saw me at the station but didn't have the wires. I went around to Hec's to se if they were there Sunday afternoon.

I'm sorry everything had to be so rushed on Saturday [wedding day] but that's what it is like all through the Air Force except at times when you wait for hours and nothing happens.

We went out to Aconleys' to drop Mr. Aconley off and pick up our grips [suitcases]. Poor Doris hadn't even finished her packing. Then we went out the Beach Highway and just took our time. We were in Selkirk before we knew what was going on but went back to Lockport. We stayed in the hotel there for the night. I would like to have gone to Kenora but it would have taken too much time. Then we came back into the city fairly early in the afternoon, had dinner and took some pictures. A third cousin of Doris's was supposed to take some at the church but I guess he didn't get much of a chance. They really got us with that confetti. I never dreamed the day would ever come that that would happen to me, but I'm still dreaming now.

We soon knew there was a sign [Just Married] all right because all the cars on the way out to 234 passed honking their horns. We took it off there and Doris has it in her room.

I'm sure glad that you liked her Mom because she is the most wonderful girl I ever hope to meet. And her parents are really nice too. They have been having an awful lot of hard luck because neither of them as been well now for some years. Mrs. Aconley has a goiter and won't have it out because she doesn't believe in operations. I think perhaps it's because a friend of hers died from a goiter operation a few years ago. It's unfortunate but she seems to be quite firm about it. Of course I never said anything to her about it.

Incidentally, Mr. Aconley is giving us a trained Labrador pup when we get settled down, if that should ever happen. I had told all the kids not to get us anything because I know only too well how hard it is, but some of Doris's friends gave us a couple of very nice silver dishes, a pair of bed lamps and some other stuff I forget. Incidentally Pulfer and Paddy

275

Poole got married at Clear Lake on Saturday at 3:30. Puddy got glasses in Rochester and can see almost normally with them. I didn't know they were holding it then until Sunday when Woods told me.

I had to laugh at Doris when she told me, in an awed sort of voice, that my Dad had "kissed her three times." As I told her, I don't think that we should have any in-law trouble. She thought I looked more like you, Dad.

Well, I have to go back into the link trainer in a few minutes so will have to close. It really was swell having both of you there; I wouldn't have wanted it at all without you, but I wish we could have had a little more time.

I was flying yesterday but not today as I have link all afternoon instead of flying. However I'll be at it tomorrow again. I think maybe I'll have caught up sufficiently to bring Doris down in two weeks. I sure do miss her a lot. Besides, she will be coming for wings parade anyway so I might just as well have her here for a little while. Somebody else just got into the link so I don't have to quit right now.

I'm not quite as anxious now to get overseas but if my number comes up I suppose there is nothing else to do. Actually I do want to go over but after all! I see I do have to go so will say good-bye for now.

Love, Clayton.

P.S. It sure seems funny to be addressing letters to Mrs. F. C. C. Bird!

CHAPTER 8

'Going All Out Now'

Yorkton, Sask.
Sept. 28, 1941

Dear Mom and Dad,

This is just a short note as I haven't much time. We are really going all out now and in addition have started night flying. It's really all right.

I haven't got the blanket and clothes yet but expect they will be along soon. We have a fairly nice room, hardly up to city standards but it's OK. It sure is swell having Doris here too. I have buttons on my shirts, she has fixed my pajamas so they fit me etc. and I get some decent meals for a change. I have a sleeping-out pass but haven't been able to be home for anything except breakfast so far. I didn't get a 48 this weekend on account of the night flying and probably won't get one next weekend for the same reason. Then by next weekend we will be starting exams. Boy the time goes fast in this business.

I got your letter on Friday or Saturday Dad and was very sorry to hear of Uncle Allan's sudden death. So far I haven't had a chance to write the girls but I will as soon as I can. He sure didn't look up to scratch last summer.

By the way, will you be able to get up for our wings parade? It takes place in about three weeks or so. It's a pretty long trip, and the way everything is I suppose it will be hard to manage. It would be nice if you could be here, although there actually isn't so much to it, and it only lasts for a couple of hours.

When we are finished I think perhaps we will come right to Boissevain for a few days anyway. I would like very much to get in some shooting – any kind. Well, I have to go right now to classes or I'll be late. Take good care of yourselves and don't worry about me because I have somebody to take the best care of me now.

Love Clayton.

[This letter contained a statement of his marks from the University of Manitoba, May 14, 1940: Calculus, 16 our of 100; Chemistry III Theory, 44 out of 125; Practical, 43 out of 75; Geology III Crystallography, 33 out of 66; Mineralogy, 28 out of 66. *As he said in Nickel Trip, his mind was on the war and enlistment (and marriage), not school.]*

Dear Mom and Dad,

I'm very sorry not to have written sooner, but really all the time we get to write letters is about half an hour after dinner and just before going to bed. Actually I am in bed now, it's after 10.

Before I forget again, Mom be sure to tell Mrs. Dunn that the sox were fine and also to thank her for the little note. They are a very pretty blue, the same as the Aussies wear. I really haven't time to write her, or even Uncle Percy down east.

Doris is coming down this weekend to stay until I leave too. I have a pretty nice room and she will be light house-keeping. One of the boys from my class who was married about five weeks ago lives there too so the girls will have company.

I am still way behind in flying and it will take a while to catch up. I had a flat tire the other day and touched a wing tip another time and boy there is a lot of red tape connected with those minor accidents. It took me a whole morning to get settled. My ground school is pretty fair now but it's going to take a lot of work. You can take it from me that anyone wearing wings has really earned them.

Incidentally, Laverne Armstrong is here and told me today about Doug Noton. Will he be able to fly again or don't they know yet? Kind of tough anyway.

Does it still feel as queer to you both to be a mother-in-law and father-in-law as it does to me to be a married man? I still find it hard to believe at times but I sure will be glad when she gets here. We can get sleeping-out passes and I think I really will be able to get more work done that way. Harbottle, the other chap, does.

And now the lights will soon be going out, so I will have to close. I only had 20 minutes to write this in so if I forgot anything, let me know.

Love, Clayton.

P.S. Can you send that green wool comforter to me?

169 2nd Ave. S.
Yorkton, Sask.

Oct. 14, 1941

Dear Mom and Dad,

I'm very sorry not to have written before but really have been busy. I haven't had a day off in over a month now and that includes Sundays.

We finished night flying a week ago and it's kept me busy ever since getting over the sleep I lost. Then we write our exams this Saturday, Sunday and Monday. Yes, we even write exams on Sunday. But I'll sure be glad to get them over with. Incidentally we may have to hang around here for a week or so after we are finished due to a change in the system.

Dorie and I are getting along fine except that we never have much time to spend at home. We are even managing to save a little money so as to have as much as possible for my furlough. I want to be able to enjoy it.

In case she has forgotten to tell you, perhaps you should open those parcels that came for us. I asked her to tell you but she may have forgotten. I would like to know what is in them. I haven't had a minute to write anybody else, this is my first one since the last one I wrote you, so I hope nobody will think me very thoughtless or anything. In a week I should be able to clean all those things up.

I will also be having wings tests in the next week or so and then (I hope) all our exams etc. are over. Right not all I feel like doing is sleeping for a week. However a couple of days will likely fix that.

I sure have missed the hunting this fall. There is some lovely hunting around here but there is no time for it. Boy, Dad, a plane is the real McCoy for spotting the ducks. This country is very wild, in fact it seems to be almost impossible to find a quarter section with no willow swamps etc on it and there are lots of little lakes and also some big ones. I was about 100 miles west the other day and there were some really beautiful, clear lakes with sandy beaches. You know, you can see the whole bottom of a clear lake from the air. But most of the lakes are muddy and we often see flocks on them. I was also quite close to Rivers twice last week. I would like to do a cross-country to Boissevain but doubt whether I can get permission.

Well I must drop a short line to Rosie and Cub who are at Prince Albert and may come down this weekend, so will have to close now. I know there are a lot of things I have forgotten but hope that you can forgive me. Take care of yourselves and don't worry about us, we couldn't be any happier.

Love Clayton.

169 2nd Ave. S.
Yorkton, Sask.

Wed. Oct. 22, 1941

Dear Mom and Dad,

We have finally finished our exams and now have a little time to do other things. I got an average of 80 per cent but don't know whether it's good enough for a commission [being made an officer as opposed to a lower paid non-commissioned man].

I also had two of wings (flying) tests today and got them OK. Only one more now but I don't get it for a while as it is *the* final and my time is still low. I have about 60 hours and will likely have 75 or hours before I do have it. Of course we have no classes now so I can get about four hours a day in.

We don't know when our wings parade is going to be held as all courses have been lengthened 12 days and they are undecided as yet whether to keep us around here for those or not. I hope they don't as I really do miss the hunting. Every day I dive down on sloughs and lakes and look at the ducks. There was a dandy big flock on one today and they never budged. I was less than 50 yards from them and only about 10 feet off the water. I have seen some geese, too.

Please don't worry about our finances. We saved $15 from my second last pay check and I still have about $25 of the last one left and it's only eight days to pay day. I don't know how Dorie does it as I spend about as much as she does, on bus fares, milk at meals, tobacco, and messing fees.

We celebrated the ending of exams last night by eating downtown, which was a much quieter way than most of the boys did.

We haven't got as nice a room as I wanted but you can't be choosey these times. It's pretty hard to get houses or rooms anywhere. But a young married couple own the house and are nice enough to make up for it, although for the first two weeks I never saw them (when we were night flying).

Dorie's just putting on the kettle for a cup of Ovaltine. It's only 9:30 but I still have some sleep to catch up on so we are going to bed early. We are both looking forward to getting home. If I go overseas, we will likely spend most of my [break?] in Boissevain as Dorie will have lots of time afterwards to see her parents. But I may be made an instructor and if so, it will likely be split up a little more evenly as I go to Trenton to train.

I hope to be home for some deer shooting too. A .303 machine gun isn't as much fun as a .22 or Savage .303. Now I had better close. Take care of yourselves. The best of love from Clayton.

169 2nd Ave. S.
Yorkton, Sask.

Oct. 26, 1941

Dear Mom and Dad,

It's Sunday night and I've just finished my first 48 since Dorie got here. I didn't do much besides sleep though, mostly because there wasn't anything else to do and also because I sure needed it.

The fine weather seems finally to have broken and I wouldn't be surprised to see snow in the morning it's so cold now. It should bring the northern ducks down in a hurry but I'm afraid it will be too much of a hurry and there won't be any left by the time I get home, which should be around the 7th or 8th.

I only have one flying test left to do and then I'm finished. But I have about 20 hours to get in, at least. We don't know yet what we are going to do or where we are going, or anything else for that matter.

My instructor has recommended me for an instructor but that won't necessarily keep me on this side. Regarding your letter, thank Mrs. Garton for us. You will have to send me Bernice Patton's address so I can write her. Dorie can't play bridge yet but expects she will learn sometime. We have both been trying to write but not making much of a job of it.

You will have to excuse us when we do get home if we act kind of foolishly for a married couple. We spend most of our time being crazy but have a wonderful time doing it. And we are both eating quite a bit, especially Dorie, so should start putting on weight.

Well it's bed-time now so will say so-long. Don't forget to save some partridge and ducks if possible, for us. Love from both of us,

Dorie and Clayton.

The following is special, the only letter we have from Doris to her new mother- and father-in-law. It was undated, but likely written in mid-October.

169 Second Ave. South,
Yorkton, Sask.
Thursday [mid-October 1941]

Dear Mom,

I intended writing sooner, but somehow didn't do it. I was out to tea again this afternoon. That's one a week and sometimes two since I've been here. When I came home there were two letters for me, one from my own mother and one from you. I said two letters for me, but meant for us.

Clay won't be home until 8:30 tonight so don't know what yours contains. We received the papers yesterday. I was so pleased to see the story section included. Somehow or other Clay couldn't find the one at the Barracks, and I did so want to read the serial. It spoils everything if a part is missed out.

We still don't know the exact date of wings parade, but it will be next week, so maybe you can expect us at the end of the week. We had intended leaving the same day, but find we can't do that, so it will be as early as possible the next day.

Clayton seems quite tired this week. He caught up on some of his sleep last weekend so hope he gets a 48 again this weekend.

We had a little snow the other morning, but it's not very cold. Hope this letter finds you well. Love to you both.

Dorie.

Yorkton, Sask.

Nov. 21, 1941

Dear Mom and Dad,

I got your little parcel this morning Dad, and thanks a lot. I remembered it after we were on the bus but of course that was too late.

It is now 3 o'clock and Doris and I are going downtown pretty soon. We have some things to pick up before I catch the train at 6:30. We had some pictures taken yesterday which were pretty good of me but not so good of Doris. But under the circumstances they are OK.

I also took the deer hides to a tailor and he is going to fix the coat for me. I don't know of course whether I will get it before I leave Halifax, though. Doris isn't coming with me as it would cost over $80 even with a warrant [?] for the ticket, so we will put the money into a Victory Bond.

She gave me a watch for Christmas and I hope it gives satisfaction. It cost $30. I don't feel much like writing just now, so this probably won't last much longer. I will try to write as soon as we get to Halifax if not sooner. I'm afraid that I'm going to be quite homesick for a while because it sure is going to be empty without Dorie. However we will get used to it I suppose.

Mac was over last night and will meet the train tonight. We haven't got around to seeing anyone else. Russ is still in hospital and they apparently don't know what is wrong. Well I guess that's it for now, folks. All my love,

Clayton.

P.S. Dorie left a ring either in my room or the bathroom. Would you please send it into her Mom? 234 Whytewold Rd., Winnipeg.

Nov. 26, 1941

Halifax, N.S.

Dear Mom and Dad,

I'm very sorry to be so long in writing, but this place is something like Manning Pool and we spend most of our time waiting in parades.

My address is Sgt. Bird F.C.C.,
R-91897

#1 Y Depot
Halifax, Nova Scotia.

They told us what to use for an overseas address and perhaps you had better use it until I tell you differently.
It is: (Can) R-91897
     Sgt. Bird FCC
     Attached to RAF
     RCAF Overseas.

I haven't felt much like writing anyone since leaving Winnipeg. I really miss that little girl of mine, Mom. I hate like the devil going over and leaving her here but I guess that's all we can do. She sure is a wonderful girl, Mom, and she means more to me than I could ever tell you.

I just received two more letters from Dorie. She is a funny girl. I knew of course that it would take her a day or two to realize just what my going away would mean. It dawned on her Sunday and you should see her letter. I would give my right arm to be able to go back to her now. I know it would be pretty hard on you and Dad if anything was to happen to me, but I honestly don't think that she could stand it. Already she's planning for furniture etc. and putting away money for it.

I took out $5,000 ordinary life on myself Dad before leaving Wpg just in case it will come in handy afterwards. It costs $70 per year or about $5.84 a month. Also $1,000 endowment to 60 on Doris at $2.10 a month, so my total assignment for insurance runs around $12.10 a month. Also we are depositing money with Northern Life just like the bank only you get 3 per cent interest. That is in addition to our premiums. I wish we could put it into some good stocks or bonds which won't be affected so much by inflation but neither of us knows a thing about that.

I will also sign some money over to you, Mom, although that may have to be done on the other side, to take care of Auntie Em.

One of my ears plugged up a couple of days ago and so I went to the MO. He seems to be much more sensible than most of them and is treating me for a cold although I really haven't got one. But I think he's right though. Don't worry about it as it is nothing serious. It wasn't even bothering me but I thought it best to get it fixed pronto. Don't tell Dorie though as it would only be so much more on her mind and there's plenty there now, the Lord only knows.

I wish she would go to Boissevain for a few days sometime Dad and let you have a look at her tonsils. I think they should be removed. Are you allowed to operate on her?

Her picture isn't very good, Mom, but I enclose it because that is just the way she looked. I think she was trying to keep from crying.

I had better close now but will write again soon. You will know that I have gone when you get no letter for four or five days. Lots of love,

Clayton.

Halifax, Nova Scotia

Nov. 30, 1941

Dear Mom and Dad,

We're still here and of course no idea when we leave. Life here is very, very routine and very, very dull. I have practically all my shopping done and it's just as well as I've spent over $20 on it.

I miss Dorie so much that I'm pretty near ready to head back to Winnipeg. If I had the money I wouldn't wait very long. Perhaps it is just as well that I haven't.

I don't imagine that my leather coat will be ready before we leave. Doris's last letter was written on Thursday and she didn't think they had even started on it then. But they are pretty busy. Incidentally she may be able to sell my sax. A friend of hers is interested in it. She said that she intended writing you today, but if she feels anything like I do, she likely won't.

By the way, my letters have been a long time getting to her and so perhaps yours are too. I'm very sorry not to have left you my Halifax address before I left but it never occurred to me. So far I haven't received any mail from you, but if my letters take as long reaching you as they do Doris, you may not have my address in time to get me here.

I'm afraid there isn't much to say. Perhaps you should send me that cartoon, Mom; I wrote Dorie 12 pages last night.

All my love,

Clayton.

Halifax, Nova Scotia.

Dec. 8, 1941

[The troop ship left Dartmouth Dec. 10 or 11, a few days after he wrote the following. It arrived in Greenock, Scotland on Dec. 18. Then they took a train to Bournemouth, arriving Dec. 19. They were given leave for Christmas and Clayton went to Driffield in East Yorkshire to visit Dorie's relatives.]

Dear Mom and Dad,

By now you probably think I'm half way across the Atlantic and I'm really sorry not to have written you more often. I was going to write this yesterday afternoon but we spend most of our time listening to the news and talking about it [the Japanese attack on Pearl Harbour, which prompted the U.S. to declare war on Japan, Italy and Germany].

We haven't done anything yet except parades every day, waiting for drafts. We hate to miss them for fear of being left off when the rest of the gang goes. I wish now that I had brought Dorie down here. Two weeks would have been worthwhile.

Most of the boys are starting to get impatient. After working so hard it is a let-down to have nothing to do and being broke doesn't help any. Most of us spent our money on things we figured we'd need when we first got here and have been pretty well broke since. Of course there is nothing in Halifax by way of amusement but at least you could have some decent eats. I've had one square meal in three days now, the stuff here is so terrible, and I bought it. We eat raisons, cheese, peanuts and chocolate bars all the time, if you can find any.

If we are still here on the 15th (payday) I've got a good mind to jump a train for Manitoba and spend Xmas at home. It's really starting to get on my nerves here. Nothing but rumours all he time and nothing to them. And there is nothing to do here but route marches or standing in parades for an hour or two at a time.

I hope you like the little brooch, Mom. Dorie thought you would like it more than a pair of cloth wings. If you would like some wings let me know, and I'll send them from the other side, if we ever get there.

I haven't been able to sign over any money to you here because of a bunch of darned fools in the Accounts section. I'm going to raise a stink about it with the accounts officer.

It's almost midnight now. I packed a lot of stuff tonight and it took quite a while. Don't expect to hear from me for awhile as I may not be able to write. But I'll send a wire as soon as I can.

I don't feel much like writing so this won't be much longer. I had one dickens of a time getting off six pages for Dorie. I've been sitting here for half an hour now and can't think of anything to say, so I might just as well say good-night. All my love to both of you.

Clayton.

CHAPTER 9

England

Sat. Dec. 27, 1941

Somewhere in England.

[Clayton got back to Bournemouth on Dec. 29. Two days later they were sent north by train to Montrose, Scotland to an FTS, a Flying Training School, where they would learn how to be flight instructors. They were not pleased.]

Dear Mom and Dad,

So far we have received no mail and it seems like such a long time since I had. But it takes a while to get it organized, and the Xmas rush was on too, so when it does start there should be plenty.

We had a quiet Christmas but it could have been much worse. We have changed billets and are in good ones now with decent beds and fireplaces (gas). They run for quite a while on a shilling. We also had a turkey dinner but I would much rather have dug into the one you had.

There were lots of invitations to private homes for the past few nights but I didn't go after any. I was supposed to go to one with Nash and Sanders on Christmas Day but slept through it and they couldn't find me. The heavy dinner had made me sleepy and I never woke up till 6:15 and was supposed to be there at 5:30. I didn't know where it was and they didn't know where I lived.

I spent all of Christmas Eve trying to write a letter to Doris but didn't make much of a job of it. Had to finish it yesterday for that matter, so I didn't get one off to you that night either. Hodgson sat beside me roasting chestnuts at our fireplace. I don't care much for them.

I haven't had any leave yet but get six days starting Monday. And I sure intend using them. We got paid this morning so I spent a while browsing around downtown and found a dandy camera for four pounds and 7/6 which is just less than $20 to us. It is just what I've always wanted and is very little more expensive that what Dorie would have paid in Canada. And it is a better make than the Kodaks. It really would be a shame to spend any time in this country without one. You will understand when I send you some pictures. There are trees etc. here which I certainly never expected to see. And the temperature is usually around 40 degrees F or better. Everything is still green.

I hope to get in some shooting of some kind on my leave. I don't know whether it is possible during the war or not but it may be. Even if it's only rabbits it will be worth a try. And it will be darned nice to have rabbit pie. I've had it once here and it sure tastes like more. Any meat does for that matter.

It's amazing to me how nice the people over here are to us. Some of the boys aren't very particular about their actions and do their worst for the rest but it doesn't seem to make any difference. They give you their invitations right on the street and if you are standing somewhere with a doubtful expression, nine times out of 10 someone will offer their help. I didn't expect anything of the kind because after all, troops are troops. They are very interested in hearing about Canada and the U.S. as regards the war. I had quite a chat with the landlord on Christmas Eve about that. They found out I wasn't going out and invited me down for their little party. He went through the Boer War and had spent 36 years in South Africa and was very interesting to talk to.

One chap who we were talking to on the street had harvested in Minto [near Boissevain] and around and we had a little get-together for a while. The only Christmas present most of us have got so far is some cigarettes from the Y and donated by the Dunlop Rubber Co. I took several packages down to the people here on Christmas Eve and you should have seen the way they went for them. English fags now aren't the quality they used to be. Everybody smokes, too. We are getting quite used to seeing obvious grandmothers strolling along with a cigarette between their lips.

Well, it's almost time for me to hit the hay. I hope some mail gets through soon because I would sure like to hear from both you and Doris. I have written some of the boys here but so far haven't heard from any of them. Of course it's only a week, which is hardly enough time. Give my regards to everybody, especially Mr. Southon and Mrs. Gaston.

All my love,
Clayton

P.S. Enclose lots of those cheap sugar candy (hard) and peanuts etc. in your parcels. Can't get them here.

Jan. 4, 1942
Somewhere in England

Dear Mom and Dad,

I'm sorry I forgot to post my last one when I wrote it, but I forgot it and one for Dorie in my hurry to get away on leave. I went to Yorkshire where cousins and aunts and uncles of hers live. Naturally I was an interesting sight to them and had a very good time. They are very comfortably fixed and are all very nice. I stayed at one place which actually was a large house divided in two. A cousin lived in one part and an uncle in the other. I had a bedroom very nearly the size of our ground floor minus the summer kitchen and the bed was huge. But fireplaces are the only source of heat and I still prefer central heating.

I stayed with a cousin of Dorie's named Lawrie Taylor. His wife Nora is blonde and very nice. They have a little girl Ann of two years three months and a baby of seven weeks, Pamela. Lawrie is OK and we used to sit up every night near the fireplace in the dining room to talk till about 2. He thought some of my Canadian expressions very very good and was using them himself when I left.

I heard from Bill yesterday. He expects to get his commission soon but is pretty tired. He has been working hard and would like a rest. But don't tell Mrs. Garton as she would only worry.

Will close now, but I'll be writing again soon.

Love, Clayton.

P.S. Have moved and am working. Wish I could have done this in Canada. Don't worry, Mom. All my love,

Clayton xxxxxx

Jan. 10, 1942
Somewhere in Scotland

Dear Mom,

As I said in Dad's part, I got my first letter from you this morning, and was it ever welcome. It's my first Canadian mail, too. It was written Nov. 28. It is little more than a month since I heard from anyone, my last letter being from Dorie.

We are working and Danny Nash and I are still together and should be for a few months. The rest of the gang has been split up all over the place. I know where some are but others I don't. However I wish I could have done this in Canada, which I could have but there were too many applied for it there. So far everything is fine but in this business first impressions don't mean a thing. We have good ships, a good mess (chicken dinner today) and fair quarters. Nash and I are together in a small room but these fireplaces are a blasted nuisance. Of course we have orderlies who clean our rooms and light our fires before we return in the evening but our hands must be washed several times an evening before going to bed, through messing around with the contraptions. We haven't hot water very often to shave with but aside from that there are no complaints.

I have written Bill Garton and Brook, and Doug Noton. So far I've heard from Bill, who is stationed not far from me. But there is little chance of us ever getting together. Maybe I'll be luckier with Doug. I was very glad to hear that his hand was affected. He always was a daredevil.

We have all had some funny experiences over here. On my leave I heard some queer brogues but last night I met a chappy who never said one word that I could understand. Must have been real Gaelic or something. Nash and I went into a bake shop the other day and got some sweets (English for desert; we got scones, etc., real Mrs. George Stevenson products). There were a couple of nice looking lassies to wait on us and before we knew it we had started joking with them. One of them gave us some real stuff, it sounded like nothing on earth. I heard something like it when on leave. Real rural Yorkshire is impossible to make out.

Another thing that strikes us is the fact that if they haven't got what we want, they apologize in a way that is really embarrassing. Everyone is really friendly and wants to know what part of Canada we come from as some friend of their wife's uncle's so-and-such was there once.

We have seen quite a bit of the country as we have done a lot of traveling and it is very nice but I prefer Manitoba. This place is too restricted.

I am waiting for the box with the cookies you mentioned to show up, Mom. It will be very welcome. We have a pretty fair mess here but by bedtime we are as hungry as wolves and consequently usually have a little stock laid by for a midnight snack. We found some peanut butter in a store the other day and it is really coming in handy.

Well I shall turn in and read for a little while before going to sleep. I am finished Leo Tolstoy's Anna Karenna which I have always wanted to read just to see what his mind really was like. My impression is that he is extremely sentimental, and also confused, or else it's myself. Maybe both of us are. I studied a bit about him in Sociology which started my interest in him. I find his sentimentalism is childish in places and very disagreeable. You will see what I mean if you read it. Or perhaps you have. I have the Everyman's Edition in two volumes, about $1.25 for the two.

Goodnight for now, Mom, with all my love,
Clayton.

Somewhere in Scotland
Sunday, Jan. 25, 1942

Dear Mom and Dad,

I got your letter of Dec. 18 which you had sent to Halifax, Dad, about a day ago. As you should know by now I had left Halifax a week before, however I guess you didn't get what I meant in my last Canadian letter.

Also I suppose I told you about getting the $2 [from the sale of his furs]. Thanks a lot but you really shouldn't have as I told you. I would use it to send you something but we can't send parcels so that's out. I don't need it over here as my pay amounts to more than that modest sum. However I am signing over a bit more pay (about $15) to take care of my insurance.

We have had a very dull time of it lately. As they say here, we are all thoroughly browned off, which means fed up. Even Halifax would look wonderful to any of us. But that feeling will clear up with the weather, I hope. It's supper time (7) now so will finish after that.

Monday: I didn't do any more writing last night so will finish this if I can before afternoon lectures start. We aren't flying yet and it's cold. Reminds me of New Year's Day last year. And I get madder every time I have anything to do with some of these d----d Englishmen. The mess especially gets me down. We have an electric gramophone in the lounge with an amplifier in the mess hall over which we often play some records by Bing Crosby and other Americans. And sure as shooting, one of these blokes will turn it off. They are higher rank as a rule than we are or we could say something about it.

And they consistently refuse to close the doors. It's a matter of pride or ignorance (I have my own opinion) with them and more often than not you can see your breath in the place. Their precious little fires are so pitifully inadequate at the best of times but with a gale blowing snow through the open doors you might as well try to keep warm off a cigarette. I've tried making pointed remarks about igloos and taking the doors off to save having them in the road at all, but nothing seems to help.

Aside from all that they are the darnedest bunch of snobs. Of course the average English sergeant is a thing of awe and respect (?) to their A.C.s. It's funny, really, to talk to some of these fellows. They stick in "sergeant" every time they possibly can. Of course there is the big difference in that we will talk to them at a dance or something where their own sergeants won't.

You may think all I have to do is grouse, but I really can't say that I am crazy about this country. I used to wonder what on earth it was that motivated the early explorers. Now I know. Even when they didn't know where they were going, the odds were still with them. The trouble with us Canadians is that we don't appreciate a good thing when we have it.

At any rate, the gist of the whole matter is that the sooner I get back to Canada the more satisfied I'll be. I've even been told (by a flight sergeant) that he'd just as soon we stayed on our own side of the puddle. I told him that was our choice too but we had no say in the matter.

I finished H.G. Wells' Brynchild yesterday. I certainly have a knack of picking real philosophical studies anyway. If the sensor leaves anything I said above, don't pay too much attention to it as I soon expect to become acclimatized.

Your loving son,

Clayton.

P.S. There must be something wrong with my mail as I've only received one letter in a week.

Somewhere in Scotland [Montrose]
Feb. 1, 1942

Dear Mom and Dad,

I received a Recorder a few days ago and another yesterday along with your letters of the 26 Dec. and Jan. 1st. But so far none of my parcels have arrived but they should get here any day now, as most of the boys have got some now. Nash got two the other day and one had some Nielsen's chocolates in it. Was it ever good. I haven't got the windbreaker yet either and sure wish it would come.

It was tough about Ted Shields. I can't remember him very well but knew Bob. Was also sorry to hear about George Crowston. I'm afraid he's a bit scatter-brained at the best of times.

I heard from Doug Noton the other day, the second from him. He was training to be an instructor too and hopes to get back at it when he is OK. His ankle was broken three times which took three operations, his wrist once and was also cut about the eyes. I don't know whether he told his parents or not, so perhaps you'd better not say anything about it to them. If his eyes are OK he'll be able to fly again. I also heard from Bill Garton and Bill Brook. Latter got your parcel OK Mom but has been very busy. Garton is also very busy and said not to write him till I hear from him again so apparently something is going on.

I haven't written Jack Moore yet but will likely get around to it when our exams are over. We write them on Thursday next. Nash is going over some patter now with our orderly. He is a Welsh boy of about 19 and we have a lot of fun with him. As a matter of fact I am having quite a time getting this written. Most of the English NCOs are a hard bunch of guys to get along with and we don't have much to do with them.

It's a perfectly miserable day and we don't go out if we don't have to. We haven't done any real work for a couple of weeks now and it doesn't look as though we will for a while (Nash is having some trouble with his patter. Our main job in learning to become flight instructors was to learn what they called 'patter.' (As Clayton wrote in *Nickel Trip* on page 62, "Every maneuver in the RAF was taught with a certain description of the maneuver and prescription for it, given by the instructor, which he at the same time did with the controls, so as to make the airplane do what he was talking about. And then the student tried to follow through on this. We had to memorize this patter, which was the slang term for this system. This was the RAF system for standardizing flying instruction so that as much standardization as possible could be achieved. Otherwise, fellows would develop their own methods, some of which would be effective and others not. We had to memorize this patter for every possible situation in training a student to fly an airplane.")

I heard from Dorie yesterday too, the first one for 10 or 12 days. Apparently she had only received one cheque up to Christmas ($26.83) but she should have received at least two more by now. I am going to sign over some of my money from here because I don't need it all. I still have 1,000 fags left though don't want to run out as some of the boys have. These English ones are horrible as a rule.

There isn't anymore news or anything. Don't worry about me. All that is wrong is that my better half isn't here. I sure do miss her.

All my love,
Clayton.

Scotland
Feb. 15, 1942

Dear Mom and Dad,

I don't know how long ago it is since my last letter, but I'm afraid that it's been some time. We have been working hard for some time and I've spent most of my time sleeping.

Nash and I were down to Dundee and Edinburgh last weekend. He has an uncle in Edinburgh and three very pretty cousins. But you can have the old cities. I don't think they are quaint anymore, just impossible. It sure would be great to be standing on Portage beside The Bay again.

We had quite a time on our 48 and it cost us plenty, mostly for hotels. We got stranded in Dundee late the last night and had to sleep in a "Sailor's Home." That was its name. It wasn't too bad for a cheap place and we never lost anything, which is more than we can say for our own quarters. Nash lost a wallet with three pounds in it a few days before we went on our 48.

The results of our ground-school exams were out today. I was fifth out of 33 with 312 out of a possible 400. If I can do as well with my flying, I'll be all set. Nash was eighth with 288. We intend taking some pictures to send you but whenever the sun stays out that long, we are sure to be flying. You're sure right, Dad. I really do miss good old Manitoba sunshine.

I got the parcel you sent to Halifax yesterday, also the W.A sent on or about Jan. 18. Thank them very much for me, but I suppose I should write them a note. Your parcel was swell – I sure appreciated the nuts and peanut brittle especially. You can't get any candy here, of course, or nuts. And the shortbread just melts, Mom. Between the two of us we should be all right. I hope our parcels alternate. The W.A. sent chocolate bars (five), razor blades, a few cigs, a half pound of cheese which will go swell with the soda crackers. Your parcel was sent to a wrong address over here and that's why it was so long in coming.

I also got your second letter, Dad, and Dorie's 28th the other day. I haven't received all of hers but the others will likely turn up soon. Mail is very irregular.

Nash and I both intended sending cables yesterday but haven't had a chance for over a week now. We haven't even been able to get our tunics from the cleaners. Mine has been there two weeks and Nash's longer.

This has been short, but I will try to write more often in the future because I know only too well how much a letter can mean.

All my love,
Clayton.

Scotland (Montrose)
March 5, 1942

It must be some time since I last wrote but we've been quite busy for the past while. I haven't had any letters for a while which for the above reason was a good thing in a way, but I sure miss them.

I heard from Miss Bradley, Emily Cherry, Bernard Birbeck and Rosie. Rosie said he was going to try to see Doris on his way to Halifax. He said that Cub was slated to be an instructor but was doing his best to get out of it. If he takes my advice he will take the job. A lot of us thought the same way about it when we didn't know any better. But we do now.

The Recorders have been coming and are rather a treat but don't tell W. V. [Udall, publisher/editor] that. Nash gets a kick out of them too as he knows some of the people. Besides, anything Canadian is worth seeing. Sending the Free Press comics was a good idea, they were OK. And you can keep the ginger snaps coming too Dad, we just gobble them up. So far neither of us has received any cigs. There definitely must be something wrong somewhere. I talked to one Canadian here who has been here a year. He has got 600 so far though four or five times that many were sent. If I find that they aren't coming through, I'll cable and tell you as there is no point in your wasting money on them. It will be hard getting used to English stuff but I would have to do that in any case if they didn't come. Although one alternative is to send half a pound of fine cut and papers. That much would do us a month and you could send it in a parcel.

I haven't heard from any of the boys though I really owe them, but I really haven't had time the past month to be writing. Let me know what Jack and Les and any of the rest of the gang are doing if you can. Tell Mrs.

Garton that if Jack still wants to learn to fly, to wait until I get home as that is my job now and I would like to teach him. I don't think I could resist the temptation of scaring the liver out of him once or twice though.

I got the lead of a gramophone and a bunch of good records of American bands and we have a jam session all the time we are in. Right now it's playing "Oh daddy, beat me right to the bar" if that means anything. Of course we only have about a dozen records so it's the same ones over and over. But that doesn't worry either of us, though some of the boys get a bit tired of hearing the same things all the time. But it helps a lot.

I bought some goggles today (three pounds) but worth all of it. They are hard to get here too. I'd have paid more for them in Canada. My others weren't protecting my eyes from the wind but these should. I was just lucky to get them as you can't walk into stores and buy them like you can in Canada.

Nash's chocolates have run out and I wish we had some more to take their place. We have some of my snaps, nuts and cake instead. Well I have a bit of work to do so perhaps had better get at it. Lots of love,

Clayton.

CHAPTER 10

Instructing at Cranwell

His first letter from RAF College at Cranwell, Scotland, suggests an urgency to get home. He deeply misses his wife. But by the end of 1942 Clayton is eager to leave instructing and get into operational flying, which means attacking German installations.

March 31, 1942

Dear Mom and Dad,

We finished our course about 10 days ago and I came straight to our new place. However there are only four of us here and Nash and I got separated. I was lucky to get the top categorization in my tests. It means, among other things, that I can go back to Canada on the first draft I can get my name on, and believe me I'm doing it. Being married gives me an edge too.

The school where I am now is kind of an elite place where all the upper 400's sons come to learn to fly. As a matter of fact one of my pupils flew with the French Air Force before the capitulation and has twice as many hours as I have. But he is still a terrible flyer. It seems funny to be teaching other fellows how when I was learning how myself such a short time ago.

I received a parcel from you the other day but there was no mouth organ in it so there must be another someplace. I forget exactly what was in it as I got one from Dorie too. Also received several Free Presses and two Recorders yesterday. The "blokes" (English chaps) get quite a kick out of the comics.

It sure was good to see that Bob Moore had managed to get out of that mess OK. He certainly was lucky.

This is kind of short but for some time I haven't felt much like writing letters. Besides there is nothing to write about over here. I wish they would put me on a Canada draft tomorrow. But I suppose I can wait a while.

All my love,
Clayton.

April 23, 1942
RAF Cranwell, Scotland

Dear Mom and Dad,

I received your last parcel and letters of March 16 yesterday, also 300 fags from Dorie. If they keep coming the way they are, I will never have to worry about smokes. Your parcel had four packages of Ogdens fine cut, papers, canned chicken, peanut butter, etc. in it. There are three Canadians, a New Zealander and an Aussie in our hut with about 10 RAF chaps. We usually pool our parcels and have big feeds in our hut or take the stuff over to the mess and have a feed there. Usually we manage to have some butter, also some jam, honey, marmalade and now peanut butter, along with biscuits, canned meats of different kinds, powdered cocoa, coffee and different things which the chaps haven't seen in some time. They really enjoy it.

Also I give my cigarette and chocolate rations to one of the boys as I don't care for them and don't need them. We are allowed 30 cigarettes and about two bars from our mess per week, so you can see how much it means to them to get a double ration. I also received four packs of English cigs from some people I met in Scotland. The Scotch are really swell on the whole. Certainly the younger people are more like our own than the English.

There are three NCO instructors in my flight and they really are OK. It is one of them that I give the rations to.

You wanted to know a bit more about what I am doing. I'm not just sure how much I am supposed to tell you, and there isn't much to say anyway. I am at the SFTS for the British Empire, supposed to be quite a break actually, instructing on Master aircraft which are like Harvards in general appearance. They are quite powerful, a lot faster than Harvards. The results of our instructors' course in Scotland, I was fifth out of 35 in ground school and one of about eight or 10 who got Q categories as instructors. There are two categories over here, C and Q. C is below average or low average and Q is average, above average or exceptional. I am an average Q which is nearly always the rating given a Q when leaving the course, but can make it above average Q if I can qualify by taking a test in a few months. Also having a Q means I can be posted to Canada.

I like my flight commander quite well and my group commander [Fl. Lieut. Foxley-Norris] very much. He just rented a nice house and told me to make it my home away from home. I haven't been around to it yet but will one of these days. He is a real guy, as a crazy as a bed-bug and his wife should be really OK though I have never met her. She likes Canadian cigarettes though.

Among my first students was a Frenchman who I told you a bit about last time. He has had a couple of long layoffs, one due to a machine-gun wound in the chest and the other to a bad accident in which the other chap was killed and so they put him through the course here. Two of his brothers had it from the Jerries and all the rest of his family, including several brothers and sisters, are in Nazi hands. Anyway, he sure was anxious to get to work against them so I worked pretty hard with him. When I first got him his flying was on the whole pretty horrible though he had almost twice the time I had. He was a Fl. Sgt. too. However he passed out above average on both his tests which is better than I did. The Flight Cmdr was very pleased with his showing, especially after his poor start.

I have three left now and one of them has more time than I have too but there are still a couple of things I can teach him. He had his tests recently and also did very well. The other two had never flown before joining up and are quite a trial. It really is a good thing that I did as much shooting, fishing and trapping as I did. They all develop your patience and believe me you need it at this job.

One good thing here is that we get plenty of time off – one day a week, a 48 every month, and seven days every three months. Today is one of my days off so I slept in this morning and am writing letters this afternoon. This coming Sunday and Monday I get my 48 and am going to fly to Driffield Saturday afternoon, weather permitting. I get my seven days starting May 4 and am planning a bike trip. I bought a bike a couple of weeks ago.

I'm in the sergeants' mess lounge listening to records on the radio-gramophone. There is a darned nice selection of American records, Bing Crosby, Glenn Miller, Jimmy Dorsey, etc.

I suppose you have been reading a lot about the commando raids the last few weeks. One of the pupils on our course, an army lieutenant, was in a commando regiment. He is a big chap, 6'3", 190 pounds and built like a Greek god. You can't make him talk about it but some of the other chaps know him and say he could talk plenty if he wanted to. He is very quiet and well-educated, and incidentally a natural-born pilot. We all like to fly with him because he really is good. He should make a name for himself in a Spit, lucky fellow.

My nicknames here are "Canada" or "Lofty" (English for slim). I am the only Canadian in the bunch. The only Jerry planes I have seen here were three captured ones used for instructional purposes. [At this point two and a half lines are cut out of the letter.] The RAF has machines of each type which can cope with them very handily and the Spit doesn't have any trouble with any of them. The only air raid I have been in was when a single Jerry tried to hit a train I was on one night. He missed by a long way and I understand a night-fighter got him a little later. Hitler has been pretty leery about sending his boys over here for some time now. It just doesn't pay him. It sure is a pretty sight to see a big bunch of Spits in formation going over. Makes a fellow darned envious too. [Two and a half more lines are cut out of the letter here.] They must be wonderful ships too, really fast. There is a Canadian Spit squadron very near here too; I am going over some day on my bike. It makes me mad when I think of coming over here and then being made an instructor. The trouble is that there is no way of getting off it onto ops [operations]. The only good point is that you really are a flyer after a year or so at the job.

Well, I've been two hours writing this and I have some others to write so had better close. Give my regards to everybody at home. I am very glad Dorie was able to stay with you for as long as she did. It was about two weeks, wasn't it?

I must go now. Don't worry about the parcels, they are coming through fine and are OK.

All my love,
Clayton

Cranwell, Scotland
May 13th, 1942

Dear Mom and Dad,

I am afraid that I haven't been writing as often as I should, but I find it very depressing over here, and I am also afraid that what letters I have written haven't been terribly cheerful. It isn't that the country is depressing, though it definitely is at times; it is more the fact of working every day knowing that the next few hundred will be the same and totally wasted as far as I'm concerned. Of course I am teaching blokes how to fly but it is a thankless job at the best and I would much rather be doing it at home. It seems to be part of my nature to be short-tempered whenever I'm restricted when doing something I don't care about and it certainly is the case over here.

A short while ago I had some very disappointing news. I hadn't written for a while hoping to have some very good news for you all, but it fell through due to the fact (apparently) that the Canadian Government has given orders to the Air Ministry to the effect that no Canadian instructors are to be posted back to Canada from Great Britain. Of course I haven't taken that without doing something and am going down to London early next week to see the RCAF Liaison Officer (and anybody else who might help) to find out the reason for such an apparently ridiculous order and to see if it can't be modified. I have spent several days trying to think of one reason, however insignificant, for it and can't find one. Unless they can satisfy me that it is for a very good reason I am going to do a bit of writing to various places.

No parcels or anything else have come through for a couple of weeks now, though quite a bit of Canadian mail seems to have got here OK. I have been out of fags for a few days and have been rolling them and smoking English ones which I don't like. The reason I run through so many is that I give so many away. I gave Doug Noton 200 and lent another 200 to another chap going on leave. Besides, all the English chaps like them. The Recorder comes very irregularly, about five since you started sending them. The Saturday Free Press comes much more regularly and I really appreciate it.

Well, there is a snooker game waiting for me so will have to go.

All my love,

Clayton.

Cranwell, Scotland
May 14, 1942

Dear Mom and Dad,

There was a letter from each of you waiting when I got back from leave, two from Doris and one from Marion Murray and today I received another from you Dad and a parcel containing ginger snaps, tobacco, peanut butter, etc. Those parcels certainly come in handy to relieve the monotony. I practically live from day to day for them now.

I had a very nice leave. Saw Cub [Brook] and Rosie [Bill Rosenberry], also several other chaps I knew and visited Doris's Aunt Edith and Cousin Dorothy.

Two days ago Doug Noton came in to visit me. He is on sick leave and hopes to be flying again in July. He looked very well, with a small mark between his eyes, the back of his left hand a bit "bumpy" where the bones were broken, and limps a bit yet though expects that will go soon [was involved in a crash landing we suspect]. I was very surprised of course to see him, though I had written him before going on leave hoping to be able to drop around and see him. But he was on leave himself and didn't get it until mine was almost over. We had quite a little chat although he couldn't stay very long.

That same night another of the boys and myself went out to our group commander's (a flight lieutenant) house about six miles away for a game of bridge and a bit of beer. That certainly is as much a national drink over here as tea. I like it OK in limited amounts. We had a rare time, his wife being away, so we cooked up our own eats. She is very pretty. He [Flight Lieut. Foxley-Norris] is a real regular fellow and I have him working on a posting home for me. I will be sorry to leave him as he really is one in a million but I think that can be made up in Canada.

A couple of days ago I flew my first Hurricane and several times since. They really are a swell kite to fly. [Bird did air tests on Hurricanes May 13, 14, 15, totaling one and three-quarter hours, according to his Log Book and Nickel Trip.]

As I told Dorie, I am pretty tired tonight so will close. Have lost my little address book and will have to start numbering letters all over again. Thanks ever so much for parcels.

Lots of love,
Clayton.

P.S. Lost Mac's Ronson lighter that he gave me one and a half years ago. Don't know how. Have a cheap one.

May 16, 1942

Dear Mom and Dad,
[A few words about receiving letters and cigarettes, just a brief addition to his previous letters.]

May 18, 1942
Scotland

Dear Mom and Dad,
We have really been going hard this last while trying to clean up a course and get them away. I got a letter from you today Mom and one and a parcel from Dorie.

Yes I am instructing all right but I wish they could have seen fit to have given me a crack at operations first. Hurricanes really are a treat to fly and Spits must be really something. Some day I am going to make a trip in one of those babies.

Paul Sander's death will have appeared some time ago I imagine, in the Free Press. That was a tough case because he really wanted to fly the type of aircraft he was flying at the time. I know some of the details but I'm afraid I can't give them, but he was almost ready to go on ops. I have heard that another chap from our course has had it too.

Personally I am getting pretty fed up with it all… and am doing all I can to get my Canadian posting pushed through.

If everything goes right I may spend a couple of days in London and perhaps see a bit of the big town. Of course I have seen part of it, but only a small part of it. The tubes are a great thing (underground railroads) and you can go almost anywhere for less than five cents. Don't worry about money, I am doing my best to save some but often some unforeseen something comes up. I have plenty for ordinary use though.

Must go do some night flying now. All my love,
Clayton.
P.S. Give Dorie all my love.

[Cranwell, Scotland]
Aug. 22, 1942

Dearest Mom and Dad,

Another parcel came today with candy, gum, peanuts, toffee, ginger snaps, raisons and cigs in it. At least I haven't been suffering from a lack of parcels. I got 1000 cigs from Mac the other day and 300 more from Dorie today. And it certainly makes a difference not being short of things like that. And don't worry about me smoking too much as I have rationed myself to15 a day. In case that sounds like a lot, it used to be 25. Besides I developed catarrh the other day and am going to take more care of myself in the future.

Actually that is pretty hard to do as our work is heavy right now. I was flying last night and am going again tonight. But I wish it was on night intrusion over German airfields. That is the kind of operational work I would like. By the time you get this I will have nearly 100 hours night flying and 600 hours total time. However I am afraid that my chances at ops are slight because of my catarrh. It is bad stuff in this game.

You have asked several times about the pen-light and batteries, Dad. I got them several months ago and thought I had told you about them. It is coming in very handy as I take it flying with me every night. You can get used to walking in the blackout and I don't need it much for that. But it is a big help when flying. I have used about six of the batteries but still have six or so left.

I am not short of anything else except sox. Several pairs of them would come in handy. I wrote Dorie about them some time ago and she replied saying she was sending them in separate parcels. I have received one pair. Also a couple of shirts and shorts would come in handy but she is taking care of them too, I hope.

It certainly was a shock to hear of Reg Noton. I had forgotten he was over here. I will try to find out what he was on. Doug hasn't written me for a while and I don't know what he is doing just now. Dorie told me she had seen Bill Garton. I wonder how long he will be staying at home.

My seven-day leave is overdue now but I will be getting it in two or three weeks. I have been off the station only once in over a month and that was the day before yesterday. Our pupils were writing exams and we had the day off. Anyway I sure need the time off.

One of my pupils off the last course was in yesterday to see us with his Spitfire. Boy are they ever a sweet kite. So far I haven't had a chance at one but I will some day.

I was disappointed to hear that no more papers etc. can come over. However it's just as well as they did take up a lot of room. There must have been thousands every week. But I was glad to hear that cigs have been limited to 1000 each month per man. Some have been doing a real business over here as they sell quite easily for more than twice what it costs you to buy them in a store. And that is taking advantage of a good thing. Talk about giving an inch and taking a mile.

Please convey my good wishes to Bernice and her hubby. If I had known where to send it I would have sent a wire, also to Eldon Bliss and Betty Bucham. There is a real pair of kids; I knew them both real well at Brandon. Pulfer and Puddy Poole, Jack Wood and Winnie, and now Bliss and Betty [getting married]. Dorie may not be a Brandonite but she's almost [having been born and raised in McGregor not far away]. She knows Woods and Winnie and Pulf real well.

I met two Brandon boys in the Beaver Club some time ago, but I doubt whether you knew them.

I'll close now but will try to add some more tomorrow. Incidentally those blue letters got through in nine to 12 days and are OK. Dorie uses them a lot too. We may be able to soon as well.

I almost forgot your telegram asking about me. It has taken a long time to reach me I'm afraid. It is stamped London Aug. 8 so presume that is the one you sent on the 6th. Will wire on Monday too.

Thanks for the parcels, take care of yourselves and don't worry about me.

Love,
Clayton.

Sunday, Aug. 23, 1942

Dear Mom and Dad,

I never got up in time to hear Jack Benny today. If you remember I never used to think much of him at home but it's sure good to hear him, Mary Livingstone and especially Rochester over here. He comes in at 12 noon, recorded of course.

Jerry was over for a short while last night but he doesn't bother us much as a rule. If you could see the night fighters we use now you would understand why not. I'd be in my element with one of those babies and all those cannon and machine guns. We heard some cannon fire last night and they were actually quite close to us as we could see the tracers only a few miles away. There was a fire a minute later on the ground so they probably got the one that bothered us. I was just on the ground when we heard his engines and then he dived. They sure make a racket. Of course we have been bothered before but only once has it amounted to anything. I wasn't on that night but apparently he dropped a couple of pills near the flare path. They didn't explode and could only be found in the morning when they could be seen.

Our kites are quite fast actually and especially so for trainers. It's quite a thrill to be travelling 250-60 miles per hour when low flying instead of about 150 that the old Harvards gave us. But I wish I was back on them as I liked them quite a bit more than these.

I received a letter from Auntie Emm a few days ago. By gosh Mom but her writing is hard to decipher. Two words were too much for me.

Time certainly flies over here, which is a blessing in a way. I've been here almost 10 months now but it doesn't seem like it. By gosh it's raining cats and dogs now and about 10 minutes ago the sun was nice and bright. I've been caught several times out in the darned stuff. But I usually get the "gen" (meaning information) from the Meteorological office before I go anywhere so as to be prepared. But the climate as a whole doesn't agree with me at all.

Well, must close now and write Dorie. Thanks again for the parcels and especially candy. You need coupons to get anything like that here (except chocolate which isn't very sweet).

Love,
Clayton.

Sept. 23, 1942

Sgt. FCC Bird
(Can) R-91897
RCAF Overseas

[This is the first Airgraph he has sent. It is stamped Oct. 3, we don't know where. These are annoyingly short letters that appear to have been copied and

reduced in size, limited to one side of one page, not good for encouraging interesting or in-depth writing, but with the advantage of being light.]

Dear Mom and Dad,

We can send these now so be sure to let me know how long they take. I am sorry you haven't heard from me in such a long time, although I'm sure that I wrote in that time. But I don't keep the dates so can't check up.

My Flight Sgt. has not come through yet but I am not worried, though it is overdue, as I have been recommended for a commission and have had one interview. In two months I either will be or won't, but I have hopes.

The last parcel you told me about came yesterday, a day after the letter. Another blue air mail came this a.m. Parcels seem to be coming through fine and so do fags.

Had a letter from Cub this a.m. asking to be reminded to you both. He is on a squadron now, lucky guy, and what a squadron. I wish I could tell you more about it. Good-bye for now and thanks for the parcels.

All my love,
Clayton.

Scotland
Oct. 25, 1942

Dear Mom and Dad,

Your parcel arrived yesterday with the shorts. Also 300 British Consols from Dorie. There has been very little mail for about three weeks now. Oh yes, thanks a lot for the Recorders.

That must have been a terrible storm to cause so much damage. I feel very sorry for the Pettypieces. If you remember I went to school with Jean and Marguerite. Jean was one year ahead of me and Marguerite died when we were in Grade X. Seems like a long time ago.

Life goes on here pretty much the same as usual, probably like good old Boissevain but I know where I would rather be. We have been here so long now that when a new Canadian instructor arrived last week, his talk actually sounded strange! It's definitely time I was sent home for a short leave but the authorities won't agree.

Jack Wilson and Syd Harrison were in on the Dieppe do. They were lucky to be able to go through it, if you get what I mean. One of my former pupils was in it too, and nearly had it when he got separated and two F.W. 190s jumped him. He was back here in his Spit a few weeks after it and

told me about it. He was reported missing about three weeks ago. A crazy type but I liked him. One of my other pupils has had it since too.
[Here the letter stops and a new date appears, Nov. 8.]

Scotland

[This is his second 'Airgraph' which is clearly too short to be of much use as a letter. If nothing else it lets those at home know he is still kicking.]

Oct. 29, 1942

Dear Mom and Dad,

Thanks ever so much for the last parcel with the shorts, candy, cheese, etc. The Kleenex was a good idea as it certainly saves on hankies.

I made inquiries at the post office and find that we can send parcels home so am going to get some Christmas shopping done on my next day off. It's a good thing I have managed to save some money. I have about $60 in the bank here but it won't go far as things are fairly expensive. Besides which I am to be best man at one of the boy's weddings on Dec. 17. Well must close now.

Love,
Clayton

Nov. 8, 1942

[Continues as part of the Oct. 25 letter.]

I'm sorry not to have finished the above when I started it, but on this night flying we usually sleep until just before we have to go out again. The nights are quite long now and it's a bit tough. I have had a bad cold into the bargain but think I have found the answer to that, a cold shower in the morning. It sounds a bit drastic and actually it is, but it sure makes me feel better and it did get the cold off my chest. The rest of the boys think I am crazy. It also keeps me from shivering all day long too. Winter in this part of England is a wet miserable sort of cold foggy weather and even with my wool underwear and sweaters I used to be cold all the time. But it's OK once I started the cold showers.

By gosh would I like to be in on some of those duck hunts on old Whitewater. Shooting is one thing that I really have missed over here.

As I believe I told you, I did a bit of hunting with a .22 on my last leave at Lawrie Tayor's but it was only target shooting. My eye is still in pretty though. He was certainly amazed to see me hit a tin can that he threw into the air. Actually he is a fair shot from prone position but pretty hopeless any other way. I am afraid he believes we still have to defend ourselves from Indians, or gophers or jackrabbits after what I showed him.

So Mac is a Second Lieut. now. Please send me his address as soon as he is settled at Shilo so that I can congratulate him. My Commission should be through before Christmas. The RCAF has orders out about air crew commissions now and the Group Captain who turned me down "because he didn't know me well enough" and told me to come back again in three months had no authority whatever to do it. The trouble was that I didn't know that. If I had known then what I know now I would have told him straight to his face and referred the matter to our Headquarters. They have had so many complaints that they are only too glad to do something about it. Anyway now that I know this I have set the ball rolling again and it shouldn't be much longer now. We have a new Group Captain who seems to be a decent type. That last one was a dim sod though. He was shocked when I told him that I had never played rugger. And I had the dickens of a time trying to convince him that there was and is such a thing as the Royal Canadian Air Force and that I belonged to it. I had the impression that he still didn't believe me when I left him. He is the one who told a negro fellow from Nigeria, a pupil here, that he couldn't have a commission because he was black and it would be difficult for white officers and NCOs when he became a flight lieutenant and in charge of a flight. But he got his pants kicked in that case as old John Thomas (the negro) was the son of a Nigerian king or emperor and had a commission about three days later. Anyway the old dimwit was posted to India very shortly afterwards and will probably drink himself to death there. He tried hard here. Well it's dinner time now so will have to change and finish this afterwards.

It is now about 5:30 and one of the boys and I have just been to the "flicks" and had tea. We saw an English film "Pimpernel Smith" starring Leslie Howard. He was as good as ever and the picture was much better than any other English film I have seen. There is a show right on our camp and they have two pictures a week. Then on Thursdays there is an ENSA show or else a different film from what has been. The Ensa is a variety affair with various stars etc. and are good once in a while but usually not so good. Most of the films they get are American and are quite good. Then on Wednesday evenings the Canadian YMCA comes over from an operational station nearby and gives us a free picture. Last Wednesday was "49th Parallel." They also distribute free comforts from the Red Cross. I got some pajamas which I needed and two pairs of sox which I definitely needed. I am OK now though as some of Dorie's have come through as well.

There is an amazing amount of game just around here. One flock of Hungarian partridges uses our auxiliary landing field as a headquarters and every evening when I go over I can hear them chirping around. Hares live right on the drome for all the aircraft that are continually taking off and landing. There are immense numbers of crows around and they are so accustomed to airplanes that we can get the wheels to within 15 feet of them. I have seen them right underneath my wing.

Then there are quite a few ducks but only in one district and they are rather hard to get at. Besides it is quite hard to get ammunition now as well as the guns. Licences don't seem to work the same here either. You have one for your gun and then you can shoot the different kinds of game when in season. At least I think that is the way it works.

I was very sorry to hear what you had to say about Mrs. Southon, Dad, but perhaps it will be for the best. The old man had to do all the work anyway. I will have to drop him a line and will do so tonight if I have time before we go out. I am glad he has had such a wonderful summer of fishing and hope he has had his share of the ducks by now. He will if they came within range of that old gun of his. It's too bad that you couldn't get in on more of the fishing Dad but maybe you will make up for it with the ducks and jumpers. I don't suppose Southon will be after them this year either, will he?

And now I must close if I'm to write any other letters. I wrote Dorie and told her about the tray you sent her Mom. She hasn't said anything about it in any of the letters I've received so apparently it didn't reach her. And now I must go.

Love,
Clayton.

Scotland
An Airgraph
Nov. 15, 1942

Dear Mom and Dad,

Your Christmas parcel with the sweater, pajamas, sox, hankies, chocs, etc. arrived safely yesterday. Oh yes, and the cake. I haven't had time to try that yet but it certainly looks good. The sweater fits fine and will be real nice when I get my commission, if I do, and the flannelette pajamas are the real McCoy for this climate.

My Christmas parcels are going to be late as I have been unable to get away to do some shopping. But I hope to soon. All my love and many thanks,

Clayton.

Scotland
Airgraph

Nov. 27, 1942

Dear Mom and Dad,

[A short note about receiving letters and not receiving Pat Herron's parcel.] "Heard from Kay Heywood in a card. Hope her baby is OK. By now, will continue in an air mail letter.

All my love,
Clayton.

Sgt. FCC Bird
Can R-91897
RCAF Overseas

Nov. 27, 1942

Dear Mom and Dad,

This letter is a continuation of the airgraph of the same date. As a matter of fact I only finished it a minute ago. Let me know which arrives first as they will be mailed together.

The Community parcel which was sent to me in August has not arrived, but I wish you would thank everybody concerned. I think Mrs. George McDonald and one of the Henderson ladies are the big noises if I remember rightly. I received one from them some time ago but believe I acknowledged it.

Really you know, there are too many parcels sent to us fellows over here and I don't want you to send me so many. It isn't that we don't enjoy getting them but it does cost a bit and besides must take up an immense amount of shipping space. Getting war-minded you see.

Kay's letter was very nice and she mentioned that she and Jack were to become parents. I certainly do wish them the best of everything and please extend my congrats in case I am a while writing them. I can only stand writing so many at a time and don't often feel inclined to write at all. I know it's a shameful thing to have to admit but it's a fact. However I do my best.

Kay mentioned that Clayton Lee was flying. I didn't know it before. From her letter he was at Fort William so was still doing elementary. I imagine by now he is in a SFTS. I would like to have someone like that I know to teach. We are getting on OK, not too much to do because of weather conditions but enough to keep in shape. I must say that anyone who can fly in this country should be able to fly anywhere. I have over 650 hours in now, about 115 of which is night flying so I really know what it means to fly by night. And it sure is dark here what with the blackout and everything. I haven't seen a great deal of enemy action yet though. I have hopes of it in the not too distant future as I am going to try to get on to ops. It will be night fighters if I can, doing intrusion work over France. However time will tell.

My sinus has largely gone but is still present as I have been subject to headaches (a rarity in me) due I think to the cold wind hitting my forehead at 160-180 mph. However I have rigged up some chamois which I taped onto my goggles and so far it has worked like a charm. It protects my forehead fine. But I don't know what it will be like when it gets wet. The other day while I was up the cloud went right down to the ground and I had to wait awhile before it had cleared sufficiently for me to come in. But I am used to things like that and they don't bother me anymore. I got caught out one night when it came down to 150 feet and I thoroughly enjoyed the chance to beat up the flare path.

Speaking of beat-ups, I am going on another Home Guard dive bombing raid on Sunday. They are a great deal of fun and I get a great kick out of them. We get so little time for amusing ourselves when flying that it is a treat to be able to do something of the kind. They consist of three airplanes as a rule flying over in formation, peeling off and then doing very steep dives on an objective, usually a junction of two streets or something similar. We come screaming down, one after the other, at about 300 m.p.h., and go whistling over the heads of the populace. And you should see the way they duck and run. Actually of course we do come quite low. On the last one I was flying level with the tops of the houses down the street pretending to be machine-gunning them. We take pupils with us and they get a big kick out of them too.

Tell Mac to write me sometime. I can't guarantee to write punctually but will do my best. I will write him through you one of these days. It's too bad that he couldn't have got on flying too, but it is darned nice that he at least has a commission. Personally I don't think I could stand the army. By the way I have only one more hurdle to pass before my commission comes through and it comes up in about a week. It will be a few weeks after that before it is confirmed. Then I am going to see RCAF HQ about getting on to ops. And I will be very disappointed if I can't make it.

I wish I could send you some pictures of our airplanes but I can't even get them printed. However I am keeping a roll or two to be printed when I get home unless I can get it done here. Of course I couldn't send them even then.

Well must close now as it is bed-time. Congrats on the ducks Dad and give my regards to Southon.

Love to you both,

Clayton.

P.S. Airgraphs cost only six cents each.

Dec. 19, 1942

To Mr. Percy Bradley,
North Gower, Ont.
Canada

Dear Uncle Percy,

This letter is to everyone who contributed towards my parcel which arrived a day ago. Thanks ever so much to all of you as parcels are so darned nice to get over here. Not that we do so badly here, but they seem to me to be a closer link to those at home. The honey was about the best thing you could have sent. I could almost live on it.

Last week I was promoted to flight sergeant and my commission will be official tomorrow. I will write again in two or three weeks. All my sincerest thanks and best wishes.

Clayton Bird.

Dec. 19, 1942

Dear Mom and Dad,

Before I say anything else, you will probably find it easier to read this with a magnifying glass.

I was promoted to flight sergeant a week ago and was told today that my commission would be officially through tomorrow or Monday. So you can start addressing your letters to P/O Bird anytime, as soon as I let you know my new number.

It was a year ago Thursday that I landed over here. It doesn't seem so long in a way and yet in another it seems like an eternity. Am going to try to get on operational flying or to get home. Best wishes to everyone at home and my love to you both.

Clayton.

[A second Airgraph was included in the envelope, same date.]

Dear Mom and Dad,

I got a letter about a week ago in which you said you had only had about two letters from me in five months. That rather shook me as I have certainly written more than that. However that was last summer before we could send airgraphs so I hope there won't be any more of that. At least I will do my best to see to it that there isn't. You should have cabled me and let me know that they weren't getting through and I would have sent you a cable once every two weeks or something. They only cost me 50 cents.

All my love,
Clayton.

CHAPTER 11

Promotion

Jan. 1, 1943
Scotland

Dear Mom and Dad,

This will only be a short note as I was too long in writing Dorie. However I got back from leave yesterday and saw the New Year in in the sergeants' mess as I didn't have my uniform.

I had a wonderful leave with Lawrie and Nora and bags of grub. To wit, one turkey, one goose, and two chickens among all the other things. Norah really splurged and we ate like kings for a week. Beyond playing a few cards I didn't do much else but sleep. I get along very well with Ann their three-year-old daughter now and we had a lot of fun. They are definitely the two best kids I've ever seen.

Previous to that I was in Bournemouth as best man at the wedding of one of the boys. He married a very nice girl, a real peach, and I had quite a good time while I was there. My sinus affected me a bit this morning on my first flight in about 10 days so I took it easy and am treating it with the nasal drops the specialist gave me. At any rate I am afraid I will have to give up my idea of going on ops and try to get a posting home. I think our dryer climate would be much better. It was cleared up sufficiently not to bother me, but it only lasted for a couple of months. However it needn't be an immediate cause for worry, though I am not going to slip up on treatment this time.

It is now some time since my commission was confirmed and I am just moving up to the College tonight. That is, the officers' mess. I haven't all my kit yet but am getting it together. I am not in too much of a hurry for some of it because I want good stuff when I do get it. Incidentally I have been a Pilot Officer since Dec. 5. Must go to tea now, will finish later. Love,

Clayton.

Pilot Officer F.C.C. Bird
Can J 16.16235
RCAF Overseas

Jan. 3, 1943

Dear Mom and Dad,

I received about five or six letters from you the other day but everything is in a bit of a shambles due to moving into the officers' mess. I don't know where they are and will have to respond to them individually.

First, thanks ever so much for the Christmas box. I have the sweater on now. It is the real McCoy for lounging in my room. Also thanks for Mac's and Charlie Palton's addresses. I will write both as soon as I can. Mac's parcel arrived too, two big boxes of chocolates and two pairs of sox. Thank him for me until I write.

I also received very nice parcels from the Boissevain Community Club (see Mrs. E. Henderson) and from Mrs. Dunn. And fags from Mr. and Mrs. Moore and Mrs. Lawlor. I think that is all. You know in the general excitement of undoing them (they were coming two or three at a time) everything gets all mixed up and it is very hard afterwards to remember who sent what.

It is very hard for me to write more than two letters an evening and if I do they are a strain and I really don't like them. I suppose it is mostly laziness but it is partly monotony as I can only say the same things more or less in each one.

Oh yes, I also got a very nice card and letter from Brandon College but don't know who wrote it though I imagine it was Miss Duncan. I sent her a card by the way. I hope my cards all got through in time. It cost me very nearly $5 to send 12 cards. Rather shakes you, doesn't it?

I was very glad to hear that you were successful with the deer, as usual. And I wouldn't worry too much about the hunting party Dad as it is pure jealousy. Some of those blokes ought to have about eight machine guns like a Hurricane. Then perhaps they would drop one themselves occasionally. I sure would have liked to have been there. However there will be plenty of time for that later.

By the way I know now that not all my mail has been getting through to Canada because Dorie asked me in one of her recent letters if I had got a water bottle she sent last spring. I had told her in several letters that I had got it, so they can't all be getting through. However now that I have a decent room I am keeping an accurate record of all my mail, including the dates when I write and when I receive mail. That starts with Jan. 1. If you do the same we can have a definite check on everything.

Now it is 11 p.m. and I must get to bed soon. I have some reading to do first though to get an idea as to my responsibilities etc. as an officer. We don't get a course like Mac did (thank goodness!) and so a new officer is sometimes left guessing. Give my regards to Southon and the Brooks and anyone else that I know particularly well.

All my love,
Clayton.

P.S. Saw Doug Noton three weeks ago. He is commissioned too and is about 16 miles from me. Tried to see him yesterday but he was away.

Jan. 13, 1943

Dear Mom and Dad,

Your 46th came today Dad, with the pictures of Mac in it. I am surprised to see he is already a full lieutenant as that seems terrifically fast promotion to me. I have another five months to go before I am the equivalent rank, flying officer.

I am afraid that I can't really tell you much about my job. We teach blokes how to fly fairly heavy airplanes, something like Harvards only considerably faster. From us they go on to an operational training unit where they go on to Spitfires etc. In other words they are solo when they leave us, having had their last dual trip and being left to their own devices.

It really can be excellent work especially when you are fortunate enough to get some decent pupils. But so many seem so stupid and others are just poor stuff quite aside from a flying point of view. As far as the flying part of it goes I am afraid it would be a bit technical and I couldn't explain it without using technical terms. Just realize how hard it would be to describe three-dimensional movement without some difficulty.

But I still enjoy it as much as ever for its own sake. It's a wonderful feeling to get away from all the restrictions that you find on the "deck" and just float around over some clouds, or on a clear day to see the country spread out for miles around. Usually of course in England there is some cloud somewhere. There are many different kinds but the ones I like are the ones that look like big pillows, or even sheep, from the ground. They look just the same when you are beside them or on top of them. They are usually found between 4,000 and 10,000 feet altitude. There are always holes through them and little gullies and caverns on their surface and I like whipping along these with cloud away over me on either side. It's similar to going down a very narrow ravine with steep walls.

That, along with certain other maneuvers, is what I call a cloud beat up, and is one of my favourite ways of relaxing. I even send pupils to do it solo when they get stale from working too hard.

I found some one night at 7,000 feet and had the time of my life. They certainly looked pretty too as they were between us and the moon which was full and made them look very mysterious. They made me feel so good that I did some acrobatics and when we got back down again the boys wanted to know what I had been up to as they could see my lights going all over the place.

However these are just the odd moments we get when we can enjoy ourselves. The rest of the time it is just hard work, showing them how a thing is done, correcting their mistakes, etc., ad infinitum until they reach the best possible standard with the time available.

I do have that trouble yet but hadn't said anything about it as I thought there was no use in worrying you with it, but since you are anyway I might just as well tell you. It happens when I've been up a few thousand feet for a while and am coming down. Usually whenever it does affect me I can just feel it at about 2,500 feet, then it gradually gets worse until it is at its worst when we land. Sometimes the pain persists for awhile, other times it goes in a short time. Several weeks ago I had a dull pain in my head for the rest of the day. It affects my ears also and I always have to blow them out. The trouble is doing that only increases the pain from the sinus, though I have to do it to clear my ears.

The RAF specialist gave me some very good nasal drops but warned me not to use them to much as they are powerful. As a matter of fact the stuff has cocaine in it and it feels as though the back of my mouth and throat were half frozen. However it causes really good drainage and helps to relieve the condition enormously, but I doubt if it will ever really get rid of it.

I haven't got a cold and I haven't had one for months now, but my nose drains in the same way as though I did have one, and all the time. I am quite convinced that the damp climate can have nothing but adverse affects on it.

At any rate I am quite useless for operational flying as it would be suicide for me to go to any height in a single-seat fighter, and mass murder to send me in a bigger ship, responsible for a crew. The trouble is that sometimes I can scarcely see when coming into land. Rather awkward as you can imagine. However I am not worried as long as I can get these nose drops and it is only at the first that most pupils can't be trusted to bring a kite down without busting something. It doesn't impair my flying in any way except that it restricts me to height. Most days my limit is about 5,000 feet. Incidentally I have 700 hours as pilot now and probably 50 to 60 as a passenger.

You might send me those cold pills you were telling me of Dad, as I am willing to try anything to get rid of the stuff.

When we are commissioned we get a 55 pound ($275) clothing grant and 240 clothing coupons which is ample to buy everything we need. But uniforms are expensive. So far I have only one but intend to get another when I get my financial affairs straightened. The jacket I have cost $47.50 and the pants $17.50. My great coat also cost $65. You can get quite decent sox for .75 cents to $1, shoes from $10 to $15, gloves around $3. But my dress hat cost $11.50. Let me know what Mac pays so I can get an idea of what things are like at home.

I have some snaps which you may not have so will enclose one or two just in case.

Spent my Christmas leave with Dorie's cousin and really enjoyed myself. We had a goose, a turkey and two chickens. Jerry is a long way from starving England out yet!

And now I must close. Please don't worry about me as it won't do anyone any good and take good care of yourselves. I hope you were able to get out home for Christmas, Dad.

All my love,
Clayton

Jan. 18, 1943

Dear Mom and Dad,

Thanks ever so much for the parcel. And you won't need to send any razor blades for a very long time to come Dad; I must have 120 or 130 of them now. I don't waste them even when I have lots.

That concentrated orange juice was a good idea. I'm afraid though that the only way I can use it is to mix a bit at a time. It may not keep either, as the directions say to keep it in a fridge.

You must have gone to a great deal of trouble to wrap everything up individually the way you did. And it really isn't necessary Dad because all of your parcels have reached me in A1 shape. And small wonder too. You have to hand it to the navy though.

I sure was glad to see the cigs as I was down to two packets again. And really you shouldn't have sent the sugar. We aren't quite as badly off as all that. We had some lovely roasted hare tonight for supper, and you know how I like that. We get it only about one a fortnight but they certainly do it up nicely, with dressing etc. I always have a good appetite and almost always go back for a second helping (like Oliver Twist, only I get it!) especially at supper.

Things are pretty dull in this particular mess and quite often I spend the evening with my old chums in their barrack block. We have a miniature ministry of aircraft production there and so far have flown (and pranged!) one Lysander, one Me 109, and one Spitfire (mine). My Spit hasn't pranged yet though. She did a beautiful loop the night before last. Also under construction are two more Spits, a Hudson, a Hampden and a Heinkel 112.

Incidentally a Jerry of some description was [*the letter ends. The censor cut out the rest*].

Jan. 27, 1943

[Another Airgraph]

Dear Mom and Dad,

Another parcel today! Now, you will just have to stop sending them so often, because I don't know what to do with everything. I'll bet that I have more razor blades than any three shops together in England. But the fruit juices are OK, I can use lots of them.

I just got back from London after spending two days there straightening out some things. And do I hate that place! Was also in sick bay three or four days previously with a spot of flu. OK now except for a bit of a head cold, the first in quite some time. Well these are pretty short, but I will write a real letter soon.

All my love,
Clayton.

Feb. 15, 1943
[Scotland, Cranwell]

Dear Mom and Dad,

Well I have received half a dozen letters from both of you in the past couple of weeks and am very sorry not to have written since Jan. 27. But will send an Airgraph tonight and will try to space them out a bit better.

The past week we have been so very busy that I haven't written anyone. We have averaged over four hours a day which in this line is hard work and so have been trying to get to bed reasonably early.

The sinus doesn't bother me as long as I use the nasal drops. They keep a steady discharge of yellowish phlegm flowing and so I can fly as I please. Without it there isn't much doubt that I would be grounded. I hope to get the situation cleared soon as I had the good fortune to meet the right officer at a mess party Saturday night and he said he would arrange a medical board for me. He took down my particulars anyway and so I am hopeful. If I am not fit for operational flying then there won't be anything to stop me being posted home. On the other hand, if I am operational there won't be any need for me to stay at this job. I figure that I've done my share of it, almost 11 months now.

About two weeks ago I went to London with one of my fellow instructors who knows London *[Edward Holbech, who was killed a little later flying a fighter and attacking a barge on the Rhine]*, and he showed me around. I was introduced to several English band leaders and a couple of head waiters. One of them never forgets a name or face. Eddie says he is the head waiter in London. It was some hotel too. Air Chief Marshall Sir Richard Courtneigh was in the bar when we stopped in for a quick one. *[Dad later said it was a real honour to meet him, but he declined to have his photo taken with Courtneigh because he didn't feel worthy of it, a decision he later regretted].*

All in all we visited quite a number of places: the Ritz Hotel, the Hyde Park Hotel, Hatchett's Restaurant and the Embassy Club. We had dinner at Hatchett's where we had a very nice table right beside the orchestra which is one of the best swing bands I've heard over here. The menu was: oysters, roast plover, and mushrooms on toast with a bottle of burgundy wine, a brandy, and coffee. It took us two hours! To be quite frank I didn't want to leave as I was really enjoying the band but Eddie and his brother said there were several other places we had to see.

Just to illustrate the kind of company I was with, the following night I took a couple of my former pupils along to Hatchett's in the hope of getting another dinner similar to the previous one. As we were approaching the head waiter he was turning away a couple who were looking for a table. But he remembered my name, asked me if I had enjoyed myself the previous evening, and gave me a table for four, though I had no reservation. I'm sure I don't know how they do it but it really is remarkable as they look after so many people. Incidentally, the meal I described cost us about $5.50 each [at least $50 in today's money]. But it was worth every penny of it.

That lasted for two days but on my next leave I think I will go down to the holidaying section of Devon which I am told is really nice. I believe there are still hunting and fishing facilities to be had, as well as swimming, tennis and dancing. I read a book on the country and it really intrigued me. If Hitler only knew how much this little island has even after three years of war he would give up I am sure, without further argument. And to think that everything in Germany not absolutely essential is being closed down!

I really like England now and wouldn't mind living here but for the climate which is unforgiveable. The people are definitely OK but they do have a sort of reserve, or rather disinterestedness towards others. However once that is overcome, and it's very easy these days, they are better than you could find in most countries. What strikes me is their absolute sincerity, amounting almost to frankness.

But I must get to bed now as I have another heavy day ahead of me tomorrow. And the next day *[Feb. 17]* is my 24th birthday. 24 years old! I wonder.

My love to you both,
Clayton.

March 24, 1943

#405 Squadron
F/O Brook, QC J 10 4 22

[This is the only letter we have from Cub Brook, a chum of Clayton's from Boissevain.]

Dear Mr. and Mrs. Bird,

Thank you very much for the lovely parcel which arrived this week. It was very kind of you to send it, and the cigarettes and all were very handy. We have had no letters from home for some time – it seems many many weeks. But I expect a bunch of mail will arrive soon.

How are you all keeping at home? It must have been a very severe winter you had in Manitoba this year. I haven't heard from Clayton lately, but both our letter writing goes in fits and starts. I was very pleased to hear that he had his commission. It would be nice to have another get-together soon.

Freddie Culbert and John Atchison are both on this station with me. There are many others from Hartney, Souris, Brandon and Winnipeg. Our squadron is practically all Canadians, from all parts of Canada.

Bill [?] has been quite busy, and hasn't had much time for writing lately. There is just a possibility that we may both get leave soon. I hope it will work out that way. This is the station that Jack Moore wrote one from last summer. I have heard nothing of him since, and so have lost track. Please give my regards to Dorie and Mac. Very sorry to hear about Rosenberry.

Best wishes, sincerely,
Cub.

The frustrations are building with Clayton, as we read below.

April 5, 1943

Dear Mom and Dad,

It's a very long time since my last one but I really have been terribly fed up with everything here for quite a while now. If I only had some reason for being satisfied here it wouldn't be too bad, but from my point of view there isn't one.

I have just returned from a week's leave which I spent in Exeter, Devon. There is some marvelous fishing there, salmon and trout, and I had a crack at both but inexperience beat me. I haven't room here to describe it but will in the very near future.

There was a letter from each of you when I got back last night, the first in almost a month, and a cable from Doris, and some from Mac, Jack and Winnie Wood (of Brandon College days), Auntie Emm and Marnie. I haven't received any fags for almost three months and am getting used to English ones though it's expensive at 50 cents for 20. Only two parcels have come through since Christmas, from you and Dorie for my birthday. Gosh it's hard to realize that I'm 24 now. Soon be middle-aged and nothing to show for it!

Will try to write a longer one tomorrow night as I have several would like to answer tonight. My sinus doesn't bother me much, but the worry is always there.

All my love,
Clayton.

June 11, 1943

Dear Mom and Dad,

Lots of mail! A letter from you Mom yesterday, one each today and parcel No. 23. And what a parcel! But you got my waist measurement a bit out. I haven't got fat enough to wear 36 yet, still 32. However my batwoman *[aid assigned to each officer]* thinks she can fix the shorts. But thanks ever so much for all the candy, marshmallows and everything else.

It's been a long time since I last wrote but we are doing night flying and it leaves us so little time for ourselves that I usually get outside to get a bit of sun, if there is any going. A while back I had managed to collect a rather good tan but it is mostly gone now.

I hope you liked the snaps. It is a pity the censor had to cut out the planes because I can't think of any reason why he should except that they are planes. I suppose they have their reasons. Film is very difficult to obtain and I may not be able to send you any more for a while.

Yes, Prince is the pet of the flight. He is a loveable little rascal and I look after him a lot when Kopecky *[Miroslav, his Czech friend]* is on leave. He is more fun than a barrel of monkeys.

I certainly was glad to hear you had the Nash. It's about time. And I hope it continues to work OK. Boy would it be nice to have a car! As it is my bike was swiped out of the mess about five weeks ago and I've given it up as lost.

The flowers have been wonderful this year. There is a big bed of roses right outside my window. Our batwoman keeps some in a vase on our table and they really do make a difference to a room. My roommate is from Kenora and knew Dr. Paton and his boys and old mother. Jimmie Paton was killed in the Air Force over here a while ago. Do you remember them? Will write a good long one soon as night flying is finished.

All my love,
Clayton.

Aug. 2, 1943

Dear Mom and Dad,

I feel like an awful cad not having written for so long. I don't know what to say as I have no reason or excuses for it, but the other fellows seem to have the same trouble. We were talking about it the other evening and the general opinion was that there is so little that one can say in a letter that they only amount to notes which we can't appreciate but which you doubtless do. On the other hand I have plenty to say. So here goes.

Mac sent me a wire and came to see me the next day about three weeks ago. He arrived about noon and had to leave about 2 the following afternoon. He could have left later if he could have flown back but he doesn't take to flying the same as I do. However we had a real good talk that night and I did take him for a short ride. He said he enjoyed it all right but his stomach is a bit too sensitive. I had a week's leave starting only a few days later but as he said he was going to be very busy on a special course for a while. I didn't go down to see him as I would only have seen him in the evenings and it would be pretty hard to get a place to stay close to his camp.

I heard from Cub a week or so ago, very unfortunately, because three days before his letter came I went up to his old station to see him only to find that he had moved and nobody on the station knew where the gang had gone. So that explained why my previous letters hadn't been answered. I was beginning to get a bit worried as Cub is always prompt.

I also saw Doug Noton when on my way back from my leave keeping very well and sent his best regards.

One of the boys recommended me to see Chester while on my leave as it was on my route. So I dropped off there for an evening and met Mrs. Bert

Grant's brother there. He owns a hotel called the London Bridge Hotel and we had quite a talk. His name is Ernest C. Bowles. Be sure to tell Mrs. Grant about it. It certainly was a coincidence and the first of its kind that has happened to me over here. I also met an army chap there who knew Brant Howell at Flin Flon, and Mrs. Rosenberry and Bill.

I spent several days in Chester and had a couple of nice afternoons on the river there in a real canoe. I had my swimming trunks and had a real good time. As a matter of fact I was in swimming this morning from 9 to 12 (my day off today) in a pool a few miles from here. But this English sun doesn't tan you the way it does at home even when it appears to be strong.

We have been working quite hard for some time now and consequently I have almost 1100 hours time in now. For a while it looked as though I might get a job on Spitfires, still instructing, but that fell through, though I have had three trips in them. And they really are wonderful. I also got a spot of instruction on a Mosquito not so long ago. Very nice indeed.

Gosh, but I would like to get home again. You might scarcely believe it, but I've almost forgotten what Canada is like. I must be quite a respectable Englishman by now. But I haven't forgotten how to shoot yet! I give Lawrie Taylor a lesson nearly every time I get up there and the other day on the range here, I did better than the instructor, and I'd never fired the type before. It was a kind of submachine gun. I hope you get some good hunting in this fall Dad. I am going to try to get some in Scotland, ducks, grouse and deer if possible.

Send Grace my congratulations and my best wishes to the Southons, Moores, Mr. Henderson and all the rest. Don't forget Mrs. Grant.

All my love,
Clayton.

Aug. 13, 1943

Dear Mom and Dad,

One letter a couple of days ago and three today, two of them the blue air mail types. It took them 11 days, but sometimes they are quicker and other times slower. It all depends on a lot of things. On the whole they are OK but a dime is a lot to stick on every letter, so I think the best plan is to send one once in a while and make the rest ordinary.

The fishing didn't materialize on the last leave as I couldn't get any tackle but I did get some canoeing and swimming in. I only wish Mac could have come with me. I wrote him the other day but haven't heard from him yet. I presume by now that he has recovered from his tonsillectomy. It struck me as being very funny at the time, but I suppose he had a different point of view and reaction to it.

I haven't had a cold since Christmas now, or been bothered with the sinus. I don't know what it's due to, but I suppose partly to being more acclimatized and also no doubt to the cod liver oil and malt extract.

I was very sorry to hear about Rosie but I suppose it was for the best. It was also a surprise to hear about Margery McCorquadale (Mrs. Albert Powell). I didn't know that she had been ill at all. Also pretty rough for Mrs. Wilbert Walker. It's to be hoped there are no after-effects from such an experience.

[The letter ends abruptly here.]

Sept. 3, 1943

Dear Mom and Dad,

Received your letter #77 of July 19th today Dad, also one from Dorie and also some cigs. Had a phone call from Mac the other day that he had seven days' leave and could I get some. Ordinarily it would have been no trouble at all, but the circumstances aren't so good at this time and it's going to be touch and go. I had some coming in two weeks too and had planned to do some pheasant shooting and perhaps some deer stalking in Scotland. Of course if I do get my leave early now, there won't be time to arrange for it. But with a little ingenuity we might work it on chance.

We had a revolver shoot (.38 Smith & Wessons) the other day and believe it or not, I got 135 out of 150 to tie for first place with an ex-army officer. About $2 in prizes for each of us. That is the second time I have shot a revolver and would like to get some more of it. All I know about it is what I read in Rod & Gun, Field and Stream etc., so perhaps it does pay to have a good theoretical background before starting the practical side.

Mac was up a couple of weeks ago and we went to one of England's old towns where I showed him some old Roman walls and gates as well as the old cathedral. It was begun in 1070 so is fairly old all right. We also had a swim in the very nice outdoor swimming pool they have there. Costs six cents to get in so it didn't break us! I don't know just where we will go if he does come up this time, but it will probably be Scotland. I still have hopes for some shooting. Well, I may add more to this later but cheers for now.

All my love,
Clayton.

Sept. 24, 1943

Dear Mom and Dad,

Am enclosing the start of two letters just to show that my intentions are good *[Aug. 13 and Sept. 3]*. Have not time right now but will be sending several letters in a few days. Had a wonderful leave with Mac (and the ghosts) in Scotland, which I will describe later.

Apologies for the two enclosures and all my love,

Clayton.

England,
Oct. 27, 1943

Dear Mom and Dad,

Your letters and parcels are arriving quite regularly though some are missing. You have mentioned things that I haven't heard of which you had written before, and the numbers are often a few shy. But most of them get here.

I was shocked to hear about poor Mr. Littler. It must have come as an awful shock to everyone. Please give Mrs. Littler and the boys my regrets.

The successful duck hunting certainly makes me envious Dad. We never got any on our leave as it is very difficult these days with so many of the men away and the shop-keepers keeping their ammunition for their regular customers. I got 25 12-guage shells in Scotland which I will use around the drome for the odd rabbit and grouse which we can get done in the mess. I made a very nice group with a .303 recently, a big nickel would cover them all, and the commanding officer has made me a rifle instructor to the troops as a result of it. That was at 25 yards.

I am keeping very fit with exercises and sports etc. but my old sinus is always lurking in the background. I have had a touch of bronchial catarrh recently and so am particularly careful. Have nonetheless given up any idea of operational flying now as I just cannot take the heights or the rapid changes of pressure involved in a fast dive. I hope to get a medical board before long, they wouldn't give me the last one as I wasn't on an operational posting, and if it's what I think, then will try again to get home.

I am still flying of course, on a new kind of airplane now, and still enjoying it as much as ever, but give me a few days in the bush! *[of Turtle Mountain]*. Well I must close now but will tell you more of our leave in the next one.

All my love,

Clayton.

Only two weeks later, Clayton writes that he's been posted to operational flying, and he seems pleased to finally get into the real war. But he is worried by his wife's situation. And so the year ends on a somewhat ominous note for the young flyer.

Dec. 11, 1943

Dear Mom and Dad,

I received a very disturbing letter from Dorie a few days ago and I want you Dad to try to help her get this business cleared up. She said that she had to give up her job at Eaton's because of "nervousness" and that is all she said. I don't like it and have asked her to write you Dad and to describe everything she thinks might be contributing. It may be just being run down but on the other hand it could be more serious and, in either case, should be seen to immediately. If it was serious I would try to get a compassionate posting home, but naturally that would be possible only if there was something really wrong.

If you could recommend a Winnipeg doctor she could see or else see her in Brandon at the clinic, whichever is best and most convenient. I think possibly tonsils and teeth are largely to blame as, so far as I know, she has had neither looked at. Anyway please let me know the full details as soon as possible, if there are any.

As I believe I told you I have been posted to operational flying and hope, before long, to be dropping some blockbusters on Berlin. But I will be able to tell you more later.

I trust the deer hunting was its usual success and would certainly like to be able to sink my teeth into a steak. As well, we had a lovely hare for dinner today. Lawrie's cousin shot it a few days ago and I skinned and butchered it last night. It certainly was nice.

Mac wrote two weeks ago to know when I could get on leave as he was getting some. I had to write and say I couldn't arrange anything, so I believe he must have tried to get some hunting on his own. Naturally I was very sorry but it just couldn't be helped.

Well, must close now so the very best of Christmases and may the New Year be your best ever. All my love to you both,
    Clayton.

CHAPTER 12

Operational Flying, 1944

As 1944 begins, Clayton is happy to be heading into operational flying.

Jan. 1, 1944

Dear Mom and Dad,

And so another year has begun, and I sure am hoping that its end sees the world restored to its senses, and a few of us strangers to our homes back where we are meant to be. Things do look bright though and if only we can produce a few statesmen of the required calibre, they should be just as bright for the days to follow.

Mac phoned me just before New Year's so I managed a compassionate 48 to get to London to see him. There wasn't much we could do as all the city theatres are booked up days ahead, but we did a lot of talking in the 24 hours we had (including a few hours sleep). Then I had to come back again.

We had quite a nice Christmas here, my first on a camp in the three I have spent here. The place was nicely decorated and we had turkey for our dinner. The troops had a real Christmas dinner too, served up by the C.O. and some of his staff. Christmas Eve there was a dance in the airmen's mess and everybody had a whale of a time. There are a lot of Canadians here, so Christmas and New Year's had more of a Canadian aspect for me than for some time. Incidentally, these Canadians take some getting used to! It's a long time since I've seen so many at a time.

No Mom, I'm not on reconnaissance now, it's bombers instead. Right now it's Wellingtons but I should be going onto four-engines soon. And am I happy about it! I really am looking forward to my first trip over "there." I haven't mentioned the sinus to anyone yet and am waiting to see how height-flying will affect it. There is nothing to worry about as I have it all taped. If it is no go, then at least I've had a try at this and perhaps they will give me a break. Am waiting to go night-flying right now.

Heard from Frankie Moore and must write him. The terrible news about Bob must have shaken Mr. and Mrs. Moore more than a little. Give them my sympathy when you can. Bob was a good friend of mine. I'll never forget the nights I used to spend there at the farm, with him, Jack and Frank.

All my love,
Clayton.

P.S. Mom, please don't write on the part near the glue as it is broken when I open the letters.

Jan. 17, 1944

[This is a post card, with no photo, the only post card among the letters. "On Active Service. Please mail this card promptly to address above. Parcel N. S3A 67490." It carries a 2 pence stamp.]

Dear Mom and Dad,

The fags have really been coming through! Am replying to Mr. Brook too who sent me 300 "flat 50s" this afternoon. Am writing a letter this p.m. also to you so won't say anymore right now.

Love,
Clayton

Feb. 7, 1944

[He is in 6 Group Battle School from Jan. 30 to Feb. 17, his 25th birthday. This was at Dalton, in Yorkshire. They were trained in escape tactics in case they got shot down over Germany. POWs who had escaped provided lectures. They did a lot of physical training, too.]

Dear Mom and Dad,

I'm sorry not to have written you for some time, but, as I explained to Dorie, I haven't a pen (she is sending me one) and it's darned hard to borrow one here. I am taking a Commando course (or the Air Force equivalent) to prepare me for throwing a Halifax around I suppose.

I spent nine days leave in London and stayed at a real home-away-from-home for Canadians. Mrs. Hancock married an Englishman and runs a really wizard place. The first afternoon I was there I got a free box ticket to the London Philharmonic Symphony concert. John Barbirolli was conducting and Albert Sammons was solo violinist. It really was good too. I'll send you the program in an ordinary letter in a few days. The rest of my time I sent to different theatres and cinemas.

By the way, the symphony was in the Royal Albert Hall which is a huge round room about 300 or so feet in diameter. Barbirolli is a funny little man with an enormous black shock of hair which bounces around when the going gets allegro, and awfully theatrical at the end of it too. But the way he controlled the orchestra and the crowd was amazing. You could hear everyone take a deep breath at the pauses between phrases. And to see all those violin bows going up and down in unison like mad. Whenever I hear symphony on the radio I can see those bows going, and the conductor's baton. But I couldn't stand too much of it. It did get dull in places, too much repetition.

I met Laverne Armstrong in a barber shop in London, too. Quite a coincidence, eh! We tried to contact Jack by phone, but couldn't. I suppose you will know by now that Mac has left. I went to see him but found that he had gone. He couldn't have been able to let me know. I tried to see Cub Brook last weekend but he had gone on leave just four or five hours before I got there. Tough luck all round there.

Well, as I am running short of space I suppose I must close. Take care of yourselves and don't worry about us.

All my love,
Clayton

Brad Bird

Feb. 9, 1944

Dear Mom and Dad,

I just received your letter Mom, written Jan. 1st – ordinary, not air mail – so it's about right *[for time in transit]*. I had heard the sad news about Auntie Emm and Bob Welch from you some weeks ago. As a matter of fact I got Auntie Emm's letter about three or four days after hearing from you that she had died, and it certainly gave me a queer feeling to read it. But it was nice that she went in her sleep instead of how she might have.

I'm afraid that my relations with Bob Welch were rather distant, but I was sorry to hear about him. I heard from Frankie Moore only a couple of months ago and he had run into Bob in London and somewhere else, and when I wrote him last about a week ago, he hadn't known. I have a letter of Frank's here that I must answer this afternoon.

Our Commando training is continuing nicely and my hands are all cuts and scratches from bramble bushes. You should see them, they grow like creepers along the ground and will go about four feet high themselves, or higher on other bushes. They are about a quarter of an inch thick and strong as steel rope and an absolute mess of prickles like gramophone needles. We did some shooting this afternoon, but not strictly target shooting, with .45 revolvers and sten guns. Yesterday we were doing field craft – stalking a man instead of an animal. Not my idea of the game but I suppose one day it may be necessary, but I reckon I can hold my own at that game.

I'm glad that the boys had a good time in old Boissevain over Christmas. Mac and I were both in camps for it but they had a party in mine which made it not too bad.

I'm afraid you're not right about my job. I did fly Spitfires for a bit, also Blenheims, but am going on heavy bombers now. I can't tell you just how that came about here, but will when I get home. Anyway I am looking forward to it, and that's the main thing.

Well, here I am at the end again. Take care of yourselves and don't worry about Mac and myself.

All my love,
Clayton.

Feb. 24th, 1944

No. 1611 Conversion Unit
Wombledon, Yorkshire.

After completion of the Battle School course, he was posted to No. 1611 Conversion Unit, Con Unit, at Wombleton, Yorkshire. "Wombleton in the Mud," they called it. Here they learned about the Halifax aircraft and flew Halifax IIs and Vs, underpowered planes which cost many airmen their lives. He flew the Mark III later on ops, a much more powerful and capable craft.

Dearest Mom and Dad *[sounds optimistic and happy even here]*,

Well, here I am on a new station, and about to enter a new phase of my service life. In a few weeks I will be flying a Halifax and from then on will be responsible for six other boys, three Canadians and three Englishmen. I wanted a mixed crew, so am looking forward to meeting them. They aren't here yet, but will be before I start flying.

By the way, as you can probably tell, I am using a dip pen as my fountain pen was swiped some time ago. Dorie is sending me another but in the meantime it is darned awkward. There was a Waterman's of mine that you gave me Dad, in the attic. It was broken while I was at College.

I bought another bike before coming here, because I knew what the place would be like, and I am right! Mud and water everywhere and I live a mile from the mess. Also bought a pair of ankle boots and soaked them in Dubbin, so between them I should keep my feet dry. Everything else is OK though of course the accommodations hardly come up to Cranwell. That place got a fellow unused to a few little hardships.

It's getting on two years since I last saw Cub (May 1942). Gosh how time flies, and yet it creeps by at a snail's pace. I wrote to Cub this afternoon and should hear from him in a few days as we aren't very far apart.

Well, we are going to have a Jack Benny picture in the mess in a few minutes so I will have to pack up for now. I haven't heard from Mac yet and it may be awhile before we do as it may be impossible for him to write us for a while.

Don't worry about us anyway, and try to get some fishing in this spring, Dad. How I'd like to ramble down the banks of the old Souris again, and go to that little lake near Clear Lake where we used to get those beautiful two pounders with Percy Chard. I wonder where he is now!

Bye for now and all my love,
Clayton.

March 7, 1944

No. 1611 Conversion Unit
Wombleton, North Yorkshire.

Dearest Mom and Dad,

There hasn't been a great deal of mail just recently but today my watch arrived from Dorie. It is a Rolex Oyster, waterproof, shockproof, anti-magnetic etc. and just what I have been needing for a long time. My other had been giving me a lot of trouble and wasn't very reliable. Dorie got this one engraved on the back, "Clay, with love, Dorie, 17-2-1944." It cost her $42.50 which was quite cheap really as she didn't have to pay tax as she was sending it to me, and furthermore got a discount on it from Eaton's.

I haven't heard from Mac yet, though perhaps you have, but I know what this moving business entails, and especially one of that size and character *[Mac and thousands of other Allied troops are preparing for the invasion of Sicily, which began July 10th. Mac is sent to join the fight later]*

I have my crew members now. Navigator is Flight Officer *[X; Bird did not want him named because he didn't work out]*, from Montreal. Bomb Aimer is Flight Sgt. Brooks, Jimmie from Dafoe, Saskatchewan. Mid-upper gunner is Pilot Officer Mosher, "Lucky," from Dartmouth, N.S. My wireless operator, Sgt. Willis or "Pee Wee" is from the Isle of Wight. The rear gunner, Sgt. "Moe" Cohen is from London and Flight Engineer Sgt. Ted Larkins is also from London. The three English boys are young, 20, 19 and 20 respectively. They're a smart bunch of kids though and darned keen. Moe and Lucky are here just now and do make it doubly hard *[to write]*. Charlie McCarthy is on the radio. The navigator has a radio, luckily. Anyway I'm sure looking forward to flying with these boys.

We were supposed to have started flying Halifaxes today but will tomorrow. They look OK to me but boy oh boy they're big!

By golly you really are roping in the blood donors Dad. Reminds me of the three I gave, only I got $10 each for them, and did it come in handy then!

Things are getting a bit difficult for letter writing right now so I might as well pack up. But I'll be writing again in a few days to let you know how we're getting along. Take care of yourselves and don't worry about Mac and myself.

Love,
Clayton.

The next letter is important as his parents' first correspondence from Clayton as an operational pilot. A crew's initial foray over Occupied France was not a bombing raid, but a diversion for a bombing raid. Sometimes the diversionary planes dropped propaganda leaflets. This "nickel" trip, as it was called by Canadians, could be dangerous, as the point was to draw fighters and flak away from the path of the real raid. On March 24, pilot Bird flew with his new and untested crew in a beat-up old plane called V-Victor on such a diversion. After enemy fighter planes appeared and flak hit the plane, their navigator quit working. A crew member told me he either had the wrong maps, or no maps, but for whatever reason ceased to do his job. Initially he got them off on the wrong track as well. In his log book, pilot Bird wrote "Bullseye France, holed by flak," adding: "Dodged four fighters one 109 one 190 two unidentified. Lost in three search lights." That hardly begins to explain the many maneuvers such as the violent downward corkscrew needed to shake off the fighters and blinding lights. Bird also wrote, "Navigator quit." But he got them home, after being lost near Paris in the middle of the night, and maybe should have been recognized. "Good show!" he wrote in his log as an afterthought. Indeed it was, for seven lives and a plane were saved. For a full account of this flight, see our book Nickel Trip.

March 27, 1944

Dear Mom and Dad,

I received two letters from you today. Yours Mom, a plain one, was mailed Feb. 24th and Dad's on March 13th. Also got some cigarettes the day before yesterday but won't be sending the card for a week or so as I just opened 200 a couple of days ago.

My crew is working out fine except for the navigator who let us down very badly the other night [March 24] so I scrubbed him and am getting a new one tomorrow. If only I could have Cub I sure would be happy, but there are regulations which prevent it. However the rest of the boys are tops and we get along fine. We will be finished here shortly and then will go to squadron.

I really have been enjoying myself here. Soon after arriving I went down to the local pub to try their beer and met one of the local lads, Tom King, and beat him up at darts which rather shook him and since then I've been around to his place several times. Had yesterday off and spent the whole day there. We've been after pigeons a couple of times, but it's like shooting ducks in the bush, you need several lakes covered before it's any good. We go after them in a bit of mixed cover but the first shot scares them all away. But we've enjoyed ourselves anyway. He's real Yorkshire and sometimes is hard to understand. We play darts with a couple or pals of his, civvies, and a couple of soldiers who are two of the cleanest-built lads I've ever seen. After 10 o'clock we go to Tom's place and his mother sets us out a bite to eat and we talk till about midnight when the soldiers have to be in.

Mrs. King is really nice and so is Tom's sister Mary. I certainly will miss them for a while when I leave here anyway, though they have made me promise that I will come back some time and see them.

The rest or my time I mend things, talk with the rest of the fellows, write letters, go to the movies occasionally, etc. I haven't been to a dance in months. I don't believe I told you before, but I told Dorie to come over if she could possibly arrange it. I got a letter from her from Toronto and only then realized just how unsatisfied she was so wrote her immediately. I sure hope it can be arranged OK. I always wanted her here naturally but thought it best not to. However it's the only thing to do now and so I hope there won't be anything to stop her from coming. That will spoil your plans for going East this summer, Mom, but I felt there was no other answer. As you will probably hear from her about it before I do, there is no need for me to say more.

Love, Clayton

April 7, 1944

Dear Mom and Dad,

I am writing this on the pad in my writing case which I received only yesterday. It is just what I have been wanting for some time, and the only thing I needed to make it complete was a pen. I still haven't got one, though I should be getting one from Dorie soon. But thanks a lot for the case anyway. It is a very convenient size to carry around and will enable me to write more often in my spare time.

I am on a squadron now, did my first trip last Friday. That makes two I have in now. *[His first was the nickel to drop leaflets; his second dickie on March 30, with Ed Northern, in which he rode along to watch, was the Nuremburg debacle in which 96 planes (each with seven men) got shot down. His third trip, his first one alone with his crew on an actual bombing run, was coming up on April 24 – Karlsruhe.]*

My crew worries are at an end I believe, now that I have a good navigator, and we should get along fine. We have really good kites, and that counts for a lot. Quite a few of the fellows with whom I have trained since leaving instructing are here too, so I am not in with complete strangers. It is a Canadian squadron anyway.

I haven't heard from Dorie for a couple of weeks now, but have put it down to my moving upsetting the mails. However I had two of yours Mom and one of Dad's the day before yesterday, so I should be getting Dorie's anytime. I sure hope she can come over here. If she can't for any reason, it will be a let-down after looking forward to it. If she sends me word that everything is OK for her to come, and is coming, I shall be busy looking for a house, and will also have to get a car or motorcycle. They are not too hard to get and, living out, I could get petrol ration easily enough.

I am afraid Mom that it is not allowed to tell you where we go, but I have been across the channel, and then some. And it is quite an experience! While I think of it, I was sure glad to see that bit about Cub because he has been at the job a long time and deserves something. And don't be surprised to see him as Fl. Lieut. Brook soon because he is also due for a promotion.

In York the other night I ran into a chap that I knew at Brandon College. His name is Ray Chant and he is stationed very near me. One of these days I will give Cub a buzz on the phone and dash up to see him as he is not so very far away either. Jack Moore is only a few miles away also but haven't seen him yet. But I will drop him a line as soon as I can and let him know where I am. Give my best regards to his mother and father when you see them.

I haven't heard from Mac yet but am glad that he has landed safely in Italy *[actually Italy was not invaded until September, and Sicily in July]*. Frankie Moore should be nearly ready for squadron by now, though of course I don't know where he will be going. What are Jack Garton, Les Maxfield and Jack Stone doing now? Was Stone called into the army? I shouldn't think that should be the best thing in the world for him with his heart.

By the way, my sinus isn't giving me the slightest trouble now, though the catarrh still runs a bit. The oxygen we use seems to have a very beneficial effect on it. That might be a line worth following up Dad, though I suppose it already has been.

So the McGregors are selling their farm. I do hope that the B.C. weather agrees with them better than ours did. Did young Gordon recover OK from those terrible nose bleeds he had?

I'm sorry that my letter telling you of my Christmas parcels has been lost, though it may turn up yet like my birthday parcel. Yes it was one of the eight, and like a darned idiot I opened them all the same day. As a matter of fact I got two from you that day. Anyway when I had finished I had no idea who had sent what, as you can imagine. But I knew your cake Mom and it was all right. However it was a lot of fun that day and made it more like Christmas as some of the other boys were digging into theirs at the same time.

There is nothing I need except the pen and a couple of pairs of sox, as the English utility sox are very short and they shrink so that they are barely ankle sox. However that is nothing to complain about as long as I have some of the heavy wool ones. Aside from that, I am fine.

I sure was glad to see 16 chocolate bars in that parcel, though I'm sorry Mac can't get any. They were all in perfect condition. And the gum was a godsend. It is good stuff to have when flying. We do get flying rations, but when you're not flying you run out of it.

Well that is about all for now. Look after yourselves and don't worry about us.

Love,

Clayton.

April 21, 1944

Dear Mom and Dad,

When I got up this a.m. I found my bike missing. After making sure that none of the boys had it, I reported it to the police, and they picked up the fellow tonight. He was riding it home from work. He is a publican *[bar owner]* and had 15 bikes in his barn when the cops looked in. But only six had been reported to our police. However it should be enough to get him a spell in jail and to lose his licence to run a pub. And I'm not having any mercy on him either.

Before I forget, if is it possible to pick up the odd can of spork, spam or whatever they like to call it, it would come in handy for the before-bed snacks we have. We live in nisson huts and have stoves on which we cook anything we can find. One of the boys has a percolator which really makes good coffee.

I bought a Luger automatic which is really a honey, Dad. It uses 9mm stuff and is quite accurate. But so far I haven't been able to draw a bead on a rabbit with it. I meant to send it home to you, but I'm afraid postal regulations don't allow it. I'll let you know if I have any luck with it. It sure is a beaut.

Thanks for the sox Mom. They are better than anything over here. I hope to be able to send you some snaps of the crew in a week or so. There are quite some good ones. And this gang of mine is really tops. My new navigator is tops in every way. We get along well now and someone who should know says his work is among the best in the squadron. Anyway we are all quite happy again, and are only waiting to finish the job now.

Don't worry about Mac and myself and do take the best care of yourselves.

Love,
Clayton.

A Halifax bomber similar to the one flown by Clayton Bird and his crew in 1944.

The nose of Daisy Mae. Clayton Bird's crew insisted he carry along his lucky
lighter when on operations. It must have worked.

CHAPTER 13

More Bombing Raids and Home

On June 6, 1944, the largest sea invasion in history took place on the beaches of Normandy, France. This was D-Day, when the Allies began their push to liberate France, Holland and other countries in a final effort to win the war. Young Bird, however, finds himself ill and in hospital.

June 7, 1944

Dear Mom and Dad,

It looks as though today is IT. We heard on the 8 a.m. news that the Germans had reported parachute landings etc. I wish I could be in on the show, but it won't be long before I can.

I'm very sorry not to have written for so long, but I had a bit of worry for a while. I am in hospital right now, but it's nothing serious. My Eustachian tubes were plugged one morning and the M.O. sent me here for a while. However nothing has turned up and I should be fit to fly again in a week or so. Right now I'm having a good rest, and, believe it or not, have picked up a bit of a tan.

I'm also using all the spare time I've had to learn French. And I'm getting along OK too so far as reading and writing are concerned. Speaking it will have to come later but as there are a lot of French Canadians on the station that shouldn't be too bad. And I'm finding it a lot of fun, a lot more than it was when in school. I'm afraid I didn't have much inspiration for

343

it there. By the way, remember Miss Malcolmson? I met her brother about five months ago, quite by accident.

Dorie sent me a beauty of a Parker Vacuumatic Pen which I am using now. So now you will definitely get more letters.

I sure hope you can get down east this summer Mom *[to visit her brothers and sisters at Gower near Ottawa]* See if you can get Dorie to go with you. The trip would do you both a world of good. Gosh but I wish I could get home to look after her.

By the way, how does Uncle Archie like being a grandfather twice all at once? It only just occurred to me this morning that Doug is an uncle. Good Lord! How time changes things.

As yet I haven't heard from Mac but I imagine he is leaving it to you to give me any news of him. It must be perfect hell fighting in the dirt that they must meet there. But all the same it must be quite an experience to enter a city like Rome.

Well there isn't much more to say except that I'm very sorry not to have written for so long, however I couldn't help it, although I know you worry a lot in spite of me asking you not to. It can't possibly do any good and besides we are in the last lap of this thing now and I know we have the odds in our favour. And the boys really feel like giving those ---------- a real pasting. And so I'll close, always

Your loving son,
Clayton.

June 15, 1944

Dear Mom and Dad,

I'm in London now, on a few days' sick leave, and not doing much besides eat, sleep and go to all the good shows I can find. That is, stage shows. I haven't been to the movies yet.

So far I've seen Arthur Askey, a comedian in The Love Racket, at the Hippodrome; Patricia Burke in The Lisbon Story at the Princes, and last night Michael Redgrave and Beatrix Lehman in Uncle Harry at the Garrick. Askey was extremely good and I almost split my sides laughing. The play was a farce of course. The Lisbon Story was a musical and there was some really good singing, solo and choral, and dancing and was also very good. Uncle Harry was a drama and I don't expect I'll ever see better acting in my life. It was incredible, that is all I can say. Tonight I am going to see another comedy in the Globe. When the Sun Shines, I believe the name is. It's supposed to be very good.

I suppose you are wondering what on earth has started all this. Well I decided it would be a good thing to see a few good shows while I had the chance, and so I am. The seats cost me around $3.50 each, or a bit more, but they are worth it. I reserve the best I can get.

I've been spending my mornings just lying around, and doing odd things I think of, and my afternoons at Eileen's Club, a little private club of which I am lucky enough to be a member. Edward *[Holbech]* first took me there. It is just off Piccadilly Circus on Fermyn St. and is really most entertaining. I have met some weird types there. Eileen herself is darned nice to me and took me in as a member when she isn't taking any more. I've seen her turn dozens of people down. Anyway it gives me a chance to mix with different kinds of people.

Well, take care of yourselves and don't worry about me. I won't be flying for a week or two yet. All my love,

Clayton.

Clayton got news that his mother's brother, his Uncle Percy, who married him and Doris, died suddenly. One or two of Percy's letters are included in this volume. If he seems nonchalant about his uncle's demise, remember that Clayton is facing empty seats many mornings where young men who didn't return from the previous night's bombing efforts once sat. The crews knew the odds were against them, but most men kept at it anyway. It was rare for anyone to refuse to keep flying, but it did happen. They were branded LMF – Lack of Moral Fiber, which Clayton thought cruel. Often those men had given greatly of themselves in many operations and simply could not go on. Still they faced LMF humiliation and toilet cleaning duties. Today they might be diagnosed with post-traumatic stress syndrome and treated. Or maybe not.

June 23, 1944

Dear Mom,

I was certainly shocked to hear of Uncle Percy's sudden death, though I had known of course of his heart condition. And it is perhaps just as well that you couldn't get there for the funeral as it would have been a terrific strain on you. Auntie Lill certainly has had her share to put up with the last few years.

Remember me to Auntie Lill, May and Emily and to Miron, Grace and Clayton when you see them. It seems ages since we were there in '40.

I haven't resumed flying yet as the M.O. figures that I am a bit run down and need a couple of weeks' rest. And was he right! But I'm getting browned-off with hanging around and sure will be glad when I can get cracking again with the boys. However it's not too bad so long as the weather is nice and I can stay outside. They were cutting hay around the mess around about the last few days. It would be all right to get a hay fork in my hands again.

I had a nice, long, news-packed letter from Jean Duncan (Brandon College), with the promise of another to follow. And are the fellows ever scattered around this old globe! Which reminds me that I got Mac's address from that letter you enclosed and will write him. I haven't heard from him myself.

We have a mascot now in the shape of a little spaniel pup who answers to Oscar. He's the cutest little devil you ever saw, and every morning we have to look for our socks and shoes outside the hut. But he is training better all the time.

And my nick-name is not Nick, it's Dick. I'll let you guess how the boys picked that. It was that darned fool of a reporter who got it wrong.

We had done nine trips, when I had to stop. Well, I'll drop Dad a line now. It must be a bit lonely at home. Am glad Southon is back but sure am sorry to hear that his legs have played out.

All my love Mom, and have a good holiday after you get the details cleared up.

Your loving son Clayton.

July 12, 1944
420 Squadron, RCAF England

Dear Mom and Dad,

I got your last Dad today, dated June 25th. There hasn't been much mail coming through for anyone lately but I expect things will break soon.

By now I presume that you are home Mom. I hope so for Dad's sake anyway, and I hope you had a good time visiting those down east though it must have been hard to dispose of the old homestead.

It is OK for you to send your mail now to me to 420 Squadron, RCAF England. They will get here quicker that way. I am with the Snowy Owl

Squadron and it really is a hot outfit. I will try to send a crest and some snaps as soon as I can.

Another 10 days and we will be on leave again. And am I looking forward to it. I intend driving in my car over to the Lakes district, around Lake Windermere. I have been told that there is really some beautiful country there, and there is also supposed to be some good fishing. Anyway I intend to do my best and am going to have better luck this time too.

The crew are all bang-on and as keen as nails. Morale on the squadron couldn't be higher, only we aren't working often enough. However our time will come, soon I hope.

I have been doing a lot of thinking and have pretty well decided to go on with the geology *[which his mother wished him to do, though his heart was never in it]*, and pick out a special line in it when I know more about everything. If this university rehabilitation scheme of the government's comes through, it shouldn't be too bad. However I am rather a long way from everything to do much except generalize.

This war has changed a lot of my ways of thinking, but not all of them, and I hope for the best where things have changed. One thing is sure, and that's that I couldn't have had better examples of how to live this life than you, Mom and Dad. And I know that Mac thinks exactly the same way though he may not have said so. I guess we are both pretty bad at expressing ourselves sometimes.

Well, I must go now, all my love and take care of yourselves,

Clayton

July 28, 1944

Dear Mom and Dad,

Well, our leave has been postponed for a few days but it shouldn't be long now. I got my car and it's a honey. It's an Opel (made in Germany by General Motors), and is a maroon coach. It has hydraulic springing and hydraulic brakes and runs like an American car.

Cub was around the other day on leave with his DFC [Distinguished Flying Cross] and second ring up. He looked good too. He took a couple of snaps of me and the car, also Oscar, so you may see them before I can get some to you.

I would like very much to keep this little car; it would be the real thing for city work at home, but that is out of the question. However it might be worth double the 100 pounds I have put into it, when peace comes. I think I will leave it with Lawrie, Doris's cousin, if I go home before then, and let me him sell it for me.

I am enclosing a few snaps of the crew and our kite "Daisy Mae." I only hope that these snaps get through *[they didn't]*. Anyway she's a great, big, beautiful gal.

And now I must be rushing. I got your ordinary letter Mom in 11 days when you addressed it to the squadron as it sure makes a difference.

My love always,
Clayton.

420 Squadron
Aug. 23, 1944

Dear Mom and Dad,

The mail is coming through fine, but sometimes it perplexes you. I just got a letter you wrote from Ottawa before going out to clear up the house, Mom. On the other hand Dad I had one of your airmails four days after you wrote it. Pretty good eh?

We have been having a rare time lately, working often and having maximum benefit from our few hours off, thanks to the car. We had several fine days and went swimming each afternoon, after getting off from the previous night's work. And we've had several good nights of darts in some of the pubs round about. Then I landed at Cranwell and spent a couple of days there before coming back and saw many old pals. But a lot of the boys have gone on ops from there.

So far I haven't managed any fishing but I think I can now, though I have to provide myself with tackle first. May do that this afternoon.

The way things are going, we should be finished by the end of October. In that case I should be home for Christmas and sure hope I am. Three years over here is long enough for one time anyway.

I don't believe I have told you about the car. It's a 1937 Opel, two-door coach, made in Germany by GM and really quite a nice job. It has knee-action front suspension, a four-cylinder engine and does about 35 miles to the gallon. And it certainly has been a boon to us. I wish I could take it home with me. It is only 11.3 h. p. but cruises comfortably at 50 miles per hour. The driving over here Dad would send you crazy after Canadian roads. Just like the old Lake Max roads, only more turns, and some places more hills. Some fun, anyway!

Well must close now. Don't work too hard on the gardens, and all my love,

Clayton

September 3, 1944

Dear Mom and Dad,

I'm really sorry for going so long without writing but here it is at last anyway. We have been going strong and have 24 trips in now. But the way the boys are going in Europe, I may not get a chance to finish my tour right. But I imagine that would be OK with most of the boys, though Jerry's air force has just about had it anyway. However as this is the fifth anniversary of England's war with Germany it would be a good idea for them to pack up.

Our pup Oscar was missing for a few days and we thought someone must have swiped him but he came back today and just about ate us all up. He has half a dozen "tank traps" dug around the hut and I have to watch and not drive the car in them as some are pretty big. He really is cute and I'll send you a snap as soon as we can get some.

We get another leave on the 29th of this month and I'll be going to see Cub. I got a letter from him a couple of days ago. He is pretty browned-off with instructing, so he may have an idea of how I felt after a couple of years of it, at least 23 months.

Pilkie just gave me an idea, and that is cigars for Christmas. I don't expect to be here for Christmas but a good Canadian cigar would taste good anyway. You can send them the same way as cigs and just leave out the cigarettes that time. By the way, I've had two lots from Scotty Clements. Thank him for me and tell him I'll be writing.

Well, as it's after 11 now I'll hit the hay. Lucky is in bed now. Pilkie is writing home too. I have had several letters from you and the big parcel too. Those olives lasted about half an hour and the Prem less. We haven't eaten the rest yet but that won't take long. Thanks a million and cherrio for now.

Love, Clayton.

Sept. 24, 1944

Dear Mom and Dad,

Your last letter Mom came about a week ago Friday and yours Dad was yesterday. I was going to write earlier in the week only I went to another station to fly an aircraft over here only it wasn't ready, so we had to hang around there for four days with no kit of any kind.

Moe and Lucky have finished their first tour now. They had to do some trips as spares while I was off, and got a bit ahead of me. I have 30 trips in now and only a few to go to finish my first tour, and then I will be coming home.

I sure was glad to hear that Doug had got home; I lost contact with him a long time ago. Did he do any ops or is he still not able to get on them? He was one fellow who certainly deserved to get home.

By the way, I've been bumped up to Flight Lieutenant, so you can put F/L instead of F/O on your letters. It means an extra $1.50 a day too. Cub will be surprised when I see him as I expect to do in about a week.

I had a letter from Mac some time ago and he should have some of mine by now. They seem to have taken a while to straighten things out over there.

Well, it sure will be great to get home again, though it probably won't mean leaving the mob for a while at least. But it's a step in the right direction. And it will be a treat to see sunny Manitoba skies for a change, too. You will be surprised to know that I burn in a very few hours' sun now, a thing I wouldn't have thought of at home. Frank Moore doesn't think much of the weather here either. As a matter of fact his views on it are rather spectacular. He has almost finished his tour though I don't know whether his folks know so would be careful when talking to them.

Am very glad everyone is keeping fine, and give my regards to Mr. Noughton, the Moores and Brooks next time. Love as always,

Clayton.

Oct. 26, 1944

Dear Mom and Dad,

Well, we've finished our first tour, except for Pilkie who was sick for two trips, and it's a nice feeling. I did 34 trips all told and the rest of the boys the same. I got the whole bunch commissioned, and I think Pilkie who is a F/O will get his Fl./Lieut. out of it too. So it's been a darned good tour as far as we are concerned.

I sold the car for 85 pounds which I paid for it in the first place, so it cost me less than $100 to run it, and boy was it worth it. When you consider that petrol cost $25, and oil/greasing etc. another $10 or so, it was OK. Licence and insurance were about $55 and it didn't take much in the way of repairs. All I ever had to get for it was a new coil ($4.50) and a second-hand tire ($3) and it sure was a honey of a car.

I lost my watch yesterday in a Turkish bath. I forgot to put it in the safety box along with the rest of my stuff, and rather than go upstairs again, stuck it in an inner pocket of my raincoat. When I was ready to go it had gone, and as the management said there wasn't much that could be done because it wasn't in my safety box. So that's what I get for being so lazy. A chap in the bank told me these pickpockets can take a match off your arm so I suppose it would be easy enough to get it out of my coat while I wasn't there. I have another one that will do.

I am on leave just now and am staying in London with Ted, my engineer. He has a real swell family and it's lots of fun. I hope to be able to let you know something definite about going home pretty soon but it looks as though I've missed the deer again.

Oh well, here's hoping,

Love,

Clayton.

Nov. 11, 1944

Dear Mom and Dad,

Well Dad, it looks as though I've had the deer again. But don't give up hope yet. I am sorry I couldn't give you any more definite word earlier so you needn't have sent my Christmas parcel, but someone will enjoy it, that's a cinch.

And it looks as though the future is as well organized as possible too. Here's the set up.

They have a new scheme in the RCAF which is a good thing. We now have officers trained as personnel counselors, and their job is to help the boys decide on their best bet for civvy street. They have three tests which they give anyone who wants them. I took them, and on ability to learn and perceptions I got 76 out of 80. In clerical aptitude, including spelling, grammar, punctuation, arithmetic etc. I got 157 out of 185. And in mechanical aptitude I got 57 out of 65. Naturally I am rather pleased at the results and I'm a cinch now for my geological engineering. All I need is the work and I'm willing.

The government will pay me $80 a month while I'm in university, and all tuition fees. Right now I am entitled to 46 months or almost seven years of U at seven months per year. If I'm lucky I can even get a post-graduate.

Within five months of discharge I will have got about $1100 in grants etc, I have $500 here and what with Dorie's savings we should be all right. I sure am looking forward to it anyway. Canada is doing one darned fine job for the boys, because everyone in uniform, regardless of rank, has the same opportunities.

Well, I'm at the end again. Gosh, I wish Mac was going to be home too. That would really make this the most marvelous Christmas I've ever had, and it's going to be!

Don't write me anymore as I won't get them. So until I see you at home, all my love, and have good shooting Dad. Your very grateful son,

Clayton.

This was Clayton's last letter home. It is the final letter at least among the letters that have survived. For me, it is sad to see them end, as the story they tell is a remarkable and fascinating one, not only because of his story but also because of the many other lives revealed in the correspondence to him since 1940. Think of Cousin Emily, Uncle Percy, and Auntie Emm, the latter two dead by 1944. Think of Wanda, the young teacher, and Ricky, the Brandon College friend trying to chart her future. There was Rivette, the fur trapper and buyer, and Cousin Clarke Bradley, the articulate young RCMP recruit. Together, these and the other letter writers create a remarkable world for us to peer into – a world of good cheer, of fortitude in the face of medical and other challenges, a world of duty and optimism. The writers of these letters, both the young and the old, had a lot of energy. They were upbeat.

The letters were written, for the most part, by happy people who made their own fun, people active in sport and gardening and social affairs. They were aware, perhaps more than we are today, of their neighbours, and seemed to sincerely care about them. They certainly cared enough to share news about them in long letters to family and friends. Emails and twitter and texting have little to offer these ghosts, who knew the importance of good communication. They also knew that even more important was actual contact with people – the act of being together -- and they got together as much as possible. In our rush to text and twitter, in our zeal to email and attach images and jokes, let us not forget that nothing can take the place of real face-to-face contact.

– Brad Bird

SECTION THREE: WAR REPORTING

CHAPTER 1

Biography of Brad C. Bird

Brad Bird (formally Bradley Curtis Bird) was born in London, Ont., on January 27, 1959, near the military airbase where his father worked. Brad grew up with his three brothers, Bil, Bob and Bruce, and sister Kim in Downsview in Toronto, mostly at 161 Grandravine Drive, where they were a happy family. This is largely because Mom, Doris Bird, stayed home and raised the kids. Brad attended nearby Stilecroft Drive Public School, Elia Junior High and then Prince Edward Collegiate Institute in Picton, Ont. Later he studied at Brandon University and the Universities of Western Ontario (MA Journalism) and Manitoba (MA Political Science/International Relations). Brad has worked for various newspapers including the *Opasquia Times* in The Pas, *Western Producer* (as a freelancer) *Winnipeg Free Press* and *Oceanside Star* and won a number of provincial awards.

A bit of an adventurer, in 2005 he completed A 1,600-kilometre (1,000-mile) mid-winter walk/run from the Manitoba-North Dakota border near Boissevain to Churchill to raise about $14,000 for the Heart & Stroke Foundation. A year later he ran as the Green Party candidate in Brandon-Souris riding. The same year he married lawyer Karen Stewart and moved to Parksville on Vancouver Island, where they live with their cats, in a house near Karen's sister Jane, husband Mike Kelly and children Megan and Jessie. Brad spends as much time as possible fishing and canoeing, when he isn't curling or doing household chores with Karen, or writing a book. With his late father he collaborated on *Nickel Trip*, about Clayton Bird's military career. Brad wrote *Me and My Canoe* after paddling across the continent in the 1990s and then put together *No Guarantees*, about the hockey career of Don Dietrich of Deloraine, Manitoba.

* * *

Trips abroad have been an important part of my life. My first overseas adventure as a foreign correspondent was in 1987 when I spent four months in North Africa. My second trip was to Basque Country in northern Spain later in 1987 to cover the separatists there. My third, in 1993-94, was to Germany to cover a visit by then-BC Premier Mike Harcourt for *The Ledge*, a now-defunct political newsletter that covered Victoria's legislature. Then I took the trip to Greece, Kosovo, Turkey and Georgia, which is detailed in this section. A few years later I returned to Greece and Turkey to research my MA thesis about the Kurdish war in southeast Turkey.

I begin this section with the Kosovo trip because the Kosovo war is recent in people's memory and easier to relate to than my earlier journeys in North Africa, which follow in later chapters. Working as a freelancer and a summer employee for Manitoba Parks, I had the freedom to get to Europe for months at a time. It was a wonderful journey for me, as I met so many interesting people, and Greece is a delightful country to fly to from Canada in mid-winter.

What I found over the years is that war reporting is 98 per cent getting there and two per cent boom boom. To give you a sense of what it was like in the four conflicts I've covered, I'm including stories that lead up to the actual reporting in Kosovo, Turkey, and the villages near Chechnya. I think they draw pictures of the people and the countries that are useful. I do the same in my treatment of North Africa, prior to my time with the Polisario in the Western Sahara.

You may find some of this amusing; I certainly do. Travel tends to create odd circumstances. It also helped that in North Africa in the mid-1980s there wasn't the same fear of terrorist attacks as there is today. Frankly, I've always felt fairly safe in the Muslim world, where I found the people mostly kind and helpful. In fact, if I were to compare the people I've met on various journeys in the Muslim world to the Americans I met while paddling the Mississippi in 1991 and 1997, I'd have to say the warm reception extended by both peoples was much the same. I wish they were as good to each other as they have been to me.

– Brad Bird

Above, Father Alexander.

Below, Capt. Marie-Catherine Marsot in Kosovo, early in 2000.

Above, the Canadian base called DK in Kosovo, 40 kilometres west of Pristina.

Below, Brad's view from a Griffon helicopter on the way to Pristina.
Bird took most of the photos in this section of the book.

Above, the Griffon lands in a soccer field in Pristina.

Below, war damage. Photos by Brad Bird.

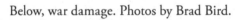

Above, editor Gilles Paquin, left, of La Presse, with interpreter.
He and Brad reported in Pristina.

Below, Brad with duffel of clothes for the poor donated by
Deloraine United Church; beside a Grizzly personnel carrier, in 2000.

Above is Zia, who helped Brad find Chechen refugees in Georgia.

Below, Brad at a NATO conference with a Turkish official, also in 2000.

Above, Ed Wadleigh, from Ontario, managed a bar in Pristina.

Below, Emzar and one of his two wives. He helped Brad in Duici, Georgia.

Above, artist Ilhami Atalay and Brad in Istanbul.
Brad studied under the master.

Below, Agnes Boucher, right, who studied piano under
the great Bela Bartok. This was in Malta.

Some of the art Brad produced under the tutelage of Ilhami Atalay.

CHAPTER 2

Arrival in Athens

"We are beginning our descent into Athens." The pilot's words jarred me from an hour's sleep, my first since beginning this 14-hour odyssey from Winnipeg through Toronto and Frankfurt. It was January 27, 2000, my 41st birthday. Athens will be my jumping-off point to the war in Kosovo.

Looking down, I saw countless islands the color of earth-tone flower pots, their jagged shorelines stark against the azure Mediterranean. The islands seemed to beckon me as they had others for centuries. The blue sea shimmered in the sunlight, and whitecaps raced across the water. The total picture was a world apart from winter in Manitoba. Greece, here I come!

On the plane I sat beside Hubert Knorr and his wife. They told me their two sons hadn't married – couldn't find "traditional" women. Hubert was born in 1939. His father, a soldier, died in 1943, before he even saw him. "Hitler was a madman, a loony," he said, scowling. "My home, Berlin, was rubble, nothing but rubble -- and this a country that produced Beethoven!" Hubert migrated to Canada in 1966, got a union job as an electrician and retired early. He and Erika, his second wife, loaned me a headset on the seven-hour flight to Greece.

On the tarmac it was beautifully warm. Palms and large green plants grew nearby and a friendly lady from Maryland, here for a cruise, told me they were aloe Vera. Marylin Jasper and Vinie Glass had told me of their healing abilities, so I broke off a bit.

In Athens I decided to find a cheap hotel in Plaka district, a place of cafes, trendy stores and antiquities. Nearby was the Acropolis and

Hadrian's Arch, a monument to Zeus. The bus from the airport was packed and took me past a business district much like any in Canada. I got off near a large park downtown, shouldered my pack and heavy duffel and walked toward a series of hotels, settling on Hotel Kimon, a small but tidy place near an old church.

"You must meet the priest," said Peter, the middle-aged Romanian clerk who greeted me. "He lives near poor village; maybe some clothes go there." My duffel was full of sweaters, scarves, pants, coats and more for the poor, donated by the Deloraine United Church. We settled on a price per night of 4,500 drachmas, about $18. I learned later, as I shivered in my bed, that that didn't include heat.

Five million people called Athens home, and this ancient city that gave us democracy hummed with commerce. A layer of black soot soon lined my nose from the exhaust fumes. Cars screeched and honked, people argued and shouted, mopeds whipped by. Quite a change from my rural home on Turtle Mountain, Manitoba. "Sorry, I don't speak Greek," I told a waiter who asked for my order. He pointed to himself, declared "I am Greek!" and stomped away.

Most waiters and others were friendly. In fact, I kissed more women here in four days (cheek to cheek) than I did in four years in Manitoba. That says something -- about me or Manitoba or Athens, I'm not sure which.

Phothitos Dimitrios, 60, wears a pencil thin moustache on his expressive face, which is made all the bigger by his baldness. A 12-year veteran of the Greek merchant marine, he says he's sailed around the world. Dimitrios manages Hotel Kimon, and is holding court with two Danish women young enough to be his daughters.

"The rich, they are crazy," he pontificates from a couch. "I work for them, captain their yachts. One time a man and woman have big dinner on deck. After, he come to me. 'Dimitry, we want to be in moonlight. But it is over there.' He points to a place beyond the boat. 'Take us there.'

"What could I say? There was no argument. I told the crew, we will chase the moon. So we did. But we did not catch it, of course. The man said later he understood. Crazy."

The priest is stout and wears a black robe, his head crowned by a round, flat-topped hat. His face is broad, his fingers fat, his eyes alive and kind, with a suggestion of deviltry.

"I must talk to you," I tell him, emerging from the alcove and thinking of the heavy duffel. Maybe he knows folks who can use this stuff.

366

"Come then, we go for coffee." He spies Peter, behind the desk, puffing on a cigarette, and stabs him with these words: "You must stop smoking! It makes me sick. So many die for nothing, at whose expense? It is a scourge!"

Poor Peter, a mousy little man who has lived under repressive Romanian rule, says nothing. This priest, I think, has moxie. Should be a good interview.

Outside it is dark, 8 p.m. Athens throbs with humanity, cats and dogs. The animals live as they can on the street. I see one homeless person, an old woman lying on a tattered sleeping bag on the sidewalk near a store. People stride past her and traffic growls as we carefully work through it toward Café Thannes.

At the back of the building we climb a steel circular staircase, like the kind on a submarine. Nearby, five teenagers chatter and flirt, annoying me. I want quiet to hear the priest! We sit and order coffee.

Father Alexander is a monk, a hermit monk, age 59. He told me that for seven years he lived alone in a cave in Israel, praying. For 18 years he has lived in a former donkey stable hundreds of years old on Mount Athos in northern Greece, where 20 monasteries are located. The walls of his home are a metre thick. But even that couldn't save him from the Albanian robbers who visited him in November 1997, leaving him scarred, he said, eager to tell his tale. But first I wanted to know what he did, now he justified receiving handouts from the monastery and people like me.

"I pray for hundreds of people, the living and the departed," he says in English learned, he claims, at Oxford. "I make thousands of photocopies of all kinds of spiritual texts, and my poems and icons, and send them to my friends in Russia. Because Russia is very poor. I give them money as well. It is my mission."

He prays a lot. "Where there is repentance, there is a new start of life. If the Lord has mercy on us, we will have mercy on others." Born and raised in Vienna, his father was Slavic ("I have a special feeling for the Slavs") and well-to-do, owning a castle.

But Father Alexander knew his destiny lay not with the material world of his father but with God. "I wanted to become a hermit from childhood. People said when I was small, 'But it is not a profession!' I said, for me it is a profession."

He abandoned his loves -- theatre and classical music -- to live the ascetic life of sacrifice led by priests, according to the wishes of the Russian

Orthodox bishop. But I wonder. The man's face is ruddy and pudgy, his body heavy, hardly signs of a man living largely on soup, as he claims.

You must have regrets, I say – no family, no car, no possessions.

No, he insists. "I had to endure many sufferings, dreadful sufferings, but I am the happiest person in the world. I have a special feeling toward my guardian angel. Thirty-two years ago he appeared to me in a cave when I was in great distress. The Israeli soldiers harassed me at night. He reproached me and said, 'Alexander, have you forgotten that spiritual joy comes only through sorrow?' I repented and stayed in the cave."

OK, I say, but tell me about those Albanian robbers. And how did you get those ugly long scars on the back of your hands?

"Four blows with ax were here, and chopped to the bone," he says, holding out his hands. One man appeared at his gate, seeking food. When he returned with food another jumped him with an ax. Father Alexander put his hands on his head to ward off the blows, hence the scars. His hands then fell to his side, weak and bleeding.

"In the very second he would have killed me, Mother of God intervened, and I am still here, but a suffering invalid. In the very second he wanted to give me the death blow, he slipped because it was raining and fell down.

"And the ax head came near my nose, can you imagine? I grabbed the ax and he stood up, afraid. The two ran away toward the border of Mount Athos and were caught by police. The one who wanted to kill me was shot in the arm." Now his home is encircled by two-metre barbed wire fence.

He has forgiven his attackers, and sends the one parcels of food and texts. The violent one has not repented and gets nothing. His grip is weak, he says; he cannot write for long. Albanians who raid Greek residents are a problem. He told me about a priest in his 80s who a month earlier was ordered to hand over 5,000 drachmas, about $20, or lose his hands to an ax. He paid.

Father Alexander learned English thanks to a European couple who visited the monastery. Troubled in their marriage, they were counseled by the priest and gratefully paid for his year at Oxford. He visits the monastery weekly to get food and news, and to speak to the pilgrims from around the world. He speaks Arabic, Russian, Greek and German.

"I love to write poems," he says. Tell me one, I insist. He calls this his poem for the new millennium.

"And God this evening embraced His earth/ And kissed it with golden shimmer/ And all the sorrow caused by sin/ In repentance will be healed by our Lord and Savior./And in grace forgiven./ Where tears have moistened the earth white roses blossom, as new life begins.

We part in peace. He wants no clothes from the duffel.

"How can I carry them?"

CHAPTER 3

Three Women, Three Lives

At age 20, Anka Niculesu was in the bloom of life, pretty, dimpled and demure. I met her as she bustled about on my floor, cleaning rooms. She was of medium height and sturdily built. Born and raised in Romania, Anka had seen hardship under the dictatorial rule of Nicalau Chauchesku. She and her father had come to Greece for employment and a better life.

As the only maid at Hotel Kimon, Anka spent 12-hour days mopping floors, cleaning washrooms and doing laundry. For that she earned four drachmas a day, about $16 Cdn. Sixteen dollars, in a country where the cost of living isn't a whole lot less than Canada's. She said she hadn't had a single day off since starting there four months earlier, as the Greek hotelier wouldn't allow it. Anka wanted a little free time to go out to shop and meet people.

She and her father, Peter, shared a flat, and after meeting with the hotel owner they gained a concession: she would get a room of her own but must continue to work the same hours. That saved her the half-hour walk home at night when she feared being robbed, or worse.

"I would like to give you some clothes," I tell her one day, as her father looks on from behind the reception desk. It is January 29, 2000. "These clothes are from Canada and I think there might be something nice for you and your father." Anka glances toward the graying, slender man for guidance.

I offer to open the bag there, but it is not a good idea, he says.

"Go to his room and see the clothes," her father says. So we go upstairs.

370

Inside the room I untie the bag and unload tops and slacks and baby's jumpers. Anka's eyes light up as she spots a little outfit. "I have a cousin who would like this," she says. She roots through the clothes and finds other items: a shirt for her father, a blouse for herself, another baby outfit for the child.

It is much like Christmas for her, I sense, as she joyfully handles the many items donated by the United Church in Deloraine. "That is what these clothes are for, to help people," I assure her. "Go ahead, put that aside too."

After the duffel is emptied and re-packed, minus the half-dozen items, her face suddenly goes cold. "What do you want me to do now?" she asks.

At first I don't understand. "What do you mean, Anka?"

"You give me these clothes. What do I do for you?"

"Nothing," I say, finally comprehending. She thought I would want a favour. "You make me happy by accepting these gifts. That is enough."

A little smile returns to her pretty face; her eyes twinkle. "Thank you."

Next day I walked to the top of the acropolis, one of the most famous places in the world. Admission was free, as it was Sunday in the off-season, so many locals were there as well. "Acropolis" in Greek means "upper city," the fortified citadels common two thousand years ago as places of refuge from attack.

The acropolis in Athens is famous for its Parthenon, that structure with many large pillars made of marble. Well, I can tell you it's even more amazing in real life than on TV, despite the damage. Apparently some nut in the 17th century blew it up and they've been trying to restore it ever since. But there are other antiquities, theatres, buildings, archways, walkways, that make the acropolis a fascinating visit.

The acropolis is a flat hill-top you can walk around in 10 minutes. It provides a wonderful panoramic view of Athens, a sprawling city that seems to go on forever. To the south is the Aegean Sea, and you can see the sparkling blue waters of the Mediterranean. While enjoying this view I met Janie von Holzen.

She was sitting beside a metre-thick rampart at the edge. Dark glasses, dark hair. "Nice view, isn't it," I ventured.

"Indeed it is."

Well, before you knew it we were chatting. She was from England, where she managed an English language school. She was here with a girlfriend for the weekend – they'd found cheap tickets on the Internet.

"It feels like a week!" she enthused. "It's so restoring. The warmth, not only of the weather, but of the people. It's just unbelievable. You learn about these places in school, but we can't believe what we've seen," she went on. "It's the things you don't know exist, like the theatres. Amazing."

We could see one from where we stood. Janie was in her 30s. She and her friend were staying at Hotel Olympus. "We pay 14,000 drachmas for a double room with bath and breakfast, and we're delighted with our choice. It's a 19th -century house with painted frescoes on the ceiling. The room we are in was obviously a salon originally. You can just see that some very wealthy family used to live there.

"In the past 24 hours I've had the best intellectual conversations I've had in four years. It's been like a gift from God, I feel. Just what I needed," and she sighed.

I sighed too. Golly.

"You know what?" she continued. "I never even wanted to come to Greece. Never. Now I want to see the islands. On Friday, my goal was to get out of London. It was 70 pounds. This has changed my thinking completely."

At home, she added, she had some bad experiences with Greek men. "Totally sexist. They treat women so badly. But here, it's been fun. It's been great."

We said our good-byes and I finished my tour of the acropolis, then headed back down to find a café for an afternoon meal and drink. Before long I was drawn toward the sound of an accordion and laughter. Near the base of the hill I found the source of the music, and many people enjoying a meal in the afternoon air – but there was no place to sit.

Then a pleasant-looking man and his friend beckoned me to join them. Thanos Kotsakis, 58, spoke good English. I pulled up the lone chair. "I am a graphic artist," he said. I reciprocated, and the word "Canadian" opened another level of hospitality.

"I think you are in the middle of the best season to come to Greece," Thanos said, "because in the summer there is a huge tourist invasion and everything changes. For Athenians, Athens becomes uninhabitable, the islands too. Every resort we used to go to, it is taken." So they flee to the lesser known islands and seaside towns.

What is this? I asked, pointing to a dish of greens in olive oil and lemon juice.

"Horta," he replied, taking a fork full off the plate. I order some too, and some meat, and dug in, famished. Horta tasted great. We talked about food, agriculture, as I have an assignment to produce a story about dry-land farming, or maybe organic farming here.

"After the Second World War, the tendency in Greece was to industrialize," Thanos said. "We have no big industry in spite of all this effort for industrialization. In the race for industrialization we abandoned agriculture. Most of the things we consume are imported."

The beef? I ask.

"Most of it. the only local meat is the lambs' meat, and the goats."

So what's the deal with the subway expansion? It had opened the day before.

It's partly to reduce the smog from too many cars on Athen's streets, and partly to prepare for the 2004 Olympic Games, he told me.

"The Olympics have been a question mark because, as you know, we have very uncertain relations with Turkey. There is an open threat that just before the Olympics, they start hostilities. If that happens, we have no profit from the Olympics but we'll be deep in debt again."

I pointed out that even then, early in 2000, Greece was behind schedule in its Olympic preparations.

"It's too much bureaucracy in Greece. Things are delayed," he said, recounting a story about the opening of the new subway lines. "The president gave a speech and said despite delays, at least we have it. It seems in Greece we have many delays, because the Temple of Jupiter started being built about 600 B.C. and ended AD 130, 700 years later! So the Metro's not so bad."

He and his friend, who didn't speak English, laughed and smiled and I greatly enjoyed his history lesson, the music, the food. It turned out that Thanos's father, Alkis, was also a newspaperman who wrote for several papers and freelanced. "I traveled all around Greece with him when I was young. He told me it was true, what I'd heard about Albanian outlaws in Greece. I mentioned Father Alexander's story.

"We have quite a problem with the Albanians. In the whole history of Greece, there were several waves of Albanians coming down to Greece. Usually they were absorbed. They do several pranks. They invade. Even in the city, Athens, we have many Albanian criminals, and they are rough, they hit and they kill."

So why not deport them?

"If they send Albanian criminals home, Albania doesn't allow Greek companies to invest there," then he adds: "Greece has already become Americanized."

He talked about America. "I have noticed that the U.S. is a very rich country, many universities, but they are very stupid. If you ask a Greek in a little village about Kashmir, he will have an opinion. If you ask an American in a city, he will ask, "What is Kashmir?"

As a boy, Thanos watched sailors from the American 6th Fleet come ashore. They asked for Coke. They were told there was no Coke here, but many local juices were available, which they refused. "They could not open their minds to trying the local juices."

Just then a pretty sprig of a girl approached and asked for money. Her dark brown hair matched her big brown eyes. Thanos talked kindly to her, and held her; her named was Bora. She was 6. She stayed until Thanos gave her 250 drachmas. "Now I'm leaving," she said in Greek.

"A gypsy," Thanos explained, from Albania. Soon I left too, but before doing so was told my lunch was on them. I thanked them very much.

The following day I took an hour-long bus ride from Athens to Corinth. It was great to see the water and the ships, and to breathe some cleaner air. In a butcher shop, an old lady pointed to a hanging carcass. I asked her if it was beef. "Baaaaaa!" she said, and we all laughed.

"I am teacher," said a stylishly dressed woman on the bus. Her name was Athina Kostarelon and she was 28. In fact I guessed her age, and her eyes widened in surprise. I've always been good at guessing a person's age.

The monthly salary for a teacher in Corinth was about $1,200 Cdn, or 280,000 to 350,000 drachmas. "It is good but not enough for a good standard of living," she said. I complimented her on her fashionable, tidy dress. "It is my style."

Athina said she had taught five years and had a boyfriend. She wanted to get married and have children. Her family was in Athens but she liked Corinth – fewer people, cleaner air.

* * *

Tonight near Old Corinth, an area of ruins near new Corinth, I dined royally. I dined with a dog.

While sitting on the marble steps of a little grocery store, with the sun setting low amongst the ruins and groves of oranges and lemons, I shared my supper with another fringe member of this society, a shaggy black and white dog.

His right foreleg was injured, for he held it up and limped. He was dirty and scruffy but humble and polite. And a good listener. These are good qualities in a dining partner.

He hopped toward me with hope in his eyes. "Hello, boy, how are you?" I said. English was obviously not his first language -- but he understood the universal language of a warm greeting. I had no food out then, but when he looked at me forlornly I produced the little loaf I had just purchased. We shared that in turn, in silence. His ragged tail wagged each time he got a piece of broken bread. What a wonderful thing is a dog.

The bread gone, he was still hungry. Around us people walked by, rode bikes, passed in cars. We ignored them. To me they were outside our little encounter, our momentary world. We had each other's company in this moment, and that was enough. I told him what a fine dog he was, and how I enjoyed his company, and he looked at me knowingly.

I brought out a yogurt cup, strawberry, and we ate that in turn, like we did the bread. He liked it. After my own mouthful I would plop a dollop on the clean marble step for him, and he gratefully licked it clean. When all was done he looked at me, wagged his tail one last time, turned and hopped away.

* * *

The fur merchants in Athens told me fur was back in fashion. Ranch mink, sheared beaver and fox especially were in demand again. Many fur shops had closed here in the last decade but those remaining were optimistic. Good news for my trapper friends on Turtle Mountain in Manitoba.

* * *

From Old Corinth I boarded another bus and headed for a place famous for its spring water and spa – Loutraki. The name was on water bottles all over this land. At the spring I met Jim Rotas, 42. Born in Australia, he had made a life here with his Greek wife and two children. He was a cook in a casino. His wife, Anastasia, sold water.

Soon after arriving there I asked a young woman for directions to the spa. Her mother scowled at me, threw me the evil eye, and muttered Greek unpleasantries.

"What is the matter with your mother?" I asked.

"She thinks you're drunk and out of your senses," came the reply. I was dumbfounded. I hadn't shaved that morning, but otherwise had certainly not been drinking.

"Tell her I'm not drunk," I shot back. "I just don't know Greek."

The spa, by the way, was very nice. Very modern, not like I had imagined. You entered a private room and they filled a tub and you soaked for 15 minutes. Felt good.

* * *

My heart beat rapidly as I neared the top of the mountain in Nafplion (pronounced NAFpleon). This beautiful town was in the Peloponnesus west of Athens. The Peloponnesus is home to Sparta and the site of the first Olympics. Let me tell you, I felt like an Olympian after walking 1,000 steps up to an ancient fortress called Palamidi. Wouldn't you know it, I found the gate locked.

So I scaled the old wall, hundreds of feet up, and was soon inside the metre-wide ramparts. It was grassy there. I roamed the ancient area where people stayed during attacks by pirates, Turks and others. I lingered at the wall and gazed at the Mediterranean far below, where a ship, just a spec, was anchored in the morning mist. Slowly the mist dispersed, like steam from a kettle, a beautiful sight. I felt I could see for 100 miles in any direction. Closer, down below, were the earth-tone roofs of old Nafplion, and a little farther away the whiteness of the new town, a lovely sight.

Later that day I actually made some money (a pleasant change!) By writing a piece of analysis about Greek-Turkish relations for the Focus page of the Winnipeg Free Press. At an Internet café I typed in the piece from my longhand. Longhand is much under rated, and in many ways better than composing on a computer, as the words seem to flow more fluently, as if you somehow know it's important to get it right the first time.

I went down to the water to watch the sun set over the Soronic Gulf, part of the Sea of Crete in the Mediterranean. It was Feb. 1, and two men went for a brief – very brief – swim. It was a warm evening with a slight breeze, and low mountains lay beyond the bay. Again, beautiful. Waves lapped at the shore and a dog that had licked my ear a minute earlier was swimming.

Next day before leaving I popped into Propileon Café near the bus stop for a bite to eat and was served by Diane Kondos. At 26, she was married to Dimitra Kondogiannopoulos who didn't speak English. Diane said she was born and raised in Saskatoon, Saskatchewan. When she was nine her parents returned to their homeland, the cold proving too much. Diane had been back twice. She loved Nafplion, where they only just arrived in July, after living in Athens.

"It's very quiet, a much better way of life," she said. She was radiant, with a personality to match.

As I rode the bus back to Athens I considered my first few days in Greece and figured I was doing OK. As it had done for countless others for countless centuries, travel fascinated me. That night, as I strolled around Plaka, I was drawn by the sound of bongo drums to an illuminated old ruins. A group of young men and women sat making music. After a while, with their approval, I took my turn at the drums. It was fun. I was indeed in tune with the beat of life in Greece.

CHAPTER 4

I meet a philosopher and natural farmer, Panos Manikis

It was 7 a.m. and the train station in Athens was almost empty. I had my pick of seats, and chose one near a window. After a few busy days I intended to enjoy a quiet trip north and take in the sights of rural Greece, including Mount Olympus.

As I settled in, a big man with a bushy salt and pepper beard entered the coach -- and sat right next to me. I was a little annoyed. There were plenty of other seats. Glancing over I saw the thick strong hands and plain clothes of a working man.

"Good morning," I said.

"Hello," he replied.

"You speak English?" I asked.

"Yes, I speak it well."

I introduced myself, pleased we'd be able to converse. Suddenly things looked a bit better. We shook hands and met each other's eyes. "I am a journalist from Canada."

"Canada," he echoed. "I am Panos Manikis, a natural farmer."

"What do you grow on your farm?"

"Peaches and cherries mostly, but also many vegetables. I am from Edessa in the north, and am headed home now."

I let this sink in for a bit, puzzling over his qualification of farmer with the word "natural." "Panos, I've never heard of *natural* farming. I cover agriculture in Canada and write for a variety of newspapers, including

378

the Western Producer. I'm sure they would like a story about it. What is natural farming?"

The question opened a floodgate of fascinating discussion. Agriculture in North America and indeed across the world was experiencing a quantum shift as high input costs, economies of scale, amalgamation of agribusiness companies and low commodity prices forced thousands off the land and out of the only way of life they and their parents had known. The question around the world was this: what types of agriculture would foster safer products, environmental sustainability, economic feasibility and the well-being of increasingly depopulated rural communities? The question was as relevant in Greece as in Canada. And here was a man with another path, another contribution to the dialogue to increase the pool of shared meaning.

Natural farming, began my 50-year-old seatmate, is based on nature's diversity. A variety of plants growing together creates harmony and keeps pests and disease in check. Natural farming uses no machines, chemicals, tillage or weeding. I found this astounding, contrary to everything I knew.

"But how does it work?"

Clay balls are the key, he said. You take a variety of different seeds and sprinkle a bunch in a container holding fresh wet clay. Mix the seeds in. Then take a bit of clay and roll it, creating a little marble-like ball. Each ball will contain one or more seeds. Make a bunch of these balls and dry them thoroughly in the sun. After that you broadcast them by hand across the land. In time, as the rains come, the clay dissolves and the seeds sprout. Meanwhile, they are protected from rodents and the burning sun. This is the basis of natural farming.

Panos blends such seeds as cabbage, Swiss chard and oriental greens with grass seed and others and tosses the clay balls across his land (I later helped him do this). They don't all germinate, but enough usually do to create ground cover, which encourages strong soils, plant and animal diversity, and self-seeding year after year.

The system produces enough vegetables for him and his friends, he said. For income he relies on his orchard of peaches and cherries. These are also maintained without chemicals or cultivation and are noted locally for their flavour, texture, and lack of pesticides, which are heavily used in Greece. In later years you spread more clay balls until enough plants take root to reproduce so that no more clay balls are needed. Ultimately, all you do is collect produce and thin things out. That, in short, is natural farming.

"There are no machines. There is nothing at all," he said. "We just make clay balls and scatter them all over the farm before the rainy season starts in September-October or March-April, and you can have forest trees and fruit trees, vegetables, green manure plants and grapes growing together in harmony.

"Scientists believe there is in nature competition and survival of the fittest, but this is wrong," said Panos, who was beginning to remind me of Socrates. "This is human mind. The ecologists believe there is cooperation. This is also human mind, this is wrong. In nature there is harmony. And this harmony is created when we have a rich variety of life, of plants, of animals. This is the only way to have harmony, and this is the only way to solve the problem of the diseases and the pests."

I found it hard to accept. No tractors? No cultivators? No combines? Surely it's a crock, I thought. "So how much money do you make?" I asked, getting right to the point. Surely his answer would prove the method a fraud.

"My farm is two hectares, about five acres. My income in dollars, it is about 400,000 drachmas, about $1,500 US per 1,000 square metres, about $13,000 US per year."

That's not bad, I thought, and he's only working five acres. That's about $20,000 Cdn, a lot more than most Western Canadian farmers netted last year, and their farms average 1,500 to 2,000 acres. Plus, Panos says – and this struck me as novel – he doesn't work very hard.

"I am a lazy farmer," he told me more than once. "I go to the spa, I watch the birds, I visit with friends. I am a lazy farmer."

And a smart one, apparently. My image of him as Socrates began to grow. He questioned so many things we took for granted.

"I think natural farming is the only way out of the standstill in agriculture all over the world because we use zero energy," he went on. "The cost of production is practically zero. So even if we sell for small prices we make profits. It's very important that we sell for the poor people as well so it not be just for the rich people. Earth is for everybody. So if we sell at high prices like we do in Greece (and Canada), what we call national products, then very few people can have them.

"We have what we call petroleum agriculture. So if petroleum is in short supply that will be the end of agriculture. The country that controls the petroleum, the energy, can control agriculture all over the world. So natural farming can be the only solution."

Grain producers in Western Canada want higher commodity prices for wheat, barley and canola, I told him. He wasn't impressed. "The answer is not higher prices. The answer is natural farming, zero cost of production, so no matter if the price be low or high, the income will be good. The important thing is that what happens in Canada is happening all over the world. In European countries you can see the same problem. The cost of production is getting higher and higher and the prices are the same as 20 years ago or worse. And of course the fertilizers and pesticides are 10 or 20 times more expensive."

I puzzled over the origins of natural farming and asked him to explain. He told me about a man named Masanobu Fukuoka who lives in Japan. He is the founder of the method.

"Fukuoka right now is 87 years old. We can say that his idea of natural farming started at the age of 27, when he had something we could call illumination, or what the Japanese call satori."

I've since read one of Fukuoka's books in which he explains what took place. It was shortly after the Second World War, and the young man left the armed forces to work with his father on the family farm. But he was troubled by what he saw — people were quickly forsaking the old and proven ways of growing food naturally and embracing chemicals and fertilizers, which they had never used before. Their American marketers, who gained understandable stature by virtue of victory over the Japanese in 1945, said the new way promised higher yields and greater profit.

One day, Fukuoka was struck by what he describes as an insight that changed the course of his life. He realized that man knew nothing at all. He came to believe that man can know nothing of the vast truth of how the universe functions. In other words, man may think he does, but he doesn't truly understand how nature works, and how and why things grow. Snippets of insights here and there, in other words, do not provide the total picture. This same realization struck Socrates two millennium ago when he said: "One thing I know: I know nothing."

But from ignorance, real instinctive knowledge begins, Fukuoka said. This is understanding that comes directly from nature. Nature is our teacher, he came to believe.

"So he came back to his village and he started trying to apply this philosophy to agriculture," Panos explained. "If he could prove that without using technology — that means machines, chemicals, fertilizers or tractors, herbicides or weeding — if he could prove that he could have good crops, then the answer would be there for everybody to see it....And he started farming this way.

"And after 60 years, at a place where there was a desert (they could only grow sweet potatoes there), we have a paradise, a jungle, forest trees and fruit trees and vegetables and grains and green manure plants grow. It's for everybody there to go and see." And the Japanese man has made a good living growing rice and other crops. I wondered how he and Panos knew which plants to seed together to create harmony.

"The only thing we know is that we know nothing at all," the Greek repeated. "So we have to collect all kinds of seeds, mix them together, make clay balls and sow them together before the seasonal rains come. Nature will show us the types of plants that can grow in that area. Or we could say that the plants will choose the place where they like to live."

In Canada, we need quantity. Five-acre farms with hand-tossed seeds just wouldn't work, I argued. And how would you harvest plants in a jungle?

He said there are people in California who have tried natural farming, like Loonberg's farm, which has 3,000 hectares. Panos said Loonberg has grown rice there successfully and has built a cooperative of 300 farmers, so the same might be done in Canada.

Natural farming sounded a lot like organic farming to me. I asked about that.

"Whether we speak of organic farming or thermoculture or biological farming or bio-dynamic farming, the difference is that in all these kinds of farming we use the human mind. Man is supposed to be the culmination of creation. In natural farming we don't use the human mind, we only make clay balls. And in these clay balls we have the four principles: no tillage, no fertilizer, no pesticides, no weeding or herbicides. Also, no pruning. So in these clay balls we could call them clay balls of love and hope. Hope for the creation of a paradise, and love of nature, for the whole of nature."

Didn't people farm a lot like that 100 years ago?

"They were not making clay balls. No tillage was applied maybe 3,000 years ago in India, for example. No, we haven't come full circle. Natural farming is not traditional farming. Natural farming is based on a different philosophy. In natural farming the only thing the farmer wants to do is serve nature, not humanity. Of course, when we serve nature, we also serve human beings. But if we try to serve humanity, what we've done so far is destroy nature."

He continued in this vein. "I think right now we have separated God, man and nature. We have separated religion, philosophy and science. I think the right time has come to that they will become one. Man, God and nature will become one. They will come back to the source where man has not been separated from these things.

"Science only will destroy nature. That unity of Man, God and nature will save the world. Otherwise, there is no hope.

I tell him some conventional farmers must laugh at him.

"Even with alternative farmers we have a strong resistance, so it is not only chemical farmers who laugh." Natural farming, he said, makes other farmers feel afraid because there is nothing to question.

It seems too simple to be effective, I say.

"Natural farming is the only answer for the re-vegetation of the desert. What we've been trying to do the last seven years is re-vegetate the whole Mediterranean region, trying to block the expansion of the desert into central Europe, and trying to made the same thing up from Tanzania to the Atlantic Ocean to create another green barrier to create a paradise on earth. The idea is that man can live happily in Eden, so we're trying to create a paradise again. Because the real beauty, truth and good, exist only in nature."

Sounds good, I say, but the fact is the earth is bound by a complex political and economic system that controls agriculture. He agreed that the bureaucrats in Brussels (head office of the European Community) or in other countries of the world have a lot of clout, and he suspected they were trying to reduce the farming population to four per cent, and to create large farms.

"But the farmer is the salt of the earth ... and going back to nature is the only answer to human problems....The time has come to create another kind of culture, we could call it natural culture. Man's only objective would be to serve nature, where he could play, enjoy the sunshine, enjoy nature, and live happily there."

This was all quite fascinating – and surprising. I wanted to know more about my new friend.

"I was born in Thessaloniki in 1950. I lived in a city to the age of 30. My father had a grocery shop. I was ill. I was, let's say, without hope. Doctors said I wouldn't live long because I had a heart problem and other health problems. So they told me that I had to live a quiet life, to study and become a scientist.

"That was at the age of 18. A moment came that I wouldn't accept the idea that man is born and has to suffer, that something we call disease exists in nature. But I was young at the time. So after spending years taking thousands of pills trying to solve my problems, all of a sudden I decided to throw them away and I tried a more natural diet.

"After one year I recovered completely, I was breathing again freely, and I said, there it is. I have the answer. So I said, what about agriculture, that was my field, what I studied at the Agricultural University of Athens for five years. Bachelors only, no masters, no Ph.D. I was lucky. That's why I said BA only!

"So I said man and animals and plants can enjoy perfect health without having to use pesticides and fertilizers. What I understand is something that other people in other times have also understood. So I started looking for books concerning this kind of farming ... and I found *The One Straw Revolution* (by Fukuoka), published by Rodale Press in Pennsylvania.

"Then I went to Japan and I worked with Fukuoka. He is a simple man. The big difference is that he realizes that man cannot understand nature, that man can really know nothing at all. And that changed his life completely. He proved it practically on his farm. Now we can say he is the richest farmer in his area, although he has done nothing at all, just sown clay balls. He has about five hectares of land. He started with only half an acre, if I remember well."

I paused, as he paused, to let this all sink in. After a few minutes I asked him more about himself, how long he has farmed.

"For the last 19 years. The last 12 years in Greece. Right now my whole life is, I want to re-vegetate the desert, to sow seeds in the desert. I want to serve nature. We need to sow seeds."

But won't nature do that on its own?

"In the barren areas there are no seeds. In other places where the animals graze year after year, there are few plants because since they graze all year round, the variety of plants is diminished. So in the end we have very few plants, soil erosion, and the desert is the final result."

It sounded a lot like southern Saskatchewan and Alberta. I told him that, and he nodded.

"It is the first 10 metres of vegetation that creates rain. It is not evaporation as the scientists believe of the lakes, oceans and rivers that creates rain. It is the first 10 metres of the vegetation, the moisture. So we need plants with large leaves to bring the rain, to call the rain. So the idea is to make 100 different kinds of plants and bushes and annual plants, make clay balls, and let nature do the rest of the work.

"If we only sow seeds of trees, we'd fail. If we only sowed seeds of annual plants, we'd fail. We have to mix all kinds of seeds."

He started talking about irrigation and salinity. "What the scientists do is use water to irrigate the plants in the desert and create farms. What happens there is the water evaporates and we have salinity increase. After five or 10 years the farms have to be abandoned. And that's happened in farms all over the world like India and Somalia and Ethiopia. Russians and Americans went there and they made the same things and had the same failures."

Diversity of plants and trees create the necessary harmony so that all can grow together and attract rainfall, he said. The problem, in other words, was monoculture – the industrial method of growing only one crop in vast fields.

Panos called monoculture scientific famine. "They believe that in nature there is competition. So they don't believe that fruit trees and forest trees and vegetables can grow together, because to them in nature we have the survival of the fittest. So they start with the wrong philosophy.

"Nature is perfect," he said. "The only thing we have to do is see and learn directly from nature. So when something goes from on our farm, we shouldn't think the problem is nature. The problem is the mind, which has interfered and created the problem. So the only thing we have to do is start from the point that nature is perfect and see what we have done to create the problem.

"All is one. We should never forget that. Everything that happens even to a butterfly is important to life. It is interconnected to our life. It is very important what happens to the Balkan countries, because all is one. That is the very reason I want to go to Romania, to Bulgaria, to Turkey, to Yugoslavia, to make clay balls with the people to create vegetable gardens, small farms, so that people can become self-sufficient. We can have no peace using arms. We can only have peace when we have beautiful nature, when people have enough food. Then we will have peace."

Panos Manikis gave me a lot to think about on that train ride north. Recently, I found this in the Nov. 5, 2001 Globe and Mail: "The greatest obstacle to discovery is not ignorance – it is the illusion of knowledge." – Daniel Boorstin.

CHAPTER 5

An Aussie Haberdasher, and Organic Farmers

As the train chugged north, and our conversation continued, I observed the passing countryside, and the scenes varied from sheer mountainsides to lush valleys to seemingly endless expanses of olive and peach trees. Greece is gorgeous.

On the plains vast orchards unfolded around us, perfect rows of endless peach or olive trees. Panos said, "Monoculture in all its glory." But the fact is peaches and olives are huge industries here, accounting for most of the country's agricultural revenues.

Panos had friends who farmed organically near a city called Larissa, in Thessaly, and he felt they would welcome me. It seemed a good story to pursue. I bid him farewell at Larissa, but not before accepting an invitation to visit him at his home in Edessa.

"Remember, all is one," he said as I rose to leave. He added: "If we are happy, if there is joy in our lives, then with this standard we can judge things of importance to us." I thanked him again for all his help and struggled off the train with my heavy load, feeling -- happy.

Only a hundred metres from the train station was Hotel Diethnes. I still had my duffel of clothes for the poor, and the thing weighed a good 40 pounds, on top of my regular pack and smaller carry-on bag with a typewriter and related materials. The proprietor was a jolly fellow in his 60s who was clearly glad to see some business walk in the door. After settling in, I toured the city and had supper at a nearby restaurant.

Next day I took a bus to a town called Sikulio where I found a busy rural market. As I wandered around the market taking in the fresh fish, vegetables, clothing and other items on display, I heard some strange words: "How are you, mate?" The voice was unmistakably Aussie. He followed that with, "What are you doing up here?" singling me out as a foreigner.

I turned to face him. The man was about 30, with a smile as wide as the Nile. He stood behind two tables flooded with women's garments. He looked like a foreigner himself.

"More to the point," I exclaimed, "what are *you* doing up here? To answer your question, I'm a Canadian waiting for a ride. How do you, an Aussie, come to flog women's underwear in rural Greece?"

He smiled.

"My parents are Greek, and I've got to make a living." His name was Nick, he said. "And I'm pretty good at this."

He was, too. Nick sold me the only men's item he had left, a pullover. His prices were less than half what most Greek shops ask, and women were pawing through his wares as I stood watching. As he chatted with them in Greek you could see he was right at home. He'd spent his early years in Australia and had come to his parents' homeland later in life.

You just never know when or where in the world you'll meet an Aussie. They're everywhere, the world's greatest travelers. I once asked an Aussie why this was so. "It's easy," she replied. "Australia is so far from anywhere, that once you get some place you want to stay awhile." Airfare to Europe from Australia costs a fortune, she noted. It's common for Australians to spend three years or more on the road, compared to a North American's or European's few weeks or months.

On this road the ride I had arranged finally came by. A dusty little car pulled up and a man about Nick's age got out. John Pazaras extended a hand and after introductions, we sped toward his home, in a village called Pournari, 20 minutes away.

John was married to Meni, and they had a small child Margareta. He had met his wife in agricultural college, and John made his living as an inspector for the Hellenic Dairy Association, visiting dairies and checking quotas. It paid him a comfortable wage and allowed him some freedom to farm on the side. They lived in the village of Pournari, population 300, northeast of Larisa.

We wound our way toward his country home, passing forests and houses in the mountains, finally arriving at his village with its narrow streets and small old houses. As in Canada, most rural folk here are elderly, and depopulation is a problem as the young leave home for jobs in cities. The Pazaras family live 150 metres up a mountain called Kissavos.

Their home, an 80-year-old stone dwelling with thick walls and a workshop built alongside, was on the edge of Pournari. They bought it and 1.5 acres of land in 1991 for six million drachma, about $24,000 Cdn. John had spent a lot of time updating and insulating, making it comfortable and secure. The windows were barred. Outside, a large black dog was on guard, for they feared thieves, and mentioned, as others had, the Albanians as prime suspects.

Over a cup of sage tea in their kitchen, heated by a wood stove, I learned about their lives. They were energetic, honest, hospitable. Meni, 36, made soap in the workshop, which she sold in 25 stores. She spoke of her choice to work at home with Margareta, 3 1/2 – a chattering, cheerful, dark-haired girl, the image of her mother -- of her hopes that John, 38, might one day quit his job to devote all his time to the farm and family; of her frustrations finding time for all their interests.

In addition to everything else, they published a quarterly magazine called *New Moon* about organic farming and natural medicines, writing the articles with others in a small group of devotees. The three-year-old magazine, written in Greek, had 350 subscribers. With no advertising, it wasn't a money maker. "Our purpose isn't the money. It is an effort to tell our experience with ecology," Meni said. "It's something that keeps us together, many friends."

Every month about 15 of them met at a home to discuss the next edition. "We eat, we drink, and children play together, sometimes fight together!" Meni said. "But it's very creative. We are in a big fight against genetic engineering. Here in Greece for two years there is a ban."

Although meaningful and rewarding, the work was adding up. And the mock-up of their latest issue of *New Moon* – with articles and artwork – had been stolen from their vehicle in Larissa. It was a huge loss, and Meni's frustrations came to the fore the second day I was there.

"We have no time because of the magazine, because of the farm, because of his work," she said. "We want to see friends. We have no time. At the moment he feels he must work at his job for security. But I want him here, because now we have two different kinds of life. They don't go very well together.

"We must do it when he's ready to do it....I do what my heart says. John is very good, very generous. He believes that I am crazy when I say 'stay here'. I believe that everything is very easy. He thinks that things are hard....(Scientists) respect him for what he is doing and because he speaks their language to prove the validity of organic farming. I believe that is his mission in life, to learn and explain this and spread the knowledge."

They had moved from Larissa, a city of 145,000, a year earlier. "I want a life without noise, without too many people, with nature, to work with my mind and body together," Meni said. Like many of us they wrestled with a basic conflict: the desire for financial security in terms of John's city job, and their quest for a simpler life on the farm.

The farm was an impressive little operation based on olives and olive oil. They had a few turkeys, some chickens for eggs, ducks, a vegetable garden and olive trees. Higher up the mountain, a short distance away, was another small plot of land with more olive trees and bee hives, which are kept for the honey and the bees' ability to fertilize the trees.

They had 200 olive trees and some apple, chestnut, walnut, peach and almond trees. They also grew many herbs such as lavender and rosemary, used in their soaps, which earned an impressive $4,000 their first year. Olive oil sales brought in $1,600, olives $1,200, and olive oil paste, $3,200. That's a total farm income of about $10,000 in addition to John's salary of $18,000. Their costs of farming and soap making were $1,200, but EU farm subsidies of $600 cut their costs in half. You can see why Meni was inclined to think the farm could support them, but John's position is also persuasive. Their income from agriculture would fall by half -- about $3,000 every second year – due to the nature of olive production.

As organic producers of oil, they made 30 per cent more per kilo than conventional farmers, and demand for their product was growing. "They want more and more from us but we don't have any more," Meni said. "The organic market is stable for us and continues to get better. We're doing what we like and we know that what we sell is good for people. We feel good about that."

People are afraid of chemicals, but most farmers continued to use them for fear their production and income would decline. Even when picking dandelions for salads, neighbours spurned their own chemically treated land and asked to pick on John and Meni's because they knew it was clean. "They are afraid to pick dandelions on their own farms," Meni said.

"We would farm organically even if we lost money because we believe in the lifestyle, the philosophy," she added. Part of their economy is bartering. In exchange for oil, soap and olives, they receive organic wheat and cheeses from friends.

John pointed out that science itself is showing the need to stop using chemical poisons, which are killing vital micro-organisms in soils, eliminating wild plants, polluting water tables and harming people. They use natural pest controls. One problem is an insect that lays its eggs in olives. To control its numbers, they use a solution of ammonia and water in soft drink containers that have been cut open to allow the insects inside. Hung with wire, one container protects three trees.

Another problem was mice that ate the roots of their grape vines. They brought in cats, which worked for a while, but then the cats left, or were shot by neighbours. To combat another insect, they used a natural micro-organism called B.T. (Bacillus Thuzigiensis), with which they sprayed their trees three times a year.

I asked them about their friend, Panos Manikis, and his philosophy of natural farming. "In Panos's case it works, but he's in a place where it is good," John said. "There are many difficulties in Greek agriculture. I'm not sure it will work if you do nothing. If you don't prune, you don't take as many olives. If I see a pest, I believe that I must do something." Added Meni: "He succeeds, but here we do something between conventional and do-nothing farming."

At the time of my visit, February 2000, the Greek Ministry of Agriculture did not support organic farming, and more than 99 per cent of production was conventional, with heavy use of chemicals. The Pazarases paid $40 a year for chemicals they didn't use, because each farmer shared the cost. Each olive grove was sprayed three times with a tractor spreading clouds of chemical to control weeds and insects. "It comes right into the house. They believe it's the only way to have good production," said Meni. Added John: "The real cost is my bees, the water, the wildlife. Larissa has a problem with water because of the many fertilizers." Still, their neighbours and government oppose their organic methods. "It isn't so easy."

Meni makes 20 varieties of soap, and what makes them special is the glycerine. "In conventional soap making, the manufacturer takes away the glycerine, but we leave it in, so it's good for the skin. They don't dry the skin....And it's natural, 100 per cent." John, sitting across from her at their beautiful kitchen table (an old outhouse door he sanded down), interjected: "But I am afraid we will lose our home to soaps!"

Next day John had a day off, so we drove to a village called Spilia and stopped at café Manthos. Spilia means "caves" and refers to the original dwellings used by people who fled an island, Hios, which was ruled by the Turks in the 1800s. Formerly a bustling town of 1,000, Spilia when

I visited had only 100 souls, "old people" they said, though the number quadrupled each summer.

They grew beans and tomatoes there, which are known for their exquisite flavour said to be due to the elevation, 700 metres above sea level. During the Second World War the Germans burned the village twice because it harboured resistance fighters.

Our server was also the owner, Niki Hrisikou, a five-foot tall grandmother with a bit of a moustache, stocky and strong, who brought us dish after dish of meat, vegetables, oil, fries, bread and drink, chatting all the while.

"I must leave here!" she said, as we idled away a couple of hours. "I eat too much, being cook for this village. If I stay here, I die!"

When she was young she wanted to live in Larissa. Now she prefers the village because her friends are here. But she still goes to Larissa, she said – to visit the discos.

Her husband, Manthos, doesn't want to leave here anymore than she does. "We're happy with what we have now. We won't change it."

CHAPTER 6

Into Macedonia, where I meet a man
Who Drove a Tank for Milosevic

My journey north to Macedonia was quiet. The train passed through some spectacular vistas, and I'm sure I caught sight of Mount Olympus, home to the mythical Hercules, a favourite childhood TV character of mine. At the Macedonian border I purchased a visa and waited for another train to leave for Skopje, the capital city of about 500,000 where the Canadian military were expecting me.

The night was dark and damp, the station grimy. As I walked to the platform, a dim illumination shone down from a few old lamps. It was enough, however, to reveal a figure sitting on a bench, a well-dressed young man with a lean intelligent face, a fresh crew cut, black leather jacket and polished shoes. He was smoking, and was much better attired than most of the people I had met. When I asked him if he would mind sharing the bench, his reply was friendly. I sat down and introduced myself.

"I am Aleksandar," he replied. "I live in Serbia." He was 26, a veteran of Slobodan Milosevic's war in Yugoslavia. He was partners with his father in a company that imported Greek food. His full name was Aleksandar Milojevic -- no relation to the dictator, in fact their spellings differ.

To jump head for a moment, the infamous Milosevic was found dead in his cell of a heart attack on March 11, 2006, in the United Nations war crimes tribunal detentions centre in The Hague, Netherlands. ICTY Chief Prosecutor Carla Del Ponte said she regretted his death. "It deprives the victims of the justice they need and deserve. In the indictment which was judicially confirmed in 2001, Milošević was accused of 66 counts of genocide, crimes against humanity and war crimes committed in Croatia, Bosnia and Herzegovina and Kosovo between 1991 and 1999. These crimes affected hundreds of thousands of victims throughout the former Yugoslavia. During the prosecution case, 295 witnesses testified and 5000 exhibits were presented to the court. This represents a wealth of evidence that is on the record," she said. "It is a great pity for justice that the trial will not be completed and no verdict will be rendered. However, other senior leaders have been indicted for the crimes for which Slobodan Milošević was also accused....Finally, I would like to share a thought for Zoran Đinđic, his wife and his family. Exactly three years ago, he was murdered in Belgrade. He is the man who had the courage to bring Slobodan Milošević to The Hague so that he could face justice."

The man beside me on the bench was on his way home from a business trip. I was fortunate to meet him, for I would soon be writing about the war in Kosovo which his former commander-in-chief engineered. Here was a fellow who had served under the war criminal.

(At this point you have to admit my good fortune in meeting interesting people. First Anka, the maid, then Father Alexander, then Panos Manikis the farmer, John and Meni Pazaras, the Aussie merchant, and now this former military man – and I'd only been in Europe a week. Would I have met such people near my home in Manitoba?)

We talked about the war. "Milosevic not good," and Aleksandar shook his finger at me. At least I knew where he stood. "I like Milo Dyukanovic, president Montenegro. A very good man and no war. Milosovic war, war, war." In March of 1999, NATO bombs hit his home in a city called Paracin. Nobody was killed, but the roof fell in. He and his father, Rade Milojevic, rebuilt the roof. NATO's attack made him angry, mainly at Milosovic, he said. Many Serbs were angry that he halted democratization.

Aleksandar himself drove a tank in the campaign against Croatia in 1991 when he was only 17. "I'm lucky, war in Croatia. But my friend, dead." In fact, he said, many friends died. In one close call, a bazooka shell fired toward them went under his tank and out the other side. It so unnerved him he spent some days in hospital for stress. It was his mother, Radmila, he said, who made him well again with her good cooking, which she delivered each day.

Now, he said, the Serbian secret police are putting dissenters in jail. A friend of his is one of them.

When I ask him how he learned his English, he replied: "English films good. Mel Gibson, Sharon Stone, CNN Live. Eurosports." We laughed. TV taught him what he knows. TV in excessive amounts may be bad for kids, but it sure helps motivated people learn English. He was a polyglot: he also spoke Serbian, German and Italian.

Kosovo was very much part of Serbia, he insisted. "Kosovo is the Serbian soul." He didn't see how Serbia would ever relinquish the territory. And he was concerned about Albanian Kosovars injuring and killing Serbs. "Albanian people not good. Steal and kill Serbs, anybody. Canadians, Italians, Germans."

He predicted Milosevic would be "kaput" by June, which proved wrong, but the leader was eventually out of power by a people's revolt. They were tired of him, his oppression, his ruthless treatment of dissenters, his wars. What we had been told in the media was largely true.

"European people good. Orthodox people good, Greek, Macedonia, Serbia, Russia. And Russian girls OK," and he winks and smiles.

Our dirty old orange and silver train soon struggled north, as we settled in for the ride. There's always an element of mystery when traveling the countries of southeastern Europe, especially at night. I had the same feelings in Yugoslavia and Hungary in the mid-1990s. These countries seem stuck in the 1940s or 50s. Few major technological or infrastructural changes appear to have taken place since then, and you feel you're in an older era. The train, as I say, was 50 or more years old, judging by its worn seats, tarnished chrome and general griminess, the residue of Communism. It didn't help that armed Macedonian customs agents were brusque and suspicious.

Fortunately Aleksandar spoke on my behalf when I was questioned by one such man. Then we were able to relax somewhat, and eat our bread and nuts as we journeyed north. The mystery was enhanced by the night, which gave us only glimpses of roadways and towns. I felt good, enjoyed it all, but my senses were always a little keener, because nothing -- absolutely nothing -- was familiar. At such times, I rarely questioned what I was doing. To get the next story the train was necessary, this ride was necessary, the only affordable way to Skopje.

The clock on the old Skopje train station has been stopped at 5:17 a.m. since the morning of July 26, 1963, when it was one of the few parts of the city that remained standing after a massive earthquake. It measured 6.1 on the Richter scale, killed nearly two thousand people, and left over a hundred thousand homeless after destroying about 80 per cent of the city.

We arrived in Skopje at 11:15 p.m. It was February 8, 2000. I disembarked, said good-bye to Aleksandar, and took a cab to Camp Maple Leaf. The cabbie knew of the Canadian base, though he spoke little English. It was on grounds leased from a trucking company, with all the big buildings and storage sheds required to feed and house 1,300 soldiers, for this was the supply base that kept satellite camps in Kosovo equipped. About 1,000 of these men and women were in Kosovo at any one time.

The young guard at the gate confirmed that I was expected and sent me in to another gate where I hoped to be posted to a tent for the night without waking anybody. I was thinking in particular of Capt. Patricia Viscount, a public affairs officer with whom I had made my arrangements before leaving Canada. I'll let my journal entry tell the story.

"It's 12:15 and I sit in a heated tent at Camp Maple Leaf in Skopje. It's three degrees C outside and a balmy five in here with 14 army cots and me the lone resident. It felt good to see the Maple Leaf and a Canadian soldier guarding the entrance to this camp. He was from Petawawa, Ont., and said things were going OK. The Albanians have been tossing the odd grenade here and there and they don't get too close to the Russians because they're shooting at them in Kosovo.

"Capt. Patricia Viscount is a slim pretty thing who was awakened to greet me and place me in a tent, despite my request this not be done at such an hour. She was hospitable. 'Mr. Bird, you arrived.' Yes, I said, but the train schedule set the hour, not me. She seemed forgiving."

I would see quite a bit of Viscount in the next three weeks and was glad to get off to a fairly good start with her. People in her position are critical to journalists, as we depend on them for interviews, scheduling, and help with everything from where to do our laundry to our meal ticket.

Next morning I learned the Canadian army truly eats well, as endless tables of fruit, cereal, breads, coffee and other items, not to mention bacon, eggs and porridge, were all available, and I didn't hold back. I gained weight, about eight pounds, during my three weeks in Kosovo and Skopje. It was one of the happiest and most productive periods of my four-month tour.

Sitting at a table, I talked to Sgt. Robert Dean, 36, who had 17 years in the service. His father before him had done the same job -- supply technician -- for 34 years. Dean grew up in Dean Settlement, Nova Scotia, named after his great-great-great grandfather. In three weeks he was going home for a break, and he was smiling about that.

"I've got two boys, Robbie, 6, and Justin, 5, and my wife, Monique. We've been together 14 years, married 12. She's constantly reminding me that it would be nice for me to be home one year without going somewhere. I've got one (six-month) tour of Bosnia, one of Cyprus, one tour of Honduras, and then my last two were in Central America for Hurricane Mitch."

His mind was fairly at ease because he knew his wife was holding the fort in his absence, and sending him precious mail. Others I spoke to did not share such confidence in their partners, and break-ups were fairly common. This was confirmed by Lieut. Navy Bob Deobald, a chaplain I also interviewed over breakfast.

"For many of these soldiers this is their fourth tour in eight years. For many others it's their sixth or seventh tour. When you add the training time in the field, the time in courses, plus the tour, that's where we see the toll on personal family relationships."

Deobald, who had been married 19 years to his wife, Deanna, was glad the Canadians were going home in June. The soldiers and their family ties were stretched to the limit. "We are going to return home with fewer families in crisis than many other rotations because it has been shortened, and because we have just an excellent support group back in Petawawa. The flip side of doing so many tours is that we've learned how to better support our families at home. We have situations where there are difficulties and we have made any patriations where we think it is necessary to help the relationship get back on an even keel."

The Canadians' mission in Kosovo, like that of the other NATO countries, was to help to sustain a secure and stable environment so the United Nations' humanitarian efforts could succeed, Deobald said. The purpose also was to help the local people rebuild their lives and communities.

This six-month tour is different than others, he said, for various reasons, one being that Prime Minister Chretien announced last fall that this would be the last six-month rotation in Kosovo.

"It seems to me that some of the brakes began to be applied before you even arrive. For instance, we didn't have the heavy-duty snow removal equipment that the engineers need, so when we did get the snow we didn't have the machines to remove it, which was a frustration for our people. These are the best soldiers in the world," he added. "They'll roll with anything."

Does knowing the date of departure hamper the efforts here?

"I think it increases the stress levels in a different way, because it means you have to think beyond the operational tasks of the mission," the chaplain said. "Normally we'd be looking at five or 10 years. Bosnia is already 10 years, I think. As the different rotations come on they build on what's already in place. We built like eager beavers with the knowledge it has to come down. What I'm trying to say is, it's a really busy tour."

Is their work succeeding?

"In my opinion, absolutely. With the majority of people in Kosovo being Albanians, we tend to hear the Albanian stories, moreso than from the Serbian side. When we came into Kosovo in June of 1999, people had been in my opinion under oppression from the authorities in power for years, and the war was certainly in part a result of the Albanian people just reaching a point of frustration and lashing back."

When they arrived there was no garbage pickup, telephones were out, there was no police service or postal service, no taxi system, vehicle registration or road maintenance. Even the schools had closed, and many shops. With NATO soldiers present 10 months later, schools are open again, power plants are up and running and the telephones work, but only in the cities. Canadians can take partial credit for the improvements, he said. Even the economy is better, he said, as stores have been repaired and reopened with better stocks of food.

Deobald said part of the problem of helping the people was making sure those who needed supplies got them, rather than profiteers. "Like any place, you have greed. There are middle people out to make a buck," but as much as possible the soldiers have found ways around this problem, he said.

He was glad to be going home in June because Canadians are already extended in Bosnia, East Timor, and other locations. "Secondly I would say that the needs of Kosovo are being very well met by the nations in much closer proximity – Italy, France, Britain, Sweden, Denmark, Norway."

He also said he and many of his colleagues were looking forward to a change of leadership in Serbia that would go a long way to stabilizing the Balkans. In fact this did happen.

CHAPTER 7

Canadian Troops in Kosovo

The following story was written on Feb. 9, 2000 and sent to various newspapers.

Soldiers feels futility as hatred reigns in Kosovo

SKOPJE, Macedonia – After almost two months, the Canadian commander of Task Force Kosovo feels a sense of futility in trying to restore peace to this troubled region.

"What my men and women are experiencing is what a policeman in a very, very crime-ridden area must feel," said Col. Ivan Fenton in his headquarters here. But police don't have to deal daily with anti-tank rocket launchers, hand grenades, land mines and automatic weapons. One soldier said he jumped out of his truck one day to learn he had landed only inches from a mine.

"I wouldn't say we're succeeding," Fenton, 49, said in an interview. "I would say we're mitigating this semi-anarchy."

He largely agreed with Tuesday's report in the *Globe and Mail* by Timothy Garton Ash, who described the Yugoslavian province 35 kilometres north of here as an "almighty mess." Fenton said that in all of Kosovo since his force of almost 1,400 arrived Dec. 15, taking over from the first Canadians here since May, there have been more than 50 murders and 120 people injured in attempted murders. Eighty homes have been burned and 13 people kidnapped. There is no functioning government.

He points out that in the Canadians' area of responsibility things are somewhat better, with six or seven murders, perhaps because it contains fewer Serbs, which limits inter-ethnic clashes. The French section, for instance, is much worse. Last week 10 died in ethnic fighting there.

"I wouldn't say for a minute that we're providing 100 per cent peace and security," which is their mandate. "If we were not here, it would be much worse than it is."

Indeed the Canadians are helping in various ways. One bitterly cold night, Canadians on patrol pulled a taxi out of the snow and delivered two teenagers home, said Chaplain Bob Deobald. "The father invited the soldiers in for tea." Others have started the first scout troop in the Balkans. "The big thing is there's 21 scouts and a waiting list of 90," said Gary Ostofi, a visiting retired reserve commander.

Here in Skopje, many Canadian troops will be running Sunday to raise money for three widows whose husbands fell as victims of the hatred, killed in ethnic clashes.

What can be done to turn Kosovo around? Fenton said that if he had a magic wand he would remove the hate chip from the people. "It's all hatred, and that's the most corrosive thing on our troops....It's like the fog here, you can taste it."

For some, that nagging sense of futility lingers. "You see that nothing's going to change," said Cpl. Jordan Wiens. "You know they're not killing each other right now, because we're here. But their attitudes don't change."

On top of this, many of the soldiers miss their families intensely. "I wouldn't be upset in the least if they sent me home tomorrow," said Master Cpl. Brian Thibeault, 39, of Petawawa, Ont., who has three children.

He said wives are the men's backbone. "As long as they are strong and take care of the home front, we can do our jobs efficiently here because it's one less thing to worry about."

Soon they will go home. Fenton said he has recommended the Canadians at Camp Maple Leaf, the supply centre and command post, and the rest of the task force in Kosovo be pulled out by May 1. He applauded the Chretien government's decision to announce last November the force would be out by June 15, 2000, the end of a normal six-month tour.

* * *

A briefing for journalists is held, and we're hit by a barrage of incoming acronyms: MNBs (multi-national brigade groups), UNMIK (United Nations Mission in Kosovo), UCK or KLA (Kosovo Protection Corps, the military arm of the Albanians fighting the Serbs), TMK (evolved from the UCK and KLA), AOR (Area of Responsibility), KFOR (Kosovo Force), APCs (armoured personnel carriers), etc.

Then we heard about the situation on the ground. In short, it wasn't good. Determined to avenge Serb atrocities, the Albanian majority was harassing the few Serbs who hadn't fled with the army. "When the snow starts to go, the blood starts to flow," said one official, adding what they feared most was inter-ethnic violence. Their job: keep a lid on it – and protect Canadian lives. "Force protection is our No. 1 priority."

Challenges abounded: there was little employment to keep the local people busy; most farm animals had been slaughtered by the Serbs; the fields needed de-mining; the few factories had been bombed out of commission; many lacked adequate food and clothes. On top of this the Albanian mafia was active in kidnapping, intimidation and smuggling of contraband weapons and drugs. Many unemployed men turned to mafia work. Even six-year-olds were put up to throwing stones at the windows of Serb-occupied apartments.

Kosovo was a gun culture where scores were often settled with violence. "It's almost a symbol of manhood," said Capt. Roger Bowden, yet he was quick to add: "There are a lot of people in Kosovo who just want to get on with their lives. They have what they want: the Serb oppression ended."

* * *

A convoy of two buses, led by a military vehicle and followed by a van, in which I ride, snakes slowly north toward Kosovo. It is the night of Feb. 9, with no hint of a moon. We're headed for Donja Kortica, DK for short, in the heart of the small, war-torn Serbian province. Kosovo would fit nicely into southwest Manitoba, and like my home turf Kosovo is an agricultural society. But this land is hilly, with steep embankments, and we negotiate mountain passes cautiously.

Suddenly a little car darts out from behind the van to pass us on a curve. The drop-off is about 350 metres. An oncoming truck leaves him no room to dart in front. He doesn't make it. Our driver, Capt. Patricia

Viscount, is unaware he is beside us, mere inches away, and somehow the three vehicles do not touch.

"That was too close," I say to the others, who offer murmurs of relief. Vance is from a weekly near Petawawa Ont, where many of the soldiers are based. Mike is from the Fredericton daily. The National Post is also here, James Cudmore, and so is the CBC.

At the Kosovo border we stop. A long line-up of trucks awaits passage through. We'll be here all night, I think. But then we detour to the left and bypass all the traffic – a lane for NATO vehicles only. There is a fairly steady stream, army trucks from different countries. As we proceed on the road to DK, shells of burned-out cars and trucks litter the roadside. Through built up areas, with some lighting, I see general dilapidation: garbage strewn about, burned-out homes, houses with no roofs, broken stone fences, cars stripped of all usable parts. This is Kosovo.

At DK half an hour later we pass through the entrance of the sprawling Canadian camp, which is nestled on a plain between two ranges of low mountains. Stepping into a chilly damp night, we trod upon large gravel stones and mud. Our ears are filled with the roar of Griffon helicopters taking off for one of their two daily missions assisting ground troops at vehicle checkpoints.

Looking around, I see rows of large dark vehicles I later learn are Bisons, personnel carriers I would soon ride in myself. I also see dozens of large domed structures called Weather Havens. These remarkably warm and weather proof shelters are new, and house everything from sleeping quarters to dining hall and kitchen. Far better than the alternative -- drafty and leaky canvas tents (which I spent my first nights in back at Skopje) – and the soldiers understandably love them.

That night, after a beer in one of the watering holes, I slept soundly.

Next morning, I entered the co-ed washrooms and showers and overheard some soldierly chat: "He said he'd lost his passport. So I said, 'How did you lose it?' He didn't know. Honestly, some of these guys shouldn't be allowed to wander Europe on their own!" Another time: "The power was off, so I said to -------, 'Go find a wood stove, would you? The dumb fuck tried. There isn't one in the entire camp, or a stick of wood."

When I returned after breakfast to do my teeth, a female soldier had hung a sign: "Women only, shower in use." I left and returned later. About one in 10 of the soldiers is female.

A briefing on mines burst any notions I had about going for walks. The place was full of "green slime," as mines were called, with 364 known mine fields and many more unrecorded. "That's how they protect their homes," said Sgt. Steve Wrathall, from Sydney, N.S. "This whole area has suspected mine fields. Even paved roads are not necessarily safe. They cut a bit out, place their mine and cover it with gravel so it looks like a pot hole."

Another problem was UXOs, unexploded ordnance. "About 20 per cent of NATO stuff didn't go off." Cluster bombs were particularly nasty, with dozens in a canister that spun out when dropped, designed to explode on Serb vehicles, spraying shrapnel. Many hadn't exploded. Twenty-two people had died from UXOs since June. Kids were picking them up and playing with them. "In the villages, people are bringing these to you," Wrathall said. "For some reason they don't go off."

One day, Michael and Vance and I headed out in a Bison with a driver and navigator to visit a sector in Kosovo where Canadians were at work. A Bison looks something like a tank, without the turret and only a fraction of the firepower. It has six large tires. By comparison, a Coyote surveillance vehicle has eight. We had originally been booked to visit a town where Serbs and Albanians co-existed, but a protest there threatened to turn ugly (it didn't, in fact) and the brass changed our route to be on the safe side.

Problem was, our driver didn't know the new route. And we got lost. We actually drove through plowed fields and over at least one farm fence, and down dirt lanes, lost. Remember, six wide tires, land mines galore. At one point a family on a cart pulled by a small horse stopped and looked at us, puzzled by our presence.

That day, my friends and I faced the very real prospect of a mine explosion. We donned our army-issue helmets and flak jackets and hoped for the best as our groaning and powerful Bison churned through mud, our navigator searching for points on the map.

It was a harrowing hour, let me tell you.

"I don't know about you, but I'm riding out on top in case we hit one of those bastards," I said to Mike. "Then at least we might be blown free." Mike came outside with me. Neither of us welcomed the idea of being pasted to the steel inside this vehicle.

Later, back at camp over supper, I questioned the navigator. "Oh," he said, "we were lost for a while, but in no real danger. Those roads had been de-mined months ago." It was hardly reassuring.

In fact, the threat of mines is constant. A few days before our briefing, an elderly Kosovar woman watched a man cross a field and lay something on a road. A car ran over it, but it didn't explode. A guy dug it out, picked it up and placed in the grass near a fence. The driver called in the

Canadians to deal with the object – an anti-tank mine (the other type is anti-personnel). "When we blew it up, she made a good bang," said Wrathall. " That guy should be buying lottery tickets."

The last time a Canadian peace keeper was killed was in Croatia in 1994. It's the engineers who run the highest risk. "The guys taking the mines out of the fields are the same guys putting new roofs on houses." In some cases, dogs are used to sniff out mines and UXOs.

That evening, as I worked in a small hut set up for Internet use for the soldiers, I met a couple of young men who gave me a hand. I'd never sent an email message before. Cpl. Joe MacDonald was from P.E.I. and belonged to an assault troop from Petawawa, Ont. He and his friend, Cpl. Kevin Malott, from Gimli, Man., had been stopping vehicles, searching for contraband, checking gun licences and the like. But they observed a lot of things besides, and they told me about them with all the enthusiasm of youth.

"We seen a cow blindfolded just the other day!" MacDonald told me. "It was in the back of a cart, so it wouldn't be spooked." Malott had a story of his own. His men were doing a check for weapons when they opened a trunk, only to find 12 live chickens. "They don't care about their animals," he offered.

"Yes they do," MacDonald corrected. "They didn't want the birds to escape. I would say these people don't have the education we have at home. This whole country is 20 years behind us."

We talked about livestock. They hadn't seen many animals. Malott mentioned most families had one or two cows. "It's like the old days when they had Betsy."

* * *

Over a meal one day I befriended the foreign editor at La Presse in Montreal, Gilles Paquin. Gilles arrived a day or two later than the rest of us, apparently via Belgrade in a bit of a harrowing taxi ride. Medium height and slender, Gilles was the old man among us, in his early 50s. He was a cool character, independent and quiet, and I liked him. Early on I grabbed a chance to eat supper with him and build a rapport. He was strongly pro-Quebec and favoured independence, and I trod softly on that subject. Being a freelancer, I wasn't a threat to him the way the CBC and National Post boys were. Naturally, he wanted the story first for La Presse. He liked the fact I'd worked across North Africa and Germany, and I decided I'd tag along if he'd let me.

"I'm going to Pristina tomorrow, by helicopter," he said. "I want to leave these spoon-fed sessions behind and see some real people." I was all for that, being tired of the bureaucratic briefings. Acronyms ran through my head like alphabet soup. Pristina, the capital, sounded like a good idea. "Mind if I come along?" He readily consented, and plans were made.

CHAPTER 8

In Pristina we meet a Canadian bar manager and two Serb grandmothers captive in their own apartment, targets of Albanian hatred and vengeance

The Griffon helicopter took off with a roar and Gilles Paquin and I were up and away, speeding over hill and dale with a bird's eye view of Kosovo and the damage wrought by war. That Saturday afternoon in February 2000 we saw many damaged homes, their roofs caved in or burned away. Craters pitted some fields and others were flooded, while others held winter wheat.

At one point we passed a sheep farm where the large barn had been leveled by NATO, which suspected it of housing Serb weaponry, the pilot said. The only thing visible was the outline of where it had stood; the rest had burned. Also notable was what we didn't see – livestock in any number, or people working the fields.

At Pristina we landed, to my surprise, on a soccer field in a stadium, and I felt a bit like a celebrity arriving to do a half-time show, though the stands were empty. Already I was glad I had attached myself to Gilles. The foreign editor of La Presse was an old pro who knew how to get around. He also had resources. This would not have been happening on my own.

The rest of the scribes had been taken on a tour of a village to see soldiers at work. I was grateful to the Canadian military -- without their cooperation I wouldn't have been there at all -- and such trips were OK, even welcome, in limited doses. They were responsible for us, and we couldn't very well be turned lose like so many cattle in a place where travel was dangerous and restricted. But I wanted some freedom to find my own stories, and so did Gilles.

We headed toward the city centre, which wasn't far off, and on the way saw youth playing soccer on a concrete pad. I took photos of this and many other sights during my time in Kosovo.

Gilles' plan was to rendezvous with his interpreter at the United Nation's media centre. As we walked down Mother Theresa Street (she was Albanian), a sign caught my eye – Bar Kurkri, Under New Management. "Gilles, let's check this out." Rock music played as a few young people sat at tables. A long bar took up the rear of the small, intimate venue. We asked to see the manager, and a stocky young man appeared. We introduced ourselves and shook hands. His name was Ed Wadleigh, and he was only 19.

"Where are you from, Ed?"

"London, Ontario."

"I was born there," I said. "Gilles is from Montreal."

"So what brings you to a place like this?" Wadleigh asked.

"I was about to ask you the same thing."

"Well, I run this bar. When I got here in September I worked for an NGO called the CIDC, the De-mining Centre. Met a Brit at a party who offered me more money and I ended up here."

"Quite a story. Mind if we take notes?"

"No problem."

Ed Wadleigh had attended A. B. Lucas Secondary in London and had been in Kosovo five months. He was enjoying himself, despite dealing with KLA extortionists and others who said they would burn the joint if he didn't start playing Albanian music. The bar was under new management because the former Serb owner had sold out and fled.

"This is one of the safe bars for Serbs. They (Albanians) don't want the Serbs coming here, and they want a cut of the profits," he said. "Saturday night four of them were in here, KLA, and carrying on." They got drunk, threatened to kill an Albanian woman (who they figured shouldn't have been in a Serb bar) and planted a KLA flag in the place. Wadleigh phoned the UN police, stationed conveniently across the street, and they shut the joint down without incident.

Another time he watched as a Serbian mother and daughter burned to death in the upper storey of a flat while a group of Albanians laughed on the street. They had set the fire.

"They screamed as they burned," he said.

Despite the horrors and harrowing risks, Wadleigh was happy. He was making good money, 500 Deutschmarks a week (currency set by the first UN commander there from Germany), and paying that much a month for a rented apartment shared by another Canadian and Brit. The money was all cash, and only one bank was operating. He worked nine hours a day, seven days a week -- and went to UN parties once a month.

"It's fun. There is a risk but I love the fun, the people I meet at the parties I go to, like German policemen, the Irish guys from Northern Ireland, the locals I get along with. A bit more fun than Ontario. Sometimes there's a small part of me that wishes for (home). It's sane, it's safer, normal. But when I'm older I'll have a lot more stories to tell."

"If you get older," I said.

"Well, yeah, I guess."

He'd been offered a job as a manager by a South African security firm. They must have figured if the crazy Canuck could manage in Pristina, then one of the most dangerous places in the world, he could succeed anywhere. "I'll likely go to South Africa and then work in Angola or Mozambique," he said, two other bastions of peace and goodwill.

As we left, I admired Wadleigh's spunk. Maybe without realizing it, he was wise to follow his heart and find his place in the world. So many good things happen when you just leave home and travel. The real pain comes from doing nothing. That's one of the reasons I was there myself. I get bored from doing nothing, or more accurately the same old thing again and again in Canada.

Moving on, Gilles and I found his interpreter. He had been trained as an engineer but was out of work, like countless others here. He was tall and polite with a fair grasp of English. Gilles' next goal was to speak to members of the Centre For Peace and Tolerance, a two-year-old organization with a name so bizarrely at odds with the region I laughed when I heard it. He wasn't laughing, however (though at other times showed a good sense of humour).

Gilles was keenly interested in the political and humanitarian dynamics of the region, though it is so complicated, with migrations and forced expulsions and massacres that it isn't clear to me which group, Moslem Albanian or Christian Serb, represents the position of Quebeckers in Canada. I'm not alone. After the Albanian-led Kosovo legislature declared independence on 17 February 2008, the following internet debate took place. This is a portion of a much longer conversation, but it sheds some light on the dynamic.

Benoît Giguère
said

I am myself a Quebec sovereigntist, so I guess my own view could
interest some in this debate.

There is simply no possible comparison between Quebec and Kosovo.

Quebec has never been the stage of ethnic cleansing. Quebec has been
so far able to develop itself and thrive as part of Canada, which has not
been the case of Kosovo. The Quebec francophone population is quite
divided over the independence question, as opposed to the Albanese
majority in Kosovo.

Therefore, I totally agree here with Gilles Duceppe: everybody should
stop making comparisons between Quebec and Kosovo at this point.

Spirit
said

I am tired of all these double standards. International law is universal
and should apply to all countries, even though they are unique. Now that
Kosovo has declared independence, Quebec, the Basque Country and
Abkhazia should follow. Why don't we recognize their independence as
well?

J.C.
said

I think the comparison came from a comment by PQ leader Pauline
Marois who praised Harper for recognizing Kosovo. She was the one
who made the comparison. It is just a ploy to start crap and stir the pot
for her own agenda. I was born and raised in Quebec and I'm sick of this
B.S. They are comparing apples and oranges.

Leo Foss
said

Wait a minute here! The Serbs migrated from Russia, not Turkey, and that was after the Roman empire collapsed. The Serbs lost 50,000 dead in Kosovo stopping a Turkish invasion of Europe 300 years ago, and since then Kosovo has been a hallowed ground for them.
After the second world war, during chaotic aftermath, hundreds of thousands of Albanians fled north to Serbia and settle illegally. After the NATO bombings, Kosovo elected a parliament now with solely Albanian representatives, and declared independence. There was no referendum. It is expected that in a year or two Kosovo will attempt to join with Albania.
What is the principle on which Canada recognizes Kosovo as independent? Are we saying that all you need is a declaration of independence from your legislature and you are independent? That's the principle Canada seems to have enshrined here.

The office of the Centre For Peace and Tolerance wasn't far away. A heap of garbage was burning in an adjacent parking lot, attended by a man with a broom. (There was no garbage pick-up.) Amidst the stench and smoke, the three of us approached an unmarked building and knocked. A young woman welcomed us quietly and showed us into a room with a wooden table. She was Sasha Ilic, 27, its coordinator. I asked if she were from Kosovo (as opposed to Serbia). She replied, "We are always from Kosovo."

About 400 Serbs remained in the city and were being harassed, beaten up, even killed, she said. About 238,000 had fled Kosovo for fear of persecution when the Serb army retreated the previous May. Many of those remaining didn't feel safe shopping for food, so supplies were delivered by the volunteer group, escorted by NATO soldiers.

"We have nothing," said Zorica Obradovic, one such volunteer. "I can't work now. Many people can't go out from apartments, house. They can't use dinars (Serb currency) here. They can't go in shops because they are Serbian. We go with KFOR police."

Verbal abuse from Albanians was common. "We don't have a problem with the old people. But the young people from other parts, from villages, are problem."

Some Albanians would like to help, Obradovic added, but were afraid to. Food was provided with aide from many European groups. Gilles pointed out that a Canadian office in Kosovo might help and supplied its number.

Ilic noted their office had no phone (because they hadn't paid the bill), and no computer. She hinted that some money came from journalists who paid for their information, but they got nothing from me. I had never paid for an interview and wasn't about to start now. I don't know what Gilles did.

Albanian girls were kidnapped by the mafia and used in prostitution, they said. She showed us a stack of papers documenting problems since KFOR arrived. Harassment, robbery, car theft, murder, missing persons, of whom there were 720. Usually they were found dead.

We learned of two Serb grandmothers sharing an apartment nearby, and one of their husbands was among the 720. He had been kidnapped. The women weren't searching for him. Prisoners in their own home, they feared going out at all. In fact, they were petrified someone would break in and kill them.

"We would like to visit these people," Gilles said, and soon we were in a locale called Dardania. The women insisted that three armed British soldiers accompany us. Their high-rise apartment had graffiti painted on its pock-marked walls. A large sign on the women's door, apartment three, declared: 'Under KFOR Protection.' We were allowed in, the three soldiers leading, followed by Gilles, his interpreter and myself.

The place was small and homey but drab and cluttered. Sand-coloured wallpaper, brown carpeting, one bedroom. They had a fridge and stove and a TV -- but didn't watch it, as it offered only Albanian language programming.

There was no phone service. Heavy curtains covered a large window, and when I pulled them aside cracks were seen in the glass, the effects of stones and a grenade. The soldiers told us it had misfired not far from their wall.

The women were Millinka Dosic, 60, and Stana Joksimovic, 65. They appeared sallow and worried. They offered vodka, Baltic Vodka according to the label, and we declined.

Man, was I pumped. Here was a decent story. My questions came quickly and the interpreter did his work well. As I pressed one point -- why didn't they go to Serbia where both had family? -- Gilles angrily motioned me to back off. When I think of it now, the question was threatening.

Their story was this. Men came for Dosic's husband Zoran, a bank employee, on June 28, 1999 while he was taking medicine upstairs to Joksimovic, who then lived on the ninth floor. She saw two men taking away her roommate's husband at gunpoint.

"After kidnapping my husband, they came in, broke in the door and took our gun," an AK-47, Dosic said. The AK-47 has one purpose, and it isn't for shooting deer. I didn't ask what her husband did when he wasn't at the bank, and wouldn't have heard the truth if I had. The Brits confirmed the abduction. No demand for money was made and Dosic didn't know whether he was dead or alive. He was almost certainly dead.

She had a son and two daughters in Serbia, so why didn't she leave?

"I stay here and wait for my husband," she replied, saying she had lived in Pristina all her life. "That is my plan. Thirty years married."

He may be dead, I point out.

"I live on hope."

Sometimes they go out, to visit the doctor. Then teenagers taunt them. "Fuck you mother Serb, why haven't you left?" one said.

"We are afraid someone will come and maybe kill us," said Dosic.

As we were about to leave, I reached into my bag and pulled out a couple of oranges, an apple, a bar of home-made soap from Greece, and gave them to her. After all, I was returning to a mess tent stacked with enough food to feed -- well, an army.

She reached for me and hugged me tight, kissing my forehead, tears in her eyes. Soon I had tears in mine. Gilles showed no emotion.

Outside, at a nearby apartment guarded by a platoon of 30 British soldiers, I spoke to one of them, Michael McDonald, 21, from Jersey, UK. Because of the hatred, he said, "It's definitely another Bosnia."

One night he and his mates came across an elderly Serb being beaten and robbed by three young Albanians. "Basically we beat the fuck out of them," he said. "If we can get away with it, we do it. These fuckers deserve it. Especially the Brits – nobody fucks with them."

When Gilles and I got back to DK, I felt guilty for having such a sheltered and privileged life. Canada was boring, but safer. I pushed those thoughts aside. There was work to do.

CHAPTER 9

On Patrol with the Canadians

Two days later, Mike, Vance and I headed for Polgrade, a town two hours southeast of DK along Serbian border. It was a long way from the main Canadian base. Near Polgrade we found the Canadian camp. It blended into the trees and shrubs of a hill, and consisted of a canvas tent and little else. There was no noise. The focal point was a Coyote, a vehicle with advanced surveillance systems and an extremely long antennae. A few soldiers -- helmetless, calm, sleeves rolled up -- monitored people as they moved along an age-old pathway now used as a smuggling route. These videos were passed along to the nearby Americans.

The American camp, called Checkpoint Apocalypse, was a study in contrast. There were no trees -- they'd all been bulldozed down. There was no hill -- it too had been scraped away. Two tanks stood guard. A dozen soldiers, all wearing helmets and flak jackets, scurried about like ants at various tasks, some noisily shouting orders. Lumber sat in piles, and we were told they were putting up a barracks.

This border area with Serbia was sensitive, and the two camps, Canadian and American, worked together. The line was only 200 metres away. Visible across it, a mile or so away, in a valley, was the village of Dobrosin. Before the June cease-fire, Dobrosin had been in Kosovo. Now it was an Albanian island in a sea of Serbs. Albanian fighters traveled into Serbia to Dobrosin, which they used as a refuge before launching attacks on railways or individuals deeper in Serbia.

"A week ago the Serbian secret police came in and executed two people," said Lieut. Chris Stewardson from Regina. "The Kosovars have a strong force in Dobrosin, splinter groups from the UCK." The Canadians were building good relations with local people, he said. "At the other checkpoint... we're sharing a farm yard with a farmer and he's giving the guys firewood and letting us use his barn....We helped him cut firewood a couple of days ago."

The Americans were also doing well. I spoke to Sgt. First Class Brad Houston, as four children from Dobrosin approached. Their faces looked much older than their five to 10 years. They appeared sullen and gaunt and were scantily dressed. "For me, when you look into the eyes of these little guys, (you realize) they're the ones who suffer most," said Houston. "Probably the biggest thing that hits home is the poverty level. At this village you're looking at an 85 per cent unemployment rate."

Under their rules of engagement, neither Canadians nor Americans were free to cross into Serbia and help the parents of those Albanian kids if the Serb police returned for more killing. For Houston, that was almost more than he could take.

"I think that anytime that you have ethnic cleansing that there's no way any force should have to sit idly by and not do anything about it.... When we declared independence, if people hadn't of felt the way our army feels today, we wouldn't be a country in existence right now."

Later we drove to a Canadian satellite camp and got to the mess, where a husky, hairy, swarthy cook in white T-shirt and apron was toiling away while a radio played a familiar tune by Stompin' Tom Connors: "Little k, little d, little l-a-n-g, her name was just plain kd lang." The grub looked pretty good – it always did at these military messes – and soon we had supper.

Over chow, I interviewed Maj. Patrick Koch, 33, commanding officer of A Company, one of two companies in the Royal Canadian Regiment. Koch was its youngest major and the second-youngest one in the entire Canadian infantry. The RCR is also known as the Duke of Edinburgh Company because Prince Phillip is its Colonel in Chief. Koch had 118 men and women under his command.

He grew up in little Moosehorn, 320 kilometres north of Winnipeg on Highway 6. His father, Clarence, was principal of Alf Cuthbert School and his mother Heidi was a teacher. When he thinks of his years as a child he thinks of security, knowing neighbours, knowing no fear. Moosehorn's population was about 250, the same size as the village he looks after now. It's name is St. Cikatovo.

"I was in Samalia as well," said Koch, a fit 200-pounder. "My litmus test is always the children. If the children are outside playing and are happy and healthy, to me that's an indication of how well we're doing our job.

"I remember as a child growing up, we would play throughout the town. When it was time to come home, our mom would stand on the front step and call out our name. You could hear her from anywhere in town. A lot of the communities around here are very small communities and very tight and work hard to help each other.

"As a child I was never afraid. It comes back to the security. While you're there you take it for granted. In Canada we do take so much for granted while we're growing up. You don't appreciate it until you see what other people live through."

Children in Kosovo didn't appear to take much for granted. Too many had seen fathers killed, brothers injured by land mines, sisters harmed. "You probably can't find a family here that hasn't lost someone to the conflict," Koch said. "Kindergarten children at school are taught about land mines. We've pulled mines out of playgrounds at other schools....We have families that lost up to 24 members. That has to have an impact on the children."

He explained why things as basic as firewood had to be provided. "In some areas, because of the mine threat, they live beside a forest but they can't go in and cut down a tree because they're worried about stepping on a mine." Some soldiers had made it a personal mission to provide the basic necessities like tents, food and firewood for the more destitute families.

Capt. Marie-Catherine Marsot, 29, was the highest ranking female officer in the 4,000-member Canadian infantry in January 2000. There were only three or four women holding such rank. She was a platoon commander, which means she was responsible for a number of sergeants and their soldiers. "These soldiers are the men you want to see," she told me. "They are our manpower."

One of them said their leader, Marsot, had a reputation for being a shit-disturber because she wasn't afraid to confront her superiors and fight for what she felt was right. "She's OK," he said. "The guys respect her because she stands up for us."

Marsot told me about a problem with language. A man from Montenegro who used the Serbian word for something was killed by Albanians who took him for a Serb. It was not an isolated story, as I heard of others succumbing to the same prejudice. Marsot said at first she and her colleagues sometimes pronounced things the Serb way instead of the Albanian.

"Just that made them really upset so we have to be really careful." Cpl. Greg Whitman, 24, from Halifax, said a Bulgarian aid worker asked for a light for his cigarette near Pristina. "I guess in Bulgarian a lot of the words are similar to, if not the same as, Serbian. They beat him to death."

Next morning Marsot, who was of medium height and stature met with five of her male subordinates, all sergeants, at a picnic table inside a tent. I sat in. Some of their comments:

"Two thousand people are moving south because of tension in their area," she said...."As of today, 136 dogs were killed," one reported....The men were worried about exposure to radioactive elements at a bombed out plant called Fernonikl which produced ore before the fighting. The Serbs used it as a place for torture and storage, so NATO destroyed it during the bombing. "Cesium is what they find. It doesn't go through the skin but affects eyes and mucus."

Wash your hands," someone said, and they laughed.

"CO's very happy with your patrol report guys, so that's awesome.... Best news of all – the gym is completed."...."When you get information from your [village] headman, don't react right away. Make sure you have a second source, so don't jump the gun."

She appeared to have a good rapport with her officers. Capt. Marie-Catherine Marsot broke ground as the first female infantry officer in the First Battalion of the Royal Canadian Regiment, which was deployed to Kosovo in December 1999. She had joined the regular force of the Canadian Armed Forces two years earlier after serving in the Reserves since 1991. I didn't know it at the time, but Marsot was having some trouble. She returned to Canada in March of 2000, shortly after I met her, because of depression, and she was granted a disability pension for post-traumatic stress disorder. A board of inquiry investigation into her concerns that she had been harassed because of her sex found that incidents occurred "on several occasions, on account of abuse of authority and discrimination." Marsot said nothing to me about it at the time, when she was trying to resolve the matter internally.

The roar of Griffon helicopters filled the tent. After some talk about plans to close up camp and go home, the meeting ended, but not before more concerns about the radioactive plant. "You've got to keep 150 metres away from the plant, eh," one said.

Later that day, with Marsot standing atop our Grizzly, looking like Patton leading a charge, I went along on a routine patrol of a couple of villages. I'd really been looking forward to this because it meant a chance to see and talk to local people in their communities. So far, all we'd really been able to do was talk to soldiers. That was fine, but I needed to see for myself how the fighting had affected rural civilians. Recent shooting incidents in other sectors prompted the brass to put the troops on a higher level of alert, so our patrol consisted of two Grizzlies rather than one.

Before leaving, I chatted to Pte. Louis Marin of St. Claude, Man. He sat atop our Grizzly in the machine-gunner's pod and prepared a belt of ammunition. I asked him if he'd actually use that weapon if required. "I am prepared to (use it), but it's a peacekeeping mission and that's what I'm here for, to keep the peace," he said.

I asked about the people he saw and their responses. "They love us here. They love Canadians. We feel like superstars. We get to know the people. Usually we play with the kids and hand out candies and stuff sent from home. When we have suckers or a box of gun, they love it."

Maj. Koch of Moosehorn, standing in the lead machine, gave the order to move out and the lumbering, six-wheeled beasts groaned into action. The day was dreary, chilly, overcast. There was no snow. The countryside was familiar to me – the same scrub oak and hilly landscape I knew from home on Turtle Mountain in Manitoba. Many of the crinkly brown oak leaves were still attached, and sometimes I was only a few arm-lengths away from reaching out and grabbing them as we lumbered along the narrow country roads -- roads more accustomed to horse-drawn wagons than armoured personnel carriers. The hills were steep in places and the farms always small, a few fields, an old wooden barn, a towering haystack such as you never see in Canada anymore. An elderly woman wielded a pitchfork at one of these. Occasionally smiling children stood by the roadside like welcoming committees and waved, and we waved back. Marin was right – they do make you feel like a superstar.

After a while we arrived at our first stop, the village of Cikatovo in central Kosovo. Some homes were roofless, others had roofs of red tiles, which is commonplace across southeast and even western Europe. Some homes had been destroyed. We pulled up to the school, which was intact. A dozen smiling children approached in the muddy yard before we'd even stopped. "Hello! Hello!" they shouted, and I began to speak to them – only to discover, sheepishly, that "hello," "thank-you" and "NATO" were the only English words they knew.

Some wore shoes four sizes too big. Others had no coat. Most were adequately dressed. You wouldn't have known that some of the children were mourning the deaths of parents buried in the cemetery – others called it a mass grave -- 100 metres away. It was decorated with bright plastic flowers and other adornments, as per the custom here.

"A lot of their parents are buried in that graveyard. It really saddens them to see that," said Master Cpl. Dwayne Byard of Halifax. "It's the first thing they see when they leave the school." At least there were no minefields here, the nearest being a kilometre away. For Pvt. Trevor Pushie, 26, from Sydney, N.S., the scene was heart-rending. "I feel sorry for the kids over here being brought up in a very war-torn environment."

There were no swing sets or slides. Money was needed for other things – food, clothing and housing. The Canadian engineers had rebuilt more than 100 roofs by the time I got to Kosovo. "A lot of them are farmers, a lot of them are getting their houses rebuilt," said Pushie. This day, the medic was with us to deal with body lice and scabies that afflict 20 per cent of the kids. There wasn't enough clean water for bathing or drinking, as the retreating Serbs dumped corpses into the wells.

Inside the school I watched a lively discussion between the headman and a couple of the troops. He wasn't happy with the job done by aid agencies: the doors didn't fit well, the lighting fixtures weren't properly seated. And he would not be easily quieted.

Next I entered a Grade 5 classroom, with wooden desks in rows, the children now quiet and still. Their young female teacher passed along my greetings from Canada, and I provided two packages of pencils. It was much like any classroom in Canada, though the children seemed better behaved than some I'd seen at home in my work in schools for the International Peace Garden.

Our two Grizzlies pulled into their final destination 30 minutes later, an especially poor village called Gradica. Half the school was the first thing you saw, because the other half was rubble, blown away, I was told, by a Serbian tank. It destroyed four schoolrooms.

The school was called Vilezerit Frasheri, or Brothers Frasheri in English. Its headmaster was a clean-cut man in a dusty suit jacket. Shaban Xhemajli, 51, said about 50 children hadn't returned since the conflict ended because they had no homes left. The families had fled, or worse.

The second thing you saw were the children, happy and smiling, right in your face. "Hello! Hello!" they shouted. We greeted them, and at first I refused to fall into the trap of conversation, which left them with smiling but quizzical looks. Then I decided to speak to them and look at them as if they understood. The best communication comes from the heart, doesn't it? Besides, it would have been rude not to try.

And these children didn't ask for anything, an American soldier told me later, unlike the kids of other places like Bosnia, he said. They just give greetings and thanks. As they milled about, engineers spoke to the headman and said they would clean up the rubble and check for mines in three days. In two weeks a Canadian doctor and dentist would be here. The headman nodded, but didn't crack any sort of a smile.

Asked if he feared the Serbs would return when NATO left, he said, through an interpreter: "Yes. We don't have weapons. We don't have anything right now. They can come back. I know that KFOR protects us. If it wasn't for them, we wouldn't be here now."

My duffel bag of clothes from the United Church in Deloraine was given to him and he stoically accepted. He had seen too much. There was no thank-you. "It all helps," he said. Three months hiding in the mountains with dozens of others had numbed him. During that time, Serbs took a 14-year-old boy and shot him to death in front of his parents, for no apparent reason.

An old man in a ragged coat shuffled up as we spoke. "Why are you leaving?" he asked, pleadingly. "We will have more trouble if you leave!"

"I want to see my children," one of the Canadians replied. The Canadians were indeed leaving Kosovo in five months, by June 15, to be replaced by soldiers from the Nordic countries. The trusted and competent Canadians were pulling out of a land at risk of becoming another Bosnia.

"You wonder how these people survive," said Marin, as he fit himself back into the Grizzly.

CHAPTER 10

A Second Patrol, and Don Cherry

On Friday, February 11, I went on a second patrol with the troops. We left at 5 p.m. in two Grizzlies, heading out into the hilly countryside of gravel roads and bur oaks.

We stopped near a creek on the side of a hill, to listen for the sounds of cars or trucks, which could be running contraband weapons or drugs. For Fifteen minutes we sit and hear nothing out of the ordinary.

We move, and at another stop I have a chance to talk to some soldiers. I ask them what they think of Kosovo.

No response.

"What do *you* think of Kosovo?" one asks.

"I think it's all fucked up," I say.

"Right on!" one says. "All fucked up!" Then he gives me what I wanted, some frank talk.

"You know what they should do with that fucking Bouchard and fucking Parizeau?"

"What?" I say.

"Bring them here and stick them in a fucking tent in the middle of a fucking minefield and see if they still want to separate! That would fix those stupid bastards!"

"It would give them pause," I say.

"It would give them a dose of fucking reality," the soldier adds. "They don't appreciate Canada."

After a minute or two we moved on down the road to a place called Glogovac, where a platoon of 30 Canucks had set up quarters in the town hall, which the Serbs had once used for the same purpose, only a short time ago. In one room I found piles of papers the Serbs had ripped from files and strewn about in a mess.

The plaster walls were chipped and broken, and a 1966 map of Yugoslavia hung on a wall. The place had an eerie, almost haunted quality to it.

Next door were UNMIK police (UN Mission in Kosovo) and on their bulletin board were various notices. One read: "Pen pal wanted. Woman, 27, cuddly and red haired (although I am gradually trying to change this). Zacqoi." On the envelope someone had scribbled: "self explanatory."

There was also a poster with a photo of a man. It was marked "Escaped." His name was Xhezir Bajrami, an Albanian male. "The suspect was arrested by the Swedish KFOR because he was involved in gun fighting in Gracanica and one person was killed and two wounded."

He had been held for 72 months.

Another notice: "Black Jeep with blackened out windows wanted in connection with the double murder at the stadium Pristina (where I'd landed in a helicopter with Gilles) on 4\12\99."

Yet another note read: "The children of Kosovo are crying for helping hand.\The children of Kosovo are dreaming of a peaceful land."

Back in the town hall, a dirty shell of what was once an administrative centre, I find a Toronto Star story from January 27 with the headline, "Leafs dinged by Wings." There are maps of Sofia in Bulgaria (where the troops do R and R), a copy of the leave schedule, and lots of food: stacks of fruit drinks, cheese and crackers, chocolate milk, white milk, all from Denmark.

There's a litre of Matilde, full cream milk, "Danish longlife milk, Denmark." In a fridge I find lemon merainge pie, blueberry pie, and apple juice.

I've got to find someone to talk to, I figure, and find W. O. Mark Brander, 38. He says Lieut. Stewart is in charge, but Stewart was out.

Brander tells me a platoon of 30 men is holding the hall to keep stability in the town. There were no Serbs left. But there are "political factions and rivalries among the Albanians," he says. "The two major parties don't get along."

Then there is the Albanian mafia, which deals in drugs and stolen goods like fuel. "A lot of the NGOs are locals, a lot of them, so of course they have their own factions. The local people have trouble trusting local officials, he said. "They come to us first before they go to them."

It all makes for instability. "How effective is any election when you start off a new government?" he asked. "We're here to see that it is done."

I'm glad when we leave this dump and head back to the main camp.

A word or two about the camp and its pending take-down, which begins April 15. Donja Koretica, or DK, which sits 40 kilometres west of Pristina, is a 25-acre compound. It's encircled by barbed wire. What sits inside it are some 200 pieces of infrastructure such as 184 Weather Havens, which are tent-like shelters used for sleeping, eating and storage. The troops like them because they're warm and dry, with great beds.

A total of 126 are used to house the men and women, providing 907 bed spaces; 18 are used for washrooms and 21 for maintenance areas. The smaller ones cost about $20,000 each.

Some older canvas tents were still being used for offices and the like but I was told most were given to local aid agencies and people because they're old.

As you enter the camp and pass the sandbagged checkpoint, you see row after row of these olive-green, dome-shaped shelters.

"They're comfortable to sleep in and they've got good beds in them too," said Sgt. Mike Jaillet, 36.

They and everything else will be packed in 400 sea containers, which are large steel boxes. The large main mess tent alone consists of $1 million worth of Weather Havens and tons of food. Each week the troops consume 10,000 eggs, 12,000 litres of milk and 180 kilos of beef.

Numerous diesel-powered generators heat the structures, and must also be cleaned and packed.

You might also be interested in what kind of help the Canadians were providing for local people otherwise. Major. Kevin Caldwell, officer commanding, support combat company, said the Canadian International Development Agency provided $750,000 to spend locally in Kosovo for things like school repairs, culvert replacements, axes so schools have wood for heat, and repairs to homes. He said they've provided 5,000 shelter kits and roof kits.

CIDA was investing $70 million total into Kosovo in 2000, and six agencies were working through the UN to channel the money as needed.

"By and large, I think the aid is getting out to everybody who needs it," Caldwell said, adding that many of the really poor families used to work for the FN plant, which NATO bombed out of commission, thinking it harbored Serbian troops.

"Ninety thousand people are receiving food aid in Kosovo, more than half the people," partly, too, because farming has been interrupted by the war, and fields laid with landmines. Canadians are among those helping to remove the mines, and peas and corn were expected to be planted in April, to relieve some food concerns.

"We're getting over the hump of the emergency phase and we're getting into reconstruction," he said.

Canadian military engineers were busy repairing people's roofs, among other things.

"They're very resilient people here. They work hard like farmers in Canada. It's just a matter of getting them started."

* * *

Hockey in Kosovo? You'd better believe it.

I was talking to Master Cpl. Brian Thibeault one day – he's in maintenance – when I learned about the hockey practices they had every Sunday morning, in Macedonia where I came through.

"On a good day there's probably 20, enough for two teams," and there are some good players – at least two played at the Junior A level, for the Sault Greyhounds and Sudbury Wolves.

"Then all of a sudden some Macedonians started playing."

The long and short of it is that a Canadian military team was scheduled to play the Bulgarian Olympic team March 4-5. "We should get our asses kicked, but it should be fun," Thibeault, who plays goal, told me.

"I'm just a lousy goalie, but I go for the fun, for the exercise. If somebody told me four or five years ago that I would be going overseas and playing hockey in a foreign country, I'd have said wrong. But it's happening."

He said they plan to film the games in Bulgaria, where the men take R and R, and try to send copies to Don Cherry.

"He's my idol," says Thibeault. "He should be commissioner of the NHL, that's what he should be. He tells it like it is, he's straight up….He says what he thinks and that's the way it should be."

* * *

I left the Canadians on Saturday February 19, after 12 days. My journal reads: "I am sad to leave the Canadian military base here, Camp Maple Leaf. What an incredibly good time I have had meeting our people, writing their stories, seeing their work in Kosovo."

Ten stories, not all from Kosovo, had sold to various papers so far on this journey, and having money coming in felt good.

As the train rolled through the mountains of Macedonia toward Greece, I was again on my own. That felt good too. I enjoyed traveling alone because I was free, unencumbered by others. Free to set my own pace, free to go where I wanted when I wanted, free to daydream or sleep. The military provides scribes with a lot of things, but freedom isn't among them.

The train went as far as Gevgelija, just north of the Greek border. Took a cab the rest of the way and walked into Greece. No bus until Sunday morning, and spent a bone-chilling night beneath some evergreens in my sleeping bag. Gee, I missed those Weather Havens! The cabbies wanted $60 Cdn for the ride to Thessaloniki, too rich for me. Next morning I compromised and took a cab for about $15 to the next Greek town, where I caught a bus south to Thessaloniki, then got on another for a city in the northwest called Kastoria. You may think I'm cheap, but I saved enough for two nights in a hotel, which is partly what makes four-month trips possible.

Kastoria took its name from beaver castor, the scented oil the animal deposits to mark its territory. The small city had been known for centuries as a fur capital of Europe. I wanted to produce an article about the place for a trade journal and make some cash. As a trapper of beaver, mink and muskrat, I was keen to see what went on there. Who knows, some of my furs may have ended up there and been made into coats, gauntlets, hats.

Arriving late in the afternoon of Feb. 1, I walked toward three hotels and was struck by the drab and rundown appearance of the place. Some stores were unoccupied. A polluted lake sat nearby. There was any colour you wanted, provided it was grey. The day was cold and grey as well, which didn't help.

Shop windows featured key rings and purses and collars of fur. Even skunk fur, tossed aside by most Canadian trappers, was prepared with plastic eyes to make "cats" dangling from key rings. Evidently my trapper's skills had prevailed and I had found the right place!

I dismissed the first two hotels as too expensive, and hoped the last one, Hotel Keletron, offered a better rate. It was only slightly better at $28 Cdn, about seven drachmas.

"Talk at Sophia," the small balding owner told me as I tried to get a lower price. This was the off season, and I wanted a lower rate here as I'd received elsewhere. The most I'd had to pay for a room in Greece was $20. "My English no good," the man said, walking away.

Sophia sat on a sofa in Hotel Keletron. Her left arm hugged the back of a sofa and her shapely legs were crossed as she faced me. The buttons of her blouse were hard pressed to contain her, and her face said Sophia Loren. She was beautiful. "Talking at Sophia" would be quite all right with me.

"Hello," I said, smiling, "I am Brad."

"Brid?" she replied, raising an eyebrow.

"Braaad," I said.

"Braaad."

"Yes. Listen, Sophia. You are not busy. This hotel is not busy. I want to pay less for a room. How about 6,000 drachmas."

She looked at me with a hint of disdain.

"No six."

"But six is good. It's only a little less than you're asking."

"No six."

OK, I could sweeten the deal. I dug into my pack and pulled out a new portable radio. I'd brought it from home and hadn't used it, didn't want it.

"Here -- I pay 5,000 and give you a radio. A gift. OK?"

She took the box and eyed it as if it were some cheap thing from China. Which it likely was. "No OK."

I didn't give up. "OK, I give you *6,000* drachmas *and* the radio. Six is good. OK?"

At this she pouted and crossed her arms over her ample bosom.

"No six," she said, looking more like Sophia Loren every minute.

Golly, it was a good deal for her. The radio worked and I was just below the rate they wanted. Every other motel I stayed at had come down in price. I tried to reason with her.

"You are not busy. Your hotel is almost empty. I want to pay six," I persisted.

"No six!"

I looked at her, dumbfounded and beaten.

"You no understand," she said. "This old man my friend. I have other friend in Thessaloniki, he give me six."

Finally it sunk in. She figured I wanted to pay her for sex.

"You are very beautiful," I said, "but it is not sex that I want. I wish to pay six, 6,000 drachmas for the room, not seven."

It sunk in for her, too. She looked hurt, apparently because I hadn't wanted to boink her. I quickly changed tack. After all, Greco-Canadian relations were at stake.

"Sophia, listen to me," I said, grasping her lovely shoulders. "You are gorgeous. Fantastic. I want you. I *must* have sex with you. OK?"

She looked up at me again, her dignity and power restored, her bosom pressing against the thin fabric of her blouse. I even felt good when the answer came, in two familiar and carefully enunciated words.

"No six."

* * *

CHAPTER 11

At Panos's Farm

Next day I toured a large mall with fur shops and officials and got my stories about fur prices.

From Kastoria I took a bus through the mountains back to Edessa, population 19,000, to link up with Panos Manikis, my natural farmer friend. Edessa was my kind of town, big enough to offer Internet cafes and anything else you needed but small enough to walk across. I spent two nights in a small hotel to give me time to write two stories about Kastoria. One of them sold, with photos, for $250 to a trapper's magazine put out by North American Fur Auctions. Then I accepted Panos's invitation to stay with him.

Panos Manikis lived in an apartment on the edge of town. George Papageorgiou, 38, a fellow I rarely saw there (he had a girl friend) was Panos's roommate and farming partner.

"He prefers 'slave' to partner," George quips. He talks about the five acres they work together. "In four years it should be full of vegetables and at the level where we don't have to do anything else except collect the harvest. The big variety of plants that are there will be aesthetically very nice. It's quite beautiful because a lot of animals are going there. It gives a good feeling." He was talking about birds and smaller animals.

Panos hosted people from all over the world who wanted to learn about natural farming, his latest visitor being Martin, a 25-year-old German. Panos's own girl friend was also there occasionally.

In a corner of the kitchen was a small wood stove that cooked meals and heated the place. Near it was a wooden table with chairs and close by were a couple of beds. Near the table was a bookshelf with a small library of Fukuoka's works and others such as *Green Spring*, piles of papers and some photographs of Panos and Fukuoka. One bedroom served as a storage room for sacks of seeds, the hallway held boxes of figs and apples, and an end room was where Panos slept. The suite had all the modern amenities but no TV, radio or computer, and we didn't even miss them. In fact it was a pleasure to be without them.

Our meals were simple and delicious. Boiled chick peas with olive oil and lemon juice. Steamed spinach, heavy brown bread and olives. Boiled leeks from the farm chopped up with celery and mixed with olive oil, lemon juice and flour. We ate lots of boiled greens from the farm, smothered in oil and lemon juice. This must have agreed with me (as did the military fare), for I felt great and hadn't been sick since leaving Canada.

We talked a lot. Panos discussed his farming, his philosophies, while Martin and I asked the occasional question. One afternoon we went to a restaurant on the edge of the cliff on which the city sat, and the view was spectacular. Far below lay many farms, each a few acres in size, hardly larger than gardens by North American standards, but maybe they had something here. It was easier and cheaper and less trouble to work them.

Edessa means "water" in Greek, and the land below had once been a lake bottom, rich and fertile. Panos pointed out his farm, and then we set out for it in the only vehicle he owned, a beat-up little pickup from the 1970s. It reminded me of my first vehicle, a 1971 yellow Datsun pickup.

On much of his land sat an orchard of peach and other fruit and nut trees. It looked like Clifford Foster's apple orchard near Picton, Ont. in Prince Edward County, where I'd worked as a youth. But the rest was new to me: I wasn't used to walking among cabbages, pea vines, grasses, herbal plants and Chinese vegetables in what otherwise looked like a typical Canadian field. You could bend down and pick a pea pod here, some Swiss chard there, among the various grasses and forage plants such as clover. We saw a rich diversity of plant life that looked like any natural forest or field. But this field was produced by humans to serve nature first, people second. And it was sowed with clay balls containing many different seeds. Somehow, diversity reduced problems with disease and pests, Panos told me again.

"We'll let this cabbage make flowers: we won't pick it," Panos said. "So next year we'll have many cabbages growing around." He strives for five to seven clay balls per square metre. We moved on to his trees. "We have seven varieties of cherries, seven of peaches, five of plums. The ideas is to solve the problem of diseases and pests. This is the pattern of how nature works; we imitate nature."

Then he mentioned his apparently delicious peaches. "You know, my peaches are not scientific ones. Religion and philosophy are included in the taste. When you eat them you feel that there is nothing missing."

Huge plantain trees served as "water pumps," he said, drawing water up to the surface. When a neighbour cut down one big old tree (to get a four-inch slab for a butcher's block) Panos cried. "It was my pride.... One day I heard a chain saw. It was too late." He tried to buy an adjacent acreage but the same man wouldn't sell. "He hates me. He says, 'Everybody is laughing at you because you won't allow cars.' It will compact the soil. In natural farming, we first take care of the soil, then the plants, then our pocket. In chemical farming it's different."

He dismisses their laughter as ignorance. "You can only serve nature. The rest is for people to see. You cannot convince them with words."

Later, we did some grafting of trees, with George's help, and sweated while clearing a grown over area of unwanted bushes and trees, and thinned peach trees of many of its smaller fruit to encourage size among the rest. So there is in fact hard work involved with natural farming.

We also made clay balls. We began with a variety of seeds in a bucket. To this we added 10 equal units of clay powder. Then we added water and made a dough-like texture, like play-dough. Finally we sat around on logs, broke off bits of the dough, and rolled them in our palms into marble-sized balls.

They dry after an hour in the sun. We scattered our balls three hours later. To test them, submerge them in water. They shouldn't dissolve in 24 hours, so tough is the clay.

In a few years the farm will be "like the fly in the milk" of the surrounding conventional acreages, says George, who grew up in a small city but had a garden, chickens and grapes at home as a boy. He met Panos four years earlier, in 1996, when he heard about him and sought him out.

The day was beautiful, warm and sunny. George's partner, Angeliki Paladzidi said that having done so many wrongs in farming over the years, people would be wise to embrace natural farming as the safest way to produce food.

She loves the sight of cherry blossoms. "When you see it in the spring, the cherry tree is like a bride, with a white wedding dress."

They call the warmer days in the middle of winter like this one the king fisher days, George said. "The king fisher was a very beautiful girl and Zeus, king of the gods, fell in love with her. His wife became jealous and tried to wreak revenge, transforming the girl into a bird, the king fisher. She cursed her to lay her eggs in the middle of winter, the worst time for young birds. Zeus tried to help by making 10 warm days for the birds. In fact, king fisher eggs hatch in April.

"This is a king fisher day."

One afternoon, we drove to a hot springs about 30 miles away. It felt great to relax in the hot healing waters. Martin and I lay in an outside pool, with the trees all around, and as the sun set we saw bats flying overhead. Other times we went to restaurants for some leisurely meals. Life was good indeed in Greece – with Panos Manikis, anyway.

Balkan people live a different schedule from what we know. They work from 8 to 1, then shut down, go home, rest, and resume work from 5 to 10 or so. Thus the evenings here throb with energy even in this small city, Edessa. The Internet Café I used rocked with music until 2 a.m. The streets were busy.

The Internet is a wonderful tool for people like me seeking to spread information. I didn't know much about it before this trip. The Canadian soldiers and journalists in Kosovo taught me a lot. Now I value the net as something that might just enable me to pay for this trip with my stories, which are reaching about six papers. As well I am able to converse with editors in ways not possible by phone because of the expense and inconvenience.

The net also enabled Canadian soldiers in Kosovo to keep in touch with their wives and girlfriends like never before. This will perhaps reduce the incidence of marital failure which besets the military. One man told me he would send his wife flowers for Valentine's Day. She would get them, he added, if she hadn't already left him. He wasn't joking.

It is sad that women who married military men would leave because of the distance. Had my mother done this to my father, absent three years while flying Halifax bombers from 1941 to 1944, I wouldn't be here today.

After a few days with Panos, I decided to move on. Turkey was next.

CHAPTER 12

Thessaloniki, Then Istanbul

I arrived in Thessaloniki on March 1, 2000, a good way to begin a new month, with a new country. Thessaloniki is a large industrial city in northern Greece, birthplace of Mustapha Ataturk, the founder of modern Turkey. I spent a couple of days sightseeing and painting.

As I walked along its busy main avenue at 6:30 a.m. to the train that would take me east to Istanbul, I saw two Japanese men emerging from a hotel. "Hello there!" I said, recognizing them as men I had seen in the station the previous night, when I had checked departure times and bought an *International Herald Tribune.*

"Oh, Canadian!" one of them said, remembering me. They smiled broadly, and we shook hands. One of them was holding his ticket firmly in his right hand, though the train didn't leave for an hour. By their own admission and laughter their names were hard to pronounce, so they spared me the hassle of trying and didn't give them to me. With no disrespect intended, I shall call them Ying and Yang.

Ying wore a new high-tech backpack; Yang wore a gray one. In dress also, they were pretty well twins. "You stay in Greece how long?" Ying asked.

"One month," I said.

"Oh! One month!"

"And you?"

"Seven days. We go Istanbul, then Singapore, 17 days total."

"Singapore hot!" Yang added, running his fingers down his face to demonstrate perspiration.

"How much you pay for your room in fancy hotel?" I ask.

"Fourteen thousand drachma," about $56 Cdn each.

"I paid five thousand. Nice place down the street."

"Oh!" they said.

When we got to the station, which had a huge old lobby, one of them shouted out, "Good-bye Thessaloniki!" as if to say good riddance. I agreed. Its 1.5 million people swarmed the streets like bees at all hours of the day and night. The city is 2,300 years old, and is thought to be where Alexander the Great decided to conquer the world. He succeeded from Greece to India, leaving about 100,000 corpses in his wake. They glorify him here, to the disgust of some of the local people. His statue or bust is everywhere, including the station lobby.

As we waited near our train, Ying approached me with his a state-of-the-art Minolta camera. They wanted my photograph, so first Ying stood with me by the red train, then Yang took his turn. Then I took a photo of them. Soon after we parted for good.

The train is a great way to see Europe, but it can be very long and tedious. Such was the trip to Istanbul, which took just under 14 hours. At one point there was a dispute between two train officials and a Turkish man who didn't have enough money for his fare. The exchange became heated, and at that point a middle-aged fellow from New Zealand, Tony O'Donnell, stepped up to offer the balance. Or rather, most of the balance.

"All I have left is 3,000 drachma (about $12 Cdn) and it's yours," he said. But the Turk was still 500 drachma short, so I made up the difference. The young man thanked us. Tony, an engineer, was traveling with his wife, Evonne. Their home was Dundin, New Zealand. They'd been traveling for 10 weeks, since visiting Madrid, where one of their four children lived. Three of them had careers that took them to Europe.

While I didn't have any family in Europe, my sister-in-law at the time, Janice, had a friend in Istanbul.

We finally arrived in Istanbul at 9:15 p.m., 14 hours later. Each time the train started from one of its many stops it was smooth; but the arrivals rocked your guts, they were so rough as the cars clanked and jolted.

I said good-bye to Tony and Evonne and set out into the night to find a kiosk for a phone card. Then I phoned Susan, the friend of a friend, and arranged to meet her and her husband next morning.

That's easy to say, but let me tell you what really happened that night. To buy a phone card you need local currency. So you haul your bags to the currency window and exchange about $20 US, ending up with a bunch of faded little bills you know nothing about and can hardly distinguish. Then you venture out to the street to find a vendor – they are numerous – who sells phone cards, and ask how much they cost. Of course he doesn't understand English. So someone offers to help, and rifles through your stash to find the right amount. It's dark, you can hardly read the numbers, up to 5,000 and 10,000 something-or-others, and you've likely handed over too much, but you end up with a phone card and hope it works.

Hauling your bags back into the station, you find a row of phones. The first few don't work. It takes some time to discover this, for none is marked out-of-order. So you move tediously from one to another, moving your bags all the while. When you find one that actually works, you insert the card -- but don't know which way. There are in fact four possibilities: both ends right side up and both ends upside down. You try them all -- it's easier said than done, with all the dialing involved -- and voila! finally hit pay dirt.

But the phone numbers here aren't like in Canada. There are many more than seven digits, and you aren't sure whether to use the prefix in the city, or whether it's just for use from afar. So you try it both ways. By now 45 minutes have elapsed since you decided to make a call. And you are a tad frustrated and hungry and tired from the ride and everything else. Around you is constant noise and commotion and you guard your bags with your life.

There. That's a more thorough picture of what happened to me that night. Ah, but the fun has just begun. After talking to Janice, I now was free to find a room. In a city of 11 million.

Back outside, streetlights sparkled on the nearby Bosporous, the strait separating old Istanbul from the newer city. I'd catch a ferry there the next day. The avenues hummed with traffic and out of the bustle a cabbie approached and offered a ride.

"How much you want to pay? $20? $30?"

"No, $10," I said. This was Turkey. The rooms could be cheap.

"Maybe $20," he replied, stroking his graying moustache. "Nice clean place, breakfast, shower."

"No. $10," I repeated.

"OK, come on."

I put my pack in his trunk and we sped off in his little yellow Opel. This was an old game for him, and a good service for many travelers. He takes you to a friend's motel in the price range of your choice and receives a commission. Unfortunately for him, I prefer very modest hotels — you might even call them dumpy. I looked more prosperous than I actually was.

"I have nice place for you, $20 or $30."

I objected again, but could see it was useless. I was now captive in his car. As we passed by a couple of run-down hotels in a street close to the station I told him to stop the car. He refused.

If a cabby refuses to stop, you have but one option. Open the door at a light and leave. So I did. Grabbing my bags, I lit out toward Hotel Kafka, the cabbie's insults ringing in my ears. I got a dirty but acceptable room for $7 US.

Hotel Kafka was old and grimy. However, men sat drinking tea and smoking in the TV room near the entrance and that meant the place had something going for it. Upstairs in my room I retrieved a couple of dirty socks and a pop bottle from beneath one of two beds and then headed back to the lobby, where tea was on the house. After my drink I headed outside in search of some food.

In a restaurant two blocks away I was surprised to see — yes, the cabbie.

"Him very bad man!" he shouted.

"Well, you're a cheat!" I said.

"What he do?" the barman asked, and I told him – he refused to stop his cab and let me out. By now a small crowd had assembled. A bunch of them laughed. It was an old game of trying hard to earn a commission.

"Him not gentleman Turk!" someone said.

"He was trying to make a living," I said. "I'm not angry. Shake hands?"

He refused. "I'm sorry I jumped out of your car," I said.

"I sorry too." We shook hands. I had a small meal and went to bed.

My visit next day with Susan, Naci and their two children went well. Naci was a bus driver and they lived in an apartment in the newer, northern part of Istanbul. They took me on quite a tour. We visited a 500-year-old old sultan's castle and had tea, and enjoyed fresh fish for supper. Their two children, Elfie, 9, and a girl, Cemre, two and a half, were well behaved good kids.

Susan was interested in what I was doing, and encouraged me to phone her father, Vedat Uras, a retired journalist who lived on the Mediterranean coast near Kemer. On the phone he and I hit it off, and he invited me to spend a few days with him and his wife. He knew the politics of Turkey and its history very well, and would enlighten me for sure. It would be a good stop before heading into the troubled southeast of the country, where the Kurdish conflict lay. In fact, his home was more or less on the way.

Naci and a friend were headed south for business the next day, so they dropped me off at Canakkale, a town near the Dardenelles. At a hostel called Anzac House I spent two nights and met Ettienne, an employee from South Africa. After a while he suggested I visit one of his favourite places, Evciler, a village at the base of a mythical mountain an hour away.

That night I slept in a room with a few other men. In the morning a favourite red shirt that I'd hung to dry was missing, apparently snatched by someone who needed it more than I. But hostels for the most part are great places to visit, and things like missing shirts are minor troubles compared to the benefits you get from meeting people from all over the world, hearing their stories, and learning key tidbits of information about places to see and eat.

Canakkale was a gut-wrenching place to visit. You could almost sense the ghosts out there on the hillsides where tens of thousands of men had died from bullet and bayonet in the War to End All Wars. Canakkale is near the Gallipoli landing site where Winston Churchill's invasion went so terribly wrong in 1915. Some 60,000 Allies and about as many Turks died that year there. The waters were red with blood and thousands of young Australians and New Zealanders arrive annually to pay their respects to buried ancestors. About 50 Canadians, Newfoundlanders, also took part.

The trenches in some places had been preserved. Typically the Turks held the upper ground, and, motivated by a desire to protect their own turf, had fought ferociously. Among their leaders was Mustafa Kemal, who was born in Thessaloniki when it was part of the Ottoman Empire. His heroic exploits won him the hearts of ordinary Turks, whom he led to independence in 1923, in defiance of Greece, Britain and France. As president of the new country of Turkey (created as a stump state from the defeated Ottoman Empire, from which Palestine and the Arabian peninsula were also carved), he took the name of Ataturk, father of the Turks. Today his picture adorns the walls of government, cafes, stores, homes, almost everywhere. A single man much of his life, but one who valued the company of friends, he typically as president had four to six people to supper each evening, when they discussed various issues and events. It kept him in touch with what others were thinking – as the faces often changed -- and helped to banish loneliness. I have a high regard for Ataturk and my master's thesis in International Relations from the University of Manitoba dealt in part with this fascinating and courageous man.

A précis of his life notes that he was the first president of Turkey from 1923 to his death in 1938. After World War I he established a provisional rebel government and in 1921–22 the Turkish armies under his leadership expelled the Greeks who were occupying part of the country. He was the founder of the modern republic, which he ruled as a virtual dictator, with a policy of consistent and radical Westernization. As president he pursued a program of Westernization that affected all aspects of Turkish life – women were given the vote, the traditional Turkish fez was prohibited, Roman lettering replaced Arabic, and European legal systems were adopted. Today, Turkey is the only democratic Moslem state in the world, though its military, defenders of Ataturk's legacy, has not been subordinate to its elected assembly, prompting some to call its democracy a sham.

In 1918, after Turkey had been defeated, Kemal was sent into Anatolia to implement the demobilization of the Turkish forces in accordance with the armistice terms, but instead he established a provisional government opposed to that of Constantinople (modern Istanbul, then under Allied control) and in 1921 led the Turkish armies against the Greeks, who had occupied a large part of Anatolia. He checked the hated Greeks at the Battle of the Sakaria, 23 August–13 September 1921, for which he was granted the title of Ghazi ('the Victorious'), and within a year had expelled them from Turkish soil.

War with the British was averted by his diplomacy, and Turkey in Europe passed under Kemal's control. On 29 October 1923 Turkey was proclaimed a republic with Kemal as first president. It was a magnificent achievement, and the country today, a long-time NATO member and friend of Israel, is remarkably stable, given its location in a volatile part of the world.

Next day I took a bus to Evciler. There I stayed at a fish farm called Karaman. Upon arriving I was approached by a young man who knew some English. His name was Mustafa Sahin, and he was 19. Evciler told me he didn't see many North American travelers. Given that, and the lack of North American TV and radio, I wondered if he knew much about American pop culture.

"Have you heard of Wayne Gretzky?"

"No," he said.

"Have you heard of Celine Dion?"

"No."

"Good," I replied. "This is my kind of place."

Mustafa Sahin's home was a remote village of maybe 400 people. I saw farmers with horses, donkeys and 1960 vintage Massey-Ferguson tractors, homes made of mud bricks, and orchards of apple and peach trees. What a refreshing change from Istanbul's 12 million people, concrete and noise.

Mustafa said he was trying to learn English, and it was slow. He wanted to be a teacher but first had to pass an exam before entering university. He had graduated from high school. We walked along a country road near his village on the Dardenelles.

As we walked, we came across a boy breaking rock with a sledge hammer to make a stone fence. His father, a lean bearded man, laid the pieces. I asked for the sledge and broke rock for a while. The father stopped and asked a question. Mustafa told him I was Canadian. That brought a smile. The sledge hammer handle I wielded was impressively hand-made from a branch of hardwood.

I spent the night at a motel/restaurant/trout farm called Karaman and left the next day. Work beckoned.

CHAPTER 13

A NATO Conference and Vedat Uras

"Balkan is the name of one of the most beautiful mountain ranges in Europe. It gave its name to the whole region, because of its beauty. Yet today, 'Balkan' is synonymous with destruction and backwardness. The countries of southeast Europe do not deserve to be balkanized anymore."

These were the opening comments of the Bulgarian Minister of Defence at the 10th International Antalya Conference on Security and Cooperation, held by the Atlantic Council of Turkey at the Mirage Park Resort Hotel. I attended from March 10-12, 2000. I'm not going to go into great detail here about what was said – that might test your patience, and that's not the purpose of this book. But I do think you would find a summary of some of the contributions interesting.

Among the speakers was the then-Secretary General of NATO, Lord Robertson, who said the opportunities facing NATO at the turn of the century outweighed the challenges, and he listed three.

First was the chance to make positive changes in Kosovo to help stabilize the region. NATO's commitment to helping Kosovo would be long-term in that "very demanding situation." But 12 months after the war ended, much had improved, he said. The refugees were returning and war criminals being caught. Crime was down. "Despite Kosovo's difficult history there are already signs of hope."

Robertson quoted Ataturk who said "peace is the most effective way for nations to obtain prosperity and happiness." Economics and security go hand in hand, Robertson said, saying that was the logic underpinning the Marshall Plan for Europe after the Second World War. "And the same logic will be and is being applied to southeast Europe."

Second, Robertson stressed that NATO must build a strong relationship with Russia. If there is to be lasting security in Europe, Russia and Europe must work together, even in difficult situations. "Russia can be an important part of the solution."As this is written, though, it seems Russia has been spurned more than welcomed by NATO.

Third, there's an opportunity to build a stronger European security and defence identity. ESDI can serve the interests of all the allies. It can take pressure off the U.S. "A stronger Europe can handle crises more effectively when the North Americans simply do not want to take a leading role.... My job as the secretary-general of NATO is to ensure that the security interests of all NATO members are met." In 2010, it is apparent that the U.S., near bankruptcy after the Iraqi war, simply cannot afford to take a leading role any longer.

Robertson said European Union planning must be as inclusive as possible of non-EU members such as Turkey. He also called for coordinated defence planning for EU and NATO. "Our security must remain indivisible.

"ESDI is not about Europe going it alone. It is about Europe doing more. A de-coupled Europe simply cannot work. An ESDI that undermines NATO is a losing proposition."

I also saw a growing spirit of goodwill, and cited the warming relations between Greece and Turkey. He said imagination, determination and goodwill are the qualities that will make NATO work in the new century to ensure the safety of future generations.

Next, Turkish President Suleyman Demirel spoke and noted this was NATO's 50th anniversary, and last year was the 10th anniversary of the fall of the Berlin Wall.

"For the first time in history the numbers of people living under democracies exceed the numbers under dictatorship," he said.

"I believe that the issues before us should be considered from the broad angle of all. Security interdependence is the new nature of all nations around the world."

He noted how the Euro-Asia region, with its multi-trillion dollars worth of oil and natural gas, is an important new geographic region after the Cold War. Establishing lasting peace there is a top priority, for Turkey and others, as Turkey is a transportation hub of the region.

The Caucasus is another key area. Today, the borders of Europe extend into this area, including Georgia and Armenia. Because of its location,

Turkey must spend a greater portion than most countries of its Gross National Product on defence. Allowing Romania and Bulgaria to join NATO would help Turkey as well.

He didn't speak, but I met and talked to Turkish General Cetin Dogan, a four-star general who briefed me on the Kurdish situation, where the PKK remains active in its violent efforts to wrest the independence of southeast Turkey, a predominately Kurdish region, from the state. I gave him a watercolour I did of the sea; I also gave paintings to Vedat and Susan.

Dogan is a stocky, strong, balding man in his late 50s. From 1997 to 99 he was in charge of the four Turkish armies in the southeast, the state's most difficult region. He comes from the northeast, where family remains.

"It is very difficult to understand form the outside," he tells me at the outset. "We have ethnic peoples here, up to 27 groups, but our overall identity is the Turkish citizenship. We have in southeast Turkey ethnic Kurds and other ethnic groups, such as Assyrians and so forth. The problem stems from the fertile ground of terror activities. But when you speak to the people they don't want separatism, they want to live peacefully. That is why we say there is not a Kurdish problem, there is a development problem, there is a terrorism problem. Outside help only exploits the situation.

"People know the PKK cannot bring anything, only tears and pain. The problem is that Turkey is a developing country and the most underdeveloped portion is that area.

"You see, I am a military man. How can I win any combat with terrorism without the support of the people? Most of the damage is inflicted by the PKK, not the Turkish military. A problem is that when outsiders come in, they first to go to the human rights groups, but they are under the control of PKK sympathizers. You must go and speak to the local people. You must find the real man, not the pro government or pro PKK."

He also invoked the need to have happy people to have peace and stability. To make them happy, their needs must be met, and they must have hope for the future. That's why the government launched the GAP project."

This is a massive effort to build dams and generate jobs, irrigation waters and electricity. In fact it was having little success in providing work or development at the time of my visit. Its record was spotty.

But enough about the conference. My hosts, who told me about the event, lived in a comfortable condominium, a gated community, by the sea in Kemer. It was developed by a Calgary company. Vedat Uras, 69, is a former diplomat who resigned 38 years ago to marry a British woman who preceded Susan in his life. For many years he has published a political newsletter about Turkey called Pulse. He is proud, cheerful and smart. We sang Bring Back My Bonnie after consuming a delicious trout lunch (and some liquid) at Limra, a hotel and resort near a fish farm in the mountains. The assistant manager, Aytac Erenler, provided personal service.

Susan, who was born and raised in England, has lived in Turkey for years and speaks perfect Turkish. She was Vedat's secretary during his diplomatic days (he was in Jordan and other places). She is pragmatic and easy going and kind. Joining Vedat and I for lunch was a British couple, Paul and Kit, who were retired and living on a 24-foot sail boat. He was an engineer, she a stewardess. She led free aerobics classes and I took part in one with Vedat one morning on a tennis court by the harbour. Imagine the snow-capped mountains in the distance and the Mediterranean Sea and the beautiful boats as we exercised. Kit also taught English for free. She nearly died of cancer two years ago and considered each day a gift to be shared. She exuded good health and inner as well as outer peace and beauty.

Vedat is an expert on Turkey and I was grateful for his knowledge and companionship. When traveling, one never knows what the next day will bring in terms of fascinating people. I stayed with them a week. We all got along well. I learned through their friend the British consul about the NATO conference. Sixteen countries were represented. Quite a bash.

Kemer is south of Antalya on the Mediterranean coast in Turkey's south. The sea was immense, blue and awesome. The snow-capped mountains seemed to grow out of it and rose 2000 metres or so. The sheer cliffs were spectacular. I actually started painting in watercolours again, inspired by those vistas, and did some good stuff. When I gave one picture to General Dogan, he said, "Do I have a friend in Canada?" with a smile.

"You do indeed" I replied. Soon I would visit and talk to Kurds in that sensitive area.

CHAPTER 14

Alayna, and an American preacher retracing the steps of Apostle Paul

From Kemer I took a bus east along the Mediterranean coast to Alanya. The view was incredible with the sea and cliffs, unlike anything I had seen before. We passed beaches that tempted me to yell at the driver to stop. As we approached Alanya, I remarked to the local man beside me about the loveliness of the place.

"Thirty years back, was more beautiful," he said. "Here was village, not city. Garden, each family. No hotels."

"Ahh, no hotels," I echoed as we passed a series of them, like you'd see in Cancun. A few moments later we passed an old castle, a relic of centuries past, its stonework crumbling, its ramparts eroded by time and weather and wind, but it stood stolid and placid -- like a true Turk.

"It is bar now," the man said, raising his eyebrows and shrugging.

At Alanya I made use of one of those new developments, Hotel Azlesu. For some hours I painted the water scenes of boats and beaches, and enjoyed my clean and inexpensive room. Then I boarded a bus for Silifke farther east, for I was eager to get to the Kurds.

On the bus I met an American named Albert Jabs. He was a 66-year-old professor with a PhD in history, race relations, which is ironic. At first he sat in the row ahead of me beside a small Turkish man who occupied the window seat. Ordinarily that seat, with its view on the world and place to lean a tired head, would have been a bonus for the local fellow. But not in this case. Albert Jabs was a big man, big-boned and heavy. The little

Turk ended up being sandwiched between the rock of Mr. Jabs and the hard place of the window.

I watched with growing amusement as the unspoken drama unfolded. Jabs was unaware or unconcerned that his large right leg, shoulder and arm were flowing over into the Turk's space. It wasn't really his fault; he simply filled a larger than usual amount of territory and made no effort to hold back. He acted as if unaware that another human being sat beside him. To the extent we should all be considerate of others, that may be held against him. Jabs made no attempt at dialogue, no eye contact, not even a glance to acknowledge the other man's existence.

Mr. Jabs shifted in his seat, adjusting himself. In doing so he increasingly compressed and antagonized the fellow in the window seat. More than once I watched the smaller man glance angrily to his left into the stolid profile of an aloof Mr. Jabs. I felt sorry for the fellow.

Then I, too, began to feel Mr. Jab's presence: he put his chair back as far as possible – right against my knees. I'm six feet three.

"Excuse me," I said. "My legs are long, and what you just did is causing me discomfort."

"Oh, sorry," said Mr. Jabs, who raised his seat a notch or two.

Hearing the big man vocalize for the first time prompted the Turkish man to my right to whisper in my ear, "German."

I whispered back, "American." It turned out we were both right. Mr. Jabs was an American of German descent. My seat-mate and I then chatted in normal voices. After listening for a bit to our English, Mr. Jabs turned and asked me: "Where are you from?"

"Canada," I said.

"What province?"

"Manitoba."

"Where?"

"Manitoba. I live two hours north of Minot, North Dakota."

"Ooohhhh. Isn't Manitoba next to British Columbia?"

"No. Albert is next to B.C."

"Then comes Manitoba?"

"No, then comes Alberta."

To be fair, I might not have been able to tell him the states adjacent to his home in South Carolina, either. The bus stopped, and the little fellow beside Mr. Jabs hurried off and did not return. We had a short break, not long enough for a washroom visit, and upon reboarding Mr. Jabs asked me to sit with him, as he hadn't spoken English at any length for some time, he explained. He ended up showing as much interest in me as he had disinterest in his previous seat mate.

I learned that Mr. Jabs was from Lexington, S.C., where he taught the history of Western Civilization. He was over here for four months, with his daughter, to teach in Lithuania. With evident pride, he said she taught mathematics and international relations. And she was only 23. I told him how impressed I was, and suggested he must be pleased by her success. He said he was. Then we sat quietly for a while.

"I think I could maybe live in some parts of Canada," he finally offered. I replied that I was sure that he could. Then he confided various impressions. He was having to reorder his image of Russian people, he said. He found his students very kind and considerate, not at all like the stereotype. "We live with illusions and spend our lives proving them for what they are," he told me. I was impressed by this admission. Panos Manikis, the natural farmer in Greece, had told me the same thing.

Mr. Jabs said his purpose was to help bring people to Christ. A lay preacher, he was on an odyssey to retrace the steps of the Apostle Paul through Turkey. "He was a man's man. You'd have to be tough to travel the vast distances he did in those days, over these mountains. He's a good role model for today's youth."

He noted that Turkey was important also because Noah's Ark is said to have come to rest on Mount Ararat in the east, and here is where Noah's children began to repopulate the Earth. The apostles were first referred to as Christians here, and by 391 the Roman Empire had adopted Christianity.

"We think home is so important," Jabs told me. "I used to think the world revolved around Connecticut, where I was raised, and Washington, D.C. But here, this is where it all began, near the Euphrates and Tigris Rivers. Travel pops some of those illusions."

Home is important, I replied. It shapes us, and holds us. It's just that most of us don't come from places that matter, in the big scheme of things. He nodded.

Then he asked me: "Do you speak Turkish?"

I told him no.

"Nor do I. Hope the driver stops for washroom breaks.

"I'm sure he will," I offered.

"But what if you have to go?"

"I suppose you could go up to the driver and gesticulate wildly," I offered straight-faced. I felt a little guilty about that, and he likely picked up on the fact I was making fun of the situation.

"Yeah," he replied. Then he sat quietly for a bit. "I've been in Turkey four days."

For him, this bus trip was a 10-hour ride to a place called Adana. We traveled through incredible mountains along the Mediterranean coast – cliffs and sea and villages, but the vistas I raved about seemed to escape him.

"I suppose this is much like the California coast," he said. "Sure hope the driver's competent. That's a long way down."

"From what I've seen, these Turks are excellent drivers and this is a new coach, so we have nothing to worry about," I said. "Just look at that view!"

"Two days ago I got off the bus at a break and then got on the wrong one," he said. "Scared the heck out of me. Realized my error at the last minute. This traveling alone is tough."

"Really? I find it pleasant."

"At Adana I go straight to my hotel for a bath. Where are you staying?"

"I don't know yet. I'm going to Silifke, which is coming up in a few minutes, and I'll find a hotel when I arrive."

"You haven't booked ahead?"

"Never do. Like it that way. It's fun and easy to find a room. I like the surprise of never knowing where I'll stay."

"I couldn't do that."

"Oh, you could. There are always cheap hotels near the bus stations. It's easy, and a lot less expensive."

We came to Silifke, a sleepy little town. The bus stopped briefly, and I bid my American friend good-bye. Shortly afterwards I found a nice room for the night. Then I thought again of Mr. Jabs, and the Apostle Paul, and the little Turk, and how people differ. And I hoped Mr. Jabs got to a washroom soon.

CHAPTER 15

Sevil

The bus pulled into Silifke at 5:15, and I said good-bye to Mr. Jabs and got off. As I gathered my bag and walked down a street a man said something in welcome, and I said, "Cheap hotel?"

He said, "Arisan," and motioned around the corner.

At the Arison I paid three million or $7.50 Cdn. Room 22 had no TV and no bath but was quiet, in the back, new, clean and large, with two beds. I expected to stay for two nights.

It was March 14. The next day was a Moslem holiday when they sacrificed goats and sheep for a feast. I looked forward to eating well, anyway.

The Mediterranean Sea was an incredible magnet for me. I felt drawn by its power and beauty and colour, in ways I never was by the Pacific Ocean when living on Vancouver Island. Partly it was the boats. Turkish boats were fascinating in their variety and character: some tiny, others huge, most respectfully aged, a few new but most scarred and peeling and creaking, all lined up like old men on coffee row.

Partly, too, the people pulled me to the sea: fishermen freshly in from a day's work, their caps dirty and floppy, their attention riveted on ropes and boxes and nets; children playing by the water, squealing and running as anxious mothers look on; women walking hand in hand, chatting earnestly to each other as the waves wash in and break on the sand and gravel. (You rarely saw men and women hand in hand, as the Moslem code frowns on public shows of affection between the sexes.)

Next day I met a girl. She was 20, beautiful, and charming. Her family owned an orange and lemon orchard near Tasucu, a few kilometres west of Silifke, where I went to paint harbour scenes. On the way home I saw a family on the bus and thought it would be good to meet a rural family and see their farm. I was writing for the Western Producer at the time and could possibly sell the story.

But I didn't get off the bus with them. I hesitated. However I noted the home, with laundry on the line, chickens, a dog, the orchard. A mile or more down the road I decided to get off the bus and go back. I stuck out my thumb after walking for 10 minutes and was picked up, then deposited close to the house.

I walked up and knocked on the door. A woman of about 20 answered my knock, a baby in her arms. A boy about eight and a girl of maybe 10 also approached. The older girl was dressed in a skirt and blouse. I didn't recall her being with the group that got off the bus, but she may have been. No matter.

"Hello," I said, smiling. "Excuse me. Do you speak English?"
She said she did.

"I am from Canada," I said. "I work for newspapers. I write about farming. You have fruit trees. May I talk to you?"

She smiled and said OK. She knew some English, she said, from working at a tourist restaurant. Her parents were not in view, but a woman she said was an aunt was cooking something in the ashes of a fire near the orchard behind the simple concrete block house. She welcomed me to follow and I went around to the back with her. She offered me cooked sheep, strips of meat and liver. Delicious. The youngsters watched me with amusement and after a bit I declined any more meat, giving half to the girl.

Her name was Sevil Bozdag. She said she was 20. "I am single," she told me. "No boyfriend." Well! I also was single, recently divorced. I decided to fetch my bag of paints. While the others inspected six of my paintings, I painted their orchard.

"The Pask!" she said, looking at my painting of a ship. "I work here."

The children, meanwhile, were much taken by all this and very supportive of my orchard scene. Then I added chickens. They asked me to add a goat (one really was tied to a tree not far away). So I did. It looked like a pig. "For you, Sevil," I said, and handed it to her. She was surprised and pleased.

Then a young neighbour man entered the scene. He didn't stay long, however, and left shortly after our introduction. I had little interest in talking to him.

Then, feeling sad about having to go but not knowing what else to do, and being aware of the cultural norms there, where strange men were not overly welcome where daughters were concerned, I prepared to leave too. But I took a good look at this lady, knowing I probably wouldn't see her again. She had high cheekbones, a perfect line of nose and chin, soft and assured movements, height and grace. She was lovely, slim and attractive with a lovely smile. Her hands were larger than those of most girls, hands that had worked at washing clothes, carrying boxes of fruit, picking and sorting and cutting their firewood, for they had no son. She was the eldest and their prize.

The next day I returned for another visit in mid-afternoon. Her younger sister, who spoke little English, seemed to be saying she was away somewhere, and didn't know for how long. I got the feeling I wasn't welcome. I never had seen the parents. I felt bad about missing her. I'd painted four scenes to show her, two of Kizkalesi Castle, a mosque and a mountainside.

I left, taking the bus to Tasucu and tried to get on the Internet but couldn't. It was a high-use time and the machine was so slow it didn't seem to be working. I had a Coke and cookies and went out to paint another scene at the waterfront.

I'd had breakfast at a castle, so I went back for soup, and there I met a family from Chechnya. This was the seaside at Kizkalesi with the castle, which sat far out in the water. The family spoke no English; there were a boy and a girl besides the parents, and I took their photo for them.

On the way back to Silifke I got off the bus twice, once to paint a mosque, and once to paint a pastoral hillside, two of my better efforts which I still have. It sure pays to break with routine and just do what seems right in the moment. It cost me a bit more to reboard the bus, and I walked quite a bit, but doing those paintings was far more important. I have them still.

Back at Silifke I walked to the waterfront and painted a boat called Yildrim. The man on the boat watched me and then invited me on board for tea.

Next day I awoke at 6 and painted the Temple of Jupiter, which is located on the main street in Silifke. It dates back to 200 AD and came complete with a stork nest, and stork, on top. Then I packed up and left the Arisan Hotel to catch the 9:30 bus to Adana but felt ill at ease without having another attempt at saying good-bye to Sevil, so I headed toward that little home. I heard they were planning to widen the road, putting that home at risk.

When I got there I met a woman who must have been her mother, an older, stout woman who emerged wearing a head scarf and dark skirt. She made it clear that my presence was not wanted. In fact she shooed me away as if I were a fly. She wielded a mean broom.

Sevil "not home," she said.

I didn't believe her. "Sevil!" No answer.

The old woman became more aggressive and came at me with the broom. I backed off further, to the road.

Still scowling, she let loose a torrent of Turkish words that left her meaning clear. I had no way to tell her that all I wanted to do was say good-bye.

I wrote in my journal: "I plunked down my pack on the roadside, sat on it, and pulled out my paints. Then I painted their home, a one-storey building made of concrete blocks. A poor dwelling inhabited by a poor family whose eldest daughter is their only jewel."

A little while later I left on a bus.

CHAPTER 16

In Sanliurfa the world seems to have stepped back in time;
I find the birthplace of Abraham and learn about GAP

While visiting with Vedat Uras, I spoke to a friend of his who worked in government and advised me to go first to Ankara before heading to the Kurdish country. He said I needed a pass to travel in the military zone. I disregarded this advice, partly because it would take me far out of my way, partly because of the travel costs and delay, and partly because I didn't think I'd need a pass.

And so from Silifke I boarded a bus headed east, toward Sanliurfa, known also as Urfa, in the southeastern Anatolian region of Turkey famous for its prophets, bazaars and traditions. This city of about 400,000 people is 9,000 years old, and it sits beside the Euphrates River in what was once Mesopotamia. According to the Bible and Quran, Abraham, the father of Judaism, Christianity and Islam, was born there, as was the prophet Job. For me, Urfa lived up to its billing and more.

The colours and sights were many. I saw women covered from head to toe in black robes, old men with scarves wrapped around their heads, their teeth broken and tobacco stained; boys like little men, wearing three-piece suits but no ties; girls bright-eyed and playful, tagging along behind their parents, some stopping to feed the carp.

I arrived here one night. It was a Sunday. I paid three million liras which was $7.50 Cdn for a room, the rate I've been paying since leaving Istanbul two weeks ago.

This is Mesopotamia, the land between two rivers, the Tigris and Euphrates, where the dawn broke on the world's first great empires. This is battle scarred country, rocky and dry and broiling in summer, but cool at 13 C when I visited in 2000. This was home for some days while I searched for Kurds who spoke English. I needed another story for the Free Press. Urfa was half the size of Winnipeg but twice as colourful because East meets West there, the peoples of the Caucasus, the Kurds, the Arabs, crossing paths with increasing numbers of Western tourists and business people, since the GAP dam and irrigation project is based here.

A castle, called a kale, sits on a hill not far from the city's centre. Urfa is full of religious significance. Abraham is said to have been born in a cave here. The pools of the sacred carp are symbolic of the story of Abraham, a great Islamic prophet, who was destroying pagan gods one day when Nimrod, the local king, took offence, and had him immolated on a funeral pyre. God intervened to save Abraham, turning the fire into water and the wood into fish. The pools sit near Urfa, filled with sacred carp.

People paraded past the two pools in vast numbers as I sat and took in the sights, the sounds, the spectacle. Thousands passed before my eyes as I sat on my coat in the shade of a tree, watching the carp break the surface as people fed them pellets purchased for the purpose. An old man with a net on a long pole fished bread from the water, thrown by children, to keep it clean. Then I heard a voice.

"Hello, English."

I looked around at this mass of humanity and saw nobody speaking to me.

"Hello English." A boy, an 11-year-old going on 42. "How are you."

"Fine," I replied.

"This is sacred pool. There on hill, Abraham's birthplace. Here, great mosques of antiquity."

This from a midget. His name was Ishmael, he said. He wore a crew cut, a green and beige coat, white pants and scuffed black shoes. He was slim and self-assured and had the eyes of a much older person.

"How did you learn such English," I ask. A smile is his reply.

"You like Urfa? My home. I teach you." He did indeed as I rose to walk along the paved path that extended from the city centre, through a market area, to the pools and castle. Soon another boy joined us. Then a well-dressed man. They began trying to teach me Kurdish. I felt like the pied piper. As if I were an odd and rarely seen insect they inspected me, plied me with questions, took joy in watching and listening to what I did and said. So I laughed and told them what a fantastic home they had. They liked that.

Eventually my retinue dispersed, and I resumed my people watching. Then an elderly man approached, talked to me in broken English and immediately pulled from his inside jacket pocket a photo album full of photos of himself: at the castle, the pools, in Harran, Istanbul, with women. I say how nice. This is Urfa; this is the old Turkey. Maybe he wanted to guide me, I don't know. He left too, after a short while.

Next day I travelled to the ancient village of Harran, near the Syrian border. Harran is the home of bee-hive shaped houses. But first I went right to the Syrian border, to the Turkish town of Kcanakale. This was on a large dusty plain, and I figured I'd capture it in watercolour.

I sat beside a concrete pillar, one of two, and could see to my left the Syrian border post with a guard. I didn't see how he could affect me at all, as I was some 200 metres or so inside Turkey on an old railway platform. I would have been fine, partly hidden by the pillar, had a gaggle of gawking men not come up and brought attention to us.

I'd seen others like them – chattering idle youth in their late teens and early 20s who have no apparent employment, but are fascinated by the labours of a visiting Canadian. Soon, of course, the Syrian took notice, and may have suspected I was spying, taking pictures.

He ordered me over in no uncertain terms, and since he wielded an automatic weapon, I didn't argue.

Approaching him, I produced a smile, my passport and the words, "Artist, no problem." He spoke to me for a minute in his language, his rifle slung level at his hip, pointed at my abdomen. I was a bit concerned. Then two colleagues joined him, similarly armed. All were about the same age, 20.

Placid and peaceful on the outside I swirled on the inside. My one thought was to get free.

They motioned me to follow them into Syria.

"No, no, no," I said. "I stay here." There was no way I was leaving my safety zone in Turkey; once they got me the few yards into Syria they could haul me away. In Turkey they couldn't do much unless I cooperated.

The first one asked me a number of questions in broken English, and I provided brief answers, but clearly something had to be done to convince them I was no threat. Think, Brad, think.

"I am a painter," I said. "I took no pictures. Look, I will show you."

I reached into my bag and pulled out half a dozen paintings. At this, one of the two newcomers took a particular interest. The first man said, "Him painter," and the artist stepped forward, lowered his gun and flashed me a grin that would make a dentist drool.

"You watercolour?" I asked. Many nods. We "chatted." The young man liked my work. He smiled and shook my hand. With that the tension magically slipped away.

451

This man had horrible teeth but wonderful judgment. His actions put his colleagues at ease and broke the stalemate.

I still wanted out. After a few more words about my travels I said good-bye and walked away, eager to be far from that border. This was the first time my art got me out of trouble but it wouldn't be the last.

In Kcanakale a woman in a tailor shop gave me a piece of blue material in which I wrapped my brushes and pencil. I have it still. I also bought a sheet of sandpaper, which is used to make texture. Now all I needed was more paper. I caught a bus north to Harran, 18 kilometres away.

At Harran I met the headman, Halil Ozyauuz, 48, and was invited to stay for supper. Eight of us sat cross-legged on colourful silk and cotton carpets inside his home, which as I say was shaped like a bee hive. Ozyauuz and his seven sons and I each were given a spoon, a bowl of yogurt and a plate of diced tomatoes, cucumbers and onions.

It was 7 p.m. The sun had set on this baked and stony land near Syria. This was an Arab home and an Arab village, evidence of the multi-ethnic culture of Turkey. A horse whinnied, and as if on cue two boys arrived with silver platters piled high with wheat and bits of boiled sheep – couscous.

The headman began the feast and the rest of us followed. In 10 minutes we were done.

Harran, one of the oldest continuously inhabited places on the planet, was poorer five years earlier, I was told, when such suppers may not have been common. When water from the Ataturk Dam flowed into their fields, their prospects improved.

At that time he drove a donkey. When I met him he drove a Toyota. His mud and stone home had six rooms, three more than before, to accommodate his large family. He had 14 children, six girls and eight sons.

"Before the dam, nothing," said Resat, 23, one of the sons. "Very tough. No money, no jobs, no farming."

Now they have 200 acres under cultivation, rotating wheat, corn, cotton and barley. Watermelons, tomatoes and peppers are among the other foods now grown more easily here, they said, and sold in Urfa.

The Ataturk Dam, 90 kilometres northwest of there, was one of 22 dams to be built by 2005 in the $36-billion US project that's been underway since the 1980s. Some say it was designed as a way to uproot Kurdish people and keep them off balance, as thousands of villagers have been displaced by the work and the reservoirs, human rights agencies say. Theirs is a story of lost land and lost hopes for a better future, as they moved to the towns and cities but often found little in the way of work.

"Perhaps the greatest concern among activists who are against the construction of the Ilisu dam is potential destruction of the livelihood of up to 78,000 people – the majority of whom are ethnic Kurds – living along the approximate 158-mile river stretches," writes one Kurdish reporter, Ercan Ayboga, in the Kurdish Herald of September 2009. "Since the legal framework for resettlement of the displaced people is inadequately recognized in Turkey, except for a handful of large landowners, most of the displaced population is confronted with poverty."

Others, like General Cetin Dogan, said GAP was intended positively as a means to promote economic development and peace in the region. They need jobs, he said, and GAP provides jobs. It affects both the Tigris and Euphrates Rivers and was expected to put an additional three million hectares of land under the plow. Almost two million people would see their incomes double or more, state brochures say.

But the long-term benefits have yet to be proven, Ayboga writes. If anything, he says, the dams do more harm than good.

"On average, during a seven-year period of dam construction, 2,300 people are employed. However, after the completion of the project, the hydropower plant only provides about 200 jobs while some 1000 [mainly agricultural] jobs are permanently destroyed in the impounded region. Such contradiction inevitably leaves impressions among locals that that the construction of dams in Kurdish provinces is a continuation of previous campaigns of forced displacement and the assimilation of the people in the region. Activists and academics who are against the construction of Ilisu dam argue that the conservation and soft-sustainable development of the cultural heritage of the city and preservation of the biodiversity in the valley could bring more socio-economic benefits."

The "city" he mentions is Hasankeyf, one of the oldest and most continuously-inhabited locations in the world with a history stretching back at least 12,000 years. Calling it a city today is stretching it, as Hasankeyf consists largely of caves dug into hillsides, from what I've seen. I was there. It's located in the Tigris valley, an important part of Upper Mesopotamia where the first settlements of human history were found. It is, indeed, a fascinating place, a true open-air museum – and if the Ilisu dam goes ahead, it would be flooded, its riches drowned forever.

And so the GAP project, or Southeastern Anatolia Project (Güneydogu Anadolu Projesi-GAP) is highly controversial, a source of international concern. The harmful effects of hydro dams are well down around the world, as dams in China and South America have been trouble as well. In

Canada, of course, the James Bay Project and others in northern Manitoba have generated similar controversy and loss of livelihood among people (Metis and Cree among them) poorly positioned to fight the bureaucrats, engineers and governments who plan such immense projects. The fact they alter nature on grand scales and play havoc with Earth's cycles and ecosystems is of little interest to those unaffected by the projects. They tend to measure success by the bottom line, especially their own; wider human issues tend to be secondary. In southeast Turkey, for instance, malaria had increased ten-fold with all the new water.

In Harran, though, the family I met were glad to have GAP. Cotton there was now white gold, I was told. "GAP has turned the southeast into Turkey's breadbasket," Vedat Uras said. Eighteen billion dollars had already been spent – borrowed money, of course – when he spoke in 2000.

Some watercolors Brad painted in Turkey.

CHAPTER 17

Police Come Knocking in Elazig

In Urfa I walked miles to see the old sights. A must-see was the bazaar, a centuries-old maze of lanes and byways filled with merchants of all kinds. For $6.25 Cdn a tailor put a new zipper on my coat and added an elastic strip at the waist. Children with wooden boxes shined shoes, so I had that done too. For a long time I just sat and watched people go by. I took a chair near the tailor, and across the cobblestone street was a shoe merchant. One boy in particular came by with the saddest looking shoes you can imagine. The rest of his attire wasn't much to look at either, but his shoes were a mess, with their soles flopping and his toes sticking out. I felt sorry for the little duffer. Here was something I could do.

I called the boy over; he might have been nine. "Would you like new shoes?"

He looked at me, then the tailor, who said something that put him at ease. To this day I don't know that he understood me, because I never got a word out of him, but I took him across to the shoe salesman and asked the man to fix him up. A minute later the lad was wearing shiny black leather shoes, a new version of those on his feet, which were discarded. This time he looked at the shoe man, who also put him at ease. I paid the man and the boy skipped out, pleased.

I remember a vast assortment of sights and colours and scents in that bazaar. And I remember liking it there. Spices in large barrels were sold there, as elsewhere in Turkey. The bazaar was a beehive of a place and had a happy air about it. Merchants shouted to advertize their wares, and a steady steam of locals passed by. Some led donkeys loaded with merchandise. The typically old men leading them looked weather worn and fit. I rarely saw anyone in this part of Turkey who didn't look well and healthy. Obesity was simply not an issue in Turkey's southeast region.

From Urfa I made my way to Mardin, where I bought a cap that I wore for years, until I left it behind in the Qualicum Beach Civic Centre during a Remembrance Day ceremony with Dad, in 2005. I liked that cap and can remember buying it, again from a male merchant. Few women sold things like that when I was there, unlike in Canada, where most clerks tend to be women.

Mardin is perched at the edge of a plateau in southeast Turkey overlooking the Mesopotamian plain 95 kilometres or 59 miles south of Diyarbakir. It's a provincial capital with about 62,000 people, an ancient town built of sandstone with some interesting old buildings, including the medieval Sultan Isa Medresesi (1385), **Kasim Pasha Medresesi** (1400s), the **Ulu Cami** (Great Mosque, 1000s), and a rambling bazaar.

But most people come to visit the Saffron Monastery (Deyrul Zafaran). This was a holy place even in pre-Christian times, but I took a pass. I needed to make my way to Diyarbakir and points north, especially Georgia.

I left the Yeni Hotel in Mardin, which was very cheap but not a good place to stay. It was dirty even by my standards and during the night I was awakened by a man who walked into my room, which couldn't be locked, to sleep in the other bed. Apparently it was a hostel-like setup but I didn't know at the time. It was cheap, 1.5 million lira, and that should have tipped me off.

I didn't lose anything and was gone early next morning at 8 on a mini-bus (or dolmage) north. In Urfa I'd stayed at a nice place, the Ugu Hotel, with a friendly and garrulous proprietor who spoke good English and was quite a happy man, about 35. I don't recall his name but he had a flair about him. And he ran a good hotel. I'd go back there for sure, and hope to one day.

The bus ride north was only about 60 miles, as I say, but took more than an hour because we passed through four military checkpoints. Here was the test – did I need that pass from Ankara?

I didn't.

Though I was taken off the bus and questioned, the soldiers let me pass. At first I found the checkpoints unnerving, to be honest. I was a little worried. But I was an artist, a traveler intent on capturing the beauty of the country in paint, and I could prove it.

Finally we arrived in Diyarbakir, the centre of Kurdish culture (and unrest) in the region. The bus stopped at Tigris University and I should have got off there, because I needed to interview people who spoke English – and knew what was going on between the PKK separatists and the state. But locals encouraged me to stay on the bus because it was a long way to the city centre and hotels, so I did. There, I immediately got on another dolmage headed back to Tigris U.

"Anybody speak English?" I asked from the front, loudly.

"I do," said a well-dressed man in his 30s, sitting at the back.

"Good. I need to talk to a history or political science professor." The PKK issue was taboo, unmentionable in public. You never knew who was listening.

"You can follow me," he said.

This was Turksel Dulgergil, an assistant professor of dentistry. We went to his office where I interviewed him about the military situation in the city and region. The day was Thursday March 23.

In his view, the No. 1 problem in the southeast was not terrorism or war but poverty. As a dentist he made many visits to rural areas, he said, and bad teeth were common. A second and related problem in his mind was unemployment. A third was pollution in the cities.

As far as the war went, "it's completely finished," he said. What brought about the end?

"The government brought into effect new measures, not military but economic and social measures," he said, sounding like a government official.

He praised the efforts of GAP, calling cotton "white gold" as others had done.

The PKK were in decline, he said, only about 400 in the mountains. This compares to some 40,000 thought to have been active five years earlier.

Dulgergil himself was 32 and was born and raised in Izmir in Turkey's west, a more affluent area. He was married and had one child. He wasn't Kurdish but he gave his daughter a Kurdish name, Nupelda, which means "trees growing up in spring."

He said few wanted separation. "The Kurdish people in Turkey never wanted to divide from Turkey. If they divided from Turkey, what will make job?"

As we talk, there's a knock at the door. It is a shoe-shine boy. The professor tosses him a coin. "This is an example of poorness of the region," he said.

He phoned a newspaper friend of his who sends a car over to get me. I meet Mehdi Tanaman, bureau chief of the Star. Tanaman was born in Diyarbakir and learned his English in school as the dentist had. But he had a point of view much like that of the dentist. He liked the GAP project. "It's very important for us." Even for the PKK, he said, because if people are rich, they can solve first the economic problem of poverty, and then the cultural problems, because people with money have power to get things done.

He likened the PKK situation to that of Northern Ireland, where conflict is all but over. Like the dentist, he said the government had taken measures, such as allowing use of Kurdish broadcasts, to show more tolerance.

"It was a very bad war for people in this are," he said. "It was war. But not now." A big reason was PKK leader Abdullah Ocalan's call for peace from his Turkish prison.

I thanked him and went into the street, where I found the owner of a pet store to talk to. He agreed with what they said. (I had a talking parrot on my shoulder.)

Down the street I asked a young man about the nearest Internet café, as I thought I might have enough to file a story. He took me three doors down to a slim man of about 60 who sold, of all things, brassieres. His tiny shop was no bigger than a typical Canadian bathroom.

"You are a newspaperman?" was the first thing he said.

"Yes. Is it that easy to tell?" I asked. He said it was. But he talked frankly, and held a much different view than the first three men. He was a PKK sympathizer whose nephew was among the fighters. Finally, some good luck.

"There is no democracy in Turkey, no. Democracy is for the generals, not for the people. Fascism. I don't care, I tell the truth."

He continued. "Brother, let me tell you this. The military people can park their car anywhere. They pay nothing. Me? I pay fines. There is no law for them. They are gods of this country."

He said if they knew he was talking to me, he would go to jail. To them, the state, I was a "very bad man. Very bad man, brother."

OK, but was the PKK finished, as the others said?

No. They lived in the mountain areas, where "they are a little bit wild, you know." He estimated 70,000 fighters, an excessive figure no doubt for this area but he may have meant all of Kurdistan, which embraced regions of Syria and Iraq as well.

I told him somebody told me only 400.

"Tell him chicken shit," he said.

Was he PKK?

"No, but I like them. My son ...(he paused). Let's put it this way, we're trying to stay away, but my heart says you must help them. So I try to help them."

How?

"I've been telling them, cool it down."

A cousin was PKK and in prison.

The man wore a respectable grey suit, grey shirt, with dark rimmed glasses. He was 64. The Kurds want their own schools, freedom to speak their language, TV stations, he said.

He was in the army himself 40 years ago, but, like others from the area, he couldn't speak Turkish, only Kurdish. "The sons of bitches would strike our faces. Why no you speak Turkish?" they asked him.

As far as Ocalan's plea for peace went, he said a political leader must say many things to survive. "Ocalan said, if you don't want them to kill me, please slow down. It's not permanent," he said. "You see they hung my grandfather too. There's a graveyard near the airbase near here."

Time was marching on and felt a need to go. I promised to keep the man's name out of print, for his safety.

"We need freedom," he said. "We are like one hand. Freedom is the other." Then he clasped his hands together.

"You must get out of this city," he said. "They will know what you are and pick you up. If you want my advice, get out soon."

I did.

At 3 I hopped on a bus for Elazig farther north, a drab old city of about 270,000. The ride was uneventful and when I arrived it was almost 7, so I took a room in a plain old hotel not far from the station. As I entered the building I saw only one person in the lobby, a slim woman in her late 30s, and our eyes met briefly, but I pulled away. I went to my room, dumped my stuff, and then went for a quick restaurant meal. She was gone when I left the hotel. Then I hit the sack, exhausted by all my travel and interviews.

Sleep was short-lived, however.

About 8 o'clock someone knocked on my door. Three knocks, in fact, and then the words, "Open! Police!"

I didn't fully awaken right away. I was in a deep sleep. Three more sharp raps rang out. "Open! Police!"

I began to regain consciousness, processed the noise, and tried to remember where I was. Oh yes, this dump of a hotel in Elazig. Now, what to do about the knocking. Well, this is my room. I paid for it. I haven't done anything wrong. And I'm Canadian; they're Turks, with their great inferiority complex. So I'd assume a position of strength.

For a third time they knocked and shouted, and that ticked me off. I'd been having a good sleep.

"What is the meaning of this!" I roared. "Cannot a man sleep in his own room?"

For some reason I did say "cannot," rather than "can't." It seemed to have more punch I guess.

For a moment or two there was silence. No more shouting. Then, "Police. Please open the door."

That's better, I thought. Some respect. "You will wait!" I said. "I have to get dressed."

I took my time, buying time to ensure that all was well with my bags, that my typewriter was buried as were my papers and anything else that would tell them my true role there – journalist. I didn't know for sure that my brassiere-hawking friend was right that reporters were keenly unwelcome, but I really didn't want to find out – or see the inside of a Turkish police station or jail. Maybe they suspected I was an arms dealer or whatever.

Assured that all was as good as it could be, and now wearing slacks and shirt, I walked to the door and opened it. Three men stood there, one large fellow and two regular-sized chaps. They did not wear uniforms.

"Now, gentlemen, what seems to be the matter."

"We would like to ask you some questions," one of the two smaller men said, flipping open a card which supposedly was his ID. I couldn't read it but there was a photo.

"Come in, then," and I turned to go into the room.

"Why are you here?" said the same fellow, who did all the talking.

"I am a traveler who paints. I am visiting this region, all of Turkey in fact, to render it in watercolour."

"I don't believe you."

"Well, it is the truth."

"Who have you talked to."

"Very few people, as I have spent most of my time at the seaside, painting. Now I am headed north to the Black Sea for the same reason."

"Your passport, please."

I handed it over. It occupied him for a minute. The others looked at it too, over his shoulder.

A number of other questions followed, such as where else I had been in Turkey, when had I arrived, when would I leave, etc., and I answered them all.

Then, "Open your bags."

This could get tricky, I thought. I carried a big blue packsack with a number of outside pockets, and these I emptied first, beginning with my dirty underwear, which I tossed onto the bed. They pulled back.

Then I turned to a smaller carry-on sack, emptying it.

"The big one," he said.

I opened another pocket, and then an idea hit me. I remembered the Syrian experience.

"Look," I said, "I can prove my story. I'll show you my paintings," and I dug into my bag and tossed a number onto the bed.

Like the border guards before them, the men took some interest in my work, going from one to another.

"OK, so you are painter. Still, open more."

So I did. Then, a minute or two later, he stopped me. He changed course. "That is enough. Sorry to interrupt your sleep, Mr. Bird."

"I understand," and then I said something fortunate: "You have a job to do."

He seized this. "Yes, we have a job to do," looking me in the eye. "Good night."

And they were gone.

I breathed a sigh of relief and went back to sleep. Next morning I was gone too, on the first bus.

CHAPTER 18

Bus ride to T'bilisi

From Elazig the bus snaked its way north to Erzurum which had a frontier flavour about it, like Calgary or Winnipeg must have been like early in the 20th century.

Erzurum is a city in the mountains of northeast Turkey and because of its elevation was cold when I arrived in the afternoon of Friday, March 24. I walked a ways and then caught a bus to the downtown area.

The hotels I expected to see didn't materialize and I plodded along for some blocks, tired, before seeing a sign, Hotel Silver Palace, which had nothing silver or palatial about it. It was a dumpy little place with beetles crawling on the floor and walls that looked like they hadn't been washed or painted in 75 years. But it was only three million lira a night, and he accepted the 2.5 million offered, so I paid $6.25 Cdn or $4 US.

I'd come down with a cold, a nuisance to be sure, and so after a quick meal at a corner eatery I went to my room to sleep. Next day I painted the scene of an old mosque and minaret in the city centre near my restaurant and hotel.

A word about the muezzin, or call of the faithful to prayer. I liked it. It connected with something deep inside me, for no matter the hour, and believe me the call would go out as early as 5 or 6 a.m., I found it pleasant. It was one of the signature sounds of Turkey, of the Middle East in general, for I'd heard the same calls in North Africa years earlier, and liked them just as much then. Say what you will, many Muslims do pray multiple times a day. I recall being awakened one morning by a fellow next door whose early prayers woke me up. For some reason that ticked me off, but the muezzin never did.

Next day, I caught the bus for Trabzon. It arrived there some hours later, at 9:30 that night, after traveling through hilly and barren country that contained few people.

Trabzon was "busy and bright and cosmopolitan," I wrote in my journal. "I felt like I fitted in, not so conspicuous. Russian women with blonde hair known as 'Natashas' – i.e. hookers – were there in number...." At one point at my hotel I was approached by a Natasha, who sought a better life in Turkey. I didn't engage their services and never have had to pay for a woman. Though some might say marriage is a pretty big investment.

I didn't plan to stick around Trabzon long, eager as I was to get into Georgia to find the Chechens who had fled from the Russian bombing of Grozny. That's a story I'd read about in the *Globe and Mail*, but the reporter hadn't been in Georgia to talk to them face to face. I think he'd written it from Moscow. But he'd sure done me a service by tipping me off as to where they were. My goal was to find the refugees and get their story in their own words.

But first I had to get there. That meant a visa, so I visited the Georgian embassy and arranged for that. It gave me 10 days there, enough, I felt, to do the job. I changed hotels before I left, wanting a hot bath, and found Hotel Anil for seven million, a nice room with TV, a view of the harbour and sunrise, and it was clean. I spent two nights there.

There I wrote an article about the Kurds for the Winnipeg Free Press and Globe and Mail, and mailed it. Because I was able to get films developed I included photos to go with the pieces. I also mailed a story to the Deloraine Times & Star, which consistently ran my articles.

On March 28 I left Trabzon on a 7 p.m. bus and prepared to travel and sleep through the night. This would be a long ride, and not an easy one. The ticket had cost me $30 US, "$5 too much," I note in my journal. The bus itself was new and comfortable.

Soon after loading I heard the unmistakable sounds of an Australian accent across the aisle. This was Glen Wakefield, of Perth, and he and I hit it off. He was a good straight shooter who had experienced many of the same things in Turkey that I had. He'd been there for two weeks, in Ankara and other locales.

Our trip to T'bilisi was interesting and worthy of some detail. There were 27 of us making the 19-hour journey. Among them was a beautiful black-haired peasant girl about 22; her mother; four Turkish engineering students who spoke pretty good English; some older men and women who lived in Georgia; maybe two or three Russian hookers; two Azerbaijanis (big boned matronly women wearing colorful head scarves and with more muscle than most Canadian men), and two drivers, who proved to be good guys.

We took our sweet time getting out of Trabzon, as the bus stopped often to pick up people. Glen and I agreed they seemed to be farting around but I guess people don't hurry much in that country. What's the use in any case. And as I later learned, from the students, the drivers were in no hurry to reach the dreaded Georgian border, known for lengthy delays.

Night fell and we soon couldn't see much except the lights in the towns we passed. We knew the Black Sea was close by on our left. The engineering boys were a jolly lot behind us who talked and drank Pepsi and offered us some. The hookers stayed near the front with the old Georgian men (don't think they got much businesss there, but you never know) while the beauty and her mom were in the seats a row ahead of mine across the aisle.

An hour from the Georgian border, the spare driver made his rounds and asked us to cough up $5 US each. The money would buy off the Georgian border officials, who the students said weren't paid regularly. Apparently they got about $12 a month,maybe. Getting out of Turkey alone took about 90 minutes, but that was nothing compared to the Georgian side: there it took us more than three hours. Here's what happened.

We were asked to get off the bus and wait in an outside compound while our passports were checked. The staff and guards seemed very jolly, considering the hour, about midnight. I found out why – vodka.

"Have you heard of Wayne Gretzky?" I asked the man who took our passports.

"Yes – Bure!" he replied, referring to the Vancouver Canucks star, who was Russian, and dubbed the Russian Rocket. One of the students had warned me they'd check the bus and our bags, so I removed my paintings and placed them in the large pocket in the back of my vest. Over that I wore a wool sweater given to me by Mac Colqhoun at Lake Metigoshe.

Now it's 2 a.m. We're allowed into another compound where the bus is parked, and we get on. But it takes 30 minutes for many boxes of fresh flowers, of all things, to be loaded up from a van. Then we are told that each non-Turkish citizen must declare his money at an office. Being at the back, Glen and I waited a long time. Then we end up not getting off the bus at all, as one of the engineers told an official we are his friends, and he maybe assumed we were Turks, or else he didn't want to bother with the work.

So we dodged that bullet and the bus moved ahead a couple of hundred feet to a gate with a guardhouse. Inside was a man who had been drinking for some time. We saw him "sleeping" on a bench.

"Look," says one of the students, animated and out of his seat. "See, he's drunk. You must see!" He will "wake up," it seems, only if we fork over another $5 each. Everyone refused to pay and we sat for another half hour or so. So it's about 3 a.m. now.

Our deputy driver, who had delivered the first sum of baksheesh totaling $135 – a princely sum in this country -- asked the man who received it how to deal with this second request for a bribe. He said sorry, it's not my business.

Finally, with no additional payment from us, we are allowed to go. By this time most of the bus is asleep. We also stopped at three or four customs checkpoints before reaching T'bilisi.

As the sun rose, we had a chance to examine the Georgian countryside, and it was pretty. Some of the hills had been carefully terraced and orchards planted. The predominant colour was green, such a change from the stony barren landscape that predominates in southeast Turkey, or the grayness of its drab cities.

Remember, Georgia had only been open to the world for 10 years, following its break from the Soviet Union. The Russians had polluted it a fair bit, but likely no worse than we do our own lands. It is largely an agricultural land and, as I say, quite lovely.

We stopped for a pee break (or as the Aussies say, a wee break) and I bought a loaf of bread for $1 US. All in all the trip was enjoyable.

When we arrived in T'bilisi at 3 p.m., Glen and I left the autogar, or bus terminal, and looked for a cheap nearby hotel. He was headed to Armenia to visit a lady he had befriended in London while working there. He couldn't have gone directly from Turkey, even though their borders meet, because the Turks hate the Armenians and vice-versa. Their border is closed. The Armenians say the Turks slaughtered thousands of their people in the First World War, while the Turks deny much of the charge. Glen and I shared a room for $5 each and went down for a bite to eat, and I had chicken. After that we had a nap – for a short while. It was 12 hours later when we awoke!

That brings us to March 30. Back at the bus station early today, I "talked" to a clerk about where to find the Chechen refugees. This involved more sign language than English, with my fingers "walking" over the mountains to escape the "Poom! Poom! of the bombs in Grozny. It worked.

"Aahhhh!" said the clerk, recognition dawning. "Ekhmeta!" And he gave me the number of the mini-bus headed that way. It left at 9 a.m. and cost $6. We were stopped at one military checkpoint, but after the trials of Turkey this was old hat. As usual I was taken off the bus. As usual I was questioned in a language I didn't understand. As usual I handed over my passport for a check. As usual I smiled and said I was a Canadian tourist. I apologized for not understanding his words. And as usual, despite the gruffness of the guard and his weapons, I was, once again, a free man.

Two locals smiled kindly as I regained my seat. The bus dropped me off in the town of Ekhmeta, where people stopped and stared as if I'd landed from Mars. I put down my bags and walked a short distance to a pharmacy. "I speak English," I said. "Refugees here?"

They shook their heads.

I was disappointed. Was the bus clerk mistaken? I'd had to trust him. There's a lot of trust involved when you're traveling as I was. You trust your gut and go with what you think is right.

He was right. But the refugees were 15 kilometres farther north, I found out, in a village called Duici.

"Can you speak English?" I asked.

The response was raised shoulders and puzzled looks.

Meanwhile, someone who'd heard my appeals went for help and came back with a piece of paper which a man handed to me: "Hello, I know little English, so follow with this man. I'm waiting for you. Tamuna."

We put my bags in his little car and he took me to the Red Cross office which had been set up to help the Chechens. But when we got there, the woman Tamuna wanted nothing to do with me and shuffled me off to the UN office a few blocks away.

There I met Zurab Elzarov, a field assistant with the United Nations Mobile Conflict Resolution team or UNMCR, there to help repatriate refugees from North Ossetia to Georgia. He was gracious, and when I asked him about a guesthouse of some kind (I'd seen no hotels, it was all houses and small shops), he suggested one two doors down.

But before I left I got some facts and arranged for a later interview. Georgia had 4.5 million people, with 1.7 million of them in the capital. We were in the Caucasus Mountains along the border with Chechnya. There are ethnic tensions in North Ossetia, this region. "Many of them fled to Russia and they want to return now," he said. But they weren't my concern. I wanted the Chechen story.

And I could find them easily, he said, at Duici, where hundreds had taken up residence with friends and family or even strangers. Most people were poor. "There is no income. The factories except a few are not functioning. Most have been looted. You need financing to start them up again and get the raw materials."

The main source of income was farming: you grow something and sell it or barter. Or, he said, you go to Turkey, buy things, and sell them here at a profit. Maybe that's what the flowers were all about.

Another thing he stressed was the integrity of the people; they were strong and honest and hard-working -- and hospitable. Soon enough I would find that out for myself.

And it all began with Zia.

CHAPTER 19

Time with Zia and a tour of Duici;
I meet some refugees and hear their stories

When I think back on it now I realize that my six days in Georgia were among the most special of my 11-week trip. Here I came to find Chechen refugees but found much more. With no guidebook and no expectations I experienced an incredible new country and people who charmed and amazed me.

I initially had misgivings about this trip to Georgia, an uncomfortable sense that it wasn't a good idea. Maybe I was pushing my luck after encounters with police and the army in Kurdish Turkey. My nerves were a little frazzled after the Elazig experience but fortunately I ignored my fears and pushed on. (This is a common theme for me in foreign travel and work – ignore your fears and push on. It's not as easy to do as it sounds, as I generally trust my gut, and figure the fears come from there.)

Next door to the UN office in Ekhmeta I booked a room in a guest house run by a whirling dervish named Zia, a human dynamo. She hustled here and hustled there and always with a smile and purpose. Zia happened to be related to an ethnic Chechen in the village 15 kilometres north to which many refugees had fled. This was quite a bonus for me. It's amazing, isn't it, how our travels unfold in logical and meaningful ways?

Zia was tall, dark, slim, attractive, and about 35, five years younger than myself. And she was a widow. I didn't get the details of her husband's demise, as she didn't speak even 10 words of English. Her two-storey home was comfortable and uncluttered. From the start, she was cheerful and eager to please. I mean she made sure my room was clean, that I had a place to work, that my meals were first rate. I took the room for four nights.

Zia had quite a dramatic flair. When I asked permission to take her photo, it wouldn't do to simply snap a quick picture of her. No no. She insisted on time to put on the right clothes, and she chose the site of her garden, where she struck a dramatic pose by a blossoming tree, as you can see from the photo. I liked her in the way a man likes a doting and eccentric younger sister. She had a boyfriend and my mind never ventured in that direction at all. I was always very focused on my work.

As I brought my journal up to date in my room, I wrote that Zia had gone for some groceries and was "starting a fire here in the kitchen stove. I pay 20 lari a night for a good room and two meals a day. That's $10 US." I always carried some US cash when abroad, and here was a time when it came in very handy.

"Bradley, Bradley!" Zia sang as she scurried from kitchen to stairway to guest room. She radiated health and good cheer. After settling in and having a supper of fresh eggs (the kind with bright yellow yolks and flavour) and wieners, I went for a walk.

Her street was paved but rough; man-hole covers were missing, stolen to be sold, as times were tough in Georgia. The country was struggling to adapt to free enterprise after decades of Communist control.

Most families had gardens, chickens, turkeys, orchards; some had donkeys, horses, cattle. More orchards of apples and cherries and small grain fields sat just outside the town limits, and the Caucasus Mountains sat in the distance. It resembled rural Hungary, Kosovo or even Greece.

Children soon found me and tagged along. "Hello!" they chimed. I smiled and laughed at their bold attempts at English – and wondered if our children would be so bold as to approach and engage a perfect stranger. None appeared malnourished, and none were overweight. Soon a dozen followed, some on battered bikes, most on foot, bright-eyed and voluble.

As we walked, we approached half a dozen women standing and talking – visiting – by the street as their children played. My entourage preceded me, chattering all about the stranger, no doubt, so I smiled and waved a greeting while still at a distance. The women responded warmly and motioned me to sit on a bench. One of them went into her house and returned with coffee and dessert, more than I could eat.

Another went and got an English phrase book. "We welcome you with open hearts," she intoned gravely, and the others laughed.

"The pleasure is all mine," I replied in kind.

"Where are you from? What is your name? How many sisters do you have?" The last one brought a belly-laugh from me and soon many of us were doubled up in laughter. Then a pretty sprig of a girl, like Mary-Lou Who from the Grinch Who Stole Christmas, appeared before me, her arms outstretched with fresh flowers. Tears came for a different reason now.

I planted that little bouquet all over my vest pockets, so as to honour it by wearing it, and the little tyke seemed pleased. Having no children of my own, I was touched in ways these mothers couldn't fathom. As I wiped away some tears and peered through the chain of youngsters around me I saw three men holding back casually across the street.

I asked one of the women, whose husband was out of earshot, if he helped with the children. A little, she said, adding that her job was the children and the house; his job was outside. Simple and clear like it used to be here.

Just then a teenage boy riding bareback came galloping down the lane toward us in an impressive show of horsemanship. "Bravo!" I said, impressed.

After a minute I walked over to the men, shook their hands and said, "Canada."

"Ca-na-da good!" one said.

"Georgia good too," I replied.

If only they knew, I thought, that their simple ordered lives, with their families and friends and home-grown food, their visits and rituals and days of toil in the fields, their lack of high-tech equipment and their modest expectations, make them better off in many ways then we are.

Had we been able to discuss it, they surely would have pointed out the flaws in their community: hydro that's only on a few hours nightly; the paucity of employment; corruption in government; the threat of invasion from Russia; a lack of running water in many areas unless you ran and got it yourself; crumbling infrastructure; petty thievery.

Still, I sensed they were strong in ways that were also very important, human relations and family health.

I slept very well that night.

Next day, March 31, Zia ordered a taxi and we drove down the road to Duici. There we met her cousin, Emzar Machalikashvili. The 46-year-old engineer was born in Duici, part of a series of villages in the Pankisi Gorge, but he lived 18 years or so in Grozny. His parents also lived there – but he lost touch with them after the heavy bombardment by the Russians a year earlier, the intent of which was kill rebels fighting for an independent Chechnya.

Emzar was no rebel, and he was among the men who led about 300 people over the mountains to get here and escape the shelling. The journey took seven days.

At Duici, we entered a different world.

I saw donkeys and horses pulling wooden carts, much like the Red River carts of old. I saw horses dragging timber home for fire wood. Horses also pulled wagons driven by men and women who were just going from place to place. In fact, animal-drawn conveyances far outnumbered motor vehicles in and around Duici. Once I saw a man in a broken down car, head under the hood, while a couple in a horse carriage passed by. As well, chickens and cows roamed freely, on the narrow unpaved streets and elsewhere. Men and boys used two-handed Swede saws to cut wood, as wood stoves were universal.

Emzar and I soon became acquainted despite his lack of English and my ignorance of Russian and Chechen. He walked me around the village, knowing I wanted to capture the culture on film. He was my ticket anywhere.

He often chatted to me in some detail as if I understood him, and I nodded from time to time to let him know I was listening. Near noon we came to a man was cutting wood. He invited us for lunch, which my host may have set up beforehand, and so we entered his home. Simply adorned with beds and carpets in the stone and plaster dwelling, the home had wooden tables and no TV or radio anywhere. A large image of Joseph Stalin, who was born in Georgia, hung high in the porch. On another wall hung a prominent picture of a great mosque in Saudi Arabia.

As the men chatted, I sat, amazed by all I was seeing and hearing. Soon our host's attractive teenage daughter brought us dish after dish and placed them on the table. One held stewed sheep liver and heart; another was greens and onions. Still others held pork bones, pita bread, pieces of beef, and scrambled eggs – and it was all delicious. I ate with keen appreciation.

Topping it off was a glass of vodka, which Emzar and I declined.

The meal and hospitality left us feeling satisfied and ready to walk some more. We left the village and went part way up a mountain to the north. With a sweep of his arm, Emzar showed me the pass that he and dozens of others had taken a year earlier to flee the war.

I was told that some 6,000 people came to this valley, arriving in groups of 200 or so over several months, though 6,000 seems high, given the valley's limited ability to absorb them. To avoid attacks by Russian jets they moved by night and slept by day. Most made it.

Silently, without warning, Russian jets came upon them strafing and dropping bombs, killing 18 in Emzar's group, an interpreter said later. It is possible the pilots mistook the line of refugees for guerrilla fighters, who use the same passes to take R and R in the village. Duici is only about 20 kilometres south of the Chechen border, and fighting sometimes raged only 30 kilometres from the village.

It all left Emzar and others bitter.

Continuing on, we heard the crackle of gunfire. Locals or refugees tested their weapons. Emzar said some of the people keep rifles close by in case the Russians move in. The war, after all, was being fought just over the mountains, and the Russians didn't take kindly to Georgia providing the rebels with rest breaks and sustenance.

Indeed, guns were also kept by the fighters at rest there. I saw some of those young men, and they had a presence and military bearing lacking in the boys and older men. They stood out as they chatted to youth on the street, but I didn't have the language, or maybe even the courage, to speak to them.

Finally Emzar took me to his home, where I met his wife Taisa, who, like him, was born nearby. And like him, she had come over the mountains months earlier.

Taisa was eager to sing me a song, which she and her husband prefaced with an explanation. I've taken their words and combined them here to express what I was told.

"Every country has its own star," they said. "But the star of Chechnya has dropped from the sky and disappeared in the mountains. Chechnya is a beautiful country with rivers and mountains and old people who want to rest on the riverbanks. They sing and they rest but now they have no chance to do this, as they died. Also, the people cannot look after their children or old people properly because of the war, so they died. The young people died before thanking their parents. Also our people had no chance to bury their fathers, mothers, brothers. By the end of the song, everything is ruined in Chechnya. They have no houses and no chance to build new ones. The people are crying."

Her plaintive guitar-like music and singing filled the little house for some minutes.

Then there was a knock at the door.

CHAPTER 20

Emzar and I see a video of the fighting,
And I meet an English translator and other refugees

A man arrived to tell Emzar that a video of some recent fighting in Chechnya was showing that evening. Emzar grabbed his coat and out the door we went. For a journalist, this was a bit of a gift.

The two of us headed toward the movie location, the streets now dark and chilly. It had rained for part of the day but now had stopped.

We entered a small room packed with about 20 people, mostly men and boys. It appeared to be a stone room with whitish walls. In the far corner to the right sat a small TV. There was much quiet chatter among them as we waited for the video to start.

As it came on, we quickly saw Chechen rebels with rocket launchers on their shoulders, firing to blow up a Russian tank from behind a stone wall. We saw the tank burning. There was no introduction, no apparent editing, no titles or anything – just raw footage that anyone might take.

The cameraman stood behind the wall amid shouting and the crack of gunfire. It was a rural location, as there weren't many buildings in sight. The fellow was understandably afraid, as the video jumped around, but much of it was clear. We saw plenty of gunfire and heard lots of shouting. We also saw men who appeared to be Russian prisoners.

At one point we watched a rebel fire his weapon into a body, presumably a Russian, a few feet away. It appeared already dead. The body jerked convulsively, sickeningly, as bullets tore into it.

This was good rebel propaganda, I thought. The youth by my side grinned broadly and said something, which might have been, "Yeah, way to go!"

The video only lasted about six minutes, but it had a powerful impact. The images were raw and gruesome. They revealed a war that some of us had only heard of or seen in glimpses on TV. This was real. As suddenly as it started it was over.

From there, Emzar hustled me over to another house down the street to see another video. This time we watched – believe it or not -- a Claude Van Dam flick called Sudden Death. The juxtaposition was too weird for me and I had to go. But just as I was preparing to leave, somebody said over my shoulder, "How are you?"

I turned to see a middle-aged woman. "You speak English?"

"Yes, I teach English to the children," she said. Her name was Leila Bagakashvili, and her three youngsters were with her.

Now we would get somewhere. I had given up hope of finding anyone to interpret for me, to help me talk to the people.

"Look," I said, "let's go into another room to talk," and we left that awful movie.

"Is this your house?"

"It is not our house," she said. "We have no house." They, too, had fled from Grozny, but not by foot. With her were three children. Islam was 10, Usubi 13, who had grinned beside me during the video's death scene, and Abdul, 3.

I turned first to Islam, a slim, dark-haired boy with short hair. He said he wanted to build houses when he grew up.

"What do you like to do?" I asked. He liked to swim at home in the Asa and Soonja rivers. He also liked to fish. "There are many fish." And he liked to eat them.

He wanted to go home, and didn't especially like this place. Then he said: "If you can do something to stop war in Chechnya, please."

Next I turned to Usubi. Though slight like his brother, he had an older air about him. If possible, he said, they would go to Germany, and his mother agreed. But a major problem for all of the refugees was their Soviet passports. A UN official said they were useless, having been issued by a defunct state. With little money and no proper ID, they were stuck.

Usubi said he wanted to learn German and English

"We have no books," his mother cut in, "no tapes to listen to and study. No dictionary. I had some books but left them in Chechnya."

Usubi said Duici was OK for now but he did not wish to live there. The house we were in had belonged to Leila's late uncle, who left it to a daughter, so there was room for them.

Islam, beside his mother, messily ate a biscuit, and Leila got after him. The boy left the room. Maybe it was just as well, because when I asked Usubi what he wanted to do, the lad was blunt. "I want to kill Putin," he snarled. "They killed our people, Chechens. "He is a professional killer. He is a goat."

It sounded to me like some of the fighters had already got to this boy.

Usubi said a few cousins and his father's cousins had been killed in the Russian bombardment and fighting. He would turn 14 on December 24. Next year, if the war was still on, he wanted to "go next summer in Chechnya, Grozny, and poom! poom!"

"No, please, you are too little for war," said his mother. The boy looked at me and ignored her. He had talked to the men here about the war. "They tell about what they see, bombs, what they see on TV, hear on radio."

Ten years earlier, Georgia had broken away from the Soviet Union and many in the Russian province of Chechnya had sought to do the same. But for Russian President Vladimir Putin the oil and natural gas reserves of Chechnya were too much to lose. And the territory was too close to the bear's heart. Besides, beating up on a few thousand rebels was good press in the presidential election. Resources, territory, image: that's what the war was about.

Changing topic, I turned to Leila and learned the hydro was on only four hours each night. There was no gas. They cooked everything on or in a wood stove.

Given the troubles across the mountains, was there trouble here that she had seen?

No.

"Our people have their own law. Old men get together, sit and discuss all problems. If something bad happens they discuss these problems. They don't call the policeman."

Petty thievery and other crimes took place there as anywhere, she said.

If someone stole a horse, the thief must give back two horses in restitution. If the theft was of household goods, the restitution was three times the value of the booty.

"If I fight and wound somebody," she said, "I must give five cows for five stitches" – a cow per stitch. "That's why there is very little stealing," she said. "They are afraid to break the law."

Their methods were much like those of the Metis in Canada during their buffalo hunts in the 1800s. Then, too, the men met in council and decided the penalties, which all knew beforehand, to encourage compliance with their code of conduct. Humiliation and restoration were major tenets of their law, as they were among the Chechens.

Wait a minute, I said. Is this a Chechen village? Are the people here ethnic Chechens?

Leila said they were, and this was later confirmed by the office manager at the UN office. The UN people called them "Georgian Chechens," he said, because they were "Georgianized." They didn't speak Russian, just Georgian, and were Muslims.

Leila told me Duici had been a Chechen village for 300 years. When the Soviet Union existed, the people of Georgia and Chechnya would visit back and forth. The population of all the villages in the Pankisi Gorge, Duici included, was about 15,000.

Emzar, who was with us, said roadblocks forced him to leave behind one wife and their child. The wife I met and their five children had got out. He said the young people with children came to Duici, leaving behind the old men to look after the animals.

Coming through the mountains last fall, they faced cold and snow and attacks from Russian planes, Emzar said, translated by Leila. Dozens died, including a cousin. The children were crying. Some rivers they crossed using ropes. The planes came every day, but the group hid in the trees and tried to sleep, traveling only at night. Fires were not possible, since they would reveal their location. When they arrived in Duici, carrying some bodies, they were wet and cold, she said. "It was terrible to look at them."

In Chechnya, Leila said, all was ruined. The Russians were using chemical weapons. "The hair comes out. The fingernails come off. Many coughs. There is nothing to eat and the water is terribly polluted." They were thankful to Georgian President Edward Shevardnadze for giving them refuge, they said.

Work is what they needed most of all, they said, besides peace.

The war had begun back in November 1992 when the Russians came in with 150 tanks. They attacked the government house and TV/radio centre.

The conflict was complicated, Emzar said, because some Chechens were supporting the Russians. "They work against the Chechen people and give information to the Russians. We are afraid the war will last a along time and we will have no chance to go home."

Then he made a plea.

"Why can't anybody help us? Chechnya is very little; Russia is big. Nobody does anything to stop the war. Not America, not England, not France. They are afraid of the Russians. Why is this so? In Kosovo they helped the Albanians; nobody helps us."

I spent two days and a night in his little house. He was born in Duici, has land there, but lived and worked for 20 years in Grozny, the way someone born in Brandon might move to Regina to live and work.

Given all that he had seen and done, I felt awkward explaining the politics of the fight, but he asked the question and deserved a square answer.

I told him it was unthinkable for NATO to intervene in Chechnya, on Russian territory. Doing so would risk a third world war. The Russians would respond with great force to protect their homeland, and China might also enter the fray. A nuclear war could result.

Kosovo had been safe for NATO to defend because Serbia was weak, and the Russians would not risk war with the North Americans and Europe to help a minor friend

In short, Chechnya was on its own and would get no help. Emzar accepted my answer and bowed his head.

* * *

Next day, with Leila, I headed out for some interviews.

Adam Mugamai, 69, was a farmer with whiskers and a black cap. He and his family had fled from their home in a village near Grozny. "They bombed our village and wrecked it all," he said. "Rockets attacked," and some people were killed.

He arrived here in mid-October, the previous fall, with his wife, a factory worker, and their six kids. They shared one room.

"With six kids, who wants to live in one room?" he asked. "We want to go to other countries but they won't allow us to."

He had built their home in Chechnya but had no desire to return while war raged. "If I have a chance to go home I will leave tomorrow, but while the war is on I cannot. I walk around this place and I listen to the radio about news in Chechnya."

He has nothing to do, he said; he has no fields.

What is the answer to the war? "If you are in a forest and you meet a bear, what do you want to do first? I have gun to shoot the bear. We are in that position."

What does he want most? "I want the people of the world to live peacefully. But if there are Russians, today their position is in Chechnya. Tomorrow it is Georgia. Some day Canada. Russians are in Cuba."

Leila and I moved on to another little house.

Miriam Aleub was 42 and had 10 children. When I approached and raised my camera to take a quick picture, a toddler in her arms began to scream. She thought my camera was a gun, so I quickly lowered it.

They and her parents were also living in a single room. Blankets on ropes partitioned it off. I saw a wood stove and wooden table and a few beds. "They sleep three or four in a bed," the mother said.

They had enough food, thanks to aid agencies such as the Red Cross and an Islamic group, but no money.

They'd sold flour and sugar for money to buy clothes, Aleub said. All told, though, this was a good place, I said. Did she agree?

"While the Russians are in Chechnya, who wants to go there?" she said through Leila, the interpreter. The soldiers took a man and killed him, she said; it wasn't clear whether this was her husband.

"Who wants to go there to die? We have no house there. Everything is ruined. And we have no money to build a house again."

Even here, she and the old man said, they felt like prisoners. They were not allowed to leave Georgia. "Imagine one month, one year, without dollars," the mother said. "It is impossible to live in such a situation.

"We wait."

* * *

On April 2 I talked to Malkhaz Kortua, office manager at the UN office. He said about 6,000 refugees had arrived in Duici and the half dozen other area villages.

"They want to move, yes, but we can't help them. One month ago (some) wanted to go to Azerbaijan, and they left, but the Azerbaijanis did not allow them in. So now they think the Georgian government is stopping it."

"The main problem is that they have no passports," he said. "They have old Soviet passports but they are cancelled....He who has money and passport can go anywhere they want, no problem."

What is their future?

Two possibilities, he said. In May, when the snow goes, they could return home. Or, they could stay put and wait out the war.

* * *

Spring was beautiful in Duici. The trees were pink and white with blossoms. The land greened up like Turtle Mountain and the winter wheat was 15 centimetres high when I left in early April.

It was a sad day. Sad for Emzar, sad for me, sad for the fact I would likely not see any of them again. Emzar and I exchanged gifts and glances and then I got aboard the waiting, ramshackle bus.

CHAPTER 21

Back to Turkey, and Nina

A large man with beefy jowls and the scent of garlic sat beside me as our bus pulled out of T'bilisi, Georgia. The struggle for the armrest was over early and the prospect of the 20-hour ride to Trabzon, in northeast Turkey, did not cheer me.

I was tired and feeling down. For some days I had been reporting on the Chechen refugees who had fled south to Georgia from the bombardment of Grozny. It was the last of many stories, a sad story, and it affected me.

I was only a week shy of flying home after traveling for eight weeks in five countries, including Kosovo and Kurdish Turkey. My plan was clear: bus it to Trabzon, fly to Athens and escape to the islands to soak in some rays.

Then I met Nina.

She boarded the bus alone, a tall, raven-haired, attractive woman in her 30s. The garlic guy to my left, whom I secretly named The Lout, was loudly engaged in a three-handed game of cards. I watched Nina as she approached in the aisle, dressed in a black leather jacket and jeans. She stopped before the card players and produced her ticket. We were assigned seats by number and The Lout was in her place. Nina said a few words and the game ended; the big man moved farther back. Nina sat down.

For me, things were looking up. But I did nothing, just sat there and peered out into the night. Then Nina asked my name. I looked at her seriously for the first time and was pleased to see a lovely face with dark mysterious eyes, a perfect nose, and full red lips.

"I am Brad," I said. "And you?"

"Nina," she said in her deep voice.

"You speak English?"

"Little."

Her languages were Georgian and Russian. Nina, I learned, was going to Sophia, Bulgaria, a long way to the west, beyond even Istanbul, to help a sister whose daughter was ill. She was not employed, but had taught school for a stint. She had a daughter, 17. Nina enjoyed being a homemaker.

"You house warm?"

"Yes," I assured her.

"Very cold, Georgia."

Times were tough in Georgia. The 10-year-old republic struggled to adjust to a free market and political independence. Pay was poor, jobs few. She asked my business and I told her.

"You have a man?" I asked, surprising myself.

"No," she said.

"Boyfriend?"

"No, no."

It seemed too good to be true. An underlying motive for my three-month odyssey was the faint hope that I might return home with a partner. My brief and unfortunate marriage had ended in divorce a year earlier, and at 41 I was sick of being alone.

Again I surprised myself when I said, slowly and deliberately, pointing with my finger: "You need me, and I need you." For good measure I repeated it. Our eyes locked and we smiled.

Midnight arrived and the interior lights went out. Nina removed her jacket and used it as a blanket. We sat back and waited for sleep. But I couldn't sleep. She was right beside me.

My arms were folded, and my right hand gripped my left arm. Her right arm touched my left one. The sensation was incredible, electric, and I couldn't help myself – I gave her arm a gentle squeeze.

I half expected a kick or slap, but none came. Instead she returned my squeeze with one of her own. That's how we became each other's squeeze.

The night passed pleasantly as we settled in for some innocent coddling like a couple of teenagers. We were in our own world, oblivious to the others, sheltered by the veil of darkness.

Still in darkness we approached the Turkish border and braced for the dreaded delays. On the Georgian side we were herded into an outside enclosure, in temperatures near freezing, where we waited from 3 to 6 a.m. On the way to T'bilisi this ordeal had soured me, but this time I bore it cheerfully, waiting with Nina while she chatted effortlessly with other women on the bus. It had been awhile since I'd felt such joy and inner peace.

At first we tried to hide our feelings for each other from the other passengers. But at about the 12-hour mark in the trip, we gave that up. And as we neared Trabzon, I told the driver my plans had changed. I'd stay on the bus at least until Istanbul, 13 more hours. He laughed loudly. They all started smiling at us: the big-boned Azerbaijani women, the driver's assistant – even The Lout, who I began to see in a more charitable light. He brought us half a magnum of vodka, saying, "Drink! Drink!"

By then Nina and I were inseparable. She wanted to come to Canada. We made plans. I promised to help her. Three times I asked her to let me accompany her to Sophia to meet her sister, but she refused. That should have raised a red flag, but I didn't see it then.

Our parting in Istanbul was tender and I felt so alone after that. I decided not to fly home as scheduled but to stay in Istanbul three more weeks and catch her on her way back; maybe I could get her a visa then. However, the phone number she gave me for Sophia was one digit short, and she got my letter too late. We did not reconnect.

Back in Canada last May, I got her a visa application and mailed all documents. She wrote back, vowing affection and saying I would have to return to Turkey and the Canadian embassy to plead her case. Largely to make this possible, in August I backed out of a teaching position with Frontier School Division, which won me no friends there. But I couldn't phone her. The lines in Georgia were busy or down. Finally, in early December, I had to act: I booked (but did not pay for) flights and got through to her sister in T'bilisi who had phoned me a few times for Nina.

"I am coming for Nina," I said.

"Oh, Bradley, Nina is back with her husband. Her daughter insisted on it."

I was disappointed to hear about the husband. She hadn't mentioned him. And I was sad that what had seemed to right, so natural, wasn't meant to be after all. I must still have some debts to pay. At least it was resolved.

I will always be grateful to Nina for giving me 33 of the happiest hours of my adult life.

CHAPTER 22

I miss a train but all's well that ends well;
Painting with Ilhami Atalay

I'm running down a railway platform with the sinking feeling that the spec of a train in the distance is not going to stop.

With it goes my bag, my coat, my food. Soon it is out of sight.

I felt something close to panic, as the worldly possessions I depended on were rapidly being separated from me.

"That train left without me!" I told the station agent. We were in northern Greece about 30 minutes from Thessaloniki, a city of 1.5 million.

"Don't worry, be happy!" the smiling Greek said. "Express comes in five minutes."

Whew.

I got into this predicament innocently enough. The train on which I had left Larissa that morning had engine trouble and we were told there would be a half-hour wait. So I got off and took my paints along.

The subject I chose was a cluster of dandelions -- a fine plant, good eating and attractive. Forty-five minutes later I looked up -- and the train was still there. Hurriedly I packed up, but not fast enough. The whistle blew, the Bird ran, and the train disappeared.

"My fault," I told the agent. "I paint, forget the time." Showed him the effort and he liked it, as did two others.

"Very nice," and much nodding of heads. Then he phoned the train with my baggage.

"Picasso here forgot to get on," he said in Greek. I picked out the word Picasso. The rest was in Greek. I ended up arriving in Thessaloniki 10 minutes before the train with my baggage, and all was well.

* * *

Hotel Argo is a humble establishment in downtown Thessaloniki. I had stayed there the first time I went through and sought it out for a second round. The others simply wanted too much money -- 7,000 drachmas or about $25. Argo let me have a room for 4,000, or $16.

It's not much of a room, mind you. No toilet. No shower. Three brutal flights up. But it docs have a sink and a window to open and it looks out onto the roof. A grey and white cat, that would have looked like my Jimmy had the grey been black, stood outside and yowled.

Sardines. I had hoarded three cans of sardines, a few hard boiled eggs and some cheese. A peeled egg, an open can of fish and cheese I presented to the cat, who scampered away when I climbed out the window.

Next morning the food was gone and two cats were present. So I went to the harbour and bought a fishing line and bait and proceeded to fish for the cats. I couldn't cook anything myself but they would be pleased. Raw fish are good for them.

While I fished, I talked to some of the thousands of people who strode by on the promenade at the harbour. Women arm in arm, young men in groups, older couples with dogs on leashes -- it's all very much like Winnipeg at the Forks, except for the arm-in-arm bit.

I thought I might meet someone to have supper with, but no luck.

* * *

John and his wife Heni and daughter Marguerita were at the Larissa train station shortly after I arrived. My message had been received and I was set for a day of not having to eat restaurant fare and being able to sleep in a real home. These beautiful people I met coming up the first time -- they are organic farmers.

"You look good," said Heni, a sturdy and sensible woman. She married John, a solid type himself, when they were in agricultural college together. Now they raise olives and chickens and geese and turkeys.

Though they don't have the heart to eat the turkeys. "Not very clever," says John. "They don't even sit to lay eggs. They drop and break." But they like them and their silly "gobble gobble gobble."

We go from the station to pick up his old school chum, Stamous. This bearded and jolly 44-year-old speaks good English and soon we are dining on a platter of mutton and horta (cooked greens) and cheese and Amstel beer. The beer's from Holland and a staple here.

The conversation hums, the food sits well and now I remember one reason why it's so important to have friends. Wish I had more my age near Deloraine. That's a problem.

* * *

Have you ever been thousands of miles from home and not wanted to return? I see some hands raised. Have you ever been thousands of miles from home and simply not got on your scheduled flight? This narrows the field somewhat.

That was my situation on April 10 as I pondered my April 11 return date. As much as I liked my home, and Lake Metigoshe, and Manitoba, and my neighbours and few friends, I did not want to go back.

So I didn't.

I stayed put in Karystos, a town on the Seaside east of Athens and I painted. And deliberately missed my flight. No guilt, no regrets. My plan was sound: return to Istanbul, take a suite for three or four weeks, and accept the offer I received.

Offer? Yes, from a master painter, to study with him, work with him, improve my painting.

It had begun simply enough. I had booked my first organized tour, a day trip around Istanbul to see the sights the last day there. While eating lunch, Gord, a 50-year-old contractor from Bristol, England, said, "Look Brad, an art gallery. Maybe you'd like to check it out."

I did. He knew of my interest in painting because I had asked the guide to stop the bus at an art supply store. I was out of paper.

Up the stairs and into the one-room gallery, whose walls were host to some of the more beautiful paintings I have ever beheld. This was not impressionistic nonsense. These were works of genius. Colours so beautifully melded, shapes so perfectly harmonious, perspective so accurate.

In a corner sat a bearded man with a white smock, a big man who watched me with interest.

"I paint a bit myself. Just an amateur." He looked over my work with a critical eye. "Needs more colour, more colour!! No, no, do not leave this white!!"

But then he said something else. "You could study with me one month. $100. You would improve."

I dismissed this suggestion at the time, but pondered it later. It made sense. I taught painting at the Peace Garden, one of the kids' activities. I needed to improve. He could teach me surely. Plus, there are worse places than Istanbul to park one's keister for a month. I could fish the Bosporus, check out the antiquities, take the bus to the country. And so I returned to Athens intending to leave, decided against it, and now make my way by train back to Istanbul. Should be there tomorrow for another adventure.

CHAPTER 23

*Back in Istanbul, I decide to postpone my departure home
and stay to paint with a Turkish master, Ilhami Atalay*

"Remember me?"

Ilhami Atalay shifts his husky body from the chair from which he
paints in the corner of his second-floor studio. We are in the heart of old
Istanbul.

"I have decided to accept your offer to be your student. Is that offer
still open?"

A smile comes to his bearded face. "Good! Yes, of course you may
paint. I teach you!"

He wears blue trousers and a green cotton long-sleeved shirt with a
black leather vest. His jet-black hair and beard strike a handsome visage
for this 50-year-old Turkish master who has sold hundreds of paintings
worldwide, including many to Canadians.

Then two visitors enter his studio and he welcomes them warmly, his
eyes alive and dancing. "We have many original works of art. This my
daughter made. This is by my son. He has his own gallery."

The South African couple are polite and pleasant and chat about things
a while. I tell them I am about to begin a three-week session as his student
to learn colour and line and composition in watercolour but also charcoal
and oil. Ilhami says it will cost me about $6 Cdn a day.

They smile a lot but buy nothing. "Shish kabob more important than
art," the master laments. "Oh well. We paint!"

My incredible first day of instruction begins without delay. This artist,
whose works suggest Rembrandt and Picasso, and whose larger oils sell for
$10,000 US, launches into a simple piece for my benefit.

Old newspapers cover his table. On these are containers of water, one lightly blackened, one of brown water. He begins with a compass-like tool and plain water using broad bold strokes to outline a sitting Moslem man. (This is a secular country but most are Moslems and the haunting calls to prayer from the minarets outside my Hanaden guesthouse begin at 5 a.m. Last call is around 11 p.m. At that time I'm finishing my daily cool one on the roof watching the ships as they pass along the Bosporus, which links the Black and Mediterranean seas. But I digress.)

With economy of stroke and deftness of touch he outlines the geometric shapes of the body and folded legs of the sitting man. This takes less than a minute. Then he dabs the tool into the medium-tone water and the man comes alive.

The third minute sees a stronger colour used and then a large brush with sweeping quick strokes that blend the colours and lines beautifully. He is a genius.

"Less than five minutes and you are done," I marvel.

"Five minutes and 50 years," he corrects. (Reminds me of Mennonite Pastor Ernie Bergen, formerly of Killarney and The Pas. When I asked him how long it took him to write a sermon he replied, "Two hours and 47 years.")

Two more tourists have seen the art gallery signs on the street below where cafes and carpet shops compete for attention. They also buy nothing. "Shish kabob more important than art," he says again, and shakes his bushy head.

"Now you do exercise," he tells me. I've been there 15 minutes. He has seen my work and knows I need work on people and anatomy. He asks me to sketch four men sitting over a chess game, then paint it.

An hour later, the job complete, he gives it his critical eye. "You can sell. I sell for you." Maybe. "Colour," he says. "Use more colour. Courage. Artist must have courage."

I tell him I feel restricted with the exercise and want to do what he did with the ink and the Moslem man sitting -- quick bold strokes.

Freedom returns as I quickly find the lines of my subject and then add the Indian ink. The picture springs into life. Some background and it is done. Six to eight I do that day. It was Sunday April 16.

I meet his assistant, Emil, who calls himself Cat. "You, Bird, in trouble," Ilhami says. "Cat here!"

Lunch is free. Olives and bread and tea. We eat in harmony. Joke and laugh. Paint in peace.

This is why I came to Europe. Here Europe meets Asia with 12 million people. The Blue Mosque and Hagia Sophia are visible from my rooftop. What a life.

* * *

"Where is my spinach? Where is my spinach?"

Ilhami Atalay tells various visitors to his art gallery-studio the story of his Canadian student who lost his bag of spinach one day.

"I do not know what is spinach!' he says. "I think maybe he lose brush!"

He is a funny man who laughs a lot but is dead serious about his art. Today he had me studying anatomy -- again. To do this I drew studies drawn by Leonardo da Vinci. Not easy. In fact tiring.

Spinach? I cook it in the kitchen there or at my guest house. In the studio, for a typical lunch, we sit around a low table. On it sits a bowl of olives, two loaves of fresh doughy bread, a bowl of honey and glasses of hot tea. Variations include cheese or greens (I bring spinach cooked and tossed in lots of olive oil and lemon juice).

Breakfast is either chorba, which is hot lentil soup and bread; or boiled eggs with cheese and bread and olives.

The mighty olive, good for the heart, is key to the cuisine here as it is in Greece. I seem to thrive on this diet which I supplement with hearts and livers from chickens and goats, or roast chicken, or beef.

A French woman, young and slim and pleasant, came into the gallery as we worked the other day. She really liked my painting of an elephant. "Oh is so nice! I would like!"

"Ten dollars and it is yours."

"But I have no money."

"Surely you have 10 dollars," I say.

"No money." She looks at me with eyes that would melt steel.

"Give me five minutes." I paint her another elephant and present it as a gift. She touches my arm and thanks me.

"You cannot give paintings to all lovely French girls Mr. Spinach," Ilhami says. "No future." I tell him you never know.

I am also painting what I call "passion pictures" of men and women on their knees appealing to God for help. God has certainly helped me on this trip. I give thanks regularly, daily, sometimes hourly. I paint Moslem women in saris (robes). And men. Horses. Dogs. Cats. Lots of cats. Flowers. They are blooming here.

Besides watercolor I am learning use of Indian ink and oil pastels and charcoal. It is a lot of work but I enjoy it. This has been a great trip but it is true -- there really is no place like home. Broke and tired I will return, I hope on May 8 into Winnipeg and then the next day or day after (sister and uncle live there) to Lake Metigoshe and Deloraine.

"Home" has such a nice ring to it.

CHAPTER 24

Strolling Istanbul by night is an illuminating experience

It is 2 a.m. one Sunday morning. I left my windowless little room in Hanedan Guest House to see some of the city by night. Having slept from 7 p.m. to 1 a.m. I am fresh -- certainly fresher than the Aussies and Kiwis who flirt and drink and laugh nearby.

Beer in hand, an Australian throws a playful kick at a Turkish garbage man as he passes by pulling a cart. A tired man in his 60s, he gives me a woebegone glance as I walk up the noisy street in the heart of Old Istanbul, while a Janis Joplin tune rings out.

Shadows fall beautifully along the street, cast by street lamps of iron and bronze, wonderfully ornate. Old Ottoman houses, wooden relics of the Turkish dynasties that ruled here from 1453, still stand, though dilapidated. For about 1,200 years, until 1453, this city, then called Constantinople, was ruled by the Romans.

When Julius Caesar arrived he is said to have exclaimed, "I came, I saw, I can't believe my eyes!" I feel the same way. It's enough to boggle the mind -- enormous mosques, incredible castles, walls of stone 2,000 years old and five metres wide, bronze doors 2,100 years old (in Hagia Sofia, a mosque and former Christian church I see from the rooftop of my guest house), the grand Blue Mosque whose many minarets I view while eating breakfast. These and other antiquities were nobly conceived and brilliantly constructed and have endured war, revolution, earthquakes.

Two cats are nose to nose yowling -- preparing to mate? My passing causes one to pull away, the trance broken. He chases a bit of the other's tail. I hear singing -- Turkish singing, a woman's sad wailing. Toward it I walk, surprised. This seems a poor neighbourhood for a nightclub.

Down an alley strewn with garbage I go and the singing gets louder. At 2:10 a.m. I simply walk in and sit down. A dining room full of middle-upper class Turks in ties and jackets, the women in everything from blue jeans to dresses, drink raki (the national drink, an anise-flavored spirit) and dance. A young man is in the early stages of making love to his date, and they kiss alone on the floor, unaware the others have sat down.

My presence attracts little attention, a few quick glances only. I stay still and unobtrusive.

The five-piece band includes keyboard, drums and two vocalists, the lovely singer who drew me here and a big charismatic fellow who takes his turn at the microphone. The floor fills again.

To my right a lady in jeans starts dancing, waving her arms and hips harmoniously in the Turkish way, sensuously, her every line apparent. The couple at her table clap and shout approvingly. She steals the show from the band.

She seems alone, this dancer. No man. I walk up casually and express my approval of her performance. I am politely received but return to my table. Half an hour later the band quits for the night and the big male singer comes to her table and sits with her.

I set out again; the night is cool but not cold, cloudy but half a moon shines down, providing good illumination. I want the Bosporus, that historic strait linking Russia and the Black Sea to the Marmara Sea in the Mediterranean. I want to see up close the freighters plying their way, the city lights. I want to hear the water lap against the rocks and maybe find a fishing spot.

I meet a fisherman. He wears white rubber boots and a tuque. His pole is four metres long and he has a fire going, a small one, on the concrete walkway beside a major road. It is 11 degrees Celsius but cold for these people. We "talk" by gesture and he has caught nothing. I move on.

Down by the narrows I pass a lighthouse. Across the water is the Asian part of Istanbul. Istanbul's 12 million people live in three sub-cities: Old Istanbul, the new city, and Asian Istanbul. Asia truly meets Europe here. Orientalism meets Christianity here. This is the Paris of the Balkans, the Jerusalem of the region, and it invigorates and soothes a restless soul. I have been on a long journey, and now my work is almost done. I can sit back and observe without stress, without urgency. The bulk of my work is done.

Farther on I go, still hunting a fishing spot. The water is too shallow; I have only line and hook. At 4 a.m. I come to a brightly lit parking lot with a grand view of the strait. The water sparkles with moonlight and city light. Monstrous ships glide by, some with coal, others with people. Lovers in cars use the ever-changing view as a reason to park. Three kiosks offer nuts and shish kabobs but I am the only pedestrian, and I don't want food.

But I see dandelions, lovely and large from the recent rains, and pick a bagful to cook and eat later. A Turk sees this from his kiosk and helps me. I add his pickings to my bag and thank him. We "talk" about how to prepare them. The older people know how but he is 20 and westernized in his eating habits.

Retracing my steps I'm back on my street at 4:45 a.m., as a couple kiss and grope where the Aussies were drinking earlier. They have left, the bar has closed. I buy a loaf of hot brown bread from a bakery whose work has just begun. Twenty cents.

Two men relieve themselves behind a car. "Hello there," I say. "The car seems to have sprung a leak."

One is an Aussie, the other is from Zimbabwe. The tall Zimbabwean talks. "I won't go home until some international force goes in. It is crazy there now under Mugabe. My family all left years ago and live in England."

OK, OK, but not now. I am not on duty.

We wave good-bye. I return to my room for apple tea and brew a pot in the terrace kitchen. At five the call of the faithful erupts from the minaret 100 metres away. I like to hear the call -- "There is only one God and He is Allah. Come and pray and give thanks." I give thanks. Eat my bread. Drink my tea, alone. Dawn breaks, and I sleep.

CHAPTER 25

Tourism police, and parents with a key

The uniformed policeman cuffs the young man sharply on the back of the head and kicks him in the shins. The slim 20-year-old culprit winces and then assumes a sheepish demeanor.

I wasn't supposed to see this but happened to be looking into the hallway at just the right moment from my chair in the senior officer's office. (After that the door was closed.) I was visiting the Tourist Police to register a complaint about an employee at the Hanedan Guest House (now a bed and breakfast). But the talk soon turned to the commander's troubles.

"We got complaints from tourists about a man selling postcards for one million lira. The correct price is 100,000. This kind of thing is a problem."

There are some wonderful Turkish people, but, like any place, some vendors seek to gouge tourists.

For me, it is a daily struggle to try to pay the proper price for everything from a room to a meal to spinach at the market. If you give up, you will end up paying as much for these things as you do at home, and that makes no sense for a lot of reasons: the product is made locally, so it should be cheap and usually is.

But when young man like the one caught gouging for postcards is multiplied, a visit to Turkey becomes tarnished.

It's a different way of doing things; they expect you to haggle. Often when you challenge them on price they will look sheepish and agree that you are right. Some would say cheating is part of this culture, but that would be harsh, though an Australian who taught English here tells me it is just as prevalent in the classroom as it is on the street.

* * *

"And she married the guy. A Turk. Well they moved into an apartment and he gave his parents a key. Can you believe it? A key to their place. They are newlyweds."

Tracy, a young woman from Australia, is telling me and another lady, Val from New Zealand, the story over a meal in a Chinese restaurant in downtown Istanbul.

"And she says, why did you give them a key? Oh it is just a gesture, he said. They won't use it. But they did. The guy's father would show up for breakfast before they were even up, let himself in and everything. His business was just down the street. They would even come over at night without knocking and watch TV. Can you believe it?

"So Krista makes breakfast for the guy, her father in law after all. Then he starts coming for lunch! Just walks in. She walked out of the shower one day with hardly a towel around her and there he was, the father in law. She screamed, told him to get the heck out and phoned her husband.

"I am packing a suitcase. You have a choice -- the key or me. Either we get the key back or I leave. Do you understand? I am fed up with this nonsense."

Well, the man had a delicate problem. He didn't want to offend his parents. But he also liked his wife. So he explained to his parents that knocking before entering was a good thing. The parents kept the key.

They complained to him that his wife wouldn't be creating trouble if she were a good Turkish girl. In the end they worked out the problem, largely because the husband was educated and understanding and able to talk to his parents. I think there is little doubt they were deliberately provoking the poor woman and trying to split them up.

CHAPTER 26

Back in Athens, it's time to count one's blessings after a long trip

I'm in Athens, and have come full circle, 100 days after beginning this trip on Jan. 27, my 41st birthday.

It's been a great trip: five countries, thousands of kilometres, about 30 stories, a dozen or so new friends, 75 paintings, and some close calls just to keep things interesting.

Anka greeted me back with a smile at Hotel Kimon here in Athens. You will recall her as the 20-year-old maid from Romania who came here with her father Peter. He no longer works at the hotel, nor does Dimetri, who is off on a ship somewhere.

Guess who else I saw. The man in black. No, not Johnny Cash, but Father Alexander! Can you believe it? He came for a visit to Athens the same day I did, yesterday. What a coincidence. He's the hermit from Mount Athos who survived an attack with an axe by Albanian bandits.

He was cheerful, the same way I left him 100 days ago. "My life story has been published in Russia!" he told me, beaming. "Yes, a publisher has made a book of it." Quite the self-promoting old priest is Father Alexander.

Went to the orthodox church this Sunday morning, the same one I attended before, and who was there in the upper deck but Father Alexander. In black. The church itself is awesome, filled with painted images of Jesus and the disciples and Mary and others I didn't know.

The service, by the way, is almost totally sung in chant, like Gregorian chant, by the priest and choir. And people stand the whole time. I stayed 45 minutes and people stood the entire time. The atmosphere is not gaudy or filled with icons as some churches are, but rather subdued with dark colours and those large paintings and candles. It lent itself wonderfully to worship, and I gave thanks for a safe trip.

It's sunny and 24 and lovely again. Near the acropolis earlier today I sketched in pencil Hadrian's Arch. The acropolis appears inside the arch, so it makes a nice picture. Yesterday I visited the National Gallery of paintings and marveled at the beauty of so many in ink, pencil, oil and watercolour.

This is it, my last dispatch. A scene from a few minutes ago: I'm sitting on a bench in a city square near a large old church. At the other end of a bench a large middle-aged woman feeds the pigeons bits of crackers. Between us sat two young men, one of whom flung his arms to frighten the birds.

Look out. She tore a strip off him, claimed he did nasty things with people I won't mention, told him to go to a very hot place, and all in all let him know the birds were under her considerable care. He and his friend left soon after. Wisely.

"Dad, I'm bored. Do we have to go?" A nine year old boy from London England says to his father and mother as his younger sister and brother dragged themselves toward the acropolis, one of the world's great sights, in the heat earlier today. When I hear the kids whine it reminds me of how fortunate I am to travel without children. Maybe some day.

Brenda Godard, a lawyer from New Brunswick, and I had supper together last night and then wine at another place after that. Dining with a nice woman is a delightful way to cap a trip to Athens. She works for the UN in the refugee department in Skopje, Macedonia, where I was for a while with the Canadian army. She found my tales of Georgia interesting too. Met her on the terrace of Hotel Kimon, the roof, where one can sit and view the acropolis.

Oh, my travel piece about Athens will run Saturday May 13 in the Free Press, the travel editor tells me by e-mail. I'm pleased. I think a lot of the stories I wrote have run or will run yet. This has been the most successful writing trip I have ever taken.

My favourite part? Kosovo. Those two weeks were filled with stories and incredible scenes and good people. The worst part? There really wasn't one.

CHAPTER 27

Landing in Morocco

My first trip overseas was to North Africa in 1987. To do this I quit my job at the Winnipeg Free Press, studied Middle Eastern Politics and set up some papers as potential markets for my work. For a young man, it was an exciting time.

Sunday Jan. 25, 1987: London, Casablanca, Rabat

This morning I was in London. Now, at 8 p.m., Sunday January 25, 1987, I'm in the Central Hotel in Rabat, the capital of Morocco. This is my first time outside of North America, and I'm pretty pleased.

This hotel is cheap, costing me about $7.50 Cdn. My room is large and comfortable, with old wooden furniture. The drapes and bedspread are a colourful red and green and white and very Arab-looking. There's also a little table, an easy chair, a double bed, side table, large closet, sink and footbath.

I had a good flight here and saw the Pyrenees Mountains while going over Spain from London. The Casa airport was very military, and I had to show my passport six times. My bags were searched. But the people were friendly.

On the bus from the airport to Rabat I saw many strange new things for a man who grew up in Toronto and Manitoba: donkeys pulling carts, herds of sheep, chickens, groves of some kind, likely olives and fruit. And the bus driver drove like the Road Warrior, passing everyone in sight. You sure know you're in a different place, especially with the donkeys pulling carts. The people wear long robes, usually dark coloured, and have tanned faces, and are usually slim and fit looking.

After an unsettled night of waking and sleeping and wondering (what the hell am I doing here – I can't speak French!), I gathered my courage and, reviewing my French phrase book, set out toward the medina, the old Arab town. The cheapest food would be there. It was overcast and about 16 C.

I was standing in the medina, bewildered by the music, the sights, the sounds, when a man introduced himself. For one and a half Dirham he got me a large chunk of brown bread filled with two mashed boiled eggs. For two D, I got "Moroccan whiskey," a glass of hot mint tea with the leaves still in it. Very good. Again, $1 Cdn is about 6 dirham, so 2 d is about 35 cents. So breakfast, including two teas, cost $1.50 US.

His name was Karim. His brother owned a store in the medina, and he works there. The medina is full of shops. He sold leather goods and carpets, as so many of them do. Karim knows some English and wants so much to learn more, so he helps me and I help him. He's about 25, medium height and slim, like most people here. He wants to show me around Rabat.

I find Hotel Central very nice at 45 D a night. I'm sitting by the open window in my room, watching a section of the narrow street walled in by white buildings. A lot of them have little balconies, French style. The big wooden chair I'm sitting in is padded and comfortable, the air here cool and clean. No screen is on the window and there's no apparent need: very few flies.

Tonight I had my first Moroccan bath in a 250-year-old bath house. Some buildings in the medina are1700 years old. I paid 4.5 d (60 cents Cdn) and entered a stone-walled change room where I stripped to my swimsuit. I put my clothes in a basket which was watched, for security, by a man who drank a Coke. The "bath" itself consisted of three rooms about 20 x 10 which are joined by walkways. Everything – floor, walls, air – is very hot. Rubber buckets are available to fill with water from taps. You fill five or six buckets and stake your territory on the floor. There were 10 or so men and boys to a room. Some friends and family members were massaging each other. I saw fathers and sons doing this. Then you wet yourself and wash your hair and rinse off, then repeat, and do the rest of your body. Karim and I stayed about an hour

It seems that Moroccans do not rush at anything. "There is no hurry," I keep getting told. At the end you rinse repeatedly and come out very clean.

499

These baths are an ancient custom that maybe the Romans brought here. There are Roman ruins near Rabat.

I returned to my room this afternoon to rest. I've decided to stay here at least a week. It's pleasant in Rabat and my French is coming along.

Today, Jan. 27, I turn 28. Hallelujah. I went out and had the same breakfast as yesterday, two eggs in bread, with spices, for 42 cents. Karim spotted me as usual and we sat at an open café at an intersection to talk and watch the people go by. A boy of about eight led a blind old man. Both were raggedly dressed, the man in a dark smock, the boy in shirt and dirty trousers. As I watched, a man sitting at a nearby table pressed a few coins into the boy's hand. I called the boy over and gave Karim told me they were very poor and probably slept in the streets. I offered the lad a 10-dirham note ($1.40 Cdn) which he snatched from my grasp. In his eyes was despair, and fleeting disbelief. The expression held as he and the blind man, with his hands on the boy's shoulder, quickly moved on. Later, I had thoughts that I should have given him more.

The medina awakens your senses. Many little shops line the dirt and brick streets. Some offer breads, others eggs, others grains and colourful spices, or meat, leather goods, silver bowls. They specialize. One offers Moroccan shoes (leather slip-ons with nothing behind the heel). A butcher sells sheep heads (a delicacy here) and other cuts. Next to him is a rug merchant, or someone selling nuts. The atmosphere is upbeat and busy, with people calling out what they offer, or approaching visitors like me. The experience is heightened by the fluid and oriental melodies of Moroccan music.

It's a colourful spectacle, and the feeling is a good one. The people here are really alive, often cheerful and clearly at ease with their daily routine. I enjoy being in the old city, or the medina. Cats are fairly common, often thin and scrawny, like some of the people. In the same breath I saw a beggar, hand out in supplication, old and thin, chanting something, and a man in his 30s, also in a robe but clearly well off, who put money into the bony hand. I snapped a photo. Another time I saw a boy with no legs. He had a wooden platform which he wheeled around with his hands, and he was begging on the sidewalk at the time. I've never seen anything like it.

The medina police do not wear guns but have batons, and are friendly to me and others. Karim introduced me to one policeman, who pulled me out of the way of small bulldozer which was digging in the street to replace what looked like sewer pipe. I couldn't hear the machine above the din of talking, shouting, music and other sounds, and was glad of his help. The medina is the market and central meeting place, like our large malls.

I left Karim at 11 a.m. to return to my hotel and on the way was stopped by a Moroccan man. I told him I knew little French. He switched to English. He was dressed in a shabby suit and shirt and lacked a tie. He claimed he thought I was Moroccan (Karim said I looked German, more plausible). And so I met my first North African con man.

He gave me a name, El Khanjausi Aziz, and claimed to live and work for the government (water and forests) in Marrakesh. Over a drink of tea he told me his wife and son were with him in a hotel here in Rabat, and they had just come from Algiers, and earlier from Spain. He claimed to be vacationing when someone broke into their car and stole his wife's purse. He needed 300 dirhams (about $40 Cdn) for gas and food and a hotel bill to get home. He invited me to visit him in Marrakesh. He said he fishes for trout in the mountains, and that hooked me. I gave him the money. He actually gave me an IOU. I figured he needed the money more than I did. I'm quite well fixed.

Well, it's 12:30 now, and I want to visit the Canadian and U.S. embassies this afternoon. As I walked down Mohammed 5 Rue toward the U.S. embassy I was again approached by a local man. This one claimed to be a music professor, and we had coffee. He spoke very little English, but I gathered he claimed to have two homes, in Rabat and Marrakesh (sound a bit familiar?). An hour later, as we walked to the U.S. Embassy, he too asked for 300 dirhams, saying he would pay me back at 5 p.m. (yeah, right). My B.S. meter finally kicked into gear and I told him no. He appealed to me, saying we were friends. I told him he was a stranger to me, and that even in Canada we do not give money freely to strangers just because they ask for it. He got all fussed up and stomped away.

I get to the U.S. Embassy, and it's built like a fortress. Its high stone walls are topped with an iron fence which is spiked. Armed Moroccan guards stand watch. The embassy is built, inside and out, to withstand a siege. Inside the gate I was stopped at the main building by a Moroccan doorman who refused me entry. The two marines in a booth were no help. While we talked, a bubbly and bold British woman came by and asked a marine for Col. Knight. He was not available.

The woman followed me out as I left, and then stopped me and introduced herself as Lorelei Sprott, wife of the British Ambassador. We walked and talked for quite a while, and she even gave me her phone number. She invited me to call her and come to visit. She said she had been here two and a half years but soon would be returning to England, as her husband had been recalled.

At 3:15, back at the hotel, Aziz (who I met this morning) phoned. He said his father is here now and will come tonight at 9:30 to pay me the 300 d. Sounds like a set-up to me. If anyone does show up I'll stay in the hotel lobby near the doorman. Chances are nobody will show at all.

I decided to take the matter to Karim. He advised that if the men showed at all, I would likely get paid, and he said he would come at 9:30 to see how things went. We walked around the new city of Rabat, which is quite beautiful, with a wide central avenue like Paris itself. The French colonized this country and their legacy remains, not only in their language but also in the architecture.

Back in the medina, a "friend" of Karim's arrived, but there was tension between them.

This guy badgered Karim as we walked along, and sometimes their voices were loud. Once, when the man was left behind us briefly at a traffic jam, Karim said to me, "He is a crazy man, very crazy." The man seemed to be begging something of Karim, who remained cool and aloof. The fellow has a face I don't like, a weasel face.

Karim reminds me of a former colleague at the Winnipeg Free Press, Dave Roberts, dependable. He is also Dave's size and shares some of his facial traits and other physical characteristics, both being slim and of medium height.

Karim told me about the five different peoples of Morocco and their character, but stopped when this other guy showed up. He doesn't like the man any more than I do.

Nobody came to Hotel Central tonight. I did meet a Swiss man, however. Patrick gave me a hand phoning home. I talked to mom and dad and told them I was well. Patrick, 22, explained many things about Morocco that will save me time and money. He's studying Arabic here, and he's seen a lot of the country.

Jan. 28, 1987

Today I finally got around to checking into the Canadian embassy. Quite a difference from the U.S. embassy: more an English tea house than a fortress. I met with Naida Lablack, in charge of cultural affairs. I also had a long and interesting chat with the vice-consul, Marcel Cloutier. He told me how to get authorization to enter the Sahara zone as a journalist. I'm working on that now, in my efforts to cover the war.

Tonight after supper in my usual café I walked through the medina amongst the throngs and saw many people begging. It's a pillar of Islam to help the poor, and that's done quite a lot here. Some restaurants provide free food, while better-off people give change, like we do in Canada.

I saw mothers kneeling with babies, begging. I also saw a deformed old man with shrunken legs, lying in the middle of the street, a pitiful sight. He was pitiful to listen to, also. It saddened me to see so many people begging. The local people were inured to it.

Jan. 29, 1987

Yesterday I typed my first letter home. I slept well last night, for the first time here, with few interruptions. Today I went to the Department of Information for permission to enter the war zone. A guy named Roger told me I needed a letter of introduction from the Canadian embassy validating me as a journalist, so I phoned them to set that up. Tomorrow I pick up the letter.

Jan. 30.

I took a taxi de l'ambasse de Canada for an 8 a.m. appointment with madam Lablack, producing my Winnipeg Free Press business card as well as Mr. John Dafoe's letter. He's the editorial page editor I'm here to write for on a freelance basis. I was working as a staff reporter for almost three years in the lifestyles department for editor Ken Gray when I decided to do this instead. Dafoe is an old hand in this business and suggested the Western Sahara as a good starting point.

My letter for the Moroccans is signed by Cloutier. An hour later I arrived at the Department of Information to see Mohamed Abderalim, chief of the press division. With me in his office was Raji Said, a very helpful man who speaks good English and interpreted for us. They approved my papers and said they would begin the process to allow me into the military zone. They said it involves transport by helicopter and has to be approved at various levels, which would take some time. Meanwhile, I'm free to visit the civilian parts of the Sahara if I so choose. And as Raji says, I might meet a colonel in a bar in La'zoun who will talk to me for an interview. To others, I say I'm a student.

As madam Lablack told me, politics are not discussed here. This is an authoritarian country under a king, Hassan II, and not a democracy. To the locals, the king rules, and so be it. There is little opposition. This is formally a constitutional monarchy, but there is no real parliament, she said, and the military is very powerful. Algeria to the east is an enemy, and so the army must be prepared for an attack. What helps them are their close ties with the United States, an ally. The U.S. supplies a lot of military material and advice.

Lablack said the Western Sahara belongs to Moroccans, according to the people here. The Polisario says it belongs to their tribes, and that's why they're mounting a guerilla war in an effort to kick the Moroccans out. Eager to fill a power vacuum and assume control of the region's valuable phosphates, Morocco invaded in 1976 shortly after Spain withdrew, after a century of control. Morocco claims nobody was living there, the Polisario are simply Algerian fighters who moved in to occupy it. In fact, Morocco does occupy the greater portion of Western Sahara, including the port cities. Their great sand walls, utilizing surveillance technologies to observe the Polisario, effectively keep the freedom fighters out. But there are skirmishes, and that's what I'm here to learn about.

After my meeting with the Moroccans (at which I wore my best shirt and tie), I returned to Hotel Central, changed, and walked back to the medina for some food and to find Karim. He showed up as I sat in the central café we use, and we greeted each other. I missed him yesterday as the weather was wet and windy, with heavy rain, and I stayed in a lot. Karim tells me he hasn't seen it rain so hard for 12 years! I sat in a café eating chicken last night and watched it pour down in sheets. The other people looked on happily, and with some surprise. I guess it's good for Morocco's farmers.

Mohammed, a young man who works here at the hotel, found me a photocopier around the corner in a cigar shop. Copies of my letters, 30 pages, cost one dirham each. I mailed them for 10 dirham each. So it all cost 85 d., about $14.45 Cdn, a fair bit. A good job done, however.

Back at the medina, Karim took me on a tour, and I took a lot or pictures. I've got my Pentax K-1000 35-millimetre camera along. A girl about seven tripped while running on the brick road and fell, but shed no tears and uttered not a word of complaint, though she was obviously in pain. Karim comforted her briefly, then she limped away.

I also saw an accident today. A truck hit a moped and knocked it down. There are lots of mopeds here, little two-wheeled motorcycles. I turned to see the moped rider gesturing and talking to the truck driver as if to say, "What's the matter with you!" Somebody broke a large window yesterday at the Air France office near Hotel Central. I suspect it was hit by a car. Repairmen fixed it the same day.

I often see women walking arm-in-arm here, or hand-in-hand. I almost never see men and women walking together. The few I did were likely married. Women in this Muslim country tend to stick together. I see them kiss each other when greeting and they often smile and laugh together on the street. Men, too, stick together, with male friends kissing each other's cheeks for a greeting and sometimes holding arms or hands. It looks queer to me, but that's what they do. I repeat that it is rare to see men and women together on the street or showing affection toward each other.

Speaking of mopeds, they must outnumber cars 100 to one. They're cheaper to buy and operate, obviously, and this is a poor country. I've seen no North American cars, only French or German models, typically Fiat or Volkswagen, Renault or Mercedes, even Audi.

A word on the medina cafes. They're cheap and clean and offer excellent and wholesome food. A lot of locals use them. Tonight for supper I had fried fish in pita break for 2.50d, plus a soup that's popular here for 1.40 d. It has a lamb stock and is thick with chick peas, beans, a few noodles, carrots and potatoes, etc. They serve big bowls of it and it's very popular. The cafes I visit are used to me now, and the owners smile when they see me and hear my pathetic French.

Most of the people I've met here are very kind – in the banks, post office, cafes, hotel. They all help. But I am suspicious of anyone who gets too friendly.

Saturday, Jan. 31, 1987

Last night Karim and I went to the cinema. We saw two movies, Dead Zone and another B flick. The spacious old theatre was built by the French in the 1920s. Loads of leg room! 'No Smoking' signs everywhere but nobody observed them. People here smoke like chimneys. Interesting too is that I saw no women whatsoever in the crowd; it was all men, mostly young men. Dead Zone and the other movie were extremely violent, and the women go to the less violent shows with their husbands, I'm told.

I studied French as usual for a bit and then went for another walk in the medina. I ran into "Jumpin' Jack," a guy who sat with Karim and I in a café last night. He's a little crazy, but claims to have been to Canada (not likely true) and speaks some English. We took a bus to a place called Temara Plage, just 12 kms south of Rabat, where there's a souk, or farmers' market. I got some good shots of people and donkeys, but photos are sensitive things here. Poor people are suspicious and don't like to see foreigners take their picture, figuring we'll profit by it at their expense. Or else that we'll steal their soul with our camera. Jack and I were followed by a man for 20 minutes, but he left when he saw a gendarme.

Morocco is unfriendly sometimes even for Moroccans. The people are more on guard and less relaxed than those in Canada, I find. For lunch we ate liver shish kebabs and tea and bread. The bread here is great, French style like so much else, of course. Then we went back to Rabat. Jack wanted to borrow money but I said no. I did pay for his bus fair and lunch.

Feb. 1, 1987

The weather today was the best I've seen here yet – warm, sunny, with just a bit of breeze. I took advantage of it too to get some pictures: a boy watching cats, a shoe-shine job, an old man, a group of tourists. A few days ago I noticed that the newspaper my breakfast was wrapped in was English, the International Herald Tribune. So I bought one, for eight D. Expensive but good. Today's issue had a story idea I might use here in Rabat: how the war is affecting people here, and how they are more concerned about daily tasks than a 12-year-old struggle in the south.

I walked through the casbah or medina and down to the river, the oued bou regreg, which empties into the Atlantic Ocean. The water was a beautiful sight. Men fished using worms and the same methods used in the Red River of Manitoba. They used a long cane pole and spinning reel, and I watched a six-inch fish being caught. Also toured the Kasbah, an old Portugese fort built around 400 years ago.

I saw Karim this evening and met his uncle, "The Haj," since he went to Mecca in 1955. This will be my final night at Hotel Central. Tomorrow I move into a medina hotel for 21 D ($3.50) instead of 45. Not as spacious, but OK for my needs. Today I also purchased a French comic book, Zembla, about a Tarzan-like character, thinking it might help me with my French.

Monday, Feb. 2, 1987

The bed here is just as good and the light is brighter! I have a desk to work on and a sink to wash in. The only things I lack are a carpet for my feet and a bureau for my clothes. It's a smaller room but quieter than my last one. This morning, however, I was awakened by a rooster crowing! I could have strangled it.

I worked on my story idea some more, and interviewed Karim. He was helpful, and I also set up an interview with Said Raji of the Ministry of Info tomorrow at 8:45 a.m.

Tues. Feb. 7

I interviewed Raji in a quiet café and wrote the story's first draft by 2. But I need to check something with Cloutier of the Canadian embassy, and he's out of town for a week. Bought eight postcards for brothers Bob and Bil and Bruce, Mark Davis, Luis Kaj, Gail Haydon, Kim Bolan of the Vancouver Sun (we went to Western together in J school), and Marion Lepkin of the Free Press. Hope to mail my article out on Thursday, then leave Rabat for Marrakesh and the Sahara.

I feel a little weak today, maybe a bit of a bug. Rested, bought a new nine-volt battery for my radio, as I enjoy the Arab music. Am reading W. Somerset Maugham's *Favourite Stories* at bedtime and enjoying them very much. I don't miss TV at all, but I do miss Herbie and Winston (two stuffed toys mom enjoys). It was 17 C today but felt colder.

CHAPTER 28

Moroccan Travels

<u>February 5, 1987</u>

Today I spent the morning carefully preparing my letters and an article for their 14 destinations. I'm writing on a manual typewriter and mailing materials home. After preparing the original, I took each one to my photocopier friend, but his machine wasn't working so I had to find another. It cost me one dirham per page, 56 total. Then I wrote a wee note to each editor on the first page. The 11 Canadian letters and articles cost four dirham each, the U.S. ones five, so the whole operation cost 115 dirham or $19 Canadian.

This afternoon I called the British Embassy and left a message for Lorelei Sprott, the wife of a British officer. Karim was on an errand for this brother in another city so I won't see him until I return to Rabat in two weeks. He sure has been a help.

This afternoon I went to the cinema and saw two more violent shows, "Hostages" and another. It seems all they get here are violent action movies of very poor quality. I picked up another *International Herald Tribune* (eight D), expensive but worth it. I got my first story idea form that journal, so it could make me hundreds of dollars.

The sky is clear tonight, so I got out my little scope and had a look at the moon. I went downstairs to the office to let "the boys" look too. This medina hotel, called Kasbah Hotel, has its rooms built around a central courtyard which is open to the weather. Hassan, the 22-year-old owner, was quite impressed with my scope. We could see the moon clearly, and its craters. Then we all squeezed into their glassed-in office cubicle to watch TV. The news came on, in Arabic of course. Then I went to bed. Harold, my name for the rooster, is sure to wake me early again.

But before I sleep let me relate for you an incident that took place this afternoon. I was walking down Mohommed V, a main avenue, when I spied a white woman looking at postcards at a sidewalk stand. Beside her, an elderly Moroccan man was chattering at her in Arabic. So I approached and said, "Parlez vous English?"

She said yes and we began to talk. Turned out she's from Boston and is traveling with two Canadian girls from Saskatchewan. She thanked me for intervening. I didn't get her name, as I didn't want to seem too forward. One tends to back off, given the suspicion we have of strangers here.

February 6

Today I was able to overcome that reluctance to get too close to people and it paid off twice. The first time was at the Rabat train station as I waited to board a train for Marrakesh. A young black man sat a few feet from me and I asked him in fractured French the direction to Marrakesh. He said he spoke English, and we were away.

Within seconds we'd exchanged names, and he was Marvin Williams from Florida. He's a U.S. Peace Corp worker based in Yemen. That's a volunteer job, and he's helping to install water tanks and pumps in that arid country. He's in the final week of a three-week vacation.

Four hours later we arrived in Marrakesh at 2:30. We decided to travel together for a couple of days. While looking for our bus, local hustlers approached us, four in succession. One guy swore at Marvin and cursed the U.S.

"Did you tell him to f--- off?" I asked," thinking that might have triggered the venom.

"No, I told him to go away, in Arabic." His tactic is usually to say nothing. From what I see this offends the people more than a simple, "No, merci," which at least acknowledges them.

We caught a bus to the medina square, called Place Djemar El Fna. More young men wanted to "guide" us. Sometimes it can pay to hire such a person, but more often than not it doesn't, and we didn't want or need help, as we weren't typical tourists but travelers.

We took a room at the Mubarack Hotel for 25 D each. It's not nice at all, but it's only for one night. For supper we had couscous, rice-like stuff covered with veggies and a little meat, chicken. With salad it cost 16 D, about $4 Cdn.. I'm including the price so that years from now we can see what things used to cost.

In the square we found snake charmers with cobras, acrobats, and some even weirder sights. Imagine this: a man sitting, with two little toddler girls beside him; in front of him a knife, a turtle, a white bird on a string and a cloth bag with a frog inside. He spoke in Arabic and had a big crowd around him. Bizarre, but it clearly had meaning to the local people.

We also saw a number of children begging, were badgered by more "guides," and then ran into some North Americans, a man and two women, Ted and Catherine from the U.S. and Karen Keddy from Vancouver. Karen told me she's 29 and a nurse-architect, who will start her architecture studies in September. We hit it off. She's blonde, 5-6. She's been traveling alone since October through Europe, mainly Spain and Italy to study the buildings (there's always a reason to see Europe!), and she met Ted and his wife a few weeks ago. She told me quietly she's sick of them, and will soon leave them in Spain.

Karen said she lives in Vancouver, where her father's an engineer, and she's always loved architecture. I bought her supper and got her address. All three are leaving by train for Tangiers, a brutal 12-hour ride. From there the ferry takes them to Spain.

We can see the snow-capped Atlas Mountains in the background here. I've had a thing for the Atlas Mountains since I was a kid, for some reason. I normally dislike mountains, they hem me in, but these appeal for some reason. By the way, the landscape from Rabat to Marrakesh changed from green to flat and stony to brown, dry, rocky and hilly. All told it's only about 200 miles.

Karen told me a cool story. She and her friends had rented a horse-drawn buggy here for a ride when a man began waving frantically to her, so she waved back. At the end, 20 minutes later, he was there, wanting to take her home for supper, etc., but she declined. She said one man offered to pay 50 camels for her hand in marriage. She said she's holding out for 60.

<u>February 7</u>

Today I must send a birthday card to Dad, as he turns 68 on the 17th. Kim has hers on the 24th, and Wally Dennison, a Free Press friend in the business department, will get a card too.

Marvin and I slept well. We each had our own bunk. His first words upon waking were: "The adventure continues." How true. He's about six feet, 185 pounds, and pleasant. I like him. This morning I was about to have my picture taken with a snake around my neck, when the guy says, "20 dirham." I put up my hand to stop Marvin, who was focusing my Pentax K-1000, to haggle the price down to five. Later Marvin told me he took two pictures, one while I was arguing, the other afterwards. Good for him.

We took a bus out to Essaouria on the coast in a rickety old bus. It was primitive. A guy wanted two D for touching my pack as it came off the roof. No way. Some of these people want money for everything.

Next day I had a quick swim in the cold Atlantic. I also set my tent up in a sandy campsite for four dirham. Marvin and I took some photos of fishermen at the port. This is a pleasant little place of about 50,000 people. My tent-site neighbours are a couple with a child from France. He noted that his trip through Morocco eight years ago wasn't nearly as good as his current one, because now he can speak French and talk to the people, who are mostly very kind. Also, he said, Berbers outnumber Arabs by 60 to 40 per cent. Yet the Arabs run the government and most businesses. The Berbers are good people, mostly quiet farmers. As I write this I'm sitting on a wooden box at a Berber family's market stall in the Essaouria medina. The man is sitting on a box four feet away. Around us are potatoes, cauliflowers, oranges, apples, tomatoes, and things I don't know. All around us are people, kids, mopeds, and many more stalls along the street. The Berber man doesn't speak French or English. He's wearing a gray gown-like thing that covers him head to toe, and a white turban, black shoes, no socks. He's about 40, with a good face and square head. No facial hair, glasses or jewelry.

On Feb. 9, as I walked into town for supper, I was approached by a guy speaking English who said he'd show me a good restaurant. "You'll want money, right?" I said. He said no. We went to the place and on the way he said he's from the Rif. Not good. A heavy drug area. A dealer, I thought. Sure enough, as I ate supper, he asked if I wanted to smoke. I said no and he left. They always want something out of you, and I know some of their tricks now. They come on as helpful and kind, but look out.

Marvin returned to Marrakesh today. I enjoyed his company, but it's good to be alone again. He was staying in a hotel. Last night I lay on the beach with my scope and watched the moon and stars. Beautiful.

The dew was heavy and my tent leaked this morning. I got cold and uncomfortable and have decided to trade or sell the tent, as small hotels work best for me. So as I pay today to leave the camp, the guy offers me 100 D for the tent! I took it. That's only $7 less than I paid for it, which was $24. Less weight to carry, more room in my pack. Good!

Beautiful weather the past few days, sunny and warm. Must buy some yogurt, fruit and water for my six-hour bus ride down the coast to Tiznit. I'm on my way to Tan Tan, in the military zone near Western Sahara. That's why I'm here, really. But I sure am enjoying all the stuff that goes with the work, such as the food.

I just ate the most delicious omelet! It had mint leaves or some other spice in it. The bread that came with it was hot. And the tea was great. I just got up from where I was sitting and walked down the avenue a bit and around the corner. The restaurant is small and simple, as the best ones here are.

The bus for Tiznit arrived late, but soon we were headed through the hills. On the way, a Moslem woman asserted herself with some men, after they took "her" curtain and left her boiling in the sun. She gave it to them verbally and yanked the curtain back as she needed it. The man beside her said not a word. Clearly not all Moslem women are submissive.

The land here is barren, rocky and dry, dotted with trees and cultivated only in places. It's also very hilly, with deep valleys. Sheep graze, donkeys pull plows. The hair-pin turns in the road make for an uneasy ride, hard on the gut. The old lady behind me isn't having an easy time. Moaning. At 2 when we stopped for a break she threw up. But she had come prepared with a can. The rest of us left the bus. There was no john at this "garage," so we all just peed in the ditch across the road. Even the women and kids. Back on the road again, and we stopped at 3. She threw up again. At 4, again. At the height of her heaving and retching, the man beside me, bless his heart, gives me an orange. I ate it, as Moroccan oranges are big and delicious. That Berber man, about 20, had given me another orange earlier.

Near Tiznit, we were stopped at a military checkpoint. Armed police let us pass.

At one point the bus stopped for a man who had to pee.

We arrived at Tiznit at 7 p.m., and the bus to La'Youn leaves at 1 a.m., but the office is closed so I'll have to spend the night and day here.

Let me tell you this is desert country like the Badlands of North Dakota, flat, dry and hilly.

Well, it turns out there is no bus to La'Youn. I have to backtrack to Agadir to catch one. I met a nice English couple in their 30s, Mike and Lynn. I filled my canteen and bought some bread to go with my carrots and peanuts, and the bus got under way at 4:30. The ride was spectacular as we wound our way along mountain ridges at a snail's pace. There were no guardrails, and many times the road wasn't paved, just a narrow dirt road and a sharp drop off thousands of feet to the bottom.

After four and a half hours we reached Tafroute, only to find its two cheap hotels full, so Mike and Lynn and I trudged up a hillside to the four-star – 89 dirham for a single, more than my usual rate of 20 or 30; 89 is only $15 Cdn, but I decided to sleep under the stars.

Near the hotel I saw a large German man with a Mercedes Benz sports car. The guy looked rich, and he had a few hangers-on around him with the fancy car. It was one of the few cars I'd seen in quite a while. It was kind of bizarre to see this expensive car and rich guy in such a poor country. I didn't approach him.

There was no sign of rain, and it was cool but not cold, so I found myself a place under a tree, but just as I got snuggled into my sleeping bag a guy walked by and gave me heck, so I had to move. I found a more secluded tree and bedded down. At 2 a.m. I awoke as the wind got up. Then it started to rain. I got up again and managed to find a dry place under a rocky ledge. By 4 the rain had dripped its way into my cave and I was wet, so I scouted around again. Farther up the mountain I climbed, searching, and finally, at the top, found a hideaway between two great rocks. Back I went to get my bag, air mattress and pack. The rest I hid. It's raining; I'm wet. Stopped twice to rest, once to answer nature's call, and I mean No. 2! Finally I collapsed, wet and weary, in my new space, and slept. At 6 the muezzins called the people to prayer, waking me. They are eerie, mystical sirens that go on for half an hour. Then the ravens began to cry. Now my new place is getting wet from windblown rain. Should have paid the lousy $15 and taken a nice room.

At a quarter to eight I head to the hotel, ready to plunk down my 89 dirham. Had to wait in the lobby an hour, till 9. Took a room and had a long, hot shower. The storm raged, with terrific winds, and the power went out. I slept.

Just spoke to a young couple who tried to get back to Tiznit but the road is blocked by three feet of water. I also found out, to my great joy, that four buses a day leave for Agadir. The couple offered me a ride to Agadir in their rental car, and I told them I'd get back to them. The room number he gave me was wrong. Good faith in one breath, deception with the next. That about sums up human relations here.

Wednesday, February 11, 1987

I'm in Agadir, and it's a madhouse, noisy as sin. Across the street from my hotel, the Dakhla, about 60 taxis are line up waiting for fares from the buses. The "gare autocar" was a crazy place to come into, but I'm OK now. This hotel is clean and cheap. The walls are yellow, the carpet clean, the bed firm. The call to prayer has begun as well, adding to the din.

It's Feb. 13 now, and let me tell you, Tan Tan is a hole. I got here after an eight-hour ride from Agadir, and I can't wait to leave for La'Youn, my final stop south, where I hope to find some military man and get an interviews for the Moroccan perspective on the war in the Western Sahara. I want to get back to the civility of Rabat as fast as I can! This is a military zone, and we were stopped again today by soldiers. They ordered four of us foreigners off the bus and examined our passports. The soldiers carried side-arms but no rifles.

Saturday Feb. 14

I took a bus to Agadir today and gave up on La'Youn. Too long a haul for too little in return. I ran into a military guy in Tan Tan and got some of what I needed. Back in Marrakesh now, and it was a noteworthy ride. It began as they all do, with a parade of salesmen tramping through the bus, but today was extra special. They came in swarms: guys hawking bananas, eggs, popcorn, towels. One guy even stood at the front of the bus and told a story, in Arabic, then canvassed for money! Gotta remember they are poor, with no government support network to pay them monthly, no welfare, no UI. They have to be resourceful or starve.

Then, of all things, a young woman came aboard and sat right beside me! She's quite a jolly thing and full of life. She's 22 and studying political economy in Marrakesh. Her name is Fatima El-Halim. She doesn't speak a lot of English but we still managed to cover a lot of ground. She gave me one of her rings and brought us a delicious lunch of baked beef and vegetables. I gave her a couple of Manitoba pins. She talked longer than

I would have liked, as I was very tired. Her father is director of a school division in Agadir. Somehow, she has money.

Feb. 16, 1987

I'm back in Rabat, thank goodness. Enjoyed the train trip, third class, wooden seats. The cars must be 70 years old. Even so, better than the bus: more room, faster, smoother, no greedy luggage boys. I snapped a classic photo of a young man with a noble bearing, and just as I did an old woman stepped into the frame. It's a great photo.

Last night in Marrakesh I pigged out on fish, eating two whole fish fried in oil and battered. Delicious. It's quite a sight at night in the square. Row after row of food stalls, all lighted by lanterns, and an endless variety of food – fish, shish kebobs, beef, sardines, etc., while musicians play and actors perform dances on stage. The darker side was children so poor they pilfered food from your plate when you weren't looking, and adults who beg openly. I gave much of my supper to some kids. You see the local people being generous all the time. Yesterday I bought a pure silk rug for 300 dirham, a burgundy and silver item I really like, and it rolls up into my pack. I'll use it on the hotel room floors to make them homey, and could even use it as a blanket.

Next day I worked on my second story, an analysis piece about why Morocco is in the Western Sahara. I also phoned home for the second time, as it was Dad's birthday. We had a good chat.

Soon after I visited the U.S. Library, where a guard with an Uzi-submachine gun stood outside. I was permitted inside, and was told the press division was down the street. There I met Peter Kovach, a friendly guy who wanted to help. Suggested I press my case with the Moroccans to enter the south on their ticket. I also connected with Marcel Cloutier of the Canadian Embassy, and he suggested I contact the Algerian officials here about visiting Tindouf and the Polisario. I did so and they said it would be no problem, just see the Ministry of Foreign Affairs when I get to Algiers.

The final word on visiting the military zone with the army is no. They say all visits have been stopped while they restructure there, something to do with the construction of another wall to keep the Polisario at bay. At least I went there on my own, and got the lay of the land as best I could.

In my remaining time here I met two Canadians, Sam and Daniel, both students. We checked out the Chellah, the old Roman ruins from the

14th century. Then I met a young German woman who is traveling alone with her baby. She is also pregnant – by a different "friend." One day she would like to have a house, garden and children "all by the same man." For now, she travels to Israel, North Africa, Europe, on the government money she gets for being a single mom. She doesn't like West Germany, thinking the natural environment is being destroyed by industry. She had run out of money and wanted 10 D, about $2 Cdn, from me. Moreover she didn't even have a passport, having given it to her "friend" to take care of, but he'd split. A strange situation, and one I want no involvement in!

February 23, 1987

Peter Kovach has set up a briefing for me with a military man. And I've purchased a plane ticket to Algiers; I leave March 3. It seems the two overland border crossings are closed; these two states aren't friends. The plane fare cost $162 Cdn.

I went to Fes, the oldest imperial city in the Arab world, on Feb. 24, Kim's birthday. It began in 792 as a village. Two hundred thousand people still live in its old medina.

The countryside in this northern part of Morocco is lush and green and filled with orchards and crops. Beautiful.

At Meknes, an elegant woman of 38 or so entered the compartment on the train and sat in the window seat across from me. She wore a black and white striped dress, gold bracelets and a large ring topped by a pearl on the third finger of her right hand. On her left hand was a large wedding ring. Her complexion was dark, her nose a bit large but otherwise she was attractive, if businesslike.

She soon took the initiative and introduced herself as Mme. Aoulad Loubidu, and she spoke only French. I said, as best I could, that I was sorry but spoke little French, Undaunted, she proceeded to use simple words I could understand, and it was most delightful to communicate solely in French. She was on a two-week vacation. She works in a bank in Paris, her home, and said she makes lots of money. She has two kids, a boy and a girl, and showed me pictures. She loves Paris. Her mother lives in Casablanca. Her flight from Paris cost her half price because of links between France and Morocco.

Mdme. Loubidu shared her dates with me, and even her home address. I said I would send her a postcard and she was pleased (I don't think I ever will). The lady was tired, and told me so repeatedly, but she constantly kept the conversation going, even after I tried to let it lapse for her sake.

She found it quite comical that I would stay in a hotel that cost only 21 dirham. Frequently during our three-hour visit she would suddenly break out chuckling and say, "Vingt et un dirhams!" This gave her much joy. She herself was staying at her mother's place for free, so maybe I wasn't the cheap one. When we parted she said, "A bientot," see you.

February 25.

Sept well last night, as usual, and dreamt about my boyhood buddy, Mark Davis. We were kids again and living in Toronto. That's all I recall. I also dreamt that I was a reporter covering President Ronald Reagan. But none of us could get anything out of him – his aides told him not to talk, just draw pictures! It was real quandary in my dream, but sure seems funny now.

Went down to the river to watch men fish and one guy caught a small silver fish. He had a six-foot fiberglass rod with a large spinning reel and 15-pound test line, so he clearly had hopes for bigger quarry. It was lovely, sunny, warm, breezy. To my left I could see the ocean waves break on shore, and hear the dull roar. Across the river was a beach, where kids swam and played. I think that's Sale. A sandy beach also ran behind us, where kids played soccer. Near the ocean was a huge Kasbah, or castle. Overhead, gulls squawked.

Returning to my hotel, I bought three more leather wallets, bringing my total to 11! Gifts. 45 D for three.

On February 26, U.S. Colonel Paul Robert Flebotte, military attaché, gave us a 45-minute briefing on the military situation. He said the Polisario had recently launched the first armored attack in two years. This is likely why the Moroccans refused to take me south.

While waiting for Peter Kovach outside the embassy gate I saw that every vehicle entering, even garbage trucks, was checked for bombs by means of a walk-around inspection using a mirror on the end of a stick. Trunks of cars were also inspected. Inside, four TV monitors are watched around the clock. They're trained on entrances and other vital points. On the embassy roof are sensors, cameras and spotlights.

Tonight I spent some time with Hassan Iazza, 22, and friends at the Kasbah Hotel, and took his photo. He and his friends are Berbers from Tiznit. This may be the last time I see them.

Man, I'm having weird dreams. Dreamt I was a kid again with Kim and our parents and we were in a horse-drawn wagon going I don't know where. I wrote another story about the war in the Western Sahara, showered and slept. Soon I would be there, with any luck.

March 2, 1987

I bused it to Casablanca to be near the airport, but took the opportunity to do some research at an excellent library. On the way I ran into a young man about 17 who spoke very good English. We talked of Canada, Morocco, religion, the war, you name it. When I asked him if the Moroccan people were afraid of King Hassan II, he said no. "The King is afraid of Moroccans," quite an insightful observation, I thought.

He's in his final year of high school and studies English, French, Arabic, Math, Physics and Philosophy. He told me they learn about Plato and others in high school. Logic too. I had to wait until university. English is very hard for him, and he finds his whole schedule rigorous and overwhelming.

The library I targeted is in a mosque. At 2 I returned to the mosque and was able to speak to the library director on the phone. I was allowed in and was able to beef up my knowledge of the area's history. Was told the library was built with Saudi oil money; it's certainly impressive. My letter from Professor St. John at the University of Manitoba, with whom I'm taking a course on the Arab World – sending back an essay as the price of not being in class – was useful here in gaining me access. At 5 I left the library – they had opened it just for me – and waited for a bus. I missed one just as I got to the stop, and was annoyed, but it turned out to be for the best, for then I was able to meet Halima, a slim and attractive young woman who came up behind me as I sat on the curb. My position was not very dignified, but I was tired. I got up, and asked her when the bus was expected. She said at 6

We chatted a bit. She was in her mid-20s, about 5-9. At 6 she tugged at my sleeve and wanted us to walk. Now that was a long way home, and I didn't even know all the turns back to my hotel. I said no, let's wait for the bus. She told me she works in a hotel near there, and lives downtown with her family. Buses came by but were so full we couldn't get aboard. Finally at 6:15 one stopped, pretty full, but we pressed ourselves into the wall of humanity, and I laughed as we did so, it was so comical, like a Charlie Chaplin movie. We pushed and pushed, they all did.

Finally downtown, I asked Halima if she would like to have supper with me. She accepted – but at first I wasn't sure she had. Her answer was long, and I was hoping for a simple "oui." I told her I had 60 D to blow tonight, and she then thought of a nice place for us to go. She took us to a little diner where we had soup and bread, not quite what I had envisioned. And then she insisted on paying for it! I told her no, but she wouldn't listen. We exchanged addresses and left the café.

As we walked to our bus stop she stopped by a man selling socks on the street and bought a nice green and white pair, I assumed for a brother or her father. They were for me!

I kissed her goodbye at the bus stop. She was sweet and nice looking. Maybe I broke the cultural code but I couldn't help it. She had to go home, but not before I showed her how I felt.

So I get back to my hotel and settle into my room. Tomorrow I fly to Algiers. I should get some rest. But there's a party going on down the hall. Quite a racket. I pull on my trousers and shirt and go down to investigate, and it turns out two old guys are sitting in their room, drinking! Now this is a Moslem country where that kind of behaviour is seriously frowned upon, but these guys don't care. One of them gets up and meets me at the door with a big smile, reaches out and hauls me in. So I join them. They had a big platter of chicken on a coffee table and a couple of bottles of wine, which they pour into a glass for me. Next thing I know I'm seriously into the chicken, since the bread and soup with Halima didn't go too far, and the wine is tasting pretty good too and their jokes are kinda funny.

Turns out they were celebrating, in their own way, the 26th anniversary of King Hassan II's ascension to power. The younger man, who had a plump face and a glazed look, told me his buddy had been a soldier at the Normandy D-Day landing on June 6, 1944. I showed him the appropriate respect, shaking his hand and nodding my head, as after all I'm there drinking their wine and eating their bird. They wanted to know if I came from Quebec – everybody here has heard of Quebec – so I tell them no, I'm from Toronto in English Canada, which didn't impress them at all.

This kind of thing goes on for another half hour, more drinking and eating, we finally finish the bird, and then I realize how dog tired I am and the wine isn't helping in that regard, so I get up to leave. It's past midnight now. They wished me well in the manner of brothers saying goodbye to a brother, I recall a hug or two, and then I ambled back to my lonely old room. Next morning my head ached and so did my belly. But I sure had fun with those guys and don't for a second regret our party.

CHAPTER 29

Algiers and the Polisario Front

It is 4 a.m. as I leave the Badre Hotel in old Algiers. To my right a cat is dining on garbage in a darkened alley. Ahead, near the courtyard of the Square du Port Said, a half-dozen people are walking around. This surprises me, given the hour. Others doze. On the sidewalk I count 10 men asleep in their clothes, some on cardboard, a few with blankets. Others sleep in the square itself, on fancy steel benches likely put there by the French years ago. So much for the notion, suggested by an official at the Canadian Embassy, that there are no beggars in Algeria. I've also seen women and children sitting and begging in the streets.

It is Friday, March 13, 1987, the Ides of March. Ronald Reagan is President of the United States. The Edmonton Oilers, led by Wayne Gretzky and Paul Coffey, defeat the Philadelphia Flyers to win the Stanley Cup. Madonna's "Open Your Heart" and Michael Jackson's "Bad" are hot tunes. Back in my hometown, the Winnipeg Free Press is still the old lady of Carlton Street and its managing editor is Murray Burt. The Internet is unheard of, though faster and better computers are coming on all the time. On this trip, though, I still carry a Remington typewriter and am faxing my stories to Mr. Dafoe.

Walking around strange cities in the middle of the night isn't a habit of mine, by the way. On this night I'm heading to the airport to catch a plane to Tindouf in the Sahara Desert. There, in Algerian territory, I'll spend nine days with the Polisario Front guerrillas, who have refugee camps there, near their Western Saharan homeland. This has all been arranged in advance, but getting there could be a problem; the airport bus doesn't arrive. A man called Ali Foudad helps me hail a taxi. It is Allah's will to help strangers, Foudad says. "Also, travelling in a foreign country is difficult. People need to help each other as brothers." He was an English teacher, as luck would have it.

I had a bit of a problem some hours earlier, too, when I misread my watch and imagined I'd missed the plane. Shocked, I jumped out of bed with a start and peed myself, not a great way to begin the day. Or end the night.

The cab pulls up at the airport, where I'm to meet a man called Lamine who has papers authorizing my visit to Tindouf. A week ago I'd walked into the Polisario's office in Algiers and said I wanted to see the war with their soldiers. "No problem," they replied, and a few days later I had clearance. All it took was my Canadian passport and the letter of introduction from Mr. Dafoe. They need the publicity and I want the story, so we need each other. That's the interdependent nature of journalism and politics.

It's an old story of colonialism, this conflict. For almost a century Spain ruled the Sahrawi people in the Spanish Sahara. Wikipedia outlines the history well, noting that after an agreement among the European colonial powers at the Berlin Conference in 1884 on the division of spheres of influence in Africa, Spain seized the Western Sahara and established a protectorate after a series of wars against the local tribes. Spanish rule began to unravel with the wave of decolonization after 1945. Spanish decolonization began rather late, near the end of Francisco Franco's rule. It rapidly and even chaotically divested itself of most of its possessions and by 1974-75 issued promises of a referendum on independence to the Sahrawi people. This pleased the Polisario Front, an organization that had begun fighting the Spanish in 1973.

At the same time, Morocco and Mauritania had historical claims of sovereignty over the territory and argued it was wrongly separated from them by the European powers. The third neighbour of Spanish Sahara, Algeria, viewed these demands with suspicion, influenced by its long-running rivalry with Morocco. After arguing for a process of decolonization guided by the UN, the Algerian government committed itself in 1975 to assisting the Polisario Front, which opposed both Moroccan and Mauritanian claims and demanded full independence.

The UN tried to settle these disputes through a visiting mission in late 1975, as well as a verdict from the International Court of Justice, which said that Western Sahara possessed the right of self-determination. On

November 6, 1975 the Green March into Western Sahara began when 350,000 unarmed Moroccans converged on the city of Tarfaya in southern Morocco and waited for a signal from King Hassan II. The Moroccans, sensing a chance to control of the territory's vast phosphate reserves, marched in and laid claim on the basis of historical ties. When Morocco moved in the Polisario Front fought back, as they had against Spain.

The issue today is handled by the UN, which has tried to set up a referendum to settle the question of whose territory it really is. Since a UN-sponsored ceasefire agreement in 1991, most of the territory has been controlled by Morocco, with the remainder under the control of the Polisario, backed by Algeria. Internationally, major powers such as the United States have taken a generally ambiguous and neutral position on each side's claims, and have pressed both parties to agree on a peaceful resolution.

During my time there in 1987, Algeria supported the Polisario with a safe zone on Algerian turf, where refugee camps were set up at Tindouf. From the camps, Polisario fighters traveled by Land Rover into Western Sahara to harass the Moroccan troops, who were lined up along a sand wall. This wall, built with U.S. help, snaked for hundreds of miles. The frontline of this "low intensity conflict," the wall was my destination.

Lamine enters the airport at 5:12 a.m. A tall thin man with a moustache and black hair, he might have been my brother, we look so much alike. And with his long grey trench coat, he might also be a figure out of a James Bond movie. As he passes by I speak his name. "Voila," he responds, smiling. He hands me a file and walks away. It states my basic passport info, plus a physical description, and is stamped and authorized by "Director of Central Military Security."

Lamine joins a group of men he obviously knows, so I keep my distance. But when I go through to the waiting area after checking my baggage he appears by my side as two policemen examine my papers. "Bon" was all one of them said as he handed them back, giving me a quick glance. No problem. This was easier than getting through the Mohammed V Casa Airport in Morocco. Lamine sits with me just long enough to confirm my date of return, March 20, and wishes me "good trip." While I wait, a nearby soldier plays Hotel California on his ghetto blaster cassette player. Western rock and pop music are big here, as they are in Morocco.

About a third of the people waiting are Algerian soldiers dressed in military fatigues. They look so young; many are in their teens. Another third of the passengers on this plane are men in civilian clothes who otherwise have a military bearing about them, so they may be solders too. The final bunch waiting to board this flight includes me and a delegation of about a dozen well-dressed Arabs, and one woman.

At 6:30 a.m. we board a bus for the plane. The sun is just beginning to rise; it is dark and misty and cool. At the plane it is every man for himself. There are no seat designations, so you sit where you can, the soldiers up front, the delegates in back, and me among the men in the middle. The heat right now, at 8:33, is stifling. The men on either side of me are asleep, one with his hand over his face.

Breakfast is served: a croissant, a bun, and coffee. No butter, jam, fruit or juice. I also ate my second last boiled egg and an orange. One of the men beside me accepts my offer of an orange. A male flight attendant says to me, "You're crazy to do down there. There's a war on." I reply: "Yes, but it's just a little one." At 8:36 we're flying smoothly in this 737 Boeing and the sun is up and bright. Ahead of me is a week in the region around Tindouf.

Above the windows of this plane are replicas of Egyptian pictographs of hunters and animals that might have been made thousands of years ago.

We land in Tindouf at 9:30. From the air, the land is an earth tone, the colour of camels, and mostly flat. I also saw hills and gulleys. This land would resemble southern Manitoba if it were green with black soil. I saw also some small trees.

We disembark and walk to a small airport. About six military trucks, one a rocket launcher, sit idle. Passing through security is easy (we've been thoroughly checked already). A smiling Polisario man takes me to a land rover, but 100 yards into our walk we turn back: in the process of being checked, I left my pack behind.

We leave the airport at 10 a.m., passing easily through two checkpoints, which are the sine quon non of military zones. The landscape becomes flatter and bleaker the longer we drive, with fewer trees and shrubs. The temperature is comfortable, about 21 C. We drive around a wet spot in the road, an artesian well I believe, and shortly after leave the road to follow tracks in the sand. These we follow for some distance, just us and the desert, which in its bleakness is beautiful.

Besides the driver, two other men ride with me in this British Land Rover. One is an Algerian engineer in his late 30s. He speaks some English and we chat.

"You must find it difficult here, not being fluent in French."

"I do. It is difficult."

"How will you talk to the people?" he asks. "How will you work here?"

"I always manage somehow. I stumble along with the French I have, or more usually find someone to translate."

He shrugs, appearing puzzled, perhaps even offended, by a reporter arriving here without fluency in French or Arabic. He said there are few English-speaking people here. I told him all I need is one.

Fifteen minutes after landing I'm greeted in English by Maria, a Sahrawi woman. She helps me fill out the mandatory arrival forms. So right off the bat, I get help. We hop into a Land Rover and less than an hour later arrive at a horse-shoe shaped compound. Its buildings are low and orange, one-storey dwellings with a wall near all the doors and an overhang above them. Along each side of the horseshoe are three rooms. I'm given one of them.

In the centre of the room, which is about 20 feet square, is a coffee table on a red-and-tan wool rug. Seven mattresses sit around the perimeter, and I put my pack near one. Soon a man brings me flask of water.

It's all mine, this room, and I welcome it. For the past five days I've been with a local family in a town south of Algiers, and although I really appreciated their hospitality and company, I do enjoy being free and relatively alone. I really prefer it this way.

At noon a Polisario man comes and beckons me to lunch. We go to a room with tables for six. My table was set for two with a bowl of dates, two types of oil and water and tea. The man returns with a plate of delicious cold potatoes, onions, carrots and olives. I made short work of that. He appeared again with a plate of hot French fries and a large portion of lamb, juicy and delicious. Remembering what Yvon Bouthillette of the Canadian Embassy told me, I left a little food on my place to indicate I was done, because the custom is to keep bringing more if you polish things off.

Five men, including the engineer I talked to during my ride here, come in and sit at a table next to mine. One of them is especially friendly, an Iraqi named Azeed. He smiled and invited me to join them, but I declined, busy with my French grammar book. After lunch we did talk for half an hour. He's about 42, and he, his wife and two children, aged seven and three, have lived for three years in Frankfurt. A geologist, he travels to Libya, Chad, Cameroon, Saudi Arabia, to help people develop water resources. He said he'd be here 10 days. He misses his family already.

"I called my daughter last night and she said, Daddy, come home."

"I said, I have to work so we can by things for you."

"She said, I don't want things, I want you."

In the courtyard of the U-shaped compound we sat in the shade under a palm-leaf shelter. Our talk turned to the Sahara Desert. According to him there are two main reasons for its aridity. One is that it is surrounded by mountains. Any moisture falls on or near the mountains, the Atlas ranges. The other reason for its dryness is global wind patterns, which also help determine rainfall. They are such that the Sahara loses out, as do the parched American deserts of the same latitude.

I asked him why the Sahara became dry in the first place. Some 6,000 years ago it was wet, with grasslands and forests. He explained that the gradually changing position of the Earth with respect to the sun reduced the intensity of sunshine here and affected global weather generally. On the question of whether the "creeping desert" phenomenon was natural or man-made, he said it was both. He added that monoculture – the exclusive use of an area for one crop, such as cotton in Chad or groundnuts in Cameroon – ruins soils. This wasn't realized or cared about by the French colonizers early last century, he said, adding that stripping the forests for fuel and lumber is also promoting desertification.

Erosion is a third problem. Farmers the world over are cutting down trees near fields to expand production. But these trees reduce erosion, which is a natural and ongoing process caused by wind and rain.

A man brings me a second glass of sweet herb tea. Their hospitality is super. I feel at ease here, and I hope they're OK with me.

I worked on letters for much of the afternoon. At 4:20 a Polisario man named Bachir Ahmed came by and offered to give me a tour of some facilities, thinking I wanted to be busy. I told him the truth – I'm tired. I tried to nap but couldn't. I've had very little sleep the last two nights. Besides, today is an Islamic holiday, as he pointed out, so there is no activity. I said I would be ready to work hard tomorrow.

"OK, that is fine," and he smiled. We shook hands again. He told me I'd be spending two days at the refugee camps and three at the front. I ask him if there is a certain risk there.

"Of course," he said. "This is war." A few European journalists have gone with them to the front, he said, but no other Canadians. I'll be the first.

* * *

525

Next day, Saturday March 14, Ahmed and I go to a fort-like compound. On display are weapons they've taken from the Moroccans. There are parts of an aircraft (with Northrop Corp, Norair Division, Hawthorne, California label on the landing gear), bomb casings, heavy machine guns, rifles, a tank, guided missile launchers.

It's quite a display of hardware. There are even land mines, both small anti-personnel ones and larger anti-tank. My photos tell the story. A Polisario man shows me how the smaller mines operate on Duracell batteries. They main and kill both adults and children, leaving limbs mangled and torn in the name of war. Kind of tarnishes the image of the Energizer bunny, doesn't it?

Also on display in this compound, which is about the size of a football field, are about 89 bedraggled men in rows -- Moroccan prisoners of war. I'm told they were taken in the Feb. 25 raid, a major attack. They wear dirty green fatigues. All are slim and bedraggled, some with beards and moustaches. The footwear varies from beat-up shoes or sandals to nothing at all. One wears a green toque, another an Arab-like head wrap, while most are bare-headed. What stands out most of all are the expressions of gloom and sadness. I understand. They are separated now from wives and family, perhaps for years. I wouldn't have enjoyed being displayed like goats at a fair, either.

One man tells me his name is El Boukafrt. He's 30, a sergeant. He said he was taken prisoner in a raid on March 6, eight days ago, at 9:30 a.m. inside the Moroccan wall. The sergeant said his home is in Meknes, where he has children aged one and a half and three. He is a sad looking man; they all are.

"Are there Moroccan soldiers who have joined the Polisario?" I ask.

"Yes," he says, adding it is a hard life for them in hot bunkers, with only one litre of water a day. He and others surrendered to the Polisario.

At the time, I doubted they were POWs. Now, as I look back at the photos and my notes, I believe they were exactly that. This reveals part of the problem of being a young reporter on a foreign assignment: It's good to be skeptical, but sometimes you can go too far. I was 28. Had I truly believed they were POWs I'd have done more interviews with the men, with Ahmed interpreting. The whole experience of being in my first war zone was a little intimidating. North Africa in general was so bizarrely different from what I knew in Canada that it was hard to know what to think of it all. It was hard to know who and what to believe. It wasn't as if I could speak freely to the men. I had to trust an interpreter, who had his own agenda to advance, and that didn't sit well with me either.

I did, however, take many photos of the men and weapons displayed. They include Belgian and Russian rifles, U.S. and Russian ammunition, French, South African and Russian tanks, American machine guns. One gun is identified on its metal plate as a "Browning Machine Gun, manufactured by AC Spark Plug Division, General Motors, Flint, Michigan USA, U.S. No. 800272." There were Chinese machine guns, Spanish heavy mortars, Toyota Jeeps (supposedly taken in a raid Feb. 25, 1987), as well as Austrian, West German and Japanese weapons. Call it a United Nations display of killing power. Ahmed Tahar is the man responsible for this collection, what they call a "museum." He appears in some of my photos, as does Bachir. This is a sobering, saddening spectacle of man's capacity to kill his fellow human beings, and it leaves me feeling disgusted.

* * *

As if they could read my mind, my Polisario hosts take me to a bit of nature to soothe my soul. We come to an agricultural enclosure of about 10 acres. It's green and alive and such a contrast to the dusty desert and gloom I've just seen. Here are row upon row of onions, lettuce, carrots, olive trees, cabbages, sugar beets. "The Jews are not the only ones who can make the desert bloom," I am told. They use only animal dung for fertilizer, no chemicals. Water is from a deep well.

An elaborate irrigation system waters the land and makes this area deliciously cool and green. Salinity of the sandy soil is a major problem, however, and they deal with it in two ways. One is to dig trenches into which the water and salt can collect. Another is to bring in sand or soil of better quality and simply cover the salty soil. Certainly the carrots I see are large and appealing, as are the dates to ripen by summer.

The garden food is distributed solely to the four or five nearby health centres, Bachir says. This garden, which lies in Algerian territory – Tindouf itself is in Algerian territory – was started in 1978. About 15 men work in it. No Polisario men are paid, he tells me. Not the soldiers, the gardeners or even the doctors.

Lunch is a cold plate of delicious potato salad, followed by a hot hamburger-like meat, besides a large helping of cold mashed potato. Clearly potatoes are a staple here, as they are in Canada. Bread and water top off our repast. Small glasses of a sweet tea are brought to me four of five times a day. This is clearly VIP treatment: not because of who I am but what I am – a journalist with the power to take their message to the outside world and influence, however slightly, their cause.

After lunch I slept. For three days a tooth has been aching in my right upper molar area, the same dull continual pain that hit the other side of my mouth just before I left Winnipeg. At that time, Dr. Stein fixed it by filing down the teeth to spread the pressure of the bite. I did the same with a nail file. First, using a flat stick of Juicy Fruit gum, I made an impression. Then I used my flashlight, mirror and file to do the job, and the pain is gone, at least for now.

At 4:30, Ahmed enters and tells me we're going on a tour of three hospitals and will spend the night in a refugee camp. I gather up my few things – camera, film, notebooks, toothbrush – and we set off by Land Rover across the open Sahara. What a bleak, empty, windy region this is. In some places there is no vegetation at all; in others, a few trees or shrubs grow.

We arrive about 5 at Smara refugee camp, home of 36,000 people who were native to the land now occupied by Morocco. I see row upon row of large canvas tents. We drive beyond it and back into the empty Sahara until we come to what I'm told is their biggest hospital here, Martyr Bachir Salea. This 196-bed facility was built in 1976, a year after the Moroccans marched into their land to the west. The hospital has sections for men, women, surgery and convalescence. Its 11 physicians work here in the morning, and then in community clinics each afternoon, on a rotating basis. Moulay Lahssen, 31, director of Martyr Bachir Salea, said that while it has enough equipment, it lacks sufficient materials of various kinds. It also has a dentistry section.

A second hospital is for gynecology. This 122-bed facility deals mainly with pregnancy and related problems. The third hospital is for children. Its 96 beds are for kids with stomach ailments, chest problems and other ailments.

* * *

Back at our guest house in Smara, Ahmed and I chat. He is 32, I learn. I ask him why his people, the Sahrawi, choose to fight instead of live under Moroccan rule. War, after all, is terrible.

"We are a people that are completely different from the Moroccans," he says. "First, we don't speak the same language. We haven't the same customs. And historically, the Sahrawi people have had a really bad impression of the Moroccans. Also there are natural borders between us and Morocco."

He tells me the Sahrawi people lived in nomadic tribes. They raised and herded cattle, sheep and goats, selling them to Moroccans in exchange for sugar, tea and dates. But the trade was often marked by ill will and uneven exchanges, he said.

"They are known among the Sahrawis as people of lies who do not respect Islamic laws. The Sahrawi people are very religious. There is a Sahrawi saying: The West is the place of money; the South, you must visit from time to time; the East is a place of fire; the North (Morocco) you mustn't see because it is evil." Still, there are some Sahrawi people who do support the Moroccans.

"We hate the Moroccans," he said bluntly, adding that civilians with ties to the Polisario were killed or taken to jails when the Moroccans invaded. Cities were bombed by Moroccan planes. There are about 200,000 Sahrawi, he said, half of whom remain in the Western Sahara. The others are in refugee camps such as this one. But they fight from the Western Sahara and in 11 years had attacked mostly military objectives.

The Madrid Agreement of 1976 gave the north to Morocco and the south to Mauritania, which the Sahrawi defeated militarily. Ahmed said he knows they cannot defeat Morocco by force. "We can make pressure on the Moroccans," who are poor, "until they can't continue the war." Polisario morale is superior, he added, because they are fighting for their homeland, while the Moroccans are not.

"The Polisario is ready to die. Why? Because his father and his brother are martyrs. Why? Because maybe his sister or friend is in Moroccan jails."

Later I'm introduced to Senia Ahmed Merhba, the governor of Smara and as such a member of the Polisario Political Bureau. With Ahmed translating, the young woman, who is about 30, explains that Smara is one of four provinces in exile, the others being Ayoune, Dakha and Auserd. Each province has six districts. In each district, five committees are set up to look after health, education, food, justice and commerce (which is local production of food, weaving, rugs, leather, etc.). Each committee has a female chair, and these top managers form the people's council, each camp's executive authority. All the directors and camp presidents form the provincial popular council.

Since the young men are away fighting, Merhba says, "Women do the work in the camps." The secret to their success is their democratic organization, she said, combined with annual assessments and adjustments.

"We have very sacred aims," she said. "Our aims are fixed. Only the methods to achieve them change. We have rights recognized by international organizations. These rights were taken away by a very oppressive country." Their No. 1 goal is to live freely in their own country.

The goals of the Polisario are freedom of choice in their homeland; prosperity, social justice, dignity, and happiness. "The war isn't our aim," Merhba says, "our aim is to achieve these rights and purposes. The war is only a means forced on us. In spite of the war, much effort is made in these areas in order to guarantee the life of our people."

They first arrived in Smara province in December 1975, she said, using tents donated by the Red Cross. At first they didn't even have the means to cook food. Now they use gas and wood from afar, she said. Are things much better now?

"We are surviving, we are not dying," she said. The children are allowed to fight when they feel ready, usually by age 16. There is no fixed age. "They have problems if they are not allowed to fight."

As a group, their problems are many. The first is being away from their homeland, she said. "All the other problems are consequences of this exile." They lack equipment and materials including health equipment, farming equipment, well-digging tools and fertilizers. "We have a lot of water in some places, small quantities in others. Here the water is deep and salty, good for agriculture but not for drinking." The wells are 150 metres deep for water used for farming. Drinking water is hauled by truck to cisterns.

Talk turns to the war. The battle of Feb. 25 she calls a major victory, as they killed many Moroccan soldiers and took many prisoners, who I've already seen, and their weapons. Their own losses, they claim, were limited.

She says it's a war of attrition that favours the Polisario. "No other country can save Morocco from this situation. If time is against you, a very great power is against you. Mostly the Moroccans are in a defensive situation, and the Polisario are free to have the initiative. We want the Moroccans to leave our homeland. We want to establish good relations with them, if they want. Our strategy is a very easy one. We are just a people who want to be independent….If the Moroccans recognize our rights, we are able to finish the war tomorrow."

CHAPTER 30

Polisario Schools

Next day, Sunday, is hot and breezy. Flies are everywhere. They go for the mouth, eyes and ears like bees to honey. They are ubiquitous, inescapable and bloody annoying, infesting the schools, the hospitals, and the living quarters. Only at night is there any escape, when they become sluggish and dormant thanks to the cooler air. In December and January it falls to below zero here at night, while the summer heat reaches to 40 C and more. Right now we're somewhere in between.

This morning I toured schools, a carpet factory, a convalescence centre for children and another large garden. Three schools serve children 4-11. The first and largest is called "June 17 School" in honour of the day in 1970 when the people demonstrated against the Spanish occupation of their homeland.

In the first classroom we enter the children greet me with, "Good morning. Either the total homeland or martyrdom." Ahmed tells me they are learning a poem about heroic men. This school, he says, was a gift from Austria. The 200 students here are educated to their cause. History lessons look at their past struggles, while civics classes study the many "martyrs" who have fallen in the fight. The school's director, Chej Ramada Nass, said they also study reading, dialogue, Islamic recitations, grammar, geography and Spanish, their second language. Their first language is classical Arabic similar to that spoken in Saudi Arabia.

The children themselves are an interesting study. The younger ones, age 3 to 5, play games, look at magazines filled with photos of Sahrawi fighters on camels, and learn local songs. Some have runny noses, but most appear happy and healthy. Their eyes are clear, their faces clean, their clothes neat. The older ones all wear the same uniform, a blue T-shirt and green pants. They are respectful and welcoming. In one large playground, with hundreds of youngsters present, many approached to shake my hand and welcome me. It was quite an experience.

The older ones are disciplined and careful in their work. When I walk into one class of nine year olds, they stand at their teacher's beckoning and sing the familiar greeting: "Good morning. Either the total homeland or martyrdom." They say it with conviction and they know what it means. From the time they are tots, these children are taught the Sahrawi ideology: fight and die if necessary to regain the homeland, for to die in the struggle is honourable. Their flag, their president's image, their many martyrs, patriotic slogans – all are proudly displayed in the schools.

As I write this, sitting cross-legged at my table in the centre of my large room, I peer out the window and see the sun is shining, while the wind howls round the building. I hear nothing else, no people, no sirens, no machines, just the howling wind. I have seen the wind blow sand so thick it looks like a winter white-out. How, I wonder, does the isolation shape these people? The only way in is by air. In these pre-Internet days, with only one TV for all the camps, they are practically marooned on a desert isle.

At school, the children receive two meals a day of bread and water or milk. Their classes run from 9 to 12 and 3 to 6. We visited a large display of student crafts, products of a recent contest like one of our science fairs among the four provinces. There were paintings and drawings of traditional Sahrawian life, showing tents, camels, trees, sand. There were many drawings of "martyrs." There were models of saddles for camels, of tents, leather pouches, even clothes made by the girls, such as sweaters and slacks. We also visited a convalescence centre for malnourished children. They are fed a special diet of milk, eggs and fish, mainly, with vegetables as well, but no fruit. There isn't enough. The kids are ill, I'm told, because there isn't enough good food to go around, the director said. At this centre they eat five times a day, at 8, 10, 1, 3 and 7.

In the carpet factory, women make wool carpets on 10 looms. They also make straw-like mats to use on the sand of their tent floors. I was shown one such tent, the home of a school principal, and it was simply furnished. Luggage sat along one wall while foam mattresses such as my own lined the other. There was one chair. The roof consists of four layers of fabric to insulate against the heat and cold. The final layer is usually cotton but sometimes camel hide. Clay walls about six feet high extend from the walls of some tents, providing some bomb-blast protection if necessary. Their fear is that the Moroccans will attack them here from the air. Because that would risk bringing the powerful Algerians into the war, it isn't likely to happen.

Late in the afternoon, a short drive from my compound, we arrive at Smara's boarding school. Surrounded by clay walls, it is a large centre comprised of many buildings. The director said about 2,000 students aged 9 to 12 study and live here. They live here because there isn't enough room in Smara's other facilities, and because there is water here. The students, I'm told, visit their families for 10-day periods.

The principal of the boarding school says the war is causing psychological problems for some children, especially those whose fathers or uncles have died. These tend to withdraw. Others have problems accepting why they are here, when told constantly their real home is to the west. All of these children were born here. It is the only home they've ever known. I ask one boy, 12-year-old El Abed Mohamed Melainine, where his home is. This boy, president of his class, pauses and looks uneasy as the translator put the question to him, and then says, "The Western Sahara." I get the feeling he wants to say his home is here. Asked if there is a martyr in his family, he says yes, his father, who was killed in 1977. He says he is proud of his father and wants to be a fighter like him. This is hardly surprising, for their education is geared to making them soldiers. Their dorms, for instance, are filled with poster-type images of "martyrs." Political slogans are also popular. "With the gun we will snatch liberty" reads one large banner in Arabic, six feet long. This hangs in a classroom for polio victims. Another poster in a dorm reads, "Freedom and self-determination for the Sahrawi people."

But they decorate with other items too, such as magazine photos of lions, giraffes, leopards and elephants, animals they've never seen. The boys and girls have contests to see who can best decorate their rooms, with the girls often making flowers from paper and material they obtain from older women. About 32 children sleep in each room on steel frame beds which they make up themselves. The rooms are neat and clean.

The director says there is nothing here for the children, in that the environment is a dusty, stony strip of desert, compared to the plants, grasses, animals, birds and even fish they knew back home. And so politics enters the teachings even of biology and zoology. "We have children who have never seen green grass outside of here," he says, pointing to a plot of green they have nurtured in a dormitory courtyard. (As a joke, some of the kids have their pictures taken by it and tell their families they've been to France.) It's no wonder there is no natural grass, by the way: It hasn't rained here in five months.

Visiting one class, I ask the pupils to raise their hands if there are martyrs in their families. Twelve do in a class of 28. The school director asks who wants to be a fighter, and they all raise their hands. At one point, 12-year-old Ab Hila Saal Amor Bachir gives me a beaded necklace she made.

Afterwards, sitting with Ahmed and the director, I ask him to summon the boy whose father had died, 12-year-old El Abed Mohamed Melainine. The slender fellow tells me his favourite game is soccer, his favourite food, eggs, and his best subjects, history and geography. Like his peers, at least by show of hands, he wants to be a soldier. But what if the war is over by the time he is old enough to fight? I ask. Then he'd be a pilot. He does not watch TV. Few do here. There is only one TV in the school, and it is reserved for the children with polio. El Abed's hero, he says, is the Polisario's General Secretary. Asked what he knows of Morocco, he says he knows nothing.

This last statement disturbs me. It is one thing to teach the children about their homeland and the reasons for leaving it, but quite another to neglect basic teachings about their adversary. The "democracy" they speak about is weak, for a true democracy is founded on freedom of speech and expression. It allows ideas to compete. Arab countries generally lack freedom of speech and discussion. It is partly this ignorance and lack of debate which breeds radical fanaticism, for there is little to counter it. A balance of opposing facts and viewpoints is needed here, as it is across the Arab world, as a moderating influence. Like youth the world over, they are eager to embrace a cause and make their mark in life, but this lack of discussion and information almost ensures a sheep-like devotion to what their elders teach.

The school's director places a wrapped gift beside the boy, El Abed. He gives it to me, a little tile plaque with a wooden form of the Western Sahara glued on. Beside this is the school's name. I thank El Abed. Then I tell him some things about Canada. He is a bright, healthy, handsome young man with a ready smile. He would, no doubt, make a good soldier some day. But I hope he doesn't have to.

Above, Sahrawi refugee children in Tindouf, Algeria.

Below, Polisario soldier Ahmed Baba, our guide, prepares tea.
Photos by Brad Bird.

From left, interpreter Bachir Ahmed, driver Sid Ahmed,
Ahmed Baba, and Houcine.

Below, settled for the night. Photos by Brad Bird.

Top, Moroccan prisoners of war held by Polisario. Photo by B. Bird.

Below, Brad Bird with Polisario Commander Aissa Ali Moussa at the front, looking toward the Moroccan wall, on March 17, 1987.

Two Polisario men with some of the weapons taken from the Moroccan army in raids. Many anti-personnel and anti-vehicle land mines, rifles, and other items were displayed with their prisoners of war in a compound close to Tindouf, Algeria, near the Western Sahara. Brad traveled with Polisario soldiers for some days, sleeping under the stars and visiting the front, where shelling took place.

Bird in Tripoli, Libya, April 18, 1987.

CHAPTER 31

Toward the front

It is March 16, a day of much activity. I'm in the Western Sahara only 40 kilometres from the Moroccan wall, which forms the front of this little war. It's 7 p.m. and we're camped in a grassy and lightly treed area, much different from the moonscape barrenness of the refugee camps. I'm with seven Polisario men and we got here by Land Rover after an eight-hour trip across the open desert, which offered up some spectacular vistas. Now I'd better back up and tell you what happened.

Ahmed approached me at breakfast to say we were heading out. He asked me to sign a waiver freeing the Polisario of any liability should I be harmed in the war zone. I did. A little thing, this, but let me tell you, as I held it in my hands, read it and signed it, it brought home the fact I'm not in Winnipeg anymore.

I tossed my blue pack into the back of their four-wheel drive British Land Rover, where two barrels of water, a box of food, blankets and miscellaneous other items already sat. This they cover with a tarp, which in turn is covered by green nylon netting for camouflage. The tan-coloured truck has no windshield, no windows of any sort, and no roof! That's so there's no reflection for the Moroccan pilots to see. It'll be a breezy ride for sure, and I've never much liked convertibles. As we load up, a few drops of rain fall, and I pull the zipper up a little tighter on my leather jacket.

Our driver is Sid Ahmed, 28, a slender man with darting eyes. He always seems to be looking, likely for those planes I alluded to. With us also is the interpreter, Bachir Ahmed, my main helper whom you've already met. Riding shotgun – literally – are the cook, Houcine, and our guide, Ahmed Baba. Baba is 36, a stocky battle-hardened fellow with an easy grin. He wears an army cap, while Houcine has the traditional Arab headwrap. All four wear coats. He and Houcine carry battle-worn Kalashnikov automatic rifles with scratched wooden stocks. Another such rifle sits directly in front of the driver where the windshield would normally be. With these men I'll spend the next nine days.

It's cool as we head out, and, like the others, I've got on practically every stitch of clothing I own. With the sun to our left, we head south southwest across a bleak and stony landscape, at a bumpy rate of 40 km/hour. At first the track in the sand is clear, but as we proceed we turn off into a less traveled area. Soon we navigate around rocks the size of your head and fist-sized stones, and slow to a crawl. Tufts of greenery begin to appear, a few trees, some grass. Then nothing; it constantly changes. Forget the classic image of sand dunes: The Sahara I see is rugged, ever changing, and we pass escarpments and boulders, at one point a small lake. Over the course of the day we descend four escarpments of 60-feet or more each.

Shortly after noon we stop near a tree to relieve ourselves, and then proceed on. Sometimes the track is clear, sometimes not. Baba bends forward to give directions to Ahmed from time to time as I sit in the front, between the driver and interpreter. They speak in their Arabic tongue. Once we bog down in sand, and the driver gets out to engage the front wheels, going to each in turn. We then churn free in four-wheel drive.

At 1:45 the men are excited as they see a flock of four partridge-like birds. We stop, and Baba gets out to shoot. The Kalashnikov assault rifle is intended for short-range killing. It's notoriously inaccurate at any distance. Baba shows no sign of disappointment as his shots go wide, about 100 metres away. The other men say nothing and I follow their example. A few minutes later we stop for lunch in a grassy area near trees. The driver soon has a small fire going and water on the boil, as tea is a staple here, as it is in Morocco. We also eat delicious brown bread and Finnish cheese from a tin (Penguin Processed Cheese). Also there is a tasty mix of noodles and sardines, from Poland. Milk comes out of a tin from France. It's a real United Nations meal!

Driving on, we soon approach our first sign of people in six hours. We see a large canvas tent and some men talking. Farther on we see six camels, which are raised for their milk and meat. Bachir Ahmed tells me these are the army's animals. At 5, the driver beside me stops on a hill and, without warning, fires a shot, momentarily deafening me. (I'm a little ticked.) There is no immediate answer.

"This is our rendezvous with the Polisario," Ahmed tells me. But soon we drive on, and then see a truck in another grassy and treed area and pull up to about 50 metres of it. Houcine gets out and talks to them and brings back coals to make a fire for tea. Always tea! The British and Moroccans have nothing on these people when it comes to tea, believe me. And it is always carefully prepared.

First the leaves are placed in a pot, which is heated over coals. They use green tea and small glasses from France, like the Moroccans. For some reason they sometimes dump the first pot of tea in the sand. A second pot is put on to boil, this one with sugar added. Then the tea is poured back and forth to air it, from up high, for maybe three minutes. This mixes the sugar, I'm told. They like it sweet, too sweet for me, and they typically drink three glasses each, sometimes as many as 10. These people do not hurry.

While they drink, I sit in the shade of a tree. We've been in the wind and sun all day. It's been darned cold at times. I used Tropic Tan oil for protection. Right now I'm warm, under this tree about eight feet high. The grass -- where there is grass -- can be three feet high, and the seeds can be eaten when dried, they say. The guide, Baba, who I've nicknamed Kit Carson, tells me through Ahmed that we're about 40 kms from the sand wall the Moroccans built to keep them out. Baba is a friendly fellow, often wearing a smile, while the interpreter is more serious. The driver's a bit spooky, always looking about, especially into the sky, as if expecting some disaster to rain down upon us. So far we've seen no planes.

Half an hour after we first saw the truck, men come over and we all shake hands. They chant to each other various Arabic greetings. "Humdalla, inchalla, hallabus" etc., over and over for about 20 seconds. Then they talk and laugh. "Hallabus" means how are you?, while inchalla means Allah is great or something like it. But this is not the party with whom we need to rendezvous. Three of the men take our truck and drive off, in search of the commander we are supposed to meet. Five of us sit and wait, drinking tea. They tell me there are snakes, lizards, scorpions, foxes and hares here. On our way we saw one hawk. Bachir Ahmed is much happier and at ease here than he was back at the refugee camp. There he was taciturn and moody, but here he smiles more and talks more and clearly enjoys being in this place and with these men. Back in the compound he would say, in response to my questions, "Later," or "You'll speak to men about that." Here he's

541

easier to be around. I told him that I camp like this back in Canada. "It is a good life," he replied.

I've been watching one of the new men. He's young, bare-footed, with bristly black hair, no moustache, no rings, no watch, like the others. He accepts my request for an interview and I learn his name is Chia Baiba, and he's 22. He comes from Awserd in the Western Sahara. He has been fighting for two years and has seen many battles. He believes he has killed a number of Moroccan soldiers. "I can't give you a number. I saw them, I fired." He is single, and doesn't have a girl friend. His father died in 1978 at age 70, while his mother lives back in Smara. He last saw her a month ago for 15 days. As a soldier he gets two weeks' leave every three months. Though some men use lucky charms, he has none. "I fight for my country, my homeland," he says, putting his luck in his cause. "I would like to return there." He and the rest of his family and village left in 1979 when he was 14. That's when Mauritania pulled out of the dispute and Morocco began to occupy the south as well as the north of Western Sahara. Baiba tells me he is happy as a soldier and is not afraid to die. "All people must die sometime." Even if the war ends soon, he wants to remain a soldier.

We talk about the big battles of February 25 and March 6, which made the New York Times and other papers. In the February fight he took one prisoner while the man was fleeing. The Polisario drove about 15 kilometres inside the wall in both battles and claim to have killed 213 Moroccan soldiers the first time, 120 the second. Their attacks came in response to Morocco's building of walls to keep them out, he said. The point was: the walls won't keep us out if we choose to breach them. I ask him what he would do if a Moroccan soldier appeared before us now. "Take him prisoner," he says, as he would be surrendering himself.

At 6:30 p.m. our truck returns. It is decided that we will eat supper here, then travel on. Ahmed shovels away a grassy spot and out comes a small snake, which he cuts in half with his spade. This is a source of mirth for him and the others. I feel for the snake.

After rice and herrings, bread and tea, we leave, at first with headlights on. Soon they they are turned off. Reading the stars, with the Big Dipper at one o'clock and the North Star at 11, I see we're heading north, closer still to the wall. Near 10 p.m. we stop on a sandy plain to make camp. We hear a "Boom!" and then another. "You hear that?" asks Ahmed. "The Polisario are shelling the Moroccans." Not "we" are shelling the Moroccans but "The Polisario," which separates him from the group, though he is one of them, I thought. Maybe he isn't. I look to Baba, and he says we are about 10 kilometres or less from the wall now. The men make a fire and keep their guns close. We lay out the large tarp and a blanket and put our sleeping bags on top. I crawl in, fully clothed, for it's cold, and will get colder. The night sky is brilliantly bright, the stars shinier and "closer" than I've ever seen them before. As I fall to sleep, the men sit and chat around their fire.

Next day, March 17, I awake at 7:30 and look around. A Kalashnikov lies two feet from me near a sleeping soldier. One man is up saying his prayers and bowing while kneeling in the Arab way. This is quite a sight in the early morning light. I get up and pack up my blankets as another man makes tea. For me, this is the ultimate camping adventure, being with guerrilla fighters in war. We're not out here fishing or hunting deer. We're here because these men wish to recover their homeland and live by their own rule. To think that some must fight and die for such a thing makes me realize how lucky we are in Canada. We take so much for granted, including the security of our territory and the friendship of our American neighbours.

After breakfast we move a short distance into hills, for we still await the rendezvous with a regional commander. To kill time, one man shows me the action and safety of the Kalashnikov rifle. Another shows me wild camoune, a spice used in tea, and we use it in ours. I decide to interview our guide, Ahmed Baba, who I've dubbed Kit Carson. This tough and stocky fellow tells me he's 36 and has been fighting for 12 years. So what's the secret to staying alive? "It depends on God," he says. He has six children and is married to a lady named Fatimetou. He last saw her a month ago, and he misses his family very much. He gives me the standard statement about fighting for his homeland, and says the Moroccans, when they moved in, killed some people he knew and took their things. A friend of his, Sidi Dof, was one of those imprisoned and then killed, he says.

Before the war, Baba raised and traded cattle. He was a merchant. He lived both nomadically and in town. Under Spanish rule "it was a bad life," he says, as "people had to work hard to guarantee their life." Many were forced out of the country for being political. Asked what he wants out of life, Baba says the first thing is to live with no faults, or sins, toward God. The next thing he wants is independence and freedom. "And I wish that you would explain this to the people." I'm trying to do that now, Baba. What he fears most is God, for he is all-powerful. I ask him if he thinks he is angering God by killing fellow Muslims. "We are not oppressors. We are oppressed. We were invaded by a foreign power," he says, "and God doesn't help oppressors." Just then two loud booms are heard in the distance. It's a quarter to 12, noon. Baba thinks the war will be won using political and military means. "Our cause is just. The legal people support us."

I don't eat much lunch, telling the men I feel a little ill. I take two Bufferin. The commander still has not arrived. The driver asks me whether Canadians know about this war, and I say some do. He asks me for the Moroccans' view of the war, and I reply that to them, this land is their land, no question. Ahmed asks me if I can stay longer than a week, and I say maybe. Right now I don't feel well.

We pack up and move on, closer to the wall. At a shelter made of thorn bushes the men pile out and pick black berries, and give a few to me. Taste good. I seize the chance to gargle with salt and water and take some vitamins. The driver brings me a green twig and shows me how to chew it and clean my teeth with it. We hear the wind in the trees and the grass but otherwise the desert is silent, but for the occasional boom! from the front. While two men curl up and nap, two others, including the translator Ahmed, walk toward the front with their rifles.

I give the guide, Kit Carson, my only orange to divide among the men. They appreciated it and insisted I eat some too. I feel good about being here. I believe I'm doing reporting that matters. Mr. Dafoe, I'm sure, will find some of what I have to offer him of value.

It was Dafoe, by the way, who suggested I come here in the first place. I'd walked into his office one day the previous summer of 1986 and told him what I really wanted to do – be a foreign correspondent, at least for a while. He understood, and suggested the "low intensity conflict" in the Western Sahara as a good place to start. He told me that if he had a chance to do it all over again, he'd spend time abroad as well. But he was about 60, and nearing retirement, a respected voice of reason and analysis. He won two National Newspaper Awards for editorial writing. For a long time he had his own political column in the Globe and Mail. Dafoe is related to the great John W. Dafoe who was editor of the Winnipeg Free Press for most of the first half of the 20th century, a respected voice on national and international affairs, the most influential Canadian journalist of his era. I didn't want to disappoint this Dafoe and do shoddy work, so I did the best I could.

He was pretty blunt that if I wanted to do something like this, I had to strike out on my own. The Free Press wouldn't send me or anyone else to a place like North Africa for reasons of cost alone. So I quit my job as an arts reporter at the end of August and enrolled in a Middle East Politics class at the U of Manitoba, and studied up on the region. Professor Peter St. John allowed me to leave his Middle East course after Christmas on the condition I write to the class regularly and mail in a research paper, so I was saddled with that as well, but did so. It might have been a crazy move to quit a well-paid job for a dream, but at least I'm here living my dream while I'm unmarried and free to do so. It feels great to be among men and women fighting for their political independence, instead of just reading about it in a political science course. Every day is rich with experiences, which is why I'm writing this memoir.

But even exciting times have dull moments, and right now we were still waiting for the commander. At mid-afternoon the driver, Sid Ahmed, wakes up from his nap. Right now he's cleaning his pipe. The cook, Houcine, is sitting and waiting for water to boil for tea. They and a fellow I don't know are wearing gray jackets with hoods, and have taken off their socks and shoes. I have too. I feel at ease in their company, and sure wish we could talk. They speak only Arabic and Spanish. I speak neither.

"What I am living here may be worthy of a book," I write in my diary. "Something to keep in mind, and I write this journal for that purpose."

Something's up. Four men in a Land Rover just arrived. One of them, the eldest at about 45 and a fine physical specimen, clearly is in command, as the rest circle around him to shake hands and greet him. This must be the Polisario leader for whom we've been waiting. I approach, shake his hand and he gives me an extra touch on the arm – he must be the boss. A minute later three of them climb back in and drive toward the front, in the direction Ahmed took on his walk. Houcine pours tea as the rest of them talk. He pours the liquid from up high, glass to glass, to mix or aerate the liquid. The men return in the Land Rover with Bachir Ahmed and the other fellow.

Now the chief is introduced to me as their commander. It is a regal moment. This man has an air of class and authority about him, and it feels special. We both cross-legged on a blanket on the ground. The men are quiet. Then he speaks, and his words are interpreted by Ahmed:

"You have come a great distance to see us, and we are honoured by your presence."

"Commander, it is my honour to meet you," I reply.

"How do you feel?"

"I feel a little ill," I say. "But your men have been kind, giving me blankets at night and berries to eat." I see the men smile when they hear this translated. The commander's face is bronzed, golden brown. His features are perfectly formed – eyes, nose, mouth, teeth, chin, everything symmetrical. He wears an olive-green turban and a gray military jacket with a hood. His moustache is silver and black. His eyes, cool and piercing, reveal warmth for only brief moments. He is stocky and about 5 feet 10, much like Pierre Trudeau. He wears green trousers and leather sandals. His name is Aissa Ali Moussa.

"Of course I was delayed. Is it possible for you to extend your stay?" he asked.

The way I felt, I didn't think so. I seemed to be worse than an hour ago. My throat was now sore and producing thick green phlegm. I had a fever. I was weak all over, especially in my legs which ached. My head ached, my eyes were sore and my nose ran like a river. Rarely in my life had I been so ill! But there was no way I was going to quit now.

"Perhaps," I said.

"Fine then. We will go to the wall."

CHAPTER 32

I Meet the Commander

Rumbling across the open desert, we came in sight of hills in the distance about 5 p.m. Arising above them in the clouds was a beautiful rainbow – a good omen. A few minutes later we stopped near two other vehicles and four more men. This was the Polisario unit I had been told about. I had expected maybe some heavy artillery, a tank, or rockets. But all I saw, besides more Kalashnikovs, were two weapons: a heavy machine gun mounted in the back of one truck, and a mortar launcher in the other. This, of course, is how a guerrilla force travels – light. Commander Ali Moussa strode over to his men. They greeted him warmly and soon I was ushered out of our Land Rover. I watched as the commander climbed the stony hillside, crouching low as he neared the top. He crawled the final few feet. Ahmed, my interpreter, followed him, and then beckoned me on. I ascended the upper part on my belly. At the top, they had dug out a small indent in the rough reddish ground and this is where we waited.

"Look, you can see the wall," said Ahmed. Taking the commander's binoculars, I breathed deeply, having been winded a bit by the crawl up, and then slowly raised my head to peer over the ridge. To me it was a heck of a ways off, about 800 metres. "We aren't close enough," the commander said through Ahmed, as if reading my mind, and after I snapped a couple of pictures and we scrambled down the hill.

I'd read and heard so much about the vaunted Moroccan video cameras that scanned the sand and showed who was about. It was American technology, of course, and it was supposed to be able to spot a man moving 40 kilometres away. "Don't they know we're here?" I asked Ahmed.

"Yes," he said.

"Then why don't they fire on us?" I waited, but no answer came just then.

Back in the truck, we drove another mile to where another truck was parked, with two more men and the same type of heavy gun in the back. My hosts greeted them and then we climbed another hill.

"We're 600 metres away now," Ahmed said. There was a "boom" In the distance, as a mortar fell on the Moroccan side. Then there was another explosion, which I witnessed, fairly close, maybe 200 metres to our left. A small mushroom cloud rose into the sky. The three of us, me the commander and Ahmed, crouched a bit lower. We waited and watched some more. It was a desolate scene, no trees in sight, just reddish sand and stone, coloured like the dirt of PEI. It was a moonscape. There were no buildings either, in fact we hadn't seen one all day. This was the wild desert, the great Sahara, and I rather relished my time out here and with these men.

It was 6 p.m. now. We got back into the Land Rover and drove off. Houcine hit a hole, throwing us about a bit. This earned him a scolding from Ali Moussa. There are many such hollows or dips in this land, like crevices, caused by rain and erosion. We drove some distance and then stopped in a grassy, treed area to camp. For some reason the atmosphere turned tense. The men didn't talk or laugh as they had. A fire was started using dead wood from beneath the trees. A large tarp was set down for us to sleep on, and the commander sat in the middle of this facing the fire, his arms folded, his back supported by a bundle of blankets. He stared straight ahead.

Maybe he was just thinking, or praying silently.

I sat and watched, as the sun fell lower in the sky and finally behind some hills. It grew darker and cooler, and I watched the men gather up and slaughter a goat from a nearby herd. They put down the tailgate of our Land Rover and used that as a table to work on as they cut up the animal. Houcine, the cook, broke the silence, thank goodness, by laughing a little. By now I'm lying on my sleeping bag not far from the commander. I'd better talk to him soon, I thought, before I get even worse. So I raised the topic gingerly. "Perhaps the commander would like to talk to me tonight," I said, with Ahmed interpreting. "If he is willing, I am able. It is up to him," I said.

He said OK. I told him that newspaper reports in North America said the battle of Feb. 25 was the biggest in two years. Was this true? Yes, he replied, though there were large battles in the 1970s as well. But since early 1986, when the Moroccans had finished 2,400 kilometres of wall, the Polisario had engaged them in a war of attrition, he said, to wear them down, increase their costs and kill both their men and morale. He also said the last few battles represented an intensification of their war effort in response to Moroccan intransigence. "Daily we ask them to leave, through international organizations, but they refuse."

Why didn't the Moroccans bomb us back there at the wall? I ask. "I don't know. They are fearful people. They fire into the desert. We are sure the morale of their soldiers is very low. They live in small, dirty bunkers. We always attack these. We have seen how they live. Also, their casualties grow yearly. And the prisoners we take tell us their morale is low."

How far behind the wall do you generally penetrate each time? "On February 25, 30 kilometres. On March 6, 15 kilometres. On March 9, 19 kilometres. These attacks lasted three to four hours each."

What kinds of equipment do you use on these raids? He didn't want to talk about that, or about how many men were involved This annoyed me a little as I wanted some numbers to add substance to my story. I tried different tacks, even suggesting my editor would doubt I was here if I didn't come up with some facts. But it's understandable why he would withhold such information. He said I shouldn't be afraid to speak frankly.

The men, who had come fairly close to listen to the interview, began to melt away, maybe sensing some tension. It didn't help that the commander would talk for about two minutes and expect Ahmed to remember all that he said. Of course I didn't get much of that in return. I didn't say anything for a while. I wasn't getting anywhere, really. Then I thanked him very much and suggested we talk again tomorrow. It was getting late and we hadn't eaten supper. But a minute later he said he'd like to continue, so we did, but again I didn't get much, largely I think because of what was lost in translation.

Ali Moussa again said he was glad I was with them and eating with them. I told him it was an honour for me to dine with such an important man. The goat was presented to us stewed, in a large deep bowl, as we sat around on our haunches in a circle. It was deliciously tender, amongst the most tender meat I've ever eaten. And remember it had only just been butchered an hour ago. I watched as they ate. When the commander was finished with a bone or piece of meat he threw it over his shoulder.

Professor St. John had said they did that. So I did the same. Pick up a bone, chew off the meat, and toss that bone away.

We sat about four kilometres from the front. After supper I went to bed and fell into a fitful sleep, feverish and unsettled. Waking up, I considered my position and decided that as much as I wanted to, I couldn't prolong my stay. It wasn't fair to the men, and I couldn't do my work properly. Disappointed, I resolved to tell Ahmed my decision in the morning.

I awoke in the chill of the early morning. The men offered medicine and I took it, something for my throat, and it helped. They were kind yet aloof (understandably wanting to avoid me) and apparently baffled. What was the matter with this guy? I rarely got sick, and this wasn't normal. It was all I could do to pack my bag and get into the Land Rover. I told Ahmed that I would have to return as scheduled.

After an hour of driving we stopped and had tea with other soldiers. Twelve of them and myself sat around a fire. They chattered and laughed and it felt good to be among happy men again. I asked Ahmed if the commander would care to continue our chat, and the big man said yes. This time I got some useful information out of him and the tenor of our talk was better. Maybe I had rushed too quickly into the meat of the matter yesterday. Today he is more relaxed. I told him I figured he was 44. Turns out he's 46. He said there's no secret to life: God gives it and God takes it away.

Soon we would leave. I told him I hoped that he and his people would soon be able to return to their homeland and live in peace. We shook hands. Soon after, he departed in another Land Rover, and we left as well, in another direction. Now, I thought, we can return directly to Tindouf where I can see a doctor. My fever was worse. When we weren't driving I rested in shade, and the men brought me food and drink and laid out blankets.

At 11 we came to a well. The guide, Baba, lowered a can on a rope which had been concealed in a bush and pulled up some silty but cool and quite drinkable water. In fact it was quite good. He refilled their plastic jug and then he and Ahmed washed themselves, pouring it over each other's hands. Then we headed on.

We stopped again a bit later and the men picked a yellow flower, I don't know why. At noon we came to a group of men and three women – an oddity out here in the battle zone. "Only the women make butter and oil from camel's milk," Ahmed said. As we sat around in a circle we were offered a large bowl of camel's milk, a Sahrawi custom for welcoming visitors, who usually have come a long way. This camel milk was very sour, and I couldn't stomach it. I also cut myself off their sweet tea yesterday, as I'm not used to all that sugar. They drink three glasses each five or six times a day. They are sickeningly sweet. It puzzles me how people who relish that sweetness can then turn around and drink this sour camel's milk.

We drove on again and then stopped for lunch, near some small trees. I sat under a tree, while the others preferred the sun, as it was about 21 C and sunny. That's warm, but still quite cool for them, as this is just the end of their cooler season. Riding in the open Land Rover is cool and uncomfortable for me, if not for them as well. At mid-afternoon we stopped twice, at 2:15 and 2:40, the latter time for goat's milk. I took a pass, which puzzled them. In my journal I note, "At 2:45 yet another blessed visit and goat's milk. At this rate I figure we'll never get back today. Ahmed had said we'd make it by midnight. I so look forward to that bed of mine in an enclosed room."

Near 4 we came to a lake, which surprised me. It was a large, shallow, spring-fed body of water like a large prairie slough. Near the water's edge a large hole in the ground had been caused by a bomb from a Moroccan fighter plane, I'm told. I take photos of all these things. We see a water truck and bomb casing. We come across these little signs of war, but so far have not seen a single plane or other Moroccan vehicle, other than the tank near the wall. We move on and come to a couple of barley fields they have sown. They are a proud people, like all people, and are proud of their accomplishments in this desolate environment. I smile as best I can and show my appreciation for their ability to make the desert bloom.

As night fell, we pushed on, rumbling across the open desert in the cold vehicle, the harsh desert air blasting our faces. We stopped to meet a camel herder, who stood out as the stoutest Sahrawi man I've seen. Most are slim, or stocky but not fat. This fellow, who had white hair, was fat. At 9:30 we camped for the night.

Back at the camp, a doctor gave me something for my fever and after a day of rest I felt better. That evening, at a dance ceremony for visitors, I met a Basque photographer named Xabi Otero. He invited me to visit him in Basque Country of northern Spain. I did. But that's another story.

CHAPTER 33

On to Tunis

<u>Friday, March 20, 1987</u>

I was too ill and weak to take notes after 4:20 p.m. Tuesday, the 17th, when the commander arrived, until today. I'm back in Algiers at Hotel du Port.

When we got back to Tindouf, my fever fell off in two hours, just as the doctor said it would after he gave me some medicine. I felt almost normal again. I washed up and shaved and last night attended a special Sahrawi musical show for the benefit of the foreigners here. It consisted of song and dance, all celebrating their fight for freedom.

Most of the people present were women and children, as the men are out fighting. I met Xabi Otero, a Basque freelance photographer from northern Spain who has produced a couple of beautiful books about these people and their land. We exchanged addresses and he wants me to visit him and write about that conflict. (In fact I did for a few weeks later in 1987 and wrote about the ETA fighters and their campaign for Basque independence.) Xabi is a bear of a man with a mild temperament and reminds me of my friend George Curry, who lives near Riding Mountain National Park in Manitoba.

I also met a Mr. M. Said, former OAU rep for the Sahrawi Democratic Republic and now their UN rep in New York. We got along well. The dancers and singers were wonderful. The show lasted an hour and I took some good photos. Today our plane took off at 10:15 a.m., though scheduled for 9. Again we had aboard a lot of Algerian soldiers, little more than kids, all pushing and crowding their way to the stairs at the foot of the plane.

I met Xabi and his friend one more time before departing. His friend had interviewed some of the POWs I'd talked to and said Moroccan morale was low. I must learn languages! But it's so hard. I just didn't realize in school how important French would be for me. So much time wasted on useless stuff like higher math, when I could have been learning a language. Maybe teachers need to sell their subjects better. To be a fully functioning Canadian today, prepared for the civil service or politics or journalism, one really does need both official languages.

Upon landing in Algiers I was lucky to catch a bus for downtown, but it took me to a station far from where I needed to be. Then an ambulance screamed to a halt 20 feet from me. I whipped out my camera but the film was full! The attendants hauled a guy out of the station and gave him CPR, then raced away. About 30 people waited for taxis ahead of me. So I walked. My bags are heavy and I'm still not 100%, so I rested here and there. At one point a guy hailed a cab and invited me to hop in, so I did. He was going my way.

At Hotel du Port, two young men were ahead of me in the lobby. I got the last room.

For two weeks, my life has been more or less run by others. After a while you want to be free again, to eat your own food, set your own hours, your own agenda, and just be alone. That's another reason I didn't extend my stay in Tindouf. I felt cornered and wanted out.

On Saturday, March 21, I moved into a cheaper room. My hotel doesn't have running water, by the way (pay 36 D). I worked hard, first on a piece about the Polisario's new offensive, and then caught up on my journal.

Bouelem Maiza, whom I met earlier before leaving for Tindouf, came by today and it was good to see him. I spent time with his family in the town they live in south of here just before going to Tindouf. We went to the post office, where I phoned home and talked to mom for three minutes. She had good news: my first article had run in the Free Press. It was from Rabat, and how the war is viewed by people there. Mom said a cheque from the Edmonton Journal arrived, so they used it too. But just knowing that John Dafoe thought it good enough to run means a lot to me. The guys I worked with only six months ago, like

Kevin Prokosh, Greg Bannister and Dave Haynes, are saying, "Well, Brad is doing it after all!"

The days following were a blur. I slept, ate and wrote, slept, ate and wrote. For the first time this trip I feel depressed. I want to return to Tindouf and do more there.

On March 23 I moved into my favourite old room, No. 5. It's a big one. Had my first shower in three weeks. Worked hard on my letter home for Professor St. John in Political Studies. But I owe him a big essay about this war in the desert.

On March 28 and 29 I completed the essay, using interviews I did with the Polisario and other sources, and mailed the original to St. John. I got an A.

March 30, 1987

It's 6 p.m. and my train is just pulling out of Algiers for Tunis, a 36-hour trip. It cost 278 dinar, less than a flight. And I'm in no hurry, in fact am ahead of schedule.

Earlier today I interviewed Richard Turcotte of the Canadian Embassy in Algiers, and he provided lots of good information about trade and economics between our two nations.

At 6:06 we're traveling beside the four-lane highway in Algiers, the sea is only 100 yards away, and I see two ships. It's a beautiful city, this. I'm traveling first class in an air-conditioned compartment, but have no table! I've had six flights so far, and it was time for a change. The border here is wide open, unlike that with Morocco.

At 6:15 we're going by old shantytowns made of tin and garbage, but not as big as the ones in Morocco. The ticket agent checked my ticket and all is fine.

At 11:10 it's snowing. Been reading *By the Rivers of Babylon* by Nelson De Mille, a good book, and sleeping on and off. It's about an Israeli peace mission, whose members are hijacked in their Concorde and taken to Babylon. They fight back upon landing, even though there's a bomb in the plane's tail section. Good read.

By 8:30 a.m. I confirm the train is Tunis bound, as I'm the last one in this section. By noon Tunisian border officials have checked my passport and cards. I had written my birth date 1/27/59. They wanted 27/01/59, so I redid it. The car is 90 per cent full again and people are getting restless. It's raining heavily.

By 2 the border business is finished, but then an official in uniform, a man of about 65, sits in front of me and asks how much money I have. I mumble something vague, like none of your business.

"Hashish?" he says to me. He wants to know if I have any.

"I don't even smoke cigarettes, let alone hashish," I tell him.

He looks through my big blue bag a little.

I was wrong about them being finished. The Algerians were finished; the Tunisians had only just begun. This official was Tunisian.

Another guy just questioned me in what amounted to an interrogation and then searched my bags more thoroughly than the Moroccans or Algerians ever did. He even found my Moroccan ring and little Canadian flags (which I give to kids).

At 3 they take my passport, then return it half an hour later.

At 5 a man in a military uniform sits down beside me and reads a paper. We begin to chat, and I find out he's Lieut. Kamoon. Then a fellow comes along and hands me a card with the name of a hotel on it, which I get rid off. Kamoon agrees. He gets up to leave; it's 6:45.

"How much farther to Tunis?" I ask.

"Twenty minutes."

He was right.

It's dark and cold and spitting rain as I leave the big modern station. I asked about the Sabra Hotel, but got no help. I walked to an area of the city with older buildings and shops, the kind of area that has the cheaper old hotels I like, even in cities like London. They're all the same, really.

I plodded on in the night, past small stores, and then it began to rain hard, so I ducked into a shop. The proprietor and his friend gave me good directions to a cheap hotel and a minute later I was there. It had no English name, just an Arabic sign. Yes, they had a bed for me for two dinar. Good. But I shared the room with two other men.

At first I hesitated, being security conscious. I didn't like it. But it was all they had. It was pouring outside and I was hungry and tired. "They are OK," the owner said. I stayed.

I slept in my clothes and had an excellent sleep, with my money belt secure on my waist and my wallet strung around my neck. Blissful sleep.

April 1, 1987

Yes, it's April Fool's Day. This was my "getting established" day, the first one in a new place. Time to find shopping, eating, cleaning, banking, phoning and photocopying. The two most important things are a cheap hotel you can stay comfortably in and local currency from a bank. I had no Tunisian dinars.

Across the street from my current place I walked into a bank, and the teller pointed down the street to one that could help me. Then she got up and walked me there! What service. About three blocks it was, to another office of the same bank, Bank Internationale Arabe de Tunisie. In minutes I had exchanged $100 US for 81,200 dinar. One US dollar is .812 dinars. Decided to change 100 of my 150 French francs here as well, which gave me another 13,370 dinar. I was rich. So now I had 93 dinars. And Tunis is only a quarter as expensive as Algeria.

Now I needed food. I'd eaten no supper. I checked out a few places and saw what the men were eating, and felt uneasy. It appeared to be slop. Mush. But finally I stopped at a place serving this stuff. The man took a bowl and ladled some chick peas and broth into it, from a large cauldron. Then he sprinkled salt on this and added a generous helping of olive oil. Finally he squeezed lemon juice into the steaming concoction and handed me a piece of bread. Now I knew why it looked like slop – the men broke their bread into it. I didn't do this. It smelled irresistibly good. It tasted great. I finished my bowl of this stuff and wiped it clean with the bread. I came to love this breakfast and had it each and every morning, like porridge in Canada.

I asked the guy beside me how much the meal cost. This was a way of finding out the truth, which the proprietor might not deal in. So what does this guy do? He shouts out, "How much is the meal?" in Arabic. Geez. I told the owner the meal was great. I hope he didn't feel offended that I might not have trusted him. Then I ordered a glass of fresh-squeezed orange juice. Delicious. The total cost? About $1.60 Cdn, about a dinar!

The owner's son entered. I looked at my change in honest befuddlement and said, "One dinar?" I told them I was from Canada. They smiled, amused by my behaviour, and we parted on a happy note.

Back at the hotel at 10 a.m. I paid the man his two dinar and asked if he had a single room. No. OK, so I pull out my map of Tunis and ask him and his friend to show me where we were. My destination was now the Sabra Hotel, which is given an excellent rating in my guide book. Turned out it was only a few blocks away. What luck. So I packed up and headed out toward the medina.

But once I reached Sabra Hotel, I got stuck in the door! My pack was too big. So a man opened the adjoining door as well. They had a room, and a young man said he would help me with whatever I needed. I needed a shower and so he took me there, a short walk away. Half a dinar, good hot water and plenty of it.

Back in my room I wrote a letter to Penny and Adrian Chamberlain. I'd worked with Adrian in the Tempo section at the Free Press and had taken him fishing and camping in the Whiteshell. We'd had some good times, and I think Adrian was a little concerned when I quite my Free Press position, so I wanted to let him know I was OK.

Then the young fellow at the hotel, Chauki, did my laundry too.

My afternoon was also worthy of note. I left to find lunch and a hair cut. I took lunch in a café near the hotel. I sat opposite a man at a small table, and ordered what he had, soup and bread. The soup was spicy and thick, but the serving was small. Then his main dish arrived – and I couldn't tell at first what it was. Something smothered in chopped onions and a lemon slice covered half his plate, with olives and lettuce and such on the other side. I looked at the beige mass. "Do you want the same?" the waiter asked in French. Then I realized what it was – half a goat's or sheep's head, skull, jaws, brains and all.

"No thanks, I'll have chicken." It was tender and the serving large. More delicious bread, too. I secretly watched as my tablemate ate his "head." First, the lower jaw, then the upper, then he spooned out the brains. They came out as a cream-coloured mass of jelly-like material. Having finished his repast he left, leaving a graveyard of bones and teeth and skull behind. It was all quite disgusting, actually, for someone not used to the sight, but I still enjoyed my meal, and I'm starting to really like olives. It cost one dinar.

If I seem preoccupied with the cost of things, there's a reason. I don't want to run out of money. And I want to live life here to the full. I'm also fascinated by the different currencies and their value vis-à-vis Canadian money. Morocco is absurdly cheap, like Tunisia. Algeria, right next door, is more expensive. Morocco is a kingdom, a liberal economy, albeit autocratic. Algeria is a one-party authoritarian state run by the military with a puppet at its head, Chadli. Tunisia, like Morocco, leans to the West and is the most stable of the three Maghreb states. I find it all fascinating, and you know the politics must help shape the economics of these countries to a great degree.

After lunch I walked on, past many little shops and restaurants until I came to a place that sold batteries. I bought some for my little razor, which does a great job. It's a little Sanyo my parents gave me as a gift. Then I found a barber who needed a client, and sat down. I like the barbers in North Africa. They really know their stuff. They're typically middle-aged men who take great pride in their craft. If you look at the photos of people here in this book, you'll notice how well groomed the men are. These little barber shops look like what we used to have in Canada in the 1920s and 30s. Lots of scissors and tools you don't see in Canada today, including razor blades, enamel sinks, old wooden chairs, only two or three to a shop, and various lotions. The man took 30 minutes to cut my hair and it cost me only 40 cents Cdn. You've got to like that. I gave him a generous tip. Now I was ready to meet the Queen.

Then I came to a newsstand. I craved an English-language paper, but they had none. Haven't read one in about five weeks. Ten minutes later, on a wide and busy avenue, I found a stand full of English papers! Heaven! I select the British Financial Times and the American Wall Street Journal. They had some British tabs and broadsheets as well, but these two would do. Too bad they didn't have my favourite paper, the International Herald Tribune. Farther on I found the American Cultural Center, where they keep the New York Times, Washington Post, and many magazines and journals. I sat and read, enthralled, for two hours, till it closed at 5:30. In the New York Times Magazine was an interesting article, "Why the Media Focus on Israel."

Hoofing it back to the Sabra Hotel I had my shoes shined by an old man. At the Sabra was told my laundry was done, and he asked me to sit a while and watch Goofy and Zoro on Walt Disney TV, which I did. All in all, a very good day.

Thursday, April 2, 1987

Did a lot of chores today, mailed letters and cards to Gaie Haydon, my former landlady in London, Ont. where I did my MA in Journalism, and Gordon Sinclair of the Freeps.

Back at the U.S. Cultural Centre I read a piece by Marsha Sinetar in The Futurist called "The Actualized Worker." It's about people like me who need more than money to be happy in their work. So I wrote to her and provided a bit of my own story. One of the librarians is an elderly man who told me his nephew wants to study commerce in Canada. He asked me which schools were good and I told him. He asked the cost, and I said $6-8,000 a year. For this I got free photocopies and envelopes.

Lunch was a plate of fried eggs, oil, spicy sauce, olives, fries, bread, tomato and Pepsi. The owner wants to live in Canada, and I told him it wasn't easy to get in. So many here have told me the same thing: they want to live in Canada.

Next day, the Canadian Embassy phoned. I have an interview Monday with the political consul about Libya and the PLO. Spent part of the afternoon with Chauki Kasbaoui, a clerk at the hotel who earns about $50 Cdn a month. He said about half of this country's seven million people are unemployed. They get no welfare or UI. Qaddafi wants to take over Tunisia when the president dies, he said. He called him the "Arab Hitler." The men do a year of mandatory military service here, to be ready. Chauki's brother Abdul also wants to go to Canada. You can't blame him, but from my point of view it would be a mistake. He would miss his true home.

Abdul was a guy with a cloud over his head. He seemed down. We walked to the Tunis Zoo, and it was a pretty cool place. I took a photo of him and you can see his unhappiness.

On April 4, Saturday, I had my breakfast again and want to list here the ingredients: boiled chick peas, two tablespoons olive oil, dash of salt, two tsps of camoune spice with lemon juice squeezed over the lot.

This day I also wrote to Randy Midzain, another Free Press colleague.

A word about my room at Sabra Hotel. It's small. I call it my jail cell suite. By standing in the middle and extending my arms I can easily touch both side walls. It's about eight feet long. But it has a table to type on, and I asked Chauki to take a photo of me working, which he did. The bed is firm, yet soft and warm, with, count'em, eight wool blankets. My red Moroccan carpet (which I later gave to brother Bruce) is on the floor, my pillow is good, and I sleep like a rock. The ceiling is 12 feet high and the air circulation is good, from three windows. I have a small mirror and shelf, but no sink or cupboard. Three hooks for clothes, two for towel and facecloth. Good clean toilet and sink outside in the courtyard. The rooms are built around a square open courtyard, with kitchen, washrooms, office. I'm happy.

CHAPTER 34

Interviewing an Ambassador

<u>Sunday, April 5, 1987</u>

Here in Tunis, I finished the fourth draft of my business piece about Algeria's economic woes. Yes, sometimes I don't get it right the first or second or even third time, and have to write successive drafts on my typewriter. But that's OK.

That evening I wrote the fifth draft. When the piece did run, April 27 on page seven in the *Winnipeg Free Press*, it looked good, under the headline, "Low oil prices hit Algeria." Richard Turcotte of the Canadian Embassy in Algiers was a big help with that one, as we had a good meeting in Algiers.

Next day, Monday, I met with Haig Sarafian, the Canadian Embassy's political consul in Tunis. He was very helpful, and gave me a contact name with the PLO. One other story I'd like to work on is about President Bourguiba, who is in his 84th year. Who will succeed him?

More pressing is a piece about Libya one year after the American attack. Tunisia's relations with Libya are cut, and there are no flights to Tripoli from Tunis; the border is closed. I have to fly either to Rome or Malta to get there.

By the way, Mr. Sarafian introduced me to the ambassador and others here. They all descended on me like seagulls on fish guts, curious about where I'd been and what I'd seen. It took some time to explain it all.

"We don't see too many Canadian journalists here, you know," Sarafian explained. Where have I heard that before? All across North Africa!

I showed him my photographs and articles about the Polisario in Tindouf, and he was very impressed.

"Why did you choose to come to North Africa?" he asked.

"Because it's neglected in the news," I said. "Because there's a journalistic vacuum here. Because I've always been intrigued by the region, as far back as Grade 4 when I did a project about the Atlas Mountains and Berber people for Mrs. McLean at Stilecroft Dr. Public School. Now I've seen the mountains and some Berber people. Because my editor, John Dafoe, suggested the Western Sahara as a good place to go. And it's Arab. Arabs are big news these days."

I think he understood.

Tuesday April 7, 1987

"Hello, the Canadian Embassy, Rome."

"Yes, I'm calling from Tunis. I'm a Canadian journalist. May I please speak to Mr. Gregoire de Blois?"

"I'm sorry, Mr. Gregoire is on vacation until April 20."

"Listen, I'm working on an urgent story about Libya. I write for the Winnipeg Free Press and other papers. There's gotta be somebody there who can talk to me about Libya."

"Just a moment, please."

Twenty seconds tick by. My time remaining on the three dinars I paid for the call is almost a third gone. The line will go dead soon. This phone booth in Tunis is cramped and dark, and I have to compete with voices on both sides of me. It's 9:53 a.m.

"Hello, this is the ambassador's office." It's a woman's voice.

"Yes, my name is Bradley Bird, I'm a Canadian journalist writing for the Winnipeg Free Press."

"Is that B-I-R-D?"

"Yes."

Click.

"Hello." A man is now on the line.

"Hello," I'm calling from Tunis. Brad Bird, journalist. I'm working on a story about Libya and don't have much time."

"Fine, Mr. Bird."

"Is there any truth to reports that a coup is imminent in Libya?"

"We were there last week and saw no evidence of that. However, it is a well-known fact that the army is demoralized as a result of the events in Chad. And some of the leaders within the army are not exactly in agreement with the operation itself."

"Have there been any coup attempts to your knowledge?"

"None that I know of, but you've heard about the executions a month ago?"

"No."

"Well, eight civilians were shot."

"On charges of planned insurrection?"

"Yes."

"Is Qaddafi losing control?"

"There is no evidence of that….He seems to still exercise control."

"The anniversary of the U.S. bombing of Tripoli is coming up. I want to hook my story on it. What was the impact of that attack on Qaddafi?"

"I think initially it was a way for Qaddafi to regroup and motivate people. But I think the news that is filtering through on the army in Chad [where losses are high] has got to be disturbing the people."

"The conditions are good for Qaddafi's overthrow?"

"Yes, they appear to be."

"Who are you?"

"Just say I'm a senior Canadian embassy official."

"What is your name?"

"I won't tell you that."

"Tell me about your visit to Tripoli."

"We spent a week there and got back last Wednesday. We visited the Canadians there. We make six such trips a year."

"How many Canadians are there?"

"Between 1200 and 1500."

"Are they in danger?"

"They're at no particular risk at this time."

"Did you meet with any Libyan officials?"

"No high officials, no."

"I want to get to Tripoli. Can I get a visa in Malta?"

"Yes, you can. A number of people have gone that route. Or you can come to Rome for it."

"Thanks. The anniversary of the bombing is coming up."

"Yes, and there will be major celebrations in Libya."

"I'm almost out of time, what else can you tell me."

"In a nutshell, I think there is no question the Chad experience has been traumatic. But there is no evidence of severe unrest, on the surface, anyway, and nobody is prepared to make any predictions."

"Thanks."

"My pleasure."

I learned later that the ambassador's name was Claude T. Charland. I thank him for his help that day, if he is alive to read this. The Canadian embassy people have always been of great help to me as a reporter, going on the record when possible, and otherwise providing background, or comments from a "senior embassy official" when necessary. For a foreign correspondent, this foreign link to home is of inestimable value, believe me. Just seeing the *Globe and Mail* newspaper lying on a coffee table is a great morale booster. As foreign correspondents we are constantly scrambling, making do, filling in for interviews that fall through, getting out and meeting people, hearing a lot of sad stories, often war related, and sometimes facing obstacles such as military guards and checkpoints. We are always conscious of being visitors in strange countries. Just seeing that Canadian flag and feeling that unstated bond of citizenship with a fellow countryman has boosted my morale on countless occasions in a great many countries. Their quality and class as individuals, like that of so many of their military counterparts I have interviewed and spent time with, frequently deepened my joy and pride in being a Canadian.

I also set up an interview with the Palestine Liberation Organization. I first phoned them yesterday, and then they then phoned my hotel to tell me to call them today at 9 a.m. I did, but the man I needed wasn't there. So I phoned again at 10:45, and had the conversation below. Each call required a walk to a public post office/phone centre.

"Hello."

"Hello, it is Bradley Bird speaking, a Canadian journalist. I would like to speak to Ahmed Abderahmen."

"This is Abderahmen."

"Good. I would like to meet with you."

"Good. Welcome to Tunis. How long are you here for?"

"Two or three weeks."

"How did you get our number?"

"I'm not supposed to tell you. Let's just say an official at my embassy was helpful."

"I see. You may speak to my assistant about our meeting."

New man comes on the line.

"Hello."

"Hello, this is Brad Bird."

"How would you like to meet?"

"Anytime soon at your convenience. Maybe at your offices."

"What is your hotel?"

"Hotel Sabra, telephone 3403-73. In the medina."

"You are in Tunis now?"

"Yes, and if you call, please identify me as a student, not a journalist."

"I can pick you up at your hotel tomorrow afternoon at 6 o'clock. You will do your interview at 6:30. OK?"

"Yes, very good. I'll be waiting at 6 for you, OK?"

"Fine, then."

"Good-bye."

I checked about plane tickets for Malta, too, no problem.

The manager of the bank I deal with came to my hotel. He tells me a mistake was made – they owe me 28,500 dinar! That's about $50 US. We go to the bank and I get the money.

That says volumes about the bank's honesty and goodwill toward visitors.

Three-thirty at the Canadian embassy I interview Peter Furesz, their commercial counselor or economics expert. He told me Canada has modest trade with Tunisia, amounting to $76 million last year, while we imported $10 million worth of goods from them. Revenues from the sales of oil were decreasing for Tunisia, and he saw the country becoming a net importer soon. He saw Canada as having a place in helping Tunisia with dairy production and irrigation in the farming sector. In terms of telecommunications, Tunisia was looking to double its number of telephone lines, but links with France and Italy in this sector were strong. The computer sector was starting to grow.

When I got back to my room, I was delighted: Chauki, an employee I befriended, had cleaned it and added a table for my papers. Tonight he helped me clean my coat and refused any payment. I asked him to clean two shirts for me and will insist on paying him. He makes only 40 dinar a month, about $68 Cdn.

Wednesday, April 8, 1987

"All flights for Malta are booked until April 14," the man tells me. That's when I want to be in Tripoli. I then phoned Rome and spoke again to the high official, who is in fact the ambassador, who tells me, "Yes, the Libyan celebrations will last three or four days, one year after the U.S. attack."

Some background. On April 5, 1986, a bomb exploded under a table near the DJ in La Belle discotheque in West Berlin. A Turkish woman and three U.S. servicemen died, while 230 others, including more than 50 U.S. service people, were injured, some permanently disabled. Libya was blamed for the bombing after telex messages were intercepted from Libya to its East Berlin embassy, congratulating them on a job well done.

U.S. president Ronald Reagan retaliated by ordering airstrikes against the Libyan capital of Tripoli and the city of Benghazi, both on the Mediterranean coast. At least 15 people died and more than 100 were injured, including many children. Qaddafi made much of the attacks for propaganda purposes and would also exploit the anniversary as a means of helping unite his people and suppressing malcontents.

Returning to the travel agent's office, I speak to a different and more helpful man. He gets me a ticket to Malta Sunday! I bought return fare for 108 dinar because I have work to do back here before flying to Libya (CIDA work, the PLO), plus I want to swim in the Mediterranean and have an open invitation to visit a man and his family in Hamamet, on the coast near here, near Tunis. He said the beaches are good there, the water warm.

I'm overjoyed to get the Malta flight. I'm half-way to Libya!

I visited the U.S. Cultural Centre and read a great story about a day in the life of Winston Churchill in a history journal. I admire Churchill greatly.

At 12:30 I was at the Canadian Embassy for my lunch appointment with Laval Gobeil, their man with the Canadian International Development Association. A distinguished fellow with goatee and sliver hair, early 50s, he has served in South Africa, Niger and New York. Knows journalist Peter Calamai well. We got along well and had a delicious lunch at Circolo Italiano, a private club. The buffet was simply fantastic. No wonder these guys look so well fed. And so much oil in the foods – stuffed tomatoes, scalloped potatoes, tender veggies, you name it. I'm cutting back on the olive oil. My skin is so oily my glasses hardly stay on my nose.

By 5 p.m. I'm back at my hotel, after the hour's walk from the embassy. The exercise does me good. Plus, I can see the local people. Man, the women here are full-bodied and beautiful.

I hang my good silk shirt out to dry and lie down to rest.

Then a knock on the door. "Brad, someone to see you," Chauki said, and he sounded worried. "A big man."

The PLO fellow was here. "It's OK, Chauki," I said. "I'm expecting him."

He was 6-3 and about 200 pounds, intimidating for little Chauki. It was 5:45. My driver was young and well dressed. He spoke excellent English and his name was Khled.

"I had trouble finding your hotel," he said, as we walked out of the medina and up the street to his little car. As we got in, I remarked that driving here must be challenging given the speed and near-collisions I saw most days.

"The drivers here are crazy," he said, as he took us northward out of Tunis.

"You said it, not me!" I said, and we both laughed.

Khled said he'd been posted all over the Arab world. Born in Lebanon, where his parents still live, he'd been to almost every country in Europe and many Arab lands.

"I'm getting tired of this place," he said of Tunis. He works in the political arm of Fatah, or PLO.

Forty-five minutes later we pulled into the town of El Marsa. Soon we were stopped in front of a little house on a quiet street. The last thing you'd suspect of this house is that it was a PLO office, a local headquarters of a terrorist or freedom-fighting organization, depending on your perspective. It looked like something Ma and Pa Kettle would live in. Across the road, sheep grazed.

Khled led me into a modest office. The walls were bare, except for a large framed photo of "The Chairman," Yasser Arafat, shown looking to the side a bit and smiling. The other notable object was a large new desk with a glass top. A newish blue sofa, two chairs and two coffee tables rounded out the furniture.

Soon a man arrived with tea for us. Khled spoke about Israeli actions catching up with them, of the world beginning to see that Israel was the aggressor and perpetrator of crimes. This would eventually help the PLO prevail and win its homeland, in his view.

Fifteen minutes later a dignified man entered the room. He wore dark-rimmed glasses, short black hair and a moustache. His rose-coloured shirt was open at the neck. Over this he wore a light plaid sport coat which looked good on him. He stood about six feet tall, and with him was an aid. This impressive-looking man was Ahmed Abdul-Rahman, the PLO's official spokesman, head of information, and secretary of the Palestinian Writers and Journalists Union.

"I'm glad you were able to come, welcome," he said, shaking my hand and clasping his left hand over both of ours.

I'm feeling pretty good at this point. I've waited a long time for such an interview. Talking to a ranking PLO official isn't something one can do in Canada. And these people had kept their word, were on time, and things looked promising. I sensed a good interview about to happen.

"It's good to be here," I said.

There wasn't much small talk. We got right to work.

Abdul-Rahman began by telling me he had fled Palestine with his mother in 1948, when the state of Israel was proclaimed and war broke out with the surrounding Arab states. He had been born in Jerusalem and was five when the fighting broke out. He grew up poor in Jordanian refugee camps. His father and a brother were killed, he says.

"We are at war with Israel, a long war," he says. "It is now 40 years and it will continue."

The U.S. is largely to blame, in his view. "They divided the world to their benefit, and we are the victims. We are weak, but we have the will to resist, because it is our right, our future. We struggle for a homeland for our kids."

He calls Israel attacks on his people "state terrorism," pointing to the day in early October, 1985, when Israeli jets screamed out of the Mediterranean sky to bomb and strafe PLO headquarters at Hammam Beach near here, killing 21 Tunisians and about 60 PLO members. It's likely the Libyan attack on the disco was partly in response to this.

"I lost some of my friends in this raid," he says. "I have an office there. It is only by chance I was not there. And the Chairman was not there."

When news of the raid got out, Arafat, who supposedly had been exercising nearby, phoned him. He drove to the scene and saw people burning to death.

The jets had come 2,400 kilometres to this North African country, proof they could strike at their enemies anywhere. After the raid, things changed for the PLO. They reduced their presence in Tunisia – word is they were ordered to by their host government.

Eighteen months later, the PLO presence here has been slashed by 75 per cent. Only 90 members remained, he said.

They had arrived here in 1983 as the invited guests of President Habib Bourguiba, after the Israeli invasion of Lebanon. (Back and forth it goes, attack and retaliation.)

"We're guests here," Abdul-Rahman says. "We do not want to make war in Tunisia."

But he's equally blunt about continuing to make war against Israel. The resistance movement in Palestine will continue because they have no choice, he said. "The question is 'to be or to be,' for us."

This could just as easily have come from the mouth of an Israeli official. Since May, 1948, when thousand of Palestinians fled from their homes or were forced from their homes, Israeli supporters have argued there can be no security for Israel while the Palestinians are resolved to return. The sense of loss that simmered in refugee camps in the 1950s came to a boil in 1964 when the PLO was created. Now, argue the Israelis, recognition of the PLO would legitimize its terror. They also say that an Arab state next door would make them more vulnerable to attacks.

But Abdul-Rahman maintains that the only road to peace is Israeli recognition of the right of the Palestinian people to a homeland, and of the PLO as the voice of the Palestinian people.

"But are you willing to give up terrorism?" I ask.

"Are they willing to give us peace and recognition and self-determination?" he responds.

Israel damaged the cause of peace by attacking as it did 18 months ago, he said, adding they have no credibility because they want to assassinate Arafat, the man they are supposed to be talking to.

"It needs a century to be solved. It will not be the land of promise," he said. "It will be the land of death for the Israelis."

Recollections of the camps he grew up in make him ill. He usually went barefoot, for there was little money and little food. "I remember the flies. I remember the bad smells, because there were no toilets. I remember these things all my life. I cannot forget it."

They were given UN food they didn't like, as they weren't used to it.

His father wanted him to be a teacher, his mother told him. He used to go in the evening to a place to learn to read. He wasn't often in school, as he had to work, in a garage. He cleaned screens of some kind with gasoline. He also fixed flat tires. He couldn't get rid of the smell of gas.

As a kid he was ordered around. "You, orphan, come here. Sometimes they called me son of martyr. But they were very cruel. They were rude to me all the time," the owners of the garage, a Jordanian.

His mother struggled too, he said, and she went many times to register for food, and to have a home when they built the camps.

"The strongest could take the benefits. We, with my mother, what could we do? I remember seeing a list, and my mother was the last one, because she is a woman."

Now, he said, the Palestinian people are the strongest in the Arab world.

"You know what I remember about the camps? There was no green. There was green in Palestine. When we left, there was no green. Palestine for me is green, and Jericho is gray."

In his teens he went to Amman, the capital of Jordan. He began to study and understand what was going on. He leaned toward the Communist Party, as he still had little to eat.

In 1956 he was put in jail for the first time. By 1967 he received military training and was recruiting volunteers. He got into radio work for the PLO as well, the Voice of Palestine.

Now, at 44, he was married with five kids.

Incredibly, we talked for three hours, interrupted by the occasional phone call.

I talked about the King-Crane Commission of 1919, and how peace would likely have come about if its recommendations had been followed.

He smiled and agreed. "Do you know what the Commission said?"

I rattled off its major points: the people of Greater Syria wish to remain united; they opposed Jewish immigration; the Arabs should be granted independence; and intense unrest would result from continued Jewish immigration into Palestine, the home of 500,000 Arab Palestinians. The predictions came true.

At this point he leaned to his left and pulled a large book off a table. It was a copy of Alan Hart's biography *Arafat: Terrorist or Peace Maker?* He asked me if I had read it

"No," I said.

"Take this. How long will you be here? It's my only copy."

"I'll have it back by Saturday."

Brad Bird

Our talk went on and on, with him sharing quite personal information about his years growing up. I couldn't use the stuff in an article but he spoke with such feeling that I couldn't help but be impressed with his story.

CHAPTER 35

Arrival in Malta

After all the interviews of recent days, I rested. By the 11th I had my story done about the PLO's presence in Tunisia; it took me only two drafts, not six like my last one. My 30-year-old Remington typewriter is providing yeoman service.

The next day I flew over to Malta in a twin Otter, an 18-seater, which took 75 minutes from Tunis. My only hope of getting into Libya is visiting their consulate in Malta for a visa. Our flight left at 9:15 a.m., and we were cramped in the little plane, but it was extremely enjoyable for me, partly because I had a window seat. The views of the sea were tremendous. Another reason was the man I met across the aisle, a Saudi Arabian businessman named Aziz Al-Buthi. In his mid-50s, he's president of MB-trac, a contracting firm that does business in North America as well as the Middle East. He spoke excellent English and told me he had three sons and three daughters, all of whom have university degrees. One son married an American girl who converted to Islam and lives now in Saudi Arabia. He has been to Toronto and has toured the U.S. with his family in a van. I took a photo of him and his friend.

I knew nothing about Malta. The man behind the Change counter told me a few things, and the fellow at the Malta Air counter told me more, such as to buy a one-way fare to Tripoli and then buy the return fare there – it's cheaper. One way is about $130 US. There are $3 US to one Maltese pound. Taxi fare to the city, Valetta, costs four pounds! This sure isn't North Africa. I took the bus, not a cab, and it cost only 14 cents. That's not a misprint. The bus cost 14 cents.

My first impression of Malta is that it's a quaint little island republic that closely mirrors British society in some ways, such as the language, though Maltese is common. Store names like Easy Come Store, Oxford House, House of Knights (metal goods), are British, as are the quaint doorless buses. A photo of Elvis Presley, his wife and child, sits in one corner of my bus, while not one but two pictures of Jesus Christ adorn the windshield. This is a Roman Catholic country of fewer than 400,000. For some reason this place reminds me of the society in the TV show The Prisoner.

In 15 minutes the bus got us into Valetta. It's wonderfully old here, with Roman ramparts and ruins seemingly everywhere. But how pleasant it is to speak to the local people in English! When I saw the British Hotel I thought I was home, but it proved to be too fancy and expensive. More in my line was the Asti Guest House just up the street – and I do mean "up" the street as it is hilly in Malta.

The proprietor, an elderly man, told me he had a bed available in a room for three. I took it for three pounds a night. I'd be snoring that night with a German and an Englishman, he said. They were seated in the meeting area. "Here's an honest Canuck to join you!" I said, and they seemed pleased. The owner gave me a lovely cool fruit drink and set me up in the room.

After a 30-minute nap, I set out to see Valetta with my camera. The day was partly cloudy and cool, about 15 C. Everywhere you looked was interesting. Looking across the blue Mediterranean waters I saw a lighthouse and a shoreline densely filled with old buildings. The water was clean and clear. From the plane we could see the bottom many metres down. Near the guest house was a garden as well, but I left all this and found, of all things, an election rally. A loudspeaker spewed out marching melodies, while the candidate sat in a vehicle plastered with flags and posters, surrounded by eager supporters.

Near there was the War Museum. At times in 1941 and 1942 the Maltese faced 280 air raids a day. "Day and night," a café owner told me. "My father was killed in the first one, in January 1940. He worked on a ship that received a direct hit." Of course the Malta Conference in January-February 1945 -- when U.S. president Roosevelt and British prime minister Churchill planned the final stages of the war -- was a major event. One thing that stood out were the suits of armor for the knights; they were small. Some 12 year olds today might fit them.

Leaving the museum, I had a cheese sandwich and tea (35 cents) at a clean little café. How different it all is from the older and dirtier cafes of North Africa, though the food there is first class. "It must have been difficult here during the war," I said to the owner, a man of about 60. That simple statement set him off on a half-hour discourse on wartime Malta that somehow segued into a melancholy summary of life under socialist rule.

"We had a heaven here and we didn't know it," he said. Sixteen years of a government-run economy had left him bitter and sad. "A man should be able to work as hard as he likes to make as much money as he likes," but he couldn't do that now, he said. "The people used to be so happy, everybody smiling and laughing, but no more. Even if you have the money, you can't buy a colour TV. There are very few. The government buys everything and sells it to the people. You have to know somebody, and pay more, to get a colour TV." The socialist party in power was being challenged in the May 10 election by the free-enterprise Nationalist Party and a new group, a splinter from the socialists, the Democratic Party, which favours a mixed economy. He said the last election was rigged. He hopes this one is not and that the Nationalists will win, so the people here can have a change. He figured the local population at a quarter million, while almost as many others live abroad, including Canada.

A few weeks ago a 25-year-old Nationalist supporter was shot and killed at a political meeting – by a government man. He resents the fact the government people have acquired the best resorts in Malta and make a great deal of money. He supports government help for the elderly and ill, but hates all the abuses under socialism and decries the loss of individual enterprise.

The German fellow in my room is Andreas Grimm. He doesn't like his last name, saying it's too short. But I tell him it's a wonderful combination of names, Andreas Grimm. I told him if anybody's names are too short, it's mine – Brad Bird. He agreed that Curtis Bird sounded better. I may use it as my byline. Andreas and I went drinking one night for three hours at a nearby bar. We each had four beers and he was paying. A kind and generous fellow, Andreas is 26. He also gave me a leather pouch to keep my passport in; it hangs from the neck. I had little to give him, but shared some stories about North Africa, and he said he liked them very much.

Andreas left for the island of Gozo, the second largest of the three than make up this tiny state. The smallest is Camino, the largest, this one, Malta.

My other roommate is a peculiar but decent chap named John Gazdula. He's in his mid-50s and lives in England, where he moved after the war. He travels all over the world now, and on this trip carried only a plastic shopping bag full of clothes. John drinks a lot of wine, which he disguises with newspapers held by elastics. He offered me some. A retired railroad man, he is simple and uncouth. Unshaven, his few straggly hairs uncombed, he also repeats himself a lot. "No single rooms, no single rooms, they tell me." Andreas and I heard that a lot! By the same token, the same man also pulled up the covers on me early one cool morning and gives me wine and invites me to visit him in England.

April 13, 1987

Today I visited the Libyan embassy, my major reason for being here. It's in a town near the centre of this island, Attard, 7.5 kms from the capital. The embassy was closed when I arrived at 1, and a guard asked me to wait, so I walked down the road to a junkyard, where across the road were three small fields surrounded by stone walls. A couple of roofed animal pens stood unoccupied, and when it began to rain I ducked inside. At 1:30 the embassy was still closed. On the house beside it a British flag flew high.

I knocked on the door and a girl of about 16 answered. I said who I was and asked about the flag. The point is to distinguish their home from the Libyan building, she said, likely in case the Americans get ideas of bombing it.

"No, we aren't afraid," she said. The Libyans didn't bother them.

After some time the embassy finally opened. A single Libyan employee worked there, from what I could see. He sat languidly behind a wooden desk, a look of suspicion on his face. What was my business, he asked. I said I was a freelance reporter from Canada who wanted to visit Tripoli. He asked me to return the next day about 10:30.

That night, Francis, the balding owner of the guest house, served us delicious huge platefuls of spaghetti, on the house! It was great. And he has something planned for Wednesday, also. This night I met a fellow Canadian, Agnes Boucher, 65, a concert pianist. We got along splendidly. We talked about this and that and she appeared to take a shine to me.

Agnes talked about her years of study with Hungarian composer Bela Bartok, one of the 20th century's greatest composers. Bartok and Franz Liszt were Hungary's greatest composers. Agnes was his only pupil, she told me. He was "a strange man with saucer eyes," she said. She was 22 in 1939 when she began her four years of study with him. He was difficult at first, she said, not allowing her to play the piano without it stuffed with carpets to dampen the sound and action. He was also very demanding, she said, but later understanding when her homesickness became acute. She was from Canada, remember. Bartok died in 1945. The true depth of their relationship I can only guess at. Her time with Bartok was clearly a life-altering period, however, given what she told me.

I noted in my journal that this was "one of the most beneficial conversations I've ever had." I gave Agnes two small bottles of oil extracts I'd picked up in Tunis, rose and jasmine, and she was pleased.

Next day the Malta bank allowed me $500 US on my Visa card, which I need for Libya. At 2:15, after waiting one and a quarter hours, the Libyan consul helped me. He said he'd telex Tripoli that day, and I might have word by Thursday about the visa. He was pleased I was a student.

Agnes had good news: she'd been looking for a flat to rent and found one, a large place with a garden. It was being remodeled. Agnes would also have her own music studio. Not only that, the landlord couple have a little boy they would like her to teach. It's in a little town she lived in years ago, and some people still remember her. "It's a miracle," she said, "a miracle." She moves in at the end of next month, which is May. Her address until then was Poste Restante, Valletta.

Later that morning I went fishing, using a pin for a hook, fish guts from the market for bait and doubled up thread for line. Not far away was a guy about 50, who had a 12-foot rod. I used a three-foot branch. This was John Piccinina. He hadn't caught anything this day but said he had before. He knew Toronto, but Winnipeg was foreign to him.

I offered John a pastry, a delicious almond bar. He declined, saying he was on a diet to slim down his waistline, which was a bit thick. He chuckled at my makeshift gear.

"Let me see if I can fix you up with something better," he said, disappearing around the corner for five minutes. He returned with a slim old three-piece rod, a beautiful bamboo rod. "This isn't much but it will do," he said, working on the line. He was gruff-looking character but kind, that was clear. He said this wasn't about money. We fished until 2, and had a great time with a friend of his who came by, even though nobody caught anything. He gave me a dough ball for bait. He asked if I would return next morning, and I said I would.

That afternoon I puttered around Valetta's tourist sites. This "city" is only 10 small blocks square, with maybe 7,000 people. What really made my afternoon was watching Walt Disney's Pinocchio, a great movie for travelers. Beware of people like the wolf and cat.

That evening we sat down to another feast at Asti Guesthouse, all 18 of us. The main plate had bread covered with a little tuna, some oil, shredded lettuce and tomato slices. We at that with pickle forks, which prolonged the pleasure. We washed this down with a red Maltese wine. In the centre of our plates was a round cake of goat cheese, which had a bite to it. Dessert was a superb custard. We talked for hours.

Next day the Libyans granted me a tourist visa. A day later at 8:45 p.m. I would fly to Tripoli. The day began with a fishing venture with John, but again no fish. At the embassy I met a Maltese couple, Albert and Connie Cockram. I had seen him previously there. His story was, he was working for the US company Halliburton in 1986 when he injured his back and they released him. No sick pay, benefits, nothing. He's working through the Libyans with his lawyer to try to get compensation, as the job was in Libya. He was there in April when the U.S. jets attacked. We didn't talk about that then. They insisted that I call on them as soon as I returned from Tripoli on Sunday or Monday.

"You are like a son to us," said Mrs. Cockram, a short woman with a big heart. "Albert will be like a father." They have two sons about my age, both married. They also have a daughter, 17,whose boyfriend's family owns a grocery store, which we visited. Albert told me very little food other than fruit in season and bread is available in Libya. And what they have is expensive, so I bought enough to last three days.

Then they drove me to Valetta, where I got my passport photos they required, and then we went back to Attard where I saw the young man, not the consul.

"You will come Saturday for your visa," he said. "But the consul told me I fly to Tripoli tomorrow," I said.

I was told to wait while he went upstairs. Fifteen minutes later he handed me my passport, visa stamps and all, and a large green card bearing personal info.

Frankly I am a bit afraid to go to Libya, but I was also afraid to go to La'Youn, Morocco, in the south, and later wished I had. So I won't back down here. These decisions are sometimes not easy. If I go I risk my health; but success would leave me feeling pretty good. Plus, my chances of selling a piece or two about Libya will be enhanced if I go there.

I phoned John Dafoe at the Free Press about 10:15 a.m. their time, 5:15 my time. I asked him to hold my Algeria piece until he got my second, revised version. He said my two Tindouf pieces ran last week, at $125 each. Great! He said he's really happy with my material, they all are. He told me the last Southam News reporter in Libya had been recently killed. That gave me pause. But I had to go, being so close. It was the right thing for me to do, being "consistent with my nature and my business," as Somerset Maugham put it in one of his books, talking about what we do and why.

That night I spoke to Agnes about Libya. She didn't want me to go. Frances, who owned Asti Guest House, wanted me to stay, as did Connie. I went for a long walk, the day before Good Friday, and the streets were full of worshippers on their way to cathedrals. They carried crosses and lanterns. It was a memorable and mystical experience.

Next day, after spending most of it with Connie and Albert and watching the processions go by and having supper, I caught a bus for the airport.

On the airport bus I sat beside a guy who had worked in Tripoli and knew the ropes. His advice: keep your mouth shut, be careful taking pictures, but go. I ran into the airport 10 minutes before the flight was to leave.

With only a carry-on bag all I needed was my boarding pass, and I went easily through customs and into the final boarding area (this was before the idiotic searches that are done today).

My plan was to find a friendly looking foreigner and maybe spend some time with him in Tripoli, as chances are he knew the ropes. I sat beside a middle-aged Brit with a good face. On the business card attached to his carry-on bag was the name, John Patterson.

"Are you Canadian?" I asked him.

"No, I'm from northern England."

"I saw your name, Patterson, and there are many in Canada."

"Actually it's Pattinson," he corrected. "And there aren't too many even in England."

"Pardon me," I said, feeling a bit dumb.

That broke the ice, anyway. He told me he was working in Libya, on Gaddafi's gigantic water system. "This is the biggest project of its kind in the world, you know."

"I've heard about it."

"It's really Gaddafi's baby, his dream. It'll have cost many billions of dollars by the time it's done in 2000 – if Gaddafi can stay in power."

I told him of the reports I'd read about how difficult things were there.

"It's terrible," he said. "Gaddafi has led them down a road of misery. There's very little to buy in the shops. They live on bread and vegetables, mainly. There's no butter, cheese, jam, etc. There are very few clothes to buy. And it's expensive," he said.

"There are guys at the company who have worked here for 20 years and more. They tell me that before Gaddafi came to power 17 years ago, the place was busy with shops and free enterprise. Now there's no motivation. There's no free enterprise. He pays everybody about 300 dinars a month to do nothing. So they do nothing. There's no incentive anymore, like there is in Tunisia. He's killed it. And the young Libyan men don't know where they're going. There's nothing for them to aim for. So they just hang around."

John paused at this point. He had been speaking quite loudly, indiscreetly, in my view. There were Libyans within earshot; I tried to warn him to lower his voice by putting my finger to my lips, but it didn't register with him. I judged him as being a potentially dangerous "friend." He asked my business and I told him I was a student.

"You drive down the streets of Tripoli and what do you see?" he continued. "Most of the shops are closed, those hole-in-the-wall operations. Now only a few bother to open. Why? Because they get paid whether they work or not, so they don't work."

Then he said something which I later learned to be false. "You can't get your watch mended, your shoes repaired, because there's nobody to do it." In fact I saw many shoe repair outfits and watch repair shops.

At this point it was 9:15. The plane was late. A Libyan Airlines 747. We boarded at 9:30. I stuck with John, despite my misgivings.

"Better to be near the emergency exit just in case," he said, as we made our way onto the plane and to some seats. "You never know, this old bird might decide to go for a swim, ha! Ha! Ha! And I've heard that these Libyan planes aren't being maintained. They used to have it done in Paris, but now that France and Tripoli are at war in Chad, that's finished. They may not be maintained at all, just keep flying back and forth. Ha! Ha! Ha! Ha!"

A barrel of laughs, this guy. And to think he's an engineer. Geez. He really picked up my spirits. Around us, dour-looking passengers got aboard. To make matters worse, the Brit sitting across the aisle from us was as nervous as a cat. His eyes were filled with fear; he clearly did not relish this trip. Maybe I should have listened to all those who warned me to stay in Malta!

John asked me more about my visit, and I told him quietly that I hoped to write a freelance piece about it for newspapers. From the tenor of my voice I hoped he would get the drift that I didn't want this stuff broadcast.

"And when you're finished your trip," he said at 30 decibels, "do you want to go back to your journalism job?"

Thanks, John.

We sat for half an hour, and then they served us warm orange soda. Nothing else.

It wasn't a long flight to Tripoli and we approached and descended at 10:30, in the dark. All was quiet.

As the wheels touched down, a chorus of cheers broke out. Many clapped. You could feel the relief. I'd never experienced this before on a plane.

We walked out onto the tarmac. There was very little activity about. We were likely the only plane arriving. Looking at the powerful lights surrounding the runway, I saw a mist in the air.

After walking down a series of halls we came to the passport check area. It was all very modern and clean. An illuminated sign read, "Partners not wage earners."

"Are you Libyan?" an official asked.

No, I said.

"Next line."

I was third last. John was well ahead. He was staying in a compound outside Tripoli and it wouldn't work for me. I needed to be in the city, as I only had a day or two.

My passport was checked. "Sit here five minutes."

A man with a moustache and dark skin walks toward me and says, "Mr. Bradley?

"Yes."

"Your green card, please."

The Southam News reporter had just been killed there a few days ago.

"Your profession?"

"Student." My green card says student/journalist.

"I see. You must exchange $500 into Libyan dinar. You have the money?"

"Yes."

"OK. Wait for the bank to open here," and he points to a booth behind us.

At the bank – it's now about 11 p.m. – I pull out the $300 US cash I have and tell the guy the rest must be in traveler's cheques. Annoyed, he phones the guy with the moustache. "See him."

Across the floor I go – I'm the only visitor left. "Look, I'll only be here two days, and I'm not going to spend much money," I say.

He talks with the banker dude. "OK, $300."

That gets me 89 dinar. So I'm in! But not yet.

Through the gate I go and then confront a sliding door that opens and shuts like a pair of jaws, like the doors on the Enterprise in Star Trek.

I walk onto the rubber mat that activates the doors. They jerk open, stop, jerk open again. As I walk forward toward them they shut, suddenly, close to my nose.

I back up and alter my position on the mat. The doors jerk open again, then close.

I feel eyes on my back, turn around, and see airport officials watching with grins.

Bird vs. the Door. Door 2, Bird 0.

I dance on the mat, testing it, seeking out its weak spots. It opens, and I step partway through – but it closes upon me, trapping my right foot in its jaws. I pull, to no avail. I'm trapped.

I hop on my left foot, trying to activate it again. No go.

Now I hear laughter, and see more smiling faces. I've drawn a crowd.

Old Arab men are giving me tips in Arabic that I can't even understand, leaning forward and urging me on.

Younger people in the lobby which I'm half into – the one I'm trying to get to – are coaching and cheering me in English, urging me to keep hopping.

After a few more one-footed steps that Gene Kelly would have admired, the door finally decides to release me.

I'm in!

Cheers and applause break out for the second time this night (remember the safe landing?)

I do what comes naturally. Smiling broadly, I take a big bow, with a flourish.

And that's how I got into Libya.

CHAPTER 36

Tripoli

My day wasn't over yet, however. I still had to find a place to sleep. I walked over to the taxi counter with the name of what I'd been told was a "cheap" hotel, the Medina. I get into a Peugeot. But this is not a taxi. "Taxis take too long to come," I'm told. To this day I'm not sure who the guy was. Maybe an airport valet.

We speed along the modern freeway for 20 minutes, and then enter an avenue. To our right is a long wall, 10 feet high, topped with barbed wire. "What's this?" I ask.

"A year ago, boom! Boom! Boom!" says the driver. This is Gaddafi's compound, where he has his Bedouin tent. A sprawling complex all walled in, one of the U.S. points of attack.

At 11:45 we arrive at a large modern hotel. "Ten dinar," says the driver.

Ouch.

Seventeen for the room. Is there a cheaper one around? No.

I pay. Nice room. I wonder what the heck I'm doing in Tripoli. It's a world away from covering arts news for the Winnipeg Free Press, let me tell you. Have I made a mistake? I think of these things as I crawl between the clean white sheets and fall asleep.

Saturday April 18, 1987

I woke up about 7 and lay there, thinking. A former girlfriend, Elizabeth, once told me I think too much, and I think she was right.

Do I dare walk around Tripoli? Sure. Why not?

I ate some cheese and crackers and jam which I'd brought along, and an apple and plum. In those days they didn't care if you carried such things on planes. Or toothpaste or drinks.

Shaved, washed. What a fancy room. When the guy said the Medina Hotel, I imagined a lower-quality place such as you find in a typical medina, not a Holiday Inn.

I set out to observe the city in all its facets. I wanted also to see the sea and look for fishermen. If I could talk to a few people, bonus.

Down in the impressive lobby I asked for the checkout time – noon – then headed out into the breaking day. It was 7:45 as I walked across a field toward the centre of Tripoli. It was a cool morning and a clear sunny day.

As I got to some streets, certain things stood out. One was the litter. Garbage was everywhere and clearly had been for some time. Cardboard cigarette packs, drink containers, oil cans, match boxes, newspapers, food – all this and more. Another thing that stood out was all the abandoned cars. Most had been stripped of useable parts.

I saw men, mostly middle-aged men, talking and laughing with each other. Some shops were open by 8:30, such as auto repair shops, machine shops, a clothing store that carried girls' dresses only. Many shop doors remained shut the entire day, and Saturday is a business day in the Arab world. In one area, a number of buildings had been demolished and the rubble left in heaps. I wondered if this was the damage done a year ago by the U.S. jets, left as a monument by Gaddafi. I saw one or two places where it was being trucked away. I took a photo of one such area.

I walked the back lanes and minor streets and major avenues. I saw few people, so took a photo at one point of what appeared to be an army barracks surrounded by a high wall.

Around 10:30 I arrived at the Green Square, a large meeting area where the recent rallies were held in celebration of Libya's "victory." Also, I learned, the buses meet here, an important fact to know as I tried to return to the airport.

A huge image of Gaddafi was strung high at one end of the square and with it a picture of the Arab world. They're big on Arab solidarity, even though it doesn't really exist. The square was about 12 basketball courts big.

From there I walked for 15 minutes to the sea. I stopped near a lone fisherman who used no rod, just a hand line. He was the first person to say anything to me, some greeting in Arabic. I reciprocated, but no further words were exchanged. The sea 10 feet down was shallow and clear. I saw small fish in schools swimming by, in the strong tidal current. We stood by the side of a road, near an old concrete railway, on a bridge of sorts. The man, in his 40s, used a big chunk of bread for bait, which he floated on the surface, and allowed to be carried by the current into deeper water. He caught nothing while I was there. I ate there, opening a tin of mackerel with veggies and juice, all of it from Malta. I offered the man biscuits and an apple, and he took them. Then I walked on.

Coming to a large hotel, which I took for my own, I entered and saw a table holding posters and newspapers and other sheets. These I would send to Professor St. John for the polisci class to check out.

But this wasn't my hotel. But they told me where I could find a Libya Air office. I decided to return to Malta tonight, if I could. I was getting all I had come for and didn't see the need for the expense of a second night. I could see the tall building in the distance.

On the way I saw a few more shops open, but most remained closed. I saw tuna sandwiches for sale, and coffee, and Kool aid type drinks. More junked cars, more dirt, more rubble. Few smiling faces, compared to North Africa, where there are many happy people, often women walking arm in arm. Not here. The thing that was missing was joy.

At 11:45 I saw – could it be? – yes, a Ferris wheel. A carnival! Maybe that would change my impressions. I went in; there was no charge. It had nine rides, but not a lot of people were there. It wasn't a busy place like a Canadian fair. But some people were having fun. Arab and other African music played over the loud speakers. Bumper cars, the Ferris wheel and a spooky house were some of the attractions.

I walked on to the Libya Air office and learned that Air Malta had a flight leaving at 6:05 p.m. that day. To get the OK from Libya Air to switch, I had to return in an hour. So I returned to the carnival across the street and bought a ticket ($1) for the bumper cars. As I stood in line, or rather in a group, a smiling stout lady said, "You play with children?"

I said sure, why not. In the first two rounds I was too slow to get a car. The little guys were fast. But on my third attempt I got on a "motorcycle" and began to ram everyone in sight. Then they all turned on me! You couldn't do any damage, but it was fun. The kids didn't laugh, however. Not when I hit them, and not when they hit me. At best, all I saw were a few smiles.

The Libyan Air office set me up for the evening flight back to Malta. Then, walking from the office north along a main avenue, I noticed a bed-sheet banner on an iron fence. It had slipped down and was still tied at each end. This was one of the banners used in the anniversary celebrations, and I could see some green writing on the crumpled white cloth, which was about 10 feet long. Dare I take it?

I untied one end, then sat down at the other end, took out my canteen and drank. I looked around at the pedestrians coming from each direction and waited. Two minutes. The sidewalk cleared. I untied the end by my hip. Still nobody. I pulled it through the railing, bundled it up and stuffed it into my bag. I took another sip from my canteen, and then left. I walked on and came to a park, where I found a shady place beneath a tree. I rested, quite pleased with myself.

Two black men, possibly from Nigeria, then approached the nearby fountain and took each other's photo. I asked them to take mine, too. This is my favourite photo from Libya. I'm smiling like the cat that just got the mouse, and in a way I had – that banner.

Then I realized I didn't have my passport – the Medina hotel had kept it. So back I went, a 15-minute walk. The man behind the desk checked a stack of passports; it wasn't there. Nor was it in the second, which had me concerned. He went into a locked office and returned a minute late with a smile on his face and my passport in his hand. We were both relieved.

By this time it was about 2:30. I headed back to the Green Square to catch an airport bus. On the way I made careful note about the shops. There was very little to buy. I saw no meat, furniture or clothes, other than home-made clothes in dress shops. People didn't approach me or hassle me as they had in Morocco. It was almost like I was invisible. But one time, this morning, I stopped to scribble down some propaganda slogans on a poster. I stood behind a pillar, partly out of sight, but a policeman in uniform and another man approached and glared at me. I finished my task and moved on.

By 3:15 I had reached the square, and five minutes later boarded an airport bus. I wanted lots of time to exchange my dinars back to $300 US.

The ride cost $2 Cdn (or .500 dinar) for the half-hour trip, very reasonable. The taxi, I recall, had cost me 10 dinar.

The airport was bustling busy. Many people were lined up but the lines weren't moving. After confirming my reservation I exchanged most of my money. The clerk wouldn't change the last five dinars ($20 Cdn) because he didn't have small bills. All he had to use were $100 bills, or so he said. I bought some food and kept three one-dinar bills as souvenirs. Kept some coins, too.

Security seemed lax, even for that time. My bag, for example, was not inspected or screened in any way. I saw no automatic weapons around. In fact I saw none in Tripoli. The two men at the airport whose job it was to inspect bags just sat back in their chairs and asked me what I had.

"Clothes and food," I replied.

They motioned me through.

Those were the days.

It sure felt good to land back in Malta, which we did at 7. I phoned Albert and Connie Cockram, and Albert said he'd pick me up at my hotel at 9:45 next day for a visit. I also phoned Agnes at the guest house and she was relieved I was back as well. I'm sure glad I went!

Sunday April 19, 1987

This was Easter Sunday, and what a gorgeous day! Albert, 53, short and stocky, picked me up for the ride to his house. I gathered a few flowers from public gardens to give to his wife; the shops weren't open.

At their house, Connie said she had prayed for me and worried like she would for her own son. To this day I don't rightly know what all the worry was for. In fact her own son was there, with his wife, and I amused them all with the story of how I got stuck in the airport door. They fed me (they always fed me, these good people) and then we toured around the island. Their daughter, Mariella, accompanied us.

Marsa is a lovely fishing village. We also visited Hassan's Cave, Vittoriosa, Cospicua, and St. Lucien Tower, returning to their home in Fgura at 7. I then went back to my room.

CHAPTER 37

Generous Egyptians

On April 21st I flew back to Tunis, where an official stopped me at the airport, suspicious of my woven Moroccan basket.

"You can't have it here," he said. I was taken downstairs in the airport and questioned, to see that I wasn't blacklisted, they said. It was all much ado about nothing, but a reminder that security at airports can be tight, if you give them any cause for concern.

Later in the week I witnessed student demonstrations in Tunis with riot police and tear gas involved. The students were opposing Habib Bourguiba's rule. They want the police out of the universities, where plainclothes officers listen to conversations and check ID cards daily. They want jobs upon graduation. They also want a free press. I witnessed riots, but none of this appeared on the local TV news. A newspaper did mention them, however. I was told that students are tortured and imprisoned and sent to work camps in the Sahara if they kick up a fuss.

A visit to Hammamet was enjoyable. I was a guest of Riadh Esmail, whom I've mentioned. His family, of Berber stock, welcomed me, and we enjoyed a meal of couscous. In the evening, Riadh left for his job as a DJ at Hotel Venus, one of 48 in little Hammamet, which is on the coast. Nearly got into a dust up with a bartender in the hotel when he poured me a glass full of foam – my beer. Told me flatly, "I hate English people." I said I was Canadian, not English.

"I hate them, too."

He was definitely the Al-Qaeda type. Why was he bitter? I don't know. If I'd had my wits more about me I'd have asked him to explain his hatred. It could have been a good story.

On April 30th I flew to Cairo. Most of my work was done; I had nothing pressing to do in Egypt, but I had arranged to fly home from there. It would be nice, I thought, to slow down and see the pyramids and a few other things as a reward.

Tunis had begun to get to me and I was feeling down. I did a lot of writing there, including a piece about the Maltese election. Speaking of down, I was very much loaded down by this time, having acquired quite a few additional items, and two extra bags to keep them in. Since Malta, I'd carried three bags: my blue packsack, a black carry-on bag, and my Moroccan basket which holds my Remington typewriter and canteen and numerous other items; it comes on the planes with me.

On May 1st I moved from the Big Ben Hotel to a cheaper one, Hotel Golden, six pounds or $3 US a night. It's the dirtiest room I've taken yet. They gave up on the floor at least 10 years ago. It's rough wood, no paint, just dirt. The washroom's pretty bad too, but hey, what do you expect for so little money? At least the bed was good.

I walked out into the heart of Cairo, and into an apparent contest to see which driver could blast his horn loudest and longest. What an uproar. And it never ceased. The sidewalks were packed with pedestrians, most of whom seemed able to ignore the constant honking.

I walked to Tahrir Square. In view along the way were plenty of soldiers with automatic weapons. They guarded all the banks and public buildings, even airline offices. The square is rimmed by an elevated walkway that eliminates the risk of being hit by a car, so I climbed up. At the top I was met by an elfish little man with white hair and silver capped teeth.

"Hello, welcome to Cairo," he chirped. "You are American?"

"No, Canadian," I said.

"First time in Cairo?"

"Yes."

"Well, have a good time. I show you what see. Here, the museum. Here, police office for passport stamp."

"Yes, I need that."

"See, I help you! Now I show you my little shop. I have large garden to grow flowers, and make oils from the flowers. Wonderful. Please come. I show you."

We descended the stairs and walked two blocks. His shop offered little bottles of oils. I was greeted warmly by a fellow who said he was the old man's nephew, and he asked me to sit down.

"Our family owns a large flower plantation outside of Cairo where we grow the flowers used to make the oils," he said. He continued on, and then I mentioned that I'd bought a bunch of oils in Tunis. But not an orange one. So I decided to get one.

They show me large bottles of the stuff; I ask for a small one. They say they don't have one. Fine, I say, thanks but I'm going.

Suddenly he pulls a small bottle out of a drawer.

"Twenty pounds," he says.

"I'll give you one pound," I say.

The men feign anger, and start threatening me. I tell them if that's how they're going to be, I'll leave.

"Two pounds," I say. They lower their demand to 15.

"Two and a half is my final offer."

He puts the bottle away. I walk out of the store.

Two blocks away the old man catches up to me and hauls me back.

"Five pounds, sir," he says.

"Three," I counter. He accepts.

That's how shopping is done in the Arab world.

I returned to my hotel to stash my oil and then headed out for something to eat.

I found a policeman and a youth trying in vain to lift a very stout person to his or her feet. Each is pulling on a massive arm as thick as my thigh.

Heeding the Cub motto of my youth to do a good deed daily, I decided to help. The upper limbs taken, I grabbed the next obvious portion – a large buttock, and hauled away for all I was worth. The individual turned out to be a woman, who turned toward me and expressed indignation that not even Arabic could mask. I dropped my pound (or two, or three) of flesh and uttered a weak apology, leaving the others to struggle on alone.

As I walked away I caught sight of a snickering boy grinning broadly at me.

* * *

The story about the persistent oil salesman reminds me of another. I met up with three other foreigners in a restaurant one night (with cats everywhere) and we decided to go to the sound and lights show at the pyramids. We'd heard it was quite impressive.

We piled into a cab and the cabbie drives us there. At one point, not far from the entrance, an Arab man with a camel approaches the cab and tells us he offers camel rides to the show. We thanked him but nobody wanted a camel ride.

"Very good price, my friends, and a nice camel."

Thanks again we said but no.

"For you, I offer…" and on and on he went. Finally we told the driver to go. Just get us away from this guy.

But the camel jockey hops onto the hood of the cab and grabs the wipers to get a grip. The cabbie goes speeding down the road like this, with the camel guy plastered to his windscreen, hanging on for dear life. We can hardly believe what we're seeing, and I'm laughing to kill myself in the back.

Finally, the cabbie stops at the point where you pay to get into the sound and lights show.

The camel jockey, without missing a beat, hops off the hood of the car, sticks his head close to the driver's window and says, "For you, my friends, a very good price."

* * *

You want hospitality?

I rented a bike one day at Luxor, to ride into the hills and see the Temple of Karnack. It's 3,500 years old and well worth the trouble. I got very thirsty in the heat, however. Cycling on a sandy path, I passed some simple homes, with a few goats and dogs about. It was 32 degrees C and I desperately needed water.

At one point, I saw a home that looked like a stone dwelling. A small tree offered some shade near the front door. A woman sat there, working at something.

"Excuse me, miss," I said. "May I please have some water?"

This didn't register, as she didn't speak English, so I motioned with my hand to show water going into my mouth.

She promptly brought me cold water, then ice water, then tea. I was grateful. But she wasn't finished.

Her husband came out of the dwelling and motioned me to enter. I did. The stone walls were about four feet thick. It was wonderfully cool inside. He and his daughter motioned me to sit. I did, and it felt like heaven. Little goats entered and walked about. So did chickens, if memory serves me well.

"Mubarak good," I said.

"Mubarak good man," the father agreed. His clothes were simple and modest, like those of the rest of his family. These were poor people.

His wife said "Nasser," and shook her fist in approval, smiling. Gamal Abdel Nasser was a great Egyptian leader, the second Egyptian president from 1954 until his death in 1970 of a heart attack.

When I finally left, they gave me a water bottle to take along and a package of wafers. Later I realized something. This was Ramadan. They were fasting all day, taking no food or water themselves between sunrise and sunset.

Yet they gave me, a total stranger, what they were denying themselves.

Another time in Cairo itself, I became quite ill after eating something from a street vendor. My insides were turning inside out and I frankly wished I were dead.

As I lay in bed in my hotel room, the proprietor, who'd got wind of my condition, knocked and entered, saying he had something for me, for a good price. It was an old papyrus paper piece of art, a beautiful old – with the emphasis on old – painting of an Egyptian woman, which I later had framed. It's hung in my home ever since, one of many mementoes of a long and fascinating adventure in North Africa.

On that positive note I'll end this memoir.

APPENDIX

"Jimmy Jock"

The Story of the Englishman Who Turned Indian

By G. H. Gunn, Saturday Nov. 8, 1930 in the *Winnipeg Free Press*.

It begins:

Rev. G. H. Gunn, who tells the story of Jimmy Jock for the Free Press, is a well-known writer and poet. Mr. Gunn, who is of the original stock of the Selkirk Settlers, was born at Little Britain, along the Red River, in the last days of the Red River Settlement. His grandfather, Donald Gunn, who had come east with Lord Selkirk's 1815 party, lived to see the birth of the province of Manitoba and the city of Winnipeg, and wrote a History or Manitoba that is today a priceless source-book on local annals. Mr. Gunn knows the west thoroughly, and as he relates, personally interviewed the famous Jimmy Jock some 40 years ago.

This unique personality it was my good fortune to meet on the banks of the North Saskatchewan in the closing days of his life; and, as I had previously heard much of his remarkable career, I gladly availed myself of the opportunity to visit his camp and hear something of his story.

"Jimmy Jock's" real name was James Bird. He was the eldest son of James Curtis Bird, Esq., chief factor of the Hudson's Bay Company, a pure-blooded Englishman of competence and culture, and one of the great grandees of the early days of the Red River Settlement. His father, the James Curtis Bird above mentioned, lived originally on the east side of the Red River in St. Paul's parish, on the lot whose frontage, in later years, was known as Keenora Park; Bird's Hill, at the eastern extremity of the lot, being so named from the Bird ownership. Later, the Birds moved to the west side of the river and occupied the lot since known as "The Lester Farm," where at White Cottage, the family residence, most of the family grew up, and where Jimmy Jock, the subject of this sketch, was reared in the same luxury and cultured surroundings as the rest. Later, when grown to manhood, he settled in St. Andrew's parish, on the east bank of the river, a third of a mile north of old St. Andrew's church; from which farm he subsequently migrated to the west, to begin that adventurous nomadic career that made him one of the most interesting and romantic figures that have thus far appeared upon the stage of our western history.

On the wide plains of Saskatchewan and Alberta, to which Jimmy Jock turned his steps, he soon became a noted figure. His stalwart build, his bravery in the face of danger, his skill in the chase, his superior intelligence and his knowledge of the Indian and the Indian character, soon brought him to the front among the wild free peoples with which he associated.

In the sketch, Tommack, in Echoes of the Red, by my late brother J. J. Gunn (Macmillans, 1930), is told the story of how, by superb Indian craft, Jimmy saved himself from the murderous vengeance of a hostile Blackfoot chief who, as a bribe to save his own scalp, gave him, among other prized articles of Indian wealth, his daughter to be his wife, thus turning hatred into friendship and cementing an alliance that was to be the beginning of an association with these fierce tribes that later was to culminate in Jimmy Jock being made chief of the Piegans, one of the most warlike and powerful clans of the Blackfoot confederacy.

So through many years of shrewd, adventurous dealing with these wild Ishmaelites of the Prairies, Jimmy Jock went on to wealth, ease and influence, measured by the standards of the primitive society of which he had become a part. But as the years went by the inevitable gradually happened. The fine culture of his early English associations gradually faded out, and he became more and more, in customs, habits of thought, in dress and even in facial features, an Indian.

It was in the summer of 1891 that I had the good fortune to make his acquaintance. I was spending that summer in Prince Albert with another brother of mine, now deceased, when, one day, some story of Jimmy Jock having been related in my hearing, I expressed a desire to meet this famous personage, of which I had heard so many strange stories. My brother replied that I could have that satisfaction any time I desired, as the hero of my dreams was then actually encamped, with a lot of other "Indians," on a woody bank by the river side, only a short distance away.

The following afternoon – the day being bright and beautiful, and suitable to such an adventure – I made my way down to the wooded bench indicated, and was soon in the presence of the famous "Chief." But, alas; there was little romance in what I found – such a way have fame and wealth of taking to themselves wings and flying away when the heyday of life's achievements are past. The camp, as I remember, consisted of some half a dozen Indian teepees, with the usual number of half-starved dogs, half-naked children and general squalor, in evidence. There was nothing to distinguish the abode of the erstwhile great chief of the Piegans from the others; and, had I not been advised beforehand, I would have failed utterly to find a trace of any white man's presence, or influence, in that meager and motley assemblage. Upon inquiry, however, I was directed to the particular teepee that this strange "throwback" of humanity, for the time being, was pleased to call his home. It was just like any of the others of those wretched, primitive structures. And the occupants were no different to all outward appearances, just an old Indian and his squaw.

They were both very old. Jimmy Jock, at this time, was a very old man and stone blind. He was comfortably enough clad (for an Indian) in white man's clothes, with moccasins on his feet. But he was no longer the stalwart figure, tall and straight, of his manly prime. He was bent and shrunk together; this condition aggravated, no doubt, by the cramped, recumbent attitude necessitated by his tent life. His face was bronzed, by smoke and exposure, to the regulation Indian hue; so that no casual observer would ever have guessed that he wasn't a pure-blooded product of the race among which his lot was cast.

His wife, the sole remaining one of four that he had simultaneously possessed in the palmy days of his Piegan chieftanship, was of pure Indian blood, and was about his own age. Telling me, in the course of our conversation, of the regal state that he had enjoyed as chief of the Piegans and of his four wives, he said: "And this ugly old thing that you see here is the only one that is left." He was no promising subject for a beauty contest himself. But the term "ugly" was by no means inappropriate when applied to his better half. Bent and bronzed, and terribly wrinkled with age, there was an air of intelligence and gentle kindliness that gave her personality a by no means unpleasing expression. I could not help but feel that underneath that smoke-grimed, homey exterior there beat a real motherly heart. I did not then know the story of "Tommack," so I did not ask him if this was the wife he had gained as the result of that famous encounter.

My interview with this interesting pair took place seated Indian fashion on the green grass in front of their tent, while nearby the leaves rustled on the trees in the gentle summer nephyrs and the great Saskatchewan rolled murmuringly at our feet.

The old gentleman, as soon as he knew who I was, became quite at his ease, expressed his pleasure at meeting me, stating that he had known my father and my grandfather and many of my relatives; and in response to my request to hear something of his adventurous past, he was very soon in the midst of interesting reminiscences of his experiences among the wild tribes of the far west and especially of his life as the great chief of the Piegans. I only wish, now, that I could remember one half of the interesting things he told me. But, foolishly, I took no notes of the interview, and the more of it has faded out of my remembrance. As I remember, however, it had mostly to do with his grand estate as the Piegan chief.

As well as being a master of many Indian dialects, he was a fluent English speaker, and, in this medium, he related to me in good narrative style – often with enthusiasm and eclate – the particulars of his erstwhile high estate. He told me not only of his four wives, of his herds of ponies and other wealth, but of the splendors of the great lodge in which he and his family were housed. This lodge was very large, and was divided off into different rooms, for the better accommodation of himself and his household. It was made entirely of dressed skins, the product of the chase, decorated in different colours, with the finest specimens of Indian art, depicting scenes of warfare, the hunt, and traditions of the tribe. And, as he recounted these former glories, he seemed to live them all over again in fancy. His face, with its sightless eyes, took on a new expression; his bent and shrunken form seemed to regain something of its youthful bearing; and the old cracked voice rang out once more with the vibrant resonance of confidence and command.

Sic transit gloria mundi. As the shadows of the afternoon lengthened to its close, I took my leave of these old relics of a vanished day and retraced my steps towards town. On that "strip of green that fringes the river's lip" the leaves still whisper to the summer zephyrs. The river still murmurs as it flows. But somewhere, long since, under those mild Saskatchewan skies, the kindly mother earth that knows no difference of white or red, rich or poor, humble or great, has gathered them again to her bosom. God rest their souls.

But for many a day to come, on the great prairies of the west, where the lordly Saskatchewan flows, where the Bow dashes down its silvery spray, where by day vistas of waving grain nod in the breezes, and the electric lights twinkle in the evening hours, over many cities and towns, will tales continue to be told of the exploits of Jimmy Jock, the Kit Carson of the Canadian plains, the Englishman who became an Indian Chief.

* * *

Editor's note: After this article appeared, James Roderick Bird wrote a letter to a Mr. Healy at the Provincial Library in Winnipeg. It is handwritten in the scrawl of an old man, on letterhead from the Department of Indian Affairs Canada – Office of Indian Agent, and stamped Provincial Library Manitoba. The letter writer was a former superintendent of Northern Indian Reserves.

Hodgson, Man.
10/11/30

My dear Mr. Healy,

No doubt you were interested in the article on "Jimmy Jock" by the Rev. H. G. Gunn in the magazine section of Saturday's Free Press.

Jimmy Jock was the man whom the Montana people were interested in and you should call their attention to the article.

Old Jimmy's father [James Curtis Bird (1773 – 1856)] was my grandfather and I have a hazy recollection of seeing him when I was a very small boy. He, no doubt, visited my father, his step-brother, once in a while.

Wonder if you could put me in touch with the Rev. W. Gunn? I would appreciate it if you would. I would like to find out from him if he had any further information of some other oldtimers.

I remember W. Donald Gunn, the Reverend's father, down at Little Brittain [sic] as I spent many happy days down there when a little boy and had many dear relatives in that vicinity.

Thanking you.

I am very truly

[signature]

James R. Bird.

The following article was included among the letters J. M. Bird carried for years. It isn't known where it originally was printed, but it certainly came out during either the First or Second World War, when magazines carried such writings.

An English Mother to Her Soldier Son

My Dearest Boy:

I don't know where you are, but wherever it is, my heart is with you day and night . . . I know that kidding you that things won't be too bad won't help you in any way . . . You are going to be called on to do tasks beyond your experience and your strength . . . Prepare yourself spiritually before you go. No war ever demanded so much courage, pitting the body against engines of steel; more indestructible than steel, however, is the immortal soul of man.

Your immortality is your strength. Do not brace yourself into a state of tension trying to build an artificial courage. This way your nerves will snap. Man cannot stand alone and should not try. Connect yourself now with the source of your being and rest secure on the only solid foundation affording a foothold now left in this world. Pray at any time about anything. Think continually "God is with me." A presence will come that will never leave you.

So, arm yourself against mental suffering at the horrors you will see, by a serene courageous attitude of mind.

Don't regard the killed as lost men, nor the crippled as defeated men, nor the bankrupt as afflicted men. These are the fears of puny hearts incapable of looking up at the starlit heavens and reading the signature of God.

You will face destruction of this temporary body, and that is the least of your troubles. Because death is nothing. Not even the loss of the pleasure of living.

You will walk through a gate and you will go on. I don't even pray you should be spared this, because I would not feel that I had lost you. A temporary separation, that is all.

Don't be afraid of fear . . . it is man's deepest instinct, and a spur to brave men. Relax and pray. Reach out for the source of all life, all courage, all good, and a hand will lead you through the dark. I don't say this to give you any false comfort. It is true – true. I have proved it – and I know.

Comfort is a drawback and not an essential to the virility of man . . . men get their strength and their delight in building, not in enjoying. So fear the future not at all.

If the new generation have to build a new world, what then? It may be impoverishment in the material sense of the word, but it will be a spiritual adventure in the greatness of living. I have never wished to give my own children a ready-made world and deprive them of the best life ever offers: the growth that comes of solving their own problems. If this is the future of the children of our whole race, they could not ask for better.

And now, dear boy, to whatever destiny your duty leads you – go with God.

Your Mother.

Fleeing the Bombing

In Canada, little has been written from the German people's point of view about the Allied bombing of Germany in the Second World War.

In May of 2009, vacationing in Germany with his wife Karen, Brad Bird interviewed a relative of Karen's in Ingolstadt, north of Munich, who lived through the bombing as a child. This article first appeared in the Oceanside Star.

Hannelori Freitmeier was born Aug. 12, 1939, "nine months after her parents married," in Straubing, a town east of Munich. A few weeks later the war broke out.

Her parents were poor fur buyers. While her father stayed at home to prepare the pelts, her mother took them to Munich to sell.

"They had nothing," Freitmeier said.

Her father was glad to give up the fur trade and work for Adolf Hitler, building roads for the Third Reich in the 1930s. A strong man, her father was pleased that a strong leader had emerged to put people back to work and restore German self-respect.

"He liked Hitler like a god. They all did," Freitmeier said. "They didn't know what happened to the Jewish people. I'm sure they didn't know... My father had been so poor. They believed what he said. They had nothing." In 1944, the early successes of the Reich began to pale as the tide turned in favour of the Allies. The bombs began to fall in Freitmeier's area. She was five, and she had two younger sisters -- twins -- often in her charge. "We had to go in the cellar," she recalled. "One time we got a bomb in the neighbour's garden." The blast blew out their windows. Paper was put up in their place. "In the evening we could see lights. My mother would say, 'Munich is burning, Nuremburg is burning,' and we really could see it, an orange glow in the sky."

Her opa and oma, grandfather and grandmother, owned a grocery, where the children often spent the day. Oma had a big garden too, so they ate vegetables and bread but rarely meat, as the war dragged on.

"It seemed like every night the bombs fell. Later, they came during the day as well. That's why my father said to my mother, 'Go to Ortenburg.'" His family, the Arnolds, lived there. It was spring of 1945, when Hannelori was six.

But going there wasn't easy. For one thing, her father left to fight on the terrible Russian front.

For another, she said, it was forbidden to leave your home to flee the bombing. The SS were the police. "They didn't want to see that we had lost the war."

It also wasn't safe to travel by day. Freitmeier said she saw Allied fighter planes shoot people.

So they traveled mostly by night. The trip to Ortenburg took three days in March 1945.

"We left by bicycle. My mother had a child in front (on the handlebars, herself) and behind. We had a maid and she took another twin." They had more money by then.

They laughed, despite the difficulties, because their mother was strong and capable, she said. "We three girls had white rabbit coats. We were rich! And she took the coats with her. We never wore them."

On the way they had trouble. It was difficult to cross the Danube River.

They found a willing helper with a boat and crossed at night, again to avoid the SS and Allied attacks.

"We had luck. My mother was so tough. She knew many things."

They were hungry, she recalls, and her mother gave them bread. As they traveled she saw no other people fleeing.

Her mother had purchased a lot of cigarettes to barter for food, but the farmers did not want them so she traded a table cloth and related items instead.

When they finally reached her father's sister's home in Ortenburg, "the Arnold relative was not very kindly to us" because of the taboo about leaving home.

But at least there was no bombing there. Her father survived 12 years in the Third Reich's army. After the war he became a prisoner of U.S. troops, who denied him and his comrades food and water. He watched friends die.

"One after another died," she said. "That's the reason he didn't like American people." He refused to visit the U.S., where a brother lived.

Freitmeier returned to Straubing in 1945, when the war ended, to find the streets filled with rubble, the old town destroyed.

"There were only pieces of houses. In these, people had to live. And later there were rats. In oma's house, in one room, lived five people."

Guerrillas intensify war against Morocco

This article appeared in the Winnipeg Free Press on April 12, 1987.

By Bradley Bird
Special to the Free Press

Tindouf, Algeria – A Polisario mortar explodes in Moroccan territory and shatters the silence of this cool desert evening. In return, a Moroccan shell strikes back, creating a miniature mushroom cloud of sand and stone, persuading three observers to crouch a little lower.

Such minor exchanges as this, witnessed from the crest of a hill near from the Moroccan wall in the Western Sahara, have characterized this low-key conflict for much of its 11-year duration – until now.

Three major offensives by the Polisario Front, on Feb. 25, March 6 and 9, produced some of the war's biggest battles. They give credence to Polisario's claim they have intensified their efforts to dislodge the Moroccans from their homeland, the Western Sahara.

"(The battles) represent a new phase of our attrition war," said Cmdr. Aissa Ali Moussa in an interview through an interpreter. He said the attacks were prompted by Moroccan intransigence at the UN negotiating table, where mediators are seeking a compromise between two polarized positions: the Moroccans refuse to leave, the Polisario demand total withdrawal.

U.S. Col. Paul Flebotte believes the attacks were triggered by Moroccan activity in the Western Sahara's south, where a final wall to the Atlantic will soon be completed. The sand and stone structures provide a defensive position for the Moroccan army.

The walls are also equipped with radar, which the Moroccans say is effective for targeting to at least 40 kilometres. But during four days of travel with the Polisario, within five kilometres of the wall, a visitor saw only one Moroccan shell land – and that some distance away.

The Polisario Front is the army of an Arab people called Sahrawi, which means nomads. They formed the Front in 1973 to fight the Spanish occupiers who had ruled them in the Western Sahara since 1886. When

Spain pulled out in 1975-76, the Moroccans moved in, quelling Sahrawi resistance with bullets and prisons.

Thousands of Sahrawi men, women and children fled east to Algeria as refugees. The men returned to fight the Moroccans, and the war has festered since.

The Polisario claim that as many as 500 Moroccans were killed in the recent pre-dawn attacks, with another 90 taken prisoner. Their own casualty figures were not released. Rows of American machine guns, stacks of Belgian rifles and ammunition and European land mines are presented as evidence of success.

"We know we can't defeat them militarily," said a Polisario spokesman, who explained they are outnumbered 10 to one. "But we can put pressure on the Moroccans until they can't continue the war."

Much of Morocco's $20-billion foreign debt is due to the war. The country has severe social problems, such as millions of poor people and a lack of full-time jobs. Moreover, Morocco's chief supporter, the United States, has reduced its financial aid from $80 million in 1984 to $34 million this year, said Flebotte.

The shortage of funds is being felt in the trenches. Moroccan PoWs interviewed said that after four to six months at the front, the paycheques often stop coming. New uniforms were not available. Corruption was said to exist. Their quarters were cramped and dirty.

Combined with their own continual harassment, the Polisario say, these factors have seriously eroded Moroccan morale. And although one Moroccan PoW denied this was true, others said morale was low.

Yvon Bouthillette, political analyst in the Canadian embassy, said that, in contrast, the appearance of high morale among the Polisario is no facade. "They believe very much in their fight," he said, and they fight for no pay.

Bouthillette suggested the Moroccan position has similarities with that of the U.S. during the Vietnam War. Their 100,000 troops outnumber the opponent, but morale suffers. They are fighting in their enemy's environment, not their own. And the Polisario are elusive, as the Vietnamese were.

Days of traveling with the Polisario revealed a determined, disciplined, confident – even happy – group of men prepared to make any sacrifice for the cause.

"The Polisario is ready to die," said Bachir Ahmed. "Why? For his homeland. Why? Because his father and brother are martyrs. Why? Because maybe his sister or friend is in a Moroccan jail."

The Moroccan cause is neither so clear nor compelling. Essentially it is a quest to reunite what it calls Greater Morocco – parts of Algeria, Mauritania and Western Sahara – which is said to have existed in Medieval times. But some scholars say the authority of Moroccan sultans was for all practical purposes ignored outside of the empire's fertile northern belt.

Others say Morocco's King Hassan II occupied the Western Sahara to win favour at home and divert attention from the country's social ills.

"He went too far in this war; he linked the Crown with the war," said Moulud Said, UN representative of the Sahrawi Democratic Republic, the political entity recognized by 67 states, of the Polisario. He said it would be politically difficult for Hassan to back down and lose face.

Indeed, by intensifying its attacks, the Polisario could precipitate a more vigorous strategy by Morocco. Hassan II may be forced to break with the defensive stance his military have taken for the past six years.

Some Polisario believe that the 160,000 Sahrawi refugees near Tindouf, in camps which produce new fighters annually, will almost inevitably become targets of Morocco's army and air force. But Tindouf is also the site of a major Algerian military base.

An attack on the camps in Algerian territory could catapult a low-key, little-known conflict over self-determination into a large-scale regional war between the Maghreb's two most powerful states, whose relations even now are dangerously strained over simmering border disputes and Algeria's substantial support of the Polisario. Northwest Africa would undergo a horrible ordeal.

Maltese hope election brings end to violence

This article appeared in the Winnipeg Free Press on May 6, 1987.

By Bradley Bird
Special to the Free Press

VALETTA – The Maltese people, who successfully held off the Turks in the Great Siege of 1565 and whose fortitude under fire from Axis bombing raids earned them high praise from Winston Churchill in the

Second World War, now encounter a new and perhaps more formidable foe – themselves.

This tiny island state, situated in the centre of the Mediterranean Sea, is in the midst of a political crisis that observers hope the May 9 general election will resolve.

In recent weeks, more than 25 people have been injured in fights between rival party supporters, incidents in which the Maltese police reportedly used tear gas, shotguns and handguns on members of the Nationalist Party, who seek to oust the Labor Government of Prime Minister Karmenu Mifsud Bonnici.

"We've been in turmoil for the past six years," said Roger Mifsud, city editor of *The Times*, Malta's only English-language newspaper. "Our island is polarized."

Appeals for calm and unity have been made by the country's acting president, Paul Xuereb, and by the bishops of Malta. Ninety-five per cent of Malta's 300,000 population are Roman Catholics. Almost as many Maltese live in Canada.

"We want that things do come forth as do honor to our Catholic island," a priest said in an interview. "We pray that the will of God will be done without violence," he added, alluding to the election, "but with mutual love and respect."

The roots of the problem go back at least to the 1981 election, said Mufsud, who is not related to the prime minister, when the two parties, Labour and Nationalist, disputed the outcome. The editor said the socialist Laborites got 49 per cent of the vote and Nationalists, who favour a more liberal economy, 51 per cent. Only 4,000 votes separated them.

Despite two per cent less support, the Labor Party formed the government because it won 34 of the parliament's 65 seats. The Nationalists took 31.

In Canada it is commonplace for a party to win fewer seats than would be directly proportionate to its percentage of voter support, and little is said about it. But in Malta, whose constitution proclaims a strictly proportional system of representation, this was cause for alarm. Nationalists accused the government, which has ruled here since 1971, of gerrymandering.

Before the election, the Labor government re-drew the boundaries of some of the country's 13 electoral districts. This concentrated Labor votes and raised Labor candidates' chances of victory. "It was strategic gerrymandering, really," said Mifsud, whose paper supports the Nationalists.

Since then, half the Maltese people have defended the government and half have called it illegitimate. Deepening the schism and causing unrest in both parties is the method by which the prime minister came to office in 1984. Even though he had never been elected to office, his predecessor, Dom Mintoff, selected him for the post.

Other issues also divide the country. Shopkeepers said socialism was ruining Malta by denying individual initiative and taxing businessmen heavily. "We had heaven here and we didn't know it," said a cafe owner of the years to 1971 before socialist rule.

"Malta is ruined," said another man who runs a bazaar near the harbour in Valetta. Until a few weeks ago it was a fishing tackle shop – which had been in his family three generations – but he was forced to close it because the government established its own tackle company which it requires fishermen to use. Now the shopkeeper, in his 50s, who refused to give his name for fear of being shot, sells soap, toothpaste and gum, with only a few hooks and lines for kids.

Other Maltese dislike the government's close ties with Libya, though these are weakening now. Col. Moammar Gadhafy came to power less than two years before the Labor Party began its 16-year domination of Maltese politics, and the countries are only 300 kilometres apart. There is a large Libyan presence in Malta, including a consulate.

Still others, said Mifsud, disagreed with the government's snuggling up to the Soviet Union and distancing itself from the West. No British or American warships have docked here since the 1970s. That means a lot of lost revenue. Now, Maltese attempts to win favour with NATO again have begun.

Mifsud himself believes the major reason for the violence was unrest in the Labor Party. Mintoff, the former primer minister, clashed with a current minister over their running in the same district. Recently the minister backed out.

"Ever since it has been resolved, the violence has stopped," said Mifsud.

Other concerns remain. A priest is bothered by reports that some Maltese police are openly siding with the government and using violence against Nationalist Party supporters. Others fear that Malta's substantial tourist trade will suffer. And some have called for an end to mass rallies, where many thousands of partisans converge in open squares.

In December, Malta's constitution was amended so that the party winning 50 per cent of the vote plus one will form the government, regardless of its number of seats.

With the election looming, people are cautiously optimistic that violence will be avoided in voting queues. What people want, said Mifsud, is a clearcut winner.

"Then, at least, we'll have a government that can be called legitimate."

'Seismic diplomacy' shakes Aegean

This ran in the Feb. 8, 2000 Winnipeg Free Press on page A9.

By Brad Bird
For the Free Press

ATHENS – Seismic diplomacy is rumbling through the Aegean as two blood rivals, Greece and Turkey, are thinking – and acting – peace.

Shocking news indeed. Green Foreign Minister George Papandreou recently returned from talks with his Turkish counterpart in Ankara, the first such meeting in 38 years. The two signed four agreements of co-operation and are even talking about a shared military exercise in May in which Turkish soldiers would "invade" a Greek island.

But today, with peace breaking out in Northern Ireland, threatening between Israel and the PLO, and with even blustery Lucien Bouchard showing a little common sense, anything seems possible.

Here in the Mediterranean, the earthquakes of last fall are being credited with achieving what humans alone could not. In response to the killer quake that took 10,000 Turkish lives in August, Greece sent crews, food, water, and medical supplies.

When Athens was struck by a smaller tremor two weeks later, leaving 150 dead, Turkey responded in kind. "We just wanted to help them," said Manolis Kadsames, a security guard at the Canadian embassy here. "That's why we are a little bit friends," and he laughs. "For a while, I think."

But it's more than just the earthquakes, says Gerard Kruitof, 38, a market analyst with Deutsche Bank Group. He says both countries are seeking membership in the EU and can smell the economic potential of working together to develop joint ventures in tourism and development.

Greek stocks are an investor's paradise and interest rates are falling, he says, as a real estate boom begins. "I think the economic considerations are dominant," he concludes in an interview.

But if history is any kind of guide, the olive branches and pretty words will dissolve, eventually. Many Greeks fear the Turkish plan in fact is to launch a war on the eve of the 2004 Olympic Games, thus depriving this country its moment of world glory, not to mention the profits it expects to see.

"There is an open threat that just before the Olympics they will start hostilities," said Thanos Kotsakis, 58, a graphic artist.

Indeed, while it talks peace, Greece continues to modernize its military and plans to spend up to $15 billion on fighter planes and tanks by 2005. This decision came only a day after the historic meeting of foreign ministers in Ankara. The two neighbours, both NATO members, have come close to war three times in the past 26 years.

And they are still at odds over Cyprus, where Canadians have helped keep the peace, and other islands in the Aegean. Interestingly, these topics were not raised in recent talks in order than progress be made in other areas.

The positive climate between the two countries is indeed unprecedented," Papandreou upon returning from Turkey. "Differences of opinion remain, such as over Cyprus, but in all other areas the progress is fast, impressive."

Turkey's foreign minister, Ismail Cem, said "we have made a new beginning which can only get better." Cem was to visit Athens early this month to continue talks. The two men will also open an important conference of Green and Turkish journalists. This is designed to encourage the media on both sides of the Aegean – and through them the broader public – to stop cultivating hateful and threatening images of each other.

In Ankara, Cem and Papandreou went further than expected. They agreed to examine a proposal for a joint bid so that the 2008 European Football Cup takes place in both countries, much on the model used by Japan and Korea for a forthcoming World Cup. In countries where soccer is the Canadian equivalent of hockey, this is indeed ground-breaking. Turkey was also invited to take part in cultural events linked to the 2004 Athens Olympics.

Newspapers in both countries have praised these developments and speak of a "love affair." "We are at the start of a beautiful road of no return in the Aegean," wrote Ferai Tinc in the Turkish Hurriyet daily. Greek daily

Ethnos declared: "We are headed for a signing of a non-aggression pact with Turkey in June."

And as observers have said, it all began with the earthquakes and mutual outpouring of public sympathy in both countries.

Politicians dubbed this seismic diplomacy and pounced on the opportunity. Most incredible of all the signs of peace here is their agreement to hold joint military manoeuvres this spring, under NATO auspices, code named Dynamic Mix. For the first time in their history the drill envisages Turkish jet fighters freely flying over Greek territory and troops actually "invading" and landing on a Greek island in the Ionian Sea.

Greece's worst nightmare has been turned into a harmless scenario for a war game. That is, if the Dynamic Mix doesn't explode.

Terrorist presence in Tunisia dwindles

This article appeared in the Winnipeg Free Press on May 7, 1987.

By Bradley Bird
Special to the Free Press

TUNIS – The walls in Ahmed Abdul-Rahman's office are bare, save for one large picture of Yasser Arafat. In it, the chairman of the Palestine Liberation Organization is smiling, as he might when considering the 50 or so assassination attempts he has survived.

Sitting behind an expansive glass-topped desk, the PLO's official spokesman, Abdul-Rahman, recalls the day in early October, 1985, when Israeli jets screamed out of the Mediterranean sky to bomb and strafe and destroy PLO headquarters at Hammam Beach, killing 21 Tunisians and about 60 PLO members. But not Arafat.

The now 57-year-old co-founder of the PLO, whose policy of terrorism has made him reviled by many around the world, was not in his office when the bombs began to fall about 9:50 a.m. He was exercising in a nearby house.

"He called me here," said Abdul-Rahman. "I was at my place where I sleep. I took my car and then drove. When I was halfway here the raid begins, so I go very quickly. I saw my friends. I saw their hands and their heads burning."

Much of the building was rubble and has since been razed.

The Israeli jets had to come 2,400 kilometres to this North African city. The significance of the distance lies in its proof that Israel has the capacity to strike at the PLO perhaps anywhere in the Arab world. The significance of the raid itself is that it dramatically reduced the PLO's presence in Tunisia and altered its strategy throughout the Arab world.

A year and a half later, the PLO presence has been slashed by at least 75 per cent. It now consists of about 90 members, Abdul-Rahman says.

Arafat and about 600 fighters arrived as the invited guests of President Habib Bourguiba early in 1983, after the Israeli invasion of Lebanon. Late last year, according to a Canadian embassy official, the Tunisian government told the PLO that its political department was welcome to stay, but its fighters must go.

Abdul-Rahman says the soldiers were transferred to Algeria and Sudan for security reasons. He cites the same reasons for the dispersal of some PLO leaders to other Arab states.

"We're guests here," he emphasizes. "We really do not want to make war in Tunisia." But he is equally blunt about the continuing PLO effort to make war in Israel. This the raid has not changed.

"We have the resistance movement in Palestine," he says. "We continue to support our people, we continue to fight and we will not stop, because we have no other option. The question is 'to be or to be,' for us."

His last sentence could as easily have come from the mouth of an Israeli official. Since Israel was proclaimed in May of 1948, Zionist supporters have argued there can be no security for Israel while the Palestinian people are resolved to return. Hundreds of thousands of them fled from their homes in Palestine in the face of Jewish attacks that same year.

(On April 10, 1948, in the village of Beir Yassin, some 260 Palestinian men, women and children were slaughtered. The attack was a combined operation by the two main Jewish terrorist groups: the Irgun, whose chief was Menachem Begin; and the Stern Gang, one of whose leaders was Yitzhak Shamir. Fear spread quickly after that.)

The sense of loss that simmered in Palestinian refugee camps in the 1950s came to a boil in 1964 with the creation of the PLO. Now, argue Israeli hardliners, recognition of the PLO would legitimize its terror. They also say the establishment of a Palestian state on or near Israeli territory would make them more vulnerable to terrorist attacks.

In this context, a pact between Arafat and King Hussein of Jordan was concluded on Feb. 11, 1985. It would have set up an independent

Palestinian entity to be confederated with Jordan – right next door to Israel. In Washington, President Reagan was showing rare signs of interest in the possible solution to the Mideast problem.

The Israelis would have none of it. Talks in Washington to discuss the pact were slated for late October, 1985. Egypt's Hosni Mubarak and Jordan's Hussein were set to take part. But since U.S. policy on the PLO is to have no contact with the organization, Arafat, as usual, was left out.

Abdul-Rahman maintains that the only road to peace for Israel is its recognition of the right of the Palestinian people to a homeland, and its recognition of the PLO as the representative of the Palestinian people.

But are you willing to give up terrorism?

"Are they willing to give us peace and recognition and self-determination?"